Early Babylonian History

Ancient Texts and Translations

Series Editor
K. C. Hanson

Robert William Rogers
Cuneiform Parallels to the Old Testament

D. Winton Thomas, editor
Documents from Old Testament Times

Hugo Radau
Early Babylonian History

Henry Frederick Lutz
Early Babylonian Letters from Larsa

Albert T. Clay
Babylonian Epics, Hymns, Omens, and Other Texts

Daniel David Luckenbill
The Annals of Sennacherib

A. E. Cowley
Aramaic Papyri of the Fifth Century B.C.

G. R. Driver
Aramaic Documents of the Fifth Century B.C., rev. ed.

Adolf Neubauer
The Book of Tobit

August Dillman
The Ethiopic Text of 1 Enoch

R. H. Charles
The Apocrypha and Pseudepigrapha of the Old Testament

R. H. Charles
The Book of Enoch

R. H. Charles
The Book of Jubilees

R. H. Charles
The Testaments of the Twelve Patriarchs

R. H. Charles
The Apocalypse of Baruch

Robert Bensly et al.
The Four Gospels in Syriac

H. B. Swete
The Gospel of Peter

Richard Adelbert Lipsius and Max Bonnet
Apocryphal Acts of the Apostles (3 vols.)

Early Babylonian History

Down to the End of the Fourth Dynasty of Ur

To Which is Appended an Account of the
E. A. Hoffman Collection of Babylonian Tablets in the
General Theological Seminary, New York, U.S.A.

Hugo Radau

Wipf & Stock Publishers
Eugene, Oregon

EARLY BABYLONIAN HISTORY
Down to the End of the Fourth Dynasty of Ur
Ancient Texts and Translations

ISBN: 1-59752-381-X

The Library of Congress has cataloged an earlier edition of this book:

Radau, Hugo, 1873–

Early Babylonian history down to the end of the fourth dynasty of Ur : to which is appended an account of the E. A. Hoffman collection of Babylonian tablets in the General Theological Seminary, New York, U.S.A. By Rev. Hugo Radau. . .

New York, Oxford University Press, American branch; London: A. Frowde, 1900.
xix, [1], 452 p. fold. tables. 25 cm.

Printed in Great Britain.
"Written as a doctor's dissertation, and submitted as such to the Faculty of Philosophy, Columbia University, New York City, N.Y., in April, 1898 . . . supplement[ed] . . . by all the inscriptions . . . published up to April 1, 1900."— Pref.

1. Babylonia—History.

DS73.1 .R2 04031179

Manufactured in the U.S.A.

Series Foreword

The discoveries of documents from the ancient Near Eastern and Mediterranean worlds have altered our modern understanding of those worlds in both breadth and depth. Especially since the mid-nineteenth century, chance discoveries as well as archaeological excavations have brought to light thousands of clay tablets, stone inscriptions and stelae, leather scrolls, codices, papyri, seals, and ostraca.

The genres of these written documents are quite diverse: receipts, tax lists, inventories, letters, prophecies, blessings and curses, dowry documents, deeds, laws, instructions, collections of proverbs, philosophical treatises, state propaganda, myths and legends, hymns and prayers, liturgies and rituals, and many more. Some of them came to light in long-famous cities—such as Ur, Babylon, Nineveh, and Jerusalem—while others came from locations that were previously little-known or unknown—such as Ebla, Ugarit, Elephantine, Qumran, and Nag Hammadi.

But what good are these remnants from the distant past? Why should anyone bother with what are often fragmentary, obscure, or long-forgotten scraps of ancient cultures? Each person will answer those questions for herself or himself, depending upon interests and commitments. But the documents have influenced scholarly research in several areas.

It must first be said that the documents are of interest and importance in their own right, whatever their connections—or lack of them—to modern ethnic, religious, or ideological concerns. Many of them provide windows on how real people lived in the ancient world—what they grew and ate; how they related to their families, business associates, and states; how they were taxed; how and whom they worshiped; how they organized their communities; their hopes and fears; and how they understood and portrayed their own group's story.

They are of intense interest at the linguistic level. They provide us with previously unknown or undeciphered languages and dialects, broaden our range of vocabularies and meanings, assist us in mapping the relationships and developments of languages, and provide examples of loan-words and linguistic influences between languages. A monumental project such as *The Assyrian Dictionary,* produced by the Oriental Institute at the University of Chicago, would have been unthinkable without the broad range of Akkadian resources today.[1] And our study of Coptic and early gospels would be impoverished without the Nag Hammadi codices.[2]

The variety of genres also attracts our interest in terms of the history of literature. Such stories as Athra-hasis, Enumma Elish, and Gilgamesh have become important to the study of world literature. While modern readers may be most intrigued by something with obvious political or religious content, we often learn a great deal from a tax receipt or a dowry document. Hermann Gunkel influenced biblical studies not only because of his keen insights into the biblical books, but because he studied the biblical genres in the light of ancient Near Eastern texts. As he examined the genres in the Psalms, for example, he compared them to the poetic passages throughout the rest of the Bible, the Apocrypha, the Pseudepigrapha, Akkadian sources, and Egyptian sources.[3] While the Akkadian and Egyptian

---

[1] I. J. Gelb et al., editors, *The Assyrian Dictionary of the Oriental Institute of the University of Chicago* (Chicago: Univ. of Chicago Press, 1956–).

[2] James M. Robinson, editor, *The Nag Hammadi Library in English,* 3d ed. (San Francisco: HarperSanFrancisco, 1990).

[3] Hermann Gunkel, *Einleitung in die Psalmen: Die Gattungen der religiösen Lyrik Israels,* completed by Joachim Begrich, HAT (Göttingen:

resources were much more limited in the 1920s and 1930s when he was working on the Psalms, his methodology and insights have had an on-going significance.

History is also a significant interest. Many of these texts mention kingdoms, ethnic and tribal groups, rulers, diplomats, generals, locations, or events that assist in establishing chronologies, give us different perspectives on previously known events, or fill in gaps in our knowledge. Historians can never have too many sources. The Amarna letters, for example, provide us with the names of local rulers in Canaan during the fourteenth century BCE, their relationship with the pharaoh, as well as the military issues of the period.[4]

Social analysis is another area of fertile research. A deed can reveal economic structures, production, land tenure, kinship relations, scribal conventions, calendars, and social hierarchies. Both the Elephantine papyri from Egypt (fifth century BCE) and the Babatha archive from the Judean desert (second century CE) include personal legal documents and letters relating to dowries, inheritance, and property transfers that provide glimpses of complex kinship relations, networking, and legal witnesses.[5] And the Elephantine documents also include letters to the high priest in Jerusalem from the priests of Elephantine regarding the rebuilding of the Elephantine temple.

Vandenhoeck & Ruprecht, 1933). ET = *Introduction to the Psalms: The Genres of the Religious Lyric of Israel,* trans. James D. Nogalski, Mercer Library of Biblical Studies (Macon, Ga.: Mercer Univ. Press, 1998).

[4] William L. Moran, *The Amarna Letters* (Baltimore: Johns Hopkins Univ. Press, 1992).

[5] Bezalel Porten et al., editors, *The Elephantine Papyri in English: Three Millennia of Cross-Cultural Continuity and Change,* Documenta et Monumenta Orientis Antiqui 22 (Leiden: Brill, 1996); Yigael Yadin et al., *The Finds from the Bar Kokhba Period in the Cave of Letters,* 3 vols., Judean Desert Studies (Jerusalem: Israel Exploration Society, 1963–2002) [NB: vols. 2 and 3 are titled *Documents* instead of *Finds*].

Religion in the ancient world was usually embedded in either political or kinship structures. That is, it was normally a function of either the political group or kin-group to which one belonged. We are fortunate to have numerous texts of epic literature, liturgies, and rituals. These include such things as creation stories, purification rituals, and the interpretation of sheep livers for omens. The Dead Sea Scrolls, for example, provide us with biblical books, texts of biblical interpretation, community regulations, and liturgical texts from the second temple period.[6]

Another key element has been the study of law. A variety of legal principles, laws, and collections of regulations provide windows on social structures, economics, governance, property rights, and punishments. The stele of Hammurabi of Babylon (c. 1700 BCE) is certainly the most famous. But we have many more, for example: Ur-Nammu (c. 2100 BCE), Lipit-Ishtar (c. 1850 BCE), and the Middle Assyrian Laws (c. 1150 BCE).

The intention of Ancient Texts and Translations (ATT) is to make available a variety of ancient documents and document collections to a broad range of readers. The series will include reprints of long out-of-print volumes, revisions of earlier editions, and completely new volumes. The understanding of an-cient societies depends upon our close reading of the documents, however fragmentary, that have survived.

—K. C. Hanson
Series Editor

---

[6] Florentino Garcia Martinez, *The Dead Sea Scrolls Translated: The Qumran Texts in English,* 2d ed., trans. Wilfred G. E. Watson (Grand Rapids: Eerdmans, 1996).

Select Bibliography

Beaulieu, Paul-Alain. *Legal and Administrative Texts from the Reign of Nabonidus.* Yale Oriental Series: Babylonian Texts 1. New Haven: Yale Univ. Press,

Beckman, Gary. *Old Babylonian Archival Texts in the Yale Babylonian Collection.* Catalogue of the Babylonian Collections at Yale 4. Bethesda, Md.: CDL, 2000.

Bergmann, E., et al., editors. *Codex Hammurabi.* 3d ed. 2 vols. Pontificio Instituto Biblico Scripta 51. Rome: Pontifical Biblical Institute, 1950–53.

Beyerlin, Walter, editor. *Near Eastern Religious Texts Relating to the Old Testament.* Translated by John Bowden. Old Testament Library. Philadelphia: Westminster, 1978.

Biggs, Robert D. *Šà.zi.ga: Ancient Mesopotamian Potency Incantations.* Texts from Cuneiform Sources 2. Locust Valley, N.Y.: Augustin, 1967.

Clay, Albert T. *Miscellaneous Inscriptions in the Yale Babylonian Collection.* Yale Oriental Series: Babylonian Texts 1. New Haven: Yale Univ. Press, 1915.

———. *Neo-Babylonian Letters from Erech.* Yale Oriental Series: Babylonian Texts 3. New Haven: Yale Univ. Press, 1919.

Dalley, Stephanie. *Myths from Mesopotamia.* Oxford: Oxford Univ. Press, 1989.

———. *Old Babylonian Texts in the Ashmolean Museum: Texts from Kish and Elsewhere.* Oxford Editions of Cuneiform Texts 13. Oxford: Clarendon, 1991.

Dijk, Jan van, editor. *Texts in the Iraq Museum.* 9 vols. Leiden: Brill, 1964–.

———, Albrecht Goetze, and Mary I. Hussey. *Early Mesopotamian Incantations and Rituals.* Yale Oriental Series: Babylonian Texts 11. New Haven: Yale Univ. Press, 1985.

Dossin, Georges, and André Parrot, editors. *Archives Royales de Mari: Textes.* Paris: Geuthner, 1942–.

Driver, G. R. *Letters of the First Babylonian Dynasty.* Oxford Editions of Cuneiform Texts 3. Oxford: Clarendon, 1924.

———, and John C. Miles. *The Babylonian Laws.* Rev. ed. 2 vols. Ancient Codes and Laws of the Near East. Oxford: Clarendon, 1960–68.

Faust, David Earl. *Contracts from Larsa, Dated in the Reign of Rim-Sin.* Yale Oriental Series: Babylonian Texts 8. New Haven: Yale Univ. Press, 1941.

Foster, Benjamin R. *Before the Muses: An Anthology of Akkadian Literature.* 3d ed. Bethesda, Md.: CDL, 2005.

———. *From Distant Days: Myths, Tales and Poetry from Ancient Mesopotamia.* Bethesda, Md.: CDL, 1995.

———, Douglas Frayne, and Gary Beckman. *The Epic of Gilgamesh: A New Translation, Analogues, Criticism.* Norton Critical Edition. New York: Norton, 2001.

George, A. R. *The Babylonian Gilgamesh Epic: Introduction, Critical Edition, and Cuneiform Texts.* 2 vols. Oxford: Oxford Univ. Press, 2003.

Glassner, Jean-Jacques. *Mesopotamian Chronicles.* Writings from the Ancient World 19. Atlanta: Society of Biblical Literature, 2004.

Goetze, Albrecht. *Old Babylonian Omen Texts.* Yale Oriental Series: Babylonian Texts 10. New Haven: Yale Univ. Press, 1947.

———. *The Laws of Eshnunna.* Annual of the American Schools of Oriental Research 31. New Haven: Dept. of Antiquities of the Government of Iraq and the American Schools of Oriental Research, 1956.

Grayson, A. Kirk. *Assyrian and Babylonian Chronicles.* Texts from Cuneiform Sources 5. Locust Valley, N.Y.: Augustin, 1970. Reprint, Winona Lake, Ind.: Eisenbrauns, 2000.

———. *Assyrian Royal Inscriptions.* 2 vols. Records of the Ancient Near East. Wiesbaden: Harrassowitz, 1972–.

———. *Babylonian Historical-Literary Texts.* Toronto Semitic Texts and Studies 3. Toronto: Univ. of Toronto Press, 1975.

———. *Assyrian Rulers of the Third and Second Millennia BC (to 1115 BC).* Royal Inscriptions of Mesopotamia: Assyrian Periods 1. Toronto: Univ. of Toronto Press, 1987.

———. *Assyrian Rulers of the Early First Millennium BC I (1114–859 BC).* Royal Inscriptions of Mesopotamia: Assyrian Periods 2. Toronto: Univ. of Toronto Press, 1991.

Gurney, O. R. *The Middle Babylonian Legal and Economic Texts from Ur.* Oxford: Alden, 1983.

———. *Literary and Miscellaneous Texts in the Ashmolean Museum.* Oxford Editions of Cuneiform Texts 11. Oxford: Clarendon, 1989.

Hallo, William W., and K. Lawson Younger Jr., editors. *The Context of Scripture.* Vol. 1: *Canonical Compositions from the Biblical World.* Leiden: Brill, 1997.

———. *The Context of Scripture.* Vol. 2: *Monumental Inscriptions from the Biblical World.* Leiden: Brill, 1999.

———. *The Context of Scripture.* Vol. 3: *Archival Documents from the Biblical World.* Leiden: Brill, 2002.

Hinke, W. J. *Selected Babylonian Kudurru Inscriptions.* Semitic Study Series 14. Leiden: Brill, 1911.

Jastrow, Morris Jr., and Albert T. Clay. *An Old Babylonian Version of the Gilgamesh Epic: On the Basis of Recently Discovered Texts.* Yale Oriental Series: Researches 4.3. New Haven: Yale Univ. Press, 1920.

Lau, Robert J., and Stephen Langdon. *The Annals of Ashurbanipal (V Rawlinson pl. I-X).* Semitic Study Series 2. Leiden: Brill, 1903.

Luckenbill, Daniel David. *The Annals of Sennacherib.* University of Chicago Oriental Institute Publications 2. Chicago: Univ. of Chicago Press, 1924. Reprint, Eugene, Ore.: Wipf & Stock, 2005.

———. *Ancient Records of Assyria and Babylonia.* 2 vols. Chicago: Univ. of Chicago Press, 1926–27.

Lutz, Henry Frederick. *Early Babylonian Letters from Larsa.* Yale Oriental Series: Babylonian Texts 2. New Haven: Yale Univ. Press, 1917.

McEwan, Gilbert J. P. *Late Babylonian Texts in the Ashmolean Museum.* Oxford Editions of Cuneiform Texts 10. Oxford: Clarendon, 1984.

Mercer, Samuel A. B. *The Tell Amarna Tablets.* 2 vols. Toronto: Macmillan, 1939.

Michalowski, Piotr. *Letters from Early Mesopotamia.* Writings from the Ancient World 3. Atlanta: Scholars, 1993.

Nissinen, Martti. *Prophets and Prophecy in the Ancient Near East.* Writings from the Ancient World 12. Atlanta: Society of Biblical Literature, 2003.

Piepkorn, Arthur Carl. *Historical Prism Inscriptions of Ashurbanipal.* Assyriological Studies 5. Chicago: Univ. of Chicago Press, 1933.

Pritchard, James B., editor. *Ancient Near Eastern Texts Relating to the Old Testament.* 3d ed. Princeton: Princeton Univ. Press, 1969.

Rawlinson, H. C. *A Selection from the Miscellaneous Inscriptions of Assyria and Babylonia.* Cuneiform Inscriptions of Western Asia 5. London: Harrison, 1909.

Reynolds, Frances. *The Babylonian Correspondence of Esarhaddon, and Letters to Assurbanipal and Sin-Sarru-Iskun from Northern and Central Babylonia.* State Archives of Assyria 18. Helsinki: Helsinki Univ. Press, 2003.

Stephens, Ferris J. *Votive and Historical Texts from Babylonia and Assyria.* Yale Oriental Series: Babylonian Texts 9. New Haven: Yale Univ. Press, 1937.

Thomas, D. Winton, editor. *Documents from Old Testament Times.* Ancient Texts and Translations. Eugene, Ore.: Wipf & Stock, 2005.

Whiting, Robert M. *Old Babylonian Letters from Tell Asmar.* Assyriological Studies 22. Chicago: Oriental Institute, 1987.

TO

THE VERY REV.

E. A. HOFFMAN

D.D., D.C.L., LL.D.

DEAN OF THE GENERAL THEOLOGICAL SEMINARY

NEW YORK CITY, U.S.A.

THIS IS AFFECTIONATELY DEDICATED

AS A SMALL TOKEN OF GREAT

GRATITUDE BY THE

AUTHOR

PREFACE

THE following pages, herewith issued, were written as a Doctor's Dissertation, and submitted as such to the Faculty of Philosophy, Columbia University, New York City, N.Y., in April, 1898. Ever since August of the same year the book has been in the press, yet I have not failed to supplement it by all the inscriptions which have been published up to April 1, 1900. Many able and scholarly histories of the period treated by me have been written. I mention among others only Tiele, Babylonisch-assyrische Geschichte, 1886–8; Hommel, Geschichte Babyloniens und Assyriens, 1885; Winckler, Geschichte Babyloniens und Assyriens, 1892; Meyer, Geschichte des Alterthums, B. i., 1884; Mürdter-Delitzsch, Geschichte Babyloniens, second edition, 1891; Maspero, Dawn of Civilization, New York, 1895; McCurdy, History, Prophecy, and the Monuments, 1894; Rogers, Outlines of the History of Early Babylonia, 1895; Ball, Light from the East, 1899; Winckler, Das alte Westasien, in Helmott's Weltgeschichte, Dritter Band, erste Hälfte, 1899.

From the above-given list it would seem as if another history were superfluous. Yet I have ventured to write another, having the following points especially in view:—

1. To arrange as far as possible the kings of the different dynasties so far known to us according to a certain chronological order. Whether I have succeeded in this remains for the reader to decide. Here I want to say that I have my doubts with regard to the dynasty of Isin as well as that of Ur III. It may very well be possible that Ishbigirra, king of Isin, belongs to another—either earlier or later—dynasty. In this case we would have to divide that dynasty, and either leave the other kings where we have placed them, or put them after Ur IV. Gungunu and his dynasty would have to undergo then, of course, the same fate.

2. To transcribe and translate—wherever it was possible—all those texts which are not to be found in K. B. iii[1]. By doing this I thought to help not only the historian, but also beginners in the study of Sumerian inscriptions, of whom I am the first and foremost. Everybody who has studied these oldest of all inscriptions knows the difficulties that are to be encountered. It would have been great arrogance on my part to have attempted to translate them, were it not for the excellent works of such scholars as Jensen, Hilprecht, and Thureau-Dangin. They—and especially the latter—have been my teachers; on the basis of their transcriptions and translations those to be found in the following pages have been made. While thus attempting to transcribe and translate these inscriptions, I first tried—wherever necessary—to identify the signs either according to T. C. or to E. C., which latter book came too late into my hands to be quoted throughout. Had it reached me earlier, it would have saved me considerable anxiety, and probably prevented my making many mistakes. After the sign in question had been identified I tried to establish its meaning, which has always been done according to Br. and H. W. B.,

thus affording a means to control the transcription and translation.

3. To give in a note under each respective king all inscriptions that belong to that king—where they have been published, where transcribed and translated. In this way I thought to help the reader in comparing the different translations so far extant with each other—in what respect they agree and where they differ. If there should be found some inscriptions already published that are not mentioned, this is due to the fact that the libraries which I was permitted to consult did not contain the books I was so anxiously looking for.

4. To presuppose some knowledge of the grammar of the Sumerian language by the reader. One may rightly expect that even a beginner in Sumerian should have studied the grammars of Haupt and Hommel before attempting to translate Old Babylonian inscriptions.

5. To avoid deductions from the inscriptions as far as possible, for every reader can himself make them from the documents, provided that the translation be correct. Whether it was possible for me to give in all cases the correct translations masters of Sumeriology alone can determine.

6. To avoid all legendary matter. This explains why I should have begun with Enshagkushanna rather than with the 'kings before the Flood.' History, if it wants to be history, must be based upon original documents, and not upon legends.

I would like to add here one word about the pronunciation *Šir-pur-la-*^{ki}. In Gudea, Cyl. B, v. 22 (and only there, as far as I know), the name of the city is written *Šir-pur-*^{ki}, without *LA*! This, no doubt, seems to speak—if we do not want to accept a mistake of the scribe—for the pronunciation *Šir-pul-la-*^{ki}, the *LA* containing only the overhanging vowel. With this, however, is not yet proved *absolutely* that we now have to pronounce, with Prof. Hommel, *Sir-gul-la-*^{ki} and to identify it with Zerghul; for *Sir-pu*$^{l}_{r}$*-la-*^{ki} is Tell-Loh, and not Zerghul. For such an interchange of *r* and *l*, see Hommel, S. L. p. 139 *h*, and comp. the Assyrian and later Babylonian *martu*, *maltu*, *maštu*; *Kardu-niaš*, *Kaldu*, *Kašdu* (כַּשְׂדִּים); see also Delitzsch, Assyr. Gram. § 51, p. 120. Hence this much only we can say: the sign for *PUR* had in all probability also the value *PUL*.

While writing the History, Hilprecht's O. B. I. vol. i. Part II. was accessible to me only with the paging it had as a part of the publication of the American Philosophical Society. The following may be of help for those who use Part II. with the new paging. Abstract in each case 214, and you get the page according to the other edition. E. g. p. 263 is = 263 − 214 = p. 49 of the new edition.

The different lists added at the end of the book may be useful. I have also prepared a glossary, giving the context, the places where the expression is to be found, and, if possible, also the translation. This glossary includes not only all the inscriptions here translated, but also those of K. B. iii[1]., Cylinders A and B of Gudea, and the Sumerian inscriptions of Ḫammurabi. It being arranged according to the signs as given in Brünnow might make it a helpful appendix to that publication. If it should be desired, I shall issue it in the near future.

If the whole arrangement of the book should be acceptable to the learned world, I purpose to treat also the other periods in the same way. The material for the history of Dynasties A–C of Babylon I have gathered already.

It only remains to thank the Very Rev. E. A. Hoffman, D.D. (Oxon.), D.C.L., LL.D., Dean of the Gen. Theol. Sem., New York City, my highly esteemed friend, for his kindness and liberality. Had it not been for his help and generosity these pages would never have been published. May he kindly accept these my 'first-fruits,' and may he be spared for the General Theological Seminary, as well as for science and research, for still a good many years to come! Also to the Rev. C. W. E. Body, D.D., D.C.L., Professor of Old Testament Literature in the Gen. Theol. Sem., New York City, my heartiest thanks are due. His assistance in acquiring and arranging the 'E. A. Hoffman Collection,' as well as his help in reading the proof-sheets, and the many other kindnesses and favours shown to me during the last five years are and always will be remembered most kindly by his friend and pupil. To express to my teacher and revered friend, Professor R. J. H. Gottheil, my sense of lasting obligation gives me special pleasure. During three years of special study his library, time, and scholarship have been most generously at my disposal.

HUGO RADAU.

MUNICH, BAVARIA,
April 1, 1900.

CONTENTS

The numbers in parentheses ( ) indicate the pages.

PAGES

I. INTRODUCTION 1–43

Chronology based upon (*a*) *incidental references* and (*b*) *palaeographic evidence* (3). Eponym Canon. List of kings. Assyrian mode of dating documents. The eclipse under Pur-Sagale (4). Date of Nabû-nâ'id. *ŠAR-GE-NA* and Naram-Sin mentioned by Nabû-nâ'id. Date of Naram-Sin. *ŠAR-GE-NA* an abbreviation of Sharganisharâli. (*b*) *Palaeographic evidence* (8). List of signs. Three great periods (9). (*c*) *Chronology of the kings and patesis of Shirpurla* (12). Dynasty of Ur-Ninâ (15). Kings preceding Ur-Ninâ. Representatives of the second period of palaeography (17). Rulers between Lummadur and Ur-Ba'u (18). Younger patesis of Shirpurla (19). Representatives of the third period of palaeography (23). Ur II. (24). Nisin (25). Ur III. and IV. (26). (*d*) *Chronological Table.* (*e*) *Dates assigned to the different rulers* (30). *Date of Gudea* according to Thureau-Dangin (31); Lehmann and Winckler (32). *Ur-Ningirsu en ki-ag (dingir) Ninâ* (35). Another arrangement of the younger patesis of Shirpurla (39). Palaeography according to Lehmann (42).

II. LORD OF KENGI 43–46

Enshagkushanna (43). O. B. I. 90–92 (45).

III. RULERS OF SHIRPURLA 46–121

A. Dynasty of *Urukagina* (47 ff.). Titles of Urukagina (46). Translations: Le Clercq, ii. pl. viii. No. 1 (48); Déc. pl. 5, No. 1 (51); Déc. 32 = Barrel-Cylinder (53). *Enĝegal* (54). *Lugalshuggur* (56). Their contemporaries are in all probability the following kings or patesis of Kish: *U-dug-?* (55, 2); *Mesilim* (55); *Lugal-da?-ak?* (56, 2).

B. Dynasty of *Ur-Ninâ* (56 ff.). Translations: Déc. 2ter, 4 (58); Déc. 2ter, 2 (61); Déc. 31, 1 (64); R. A. iv. p. 122, 1 (64); R. A. iv.

PAGES

p. 106, 11 (65); Déc. 2bis, 2 (66); Déc. 3ter, 1 (66); Déc. 2bis, 1 (68). *Akurgal* (65). *The other sons of Ur-Ninâ* (70). Titles of Ur-Ninâ, Akurgal (70), and Eannatum (71). *Enannatum I.* (72). Translations: R. A. iii. p. 31 (14); Comptes Rendus, 1899, p. 348, pl. ii. (72). *Eannatum* (71 ff.). Stèle des Vautours compared with Cône of Entemena and Galet A (74). Treaty with Gishban (74 ff.). *Mesilim, Ush, Gunammide, Enakalli* (75). Inscriptions recording the treaty: Déc. 3 A, col. i. (76); Déc. 3 A, col. iii. 4, Déc. 3 A, col. iv. 1, and Déc. 4ter, F[2], col. iv. 2 ff. (77); Déc. 3bis, D[1], col. i. 1 ff. (78); Déc. 4ter, F[2], col. iii. 4; Déc. 3 A, col. ii. 2 (80); C. T. 23580 (81, note 1). Name of the stèle (81). Eannatum's victory over different cities (82). Becomes king of Kish (82). Eannatum as administrator and builder (83). Galet A (83). Déc. 4bis, D[2], col. iii. 7–15: *Gunammide* (87 note). R. A. iv. p. 122, No. 2 (= Déc. 2ter, fig. 5) (87 note). Déc. 31, No. 2 *a*, *b* (93). Gishban invades the territory of Shirpurla again (95). *Urlumma. Enannatum I.* (95). *Entemena.* Victory over *Urlumma. Ili* becomes patesi of Gishban (96). Subscription of the Cône (97). The Cône of Entemena (97 ff.). Situation of Gishban (110), Guedin (111), and Kish (112). The building inscriptions of Entemena. Translations: Tablette A = R. A. ii. 148, 149 (112); Déc. pl. 5, No. 2 (116); Déc. 43 and 43bis (Vase d'argent) (116); Déc. 5bis, No. 2 (Dudu) (117); C. T. part V. No. 12061 (= A. B. K. No. 4) (117); O. B. I. 115 (118); O. B. I. 117, 116 (119); Déc. 31, 3 (= R. A. ii. 87) (13). *Enannatum II.* (119). Inscriptions translated: Déc. 6, 4 (13); C. T. 23287 (120). *Lummadur* (120). Inscription (15, 1).

IV. Kings of Kish and Gishban 121–150

A. Kish:

U-dug-? (121, 1). *Mesilim* (121). His inscription (16, 143, 144). *Lugal-da ?-ak ?* (121, 2). *Enne-Ugun* (121). Inscriptions: O. B. I. 103, 104 (123); 102, 110, 105 (124). *Urzaguddu* (125, 151). *Lugaltarsi* (125). The meaning of the titles *lugal KIŠ* and *lugal KIŠ-ki* respectively (126). *Manishtusu* (127). *Âlusharshid* (127). Translations: O. B. I. 5 (128); O. B. I. 6, 7, 8; Déc. 5, 4 (128, 2). *An unknown king*: O. B. I. 118 (129, 3).

B. Gishban:

Ush (74). *Gunammide* (?) (75, 87 note). *Enakalli. Urlumma* (95). *Ili* (96). *Ukush* (130). *Lugalzaggisi* (130). Becomes 'king of Erech and of the world.' His inscription: O. B. I. 87 (131). The time of Lugalzaggisi (11, 144). His nationality. The question of Sumeriology as such. Hilprecht's view (142). The oldest kings bear good Semitic names (142, 1). Semitic phrases (145, 2), and

PAGES

Semitisms in Sumerian inscriptions (145, 3). Thureau-Dangin's view (148). Where was the original home of the Semites, and at what time did they invade Babylonia? (149). *Ezuab* (150, 4).

V. The First Dynasty of Ur 150–153

Lugalkigubnidudu (150). Becomes 'lord' (151), and later on even 'king of Erech' (152). Translations: O. B. I. 86 (151); O. B. I. 23, 24, 25 (152, 15). *Lugalkisalsi*, his son. Mentioned on O. B. I. 86, pl. 37 (152); O. B. I. 89 (153, 6).

VI. The Patesis of Shirpurla between Lummadur and Ur-Ba'u 153–154

Lugalanda. R. A. iv. No. 3, pl. iii. No. 9 (16). *Lugalushumgal*. His inscriptions (153, 1). His son (?) *UR-E* (20), both being contemporaries of Sargon I. and Naram-Sin (see p. 7, and *sub* 'kings of Agade'). A *nam-patesi* of *Ur* is mentioned at this time. Was it *Ur-(dingir) Utu* (?) who held the patesiate of Ur? (154).

VII. Kings of Agade 154–175

Sharganisharâli, the son of *Itti-Bêl* (154). The legend (155). Tablet of Omens (156). The historicity of the Tablet of Omens proved by inscriptions of Sharganisharâli and Naram-Sin: victory over Elam (158 *a*); over the West-land (159 *b*); over Gutim (159 *c*); over Erech and . . . . *su-ki* (160 *d*). Other dates of Sargon I. and Naram-Sin (160, 3). Cities mentioned in the inscriptions (161). *Lugalushumgal*, patesi of Shirpurla, their contemporary (7, 162). The extent of Sargon I.'s and Naram-Sin's dominion (162). Titles of the two kings respectively (163). *Šar kibrat arba'i*, *lugal-kalamma*, *lugal an-ub-da tab-tab-ba*, *šar kiššati* (165). Sargon I. and Naram-Sin as administrators (164). The sign *ilu* before their names (164). The Nimrod-Epos (166). The tree of life (167). Inscriptions of Sargon I. translated: R. A. iv. p. 8 (7); R. A. iv. p. 3 (. . . *ne-šu-in-ta*) (154, note 2); Hommel, Geschichte, p. 302 (*Ib-ni-šarri*) (155 note); R. A. iv. No. iii. pl. vi. No. 16 (158 *a*); ibid. pl. vi. No. 17 (159 *b*); ibid. pl. v. No. 15 (159 *c*); ibid. No. 13 (160); Compt. Rend. 1896 (Reprint), p. 10, No. 4 (160 *d*); R. A. iv. No. iii. pl. v. No. 14; ibid. pl. vi. No. 18 (160, 3); O. B. I. 1 (167); O. B. I. 2 (169); O. B. I. 3 (161).

Naram-Sin, son of Sargon I. (170). Translations: R. A. iv. p. 11 (7); ibid. No. iii. pl. vi. No. 19 (160, 3); Comptes Rendus, 1899, p. 348, pl. 1 (162); R. A. iv. No. iii. pl. vii. Nos. 22, 23, 26 (165); Rec. Trav. xix. p. 187 (166); O. B. I. 120 (171); Déc. 44, fig. 1, and O. B. I. 4 (171 note).

PAGES

Binganisharâli, son of Naram-Sin (173). Hommel, Gesch. p. 299 (173); Comptes Rendus, 1897, p. 190 (173, 1). *Nabe-?-mash*, patesi of Tutu, brother of Binganisharâli (173). *Lipush-Iaum*, daughter of Nabe-?-mash (173). Comptes Rend. 1899, p. 348, pl. 1 (173).

VIII. THE KINGS OF GUTI AND LULUBI 175–180

Lasirab, king of Guti (175). His inscription: Z, A. iv. p. 406 (175). *Anu-Bânini*, king of Lulubi (176). His inscription: Rec. Trav. xiv. pp. 100–106 (177). The Semitic dynasties in Babylonia (178). The invasion of the Semites (179). Language of the Semites and Sumerians (179).

IX. THE SO-CALLED LATER PATESIS OF SHIRPURLA . 181–215

On whom were these later patesis dependent? (181). *Ur-Ba'u*. Translations: Déc. 27, 2 (182); Déc. 37, 1, 2 (183); ibid. 38, 2; E. A. H. 112, 113 (185). *Nammaǵni* (185), Ur-Ba'u's son-in-law (186). Translations: R. A. ii. p. 79 (19); C. T. 96-6-15, 1 (186). Names of statues, &c. (187, 12). Nammaǵni's successors (187). *Gudea*. Gudea's dream (189). His buildings (191). Extent of realm (192). His wars. Translations: Déc. 25bis, 1 *b* (191); P. S. B. A. 1890, p. 63, No. ii; Déc. 37, 4; E. A. H. 114, 115 (194); Déc. 38, 1, 3, 6; 29, 1 (195); Déc. 26, 2; 44, 2 (196). Statues of Gudea (196). Statue A (197). Statue C (199). Statue E (202). Statue H (209). *Ur-Ningirsu*, son of Gudea (210). *Ur-Ninsun* (211). His inscription: R. A. ii. 79 (21). (*Ga*)*lukani I.* How many patesis, (Ga)lukani by name, are known? He is dependent on Dungi I. (212). His inscription: Déc. 21, 4 (21). History of Shirpurla recapitulated (212). Meaning of the titles *lugal-kalamma* (214), *lugal an-ub-da tab-tab-ba* (*šar kibrat arba'i*), *šar kiššati* (215).

X. THE SECOND DYNASTY OF UR 215–225

Meaning of the title *lugal Ki-en-gi-ki-Urdu* (216). Why did the kings adopt that title? (218). Pognon's, Winckler's, and Lehmann's views with regard to the meaning of the title (221). *Ur-Gur*. Translations: O. B. I. 121; 122; 14 (222). *Dungi I.*, son of Ur-Gur (223). His buildings. Translations: O. B. I. 16; 123; C. T. 7287 = A. F. p. 547, 8 (224).

XI. KINGS OF ERECH 225–228

Singâshid and his inscriptions (225). *Singâmil* (226). *AN-A-AN-Giš-dub-ba. Ilû-ma*, O. B. I. 26 (226, 2). *Bil-Gur* (227).

PAGES

XII. Kings of Isin 228–234

Ia-lu-un-a-šar, R. T. xix. p. 48 (229). *Libit-Anunit* and his inscriptions (229, 1). *Iš-pi-gir-ra*. *Ur-Ninib* and his inscriptions (230). Translation of O. B. I. 18. *Bur-Sin II*. Translation of O. B. I. 19 (231). *Idîn-Dagan*. His inscription, R. T. xvi. p. 187, translated (232). *Ishme-Dagan* (233).

XIII. The Third Dynasty of Ur 234–237

Gungunu (25, 234). *Enannatum*, son of Ishme-Dagan. *Ur-Gur II.* (?). *Dungi II.* (235). Translations: O. B. I. 15 (236); R. A. iv. p. 90 (22); U. A. G. p. 157, 9 (37).

XIV. The Fourth Dynasty of Ur 238–287

Are Dungi I., II., and III. one and the same person? Winckler's theory (238–249). *Dungi III.* (249). Translations: R. T. xviii. p. 73 (250); A. B. K. 37 (251); E. A. H. 61 (251); C. T. 17288 (252). *Dates of Dungi III.* O. B. I. 125 (254, 6 ff.). *Dates of Bur-Sin II.* (266). Translations: O. B. I. 127 (266, 1 ff.); R. T. xx. p. 67 (269, 11); O. B. I. 20 (270); O. B. I. 21 (271); E. A. H. 26 = C. T. 12156 (273); R. A. iv. pl. xxxi. No. 80 (240, 1). *Ur-Ba'u II.* (274). R. T. xix. p. 49. *Dates of Gimil-Sin* (275). O. B. I. 127 (276); Peters, Nippur, ii. p. 239 (277); R. A. iv. pl. xxxi. No. 81 (240, 1). R. T. xix. p. 186 (315). *Dates of Ine-Sin* (278). R. A. iv. pl. xxxi. No. 82 (240, 1). *Uncertain Dates* (279). Progress of history from Ur IV. till the time of Ḫammurabi (282).

XV. The Names of the Months 287–307

The months at the time of Sargon I and of Ur IV. (287). The Canaanitish months (289). E. A. H. 134 (291); v. R. 43 (294). Of how many days consisted a year? (303). The intercalary months. The days of a month (306). Comparative table of the names of the months.

XVI. The sign of 'god' before certain Proper Names 307–317

XVII. APPENDIX: The E. A. Hoffman Collection of Babylonian Clay-tablets 319–434

General survey (321). The *mu-gub zig-ga* tablets (333). Other tablets, similar to the preceding (366). Accounts of wool (384). Officials (409). Patesis of Ashnunna (433).

XVIII. INDICES 435–452

List of Proper Names (435). List of gods (442). Buildings (446). Cities and lands (448).

The following tablets of the E. A. H. Collection have been translated:—

	PAGES
E. A. H. 14	265, 50 *a*; 333 ff., 354
19	265, 50 *b*; 333 ff., 356
26 (Bur-Sin II.)	273
27	266, 1; 423
33, 34	266, 2; 366 ff.
33	372
34	376
35, 37	266, 3; 333 ff.
35	358
37	360
47-49	266, 3; 384 ff.
47	386
48	388
49	390
50, 51, 53, 54	266, 3
50	394
51	396
53	398
54	426
56	267, 4; 399
E. A. H. 61	251; 267, 4
87	269, 9; 421
96, 109	416
96	260, 34 *a*; 418
100, 102	430
100	261, 41; 431
102	432
104	362
106	428
107	404
108	327
109	280, 4; 420
110, 111. Ur-Ningishzidda	433
112, 113. Ur-Ba'u	185
114, 115. Gudea	194
121	380
122	384 ff.; 392
134. Months	299
152	407

Transcriptions and translations of inscriptions to be found in E. de Sarzec, Découvertes en Chaldée (Déc.).

Déc. 2, 1. Ur-Ninâ	59, 16
2bis, 1. ,,	59, 16; 68
2bis, 2. ,,	66
2ter, 1. ,,	66
2ter, 2. ,,	12; 59, 16; 61
2ter, 4. ,,	58
2ter, 5 (= R. A. iv. p. 122, No. 2). Eannatum	87, note
3 A. ,,	76, 77, 80
3bis, D^1. ,,	78
3bis, E^1. ,,	71, 1; 82, 3
4 A. ,,	71, 1
4bis, D^2 (Gunammide?)	87
4ter, F^1. Eannatum	82, 2, 4
4ter, F^2. ,,	77; 80; 80 note
5, 1. Urukagina	51
5, 2. Entemena	116
Déc. 5, 3. Ezuab	150, 4
5, 4. Âlusharshid	128, 2
5bis, 1 *a* (= R. A. ii. 148, 149). Entemena	112
5bis, 2. Dudu	117
6, 4. Enannatum II.	13
9. Statue D of Gudea	60, note
10 and 13, 1. Statue C of Gudea	199
11 and 13, 2. ,, E ,,	202
13, 4. Statue H of Gudea	209
16 ff. ,, B ,,	136, 32; 197; 410
20 and 15, 5. Statue A of Gudea	197
21, 4. Gala-Lama	21
25bis, 1 *b*. Gudea	191
26, 2 ,,	196
27, 2. Ur-Ba'u	182

PAGES

Déc. 27, 3 (= E. A. H. 114, 115). Gudea 194
29, 1 (= A. B. K. p. 4, No. 9). Gudea 195
29, 4. Dungi I. 224, 4
31, 1 (= R. A. iv. p. 91). Ur-Ninâ 64
31, 2 *a*, *b*. Eannatum . . . 93
31, 3 (= R. A. ii. 87) Entemena 13; 104, 21
32. Barrel-Cylinder of Urukagina 53
Dec. 37, 1, 2. Ur-Ba'u . . . 183
37, 3, 4. Gudea 193
37, 8. *Ur-Ningirsu en (dingir) Ninâ* 37, 1
37, 10. Nammaǵni . . . 185, 1
38, 1, 3, 6. Gudea 195
38, 2. Ur-Ba'u 183
43, 43bis. Vase d'argent of Entemena 116
44, 1. Naram-Sin . . 171, note
44, 2. Gudea 196

Transcriptions and translations of inscriptions to be found in H. V. Hilprecht, Old Babylonian Inscriptions, chiefly from Nippur (O. B. I.).

No. 1. Sargon I. 167
2. „ 169
3. „ 161
4. Naram-Sin . . . 171, note
5. Âlusharshid 128
6–8. „ 128, 2
14. Ur-Gur 222
15. Dungi II. 236
16. Dungi I. 224
18. Ur-Ninib 230
19. Bur-Sin I. 231
20. Bur-Sin II. 270
21. „ 271
23, 24, 25. Lugalkigubnidudu 152, 15
26. Ilûma 226, 2
43. Kurigalzu 236
49. „ . . . 208, ix. 2
61. Kaddishman-Turgu (*sic*) 208, ix. 2
63. Kadashman-Turgu . 161, 1; 169, 24
86, pl. 36. Lugalkigubnidudu 151
86, pl. 37. „ and Lugalkisalsi 152
87. Lugalzaggisi 131
89. Lugalkisalsi . . . 153, 6
No. 90–92. Enshagkushanna . 45
93. Urzaguddu 125, 1
94. Ur-Enlil . 30, 1; 44. 4; 410
95. Ur-Mama . . 30, 1; 410
96, 97. Ur-Enlil 30, 1
102. Enne-Ugun 124
103, 104. „ 123
105. „ 124
108, 109. Udug-? . 55, 2; 121, 1
110. Enne-Ugun 124
111. Lugalshir(ge?) . . 89, 22
112. *dumu Adda-ge* . . 89, 22; 114, v. 5
113. . . . . . . 114, v. 5
115. Entemena 118
116, 117. „ 119
118. Unknown king of Kish 129, 3
119. Unknown (?) king of Agade 154, 2
120. Naram-Sin 171
121, 122. Ur-Gur 222
123. Dungi I. 224
124. . . . . . . 27; 333 ff.; 366
125. Dates of Dungi III. 254, 6 ff.
126. . . . 267, 5; 333 ff.; 412
127. Dates of Bur-Sin II. and Gimil-Sin . . . 27; 266 ff.

Transcriptions and translations of inscriptions to be found in C. T.

PAGES

96-6-12, 3 (=R. T. xxi. 125). (*Ga*)*lu-* (*dingir*) *Utu* 30, 1; 300, iii.

96-6-15, 1. Nammagni (Ninkagina) 186

7287 (=A. F. p. 547, 8). Dungi 224

12033. Bazi 30, 1

12061 (=A. B. K. No. 4). Entemena 117

PAGES

12146. King of *Ma-uru-ki* 30, 1

12155. Lugaltarsi . . . 125, 3

12156 (=E. A. H. 26). Bur-Sin II. 273

12217. (*Ga*)*lu-ligir-e* (Dungi) 237, i.

17288 (=A. F. vi. p. 547, 7). Dungi III. 252

23580. Eannatum . . . . 81, i.

(For the subscriptions to be found on certain tablets of this publication, see among other places also pp. 74, 1; 245; 246; Notes to dates of Dungi III., Bur-Sin II., Gimil-Sin, Ine-Sin, Uncertain dates, pp. 252-281; 288, 1, and 315, 1.)

Transcriptions and translations of inscriptions to be found in Revue d'Assyriologie et d'Archéologie Orientale (R. A.).

R. A. ii. p. 79. nin-Kandu . 19
ii. p. 79. Ur-Ninsun . . . 21
ii. pp. 87 (= Déc. 31, 3). Entemena 13
ii. pp. 148, 149 (= Déc. 5bis, 1 *a*). Entemena 112
iii. p. 31. Enannatum I. . . 14
iii. p. 55 and No. ii. pl. iii. (=R. A. iv. p. 35). Mesilim 16; 143; 144
iii. p. 144 278
iv. p. 3. Sargon I. . . . 154, 2
iv. p. 8. ,, . . 7; 154, 2
iv. p. 11. Naram-Sin 7; 171, note
iv. p. 22 ,, . 160, 3
iv. p. 35 (=iii. p. 55). Mesilim 16; 143; 144
iv. p. 90. Dungi II. (Ga)lukani II. 22
iv. p. 91. Ur-Ninâ 64
iv. p. 105 *b* ,, ... 59, 16
iv. p. 106, 11 ,, ... 65
iv. p. 111. *Lugal-da ?-ak ?* 121, 2
iv. p. 122, 1. Ur-Ninâ . . 64
iv. p. 122, 2 (= Déc. 2ter, 5). Eannatum 87
R. A. iv. p. 142. (Dates). . 27
iv. No. i. pl. i. Galet A of Eannatum 12; 83
iv. No. ii. pl. ii. Cône of Entemena 97
iv. No. iii. pl. iii. No. 9. Lugalanda 16
iv. No. iii. pl. v. No. 14. Sargon I. 160, 3
iv. No. iii. pl. vi. No. 13. Sargon I. 160
iv. No. iii. pl. vi. No. 15. Sargon I. or Naram-Sin . 159
Ibid. No. 16. Sargon I. . . 158
Ibid. No. 17. ,, . . 159
Ibid. Nos. 18, 19 (= R. A. iv. p. 22). Naram-Sin . . 160, 3
iv. No. iii. pl. vii. Nos. 22, 23, 26. Naram-Sin 165
Ibid. pl. ix. No. 31. Patesi of Ur . . 20, 3; 154; 249, 1
Ibid. pl. xxxi. Nos. 80 (Bur-Sin II.), 81 (Gimil-Sin), 82 (Ine-Sin) 240, 1

Inscriptions to be found in Recueil de Travaux relatifs à la Philologie et à l'Archéologie Égyptiennes et Assyriennes (R. T.), *cited in this book.*

PAGES

R. T. xiv. p. 100 ff. Anu-Bânini 177
xvi. p. 187. Idîn-Dagan . . 232
xviii. p. 64 ff. . . 244; 247; 312
xviii. p. 73. *Lugal-aš(?)-tur-ri* 250
xviii. p. 74. Utua 211; 238; 243
xix. p. 48. Libit-Anunit . 229
xix. p. 49. Ur-Ba'u II. . . 274
xix. p. 50, 9. Allamu . 212, 1
xix. p. 59, No. 338. Date of Bur-Sin II. 270, 12

PAGES

R. T. xix. p. 61. 281
xix. p. 63. Ur-Nesu. 111; 300, iii.
xix. p. 186. Gimil-Sin . . 315
xix. p. 187. Naram-Sin . . 166
xx. p. 67. Bur-Sin II. . 269, 11
xxi. p. 125 (=C. T. 96-9-12, 3) (*Ga*)*lu*-(*dingir*) *Utu* 30, 1; 300, iii.

Inscriptions to be found in Comptes Rendus des Séances de l'Académie des Inscriptions et Belles-lettres (Comptes Rendus).

Comptes Rendus, 1896 (Reprint), p. 10, No. 4 . . . . 160, *d*
1897, p. 190. Binganisharâli 173, 1
vol. iv. 25, p. 424. Lummadur 15, 1

Comptes Rendus, 1899, p. 348, pl. i. Naram-Sin . . . 162
Ibid. Lipush-Iaum . . . 173
Ibid. pl. ii. Enannatum I. . 72

Inscriptions to be found in H. C. Rawlinson, Cuneiform Inscriptions of Western Asia, vols. i.–v. (R.).

i. R. 1, 1. No. 10. *Ḫashḫamir* 30, 1; 235
i. R. 2, No. vi. 1. Gungunu . 25
i. R. 36, No. 2. Enannatum, son of Ishme-Dagan . . 25
i. R. 68, No. 1, vol. i. 12 ff. Ur-Gur 24

ii. R. 49, 1, cols. 1, 2, ll. 7 ff. Months 292, 1
iii. R. 4, No. 7. Legend of Sargon I. 155
iv. R². 34. Omina of Sargon I. and Naram-Sin . . . 18; 157
v. R. 43. Months 294

Inscriptions to be found in other publications.

(*a*) A. B. K.:
No. 9 (= Déc. 29, 1). Gudea 195
No. 10 (= E. A. H. 114, 115). Gudea 194
No. 16 (= U. A. G. p. 156, No. 7). Mutabil 30, 1; 255, 12
No. 35. Subscription . . 312, 4
No. 37. Dungi III. . . . 251
No. 65 (= Hommel, Geschichte, p. 302). Ibnisharri . . . . . 155, note

(*b*) U. A. G.:
P. 156, No. 7 (= A. B. K. No. 16). Mutabil. 30, 1; 255, 12
P. 157, No. 8. *Ip-ša-*(*dingir*) *Innanna-Erin-ki* . . . 30, 1
P. 157, No. 9. *Ur-Ningirsu en* (*dingir*) *Ninâ* 37

PAGES

(*c*) A. F.:

P. 545, 3. . . . *ši* patesi of . . . *mu-tuk* . . . *ki* . . . 30, 1

P. 545, 4 (= C. T. 12033 ?). [Ba]-zi king of Al . . . 30, 1

P. 547, 7 (= C. T. 17288). Dungi III. 252

P. 547, 8 (= C. T. 7287). Dungi I. 224

(*d*) Hommel, Geschichte Babyloniens und Assyriens:

P. 290. *Iš*(?)-*mà-i-lum*, patesi of *Dun-til ki-la* 30, 1

P. 293. . . . *da*, patesi of *Šit-tar-ki* 30, 1

P. 299. Binganisharâli . . 173

P. 302 (= A. B. K. No. 65). Ibni-sharri . . . 155, note

P. 308. Apil-Ishtar (?) 171, note

P. 334. *Ur-*(*dingir*) *AN-MAĜ* and *Lugal-kal-la*, patesis of Nippur. 30, 1; 223

(*e*) P. S. B. A.:

1890, p. 63, No. i. Alzuzua 82, 4

PAGES

1890, p. 63, No. ii. Gudea. 193

(*f*) Le Clercq:

i. pl. v. No. 461 (= A. B. K. 65). Ibni-sharri . . 155, note

ii. pl. viii. No. 1. Urukagina 48

ii. pl. x. No. 6. Urlumma 95, 1

(*g*) Z. A.:

iv. p. 406. Lasirab . . . 175

xii. p. 267 423

(*h*) Ménant, Glypt. orient. i. p. 104. Bilgur . . . 227

(*i*) Constantinople 622. Dates of Dungi III. and Bur-Sin II. 253

(*k*) Abel und Winckler, Keilschrifttexte, p. 40, col. ii. 46 ff. Nabû-nâ'id . . . 5

(*l*) Peters, Nippur, ii. p. 239. Gimil-Sin 277

(*m*) Muséon, 1892, p. 253, Nos. i-iv. Patesis of Ashnunna 433; 434

SOME ABBREVIATIONS USED IN THE TEXT

A. B. K. = HUGO WINCKLER: Altbabylonische Keilschrifttexte.
A. B. P. R. = BRUNO MEISSNER: Beiträge zum Altbabylonischen Privatrecht.
A. F. = HUGO WINCKLER: Altorientalische Forschungen.
A. L^3. = FRIEDR. DELITZSCH: Assyrische Lesestücke; 3rd edition.
B. A. = FR. DELITZSCH und P. HAUPT: Beiträge zur Assyriologie.
B. O. R. = Babylonian Oriental Records.
Br. = R. E. BRÜNNOW: A Classified List of all . . . Cuneiform Ideographs.
C. T. = Cuneiform Texts from Babylonian Tablets, &c., in the British Museum, Parts i–viii.
Déc. = E. DE SARZEC: Découvertes en Chaldée.
E. A. H. = E. A. Hoffman Collection.
E. C. = F. THUREAU-DANGIN: Recherches sur l'Origine de l'Écriture Cunéiforme.
E. S. = FR. DELITZSCH: Entstehung des Altbabylonischen Schriftsystems.
H. W. B. = FR. DELITZSCH: Assyrisches Handwörterbuch.
J. A. O. S. = Journal of the American Oriental Society.
K. B. = Keilinschriftliche Bibliothek.
O. B. I. = H. V. HILPRECHT: Old Babylonian Inscriptions, chiefly from Nippur.
O. L. Z. = Orientalische Litteratur-Zeitung.
P. S. B. A. = Proceedings of the Society of Biblical Archaeology.
R. = RAWLINSON: Cuneiform Inscriptions of Western Asia.
R. A. = Revue d'Assyriologie et d'Archéologie Orientale.
R. P. = Records of the Past.
R. R. B. L. = H. V. HILPRECHT: Recent Research in Bible Lands.
R. S. = Revue Sémitique d'Épigraphie et d'Histoire Ancienne.
R. T. = Recueil de Travaux relatifs à la Philologie et à l'Archéologie Égyptiennes et Assyriennes.
S. L. = FR. HOMMEL: Sumerische Lesestücke.
T. C. = A. AMIAUD et L. MÉCHINEAU: Tableau Comparé des écritures Babylonienne et Assyrienne.
U. A. G. = H. WINCKLER: Untersuchungen zur Altorientalischen Geschichte.
Z. A. = Zeitschrift für Assyriologie.
Z. D. M. G. = Zeitschrift der Deutschen Morgenländischen Gesellschaft.
Z. K. = Zeitschrift für Keilschriftforschung.

(All the other abbreviations used are self-evident.)

EARLY BABYLONIAN HISTORY

لَيْسَ بِإِنْسَانٍ وَلَا عَالِمٍ   مَنْ لَمْ يَعِ ٱلتَّارِيخَ فِي صَدْرِهِ
وَمَنْ دَرَى أَخْبَارَ مَنْ قَدْ مَضَى   أَضَافَ أَعْمَارًا إِلَى عُمْرِهِ

Der ist kein Mensch, noch gar ein gelehrter Mann,
Wer die Geschichtsdaten nicht auswendig kann;
Doch wer von der Vorzeit kann Kunde geben,
Fügt neues Leben zum eigenen Leben.

No nation can look back upon such a long time of recorded history as can the Ancient Babylonians. Recent excavations have brought to light tablets, which show us that in the land between the Tigris and the Euphrates there existed a highly civilized nation as early as 5000 B.C., a nation which had its own language and its own system of signs in which to express it. This fact alone would make the study of old Babylonian history full of interest. The study, however, is not only interesting, but also of great historical moment. We are informed by the Bible that Abraham, the ancestor of the Jewish race, came from Ur of the Chaldees. If we want to follow up the history of Abraham and his ancestors we are at once thrown into contact with Old Babylonia. Abraham, according to Archbishop Usher's chronology, lived at about 1900 B.C. At this time Babylonia had long outgrown its infancy. Amraphel, king of Shinar (the Babylonian Ḫammurabi), does not merely claim authority over Babylon, but he bears the proud title 'king of the four corners of the world,' thus showing that the countries north and south, east and west of Babylonia were subject to him. This Ḫammurabi records his mighty deeds in inscriptions written in two different languages. We are therefore led to conjecture that there must have been two different peoples in the country, differing from each other in speech. These two languages vary widely in grammatical construction and arrangement. They have been called by scholars the 'Sumerian' and the 'Semitic-Babylonian' languages respectively. An examination of them shows that the Sumerian was the original one in Old Babylonia. The Sumerians must consequently have been the people who invented this system of writing, called the 'Cuneiform Script.' If this is so—and it can hardly be denied—it would follow that there must have been a time when the Sumerians were the sole possessors of Babylonia. And if the Sumerians were the originators of this system of cuneiform writing and the original inhabitants of Babylonia, the question arises, when did the 'barbarians,' who adopted the Sumerian mode of writing in order to express their Semitic language, invade the country? Whence did they come? Did they come from the north or from the south? If they came from the north, where was their original home? If they, on the contrary, came from the south, from what part of the south? These are all questions difficult to answer. A due consideration, however, will be given to them, when we come to consider the times of Lugalzaggisi.

True, it has been maintained by very eminent scholars during the last twenty years, that we should not look for two distinct races in Babylonia, but only for *one race*, using two *different modes of writing*, this race being asserted to be the *Semitic*. But, if we postulate only one race, using two different 'modes of writing,' how well educated must the people have been at so early a time as 4000 B.C. to be *able* to *use* two such widely differing 'modes of writing'! That would presuppose a development of at least two to three thousand years and a civilization which would be without parallel in the history of mankind.

The most difficult question, however, in this history is that of its *chronology*. Here we have almost no basis to stand on; nay, we are often at a loss to tell which dynasty of rulers preceded or followed another dynasty, and even within the dynasties we sometimes do not know which ruler is to be placed first and which last.

And yet, thanks to the excavations made at Telloh and Nippur, and to the diligence of such scholars as Hilprecht and Thureau-Dangin, we are now able to bring at least some light into this darkness.

We know that it is possible to reconstruct the chronology of the Assyrian empire on the basis of the historical inscriptions which have been found. If we had similar documents for the period which we propose to discuss, the task would be a simple one. But not having this assistance, we must content ourselves with other means. These are:

1. Incidental references in some particular inscription to a certain king, who is thus shown to be contemporary with the events narrated in that inscription.

2. Palaeographic evidence. This latter, however, must only be employed where the former is wanting.

As soon as some of the cuneiform inscriptions had been deciphered and the meaning of the signs established, scholars were able to verify the results so far obtained by facts derived from other sources. Thus the principle employed in reading cuneiform inscriptions was proved to be correct. Among these inscriptions brought to light were also some tablets which proved to be 'lists of officers' and 'lists of kings.' Each officer was appointed for a particular year, and gave his name to it, like the ἄρχων ἐπώνυμος of Athens. Hence this official list was called by George Smith 'The Eponym Canon'; and this title is still retained by scholars. It was customary for the Assyrian kings to date their documents by these eponym-years. When they did so, the expression usually used was: *ina lîmi* X.X., i.e. 'in the eponym of a certain officer,' or 'when a certain officer was eponym.' Some documents, however, are arranged according to the years of the king's rule, as for example: 'in the first, second, &c., year of my reign I did a certain thing.' In some cases both methods were combined. In the Black Obelisk of Shalmanassar, e.g., we read: *Ina šurrat šarrûtia*, i.e. 'in the beginning of my kingship' (l. 20); then in l. 26: *ina ištên palia*, 'in the first year of my reign'; *ina šani-e palîa*, 'in the second year of my reign' (l. 32); *ina šalši palîa*, 'in the third year of my reign' (l. 35); but in l. 45 he does not say 'in the fourth year of my reign,' but *ina lim-mu Dâin-Ašur*, 'in the eponym of Dâin-Ashur.' Hence the eponym of Dâin-Ashur is identical with the 'fourth year of his reign.' Probably as many as thirty different officers could be eponyms. When the list was exhausted the series was recommenced. This series was headed by the king (*šarru*), then came the tartan (*turtânu*), then the military commander (*rab ummanâti rapšâti*), then the *rab ekal*, the 'chief of the palace,' and so on. These lists of eponyms were kept with the greatest regularity. A new reign was marked off from the preceding one by a dividing line. Seven of such canons have been brought to light; unfortunately none is complete, but in many cases they confirm and supplement each other. Some of these canons only give the names of the different eponyms that followed in an unbroken line; others, again, are accompanied by brief historical notices of some event or events which occurred each year. These brief notices, curiously enough, became the means of reducing the Assyrian chronology to 'exact terms of our own.' And if we succeed in fixing precisely the date of one eponym, we can generally fix all the others which either precede or follow, provided the line is unbroken.

The remarkable statement which gives us the key to the whole Assyrian chronology runs thus:

'Pur-Sagale of the land of Gozan. Revolt of the city of Ashur. In the month Sivan the sun suffered an eclipse.'

This eclipse has been calculated by the celebrated Mr. Hincks to be that which occurred on June 15, 763 B.C.; and this date has been generally [1] accepted as that of this eponym. Pur-Sagale was the eighth eponym in the reign of Ashurdanan [2], king of Assyria; consequently Ashurdanan began to reign in the year 771 B.C.[3] Having now fixed the date of one king, we can, with the help of the 'list of the kings' and other inscriptions, determine the date of all the others. In this way we calculate that the date of Nabû-nâ'id, king of Babylonia, is 555–539 B.C. This king mentions in one of his inscriptions ('the great cylinder from Abû-Habba' [Sippar], v. R. 64; Abel und Winckler, Keilschrifttexte, p. 40 ff.) a certain Naram-Sin, the son of *ŠAR-ĢE-NA* (read in Assyrian *Šarru-kênu*). This text is of the greatest historical importance and reads as follows (col. ii. 46 ff.):

'For Shamash, the judge of heaven and earth, Ebarra, his temple, which is in Sippar, and which Nebuchadnezzar a former king had built, and whose old foundation stone he had sought but not found—that temple he had built, and after forty-five years the walls of that temple had fallen down. I became frightened and humble, was terrified, and my face became confused. I caused Shamash to go out from it, making him to dwell in another house. I tore down that temple and looked for its old foundation stone. Eighteen cubits of ground I removed [4], and the foundation stone of *Na-ra-am-*(*ilu*) *Sin*, the son of *ŠAR-GE-NA*, which during 3,200 years no king that went before me had found,—Shamash . . . showed to me.'

In this inscription Naram-Sin, the son of Shargena, is said to have lived 3,200 years before Nabû-nâ'id. This statement would put the date of Naram-Sin at 3750 B.C., and that of his father at about 3800 B.C.[5]

[1] Oppert's contention (P.S.B.A. xx. p. 26) that this eclipse in the reign of Pur-Sagale (he reads this name *Ezid-sēli-igbi*) did not occur on June 15, 763 B.C., but on June 13, 809 B.C., *may* be of importance for Biblical chronology, but does not affect our reckoning.

[2] Oppert, l. c. p. 25, reads this name *Assur-edil-el.*

[3] Comp. K. B. i. p. 211 and p. 206.

[4] Lit.: Eighteen cubits of ground I made deep (sc. my digging = *ḫirûtu.*)

[5] For Lehmann's contention (Zwei Probleme) that we have to read 2,800 instead of 3,200, see below.

When we compare this statement of Nabû-nâ'id with the results of Babylonian excavations, we find that we actually possess inscriptions of Naram-Sin and of a certain Sharganisharâli. The original inscriptions, however, do not shed any light on the statement of Nabû-nâ'id, that this Naram-Sin was the son of Sharganisharâli, nor do they absolutely prove that this Sharganisharâli is identical with the Shargena of Nabû-nâ'id. Indeed, the name Sharganisharâli itself was for a long time a bone of contention among scholars. Some maintained that this Sharganisharâli had nothing to do with the Shargena of Nabû-nâ'id, and they even read the name Binganisharâli (Oppert)[1]. Others again, anxious to maintain the identity of Sharganisharâli with Shargena, read Shargani shar âli, taking the shar âli as a title, i. e. 'Shargani the king of the city' (Hommel, Gesch.). This, however, is not possible; because if such were the case the two elements Shargani and shar âli would be separated by a dividing line (see O. B. I. p. 17).

Hilprecht has maintained the identity of Sharganisharâli with Shargena for the following reasons:—

1. We find—at least in the last 2,500 years of Babylonian history—abbreviated forms of the same names in use. It is therefore highly probable that at some future time we may find the abbreviated form Shargâni even on his own monuments.

2. It is natural that the long name of such a famous king and hero of popular story should be abbreviated, and when it had ceased to be intelligible, explained after the method of 'folk etymology,' as Sharru-kênu, 'the true king.'

True and reasonable as these arguments were, yet they are only indirect. We should still be justified in doubting the identity of Sharganisharâli with Shargena. But this is no longer possible.

Léon Heuzey has published in R. A. iv. p. 1 ff., several seal-cylinders of Sharganisharâli and Naram-Sin. Among these, two are of special importance; one on p. 8 reads:—

[1] It was also read *Šar-ga-ni-šar-luḫ* (Ménant); *Šar(Bin)-ga-ni-šar-imsi* or *Šar(ḫir, bin)-ga-ni-šar-ali* (Oppert); *Šar-ga-ni-šar-maḫāzi* (Winckler).

Col. 1. *Šar-ga-ni-šar-âli*	i. e. Sharganisharâli,
da-num	the mighty
šar	king
A-ga-de-^{ki}	of Agade,
Col. 2. *Lugal-ušum-gal*	Col. 2. Lugalushumgal,
pa-te-si	patesi
Šir-pur-la-^{ki}	of Shirpurla,
arad-ka (*NITAĜ-ZU*)	(is) thy servant.

The other, on p. 11, reads:—

(^{ilu}) *Na-ra-am-*$^{(ilu)}$*Sin*	i. e. Naram-Sin,
da-num	the mighty
ilu A-ga-de-^{ki}	god of Agade,
šar	king
ki-ib-ra-tim	of the four corners
ar-ba-im	of the world,
Lugal-ušum-gal	Lugalushumgal,
dup-sar	the scribe,
pa-te-si	patesi
Šir-pur-la-^{ki}	of Shirpurla,
arad-ka (*NITAĜ-ZU*)	(is) thy servant.

From these inscriptions we see that Lugalushumgal, the patesi of Shirpurla, lived during the reigns of Sharganisharâli and Naram-Sin, during both of which reigns he was their servant. Hence it follows that Sharganisharâli and Naram-Sin were successive kings, and therefore, in accordance with the inscription of Nabû-nâ'id, father and son, living at 3800 and 3750 B.C.[1]

From this point we can now proceed to consider the date of the other rulers of Babylonia. It is true, for the date of the other kings we cannot adduce the testimony of *so great* and *trustworthy*

[1] See also below, s. v. 'Kings of Agade,' and compare for the present Hilprecht, O. B. I. p. 235, and Maspero, Dawn of Civilization, p. 599, note 4: 'There is at the present,' he says, 'no serious reason to question its accuracy, at least relatively, except the instinctive repugnance of modern critics to consider as legitimate, dates which carry them back further into the past than they are accustomed to go.'

a witness as Nabû-nâ'id, but we must fall back upon the argument derived from the study of 'palaeography'—a precarious argument, no doubt, but notwithstanding a helpful one.

In order to get a clear view of the palaeographic problems connected with the earliest inscriptions down to the time of Ur-Ba'u, we may select some characteristic signs, which most frequently occur, and which may be taken to represent their specific epochs. (Compare the signs given on the opposite page.)

In the inscriptions of this early period we have to distinguish—

1. Between the writing as exhibited in the so-called historical inscriptions, in votive tablets, &c. (this writing, no doubt, is in the most cases artificial; it is, if we may call it so, a 'Gothic style' of writing);

2. And the writing used in 'everyday life,' to be found on the 'contract-tablets.'

We may use as a basis for our comparison the 'contract-tablets' of the time of Sargon I., published by Thureau-Dangin in R. A. iv. No. iii. No. 13 ff., and the 'contract-tablets' of the time of Urukagina (see column A), published by the same scholar, l. c. Nos. 8–12[1]. All these 'contract-tablets'—those of Sargon I. as well as those of Urukagina—'*provviennent pour la plupart de Telloh.*' As far as I know, no 'contract-tablets' from the time of Eannatum have as yet been published. Of this latter ruler we only have historical inscriptions, which are all written in the 'Gothic style.' In order therefore to be able to compare the inscriptions of Eannatum with those of Urukagina, it is necessary—if we wish to have a common basis of comparison for the inscriptions of both of these rulers—to use also the 'Gothic' signs of Urukagina (see column B). With these 'Gothic' signs of Urukagina and Eannatum we can also compare the 'Gothic' signs as exhibited in the inscriptions of Enne-Ugun (O. B. I. 103, 110, 104, 105, 102), Urzaguddu (O. B. I. 93), and Lugalzaggisi (O. B. I. 87). The whole table of comparison I have headed with two signs taken from the

[1] We have to compare the writing as exhibited on the 'contract-tablets' of both of these rulers, because it is hardly possible to use the 'Gothic style' of Sargon I as a basis for comparison with the 'Gothic style' of Urukagina.

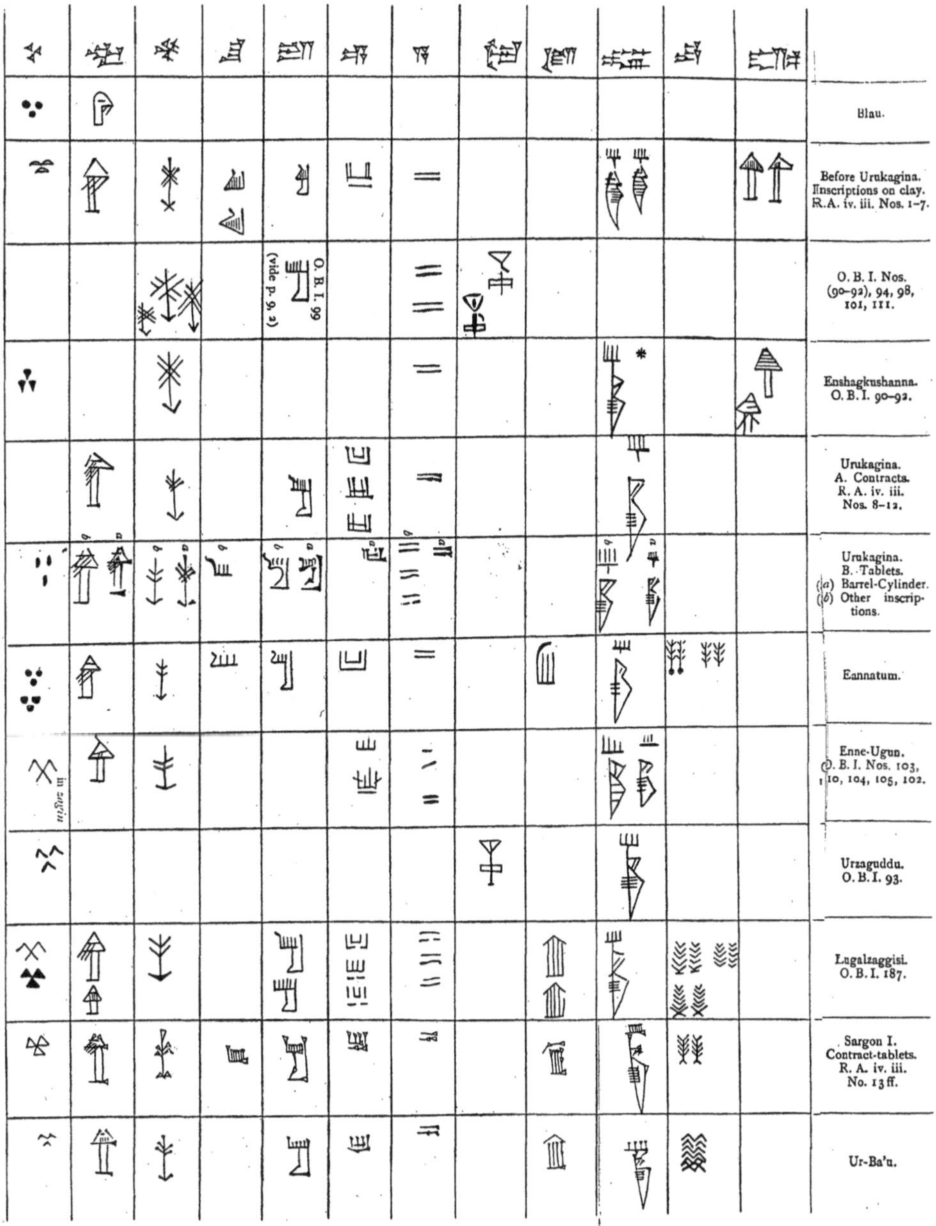
Blau.
Before Urukagina. Inscriptions on clay. R.A. iv. iii. Nos. 1–7.
O. B. I. 99 (vide p. 9, 2)
O. B. I. Nos. (90–92), 94, 98, 101, 111.
Enshagkushanna. O. B. I. 90–92.
Urukagina. A. Contracts. R. A. iv. iii. Nos. 8–12.
Urukagina. B. Tablets. (a) Barrel-Cylinder. (b) Other inscriptions.
Eannatum.
in ugin
Enne-Ugun. O. B. I. Nos. 103, 110, 104, 105, 102.
Urzaguddu. O. B. I. 93.
Lugalzaggisi. O. B. I. 187.
Sargon I. Contract-tablets. R. A. iv. iii. No. 13 ff.
Ur-Ba'u.

* This sign is remarkable. That the two elements are connected is probably due to carelessness of th

Monument Blau[1], confessedly the oldest document we possess. The second line exhibits certain signs taken from 'contract-tablets' published by Thureau-Dangin in R. A. iv. No. iii. 1–7. This scholar has himself said that these signs are '*signes ayant des formes particulièrement archaïques.*' The next two lines give signs of O. B. I. Nos. 94, 98, (99[2]), 101, 111, and of O. B. I. 90–92 (Enshagkushanna).

A careful consideration of the signs above given clearly exhibits the following three great periods:—

(1) From the oldest times down to Urukagina,

(2) From Urukagina to Lugalzaggisi.

(3) From Lugalzaggisi to Ur-Ba'u.

1. The *first period* apparently is governed by the peculiar sign for *MU*: 'the two pairs of parallel lines found at or near the middle of the horizontal line cross each other.' At the time of Urukagina we find, however, that this 'crossing' is not always the case. Hence Urukagina belongs to the end of the first, and also forms the beginning of the second period. It will be noticed that in the oldest period (line 2) not only the parallel lines near the middle of the horizontal line cross each other, but also the two lines at the beginning[3]. At first these lines at the beginning were shortened, and later on also those near or at the middle of the horizontal line.

2. The *second period* is governed by the signs *DA* and *ŠU*. Notice the development. In the oldest times the 'thumb' is 'curved' and 'pressed on the fingers.' In the age of Urukagina, the thumb, although still curved, is removed from the fingers; at the

[1] See p. 11, n. 3.

[2] I would not class O. B. I. 99 among these inscriptions as Hilprecht does; the form for *DA* shows this clearly. See opposite page.

[3] Hilprecht's statement (O. B. I. p. 249), therefore, that 'the original picture for *MU* is an *arrow* . . . whose cane shaft bears the same primitive marks or symbols of crossed lines as are characteristic of the most ancient form of arrow used in the religious ceremonies of the North American Indians,' does not hold good. Comp. also Delitzsch, Schriftsystem, pp. 34 f., 114–120. Thureau-Dangin's contention, E. C. p. xiii. n. 2, that this 'crossing' is due '*au mouvement rapide imprimé au calame*' is disproved by the very occurrence of this *MU* on *stones*.

time of Lugalzaggisi, however, we find that the 'thumb' is not only taken away from 'the fingers,' but is sometimes *curved* and sometimes *straight*. Lugalzaggisi therefore belongs to the end of the second period, and forms at the same time the beginning of the third [1].

Hilprecht, speaking about the palaeographic evidence of the inscription published in O. B. I. 90–92, 94, 98, 99, 101, 111, says (O. B. I. p. 250): (1) 'Urukagina [2] lived before the ancient kings of Shirpurla;' (2) 'The inscriptions above referred to are older than Urukagina.' This is true, if we except O. B. I. No. 99. But when he goes on (p. 254) to say: 'Nos. 86, 87 (i.e. inscriptions of Lugalkigubnidudu and Lugalzaggisi) . . . show all the characteristic features of the inscriptions of Urukagina, Ur-Ninâ, and Eannatum (*sic!*). But besides they exhibit a number of palaeographic peculiarities which are altogether absent from the inscriptions of *Telloh*, and must be regarded as characteristic features of an earlier stage of writing. They will be treated in full at another place,' he overstates the facts. Lugalzaggisi (and consequently also Lugalkigubnidudu, Hilprecht, O. B. I. p. 271) is by *no means* to be placed before Eannatum [3]. Compare for instance the sign *KA*, of which Thureau-Dangin says (R. S. 1897, p. 269): '*Le signe KA présente déjà la forme symétrique qu'il doit garder et dans laquelle il n'est plus possible de discerner* (*ainsi que dans la forme d'Eanadou et mieux dans celle du Monument Blau*) *le profil humain tourné vers la droite.*' Compare also the signs for *KUR*, *E* (not *mà* or *ga*, as Hilprecht reads); the sign *ĠUL* of Eannatum has still a curved line in front, which curved line becomes a *broken* one at the time of Lugalzaggisi. Compare also the sign *LUGAL*. In Eannatum's inscriptions it is always written *gal* + (*ga*)*lu*, while in Lugalzaggisi the two elements are joined together.

[1] This is also the reason why I would refer O. B. I. No. 99 to the end of this second period, viz. because the 'thumb' is straight, although the sign *MU* has the *old* form.

[2] Heuzey (Comptes Rendus, 1897, 238, 240) and Thureau-Dangin (preface to E. C. p. xiv, note) put Urukagina after Lummadur. Scheil, R. T. xxi. 125, says that Urukagina is a vassal of Manishtusu, king of Kish.

[3] So already Thureau-Dangin. See R. S. 1897, p. 268 ff., where that scholar came to the same result by a comparison of certain signs.

Hence, there can be no doubt that Lugalzaggisi is younger than Eannatum, and not 'surely older' (*sic!* Hilprecht, l. c. p. 258). Enne-Ugun is older than Lugalzaggisi (comp. the signs of *LUGAL* and *E* with those of Lugalzag.), but probably (?) younger than Eannatum (see the sign for *KA*, which in Enne-Ugun's inscription already has the 'symmetric' form). Whether Urzaguddu is older than Lugalzaggisi is uncertain, if we try to determine his date only from 'palaeographic considerations.'

3. The third period, beginning with Lugalzaggisi, is governed by the peculiarity that original curved lines are broken (comp. *ĠUL*), complete lines are divided (comp. *E*), the 'thumb' in *DA* and *ŠU* is straightened, the sign for 'king' no longer exhibits its original two elements, but they form *one* sign. *KA* throughout has the symmetric form. To this third period Sargon I. belongs.

From these considerations it follows that Sharganisharâli[1] is not by any means the earliest king of whom we have inscriptions, but that he belongs to the third period, which begins with Lugalzaggisi. If we claim for each period a space of only 500 years[2]—which is surely not exorbitant—we would come to the great age of about 5000 B.C. We may safely assert that the difference of the signs on the Monument Blau[3] from those in R. A. iii. 1–7 (comp. second line of signs, opposite p. 8) is so great, that we may

[1] Hilprecht (in O. B. I. i. p. 19) has come almost to the same result, i. e. that the early kings of Shirpurla (of whom Eannatum may be called the representative) antedated Sargon. His argument, however, although right, was precarious at the time when he wrote his statements. It is in substance this:—

During the excavations at Nippur there was found in the same deep-lying stratum as the inscriptions of Sargon and Âlusharshid, and close by them, a fragment of an inscription saying that 'Entemena, patesi of Shirpurla,' presented a vase to Bêl at Nippur. From this he concludes—(1) that the date of the oldest Semitic rulers of Babylonia is approximately the same as that of the earliest patesis of Shirpurla, i. e. about 3800 B.C.; (2) that the kings of Shirpurla were earlier than Sargon I. (or Âlusharshid).

[2] This supposition is chiefly based upon the number of rulers that make up each period; see further below.

[3] The 'Monument Blau,' so called from its possessor Dr. Blau, was first published in the Proceedings of the American Oriental Society, Oct. 1885, and republished in R. S. 1896, with a translation by Thureau-Dangin.

add about 500 years more, i. e. 5500 B. C., which would be the approximate date of the Monument Blau[1].

The Chronology of the Kings and Patesis of Shirpurla (Lagaš).

Having seen that Urukagina, who is called in his inscriptions 'king of Shirpurla,' must have preceded Eannatum (p. 9), who calls himself 'king' as well as 'patesi of Shirpurla,' and that this latter again antedated Ur-Ba'u, another patesi of Shirpurla, it will be necessary here to treat more specifically of the chronology of these kings and patesis.

Eannatum calls himself in the 'Galet A,' col. viii, ll. 1–7, the

dumu A-kur-gal	i. e. the son of Akurgal,
pa-te-si	patesi
Šir-pur-la-ki-ge	of Shirpurla;
pa-giš-bil-ga-ni	his ancestor
Ur-dingir Ninâ	is Ur-Ninâ,
pa-te-si	the patesi
Šir-pur-la-ki-kam	of Shirpurla.

If we compare this statement with the Stèle des Vautours, where he calls himself 'the son of Akurgal, the king of Shirpurla, the son of Ur-Ninâ,' it will be evident that the expression *pa-giš-bil-ga-ni* means in this case 'grandfather,' and hence Eannatum is the grandson of Ur-Ninâ. Ur-Ninâ again speaks of himself in Déc. pl. 2 ter, No. 2, col. 1, ll. 1–5, as follows:—

(Dingir) Ninâ + UR	i. e. Ur-Ninâ,
lugal	the king
Šir-pur-la	of Shirpurla,
dumu Gu-ni-du	the son of Gunidu,
dumu Gur-ṣar	son of Gursar.

We would get then so far the following genealogy:—

1 To this same period belong also the tablets published in Déc. 1 bis, No. 1 a.b; Déc. 1 ter, Nos. 5 and 6 a.b, and a tablet recently acquired by Dean E. A. Hoffman, which seems to antedate even the Monument Blau.

Gur-sar
|
Gu-ni-du
|
Ur-Ninâ (king)
|
A-kur-gal (king, patesi)
|
E-an-na-tum(a) (king, patesi).

But further, Jensen, K. B. iii[1]. p. 17, translates an inscription of a so-called Enannatum(a), patesi of Shirpurla, which is published in Déc. pl. 6, 4, in which inscription we read:

l. 3.	*En-an-na-tum(a)*	i. e.	Enannatum(a),
l. 4.	*pa-te-si*[1]		patesi
l. 5.	*Šir-la-pur-ki*		of Shirpurla,
l. 10.	*dumu En-teme-na*		the son of Entemena
l. 11.	*pa-te-si*		patesi
l. 12.	*Šir-la-pur-ki-ka-ge*		of Shirpurla.

Also of this Entemena mentioned here we have several inscriptions, in one of which he gives his genealogy as follows:—

Déc. 31, 3 (R. A. ii. 87):

	En-teme-na	i. e.	Entemena,
	pa-te-si		the patesi
	Šir-la-ki-pur		of Shirpurla,
	dumu En-an-na-tum(a)		the son of Enannatum(a)
	pa-te-si		the patesi
Col. 2.	*Šir-la-ki-pur-ka*		of Shirpurla,
	dumu-ka[2]		the grandson
	Ur-dingir Ninâ		of Ur-Ninâ
	lugal[1]		the king
	Šir-ki-la-pur-ka-ge		of Shirpurla.

If we compare this inscription with the preceding, we find that we have here two persons with the name of Enannatum(a); the

[1] For the meaning of the terms *lugal* and *patesi*, see below.

[2] We must read thus, not *SAG*, as Jensen does, K. B. iii[1]. p. 75, n. ii. The sign is clear. It cannot be read *SAG*, because this latter sign differs considerably from the sign *KA*.

one being *the son* of Entemena (Déc. 6, 4), while the other is the father of Entemena (Déc. 31, 3). In order to distinguish these two patesis, we shall call the latter (i. e. Enannatum(a) the father of Entemena) Enannatum(a) I., the former (i. e. Enannatum(a) the son of Entemena) Enannatum(a) II. However, one difficulty remains unexplained, viz. the expression *dumu-ka.* Jensen, who transcribed the inscription (see note 2, p. 13), read *SAG* and translated '*der erstgeborene Sohn*'; he apparently followed Heuzey, who translated '*fils aîné*.' If these translations be correct, then Enannatum(a) I. would be the firstborn of Ur-Ninâ, consequently a brother of Akurgal. That this is not the case, an inscription of Enannatum(a) I., published by De Sarzec in R. A. iii. p. 31, clearly proves. There we read:

(dingir) Nin-gir-su	i. e. To Ningirsu
gud (dingir) En-lil-ra	the hero of Enlil,
En-an-na-tum(a)	Enannatum(a),
pa-te-si	patesi
Šir-la-ki-pur	of Shirpurla,
kur-gu-zal-zal [1]	the conqueror of all the lands for
[*(dingir) Nin*]*-gir-su*	Ningirsu,
[*dumu*] *A-kur-gal*	the son of Akurgal
[*pa-te-*]*si*	the patesi
Šir-la-pur-ki-ka-ge	of Shirpurla.
(dingir) Nin-gir-su-ra	To Ningirsu
bur-še(sic) [2]*-gaz*	this vase to crush the grain
mu-na-gim (= *epêšu*)	he has made.
nam-ti-la-ni-ku	For (the preservation of) his life
[*dingir*] *Nin-gir-*[*-su*]*-ra*	to Ningirsu
[*E-n*]*innû*	the Eninnû
mu-[*na-ru*]	he [has built].

This inscription proves clearly that Enannatum I. was a son of Akurgal and therefore the brother of Eannatum.

We are now in a position to understand the expression *DU-*

[1] For this expression see Eannatum, Galet A.

[2] The copy gives *SUM*, the ideogr. for *nadânu*.

MU-KA, which Entemena applies to his father Enannatum(a) (Déc. 31, 3); it apparently means 'the grandson.' Thus, then, Entemena says he is the son of Enannatum(a), and this latter is the *dumu-ka*, the 'grandson,' of Ur-Ninâ. And this Enannatum(a) the grandson of Ur-Ninâ we have already seen to be the Enannatum(a) the son of Akurgal (R. A. iii. p. 31), the brother of Eannatum(a). We have thus established, with De Sarzec, R. A. iii. p. 32, the following genealogy:

Gur-sar
|
Gu-ni-du
|
Ur-Ninâ (king)
|
A kur-gal (king and patesi)

E-an-na-tum(a) (king and patesi)

En-an-na-tum(a) I. (patesi)
|
En-teme-na (patesi)
|
En-an-na-tum(a) II. (patesi)
|
Lum-ma-dur[1]

Above, on page 9, we have seen that the inscriptions of Urukagina belong not only to the end of the first period of old Babylonian writing, but also to the beginning of the second, of which second period the inscriptions of Lugalzaggisi form the end. Each period, it was argued, comprised about 500 years. If this is true, then Urukagina must have lived about 500 years before Lugalzaggisi. Can we maintain this statement—apart from palaeographical evidence—by other considerations?

Entemena in his 'Cône historique' (see Thureau-Dangin, R. A. iii. p. 42 ff.) mentions a certain Mesilim, king of Kish, who in the quality of lord paramount fixes the boundaries between the country of Shirpurla and Gishban[2] (?), signifying this boundary by a statue which he erects. Fortunately we have an inscription of this very

[1] *Lum-ma-dur* | *dumu En-an-na-tum* | *pa-te-si* | *Šir-pur-la-ki* is mentioned by Heuzey, Comptes Rendus, vol. iv. 25, p. 424, whose inscription is preserved in the Museum of Constantinople.

[2] The reading of this name is not certain; probably it should be read Gishuḫ.

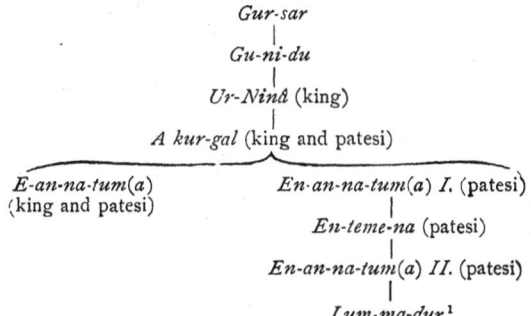

Mesilim, king of Kish; see R. A. iii. No. 2, pl. iii. and p. 55; comp. R. A. iv. p. 35. It reads:

Me-silim	i. e.	Mesilim,
lugal		king
Kiš		of Kish,
sa+ga[1]		the high priest (?)
(*dingir*) *Nin-su-gir*		of Ningirsu,
(*dingir*) *Su-nin-gir*		to Ningirsu
mu-gub		has presented it,
Lugal-		Lugalshuggur
šug-gur[2]		
pa-te-si		(being) patesi
Šir-la-[*pur-ki*]		of Shirpurla.

Here then we have a new patesi of Shirpurla, viz. Lugalshuggur, a vassal of Mesilim, king of Kish—which latter is put by Entemena in his 'Cône inscription,' col. 2, 6–8, before Eannatum. And since it is hardly possible to imagine that Ur-Ninâ should have a counter-patesi ruling over the same city as he, we are by necessity forced to put Lugalshuggur before the time of Ur-Ninâ. This argument is also strengthened by the palaeographic evidence; see Heuzey, R. A. iii. p. 57. In this same period I would like to place also another king of Shirpurla, viz. Enǵegal, mentioned by Hilprecht in Z. A. xi. p. 330 f., who says that '*die Abfassung der Tafel genau genommen sogar noch vor Ur-Ninâ anzusetzen sei*,' ibid. p. 331. And if we add to this list of kings and patesis of Shirpurla another patesi who is mentioned in R. A. iv. No. iii. pl. iii. No. 9 (comp. Thureau-Dangin, ibid. p. 70), as follows:

ud-ba	i. e.	At that time
UR-E-INNANNA-GE		*UR-E-INNANNA-GE*[3]
di-bi-ni-kud		judged,
Gal+(ga)lu-an-da		(and) Lugalanda
pa-te-si-kam		being patesi

[1] So Hilprecht! Possibly it may be read *E+RU* = 'the builder of the house of.'

[2] Reading doubtful; see below.

[3] Thureau-Dangin reads this name *UR-E-ninni-GE*, ibid.; cp. E. C. No. 294.

and who, according to that scholar's opinion, '*doit sans doute prendre place parmi les successeurs d'Enanadou II.*[1],' we might be able to fill up the 500 years which were claimed to lie between Urukagina and Lugalzaggisi, especially if we allow for every king about twenty years, and for the lacunae which exist between certain kings some twenty to fifty years[2]. The succession of governors during these 500 years would then be:

Kish.	Shirpurla.	Erech.
	Uru-ka-gi-na (king)	
	. . .[3]	
	En-ĝe-gal (king)	
O. B. I. 108	. . .	
. . .	. . .	
Me-silim	*Lugal-šug-gur* (patesi)	
. . .	. . .	
Lugal-da?-ak?	. . .	
. . .	(*Gur-sar*)	
. . .	(*Gu-ni-du*)	
	Ur-Ninâ (king)	
	A-kur-gal (king and patesi)	
Al-zu-zu-a	*E-an-na-tum(a)* (king and patesi); *En-an-na-tum(a) I.* (patesi)	
	En-teme-na (patesi)	
En-ne-Ugun	*En-an-na-tum(a) II.* (patesi)	
	Lum-ma-dur (patesi)	
	. . .	
	. . .	
	Lugal an-da (patesi)	
	. . .	
	. . .	*Lugal-zag-gi-si*

On p. 9 it was pointed out that the period from Urukagina to Lugalzaggisi preceded that to which Ur-Ba'u belongs. It remains

[1] Compare the *DA*, which still exhibits the curved thumb, and the sign for *lugal* = *gal* + (*ga*)*lu*.

[2] This allowance we have to make because from the material on hand we do not know how many rulers, for instance, may have reigned between Urukagina and Enĝegal, and how many between Lummadur and Lugalanda, &c.

[3] The dots signify lacunae.

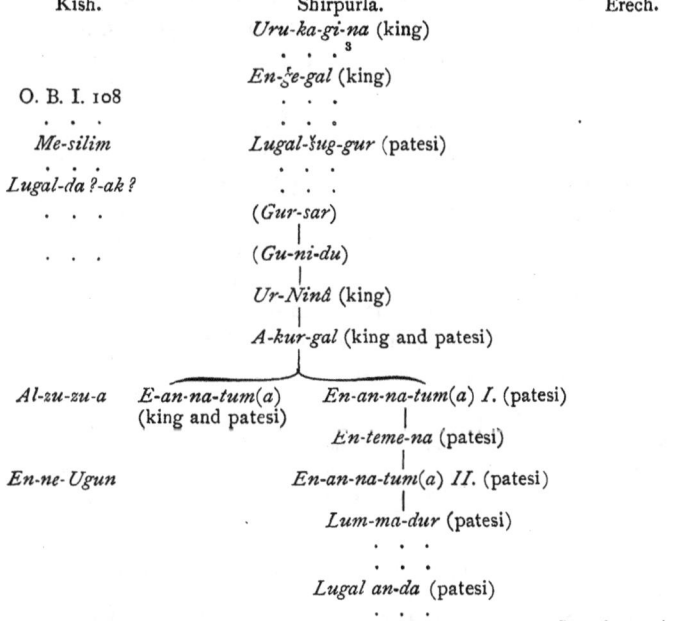

only to state here, in what succession the various rulers of the different dynasties may have followed which have to be placed between Lummadur and Ur-Ba'u.

A good starting-point for doing this is furnished by the inscription of Sharganisharâli. If we compare the so-called Gothic inscriptions of this king with those of a certain Âlusharshid and Manishtusu, both kings of Kish, we shall find that they belong approximately to the same period. If we can trust Hilprecht's[1] emendation of a certain omen of Sargon I., published in iv. R^2. 34, ll. 7–10, we must place Âlusharshid and Manishtusu before Sargon I.

This, however, is a matter of minor importance.

In O. B. I. pl. 36 and 37, are published two fragments of an inscription belonging to a certain Lugalkigubnidudu and his son (?) Lugalkisalsi. Hilprecht, speaking of these texts, says (l. c. p. 271): 'They belong doubtless to the same general period as No. 87 (i. e. the inscriptions of Lugalzaggisi); a detailed examination of their palaeographic peculiarities leads me to place them somewhat later[2].' Following Hilprecht, we shall place Lugalkigubnidudu and his son after Lugalzaggisi[3].

[1] Hilprecht (O. B. I. p. 26) restores that much-mutilated passage as follows:—'*Šar-ge-na ša ina ŠIR an-ni-i Kiš-šu* [*ki*] *Bâbiluki i-*[*šú-*]*šum-ma eprê ša šal-la bâbu ṬU-NA is-su-ḫu-ma* . . . [*ina lime ?-*]*tu A-ga-deki âlu i-bu-šu-ma* [*UB-DA*]*-ki šum-šú im-bu-u* . . . [*ina lib-*]*bi u-še-ši-bu.*' 'Sargon, who under this omen brought sorrow upon Kish and Babylon, tore away the earth of . . . and built a city in the vicinity of (*or* after the pattern of?) Agade, called its name "place (city) of the world," and caused the inhabitants of Kish and Babylon (?) to dwell there.' From this he infers that the dynasty of Kish was overthrown by Sargon I., and that therefore Âlusharshid and Manishtusu are to be placed before Sargon I. Thureau-Dangin, R. A. iv. 74, thinks that these kings of Kish are '*probablement postérieurs à Naram-Sin.*'

[2] So far Hilprecht is undoubtedly correct. He however continues, 'and to regard it as about contemporary with the inscriptions of the kings of Shirpurla, especially with those of Edingiranatum (*sic*).' We have already seen that the inscriptions of Lugalzaggisi do not antedate Eannatum, but are, on the contrary, later. And if Lugalzaggisi is later, Lugalkigubnidudu must be later also.

[3] In the Chronological Table given below, I placed Lugalkigubnidudu before

To the same period may belong also the predecessors of Gudea and his successors. Hommel, with his natural insight, when writing about the period of the so-called later patesis of Shirpurla, uttered these remarkable words, showing that he was undoubtedly right in his conclusions (Gesch. p. 312): '*In weitem Abstand von ihnen* (i.e. from the older patesis such as Eannatum, see above) *stehen der Kunst- und Schriftentwickelung nach drei spätere Patesi von Sirgurla Ur-Ba'u, Gude'a und dessen Sohn Ur-Ningirsu.*' And a little further down: '*Unter dieser jüngeren Gruppe aber . . . klafft doch auch selbst wieder eine kleinere Lücke von gewiss mehreren Generationen, also unter Umständen* 100–200 *Jahren, nämlich zwischen dem ersten derselben, Ur-Ba'u, und den übrigen, Gude'a und seinem oder seinen Nachfolgern.*' Thanks to the excavation at Telloh and the industry of the French scholars, we can in a measure fill up the gaps which exist between the older patesi Lummadur and the younger Ur-Ba'u, as well as those between Ur-Ba'u and Gudea.

Heuzey, in R. A. ii. p. 79, published an inscription which reads (comp. Jensen, K. B. iii[1]. p. 75):

[Dingir Nin]-gir-su	i.e.	Unto Ningirsu,
gud-lig-ga		the mighty hero
(dingir) En-lil-la(l)		of Enlil,
lugal-a-ni		her king
nam-ti		has for the life
Nam-maǧ-ni		of Nammaǧni,
pa-te-si		patesi
Šir-pur-la-ki-ka-ku		of Shirpurla,
nin Kan-du		the lady Kandu,
dumu Ur-(dingir) Ba-u		a child of Ur-Ba'u
pa-te-si		the patesi

Sargon I. This, however, is very doubtful. I myself would prefer to place this king before Ur-Ba'u, but after Sargon I.; thus making a closer connection between the first and second dynasty of Ur. The palaeographic evidence seems to tell more for this latter than for the former arrangement.

Šir-pur-la-ki-ka	of Shirpurla,
dam-ni	his wife
šà nam-ti-la-ni-ku	also for her life
a-mu-na-[*šub*]	presented (this object).

Here then we meet with a certain lady Kandu[1], who is the child (daughter) of Ur-Ba'u, but also the wife of Nammaǵni, a patesi of Shirpurla. This Nammaǵni consequently must—if he could marry a daughter of Ur-Ba'u—have ruled either immediately or not very long after Ur-Ba'u. Thus the gap of 'several generations' between Ur-Ba'u and Gudea is somewhat diminished (comp. above, p. 19).

We are now also in a position to fill up somewhat the '*weiten Abstand*' (p. 19) between Lummadur, the last of the older patesis of Shirpurla, and Ur-Ba'u. Above, on p. 16, we saw that a certain Lugalanda[2] must be placed after successors of Lummadur. And on page 7 ff. we heard of a certain Lugalushumgal, patesi of Shirpurla, a contemporary both of Sargon I. and Naram-Sin. This latter patesi must undoubtedly, since he is a contemporary of Sargon I., be placed before Ur-Ba'u. But further, in R. A. iv. No. iii. pl. ix. No. 31, Thureau-Dangin has published a tablet, on the *revers* of which a certain *UR-E*, patesi of Shirpurla, is mentioned. It is possible that we have here, as Thureau-Dangin has pointed out, l. c. p. 78, a certain *UR-E* who followed his father (?), Lugalushumgal, as patesi of Shirpurla[3]. If that be true then this *UR-E* must be put before Ur-Ba'u. Hence Hommel's statement above, p. 19, has proved itself to be correct. To the line of the younger patesis of Shirpurla, and after Ur-Ningirsu, the son of Gudea (K. B. iii[1]. p. 67 *a*, col. 1, 8),

[1] So I would like to read with Heuzey. Jensen takes Ninkandu as the proper name of the wife of Nammaǵni.

[2] Although Lugalanda does not belong to *this* period I mention him here in order to show that Hommel was correct in claiming such a great interval between the older and younger patesis of Shirpurla.

[3] This *Ur-E* also must have been a contemporary of a 'patesi of Ur,' mentioned on the same tablet, *Ur-(dingir) Utu* (?) by name.

have to be added also the two following, of which Hommel, at the time of writing his history, was not aware, viz. Ur-Ninsun and Ġala-Lama.

The portion of the inscription of Ur-Ninsun (published in R. A. ii. 79; comp. Oppert, ibidem, and Jensen, K. B. iii[1]. p. 77), so far as we are concerned with it here, reads:

(Dingir) Nin-gir-su	i. e. To Ningirsu,
gud-lig-ga	the mighty hero
(dingir) En-lil-la(l)-ra	of Enlil,
lugal-a-ni	his king,
Ur-(dingir) Nin-sun	Ur-Ninsun,
pa-te-si	patesi
Šir-pur-la-ki-ge	of Shirpurla, for his
nam-ti-la-ni-ku	life
a-mu-na-šub	has presented it.

The inscription of Ġala-Lama (Déc. pl. 21, No. 4, and Jensen, l. c. p. 70) reads:

Column I.

[Am] Šir-[pur-la-ki]-ra	i. e. To the mother of Shirpurla,
[dingir] Ba-u	viz. to Ba'u
[nin-a]-ni	his mistress,
[nam-]ti	for the life
[dingir Du]n-gi	of Dungi,
[lugal li]g-ga	the mighty king,

Column II.

lugal Uru-um-ki-ma	the king of Ur,
lugal Ki-en-gi-ki-Urdu-ka-ku	king of Shumer and Akkad,
Ġa-la-(dingir) Lama	Ġala-Lama,
dumu (Ga)lu-ka-ni	the son of (Ga)lukani,
pa-te-si	the patesi
Šir-pur-la-ki-ka-ge	of Shirpurla.

This inscription clearly proves that :

(1) (Ga)lukani must have been the last patesi of Shirpurla, for his son Ġala-Lama does not call himself patesi of Shirpurla.

(2) That the immediate successors of the patesis of Shirpurla were the kings of Ur, to which Dungi belongs; hence the dynasty of the later patesis of Shirpurla was overthrown by these kings of Ur, who apparently were partly their contemporaries.

(3) That Ur-Ninsuñ has to be placed before (Ga)lukani, and not, as Jensen (K. B. iii[1]. p. 77) does, '*nach der Inschrift Ġala-Lama's.*'

Of quite another (Ga)lukani, who also confesses his dependence upon a certain Dungi, king of Ur, we hear in an inscription recently published by Heuzey in R. A. iv. p. 90, which reads[1]:

(dingir) Nin-gir-su	To Ningirsu,
gu[d-lig-]ga	the mighty hero
(dingir) [En-l]il-la(l)	of Bêl,
lugal-a-ni	his king,
nam-ti	for the life
Dun-gi	of Dungi,
nitaĝ lig-ga	the strong hero,
lugal Uru-um-^{ki}-ma-ka-ku	the king of Ur,
(Ga)lu-ka-ni	(Ga)lukani,
pa-te-si	the patesi
[Šir-pur-la-^{ki}-ge]	of Shirpurla,
[a-mu-na-šub]	has presented it.

This tablet is important in more than one respect. It not only shows that we have to distinguish between Dungi, 'king of Ur, king of Shumer and Akkad,' and Dungi, 'king of Ur,' but also between (Ga)lukani the father of Ġala-Lama, and (Ga)lukani a contemporary of Dungi, 'king of Ur.' The former Dungi we call Dungi I.[2] and the latter Dungi II.

This latter inscription, therefore, does not belong to our second

[1] Winckler's and Lehmann's view, that Dungi I. was a contemporary of Ur-Ningirsu and Gudea, is erroneous. See below.

[2] Notice the difference in the titles of Dungi; and see p. 37, note 2, and *sub* 'Fourth dynasty of Ur.'

period, viz. to that from Lugalzaggisi down to Ur-Ba'u and his successors. If we try to arrange this period according to the chronology above indicated, and allow for the different 'gaps' which exist between certain rulers about twenty to fifty years, we shall see that this period may very well cover a space of about 800 years (500 years to the time of Ur-Ba'u and 300 years from Ur-Ba'u to Ġala-Lama).

Erech.	Ur.	Kish.	Agade.	Shirpurla.
Lugal-zag-gi-si				
. . .				
	Lugal-ki-gub-ni-du-du			
	Lugal-kisal-si			
E-zu-ab	. . .			
	. . .	*Ur-zag-ud-du*		
		. . .		
		Lugal-tar-si		
		. . .		
		O. B. I. 118		
		. . .		
		Ma-an-iš-tu-su		
		. . .		
		Âlu-ušaršid		
	. . .	. . .	. . .	
	. . .	. . .	*Sargon I.*	*Lugal-ušum-gal*
	Ur-(dingir) Utu (?)		3800 B.C.	*Ur-E*
	(patesi)		*Naram-Sin*	. . .
			3750 B.C.	. . .
			Bingani-šar-âli	. . .
			(comp. R. A. iv. p. 76)	. . .
				Ur-Ba'u
				Nam-maḫ-ni
				. . .
				. . .
				Gu-de-a
				Ur-Nin-gir-su
				. . .
				Ur-Nin-sun
				. . .
				(*Ga*)*lu-ka-ni I.*
				Ġa-la-Lama (contemporary of Dungi I. of Ur)

The inscription quoted on p. 21 (see especially point 2) gives us, as we have seen, a basis for determining the date of the immediate successors of the later patesis of Shirpurla. These successors are the kings belonging to the *second* (not first[1]) dynasty of Ur. Of one of these kings of Ur we have heard already, viz. Dungi, the contemporary of (Ga)lukani (?) and Ġala-Lama. This Dungi, as we know from an inscription of Nabû-nâ'id, was the son of a certain Ur-Gur, king of Ur. The passage referred to is found in i. R. 68, No. i. (translated by Peiser, K. B. iii^{2}. p. 95). It reads (Col. i. l. 12): 'In the inscription of Ur-Gur and of Dungi his son I (i. e. Nabû-nâ'id) found that Ur-Gur had built that ziḳḳurrat, but not completed it. Dungi his son completed its building[2].' This Ur-Gur must therefore have been the contemporary of the predecessors of (Ga)lukani. This second dynasty of Ur ('king of Ur, king of Shumer and Akkad') must, however, not be confused with the other dynasties of the same city, for it will be seen that the rulers of the third and fourth dynasties bear quite different titles from those of the second. The former rulers (i. e. dynasty of Ur III.) invariably call themselves *lugal Uru-um-^{ki}-ma*, 'king of Ur[3].' The representatives of the fourth dynasty of Ur, on the other hand, have *without exception* the title '*lugal Uru-um-^{ki}-ma lugal an-ub-da tab-tab-ba-(ge)*,' i. e. 'king of Ur, king of the four corners of the world.'

Assuming the adequacy of this distinction, we are obliged to refer the Semitic-Babylonian inscription published in Z. D. M. G. xxix. p. 37 (cp. K. B. iii^{1}. p. 83), which Winckler places among the inscriptions of Dungi (i. e. Dungi I.) of the second dynasty, to a certain Dungi (called Dungi III.) of the fourth dynasty of Ur.

[1] The first dynasty of Ur, as Hilprecht has pointed out, O. B. I. p. 272, is represented by Lugalkigubnidudu and his son (?) Lugalkisalsi. See p. 23.

[2] 12 *I-na mu-sa-ri-e ša Ur-(ilu) Gur* (so read) 13 *u (ilu) Dun-gi mâri-šu a-mur-ma* 14 *ša ziḳ-ḳur-rat šu-a-ti* 15 *Ur-(ilu) Gur i-pu-šu-ma* 16 *la u-šak-li-lu-uš* 17 *(ilu) Dun-gi mâri-šu ši-pir-šu* 18 *u-šak-lil.*

[3] Comp. Ur-Gur, i. R. 1, No. 1; ibid. No. 3; iv. R. 35, i.

The same is true also of O. B. I. 124, which Hilprecht refers to Dungi I.; see Thureau-Dangin, R. S. 1897, p. 74[1].

Before, however, we try to arrange the kings of the third and (fourth) dynasties of Ur, we must first consider the so-called kings of Isin. These kings undoubtedly preceded those of the third dynasty of Ur, as is evident from an inscription published in i. R. 2, No. vi. i. (comp. Winckler, K. B. iii^{1}. p. 86), where we read:

l. 1.	*(dingir) Utu*	i. e.	For Shamash
	. . . . . .		. . . . . .
l. 7.	*lugal-a-ni-ir nam-ti*		his king, has for the life
l. 8.	*Gu-un-gu-nu-um*		of Gungunu,
l. 9	*nitaĝ lig-ga*		the mighty hero,
l. 10.	*lugal Uru-um-ki-ma-ka-ku*		king of Ur,
l. 11.	*En-an-na-tum-ma*		Enannatum(a)
l. 12.	*en (?)-zi (dingir) Nannar (URU-KI)*		the *en* (?)-*zi* of Nannar,
l. 13.	*en (dingir) URU-KI*		the *en* (high-priest) of Nannar,
l. 14.	*šag Uru-um-ki-ma*		in Ur,
l. 15.	*dumu Iš-me-(dingir)-Da-gan*		son of Ishme-Dagan,
l. 16.	*E-ĜI-LI*[2]*-a-ni-in-ru*		
l. 18.	*mu-na-ru*		built the temple *E-ĜI-LI-a*-ninru.

This Ishme-Dagan, the father of Enannatum(a), is no other than *Išme-Dagan, en Unug-ki-ga lugal Ni-si-in-ki-na lugal Ki-en-gi-ki-Urdu*, i. e. the lord of Erech, king of Isin, king of Shumer and Akkad (comp. also i. R. 36, 2, where the same Enannatum(a) calls himself the '*dumu (dingir) Iš-me-(dingir) Da-gan, lugal Ki-en-gi-ki-Urdu*, i. e. the son of Ishme-Dagan, the king of Shumer and Akkad). From this it follows that:

[1] The same may be said also of the Semitic inscription published in C. T. part iii. No. 17288, although the title of king Dungi in this inscription is unfortunately broken off.

[2] *ĜI-LI*: pronounce *SAR-GUB*, and see Scheil, R. T. xix. p. 56.

(1) Ishme-Dagan was the last of the rulers of Isin, because his son does not call himself lugal or even patesi, bearing only religious titles.

(2) That the dynasty of Isin was overthrown by Gungunu, king of the third dynasty of Ur.

(3) If this dynasty was overthrown by Gungunu, then all the other kings belonging to the same dynasty as Ishme-Dagan must have preceded Gungunu.

Of the kings who call themselves 'king of Isin [1],' we have found so far the following:—

(*Ia-lu-un-a-sar*)
|
Libit-Anunit [1]
. . .
Iš-bi-gir-ra [1]
. . .
Ur-Ninib
. . .
Bur-Sin I. [2]
. . . [3]
Iš-me-Dagan
|
En an-na-tum(a), contemporary of Gungunu.

With this Gungunu, who is called 'king of Ur' only, have to be classed Dungi II, and Ur-Gur II.[4], because they all bear one and the same title. After a gap of about one hundred years (p. 40 f.), we arrive at the fourth dynasty of Ur, headed by Dungi III. The rulers that belong to this latter dynasty bear the proud title, *lugal*

[1] Notice the difference in the titles of these rulers. Ialunasar has no title; Ishbigirra calls himself 'king of Isin' only, while the others term themselves 'king of Isin, king of Shumer and Akkad'; Enannatum has no title again.

[2] Called Bur-Sin I. in order to distinguish him from Bur-Sin II. of the fourth dynasty of Ur.

[3] The dots indicate that we do not know whether one ruler was the son of the other. It is possible that between the different rulers other kings have to be placed.

[4] About Ur-Gur II. I have my doubts, for it may be possible that he is the same as Ur-Gur I.; see *sub* 'Third dynasty of Ur.'

Uru-um-ki-ma lugal an-ub-da tab-tab-ba (comp. p. 39), and are the following:—Dungi III., Bur-Sin II., Gimil-Sin, Ine-Sin, Idîn-Dagan (Hilprecht, R. R. B. L. p. 84. See, however, *sub* dynasty of Isin).

In O. B. I. No. 127, rev., last two lines, we find the following date:—

Mu (dingir) Gimil-(dingir) Sin	In the year when Gimil-Sin,
lugal Uru-um-ki-ma-ge	king of Ur,
ma-da Za-ap-ša-li-ki mu-ḫul-a	brought evil upon the land of Zapshali.

The earlier part of this tablet contains notices about the reign of Bur-Sin II.; we conclude, therefore, that Gimil-Sin was probably a successor of Bur-Sin II.

This conclusion may be confirmed by the dates of a tablet published by Thureau-Dangin, in R. A. iv. p. 142. On that tablet we find the following dates in succession:—

1. *Mu En Unug-ki-ga ba-a-tug*
2. *Mu En (dingir) Uru-ki-KAR-ZI-DA ba-a-tug*
3. *Mu (dingir) Gimil-(dingir) Sin.*

Nos. 1, 2 occur also on O. B. I. No. 127, obv., 8 and 9, belong therefore to Bur-Sin II., while No. 3 shows that Gimil-Sin must have followed Bur-Sin II.

Thureau-Dangin, in R. S. 1897, p. 74, has shown that Dungi III. was the immediate predecessor of Bur-Sin II., by restoring the historical inscription in O. B. I. No. 124, pl. 54, col. vi., as follows:—

[Ur-] Lama [1]
[pa-te-]si
[mu dingir Du]n-gi
[uš-kalag]-ga
[lugal U]rum-ki-ma

[1] Compare now also C. T. part v. Nos. 12913, 12231, 18933, 19024, and especially 18346, rev. col. viii, where all the signs are clear, and where we read: *Ur-(dingir) KAL (= Lama), pa-te-si, mu (dingir) Dun-gi, lugal Uru-um-ki-ma, lugal an-ub-da tab-tab-ba-ge, Ki-maš-ki Ḫu-mur-ti-ki, šà ma-da-bi ud-ru(m) mu-ḫul, mu-uš-sa-a-bi.*

[lugal-a]n-ub-da-[tab-la]b-ba-ge
. . . . *ki* . . .

With this he compares a contract-tablet of the Louvre (A. O. 2512), which has the following inscription:—

Ur-Lama pa-te-si mu Bur-Sin lugal.

'*Il devient,*' he says, '*par-là infiniment probable:* 1°, *que le roi qui a précédé Bour-Sin s'appelait Doungi*; 2°, *qu'il ne doit pas être confondu avec Doungi l'Ancien, roi de Shoumer et d'Accad.*' (Comp. also above, p. 24.)

In R. A. iv. p. 144, the same scholar has published another tablet having these dates:

mu mà-gur-maǧ ba-gim
mu e-(*dingir*)*-? ba-ru*
mu (*dingir*) *I-ne-*(*dingir*) *Sin.*

The two former dates preceding the reign of Ine-Sin he refers, with the help of Constantinople, No. 831, to Gimil-Sin, thus making Gimil-Sin precede Ine-Sin. (See on the whole subject, Thureau-Dangin, R. S. 1897, p. 72 ff.[1]) The succession of the kings of the third and fourth dynasty of Ur would then be:—

Third Dynasty.
Gungunu
. . .
Ur-Gur II. (?)
. . .
Dungi II.
. . .
Fourth Dynasty.
Dungi III.
Bur-Sin II.
|
Ur-Ba'u II. (see below)
. . .
Gimil-Sin
. . .
Ine-Sin
. . .
Idin-Dagan

[1] Now also O. L. Z. i. 167 ff.

The rulers and representatives of the different dynasties in this period might be arranged as follows :—

Shirpurla.	Ur.	Uruk-Amnanu [1].	Isin.
(Ga)lu-ka-ni I.	*Ur-Gur*		
Ĝa-la-Lam(a)	*Dungi I.*		
	. . .	*Sin-gâmil*	
	. . .	. . .	
	. . .	*Sin-gâšid* [1]	. . .
			(Ia-lu-un-a-sar)
			Libit-Anunit
			. . .
			Iš-bi-gir-ra
			. . .
			Ur-Ninib
			. . .
			Bur-Sin I.
			. . .
			Iš-me-Dagan
	Gungunu [2]		*En-an-na-tum(a)*
. . .	. . .		
	Ur-Gur II. (?)		
	. . .		
(Ga)lu-ka-ni II.	*Dungi II.*		
. . .	. . .		
	Dungi III.		
	Bur-Sin II.		
	Ur-Ba'u II.		
	. . .		
	Gimil-Sin		
	. . .		
	Ine-Sin		
	. . .		
	Idîn-Dagan		

[1] The date of this small kingdom, to which the above-named two (*sic*) rulers belong, is very doubtful. Winckler (Altorientalische Forschungen, pp. 231, 232) places them 'at about the same period' as Ur-Gur, while Hommel (Geschichte, p. 206) wants to put them *before* the second dynasty of Ur, but '*um einige Jahrhunderte später als* 3800 B. C.'; Lehmann (Zwei Probleme, p. 175), even after the fourth dynasty of Ur. I am inclined to place them with all reserve after Dungi I., but before Ur-Ninib; see what is said about these rulers further on.

[2] Whether the dynasty of Gungunu preceded that of Dungi III. is very doubtful.

A Chronological Table, containing the names of all[1] rulers of Old Babylonia from the oldest times down to the time of Ḫammurabi, the contemporary of Abraham, will be found opposite. A few words of explanation would seem necessary as regards the dates which are there assigned to the different rulers[2].

The starting-point of the calculations is Sargon I., 3800 B.C. According to p. 9, Sargon I. belongs to the third period of

[1] With the exception of a certain *KU?-URU* (see O. B. I. 87, ii. 32, 34)-*(dingir) Utu*, who calls himself *lugal Ma-uru-ki pa-te-si gal (dingir) En-lil*, i. e. king of *MA-URU*, the great patesi of Bêl; C. T. part v. No. 12146. This king no doubt belongs to the time between Urukagina and Lugalzaggisi. The patesis of Nippur have not been mentioned, because they probably held only religious positions, i. e. they were patesis of Bêl rather than of Nippur. Comp. however O. B. I. 94, where Ur-Enlil calls himself *dam-kar-gal*, with O. B. I. 96 and 97, where he has the title *pa-te-si En-lil-ki-da*. If, however, Ur-Enlil was a patesi of Nippur in the secular sense of the term, he must belong to the period preceding Urukagina. The same may be true of *Ur-Ma-ma*, the *dam-kar-gal* of Bêl, O. B. I. 95, and ibid. p. 262, 6. Two other patesis of Nippur, living at the time of Dungi, the *nitaǵ lig-ga lugal Uru-um-ki-ma lugal Ki-en-gi-Urdu* (i.e. Dungi I.), are *Ur-(dingir) AN-MAǴ* (?) and his father *Lugal-kal-la* (Hommel, Geschichte, p. 334). *Ḫa-aš-ḫa-mi-ir*, patesi of *Iš* (?)-*ku-un-Sin*, may belong either to the time of Ur-Gur of the second dynasty of Ur, or to an unknown Ur-Gur of the third dynasty (comp. p. 37, note 2), for in the inscription referred to (i. R. 1, i. No. 10) Ḫashḫamir calls Ur-Gur only *nitaǵ lig-ga lugal Uru-um-ki-ma*. Other patesis may belong to the period covered by our Chronological Table, as e. g. a certain *ÌP-ŠA-(dingir) INNANA-ERIN?* patesi of *INNANA-ERINki*—a city frequently mentioned in tablets of the fourth dynasty of Ur—who at the same time is a *šakkanâku ma-ti Elamti* (U. A. G. p. 157, No. 8; Hommel, P. S. B. A. 1896, 23); a certain *(ilu)-Mu-ta-bil*, a *šakkanâku* of *Dûr-ilu-ki* (ibid. p. 156, No. 7); a certain . . . *ši*, patesi of . . . *mu-tuk* . . . *ki* (A. F. p. 545, No. 3); a certain . . . *zi*, *lugal AL* (or *GIŠDIN*, not *TE!*) (ibid. No. 4, probably the same as *Ba-zi lugal Al*, C. T. part vii. No. 12033); and a certain *(Ga)lu-(dingir) Utu* (Amêl-Shamash), patesi of *Gišuḫ-ki* (T. C. part i. p. 50, No. 96-6-12, 3). Very old are also the two seal-cylinders published by Hommel, Geschichte, p. 290: *Iš(?)mà-ì-lum, dumu* . . ., *pa-te-si, Dun-til-ki-la*; and p. 293: . . . . *da, pa-te-si ŠIT-TAR-ki*. All these names have not been mentioned in our Chronological Table, because they were not important for our chronology.

[2] It is hardly necessary to say here, that these dates are only approximate and *tentative*—thus differing essentially from those of Lehmann, which are given as absolutely certain; so certain that Nabû-nâ'id's statement has to give place to the calculations of that scholar.

CHRONOLOGICAL TABLE.

Ki-en-gi (= Lagash ?)	*Kish* (written: *Kish-ki* or only Kish)	*Gir-su-ki* or *Shir-pur-la-ki* (= Lagash, Tell Loh)	*Gish-UH (?)-ki* (= Djokha ?)	*Uru-um-ki-ma* (= Ur)	*A-ga-de-ki* (Akkad)	*Gu-ti-um-ki*	*Lu-lu-bu-um-ki*	*l*	*Ni-si-in-ki-na* (= Isin)	*UD-KIB-NUN-ki* (= Larsa)	*KA-DINGIR-RA-ki* (= Babylon)	*Nim-(ma)-ki* (= Elam)
En-shag-kush-an-na, before 4500 B.C. (the 'lord' of Kengi)	. . . . *U-dug-?* (patesi, O.B.I. Nos. 108, 109) . . . . *Me-silim* (king) . . . . *Lugal-da ?-ak ?* (king)	. . . . *Uru-ka-gi-na* (king) 4500 B.C. . . . . *En-ḫe-gal* (king) . . . . *Lugal-shug-gur* (patesi) . . . . *Gur-sar* | *Gu-ni-du* | *Ur-Ninâ* (king) 4300 B.C.	*Ush* (patesi)									
Lid-daMu-ri-kur-ta, À-ni-kur-ra, Lugal-shir, A-kur-gal, Nun-pad, E(?)-ud-bu, Ninâ-ku-tur-a (king and patesi)												
	Al-su-su-a (king) . . . . *En-ne-Ugun* (king) . . . . *Ur-zag-ud-du* (king of Kish and king of -?-) . . . . *Lugal-tar-si* (king) . . . . O.B.I. 118 (king) . . . . *Ma-an-ish-tu-su* (king) . . . . *Âlu-usharshid* 3850 B.C. (king)	*E-an-na-tum* 4200 B.C. (king and patesi); *En-an-na-tum I.* (patesi) | *En-teme-na* (patesi) | *En-an-na-tum II.* 4100 B.C. (patesi) | *Lum-ma-dur* . . . . *Lugal-an-da* (patesi) . . . . *Lugal-ushum-gal* 3800 B.C. (patesi) | *UR-E* (patesi) . . . . *Ur-Ba'u* (patesi) 3500 B.C. | (?) *Nam-mag-ni* 3450 B.C. (patesi) . . .	*Gu-nam-mi-de* (patesi) *En-à-kal-li* (patesi = king of *TE* ?) | *Ur-lum-ma* (patesi = king of *TE* ?) *Ili* (patesi) *U-kush* (patesi) | *Lugal-zag-gi-si* 4000 B.C. (king of Erech) . . . . *E-zu-ab* (king)	[Title: 'King of Erech, king of Ur'] *Lugal-ki-gub-ni-du-du* 3900 B.C. (king) | (?) *Lugal-kisal-si* (king) . . . . esi)	*It-ti-Bel* | *Shar-ga-ni-shar-âli* 3800 B.C. (king) | *Na-ra-am-Sin* 3750 B.C. (king) *Na-be-?-mash* (patesi of *Tu-tu-ki*) | *Li-pu-ush-?-a-um* (his daughter) *Bi-in-ga-ni-shar-âli* 3700 B.C.	*La-si-ra-ab* (king)	*An-nu-ba-ni-ni* 3850 B.C. (king)	*Lugal-z* 4000 B. . . . *Lugal-ki-g* | *Lugal-*				

	. . . . *Gu-de-a* 3300 B.C. (patesi) | *Ur-Nin-gir-su* 3250 B.C. (patesi) . . . . *Ur-Nin-sun* (patesi) . . . . (*Ga*)*lu-ka-ni I* 3150 B.C. (patesi) | *Ga-la-Lama*		[Title: 'King of Ur, king of Shumer and Akkad'] . . . . *Ur-Gur* 3200 B.C. (king) | *Dun-gi I.* 3150 B.C. (king)	. . . .	. . . .	. . . .	[Ti ... ch']	[Title: 'King of Isin,' or 'king of Isin, king of Shumer and Akkad'] (*Ia-lu-un-a-sar* ?) | *Libit-Anunit* 3000 B.C. (king) . . . . *Ish-bi-gir-ra* (king) *Ur-Ninib* (king) . . . . *Bur-Sin I.* (king) . . . . *Idin-Dagan* (see *sub* Ur) . . . . *Iš-me-Dagan* (king) | *En-an-na-tum* 2800 B.C.		
	(*Ga*)*lu-ka-ni II* (patesi) *Al-la-mu* (?) (patesi) . . . . *Ur-(dingir) KAL* (patesi) *Gu-de-a II* (?) (patesi)	*Ur-Ne-sù* (patesi) . . . . (*Ga*)*lu-Utu* (patesi)	[Title: ' ... Ur' *Gu-un* . . . *Ur-Gur* (?) *Dungi* (?) . . . . [Title: 'King of Ur, king of the four corners of the world'] *Dun-gi III.* 2700 B.C. (king) *Bur-Sin II.* 2650 B.C. (king) | *Ur-Ba'u II.* (?) 2630 B.C. (king) | *Gimil-Sin* 2600 B.C. (king) | *I-ne-Sin* 2580 B.C. (king) . . . . *Idin-Dagan* (king) (according to Hilprecht; see *sub Ni-si-in-ki-na*)	[*Ur-Ningirsu en Nina*]	. . . .	. . . .	. . . .	. . . . 2300 B.C.	*Nûr-Ramman* (king) | *Sin-i-din-na* (king) . . . . *Rim-Sin* (king) (=*Eri-Aku*= אַרְיוֹךְ)	*Zabû* 2350–2336 B.C. (king) *Apil-Sin* 2336–2318 B.C. (king) *Sin-muballit* 2318–2288 B.C. (king) *Hammurabi* (=אַמְרָפֶל) 2288–2233 B.C. (king)

Radau, *to face p.* 30.]

cuneiform writing, which begins with Lugalzaggisi, and ends with Ur-Ba'u. According to the list on p. 23, Sargon I. and his son Naram-Sin come in the middle of this period, which period was said to extend over a space of 500 years. Hence Lugalzaggisi probably lived at about 4000 B.C., and Ur-Ba'u at about 3500 B.C. In the middle stands Naram-Sin at 3750 B.C.

In making the date of Naram-Sin and Sargon I. the starting-point of our calculation we differ essentially from Thureau-Dangin and Lehmann, both of which scholars make Gudea, as it seems, the starting-point. They fix first the date of Gudea—a date which is arrived at by supplying a 'goodly lot' of 'ifs'—and then they manufacture the date of Sargon I.; and, as we should naturally expect, the result of so precarious an argument is a denial of the accuracy of Nabû-nâ'id's statement. In this they are, however, not alone. The date of Naram-Sin was rejected by Eduard Meyer, Geschichte des Alterthums, i. (1884) § 133; Winckler, U. A. G., p. 44 ff., and A. F. p. 550: '*Kurz vor der Dynastie von UR I.*' Thureau-Dangin (R. A. iv. p. 72) writes: '*Entre l'écriture des tablettes* (i. e. the contract (?)-tablets (*sur argile*) of Sharganisharâli and Naram-Sin) *et celle des inscriptions de Gudéa, par exemple, il existe des différences assez profondes, ces différences ne peuvent correspondre en aucune façon à* l'énorme intervalle d'environ mille ans *qui s'impose au cas où on accepte les données de Nabonide. Force est donc de rabaisser dans une large mesure la date généralement attribuée à Sargon et à Naram-Sin, et de placer la domination d'Agadé non pas dans la première, mais dans la seconde moitié, peut-être même vers la fin de la seconde moitié du quatrième millénaire.*'

According to this statement Thureau-Dangin would be satisfied if there existed between Sargon I. and Gudea only about 500 years. Instead, however, of putting Sargon I. further down in time, thus questioning Nabû-nâ'id's statement, that scholar should revise his date of Gudea. Gudea lived, not at 2800 B.C., but at 3300 B.C. (see Chronological Table). A date so uncertain as that of Gudea at present is should not supersede the certain date of Sargon I.

Last of all, the date of Naram-Sin seems to have found a determined enemy in Lehmann, Zwei Hauptprobleme der altorientalischen Chronologie, Leipzig, 1898, p. 175 ff.

This scholar finds the same difficulty as Thureau-Dangin (see above, p. 31), viz. that between Gudea and Naram-Sin there exists a space of a thousand years, which is, as he expresses it, 'ein Jahrtausend völliger Leere—*ein absolutes Vacuum*' (p. 179). But how does that scholar know that Gudea lived exactly at 2700 B.C.; a date which he considers so trustworthy that the one given by Nabû-nâ'id for Sargon I. has to be rejected? He argues:

The date of Kudurnanḫundi I, probably the immediate predecessor of Kudurnuḫgamar (= כְּדָרְלָעֹמֶר, Gen. 14) is 2280 B.C. (or 1,635 years before Ashurbanabal). Kudurnuḫgamar[1] was, he says, a contemporary (??) of Ḫammurabi (אַמְרָפֶל), who reigned, according to this scholar's view, from 2248–2194 B.C., or forty years later, as we have proposed. Forty years, indeed, is not a great difference. This date *might be* accepted, *but* not the dates which he assigns to the dynasties preceding this Elamite invasion under Kudurnanḫundi. Having fixed this date, he says: '*Von dem Elamiten-Einfall zurück bis hinauf zu der bisher sogenannten "ersten Dynastie von Ur"* (i.e. the second dynasty: Ur-Gur and Dungi I.) *haben wir* eine einigermassen (*sic*) *fortlaufende Kunde, so dass sich die Zeit "der ersten Dynastie von Ur" mit* einiger Annäherung (notice his wording!!) *berechnen lässt*' (ibid. p. 175). The dynasties which preceded the Elamite invasion are (ibid. p. 175) that of Erech, second (i.e. third) of Ur, Isin, first (i.e. second) of Ur. He also ascribes certain years to these different dynasties, saying: *if* we attribute to the dynasty of Erech fifty years, then we get to the year 2330 B.C. (2280 + 50). *If* we attribute to the second dynasty of Ur at the very most 120 years, then we arrive at the year 2450 (2330 + 120), and 'gehen wir *dann weiter zu der Dynastie von Isin, von der uns fünf Herrscher bekannt sind,* und rechnen, wiederum reichlich, 150 *Jahre,* so

[1] For the correct reading of this name see I. A. Knudtzon and Fr. Delitzsch in B. A. iv. p. 88 ff. against V. Scheil in R. T. xix, 1896, pp. 40–44. It should be read: Kudur-Dugmal(?) = Kudur-Lagamar (Hommel, P. S. B. A. 1896, p. 24).

erreichen wir *das Jahr* 2600, *und wollen wir einen Spielraum für uns unbekannte Herrscher annehmen, ca.* 2650. *Der Dynastie von Isin ist die "erste von Ur" vorausgegangen, von der uns zwei Herrscher bekannt sind. Es mögen deren noch mehr gewesen sein,* aber ein Jahrhundert ist nach unseren jetzigen Nachrichten schon ein überreicher Ansatz. *Der Beginn der "ersten Dynastie"* fiele also *frühestens ca.* 2700 (2750) B.C.' (p. 176). And Gudea, being only one generation ahead of Dungi I., must have reigned therefore '*ebenfalls um oder kurz vor* 2700 (2750) *höchstens*.' This is the way Lehmann manufactures the date of Gudea!! It is so certain Gudea reigned at 2750 that there cannot be any doubt, so *absolutely* certain that even the dates of Naram-Sin and Sargon I., testified to by Nabû-nâ'id, have to give way. But he continues (p. 179): '*Somit haben wir nun folgenden Thatbestand* (indeed!?): *Um* 2700 *Gudea und kurz vor ihm Ur-Bau. Um* 3750 *nach Nabonid's Angabe Naram-Sin und Lugal-ušum-gal. Zwischen beiden also ein Jahrtausend,* ein Jahrtausend völliger Leere—*ein absolutes Vacuum*.' This, however, as he rightly says, cannot be possible, and thus, his conclusion is, Nabû-nâ'id's statement *must be wrong* (pp. 179, 185). But how does he get over this difficulty? If we read, he tells us, instead of III.M.II.C. (3200) simply II.M.II.C. (2200) in Nabû-nâ'id's statement, where these figures are very clearly written, '*so sind alle Schwierigkeiten behoben*' (p. 187). He, however, feels that there must be a somewhat greater space between Naram-Sin (2750) and Gudea (2700) than only fifty years, and thus 'nehmen wir *in Nabonid's Angabe den im vorliegenden Fall, bei der Höhe der Zahl,* vielleicht *etwas niedrig gegriffenen Spielraum von* 25 *Jahren nach oben und unten an,* so ergiebt sich, *dass Naram-Sin nicht vor* 2779 *zu regieren aufgehört haben und nicht später als* 2713 *zur Regierung gekommen sein kann*' (ibid. p. 189).

This is that scholar's argument—an argument which required a good deal of *liberality* on Lehmann's part in order to find out the *exact date* of Gudea, 2700 B.C. It would hardly seem necessary to say very much against a date which was established and made an absolute fact (*Thatbestand*) by premises introduced by mere 'ifs.' But the position of that scholar in the learned world constrains us to answer him.

1. According to Lehmann's calculation the date of Gudea was '*um oder kurz vor* 2700 (2750) *höchstens* B.C.' (p. 176). Shortly before Gudea (p. 179, note 4) we must place Ur-Ba'u and Nammaĝni. Suppose, for the sake of argument, both these rulers reigned only twenty years together, Ur-Ba'u would therefore have begun to reign either about 2720 at the very least, or about 2770 at the most.

Now Naram-Sin, according to Lehmann's argument, must have reigned somewhere between the years 2713 and 2779 (p. 189). Hence, if these calculations are correct, Ur-Ba'u and Nammaĝni must have been contemporaries of Naram-Sin. But from inscriptions we know that a certain Lugalushumgal, patesi of Shirpurla, was the contemporary of Naram-Sin. This fact alone shows how utterly groundless Lehmann's calculations are. Or does he believe that at the time of Naram-Sin there were two, or possibly three, patesis in Shirpurla, who were all contemporaries of Naram-Sin? But further, Thureau-Dangin, in R. A. iv. No. iii. pl. ix. No. 31, published a remarkable tablet from the time of Naram-Sin (rev. l. 1), on the reverse of which (l. 5) a certain *UR-E*, patesi of Shirpurla-^{ki}, is mentioned. The same tablet also mentions on the obverse (l. 9) a patesi of *Uru-um-^{ki}ma* (= *Ur*), whose name probably was *Ur-$^{(dingir)}$ Utu* (*Kalbi-Shamash*) [1].

Now let us make a diagram according to Lehmann's chronology:

Lugal-ušum-gal [between 2779 and 2713]	*Ur-Ba'u* / *Nam-maĝ-ni* } [between 2770 and 2750 (2720 and 2700)]		*Naram-Sin* [between 2779 and 2713]
	Gu-de-a 2700 [2750]	*Ur-Gur*	
	Ur-Nin-gir-su [*c.* 2700 (2750)]	*Dungi I.* [*c.* 2700 (2750)]	

[1] The two lines in question read:

Ur-$^{(dingir)}$ Utu-ge

[*na*]*m* (?)-*pa-te-si Uru-um-^{ki}-ma*

The *NAM* before *pa-te-si* may make it doubtful whether *Ur-$^{(dingir)}$ Utu* was the

But to this diagram have to be added *UR-E*, patesi of Shirpurla, contemporary of Naram-Sin and the patesi (*UR-*$^{(dingir)}$ *UTU?*) of Ur[1]. Thus we would have reigning at the time of Naram-Sin (between 2779 and 2713) four patesis (Ur-Ba'u, Nammag̃ni, Lugal-ushumgal, and Ur-E) in Shirpurla; one king (Ur-Gur), and at the same time one patesi (*Ur-*$^{(dingir)}$ *UTU?*) in Ur!! This is the historical solution at which Lehmann arrives!! Indeed, instead of clearing up the subject, Lehmann has only confused it worse than it was before his book was written. This alone would make a further argument unnecessary, but in order to corroborate our position and to show why we assigned to the kings of the different dynasties the dates as given in our Chronological Table, we proceed.

2. Lehmann (ibid. p. 176) makes the statement: '*Sein Sohn* (i. e. Gudea's son) *Ur-nin-gir-su ist Dungi's I. Vasall.*' As authority for this statement he takes Winckler, U. A. G. p. 42. On account of the importance of that passage we quote it in full: '*Dass zwischen Dungi und Gudea ein Zeitraum von mindestens* 103 *Jahren liegen müsse, galt bisher als sicher* (*Hommel, Geschichte, p.* 319), *durch eine Inschrift des British Museum lässt sich indessen mit* Sicherheit (sic!?) *anders die Frage lösen. Dieselbe steht auf einem zum Kopfaufsatz einer kleinen Statue bestimmten Gegenstande aus grünem Stein* (78, 12–18, 1) *und darin widmet "für das Leben Dungis, Königs von Ur" Ur-nin-gir-su in ki. aga an Ninâ gid, der Ninlil jenen Gegenstand. Dieser Ur-nin-gir-su findet sich nun mit demselben* Titel (welcher wahrscheinlich irgend eine priesterliche Würde bezeichnet) *auf Backsteinen und einer steinernen Schale aus*

person that held the patesiate of Ur at the time of Naram-Sin. So much however is certain, that at the time of Naram-Sin there was a [*na*]*m-pa-te-si* of Ur, hence also a patesi.

[1] Lehmann's statement therefore (ibid. p. 183): '*Zwischen Ur-Gur von Ur und Dungi von Ur* (*in Nippur*) *und den* ungefähr *gleichzeitigen* (ibid. p. 176) *patesi's Ur-Ba'u und Gude'a* (*in Lagaš = Shirpurla*) *auf der einen Seite, Naram-Sin und Lugal-ušum-gal auf der anderen Seite, ist in Nippur wie in Lagaš nicht* ein *Herrschername erhalten,*' betrays ignorance. See our Chronological Table.

Telloh wieder (Heuzey, Revue arch. 1886, pl. 2; Sarzec, Déc. pl. 37, 8) und es kann keinem Zweifel unterliegen, dass er derselbe ist, welcher auf einer Steininschrift (Déc. 37, 9) sich "patesi von Sir-pur-la," Sohn Gudeas, nennt. Er wird bei Lebzeiten seines Vaters eine Priesterwürde bekleidet haben und ist denn nach dessen Tode patesi geworden. Wir erhalten so für die Zeit Dungi's im ganzen mindestens drei von ihm abhängige patesis:

Gudea,
Ur-nin-gir-su, sein Sohn,
Lu-ka-ni (oder Gal-ka-ni).

Wir wissen nicht, welches die Reihenfolge dieser drei war. Wenn Gudea der erste von ihnen war, so wird er noch in die Zeit Ur-gurs von Ur hineingereicht haben, andernfalls würde dies für Gal-ka-ni eintreffen.' This is the *locus classicus*, on which Lehmann partly builds his chronology.

(*a*) If this be true, then Dungi I. must have been a contemporary of at least the following four persons [1]:

Gudea,
Ur-Ningirsu, his son,
(Ga)lukani, and
Gala-Lama, his son.

Dungi I. must clearly have lived to a fabulous age!

(*b*) Even if in this inscription Ur-Ningirsu had, according to Winckler, a '*priesterliche Würde*,'—for *en ki-ag* may be translated by 'beloved high-priest,' see Dates of Dungi III.—but then it would not follow as yet that he exercised that priestly function during the life of his father, who is said to be Dungi, 'king of Ur, king of Shumer and Akkad.' If Ur-Ningirsu was high-priest at all, he was it during the time of 'Dungi, king of Ur.' Winckler must first prove that those two Dungis are one and the same person.

[1] We say 'at least,' for there possibly may be discovered another patesi who lived between Ur-Ningirsu and (Ga)lukani (see Chronological Table).

Lehmann himself ought to have seen Winckler's curious argument, and not have followed him blindly.

(*c*) In the inscription above referred to Winckler says that *Ur-Ningirsu dedicates* that '*Gegenstand*.' However, the fact is not so; neither does *Ur-Ningirsu* dedicate, nor does he *dedicate*, but 'lady *Ba'u-ninan makes* something for Ninlil.'

The whole inscription reads (comp. Jensen, K. B. iii[1]. p. 68 ii.):

Nin-lil	For Ninlil
nin-a-ni	his mistress
nam-ti	has for the life
(*dingir*) *Dun-gi*	of Dungi,
nitağ lig-ga	the strong hero,
lugal Uru-um-ki-ma-ka-ku	the king of Ur,
(*dingir*) *Ba-u-nin-a-an*	Ba'u-ninan
ZABAR-KU	the *ZABAR-KU*
Ur-(*dingir*)*Nin-gir-su*	of Ur-Ningirsu,
en-ki-ag (*dingir*) *Ninâ-ka-ge*	the beloved lord of Ninâ,
ĞI-LI nam-sal-ka-ni	(for) a *ĞI-LI* (= ornament = *sar-gub*) of her (=Ninlil's) womanhood
mu-na-gim	made.

One can see instantly that this Ur-Ningirsu is no other than Ur-Ningirsu of Telloh, who later on became patesi. Lehmann, of course, is of the same mind as Winckler. This fitted well into *his* chronology. No, the inscription above quoted shows clearly that this Ur-Ningirsu (together with that mentioned in Déc. 37, 8[1]) was a contemporary of 'Dungi, king of Ur,' i. e. of Dungi II. and not of Dungi I[2].

(*d*) The very fact that Ur-Ningirsu here, as well as in Déc. 37, 8, has not the title 'patesi,' which we find in all the other

[1] That inscription reads: Ur-Ningirsu, the *en-me-zi* of Anna, the *me-ad-azag* (probably = an attribute to Anna), the 'beloved high-priest' of Ninâ. (See on the other hand Jensen's translation in K. B. iii[1]. p. 67.)

[2] For it will be noticed that the Dungi here has exactly the same title as Gungunu (i. R. 2, No. vi. 1), viz. *nitağ lig-ga lugal Uru-um-ki-ma-ka*.

inscriptions of Ur-Ningirsu, patesi of Shirpurla, is reason and proof enough that he cannot be identical with that well-known patesi, the son of Gudea, and also that Gudea himself was not a contemporary of Dungi I.

The result then is:

In the inscription there is not one syllable to prove that the Ur-Ningirsu there mentioned is Gudea's son. The very fact, however, that in case Ur-Ningirsu were a contemporary of Dungi I. —which Winckler wants to prove and which Lehmann accepts as proved—we should have at least four patesis[1] during the lifetime of Dungi, shows clearly enough that Winckler's hypothesis is improbable, yes, impossible.

3. Above (p. 21) it has been shown that Ĝala-Lama, together with his father (Ga)lukani I., were dependent upon Dungi I., son of Ur-Gur. At the present we, however, do not know if Ur-Ningirsu was the father of (Ga)lukani, and thus a contemporary of Ur-Gur. As long as we do not know this we are justified in placing a 'gap' between Ur-Ningirsu and (Ga)lukani. This 'gap' would remove Ur-Ningirsu at least one generation from (Ga)lukani, and thus put him also before Ur-Gur. In our Chronological Table we placed Ur-Ninsun between (Ga)lukani and Ur-Ningirsu. Whether he belongs

We must therefore place this Dungi after Gungunu, and thus distinguish between the following three Dungis:

Dungi I. (II. Ur): *lugal Uru-um-ki-ma lugal Ki-en-gi-ki-Urdu*;

Dungi II. (III. Ur): *lugal Uru-um-ki-ma-ka*;

Dungi III. (IV. Ur): *lugal Uru-um-ki-ma lugal an-ub da tab-tab-ba-ge*, or in Semitic: *šar Uri šar ki-ib-ra-tim ar-ba-im*. Whether we ought to distinguish also between Ur-Gur I. (II. Ur), *lugal Uru-um-ki-ma lugal Ki-en-gi-ki-Urdu*, and Ur-Gur II. (III. Ur), *lugal Uru-um-ki-ma*, is doubtful. For a discussion of the question whether Dungi I. may not be the same as Dungi III. (comp. Winckler, O. L. Z. i. 238, and Thureau-Dangin, ibid. p. 174), see *sub* 'Fourth dynasty of Ur.' We believe that we have to distinguish between these rulers according to their titles. In our Chronological Table we have indicated this sufficiently.

[1] And these patesis themselves must have lived quite a number of years, especially Gudea and Ur-Ningirsu.

there or not does not affect our argument. If he does not we would have to place him before Gudea, supplying between this latter ruler and the former again a 'gap.' In this case Ur-Ninsun simply would reduce the gap between Ur-Ba'u and Gudea[1]. Further, we do not know whose son Gudea was. Consequently we must supply a gap between Gudea and Ur-Ninsun and between Ur-Ninsun and Nammaĝni. We obtain then the following succession :—

Ur-Ba'u
| (?)
Nam-maĝ-ni
. . gap . .
Ur-Nin-sun
. . gap . .
Gu-de-a
|
Ur-Nin-gir-su
. . gap . . *Ur-Gur I.*
|
(Ga)lu-ka-ni, |
| } contemporaries of *Dungi I.*
Ĝala-Lama |

This shows clearly that Ur-Ningirsu cannot have been the contemporary of Dungi I. In our table we assigned to Gudea a reign of about fifty years on account of the many buildings he executed, the material for which buildings he got from the most distant places — all which must have consumed much time. Between Ur-Ba'u and Gudea we claimed a space of about 200 years[2] on account of palaeographic evidence—the sign for *KA* shows that clearly. Thus it will be seen that our arrangement is *true* to the present state of science, claiming 'gaps' where we do not know the succession of rulers, and where palaeography enjoins us to do so. If we bear

[1] This however would prove fatal again. For, if this arrangement were correct, then Naram-Sin would be a contemporary of *at least* five patesis of Shirpurla, viz. Ur-Ba'u, Nammaĝni, Lugalushumgal, *UR-E*, Ur-Ninsun—all living between the years 2779 and 2713 B.C.—and a contemporary of one patesi of Ur and also of king Ur-Gur of Ur!! See p. 34.

[2] See p. 19.

this in mind, we are fully justified in assigning for the space between Ur-Ba'u and (Ga)lukani about 350 years.

Lehmann very generously ('*überreichlicher Ansatz*') ascribes to the dynasty of Isin 150 years; we, 200 years. Lehmann again forgets that we have to allow for unknown rulers and for the gaps existing between them (comp. also his 'Tabelle I: *Reihenfolge unbestimmt*') some more years; thus *two hundred years* at least must be ascribed to this dynasty.

Isin was overthrown by Gungunu. Further below it will be shown that there is an important difference in the titles of Gungunu and Dungi III.; the former *being called* only *king of Ur*, while the latter is always termed *king of Ur, king of the four corners of the world*. This difference is a very marked one. Had Gungunu been also 'king of the four corners of the world'—thus belonging to the same dynasty as Dungi III.—surely Enannatum(a) would not have dared to attribute to his lord so humble a title. Again, we do not know that Dungi III. was the son of Gungunu; thus we are forced by necessity—if we wish to be scientific—to claim another gap between these two rulers [1]; and since their titles are so very different, it follows that this gap must be a considerable one; nay, it seems to show that Gungunu belongs to a different dynasty. And even *if* this were not the case, the very fact that Dungi III. must have conquered the four corners of the world before he could assume this title—a feat not achieved in a few days—is reason enough to claim for this gap 100 years. (Comp. also Sargon I., who conquered the four corners of the world, but only Naram-Sin, his son, called himself '*šar kibrat arba'im*.')

As regards the succession of the rulers of the fourth dynasty of Ur, it is, even according to Thureau-Dangin (against Lehmann, p. 174), Dungi III., Bur-Sin III. (Ur-Ba'u, son of Bur-Sin II.), Gimil-Sin, Ine-Sin, and according to Hilprecht also, Idîn-Dagan.

Lehmann assigns to this dynasty—again very generously ('*sehr reichlich*')—about 120 years, although he is able to ascribe *with certainty* to the four rulers of this house only 67 years (see Tabelle I:

[1] Comp. also Winckler, U. A. G. pp. 39, 40.

12 + 5 + 9 + 41 years), thus making their dynasty last about twice as long as he can prove.

Further on it will be shown that we can ascribe to the different rulers of this dynasty with *certainly* the following number of years :—

to *Dungi III.:*	51	years.
Bur-Sin II.:	13	,,
Gimil-Sin:	10	,,
Ine-Sin: at least	2	
not classified dates :	10	years—total[1] 86 years.

Doubling, as Lehmann does, this number, we would get about 172 years, and allowing for Ur-Ḅa'u, son of Bur-Sin II., and Idîn-Dagan only 20 years, we would be able to fill up the 200 years for this dynasty. But all the rulers of this dynasty are not yet known, nor do we know whether one was the *immediate* successor of the other ; thus we may take Lehmann's 50 years for the '*Spielraum für uns unbekannte Herrscher*.' This would make this dynasty rule for about 250 years[2].

For the two rulers of the dynasty of Erech, who are *not said* to have been father and son, we ascribe 100 years—50 years more than Lehmann does. It is hardly possible to imagine that only these two rulers should have reigned in Erech.

In regard to our difference in fixing the date of Ḫammurabi, we need not spend many words, for this difference is only one of 40 years.

The predecessors of Ḫammurabi reigned 112 years.

[1] Since the publication of 'Cuneiform Texts from Babylonian Tablets, &c., in the British Museum,' Parts I–VIII, we are able to increase this 'total' by about ten years more. See *sub* 'Fourth dynasty of Ur.'

[2] As is apparent from our Chronological Table, we have divided the so-called third dynasty of Ur into two: viz. the third and the fourth. Six rulers we were able to enumerate as belonging to the latter dynasty. Claiming an average reign of twenty years for each king, we would get about 120 years. But we know that Dungi III. alone reigned fifty-one years at least; we have to add therefore thirty years to those 120 years. Furthermore, we ought to allow about 100 years for the gaps and for the unknown rulers. Thus we may very well be allowed to make this dynasty rule about 250 years. See Chronological Table.

Now let us count up these figures and see where we can put Ur-Ba'u.

2288 (date of Ḫammurabi)[1] + 112 years = 2400 B.C.: beginning of the first dynasty of Babylon in the north and that of Larsa in the south, both of which dynasties divide 'the kingdom of the four corners of the world' under Ur IV.[2] These troubles must have been of grave consequence, for they bring another people (the Elamites) into Babylonia under Kudurnanḫundi, who undoubtedly tried to take advantage of the confusion in Babylon. Probably there was even anarchy in Babylonia before Babylon I.[2] acquired the dominion.

2400 + 250 (= number of years during which Ur IV. reigned) brings us to about 2650, and including the anarchy, to 2700 B.C. Between Dungi III. and Gungunu lie about 100 years = 2800; 200 years for Isin = 3000 B.C.; 100 for Erech = 3100 B.C. At this time reigned, or better *ceased* to reign, Ur II. (Dungi I.); (Ga)lukani, his contemporary, *began* to reign at about 3150. Between (Ga)lukani and Ur-Ba'u are about 350 years, hence Ur-Ba'u probably reigned at about 3500, and Naram-Sin at 3750—only a space of about 250 years (!). These 250 years are partly covered by Ur-E, patesi of Shirpurla, and Ur-Utu (?), patesi of *Uru-um-ki-ma* (Ur).

Where does Lehmann's *vacuum* remain? Thureau-Dangin was satisfied to claim a space of about 500 years between Naram-Sin and Gudea. Will Lehmann be content with 250 years—just one-half of Thureau-Dangin's concession?

Indeed, 250 years is not much, if we remember that we are only *beginning* to know something about Old Babylonian history and chronology.

4. Lehmann, however, tries to argue from palaeography that Naram-Sin cannot have lived before 2750 B.C., saying (p. 177):

[1] For the different dates assigned to Ḫammurabi see Fr. Hommel, Altisraelitische Überlieferung, pp. 120, 121; J. Orr, Expository Times of March, 1897, pp. 161-177; Fr. Hommel, ibid., March, 1899, p. 278.

[2] Short expressions for 'Fourth dynasty of Ur,' and 'First dynasty of Babylon,' which latter generally is called the 'Ḫammurabi dynasty.'

'*Es wird Manchem ergangen sein wie mir, den bei einem Vergleich der Schriftzeichen auf der Vase Narâm-Sin's mit den Strichfiguren der älteren und ältesten Documente aus Telloh stets ein Gefühl völliger Rathlosigkeit beschlich, wenn er sich danach den* Gang der Entwicklung, zunächst auf palaeographischem Gebiet, *klar machen wollte. Auf der einen Seite wohl entwickelte Formen vollendeter Keilschriftzeichen, die aus dem Jahre* 3750 *stammen sollen, auf der anderen Seite ungleich primitivere Strichfiguren, die* um das Jahr 3000 in Gebrauch sein müssen.'

One may well ask, how does Lehmann know that the signs in the *older* and oldest documents from Telloh *must have been in use* at about 3000 B.C.? On the contrary, on the authority of Nabû-nâ'id, we know that the writing as exhibited on the tablets of Sargon I. *must have been in use* at 3800 B.C.; hence '*die ungleich primitiveren Strichfiguren*' of the oldest rulers in Telloh must be older, must antedate Sargon I., as has been shown above.

It is impossible to follow Lehmann's arguments. We must hold to the accuracy of Nabû-nâ'id's statement, and not give it up for a doubtful date, as that of Gudea necessarily must be. Naram-Sin then reigned at 3750 B.C.[1], and Gudea at somewhere about 3300 B.C.

King of Kengi.

The oldest king of Babylonia, of whom we have any record, is Enshagkushanna[2], whose date we have placed before 4500 B.C. He

[1] So also Oppert, Journal Asiatique, 1883, i. p. 89; Latrille, Z. K. ii. 357; Tiele, Geschichte, 114; Hommel, Geschichte, 166, 309; Delitzsch-Mürdter, Geschichte[2], 72; Maspero, Dawn of Civilization, p. 599; Hilprecht, O. B. I. p. 241.

[2] That this is the right pronunciation of the name—and not *En-šag-sag-an-na* (Hilprecht)—has been shown by Thureau-Dangin, R. A. iv. p. 70, note 6. *KUŠ*, see E. C. 192. *SAG* differs considerably; comp. T. C. 221 and E. C. 191. The name may mean 'Wise (*šag-kuš*, Br. 8049, *muštâlu*) is the lord (*en*) of heaven' (*an-na*). Hilprecht translated the name according to his reading, 'Lord is the king of heaven.' His inscriptions are published in O. B. I., Nos. 90, 91, 92; comp. Hilprecht, l. c. p. 261 ff.

calls himself 'lord of Kengi[1],' the southern (?) part of Babylonia. As to his nationality, whether he was a so-called 'Sumerian' or a 'Semite,' we have no means of knowing[2]. Besides 'lord of Kengi,' he seems to have had another title, viz. 'king of . . .' The lacuna probably contained the name of the capital of the kingdom[3]. He must have waged war against Kish in Northern Babylonia, which city he terms 'wicked of heart.' He was the victor, and presented the spoil to 'Enlil, king of the lands.' Enlil—the later Bêl—was the chief god in Nippur; Nippur accordingly was called *En-lil-ki*, the 'city of Enlil.' Hence Enlil of Nippur seems to have been the god who wielded the chief influence over the inhabitants of Early Babylonia. From inscriptions of certain patesis of Shirpurla, as well as from those of Lugalzaggisi, we know that this temple was under the control of the king, who called himself accordingly *patesi-gal*, 'the great patesi.' But it also had its own 'chief local administrator,' the *dam-kar-gal*[4], who in his turn had several minor priests or patesis under him. The cult of this god seems to have been well arranged; the king, being the *summus episcopus*, had a host of other officers (priests) under him, who exercised the ordinary functions of the so-called 'priesthood' of Bêl.

[1] See O. B. I. 90, l. 4 and note; p. 58, note 6; and Hommel, P. S. B. A., 1894, p. 209.

[2] But see under Lugalzaggisi.

[3] Hilprecht, O. B. I. p. 262: 'In all probability it was Erech'; and l. c. note 2: 'The traces do not point to the ideogram of Unug, more to kalama.'

[4] Comp. for instance O. B. I. No. 94, and l. c. p. 262, 6:

1. (*Dingir*) *Nin-din-dug* or better (*dingir*) *Innannà-Edin* (Hommel)	i. e.	To Ba'u
2. *Ur-*(*dingir*) *En-lil*		Ur-Enlil
3. *dam-kar-gal*		the damkargal
4. *a-mu-šub*		presented it.

That this inscription belongs to this period, see above, p. 19. Ba'u, see Br. 11084, is called there the *be-el-tum mu-bal-liṭ-ṭa-at mi-i-ti*, which does not mean 'the goddess who destroys life' (Hilprecht), but 'the goddess who restores the dead to life'—a difference! See O. B. I. p. 252, note 6. For *dam-kar-gal* see Hilprecht, O. B. I. p. 262, note 6, = 'the chief agent'; *a-mu-šub*, see Lugalzaggisi, iii. 40, note.

This inscription is found on a stèle with human figures on it, 'which show the characteristic features of a mixed race.' Hilprecht promptly concludes: 'The Semites must have been at this time in the country.'

The inscription of this oldest of all kings reads:

O. B. I. No. 90.

Comp. Hilprecht, l. c. p. 264, note 1, and Winckler, A. F. p. 372.

(*Dingir*) *En-lil*	i.e.	To Enlil,
lugal kur-kur-ra		king of the lands,
En-šag-kuš-an-na		Enshagkushanna,
en Ki-en-gi		lord of Kengi,
lugal		king of . . . . .

O. B. I. No. 91.

[*dingir*] *En-lil-la*	To Enlil
En-šag-kuš-an-na	Enshagkushanna
. . . *ga Kiš*-^{ki}	[the spoi]l of Kish

90, l. 4. *Ki-en-gi*, according to ii. R. 39, 9; v. R. 29, 45–47; A. O. V. 1887, p. 20, No. 7, means = *mâtu*, 'land, lowland.' See also V. A. Th. 276, 2460, where *Ki-en-gi-ra* (the *RA* not being post-position) is also translated by *ma-a-tum*. The meaning of *Ki-en-gi*, 'the land of canals and reeds' (Hilprecht, O. B. I. p. 252, note 9), rests solely on the supposition—(1) that *Ki-en-gi* is = *Ki-e-gi*; (2) that *e-gi* are the constituents of *kalam*; see Lugalzaggisi, col. iii. 29. According to Delitzsch, on the other hand, *Ki-en-gi* would mean, '*das Land des grossen Gefüges von Leuten.*' In the bilingual inscriptions of Ḫammurabi the expression *Ki-en-gi*-^{ki}-*Urdu* is translated by: *mâtu Šumeri û Akkadi*. On account of which translation scholars have derived '*Šumer*' from '*Ki-en-gi*,' or '*Ki-en-gin*.' See Lehmann, Šamaššumukîn, p. 86; Hommel, Geschichte, p. 234, note 1; and especially further below, *sub* 'Shumer and Akkad.'

O. B. I. No. 92.

dig-ga Kiš-^{ki}	the spoil of Kish,
ḫul-šag	wicked of heart,
a-mu-na-šub	he presented.

92, l. 1. *dig-ga*, Br. 5320, *narâbu*, H. W. B. 480 = that which is torn off = spoil. Br. 5324, *rukḳu*, H. W. B. 627 = *Beutestucke, Tributstücke.*

2. *ḫul* = *igi* + *ur* = *înu* + *nakru* = eye + evil, inimical. Delitzsch, Schriftsyst., p. 49.

These three fragments apparently supplement each other. The complete text probably ran as follows: To Enlil, the king of the lands, Enshagkushanna, lord of Kengi, king of . . ., presented the spoil of Kish, wicked of heart.

Few as the historical notices are, yet they enable us to get an insight into the condition of the land and of the people at this remote time. They show us that a struggle went on between the south (Kengi) and the north (Kish), which struggle lasted undoubtedly for several centuries.

Prominent cities at this time were the capital of Kengi (i.e. Shirpurla-Girsu, as we shall see later on; not Erech (Hilprecht)), Nippur, and Kish.

It is necessary, however, before tracing the different steps in the development of Kish, to turn our attention to a kingdom called in the inscriptions 'Shirpurla.' The inscriptions of the rulers of this kingdom give us an impression of a power and might which presuppose *centuries* for its development. All that we know of its art[1] and civilization tends in the same direction.

The Rulers of Shirpurla.

Shirpurla is the modern *Tell-Loh* (or Telloh), where De Sarzec found the inscriptions relating to the rulers of this dynasty. It is situated fifteen hours north of Mugheir, on the east side of the Shatt-el-Ḫai, and about twelve hours east of Warka. At this early time the city of Shirpurla seems to have included four component parts, viz. Girsu, Ninâ, Uruazagga, Erim. Thus it happened that one and the same king might call himself either 'king of Shirpurla' (comp. Urukagina, Clercq, ii. pl. viii. col. i. 4, 5), or 'king of Girsu' (comp. Barrel-Cyl., col. i. 4, 5). These suburbs were built by various rulers in honour of their favourite gods or goddesses. Whether Shirpurla is the right reading, or Sirgulla (Hommel), we do

[1] See the so-called 'Vase d'Argent' in Déc. pl. 43 bis, with the emblem of Shirpurla: the lion-headed eagle with outspread wings, having put its clutches into the back of two lions, whose hinder parts are turned towards each other. Sometimes this eagle appears alone. See Heuzey, Les Armoiries Chaldéennes.

not know. According to Pinches, Guide to the Kouyunjik Gallery, p. 7, London, 1883, and Babyl. Records, iii. p. 24, Shirpurla may be read Lagash, which reading is adopted throughout by Jensen in K. B. iii[1]. We retain the old reading Shirpurla, because this writing occurs most frequently in the monuments.

The rulers of Shirpurla may conveniently be grouped under four divisions:

(1) The dynasty of Urukagina—beginning with this ruler or his predecessor(s)[1] and ending with Lugalshuggur and his successor(s).

(2) The dynasty of Ur-Ninâ, ending with Lummadur.

(3) The patesis between Lummadur and Ur-Ba'u.

(4) Ur-Ba'u and his successors, ending with Ĝala-Lama.

Dynasty of Urukagina.

To Urukagina[2], the oldest member of the first dynasty of Shirpurla, we have assigned the approximate date of 4500 B.C. His greatness consisted not so much in successful wars against the neighbouring cities, as in securing a peaceful administration for his country and

[1] It is very probable that Urukagina had some predecessors. The classification is made only on the basis of the inscriptions so far extant. It also may be possible that Enĝegal preceded Urukagina. Without being able to prove either one or the other, we content ourselves with the above-given arrangement.

[2] For the meaning of this name, see note to l. 39 of Déc. pl. 5, No. 1. His inscriptions are:

Clercq, ii. pl. viii., translated by Oppert, ibid. pp. 72, 77; see also Oppert, Acad. des Inscriptions, 1884, février; Amiaud, R. P. i. p. 68, and Déc. p. xxx.; Hommel, Z. K. ii. p. 182; Halévy, R. Arch. 1884, i. 109 ff.

Pierre de Seuil, Déc. 5, fig. 1; Amiaud, ibid. p. xxx.; R. P. i. 69 f.

Barrel-Cylinder, Déc. 32; Amiaud, ibid. p. xxx., and R. P. i. p. 17 ff.; Jensen, K. B. iii[1]. p. 10.

British Museum, A. H. 82, 7-14; comp. Winckler, Untersuchungen, p. 43, A. 1, now published in C. T. No. 12030 (part vii. p. 3).

Winckler, A. B. K. No. 2.

R. A. iv. No. iii. pl. iii. No. 8.

About a Cône not yet published, see Heuzey, Comptes Rendus, 1879, p. 428 ff., and Thureau-Dangin, preface to E. C.

city. As 'king of Girsu-Shirpurla,' he devoted his energy to the building of different storehouses, that should take up 'the abundance of the countries,' and erected temples for different gods—thus showing his devotion and piety. He built 'for Ninâ the beloved canal, the canal *Ninâ-ki-tum-a*,' and thus supplied his city with water (see note to Déc. 32, col. iii. 6). Bêl of Nippur still exercises the highest influence. Ningirsu ('the lord of Girsu') is the chief city god, under whose control the capital stands. He is the *GUD* or 'hero' of Enlil. In somewhat later inscriptions, Ningirsu has the title *gud lig-ga*, 'the strong hero' of Enlil. Many other gods are mentioned in his inscriptions; for particulars the reader may be referred to the inscriptions which follow:—

Clercq, ii. pl. viii. No. 1. Comp. Oppert, ibid. pp. 72, 77.

Col. I.

(*Dingir*) *Nin-gir-su*	For Ningirsu,
gud (*dingir*) *En-lil-la*(*l*)-*ra*	the hero of Enlil,
Uru-ka-gi-na	Urukagina,
gal-(*ga*)*lu*	king
Šir-la-pur-ki-ge	of Shirpurla,
e-ni	his house
mu-na-ru	he has built.
e-gal Ti-ra-aš-ka-ni	The palace of his Tirash
mu-na-ru	he has built.

Col. II.

An-ta-sur-(*ra*)*-ra*	The Antasurra

I. 8. Tirash is called in Déc. 2, 1, col. iii. 1; Déc. 5, 1, l. 9, only *E*. Comp. also Barrel-Cyl. i. 6–9. See also the proper name, *Lugal-Tiraš* (Ur IV.).

II. 1. *An-ta-sur-ra* is explained in the Barrel-Cyl. col. i. l. 7 and in Déc. 5, 1, l. 7, by *e-ĝe-gàl-kalam-ma*, 'the house of the abundance of the lands.' The first *RA* seems to be an erasure. Comp. also Cône of Entemena, col. iv.

mu-na-ru	he has built.
E-giš-me-ra	The Egishmera
e-ne-bi-kur-kur-ra-ku	to be an Enebi-kurkura
mu-na-ru	he has built.
E-KAŠ + GAR-bi KAK-gal-kur-ta-DU-a	His storehouse . . . .
mu-na-ru	he has built.
(*dingir*) *Dun-šag-ga-na-ra*	For his god Dunshagga
ki-akkil	the Kiakkil

Col. III.

mu-na-ru	he has built.
(*dingir*) *Gàl-alim-ma-ra*	For Galalim

30, and Galet A of Eannatum, col. v. 2–7; vi. 21; vii. 2. This Antasurra seems to have been a very celebrated storehouse, for we find its name even at the time of Ur IV.; comp. E. A. H. 91.

3. *E-giš-me-ra* is explained here by *E-ne-bi-kur-kur-ra*; comp. Déc. 5, 1, ll. 33, 34, where we have *E-me-ne-bi-kur-kur-ra* explaining *E-bar-ra*. It seems therefore probable that, if *E-ne-bi-kur-kur-ra* = *E-me-ne-bi-kur-kur-ra*, *E-giš-me-ra* = *E-bar-ra*. In 'Tablette A' of Entemena, R. A. ii. pp. 148, 149, rev., col. i. 1, 2, *E-me-ne-bi-kur-kur-ra* explains *An-ta-sur-ra*. But *An-ta-sur-ra* is explained above (note to col. ii. 1) by *e-ḫe-gàl-kalam-ma*; hence *E-(me)-ne-bi-kur-kur-ra* has the same meaning as *e-ḫe-gàl-kalam-ma*, i. e. 'house of the abundance of the lands,' and because *E-giš-me-ra* = *E-barra* = *An-ta-sur-ra*, it follows that all three are similar buildings. See also R. A. iii. p. 120, note 1, and especially Barrel-Cyl. i. 6–9.

6. The second sign is *KAŠ* (*bi*) + inserted *GAR*; see also Déc. 6, 4; Jensen, K. B. iii[1]. p. 18, note 2, '*Nahrungshaus*'; Thureau-Dangin, '*maison de vivre*,' R. A. iii. p. 119. Comp. also 'Tablette A' of Entemena, rev., iii. 3.

The expression *KAK-gal-kur-ta-DU-a* is difficult.

KAK = *du*, Br. 5256; *kalû*, H. W. B. p. 329: '*Gesammtheit*.' *gal*, Br. 6841; *butuḳtu*, H. W. B. p. 191; '*Überflutung*' = fig. for *ḫigallu*.

Du = iii[1] of *alâku*, H. W. B. p. 68.

We might translate: his storehouse (*e-kaš-gar-bi*), which bringeth (*DU*) all (*KAK*) the abundance (*gal*) into the land (*kur-ta*); or better: 'into which goeth all the abundance of the land.' Amiaud: '*qui met l'abondance* (?) *dans le pays*.'

9. See Gudea votive tablet 8, Br. 2708: *ikkillu*, H. W. B. p. 55: 'the house of lamentation.'

III. 2. *alim*, T. C. 208; Br. 8882.

E-me-gal-kiš(ĝuš)-an-ki	the Emegalkishanki
mu-na-ru	he has built.
E-(*dingir*) *Ba-u*	The house of Ba'u
mu-na-ru	he has built.
(*dingir*) *En-lil-la*	For Enlil
E-ad-da	the Eadda
im-sag-ga-ka-ni	of his imsagga

Col. IV.

mu-na-ru	he has built.
Bur-sag	The great 'Vase,'
E-SA-DUG an-na-bi-ni-ga-sag-a	the house of the sattûku, the top of which goeth very high,
mu-na-ru	he has built.
Uru-ka-gi-na	Urukagina,
gal-(ga)lu	king
Šir-la-ki-pur	of Shirpurla,
(ga)lu E-ninnû	who the Eninnû

3. *kiš*, T. C. 204; *ĝuš*, T. C. 206; these two signs have been very often confounded. The whole expression may signify: *bît ma'dûti rabîti ša kiššat šamê u irṣiti.*

8, 9. Comp. Tablette A of Entemena, rev. i. 5, 6.

IV. 3. *E-SA-DUG*, written *E-DI-KA*, see. H. W. B. p. 513: *di-ka=sa-dug=sattûku, sattukku, 'festgesetzte Tempelabgabe.' an-na-bi-ni-ga-sag-a* may mean: high (*an-na-bi*; *bi*=adv. Br. 5139) goeth (*ni-ga*, Br. 6108) its top (*sag-a*). Amiaud translates the whole line: '*son temple qui s'élève jusqu'à l'approche des cieux*?' Comp. Déc. 5, 1, l. 13.

8. *E-ninnû*, i.e. 'the house of the number 50.' Fifty is the sacred number for Ningirsu-Ninib, see v. R. 37, 18. This Eninnû is also said (Déc. 7, 8, col. iii. 6) to be that of (*dingir*) *Im-gig(mi)ĝu-bar-bar*, which Jensen, K. B. iii[1]. p. 23, note *†, explains as the house of that god '*welcher den finstern* (*gig*) *Himmel* (*im*) *erhellen* (*bar-bar*) *möge* (*ĝu*), *und spielt auf Ninib als die Frühsonne an.*' That this was the temple of Ningirsu-Ninib is evident from Gudea B, v. 12 ff.; (*dingir*) *Nin-gir-su lugal-a-ni nig-du-e pa-mu-na-ud-du E-Ninnû-*(*dingir*) *Im-gig-bar-bar-ra-ni mu-na-ru*; comp. also Gudea D, ii. 7 (Déc. 9). It had a so-called *gi-gunu*, which was built out of cedar-wood: Gudea B, v. 18; D, ii. 9; Jensen, K. B. iii[1]. p. 33, note †*. Gudea, Ur-Ningirsu, and some later patesis repair the Eninnû as well as the *gi-gunu*, Déc. 37, 9, ii. 5.

ru-a	has built,
dingir-ra-ni	his god

Col. V.

(*dingir*) *Nin-Šul-li(l)*	is Ninshuli.
nam-ti-la-ni-ku	For (the preservation of) his life
ud-ul-la-ku	for ever
(*dingir*) *Nin-gir-su-ra*	to Ningirsu
ka-šú-ĝe-na-gàl	may he bow down his face.

V. 1. Amiaud :, (*Dingir*) *Nin-shul* (*ou Nin-doun*).

3. *ud-ul-la-ku* = *ana ûmê ullûti* = Semitism.

5. *ka-šú-gàl*, Br. 714 ; H. W. B. 369 = *appa labânu*. The subject is Urukagina, not Ninshul (Amiaud).

URUKAGINA.

(Bloc de seuil ou de support.)

Déc. pl. 5, No. 1. Comp. Amiaud, Déc. p. xxx.

[*Dingir Nin-su-gir*]	i. e.	For Ningirsu,
[*gud En*]-*lil*-[*la*]-*ra*		the hero of Enlil,
[*Uru*]-*ka*-[*gi*]-*na*		Urukagina
[*lu*]*gal*		the king
[*Gir-su*]-*ki*-*ra*		of Girsu,
[*An-ta*]-*sur-ra*		the Antasurra,
[*E*]-*ĝe-gàl*-[*kalam*]-*ma-ni*		the house of the abundance of his lands,
mu-na-ru		he has built.
[*E-gal*] *Ti*-[*ra-aš*]-*ka-ni*		The house of his Tirash
[*mu-na-ru*		he has built
[2 lines mutilated]		. . . .
13 (*dingir*) *Gàl-alim-ma*		For Galalimma

6. See le Clercq, col. ii. 1.

9. See le Clercq, col. i. 8, where it is called *e-gal*, the 'great house' (*sic*) not 'temple'; comp. Barrel-Cyl., col. i. l. 8.

13. After this line we probably have to supply, according to le Clercq, col. iii. 3 : *E-me-gal-kiš* (or better *ĝuš ?*)-*an-ki*.

	[3 lines mutilated]	. . . .
17	. . . . *ni*	. . . .
	[3 lines mutilated]	. . . .
	[*mu*]-*na-ru*	he has built.
	[dingir] *Nin-sar*	For Ninsar,
23	*šag ?-lal*	the *šag ?-lal*
	(dingir) *Nin-gir-su-ka-ra*	of Ningirsu,
25	*e-ni*	his house
	mu-na-ru	he has built.
	[dingir] . . . . . *gir*	For . . . . . *gir*,
	[*ki*]-*ag*	the beloved
	(dingir) *Nin-gir-su-ra*	of Ningirsu,
30	*e-ni*	his house
	mu-na-ru	he has built.
	[dingir] *Nin-gir-su-ra*	For Ningirsu
	E-bar-ra	the Ebarra (sanctuary),
	e-me-ne(*lam*)-[*bi*]-*kur-kur-ra*	the Emenebikurkura,
35	*mu-na-ru*	he has built.
	e-ab	The *E-ab* . . . .
	(dingir) *Nin-gir-su-ra*	for Ningirsu
	mu-ru	he has built.
	Uru-ka-gi-na	Urukagina,
40	(*ga*)*lu e*	who the house
	(dingir) *Nin-gir-su*	of Ningirsu
	[*ru-a*]	has built.
	. . . .	

23. The first sign = *šag*? 'heart-bearer'? = beloved? Amiaud, *porte-*[glaive?].

33. *bar* = T. C. 125 = sanctuary (*parakku*). It is explained here by *E-me-ne-bi-kur-kur-ra*; comp. le Clercq, col. ii. 3, 4, and note to it. It would seem, therefore, that Egishmera is a sanctuary.

39. Means: city (*uru*), mouth (*ka*), true (*gina*) = the city of the true mouth. Jensen: '*Stadt der Wahrheit*' *oder* '*in der Stadt ist Wahrheit*' (?).

43 ff. Have probably to be supplied according to le Clercq, col. iv. 10 and col. v.

(Barrel-Cylinder.)

Déc. 32. Comp. Amiaud, Déc. pp. xxx and xxxi.

Col. I.

[*Dingir Nin-gir-su*]	i. e.	For Ningirsu
[*gud*] [*dingir*] *En*-[*lil-la*]-*ra*		the hero of Enlil,
Uru-ka-gi-na		Urukagina,
gal + (*ga*)*lu*		king
Gir-su-ki-ge		of Girsu,
An-ta-sur-ra		the Antasurra,
E-ȟe-gàl-kalam-ma-ni		his house of the abundance of land(s),
e-gal Ti-ra-aš-ka-ni		(and) the great house of his Tirash,
mu-na-ru		he has built.
E-(*dingir*) *Ba-u*		The house of Ba'u
[*mu-na*]-*ru*		he has built.

Col. II.

. . . . . .		. . . . . .
mu-[*na-ru*]	i. e.	he has built.
(*dingir*) [*Dun-šag*]-*ga*-[*na-ra*]		For his god Dunshagga
ki-[*akkil*]		the Kiakkil
mu-[*na-ru*]		he has built.
(*dingir*) . . . . *šag*		For . . . . *šag* . . . .
giš . . . . *ba-ṭug* ?		the hero (*giš*) ? . . . . *ba-ṭug* ?
e-ni mu-na-ru		his house he has built.
šag-ba		In its midst
(*dingir*) *Za-za-ru*		for Zazaru,
(*dingir*) *Im-pa-ud-du*		Impauddu,

I. 3–5. Urukagina calls himself 'king of Girsu.' So probably also in Déc. 5, No. 1, while in le Clercq, ii. pl. viii. col. i. l. 5, he has the title 'king of Shirpurla.' Girsu and Shirpurla are therefore only two different names for the same place!

8. The *e-gal Ti-ra-aš-ka-ni* here seems to be co-ordinate to Antasurra, and has therefore to be translated as above. Comp. also le Clercq, cols. i. and ii.

II. 10. *dingir Za-za-uru* (*sic*). Comp. this with Gudea, Cyl. B, col. xi. 4 in R. A. ii. p. 134, where this very same god is written (*dingir*) *Za-za-RU*. This proves that *URU* has also the phonetic value *RU*. Comp. also '*kur-kur-*

(dingir) *Gim-nun-ta-ud-du-a*	Gimnuntauddua,
e+mu+ne+ni+ru	their apartments he has built.
(dingir) *Nin-sar*	For Ninsar,
[. . . . dingir] *Nin-su-*	the . . . . of Ningirsu
[*gir*]-*ra*	(comp. Déc. 5, l. 22, 60).

Col. III.

[(dingir) *En-lil-la*]	i. e. For Enlil
[*e-a*]*d-da*[*i*]*m-sag-ga-ka-ni*	the Eadda of his imsagga
mu-na-ru	he has built.
(dingir) *Ninâ*	For Ninâ
id ki-ag-ga-ni	her beloved canal,
(id) *Ninâ-ki-tum-a*	the canal '*Ninâ ki-tum-a*,'
?-*mu-na-ru*	he has built.
ka-ba e	At its mouth a house
ni	. . . .
na . . . *ud*	. . . .
mu	he [has built].

12 ff.

To this oldest dynasty of Shirpurla belongs also a certain Engegal ('lord of abundance' or 'very rich [1]'). He, like Urukagina,

URU=kur-kur-ru, Galet A of Eannatum, iv. 23; *dingir-dingir-URU=dingir-dingir-ru*, Cône of Entemena, i. 3. This very same sign is also used as a verbal prefix (for *RA* ?), especially when preceded by *mu*; comp. Lugalzaggisi, ii. 32.

III. 5. *id*, Br. 11647=*nâru*.

6. Has the name of this canal to be translated: 'that goeth out from Ninâ'? Thus it would be a proof that *Ninâki*, another part of Girsu-Shirpurla, existed as early as this. Hommel, P. S. B. A. 1895, p. 207, proposes to read for *Ninâ-ki=Ghanna-ki*, in order to identify this city with the Biblical חֲנוֹךְ, which was built by Cain for his son Khanôk, Gen. iv. 17.

7. The first sign is that of T. C. 91 (*al*), without the last stroke, or is it = *NI-TUG = rabiš* ?

12 ff. Amiaud adds: '*Restent encore les fragments de quatre colonnes, dont il ne m'est pas possible de donner une traduction.*'

[1] This king is only known from a communication of Hilprecht in Z. A. xi. p. 330.

calls himself '*lugal Pur-šir-la*[1],' 'king of Shirpurla.' Besides this he bears the proud title '*lugal ki-gal-la*,' 'the great king,' and terms himself *šib* ^(dingir)^ *Nin-gir-su*, 'the priest of Ningirsu,' a title similar to that of patesi-gal. From the title 'the great king' we may venture to conclude that he, unlike his predecessor, must have carried his arms successfully against his enemies[2], who had previously succeeded in plundering Shirpurla, but fate decreed that his *royal* capital should be reduced to the seat of a patesi. Kish, having been defeated some time before by Enshagkushanna, seems to have acquired new strength. Its king, Mesilim[3], became lord paramount of Shirpurla, thus reducing its rulers to mere patesis[4].

[1] Thus the name is written in this inscription according to Hilprecht. Comp. also the same or similar sequence of signs in the inscriptions of Ur-Ninâ, &c.

[2] That is, against Kish. This is probably indicated by O. B. I. Nos. 108, 109 (Hilprecht, ibid. p. 263, 2), where we have an inscription of a certain *U-dug ?*, patesi of Kish, who presents (*sag* [*ku*] *mu*-[*pa*]-*kab*-[*du*] = *ana širikti išruḳ*, O. B. I. 109, 4) certain things to (*dingir*) *Za*-[*ma-ma*].

[3] See his inscription on p. 16. For a more detailed account of this king's power, see Cône of Entemena.

[4] In this sense I take patesi with Winckler, Altorientalische Forschungen, iii. p. 234: '*die gebräuchliche Bezeichnung für die unterworfenen Könige ist in Babylonien patesi.*'

What patesi really means we do not know. Two explanations may be offered:

(1) It means 'one that is filled (*si*) with power (*pa*).'

PA = (*a*) staff, sceptre, (*b*) name of any higher officer = *šâpiru*, *aklu*.
SI = horn, sign of fullness, strength, then 'to fill.'
TE = *ta* (?), prefix which helps to form the conjugation.

(2) Or: a governing, leading *šâpiru* = סַפִּר.

PA = *šâpiru*.
SI—*šutèšuru*, 'to govern, to lead.'
TE = *ta* (see Jensen, K. B. iii[1]. p. 6).

The difficulty, however, with both of these explanations is, that it is not yet proven that *TE* = *TA*.

The Assyrians translated *pa-te-si* as well as *SI* by *iššakku*. In inscriptions the following patesis are mentioned:—

Patesi of a god.
Patesi of a city.
Patesi of a king.
Patesi of men in general.

The name of only one of these earliest patesis is preserved to us, i. e. *Lugal-šug-gur*[1], who is mentioned in the inscription of Mesilim. The sovereignty of Kish over Shirpurla does not seem to have lasted very long[2]. Shirpurla regained its former glory under a new dynasty, namely, that of Ur-Ninâ.

Dynasty of Ur-Ninâ.

With Ur-Ninâ begins a new dynasty, probably the mightiest of Early Babylonia, the duration of its sovereignty extending from 4300 B.C. to 4100 B.C. Looking at the art and the inscriptions of these kings, we cannot help thinking that in Shirpurla civilization must have been far advanced, so far advanced as to force upon us the conclusion that 'several centuries have elapsed before men could reach this stage of civilization.' The greater number of these art treasures are preserved in the Louvre; the inscriptions found on them have been published in Découvertes en Chaldée and in the Revue d'Assyriologie.

Patesi of a so-called *bît tîmi*.
Patesi of a 'festival.'

From the fact that kings (*lugal*) very often term themselves patesi or patesi-gal of a certain god, it seems to be evident that patesi in the first place is purely a *religious title*, signifying the highest official of a god, having the care of that god's temple and jurisdiction over that territory, over which the god extends his influence. It is, however, evident that patesi, apart from its religious sense, has also its '*secular meaning*.' On page 7 we heard of an inscription of Naram-Sin, in which a certain Lugalushumgal, who was patesi of Shirpurla, is called 'scribe' (=ספר = *šâpiru*) and servant, thus clearly indicating that this patesi was dependent on Naram-Sin, and was *a mere secular official*. The argument of Hilprecht in O. B. I. pp. 262, 263 and note 1, is precarious, because based on an incorrect translation of the inscription of Mesilim.

[1] Thus this name should probably be pronounced (R. A. iv. p. 35). As such it is equivalent to *Lugal-kurum* (Br. 9929) -*zikum* (Br. 10219), (Hilprecht, O. B. I. p. 263, note 1). Thureau-Dangin (R. A. iv. p. 70, note 9) proposes to read *Lugal-šag-gur*.

[2] Only one other king of Kish has come down to us, who belongs to this period. This king is *Lugal-da?-ak?*, *lugal Kiš*; see R. A. iv. p. iii.

The first king of this dynasty was Ur-Ninâ[1] (servant of Ninâ). The dynasty of Urukagina must have been reduced to mere nothingness by the kings of Kish, so that Ur-Ninâ found it easy to take possession of the throne. He must have been of an old family, for he mentions the name of his father and grandfather, who have the title neither of patesi nor of king. He, like his predecessors, seems to have been great in peace. He built temples and various storehouses. A passage in his inscriptions (viz. Déc. 2ter, No. 2, col. iv. 5, 6; comp. Déc. 2, No. 1, col. iv. 4, 5), where he records the building of the 'wall of Shirpurla,' suggests that the old enemy, Kish, was still troublesome, so that he found it necessary to fortify his capital against the deadly enemies from the north. For further details see the inscriptions which follow.

[1] Hommel (Geschichte, p. 284) read this name Ur-Ghanna, in order to identify him with the old Orchamus in Ovid, Metamorph. 4, 212 ('*Rexit Achaemenias urbes pater Orchamus; isque septimus a prisci numeratur origine Beli*'); now he reads it Kalab-Ghanna, see P. S. B. A. 1899, p. 132, and ibid. 1895, p. 207. Jensen, K. B. iii[1]. p. 10, note 3, says that this reading '*entbehrt jeglichen Grundes.*'

His inscriptions are:

Déc. pl. 2, No. 1; see Jensen, K. B. iii[1]. p. 10 ff.; Hommel, Geschichte, p. 287. (The translation and transcription of Jensen are based upon the whole literature which preceded his, an account of which is there given.)

Déc. pl. 2, No. 2; Jensen, ibid. p. 14; A. B. K. No. 1.

Déc. pl. 1, No. 2; Jensen, ibid. p. 14; Hommel, Geschichte, p. 285.

Déc. pl. 2bis, Nos. 1 and 2; see R. A. iii. 13 ff. and R. A. iv. p. 103 (Ur-Ninâ and his family).

Déc. pl. 2ter, No. 1; see R. A. iii. 18 ff. (Heuzey).

Déc. pl. 2ter, No. 2; see R. A. ii. 147, Oppert's translation, ibid.

Déc. pl. 2ter, No. 4, and R. A. iv. p. 98.

Déc. pl. 31, i (brick); R. A. iv. 91; see R. A. ii. 85 (Oppert).

See also R. A. iii. 13 ff. (Nouveaux Monuments du roi Ur-Ninâ, par Léon Heuzey).

R. A. ii. 78, Généalogies de Sirpourla, par Léon Heuzey; comp. with this R. A. iii. p. 32 ff., by the same author.

Déc. 26bis, fig. 4.

R. A. iv. 87 ff., and especially ibid. pp. 97 and 122, i; p. 105, fig. 10 *a*, *b*; p. 106, fig. 11; p. 114, fig. 22 (L. Heuzey).

R. A. v. 26 (L. Heuzey).

L. Heuzey, Les Armoiries Chaldéennes de Shirpurla.

UR-NINÂ.

Déc. 2ter, 4.

(Dingir) Ninâ + UR	Ur-Ninâ,
gal + (ga)lu	king
Šir-pur-la	of Shirpurla,
dumu Gu-ni-du	the son of Gunidu
dumu Gur-sar	son of Gursar,
E-Nin-su-gir-(dingir)	the house of Ningirsu
mu-ru	he has built.
E (dingir) Ninâ	The house of Ninâ
mu-ru	he has built.
E-Ga-tum-dug+(dingir)	The house of Gatumdug
mu-ru	he has built.

1. Read *Ur-(dingir) Ninâ*, and comp. *gal* + (*ga*)*lu* = king. Eannatum writes always *Ur-(dingir) Ninâ*. It means 'servant of Ninâ.' Ninâ is the sign *ab*, + inserted *ḫa* = fish, the later ideogram for the Assyrian capital, Nineveh; it may be pronounced either Ninâ or Ninua.

3. *Šir-pur-la* without *ki*! So also in Déc. 2ter, No. 2, col. 1.

4. *Gu-ni-du*: so has to be read, not *Ni-ĝal-ni-du* (Jensen) or *Ni-ni-ĝal-din* (Amiaud); comp. Thureau-Dangin, R. S. 1897, p. 272, note 8. *Ni* + *ĝal* when written together is *gu*.

6. Very interesting is the sequence of the signs in this line, i. e. *Nin* + *su* + *gir*. The same sequence also occurs in Déc. pl. 2, 1; see Jensen, K. B. iii^1. p. 10, col. i. 5. This name generally is written *Nin-gir-su*. The sign *SU* may also be pronounced *SUN* (Hommel, S. L. No. 7). It is possible, therefore, that the original name of the god from whom the city got its name (or vice versa) was *Nin-sun-gir*, and the city originally was called *Sun-gir*. Whether the latter reading or that of Girsu is the correct one cannot be made out at the present, but compare what has been said about the title 'king of Shumer and Akkad.' On account of the sequence *SU*(*N*)-*gir*, some scholars wish to derive from it the later 'Shumer,' which in the bilingual texts of Ḫammurabi translates the word Kengi (see under Enshagkushanna, p. 45, note 4). For a derivation of Shumer from Sungir we could refer to the Hebrew שנער, Gen. x. 10, which should be pointed שִׁנְעָר (?). For the pronunciation of Hebrew ע as *g*, comp. עֲמֹרָה LXX. Γόμορρα.

10. Jensen reads her name *Ga-sig* (? *zib*, *zib*, &c.) *-dug*; comp. Gudea B, col. ii. 17, and note 2; K. B. iii^1. p. 28. She is the mother of Shirpurla; comp. Gudea B, col. viii, 56: *am Širpurla-ki azag (dingir) Ga-tum-dug*; and as such she would be the same as *(dingir) Ba'u*, see above, p. 21.

e-dam	The house of his wife
mu-ru	he has built.
E-Nin-Mar-^{ki} + $^{(dingir)}$	The house of the *Nin-Mar-*^{ki}
mu-ru	he has built.
Mà-al	From Ma'al
kur-ta	the mountain,
gu-gàl-giš-MU	with all kinds of wood,

12. The same building occurs also in Déc. pl. 2, No. 1, col. ii. 5. Jensen, K. B. iii[1]. p. 12, makes a note of interrogation for the second sign. Oppert reads it = '*AR*'; comp. R. A. ii. 147, but the more probable reading is *DAM* = *aššatu, ḫirtu.*

14. $^{(dingir)}$ *Nin-Mar-*^{ki}, i. e. the mistress of 'Mar' (a city). She is the 'first-born of Ninâ'; comp. Ur-Ba'u, Déc. 7, 8, col. v. 8 : *dumu-sag* $^{(dingir)}$ *Ninâ-ra.*

16–19. The interpretation of these lines is rather difficult, owing to the difficulty of identifying the second sign in l. 16 and the correct interpretation of the phrase *gu-gàl-giš-MU.*

Amiaud (R. P[2]. i. p. 65), Oppert (R. A. ii. p. 147), and Heuzey (R. A. iii. p. 17, and Déc. p. 170) read this sign *GAN*(*KAN*), thus identifying it with that to be found in Gudea D (Déc. pl. 9): *Mà-GAN*^{ki}*.* Jensen, in K. B. iii[1]. p. 12, simply gives a '?.' Hilprecht (O. B. I. p. 253, note 1) transcribes this sign by *GIŠ-DIN*, and reads and translates Déc. 2, 1, col. iv. 10 ff., as follows:— *ma giš-din kura-ta gu-giš-gàl mu-tum ?* i. e. 'a ship (laden) with wine he brought from the country which possesses every kind of tree.' Thureau-Dangin, on the other hand, identified this sign with *AL* (R. A. iv. p. 71, note 1). In E. C. No. 325 he, however, leaves it unidentified, but comp. also E. C. No. 377. That Hilprecht's proposed explanation cannot be correct is evident from a comparison of all those places of Ur-Ninâ's inscriptions where this same sign occurs:

R. A. iv. p. 105 *b* : 1, *mà-*[*al*]; 2, *kur-*[*ta*]; 3, *gu* . . .

Déc. 2, 1, iv. 1 ff.:

1, *mà-al*; 2, *kur-ta*; 3, *gu-gàl-giš-mu* (*sic*! nothing else); 4, *bad pur-la-šir*; 5, *mu-ru.*

Déc. 2ter, 2, v. 3 ff.:

3, *mà-al*; 4, *kur-ta*; 5, *gu* + *giš* + *gàl*; 6, *mu—?* (= *lal* ?)

Déc. 2bis, 1, lower half:

mà-al | *kur-ta gu-gàl-giš-mu* | *DU-DU.*

And especially the passage in question (Déc. 2ter, 4, 16 ff.):

16, *mà-al*; 17, *kur-ta*; 18, *gu-gàl-giš-mu*; 19, *Ib-gal*; 20, *mu-ru.*

How would Hilprecht translate this passage? Line 18 shows that that scholar's emendation (viz. to read *tum* (?) after *mu*) is without warrant. If we had to supply a verb after *MU* we would—according to the analogy

Ib-gal	the Ibgal
mu-ru	he has built.
Dul-nir	The Dulnir
mu-ru	he has built.

of the inscription above referred to, and according to Déc. 2bis, 1—expect *MU-TUM* (?) to form a line by itself; but it does not.

Dismissing, therefore, Hilprecht's emendation, we could translate this passage —again if that scholar's assimilation of *AL* = *GIŠ-DIN* is correct—only as follows:—[With] a ship (laden) with wine from the country which possesses every kind of tree he built the Ibgal. But this is absurd. The *TA* in line 17 has to be connected with line 16, which latter line contains the name of the *KUR*, and therefore line 16 has to be read *mà-al*: 'from (*ta*) *MÀ-AL* the mountain.' *GU* = Br. 3220, *napḫaru*; *gàl* = *bašû*; but how is the *MU* to be explained? Hilprecht (personal communication) sees in this *MU* some kind of a participial construction, and wants to translate: 'From *Mà-al* the mountain all kinds of wood having *MU* (= brought),' thus supplying for *MU* an unknown meaning. The correct interpretation of this passage is given on hand by Gudea D, iv. 6 ff.: For Gudea . . . Magan, &c. . . . *gu-giš mu-na-gàl-la-a-an mà giš ru-a-bi Šir-pur-la-*^{ki}*-ku mu-na-tum*, which can be translated only (against Jensen, K. B. iii^1. p. 53, and Hilprecht, O. B. I. 253, 1) by: 'For Gudea have brought Magan, &c.—each of which (*a-an*) possesses every kind of tree—a ship (laden) with wood (for) his (*bi*) buildings in (or to) Shirpurla.'

gu-gàl-giš-mu therefore has to be read *gu-giš mu-gàl*; comp. Déc. 2ter, 2, v. 3 ff. Such transpositions occur very often in our texts: Déc. 3bis, D^1, col. 1, 8: *bal-mu-e* = *mu-bal-e*, ibid. l. 3; Déc. 32, ii. 13: *e* + *mu* + *ne* + *ni* + *ru* = *e-ne-ni mu-ru*; comp. also Déc. 31, 1; Déc. 3 A ii. (= *ud-da inim-ba ni-šu-bal-e*); Lugalzaggisi, iii. 33.

Our whole passage must therefore be translated as has been done above, and its meaning is: he built the Ibgal with all kinds of wood (which is or comes) from the Ma'al mountain. Déc. 2, 1, iv. 1 ff. can be rendered only by: 'with all kinds of wood (which is) from the Ma'al mountain he has built the wall of Shirpurla.'

Line 6 in Déc. 2ter, v., has to be completed according to Déc. 2bis, 1, i. e. has to be read *mu-DU* = Shaphel, or probably also *mu-lal* (= *ṣabâtu*).

It would seem, if we compare E. C. 325 with E. C. 377, that both these signs are identical, but differ essentially from the sign *GAN*. The sign *AL* occurs also in A. F. p. 545, No. 4, l. 3.

19. *Ib-gal*, Jensen, l. c. '*Innenraum*?'; comp. Déc. 2, 1, col. i. 7. Also mentioned in A. V. 2100.

21. The *Dul-nir* mentioned here, and R. A. iv. p. 122, 5, l. 13, and in Déc. 2, 1, ii. 1, may be read also *KI-U*; so at least here! *U*, Br. 6025, *rêtu* = 'place of pasture' = pasture. Comp. Jensen, K. B. iii^1. p. 12, note 1.

E-pa	The Epa
mu-ru	he has built.

23. Occurs also in Déc. 2, 1, ii. 7, and Déc. 2ter, No. 2, col. iv. 3, and is explained in Gudea D, col. ii. 11, and in Gudea G, i. 13, as the *e-ub imin-na* (Jensen: '*Siebenweltraumhaus*,' K. B. iii[1]. p. 51, note **o, and Kosmologie, p. 201 ff.) of Ningirsu.

Déc. pl. 2ter, No. 2.

Col. I.

(*Dingir*) *Ninâ-UR*	Ur-Ninâ,
lugal	king
Šir-pur-la	of Shirpurla,
dumu Gu-ni-du	the son of Gunidu,
dumu Gur-sar	son of Gursar,
E-Ninâ-(*dingir*)	the house of Ninâ
mu-ru	has built.

Col. II.

(*dingir*) *Ninâ*	The (image of) Ninâ
mu-tu	he has renewed,
min alan (?)	2 statues
mu-dun	he has digged (= cut, carved, sculptured);

II. 2. *mu-tu*; *tu* evidently the sign in T. C. 179; it occurs again in Déc. 2, No. 1, col. v. 2. Jensen transcribes it with *tur*, and thinks it is that given in T. C. 181—but wrongly. *tu*, Br. 1069 = *edêšu*, H. W. B. p. 30. In connection with this compare such expressions as '*ṣalam ilâni rabûte uddiš*,' or '*anḫusunu uddiš*': also used of temples, '*uddušu ešrêtim*.' Here undoubtedly the former meaning is the correct one, viz. = '*ṣalam Ninâ uddiš*.' Jensen translates '*hat hineingebracht*.' Déc. pl. 2, No. 1, col. v. 1, 2, ought to be translated: 'the house (*e* = *ešrêtim*) of Ninâ the mistress he renewed.' Oppert, R. A. ii. p. 147, '*il a sculpté la déesse Ninâ*.'

3. *alan*? So Amiaud and Jensen. Thureau-Dangin, E. C. 107: 'probably identical with *alan*.'

4. The second sign is here clearly that of T. C. 188. It is also found in Déc. 2, No. 1, col. v. 4. Jensen (= *azag*, see K. B. iii[1]. p. 14) and Amiaud

(*dingir*) *Ninâ*	Ninâ's
alan	statue
a-mu-na a-ag (?)	for the declaring of her (his?) name

Col. III.

Ap-ir	(on the side of?) the Apir
mu-tu	he has renewed.
40 *ur*	40 servants
dam	of his wife
(*dingir*) *Ninâ*	for Ninâ
maš-bi-pad	that called him to be her prince

(who translates it 'he has set up' = *du*?) misread it. *dun*, Br. 9868 = *ḫirû*, H. W. B. p. 289 = 'to dig' (cut), hence when used of a statue = to sculpture. So also Oppert, l. c. Déc. 2, No. 1, col. v. 4, has to be translated: 2 statues he digged, i. e. sculptured, and not as Jensen: *hat zwei Statuen? gereinigt? (geweiht)?*

7. *a mu-na a-ak*, written here *a* + *mu* + *a* + *ag?* (= a ligature) + *na* (under it). If the last but one sign is *ag*, T. C. 2—which however is very doubtful, comp. E. C. 558—then see Br. 2785 and H. W. B. p. 441: *nabû*. The '*na*' then would be the pronominal suffix to *mu*, or the prefix to *ag*. It ought to be translated: (Of) Ninâ a statue to declare her name (on the side of) the Apir he renewed. The *na*, however, may also refer to the king himself. Oppert translates: '*(Il a sculpté la déesse Ninâ): deux statues pour célébrer le nom de Ninâ, une statue à côté du bassin Ap-ir, il les a sculptées.*' How he substantiates this translation is not clear.

III. 1. The *Ap-ir* is probably a similar construction to the *zu-ab-gal*, Déc. 2, 1, col. iii. 5, or the *zu-ab-tur-da*, Déc. 2, 1, col. iv. 6; Déc. 2ter, No. 1. Comp. also the *ab-gi* in Déc. 31, No. 3, col. iii. 2, and the *e-ab* . . . in Déc. 5, No. 1, l. 36. See also note to l. 4 of Dec. 31, No. 1; and to C. T. 12061, l. 9.

3 ff.: The sense is: Ur-Ninâ commanded forty servants of his wife that they should build for Ninâ, who called him (Ur-Ninâ) to be her prince, two bamoth. Because Ur-Ninâ enumerates the buildings he himself had built, we have to translate *mu-ru* not by 'they built,' but 'he caused them to build.'

6. *maš*, Br. 1739, *ašaridu*, H. W. B. 149: 'prince'; *bi* = pron. suffix; *pad*, Br. 9420, *zakâru*. *PAD* is here only shorter expression for *šag pad-da*, i. e. 'called by the heart,' sc. to be her prince (*maš-bi*); hence also the king's name: Ur-Ninâ = servant of Ninâ. Thureau-Dangin, O. L. Z. i. p. 167, 4, takes *MAŠ-PAD* in the same sense as *PAD* (comp. Gudea B, iii. 14: *šig maš-e-ni-pad: des briques je choisis*), and translates our passage: '40 *hiérodules époux de la déesse Nina j'élus.*' Comp. also O. B. I. 125, obv. 11.

min edin	2 bamoth
mu-ru	he caused to build.

Col. IV.

nin-ni	(The statue of) his mistress
mu-ru	he has built.
E-pa	The Epa
mu-ru	he has built.
bad Šir-pur-la	The wall of Shirpurla
mu-ru	he has built.

Col. V.

gal + (ga)lu dingir uru	(The image of) the king, the god of the city,
mu-tu	he has renewed.
Mà-al	From Ma'al
kur-ta	the mountain
gu-gàl-giš	all kinds of wood
mu—	he has (brought ?).

7. *min edin.* The sign for '*edin*' is undoubtedly here the same as in Galet A of Eannatum; comp. R. A. iv. No. 1, pl. 1, col. iv. 4, where *edin* is determined by *GU*. That this *gu* = land (*mâtu*) is clear from the parallelism: (*dingir*) *Nin-gir-su-ra* a-šag *ki-ag-ga-ni Gu-edin-na šu-na mu-ni-gì*, l. c.; see also the note to it. And because the *edin* has not the *gu* (=land) before it, it is very probable that we have here the במות of Ninâ, as we have in the Galet A those of Ningirsu. Hommel, P. S. B. A. 1895, p. 206, reads *A-idinna* and translates: 'the town *A-idinna* he has built,' and because *A-idinna* is translated by the Assyrians with *nâdu*, 'leather-bag,' he concludes that *A-idinna* = *Nâdu* = Heb. נוֹד. See Gen. iv. 16: 'Cain dwelt in the land of Nod, on the east of (or better, before) Eden (*Idinna*).'

IV. 1. sc. *ṣalam*.

3. For *E-pa*, see Déc. 2ter, 4, note to l. 23.

V. 1. *Lugal dingir uru* is probably (*dingir*) *Ningirsu*, the god (*dingir*) of Girsu (the royal capital). It is interesting to see that Ur-Ninâ, king of Shirpurla-Girsu, calls his god here *lugal* (king).

3 ff. See Déc. 2ter, 4, note to ll. 16, 18.

6. The last sign is not clear, probably = *DU* or *LAL* = he has brought (taken); comp. Déc. 2bis, No. 1.

(Brick of Ur-Ninâ.)

Déc. pl. 31, No. 1, and R. A. iv. p. 91.

(Dingir) Ninâ-Ur	Ur-Ninâ,
lugal Šir-pur-la	king of Shirpurla,
dumu Gu-ni-du	son of Gunidu,
Ab-Gir-su	the Ab-Girsu
mu-ru	he has built.

4. What this *Ab-Girsu* was is difficult to tell. It may be a similar construction to that mentioned in Déc. pl. 2ter, No. 2, col. iii. l. 1 (see the note), and also similar to the *zu-ab-tur-da* and the *zu-ab-gal*, which latter two Jensen, in K. B. iii^1. p. 12, translates with '*das kleine Weltmeer*' and '*das grosse Weltmeer*.' Oppert may be right when he remarks, in R. A. ii. p. 85: '*On y a vu des bassins d'ablution, ayant un usage analogue à la fameuse mer du temple de Jérusalem. Il faudrait se demander si l'ap-Girsu ou mieux l'ap de Girsu ne pourrait pas rentrer de près ou de loin dans la même catégorie*.'

(' Seuil-Borne.')

R. A. iv. p. 97, fig. 5, and p. 122, 1.

(dingir) Nin-su-gir	To Ningirsu
(dingir) Ninâ-Ur	Ur-Ninâ,
gal-(ga)lu	the king
Šir-pur-la	of Shirpurla,
dumu Gu-ni-du	the son of Gunidu
ud ab-Su-gir	—when the Ab-Girsu
mu-ru	he had built—
a-mu-šub	he presented it (i.e. the *seuil-borne*).
e-(dingir) Ninâ	The house of Ninâ
mu-ru	he has built.
Ib-gal	The Ibgal
mu-ru	he has built.
Dul-nir	The Dulnir

mu-ru	he has built.
Igi-e-ni	The Eigini (lit. house of his eye)
mu-ru	he has built.
e-dam	The house of his wife
mu-ru	he has built.
e Ga-tum-dug	The house of Gatumdug
mu-ru	he has built.
Ti-aš-ra	The Tirash
mu-ru	he has built.

15. For this building, comp. Jensen, K. B. iii[1]. p. 12, notes 2 and **: '*Hochbau, Etage.*' Better perhaps = *maṣṣartu*, H. W. B. p. 478, or *bît tamarti*, Del. A. L[3]. p. 122, No. 3, l. 15 = 'watch-tower,' √ אמר.

(Coupe d'Our-Nina.)

R. A. iv. p. 106, fig. 11.

(*Dingir*) *Ba-u*	To Ba'u
(*dingir*) *Ninâ-Ur*	Ur-Ninâ,
lugal	king
Šir-pur-la	of Shirpurla,
dumu Gu-ni-du	son of Gunidu,
a-mu-šub	has presented it.

The son of Ur-Ninâ, who succeeded him upon the throne of Shirpurla, was *Akurgal*[1]. As yet no inscriptions of this monarch have been found. All that is known about him is gathered either from the inscriptions of his son (Eannatum) or from those of his father (Ur-Ninâ). Owing to the importance of those inscriptions in more than one respect, it will be well to give a transcription

[1] The meaning of the name of this king is not quite clear. Jensen (K. B. iii[1]. p. 16, note 3) explains it as 'son of the great mountain,' i. e. of Enlil-Bêl (?). He also admits that it is possible to take the '*a*' in the sense of 'man.' According to this the meaning would be: 'the man of Enlil-Bêl.' Comp. also *a-zu* = *asû*, Br. 11377 = physician; lit. 'a knowing one' (as Arabic طبيب and حكيم), from *zu*, 'to know.'

of them here. They are published in Déc. pl. 2ter, No. 1, and especially Déc. pl. 2bis, No. 1 and No. 2.

Déc. 2bis, No. 2 [1].

(dingir) Ninâ-Ur gal + (ga)lu Šir-pur-la
dumu Ni + gu + du

E Nin-gir-su	*À-ni-ta*
mu-ru	*A-kur-gal*
Lugal-šir	*dumu*
Ni-ĝal-la	*Luĝ + bar + ĝe +*
	gid ? + dul

Déc. 2ter, No. 1 [1].

?-tum	*(dingir) Ninâ-Ur*	*A-ni-ta*
Lugal-šir	*gal + (ga)lu*	*Ba-lip*
dumu	*Šir-pur-la*	*?-du-du-gal*
	dumu Gu-ni-du	
Mu + kur + ta + ri	*E Nin-su-gir*	*A-kur-gal*
dumu	*mu-ru*	*dumu*
	E (dingir) Ninâ	
Ǵar-sag-	*mu-ru*	*Nam-tum*
ku-al	*zu-ab-tur-da*	*(ga)lu*
	mu-ru	*dup-sar*
	uru-ni mu-ru	

Déc. pl. 2bis, No. 1, is the most important, because it gives us Ur-Ninâ and his whole family. I shall give the description [2] of Léon Heuzey in R. A. iii. p. 14 ff. *in extenso:*

'*Ici les figures forment deux processions superposées, marchant en sens inverse, au-devant d'un personnage beaucoup plus grand que les autres, ce qui évidemment marque son rang exceptionnel. Le*

[1] A translation of these inscriptions is not necessary. See, however, the notes to Déc. 2bis, No. 1.

[2] Comp. also Hilprecht, O. B. I. p. 253, note 1.

nom, gravé tout près du profil, ne permet pas de douter que ce ne soit l'image d'Our-Nina, deux fois répétée.

'*En regard de la file supérieure, le roi se tient debout, le torse nu. Le châle de kaunakès, rendu de la façon sommaire . . . entoure ses reins. C'est le costume de l'action et du travail. En effet, le souverain de Sirpurla se montre à nous dans une attitude qui est faite pour nous surprendre : sur la tête, complètement rasée, il soutient de la main droite une grande corbeille ; . . . le roi Our-Nina . . . humble . . . dans sa dévotion tient à honneur de remplir le rôle de porteur d'offrandes, de néocore, ou mieux l'office de manœuvre chargeant sur sa tête les matériaux pour la construction du temple. . . . En arrière, un petit personnage, tenant par le col une aiguière apode, à bec long sortant de la panse, représente l'échanson royal.*'

The king in the upper row looks toward the right, while the other figures, five in number, march towards him. '*Le premier,*' Heuzey goes on (p. 15), '*est plus grand de proportions, et plus richement vêtu que ceux qui le suivent, sans doute pour marquer la dignité de fils aîné. . . . Les quatre petits personnages qui viennent ensuite et dont la taille va crescendo sont complètement rasés et portent le châle simple, roulé en jupon entour des reins.*' In the same fashion are also clad the servants of the king.

Of the second row of figures, Heuzey says (p. 16):

'*(Le) second registre de figures (est) disposé en sens contraire du premier. Le roi, assis maintenant, se repose après la tâche terminée. Toujours plus grand que les autres personnages et portant le kaunakès enroulé autour de la taille, il lève un vase à boire en forme de cornet. Derrière son trône à dossier, . . . un nouvel échanson tient l'aiguière. En avant, comme première figure, plus haute que les suivantes, un dignitaire étend la main et semble parler à son maître.*' In the upper row all the figures have the sign for 'son' behind their names, while in the lower row only the last three are honoured with it.

The inscription of this remarkable monument—which I shall give exactly in the same sequence in which it is found on that tablet—runs as follows:—

Déc. pl. 2bis, No. 1.

Mu + *ta* +
ri + kur
dumu

À + *ni* +
kur + ra
dumu

Lugal +
šir
dumu

A-kur-gal
dumu

dumu
Lid-da

Šir-pur-la
lugal
UR
(*dingir*) *Ninâ*

Sag-
an-tug

Mà-al

kur-ta gu-gàl-
giš MU
du-du
Ba-lip

Nun-pad
dumu

e
(*dingir*) Nin-su-gir
mu-ru

E(ge ?)ud-bu
dumu

Šir-pur-la dumu Gu-ni-du dumu Gur-sar
gal + (*ga*)*lu*
(*dingir*) *Ninâ* + *UR*

Ninâ-ku-tur-
à
dumu

e (*dingir*) *Ninâ*.
mu-ru

Zu-ab-tur-da
mu-ru

À-ni-ta

Mu-ta-ri-kur. In Déc. 2ter, No. 1, this son of Ur-Ninâ is mentioned again. The signs there have the sequence: *mu-kur-ta*, and under them *ri*. It is possible that this name has to be read *Mu-ri-kur-ta*.

À-ni-kur-ra. *À* has to be read, not *da*. The *ni* may belong after the *ra*, and the whole name may be pronounced *À-kur-ra-ni*.

Lugal-šir(*ezen*). So I would like to read the name of this son. He is mentioned also in Déc. 2bis, No. 2.

A-kur-gal. '*Tient une aiguière comme s'il remplissait auprès du prince héritier qui le précède le rôle d'échanson*' (Heuzey, R. A. iii. p. 16).

Lid-da, the last sign, may also be *ŠU*. He is the 'firstborn,' while Akurgal —to conclude from his height—may be the youngest son. It is hardly possible to imagine that *Lid-da* would be = *lêtu* = לֵאָה — a feminine, although the sign '*dumu*' does not speak against this. If this were true, '*il resterait*,' says Heuzey, R. A. iv. p. 104, note 2, '*à expliquer comment, d'après les usages orientaux, une femme pourrait occuper ici la première place, avant les enfants mâles, même avant le prince héritier*.'

Gu-ni-du. In Déc. 2bis, No. 2, written *Ni* + *gu* + *du*.

(*dingir*) *Ninâ-Ur*. So written here; in the second row, however, the name is written *Ur-*(*dingir*) *Ninâ*. Eannatum, too, in his 'Stèle des Vautours,' writes the name Ur-Ninâ; comp. Déc. pl. 4, col. ii. 11.

À-ni-ta (Hilprecht, O. B. I. 253, note 1, reads *Da-ni-ta* = 'at his side' =

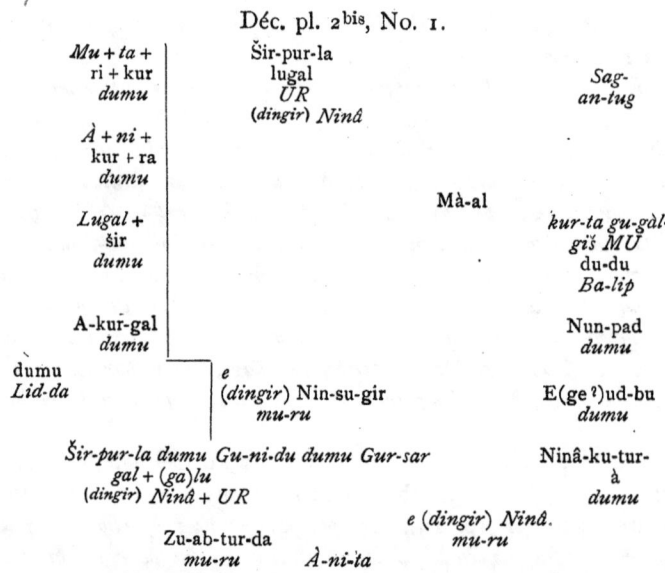

The whole may be translated, beginning from the left (on the right side of Ur-Ninâ):

Ur-Ninâ
king
of Shirpurla, son of Gunidu, son
of Gursar.

Lidda
the son,

the son
Akurgal,

the son
Lugalshir,

the son
Akurrani,

the son
Murikurta.

On the left side of the king:

The *ZU-AB-TUR-DA* Anita.
he has built.

The middle part:

The house of
Ningirsu
he has built.

Second row, behind Ur-Ninâ (to be read from the left to the right):

'*Ur-(dingir) Ninâ*,
king Sagantuk.
of Shirpurla.'

In front of Ur-Ninâ (to be read from the right to the left):

'From Ma'al
the mountain all kinds of
wood
he brought.
Balip,

Nunpad
the son,

E(ge ?)-ud-bu
the son,

Ninâkutura
the son,

the house of Ninâ
he has built.

page) and *Sag-an-tug* (Hilpr. l. c. = 'he is chief') are servants or officials of the king; so is *Ba-lip*. The latter is mentioned also in Déc. 2ter, No. 1, where this name is followed by ?-*du-du-gal* (the ? is the same sign which is found in the name of the god mentioned in Galet A of Eannatum, col. vii. 18; which see). Among other servants of the king may be mentioned a certain *Ġar-sag-ku-al* (Déc. 2ter, No. 1), *Ni-ǵal-la*, *Luǵ-bar-ǵe-gid(?)-dùl*, and *Nam-tum*, the scribe (Déc. 2bis, No. 2).

?-*ud-bu*. The first sign is not clear. It looks as if it were *e* (*bîtu*).

Mà-al. The *al* is quite clear here, and no other sign than T. C. 91. For the whole expression, see Déc. 2ter, No. 4, ll. 16–18. The signs *du-du* contain the verb. They—or only one *du*—probably have to be supplied in Déc. 2ter, No. 2, col. v. l. 6.

Among the buildings mentioned here are the *Zu-ab-tur-da* (comp. also Déc. 2ter, No. 1), the house of Ningirsu (ibid. and Déc. 2bis, No. 2), and the house of Ninâ (ibid.). In Déc. 2ter, No. 1, also a certain '*uru-ni*' is mentioned, which also occurs in Déc. 2, 1, col. ii. 9. Jensen, K. B. iii[1]. p. 12; translates it '*sein Observatorium*.' See notes 4, 6, and * ibidem.

In this inscription eight sons of Ur-Ninâ are mentioned. If we classify them according to their height, and take this as a basis for determining their age, we would get the following result:—

Ur-Ninâ

(1) *Lid-da*, (2) *Mu-ri-kur-ta*, (3) *À-ni-kur-ra*, (4) *Lugal-šir*, (5) *A-kur-gal*, (6) *Nun-pad*, (7) *E-ud-bu*, (8) *Ninâ-ku-tur-a*[1].

It is remarkable that the firstborn, Lidda, is not mentioned in any of the other inscriptions. Did he never succeed his father upon the throne of Shirpurla? Did Akurgal, his fifth son, in preference to all the others, inherit the royal sceptre, and thus become the immediate successor of Ur-Ninâ? Interesting as these questions are, we are yet, with the means on hand, unable to decide them[2]. This much only we know, that both Eannatum and Enannatum I. call themselves 'son of Akurgal.' Another interesting fact is that Eannatum, in his 'Stèle des Vautours,' calls his father *lugal* ('king[3]') of Shirpurla, while in his other inscriptions he only terms him 'patesi of Shirpurla[4].' Not very much can be concluded from this, because even Ur-Ninâ is styled by Eannatum 'patesi of Shirpurla' (comp. Galet A, col. viii. 4–7)[5]. The translation of this latter passage, however, is uncertain[6]. Ur-Ninâ's successor, however —either Lidda or Akurgal—may have lost the title 'king' in consequence of an unsuccessful war. Eannatum, on the other hand,

[1] Hilprecht, O. B. I. p. 252, reads this name: *Ninâ-šu-banda*.

[2] We are inclined to believe that Akurgal was not the direct successor, but probably followed upon the reign of Lidda. If this is true, then we would have here a similar case to that of Eannatum and Enannatum I.—both sons of Akurgal.

[3] Comp. Déc. 4 A, col. ii. 8–10.

[4] Comp. Galet A, col. iii. 1–3; viii. 1–3.

[5] Entemena, on the other hand, calls Ur-Ninâ a king; see R. A. ii. p. 148, obverse, col. ii. 2, '*dumu-ka Ur-(dingir)-Ninâ lugal Širpurla-ki-ka-ge*,' i. e. 'the grandson of Ur-Ninâ, king of Shirpurla.'

[6] Probably we have to translate col. viii.: He (i. e. Eannatum) is the son of Akurgal, &c., and begin a new sentence with l. 6: He (i. e. Eannatum) is (*kam*) patesi of Shirpurla. If this explanation is right—which is highly probable—then Ur-Ninâ alone would have been king of Shirpurla, his successors being again reduced to mere patesis.

being more successful, resumes again for a short time the title 'king' after his victory over Kish. This latter fact is very important. Eannatum expressly tells us that Innanna gave him the *nam-lugal Kîš-ki*, 'the kingship of Kish' (Galet A, col. vi. 5), while as ruler of Shirpurla he was only patesi (ibid. l. 2). The state of affairs then was as follows:—

Ur-Ninâ, a usurper, was able to constitute himself *king* of Shirpurla in consequence of the weakness of the patesis of Shirpurla who preceded him, they having been reduced by the kings of Kish (comp. Mesilim) to complete powerlessness. Ur-Ninâ's successors, however, were not able to retain the title of their father. Was it internal disharmony between the sons of Ur-Ninâ which caused this? They lost the title 'king,' and had to accept that of patesi. Undoubtedly they were forced to do this by one of the successors of Mesilim, i. e. by a king of Kish. Eannatum—a great hero—was able to overcome the old enemy Kish. He even was so fortunate as to add to his old title, 'patesi of Shirpurla,' that of 'king' (sc. of 'Kish'), and by a stretch of this latter title he may have called himself also 'king of Shirpurla [1].' The successors of Eannatum called themselves, and are called without any exception, 'patesis of Shirpurla.'

After these preliminary remarks about the titles of the different members of the dynasty of Ur-Ninâ, we now turn our attention to Eannatum [2] (i. e. 'The house of heaven is stable,' see Galet A, note

[1] This, however, is very doubtful. We find only two places in all the inscriptions of Eannatum which might prove that he was 'king of Shirpurla': Déc. pl. 4 A, col. i. ll. 5, 6, *gal + (ga)lu Šir-la-pur-ki-ge*, and Déc. 3bis, E[1], col. 1, *E[annatum] gal + (ga)lu Šir-la-pur-ki*. Then follow the same titles as given in Galet A, i. 5 ff., with few variations.

[2] His inscriptions:—

Déc. pl. 2ter, fig. 5: see R. A. iv. p. 39, note 2 (Thureau-Dangin), and R. A. iv. p. 122, 2.

Stèle des Vautours: comp. Heuzey, R. A. iii. 1 ff., and especially Thureau-Dangin, Comptes Rendus, 1897, p. 241 ff., and Heuzey, ibid. 1892, p. 236 ff., and 1895, p. 340 ff.

Déc. pl. 3 A: Jensen, K. B. iii[1]. p. 16, No. ii.; Thureau-Dangin, R. A. iv. p. 38, note 3, and ibid. iv. pp 124, 125.

†

to i. 2), the son of Akurgal himself. Whether he reigned contemporaneously with his brother Enannatum I. or not, we cannot tell. The fact that the sons of Enannatum I. succeeded upon the throne of Shirpurla, and not those of Eannatum, makes it reasonable to suppose that Eannatum preceded Enannatum I. This latter ruler seems to have played only a minor *rôle* in early Babylonian history. Only two of his inscriptions have so far come down to us. One of them has been translated above on p. 14; comp. also R. A. iv. p. 122, No. 3. The other was published recently by Thureau-Dangin in Comptes Rendus, 1899, p. 348, pl. ii., and reads:

Col. I.

En-an-na-tum	Enannatum,

Déc. pl. 3 B.
,, C.
,, 3bis, D[1]: Thureau-Dangin, R. A. iv. p. 39, note 1; and ibid. iv. p. 124.
,, E[1].
pl. 4 A.
,, B.
,, C.
pl. 4bis, D[2]: Thureau-Dangin, R. A. iv. p. 39, note 3 (col. iii. 7–15); also published in R. A. iii. No. i. pl. ii. (*estampage*).
,, E[2].
pl. 4ter, F[1]: Thureau-Dangin, R. A. iv. p. 40, note 2 and note 1.
,, F[2]: Thureau-Dangin, R. A. iv. pp. 124, 125.
C. T. 23580, part vii. pp. 1 and 2.

'Briques':—
Déc. 31, No. 2 *a* and *b*. Also published in R. A. ii. p. 81, and translated ibid. by Oppert, p. 86.

Other inscriptions:—
Berlin Museum, No. V. A. 2599: Jensen, K. B. iii. p. 15, i.
V. A. 2100 (unpublished).
Inscription of London, P. S. B. A., Nov., 1890, p. 63.
Les Galets: see Thureau-Dangin, R. S. 1897, p. 66, note 1.
A: published in R. A. iii. No. iv. pl. v.; revised edition in R. A. iv. No. i. pl. i., translated by Thureau-Dangin in R. S. 1897, p. 66 ff.
B: not yet published, is in the museum of Constantinople.
C: published in Déc. 2ter, No. 6.
D: published in Déc. 2, No. 3.
E: unpublished, in Constantinople.

pa-te-si	patesi
Šir-la-pur-*ki*,	of Shirpurla,
dumu A-kur-gal	son of Akurgal,
5 pa-te-si	patesi
Šir-la-pur-*ki*-ka-ra (?)	of Shirpurla—
ud (*dingir*) Nin-gir-su-ge	when by Ningirsu's

Col. II.

šag-gi ba-pad-da-a	true heart he had been called,
erin laǵ-laǵ	(then) bright cedars
kur-ta mu-na-ta-*DUL-DU*	from the mountain (= hardly the Lebanon, more probably = the Elamitic mountains!),
e-ku mu-na-sig-sig-ga-a	(and when) in (?) the temple he had been filled with power,
5 sag-šú-bi	(then) the (lit. its) coverings (ornaments)
erin laǵ-laǵ	of the bright cedars,

Col. III.

mu-na-ni-gub	he put them on.
Ur-Ġa-lu-ub	Ur-Ġalub
ni-gab-ku mu-na-*KU-KU*-na	as guardian he installed,

I. 6. *RA* doubtful. We would expect *GE*.

II. 3. For *DUL-DU*, see Br. 9593.

4. This line is parallel to l. 1, and dependent on i. 7.
SIG-SIG-GA = to fill (*malû*) with strength (*SIG* = *karnu*, comp. Heb. קרן). Or, when in a house he had filled them up, i. e. stored them (the cedars) away.

5. For *sag-šú* see H. W. B. p. 316 *sub kubšu*: *Kopfbinde, Kopfbedeckung und dergl.* Here probably = coverings, ornament. Thureau-Dangin translates ll. 4 ff.: *et (lorsque) dans le temple il l'eut transporté* (?) *dans ... ce bois de cèdre brillant il plaça*.

6. Might also be translated: ' And when in the temple he had stalled them up (lit. into the temple ... had filled them up).'

III. 3. *Ni-gab*, Br. 5352 and H. W. B. 584 (*amtlu*) *kepu*.
KU-KU-na has probably to be read *durun-durun-na*, see Br. 10532 = *ušešib*.

gal + (ga)lu ki-an-na-ag-ni	to his king, who loves him,
(*dingir*) *Nin-gir-su-ra*	viz. to Ningirsu,
mu-mu-na-gar	he presented them.

6. *GAR.* See Br. 11982 and H. W. B. 691 : *šarâku.*

Eannatum, his brother, on the contrary, is the greatest of the whole dynasty. The deeds of this monarch have been preserved to us on different monuments, among which the 'Stèle des Vautours' is the most important. In order to obtain a full conception of his time we must compare this 'Stèle' with the so-called 'Cône' of Entemena. Those monuments, in connection with the Galet A, give us the following interesting piece of history:—

The god of Shirpurla (Ningirsu) and the god of Gishban, at the instigation of Enlil (god of Nippur), agree to settle the boundaries between their respective territories (Cône, i. 1–7). Mesilim, king of Kish—a contemporary of Lugalshuggur, patesi of Shirpurla; see above, p. 16—in the quality of lord paramount of Shirpurla corroborates the result of 'this settling of boundaries,' and erects a statue on the junction of the two territories, to mark out the boundaries of the territory of Shirpurla on the one side and of Gishban[1] on the other (Cône, i. 8–12). Ush, however, a certain ambitious patesi of Gishban, is not satisfied with this decision. He takes away the statue which Mesilim had erected, and then invades Shirpurla undoubtedly to extend his territory beyond the boundary previously fixed (13–21). A war between Shirpurla and Gishban ensues.

Mesilim, who feels dishonoured by this action of Ush, takes the side of Shirpurla and defeats Gishban (22–31). Gishban in

[1] It should be borne in mind that the better reading of the name of this city is *GIŠ-UḪ—UḪ* being the second half of the sign reproduced in Br. 8124. Comp. Winckler, A. F. p. 373, note 3, and the note to the reading of the city *Ḫu-uḫ-nu-ri-ki* further below, and see for the present C. T. 94-10-16, 2 : *mu uš-sa Ḫu-ḫu-nu-ri-ki*, and C. T. 94-10-16, 4 : *mu-uš-sa Ḫu-UḪ-nu-ri-ki*, which shows that the sign in question has to be pronounced either *ḪU* or *UḪ*. *GIS-UḪ* is the modern Djokha, which latter might be a variant of the former.

course of time again becomes restless. It invades, under its patesi Gunammide, the territory of Shirpurla, and more specifically the Guedin, a district sacred to Ningirsu. 'Gunammide, the patesi of Gishban, according to the command of his god . . . the Guedin, the beloved territory of Ningirsu, he destroyed' (Déc. 4bis, D^2, col. iii. 7–15; see note to Galet A, iv. 4). Eannatum, after having fortified Shirpurla sufficiently ('the wall of Uruazagga he built,' Galet A, iii. 7), and having led his armies victoriously against Elam and Gishgal (Galet A, iii. 13–19), feels himself strong enough to deal a deadly (?) blow at Gishban. 'Gishban he put under the yoke, twenty of its dead ones he buried' (ibid. iii. 24 ff.). Having done this, he restores the sacred territory, the Guedin, to Ningirsu (Galet A, iv. 2 ff.); concludes a treaty with Enakalli, (one of) the successor(s) of Gunammide; digs a canal 'from the great river (i. e. Euphrates?) to the Guedin' (Cône, ii. 1 ff.), thus establishing a boundary between the two territories. By the side of this canal he erects a statue of himself, restores the statue of Mesilim to its old place (Cône, ii. 4 ff.), and makes the Gishbanites swear never to invade the sacred territory of Ningirsu again, nor to trespass this boundary.

'In the future time the territory of Ningirsu, when (the Gishbanites) should invade it again, the dyke and the canal, if they should trespass it, the statue, if they should take it away—at that time when they invade it, then the *sa-šuš-gal* (i. e. Eannatum) of Utu, the powerful king, by whom they have sworn [1], shall arise against Gishban' (Déc. pl. 3bis, D^1, col. i.).

The 'Stèle des Vautours' has for its main object the commemoration of this treaty with Enakalli, patesi of Gishban, after the latter city had been defeated by Eannatum [2].

The places of the 'Stèle des Vautours' which mention *this treaty* have been arranged by Thureau-Dangin (R. A. iv. p. 124) as follows:—

[1] Comp. also Galet A, i. 2, note.

[2] And not to commemorate the defeat of Gishban (Hilprecht, O. B. I. p. 271), which preceded the erecting of the 'Stèle des Vautours.'

Déc. 3 A, col. i.

E-an-na-tum me	i. e.	Eannatum I am,
sa šuš-gal		the scourge
(*dingir*) *Utu*		of Shamash,
gal+(ga)lu zal si(g)-ga-ka		the king filled with splendour;
(ga)lu giš-BAN-ki-ra		unto the Gishbanites
e-na-sum		I have given an oath
nam e-na-ta-kud		and sworn.
(ga)lu giš-BAN-ki-ge		The Gishbanites
E-an-na-tum-ra		to Eannatum

1. *ME*, Br. 10358: *anaku*; comp. Déc. 7, ii. 4; *Ur-*(*dingir*) *Ba-u me.*

2. *SA ŠUŠ-GAL.* Jensen, K. B. iii[1]. p. 16, and Thureau-Dangin, R. A. iv. p. 38, note 3, read *sa-u-gal*, which the latter translates '*serment*.' In R. A. iv. p. 124, the latter, however, reads *sa-šuš* (Br. 8643)-*gal*, and compares iv. R. 27, 58 *a* (*sa šu-uš-gal*), and ii. R. 19, 3 *b* (*sa šu-uš-kal*). Comp. also Br. 7166 and 7167. For *šuškallu*, see H. W. B. p. 694. It is a title which even later Assyrian kings apply to themselves, viz. Tiglath-pileser (col. iii. 33) and Sargon (Lay. 33, 10). According to Thureau-Dangin, l. c., this expression signifies '*l'épervier*,' '*le filet*,' while Delitzsch, l. c., translates it by '*Fallstrick, Fangnetz*.' Comp. K. 133, obv., 7, 8: *Ninib ḳarradu ša šú-uš-kal-la-šu* (=*giš SA ŠÚ-UŠ-KAL-bi*) *a-a-bu i-saḫ-ḫa-pu*. This latter writing shows that *SA ŠÚ-UŠ-*$\frac{K}{G}$*AL* = *ŠÚ-UŠ-*$\frac{K}{G}$*AL*.

The best way to translate this expression would be by 'rod,' 'reed'—on account of *giš*—i. e. *eine* (*Zucht*)-*Rute*, a 'scourge.' This is evident from l. 29, where the *sa-šuš-gal* is said to *an-ta ge-šuš*, 'to cast down,' 'to overpower' his enemies. This expression occurs also in Cône of Entemena, i. 29, vi. 22.

4. *ZAL*, Br. 5319: *namâru*; *ZAL-ZAL*, Br. 5359, *kamû ša nabli*; *SIG*(*-GA*), Br. 3393, *malû*; the whole might be translated 'king, filled with light' (splendour). Comp. also Gudea B, viii. 62, 63.

For lines 1–4, comp. also Jensen, K. B. iii[1]. p. 16, No. ii.

6. *SUM*, H. W. B. p. 450: *nadânu*: '*einen Eid leisten, angeben, kundthun, zeigen*'; comp. also ii. R. 65, obv., i. 4: *mamîtu iddinû*.

7. *KUD*, Br. 390; *tamû*, H. W. B. 708. *NAM . . . KUD*, according to Thureau-Dangin, l. c.: '*paraît avoir ici un sens analogue à NAM ERIM . . . KUD-*(*DA*)'; see Br. 2182 (written: *nam-ne-ru . . . kud-da*) = *mamîtu tamû*; comp. H. W. B. p. 415 *sub mammêtu*.

9. The *RA* here, as well as in l. 5, is postfix, dependent upon *sum* and *kud*—and not an essential part of the name of Eannatum, as Jensen, K. B. iii[1]. p. 14, note 13 (*E-dingir-ra-na-gin*, see Galet A, i. 2), supposes.

nam mu-na-kud-du	have sworn—
zi (*dingir*) *Utu*	by the life of Shamash
[*mu-ni-pad-de* (comp. Déc. 3 A, iii. 4)]	they have sworn.

Déc. 3 A, col. iv. 1, and 4ter, F[2], col. iv. 2 ff.

(*g*)*uru ni-kù*	A (boundary)-canal I have made,
e til-zi(*d*) *na-e*	and to keep (them) back I filled it with water,
da-ur da-gal-la-ku	in order that for ever

12. *PAD*, Br. 9417 : *tàmû*.

13. The first sign occurs again in Gudea D, iii. 3 : *mà-*(*g*)*uru ki-ag-ga-ni*, and *passim*. Comp. Jensen, K. B. iii[1]. p. 52, note 1 and * : '*meine geliebte Barke*'; T. C. 201 ; and Hommel, P. S. B. A. 1896, p. 20.

NI-KÙ. This *KÙ* occurs again on the Cône of Entemena, ii. 23 : *ĝar-ku ni-kù*, where it is parallel to *kud-du ba-uš*. But *UŠ*, according to H. W. B. p. 80, is = *emêdu* ; (*g*)*uru ni-kù* then may be = *uṣurta* (sic) *êmid*, i.e. '*eine Umschrankung* (H. W. B. 122) *errichtete, legte er an*' = a boundary-canal he made, thus identifying T. C. 201 with T. C. 194. In later times these two signs were separated. If this be true, then a *mà-*(*g*)*uru* is only a small boat, such as is used only on a canal, in contradistinction to a *mà* *κατ' ἐξοχήν*.

14. *NA-E*. *E*, Br. 5844 : *mû*, 'water,' as verb 'to water, to fill with water'; comp. O. B. O. 87, ii. 36, 37 : *a-ne ĝul-la mu-da-e*, 'with waters of joy he watered,' i. e. filled. The same meaning has to be postulated here.

(*E*)-*TIL-ZID*. According to Br. 1577 = *TIL-ZID-DA* = *nîtu*, H. W. B. 460. According to this lines 13 and 14 might be translated: '*eine Umschrankung legte er an und füllte sie mit Wasser* (*na-e*) *als Zurückhaltung* (*nîta* or *nîtiš*),' i. e. he filled the boundary canal with water in order to keep away the Gishbanites. This would actually agree with Cône of Entemena, i. 32–ii. 3 : Eannatum, patesi of Shirpurla, *e-bi id-nun-ta gu-edin-nà-ku ib-ta-ni-ud-du*, 'a canal from the great river to the Guedin he made to go.' This canal (*e-bi*), called here (*g*)*uru* (*Umschrankung*), was then filled with the water from the great river (הנהר הגדול), the Euphrates. Thureau-Dangin, l. c., translates lines 13 and 14: *Un fossé . . . . j'ai creusé.*

15. *da-ur* = Semitism for *dârû* or *dûru*, H. W. B. p. 213. Comp. O. B. I. 261, note 4.

DA-GAL-LA-ku. That *da-GAL* = *da-mal*, see Hommel, Sum. Lesestücke, p. 137 *b*.

ki-sur-ra [comp. Déc. 3bis, D^1, col. i. 1 ff.]	the territory
(dingir) Nin-gir-su-ka-ge	of Ningirsu
ba-ra-mu-bal-e	they may not invade;

Déc. 3bis, D^1, col. i. 4 ff.

[e]-kur + e-bi	and the canal
šu-bal ba-ra-ag-ge	they may not cross over,
na-ru-a-bi	and that stèle
ba-ra-pad-du	they may not take away.
ud-da mu-bal-e	On the day when they should cross over,
sa šuš-gal	then the scourge

DA-MAL-LA, Br. 6679–6681, which latter again is dial. equivalent of *DAGAL*, Br. 5446; *rapâšu, rapšu*, H. W. B. 626.

DA-UR DA-GAL-LA-ku = *ana dûri rapši*, i. e. for ever = *ana dûru umê*, v. R. 65, 23 *b*.

16. Lines 16–18 are identical with Déc. 3bis, D^1, i. 1–3, and supplement each other.

For *ki-sur*, see Cône of Entemena, i. 7; vi. 10, 12.

18. *BAL*. See Cône of Entemena, vi. 16: *an-ta bal-e-da*. *BA-RA*, Br. 123: *lâ* = negation.

19. Thureau-Dangin reads this line [*e*]-*kùr-e-bi*, and says, l. c., note 11: '*le signe kùr est emboîté dans le signe e*.' This very same sign we find also in Tablette A of Entemena (R. A. ii. p. 148), face, iv. 8: *zu-ab E* (= *kùr-e*) *GID-RA*.

E (Br. 5841) as well as (*E*)-*KÙR* (written *BAB*)-*E*, see H. W. B. p. 51, and iv. R. 14, No. 3, 11, 12 *a, b*, signify = *iku* and *palgu*, '*Bewässerungsgraben und Kanal*.' R. A. ii. p. 148, col. iv. 8, therefore, has to be read and translated: *zu-ab kùr-e SIR-ra*, i.e. unto Enki he built an *ab-zu* for (*ra*) the long (*gid* = *arâkû*) canal (*kùr-e*).

20. The first sign is not clear; it may be either *KI* or *ŠU*. Both as prefixes form nouns, Hommel, S. L. p. 141, 2 *b*.

KI-bal or *ŠU-bal* = the going over, the crossing; see above, l. 18.

Ba-ra = *lâ*; *ag-ge* = *epêšu*. Word for word: a crossing not to make.

21. *na-ru-a-bi*. This stèle was erected by Mesilim on the boundaries of Kish and Shirpurla (Cône of Entemena, i. 12); Ush, the patesi of Gishban, removes it (ibid. i. 19), and Eannatum restores it again to its former place (ibid. ii. 6-9).

22. *PAD*. See Cône of Entemena, i. 19.

(dingir) Utu	of Shamash,
lugal zal si(g)-ga-ka	a king filled with splendour,
nam e-ta-kuḍ-du	by whom they have sworn,
giš-BAN-ki-a	over the Gishbanites
an-ta ĝe-šuš	may it come.
E-an-na-tum me	Eannatum I am,
gal-na-ga-mu-zu	may I be very wise:
tu-ĝu NAMṢABU-2,	two doves,
igi-ba KAŠ-ŠIG ba-ni-gar	upon them I poured wine
ùr-sag-ba ni-mi-gab	and sacrificed them.

29. *AN-TA* = *eliš* (Br. 459); *ŠUŠ*, Br. 8700: *katâmu*. The subj. is *sa-šuš-gal*, l. 24. This line shows that the meaning of *sa-šuš-gal* can be only that which was given above, viz. 'scourge'; a *šuškal la mâgirê* is 'a scourge for the not subservient ones' (Tiglath-pileser, Sargon); *an-ta ĝe-šuš* can only be translated by 'may (*ĝe*) the scourge (*sa-šuš-gal*) of Shamash come (*šuš* = *katâmu*, H. W. B. p. 362) over (*an-ta*) the Gisbanites.' Comp. also *sa-šuš-gal ne-šuš* (Cône of Entemena, i. 29) and *sa-šuš-gal-ni šà-ni-šuš* (ibid. col. vi. 22, 23).

31. *GAL* ... *ZU*, according to Thureau-Dangin, l. c. note 17 = *GAL-AN-ZU* (Br. 6853; H. W. B. p. 139): *iršu*; comp. also Cyl. B, ii. 8; xiii. 13. *NA-GA-MU* is the prefix to *ZU*. *ZU*, Br. 130: *mudû*.

32. *tu-ĝu*, Br. 1084; *summatu*, H. W. B. 503.

namṣabu = *iṣṣuru*, Br. 2232. Thus we should probably read, and not *NAM*.

33. The third sign is not clear. Thureau-Dangin thinks (l. c. note 19) that it is composed of *BI* + *SIG* (= *IGI-GUNÛ*, E. C. 391). For *igi-gunû* comp. Br. 7005 and 7373. The latter has also the meaning *dannu*, *rabû*, and *dummuḳu*. Probably in these old times *igi-gunû* was = *igi-êrinnu* (*ŠIG* = *damḳu*, Br. 9446). For *KAŠ* (*BI*)-*ŠIG* comp. R. A. iii. p. 136 = *šikaru damiḳtum*. *GAR* = *šakânu* (Br. 11978). The whole line may be translated literally: Upon them (*igi-ba*, i. e. upon their faces) I placed (*ba-ni-gar*) wine (*KAŠ-ŠIG*), i. e. I poured upon them wine, apparently a ritual observance.

34. The first sign is that for *ÙR* with inserted *gunu*-signs. Because *GAB* = *pitû*, *paṭâru* (Br. 4488): *spalten, zerreissen, durchbrechen*, we would not be far from the correct interpretation if we explain this line by: their *ùr-sag* I pierced through, destroyed. But *ÙR-SAG* means *ḳaradu*, *ḳarradûtu*, which when put into the *gunu*-state may very well stand for 'life' or 'heart.' In l. 33 he pours upon the doves wine; in this line he states that he destroyed their vital (= *gunu*-signs) strength, i. e. he killed, sacrificed them. Lines 29 ff. seem to indicate that his wish (*ĝe*) will surely

[(*dingir*) *Utu*]	For Shamash,
gal + (*galu*) [*zal*] *si*(*g*)-[*ga-ra*]	the king filled with splendour,
UD-UNUG-ki	in Larsa,
E-BAR-BAR	in (the temple) *E-BAR-BAR*,
ninda-gud ku-an-kù	young oxen I offered.

Déc. 4ter, F^{2}, col. iii. 4.

E-an-na-tum me	Eannatum I am,
ka-a-kud-du	obedient
lugal-mu	to my king
(*dingir*) *EN-KI-ra* (we would expect here the god *Utu*)	Ea.
ab-ba dug-ga-na (cp. Déc. 3 A, col. ii. 1)	If any proud one

Déc. 3 A, col. ii. 2.

a-ba šar-ra-na	(or) any powerful one

be fulfilled, i. e. that he will punish the Gishbanites if they should trespass the boundary canal. It is, so to speak, an oath corroborated by this sacrifice of two doves. Apparently the king had such sacrifices instituted all over the country, in order to celebrate in the right manner his treaty with the Gishbanites. This is evident from Déc. 4ter, F^{2}, col. v. 2; where we are told that four other doves were sacrificed, two of them in the city of Ur for Nannar: *E-an-na-tum me gal-na-ga-mu-zu tu-ĝu* 4 *igi-ba KAŠ-ŠIG ba-ni-gar ùr-sag-ba ni-mi-gab* 2 *NAMṢABU Uru-unug-ki-ku*.

39. *NINDA*, T. C. 53; Ur-Ba'u, iii. i. *NINDA-GUD* probably = *GUD-NINDA* = *bîru* in the sense of *bûru*, 'young ox,' H. W. B. p. 169.

KU-AN-KÙ. *ku* = verbal-prefix. For other examples, see Lugalzaggisi, iii. 33; *mu-tar-ri-KU-a* (read: *mu-ku-tar-ri-a*); Cône of Entemena, iii. 21: *e-ku-kid*; Déc. pl. 31, No. 3, col. iv. 5: *ĝe-na-ku-tum*.

KÙ = *akâlu* (Br. 882), here = *Shaphel*, 'to give to eat' = to sacrifice to somebody. *KÙ* is used here for 'to sacrifice,' because the *ninda-gud* were 'given to eat' to the priests of Shamash.

41. *KA* . . . *KUD*, Br. 561; *dalâlu*, H. W. B. p. 219, and K. 257, rev., 17, 18: *edlum muddallum* (written: *KA-TAR-RA*) = obedient (to the gods).

44. *AB-BA DUG-GA-na* may be best explained by 'hero (comp. Br. 3820, *amêl AB* = *nasîku*, H. W. B. 472) of his (*na*) mouth' (*DUG-GA* = *pû*) or 'hero of his words' (*ḳibîtu*) = 'a proud person,' '*ein Maulheld*.'

45. *a-ba*, Br. 11370; *mannu*, H. W. B. 419: '*wer immer*.' Is this *a-ba*

(ga)lu [giš-BAN-ki-a]	of the Gishbanites
enim da-gur-ra-da-an	should break his promise,
ud-a-ru	or in future time
ka-an-gàl	should want to take it back,
50 ud-da enim-ba šu-ni-bal-e	on that day when he breaks his promise
sa šuš-gal	the scourge
(dingir) Utu	of Shamash,
lugal zal si(g)-ga-ka	the king filled with splendour,
nam e-ta-kud-du	by whom they have sworn,
55 giš-BAN-ki-a	over the Gishbanites
an-ta ge-šuš	may it come [1].

identical with the *ab-ba* in l. 44? The third sign, according to Thureau-Dangin, l. c. p. 125, 2, is that for *ŠAR* = 3600. As such it is that of Br. 8981: *birku*, 'knee.' He translates *šar-ra-na* by '*par sa puissance*?' thus considering the ברך as the 'seat of power.' For the reading of this sign (= *šar* instead of *DUG*), see also Meissner, A. B. P. R. pp. 98, 99.

47. *enim da-gur-ra-da-an* may mean: whosoever (*a-ba*, l. 45) shall turn (*da-gur-ra* = *târu*, S^b 209) against (*da*, Br. 6655: *ana* = Hebr. אל) his (*an*? for *na*?) word (*enim* = *amâtu*) promise. As such it would be like l. 50, which see.

48. *ud-a-ru*, probably = *ud-ul-ru-(a)* = *ûmê ṣâti*, Br. 7939.

49. *ka-gàl*, Br. 611, *puḳurrû*, H. W. B. 537: '*Reklamation, Anspruchserhebung*.' Here = verb, on account of *an* = *paḳâru* = *ipaḳḳar*, 'he claims.'

50. Lit.: On the day when (*ud-da*) he transgresses (*šu-ni-bal-e*; *bal* = *nabalkutu*) his promises, or destroys, breaks (= *naḳâru*) his promise.

It bears the significant subscription: 'Stèle: Its name—nobody has ever seen its name—is: *Nin-girsu en menluma namti(id) Kiš-*

---

[1] This formula is repeated several times, only the gods, by whom Eannatum and the Gishbanites sware, change. Among the gods we find, besides Utu, also Enlil (see C. T. 23580, col. ii. 6 ff.: (*ga*)*lu giš-BAN-ki-ge* | *E-an-na-tum-ra* | *nam mu-na-kud-du* | *zi* (*dingir*) *En-lil* | *lugal an ki* (sic; not *DI*, as King copied)-*ka*; comp. also Déc. 4ter, F^3, col. vi.); Ninḫarsag, whom Eannatum calls his mother (C. T. ibid. col. iv. 1 and Déc. 4 B, col. iii.; Déc. 4ter, F^3, col. ii.); Enki (see above, and Déc. 4 B, col. iv.); Ninki (Déc. 3 A, col. iii.; Déc. 3bis, E^1, col. i.); and Enzu (Déc. 4 B, col. vi.).

edina[1]; stele of Guedin, the beloved territory of Ningirsu, which Eannatum has consecrated to Ningirsu[2].'

But Eannatum was not satisfied with this; he imposes a heavy tribute upon Gishban, consisting of one karu of grain for Ninâ and one karu for Ningirsu, besides 144,000 (?) great karu (Cône, ii. 19 ff.).

After having reduced Gishban to tranquillity, Eannatum also carries his victorious weapons against Erech (Warka) and Ur (the Ur of the Chaldees), Ki-Utu (Larsa?) and Az (on the Persian Gulf)—the patesi of which latter city he kills—against Melimme and Arua[3]. These latter cities were all in the neighbourhood of Shirpurla. Last of all, he crushes and defeats Zuzu, king of Uḫ (Galet A, iv. 6–v. 8). But even this does not exhaust the record of his victories. He becomes *king of Kish*—Kish, which for so long had itself been sovereign over Shirpurla. How this victory was accomplished is not evident from the inscriptions so far extant[4]. Probably at some future time we may find an account of this war.

[1] The name, according to Thureau-Dangin, means: '*Ningirsu, seigneur de la tiare magnifique, fais vivre le canal Kish-édina*,' l. c. p. 40, note 1.

[2] Déc. pl. 4ter, F^1: *na-ru-a* | *mu-bi* | (*ga*)*lu-a nu mu-bi igi-e* | (*dingir*) *Nin-gir-su* | *en-men-lum-ma* | *nam-ti* | (*id*) *Kiš-edin-na* | *na-ru-a* | *gu-edin-na* | *a-šag ki-ag* | (*dingir*) *Nin-gir-su-ka* | *E-an-na-tum me* | (*dingir*) *Nin-gir-su-ra* | *šu-na mu-ni-gì-a.* |

[3] Here probably belongs also Déc. 3bis, E^1, col. iii., where upon *A-ru-a-ki mu-ĝa-la* follows *ŠU-UD-DU Ki-en-gi*. The verb is not given—we expect however some such expression as *ṭu-ku bi-sig* or *mu-ĝa-lam* or *sag-ba-mu-du*. We then would have to translate the *ŠU-UD-DU* (*ŠU* = *ḳâtu* = portion or side, H. W. B. 599; *UD-DU* = Br. 7876, *elû* or *ṣîtu*, hence either = the upper (northern) or eastern (*ṣît*) portion) of Kengi (sc. he subdued).

[4] The king of Kish whom Eannatum overcomes was in all probability a certain *Al*-[*zu-zu-a*] *gal* + (*ga*)*lu Kiš*[-*ki*], mentioned in Déc. 4ter, F^1, col. iii, and especially in P. S. B. A. Nov. 1890, p. 63, where we read in part, col. iii. 3 ff.: *gal* + (*ga*)*lu Kiš-ki bi* | *na-dib-bi*, i. e. the king of Kish he captured, and further below, col. iv. 2 ff.: *giš-tug* (-*pi*)-*ni* | *Al-zu-zu-a* | *mu-sar-ra-bi* | *ab-ta-gir-a* | *giš-tug*(-*pi*)-*ni* | *Al-zu-zu-a* | *bil mu-ba-sum*, i. e. 'of his vassal (*der Hörige*) Alzuzua, his inscription he burnt, his vassal Alzuzua (himself) he cast into the fire'; and again, ibid., col. v. 2 ff.: *giš-tug*(-*pi*)-*ni* | *Al-zu-zu-a igi* (*dingir*) *Ninâ-ku* | *dingir-ra-ni* | *na-dib-bi* | *a-ne na-dib-bi*, i. e. 'of his vassal Alzuzua before Ninâ, his god(s) he captured and threw him (them) into the water.'

Eannatum was not only a hero in war, but also a wise administrator. He not only renewed three suburbs of his capital (Galet A, iii. 5 ff.), one of which—Uruazagga—he even surrounded by a wall, but also improved the condition of Shirpurla itself by digging different canals, which he consecrated to his god Ningirsu: the Kishedin, which probably marked the boundary between the Guedin and Gishban, and which the Gishbanites had to swear never to cross; the Lummagirnuntashagazaggipadda along the territory of Ningirsu (Déc. 2ter, fig. 5); and the Lummadimshar (Galet A, vii. 4).

Urukagina, we have seen, was the first to build a canal, viz. one for Ninâ, which he called *Ninâ-ki-tum-a*. In the Cône of Entemena are also mentioned the canal Lummaṣirta (iii. 20), the Imdubba (ii. 11), and the Namnundakigarra (ii. 13, *et passim*). Here then we have the beginning of the most characteristic feature of Babylonia. Babylonia becomes 'the land of canals,' such as the Psalmist had in mind when he wrote that touching psalm: 'By the rivers of Babylon we sat down and wept.' Further, Eannatum was not unmindful of his duty to the gods. He confesses in the opening of Galet A that all that he is and that he has comes from his gods. Accordingly, he shows his gratitude by erecting sanctuaries for Enlil, Ninḫarsag, Ningirsu, and Utu, and by restoring old buildings, which had been erected by his predecessors in honour of the gods, among which is to be found the Tirash.

The greatness of Eannatum as a mighty warrior, wise administrator, and faithful servant of his god may be best understood from his own words:

GALET A OF EANNATUM.

Comp. Thureau-Dangin, R. S. 1897, p. 66, and R. A. iv. No. 1, pl. 1.

Col. I.

(Dingir) *Nin-gir-su-ra*	For Ningirsu—
E-an-na-tum	Eannatum

I. 2. *E-an-na-tum*. This is the correct reading of the name. The argu-

pa-te-si	patesi
Šir-la-ki-pur-ge	of Shirpurla,
mu-pad-da	he who was chosen (called)
(*dingir*) *En-lil-ge*	by Enlil,
à-sum-ma	to whom power was given
(*dingir*) *Nin-gir-su-ka-ge*	by Ningirsu,
šag-pad-da	he who was chosen by the heart

Col. II.

(*dingir*) *Ninâ-ge*	of Ninâ,
ga-zi-kù-a	he who was nourished with the milk of life
(*dingir*) *N[in]-ḫar-[sag]-ka-ge*	by Ninḫarsag,
mu-šag-sa-a	he who was called by the heart
(*dingir*) *Innanna-ka-ge*	of the goddess of Innanna,
giš-tug(-pi) sum-ma	to whom intelligence was given
(*dingir*) *EN-KI-ka-ge*	by Enki,
ki-ag	the beloved
(*dingir*) *Dumu-zi-zu-ab-ka-ge*	of Dumuzizuab,

ment of Jensen (K. B. iii[1]. p. 14, note 13) that, because such forms as *E-AN-na-ra-du* (see Déc. 3 A, col. 3, 5) and *E-An-ra-na-du* (see Déc. 3 A, col. i. 9; Déc. 4 A, col. v. 5) occur, the name has to be read *E-dingira-na-DU* is based upon a misunderstanding of the text. In both cases *RA* is post-position, depending upon *kud*: 'to Eannatum (*RA*) they have sworn.' That we have to pronounce *DU* as *tum* is apparent from col. v. 10: *E-an-na-tum-ma*. *TUM*, Br. 4884, *kânu*, *kênu*. The whole name then would be *Bît-šamê-ukîn*, 'the house of heaven is stable,' just as *En-anna-tum* is *Bêl-šamê-ukîn*, 'the lord of heaven is stable.' For *Du* with the pronunciation *tum* = *kânu*, *kênu*, comp. Cône of Entemena, vi. 8, *ĝe-na* + *me* + *tum*, probably to be read *ĝe-na-tum-me* (comp. also *ĝe-ĝa-lam-me*, ibid. l. 20), and the name *En-an-na-tum(a)*.

5. Comp. Lugalzag. i. 19.

7. *à*, Br. 6547, *emûḳu*; *sum* = *nadânu*.

II. 2, 3. Lugalzag. i. 28, 29.

4. The arrangement of signs is *mu* + *šag*, and under the *šag* the first part of *sa*, and under this latter the second part of *sa* + *a*. *sa*, Br. 2290; *nabû*, H. W. B. p. 441. Thureau-Dangin reads: *mu-sa-a*. But why? The traces of *šag* are clear on both copies. For *šag* we might also read *dug* = called with a good name.

5. *ka-ge*, double genitive! Compare also Amiaud, R. A. ii. p. 12.

6. Lugalzag. i. 17.

iti (*ti*)	the abarakku
(dingir) *Pa-sag-ka-ge*	of Pasag,
ku-li ki-ag	the beloved friend
gal + (*ga*)*lu* + (dingir) *Erim-ka-ge*	of Lugal-Erim,

Col. III.

dumu A-kur-gal	the son of Akurgal
pa-te-si	patesi
Šir-la-[ki]*-pur-*[*ge*]	of Shirpurla—
[(dingir) *Nin-g*]*ir-su-ra*	for Ningirsu
*Gir-su-*ki	the city of Girsu
[*ki-b*]*i mu-na-gì*	he has restored,
bad Uru-azag-ga	the wall of Uruazagga
mu-na-ru	he has built.
(dingir) *Ninâ*	For Ninâ
*Ninâ-*ki	the city of Ninâ
mu-na-ru	he has built—
E-an-na-tum-e	Eannatum,
Elam-ḫar-sag igi-e (sic)*-ga*	Elam, a mountain higher than a temple,

10. *ŠI-UM* = *iti* = *abarakku*, H. W. B. p. 12; Br. 9427. Here with phonet. compl. *ti* = Semitism.

12. *ku-li*, Br. 10579; *ibru*, H. W. B. 10.

13. The third sign is found in T. C. No. 58, and has to be identified, not with *gišgal*, as Amiaud, Thureau-Dangin (E. C. 359), and Hommel (P. S. B. A. 1893, p. 1) do, but with Br. 949, *Erim*. So also Jensen. *Gišgal* occurs in col. iii. 17; comp. also Ur-Ba'u, col. ii. 2, in de Sarzec, Déc. pl. 7 and 8: *uru ki-ag* (dingir) *Lugal-Erim-ki-ka-ge*. (dingir) *Lugal-Erim* is the god who is king of the city Erim, just as Ningirsu was the lord (*nin*) of Girsu. Erim was one of the parts of Shirpurla. A king of Erim is mentioned also in Déc. 30bis, No. 21.

III. 6. *ki-bi* . . . *gì*, Br. 2405. v. R. 44, 39 *c*: = *ana ašrišu-itûr*.

7. *bad*, T. C. 71; Br. 4386, *dûru*. *Uru-azag-ga* is here a proper name, another part of Shirpurla; it means 'the holy city.'

8. *ru* = *banû*, Br. 5248.

13. *Elam*, Br. 9009; *ḫar-sag*, Br. 8553, *šadû*.

igi-e-ga. So read, not *igi-ge-ga*, and comp. Gudea, Cyl. B, i. 4 in R. A. ii. p. 126. The first copy has *e* instead of *ge*! (see R. A. iii. No. iv. pl. 5). The whole phrase: *igi* (Br. 9265; *maḫar*, H. B. W. 403) higher than a house (*e* or

ṭu-ku bi-sig	under the yoke he has put.
saǧar-dul-tag-bi	Its dead ones
mu-dub	he buried.
šu-nir Gišgal-^{ki}-ka	The emblem of Gishgal
pa-te-si-bi	(and) its patesi
sag-ba-mu-du	he subdued
ṭu-ku bi-sig	(and) put under the yoke.
saǧar-dul-tag-bi	Its dead ones
mu-dub	he buried.
giš-BAN-^{ki}	Gishban
ṭu-ku bi-sig	he put under the yoke;
*saǧar-dul-tag-bi-*20	20 of its dead ones

Col. IV.

[*mu-d*]*ub*	he buried.
^{dingir} *Nin-gir-su-ra*	To Ningirsu
a-šag ki-ag-[*ga*]*-ni*	his beloved territory,
gu-na + edin	the Guedin,

temple) it goeth (*ga*, Br. 6108, *alâku*) = a mountain (or mountains) that is higher than a temple.

14. *ṭu*, Br. 11905; *apâšu*, H. W. B. 116; it may probably also stand for *apšânu*, yoke, H. W. B. ibid.; *sig*, Br. 4420; *sapânu*, H. W. B. 508; comp. also Br. 4417, *nadû*, and 4418, *nadânu*. Lit. yoke + to + he subjugated. See also Thureau-Dangin, R. A. iii. 132, note 1.

15. See Cône of Entemena, i. 30.

16. *dub*, Br. 3927; *lamû*, H. W. B. 379. Comp. Sanh. i. 59: their corpses I hung up on staves and *siḫirti âli ú-šal-me*. Is the same idea to be found here? Comp. however l. 15. *DUB* may also be = Br. 3931; *šapâku*, H. W. B. 679.

17. *šu-nir*, Br. 7198 = *šurinnu*, H. W. B. 691. Thureau-Dangin: '*tour*'? *Gišgal*. See ii. 13. Hommel (P. S. B. A. 1893, p. 108) thinks that *Gišgal-^{ki}* is Babylon!

19. *sag . . . du*, Br. 3576; *sanâḳu*, H. W. B. 504. This line has to be read as a verb on account of the parallelism: *šu-nir Gišgal-^{ki}-ka sag-ba-mu-du* and *pa-te-si-bi ṭu-ku bi-sig*. There is no proper name (Thureau-Dangin: '*et son patesi Sagbamoudou il renversa sous le joug*').

IV. 3. *a-šag = eḳlu*.

4. *Gu + na + edin*. Read *Gu-edin-na*. *Gu-edin* = proper name. Comp. Déc. 2ter, No. 2, col. iii. 7. That *edin* cannot be taken here as meaning simply *ṣêru* (Br. 4529), seems to be evident from the expression *mu-ru* in the inscrip-

šu-na mu-ni-gi	to his hand (power) he restored it (again).
Unug-ki	Erech

tion above cited: 49 *ur dam* (*dingir*) *Ninâ maš-bi-pad* 2 *edin mu-ru*. The *gu* in *Gu-edin* may be taken as meaning *mâtu* (Br. 3216). As such it is parallel to *a-šag*. *Edin*, according to Br. 4527, may mean *bamatu*, H. W. B. p. 177. Comp. with this the Hebrew בָּמוֹת, and with *Gu-edin* the בית הבמות. Have we here the bamoth of Ningirsu, as we have in Déc. 2ter, No. 2, the bamoth of Ninâ? Compare also the name (*dingir*) *Innanna-Edin* (Hommel). This seems to be reasonable:

(1) This *gu-edin* is called an *a-šag ki-ag-ga* = *narâmu*, a territory sacred to Ningirsu.

(2) It had been lost for Ningirsu; comp. Déc. 4bis, D[2], col. iii. 7–15:

Gu-nam-mi-de (?)	Gunammide,
pa-te-si	the patesi
giš-BAN ki	of Gishban,
me dingir-ni-ku	according to the command of his god
(*ga*)*lu* . . . *da* . . .	. . . . . .
gu-edin-na	the Guedin,
a-šag-gan ki-ag	the beloved territory
(*dingir*) *Nin-gir-su-ka*	of Ningirsu,
e-da-kù-e	he devoured (destroyed).

Eannatum restored it (*gi*) again to his (Ningirsu's) power (*šu-na*).

Hence I am prepared to accept Thureau-Dangin's view, l. c. p. 69, note 1: '*Elle* (i. e. the expression *gu-edin*) *doit être prise comme un véritable nom propre désignant un territoire déterminé spécialement consacré à Ningirsu*.' Another passage relating to the same event is found in Déc. 2ter, fig. 5 (comp. R. A. iv. p. 122, No. 2). The whole inscription reads:

Col. I.

(*dingir*) *Nin-gir-su*	To Ningirsu,
gud (*dingir*) *En-lil-ra*	the hero of Bêl,
E-an-na tum	Eannatum,
pa-te-si	patesi
Šir-pur-la-ki	of Shirpurla,
šag-azag-gi pad-da	called by the glorious heart
(*dingir*) *Ninâ*	of Ninâ,
nin-en-na-ge	his mistress,
kur-gu-zal-zal	the one who subdues all the lands
(*dingir*) *Nin-gir-su-ka ge*	for Ningirsu,
dumu A-kur-gal	the son of Akurgal,
pa-te-si	patesi

5. *šu*, Br. 7069, *emûku*; *gi*, Br. 6331, *târu*.

ṭu-ku bi-sig	he put under the yoke.
Unu(g) + ^{ki} + *Uru*	Ur
ṭu-ku bi-sig	he put under the yoke.
ki-$^{(dingir)}$ *Utu*	Ki-Utu (=Larsa ?)
ṭu-ku bi-sig	he put under the yoke.
uru Az-^{ki}	The city of Az
mu-ĝul	he destroyed;
pa-te-si-bi	its patesi
mu-til	he killed.
Mi-lim-^{ki}*-me*	Milimme
mu-ĝul	he destroyed.
A-ru-a-^{ki}	Arua
mu-ĝa-lam	he blotted out.
E-an-na-tum	Eannatum
Šir-pur-la-ki-ka-ge	of Shirpurla,
[Several lines broken away]	. . . .
giš-BAN-ki	Gishban,
Gu + na + edin	which to the Guedin

Col. II.

II. *ba-du-a*	had come,
mu-ĝal-lam-ma	he blotted out.
(*dingir*) *Nin-gir-su-ra*	For Ningirsu
a-šag-gan ki-ag-ni	his beloved territory,
Gu + na + edin	the Guedin,
šu-na mu-ni-gì	he restored it again tò his power.
ki-sur-ra	The boundary canal
gu-gu Gir-su-ki-ka	alongside of Girsu
(*dingir*) *Nin-gir-su-ra*	to Ningirsu
šu-na mu-na-gì-a	to his power he restored it again.
Lum-ma-gir-nun-ta-	*Lum-ma-gir-nun-ta-šag-*
šag-azag-gi-pad-da	*azag-gi-pad-da*
mu mu-na-sà-a	he called it.

(The rest is broken away.)

12. *Az*, T. C. 209. See also iv. R². 36, No. 1, col. ii. 17, and Hommel, P. S. B. A. 1893, p. 110, who identifies it with *Azu-pirâni*, i. e. the Azu of the elephants.

13. *ĝul*, Br. 9506; *šulputu*, H. W. B. 383.

15. *til*, Br. 1519; *mûtu*, H. W. B. 395; comp. also note to E. C. ii. and 278.

19. *ĝa-lam*, Br. 11850; *ḫulluḳu*, H. W. B. 280. Comp. Cône of Entemena, vi. 20.

mu-pad-da	chosen (called)
^(dingir)^ *Nin-gir-su + da + ka*	by Ningirsu,
kur-kur-ru	upon (those) lands
sag-e-ru-sig	he brought distress.
mu gal + (ga)lu Uḫ-ki-ka	In the year when the king of Uḫ
ni-zig-ga-a	came (for the purpose of making war),
E-an-na-tum	Eannatum
mu-pad-da	chosen

Col. V.

(dingir) *Nin-gir-su-ka-ge*	by Ningirsu,
An-ta-sur-ra	from the Antasurra
(dingir) *Nin-gir-su-ka-ta*	of Ningirsu,
Zu-zu	Zuzu,
gal + (ga)lu [U]ḫ-ki	the king of Uḫ,
Uḫ-ki-ku	to Uḫ
mu-gaz	he crushed him
mu-ĝa-lam	and blotted him out.
ud-ba	At that time

22. *DA* apparently stands here for *ge*; comp. iv. 27, 28; v. i. *DA* even stands for *KU* = *ana*, 'for,' 'unto.' Comp. O. B. I. 86, 4 ff.: *ud* (*dingir*) *En-lil-li gu-zi e-na-de-a nam-en nam-lugal-DA* (= *ana šarrûti*) *e-na-da-tab-ba-a*; and O. B. I. iii. 1 ff.: (*Dingir*) *Nin-din-dug-ga am nin dam* (several lines missing) *Lugal-šir-ge nam-ti dam-dumu-na-Da a-mu-šub*, 'for the life of his wife and child.' O. B. I. 112 shows clearly that *DA* = *KU*: (*Dingir*) *Nin-lil* (*dingir*) *En-lil-la*(*l*) *dumu Ad-da-ge ga* (for *gan*, Br. 4039) *til-la-ku nam-ti dam-dumu-na-KU a-mu-na-šub*, 'To Ninlil and Enlil the son of the Ada (= the temple of Enlil, O. B. I. 113, 6 ff.) presented it for abundance of life, for the life of his wife and child.'

23. *kur-kur-ru*. See Barrel-Cyl. of Urukagina, ii. 10, and Lugalzag. ii. 32.

24. *sag . . . sig*, Br. 5565, *maḫâṣu*, H. W. B. 398; Br. 5587, *šaḫâḫu*, H. W. B. 649. For *URU* = *ru*, see Lugalzag. ii. 32.

26. *zig-ga*, Br. 2335; *tebû*, H. W. B. 698; comp.: *itbâ ana epuš kabli u taḫâzi*. Thureau-Dangin, *zig-ga* = *zâḳu*; see R. A. iv. 74, 11.

V. 2. *An-ta-sur-ra*. See le Clercq, ii. pl. viii. No. 1, col. ii. 1.

7. *gaz*, Br. 4721; *ḫašâlu*, H. W. B. 294. '*Up* to *Uḫ*,' i.e. all the way from the Antasurra to Uḫ he smote and defeated him. *Uḫ-ki* is mentioned between *Giš-uḫ-ki* and the *Mà-gan-ki* in iv. R^2. 36, No. 1, col. i. 12.

E-an-na-tum-ma	Eannatum—
E-an-na-tum	when Eannatum
mu u-?-ma-ru	had done . . .
mu ne-ne-ni	and when his power
lum-ma-a	had sprouted—
(dingir) Nin-gir-su-ra	for Ningirsu
a-ne(bil ?)	water (a new canal ?)
mu-na-dun	he digged.
Lum-ma-dim-šar	Lummadimshar
mu mu-na-sa	he called it.
E-an-na-tum	To Eannatum,
(ga)lu enim-ma sig-ga	he to whom eloquence is given
(dingir) Nin-gir-su-ka	by Ningirsu—
E-an-na-tum	to Eannatum,
pa-te-si	patesi
[Šir]-la-[ki]-[pu]r-ra	of Shirpurla,
(dingir) Innanna-ge	by Innanna,

Col. VI.

ki-an-na-ag-ga-da	who loves him,
nam-pa+si+te	the patesiat

12. The third sign not clear. Thureau-Dangin reads: *mu u-ru-m[a]-r[u]-[a ?]*, which he translates: '*lorsque puissant il fut devenu*,' but adds in a note: '*lecture et traduction incertaines.*' Thureau-Dangin's translation of ll. 9–13 is improbable: ['*En ce jour-là* (*c'est lui*) *Eanadou* (*qui a fait ces choses*) *Eanadou lorsque puissant il fut devenu et lorsque*,' &c.].

14. *lum-ma*, Br. 11186; *unnubu*, H. W. B. 97, and Br. 11187; *uššubu*, H. W. B. 141.

16. *a-ne* = water. Galet B has *id* (Br. 11647)-*bil*; *bil* = *eššu*, 'new.'

17. *dun*, T. C. 188, Br. 9864; *pitû ša nâri*, H. W. B. 552: also = *ḫirû*, H. W. B. 289.

18. *Lum-ma-dim-šar.* This canal is also mentioned in R. A. iv. p. 25, on a tablet from the time of Naram-Sin. Here it is recorded that it was digged, while on the tablet of Naram-Sin it is mentioned as already existing. Naram-Sin lived after Eannatum.

21. *enim*, Br. 508; *amâtu*, H. W. B. 81.

VI. i. *ki-an-na-ag-ga-da*. *da* parallel to *ge* in v. 26; comp. iv. 22. *an-na*, infix signifying the object. Translate 'who loves him,' not 'loved by him'; comp. R. A. ii. p. 149, rev., iii. 1; Cône of Entemena, v. 14.

Šir-la-ki-pur-ta	of Shirpurla
nam-gal+(ga)lu Kiš-ki	and the kingship of Kish
mu-na-ta-sum	were given.
E-an-na-tum-da	By (of) Eannatum
Elam sag-e-ru-sig	distress was brought upon Elam.
Elam kur-ra-ṇa bi-gì	Elam to its mountains he made to return.
Kiš-ki [sag]-e-ru-sig	Upon Kish he brought distress.
gal+(ga)lu Uḫ-ki	The king of Uḫ
kur-ra-na (sic) *bi-gì*	to his land he made to return.
E-an-na-tum	Eannatum,
pa-te-si	patesi
Šir-la-ki-pur-ge	of Shirpurla,
kur-gu-zal-zal	the conqueror of the totality of lands
(*dingir*) *Nin-gir-su-ka-ge*	for Ningirsu.
Elamtu Šaḫ-ki	Elam, Shaḫ,
Gišgal-ki	Gishgal,
A-suḫur ?-ta	in the Asuḫur (neighbourhood?)
ṭu-ku bi-sig	he put under the yoke.
Kiš-ki Uḫ-ki	Kish, Uḫ,
Ma-ḳal-ki	Makal,
An-ta-sur-ra	in the Antasurra

Col. VII.

(*dingir*) *Nin-gir-su-ka-ta*	of Ningirsu,
ṭu-ku bi-sig	he put under the yoke.

15. *kur-gu-zal-zal* (*sic*), not *kur-gu-gar-gar* (Thureau-Dangin). *NI* is clear. *gu*, Br. 3220, *napḫaru*. Comp. iv. R. 23, 136: *ug u-kalam-ma* = *bêl napḫar mâti*. *zal-zal*, Br. 5359; *ḳamû*, H. W. B. 587. Whole expression = *ḳâmû* (*ḳâmi-u*) *napḫar* (*gu*) *mâti* (*kur*). Comp. also Enannatum I. in R. A. iii. p. 31, l. 6; Déc. 3 bis, D[1], col. ii. 2.

19. The second sign is not clear to me. Does Thureau-Dangin, who reads *šuḫur*, identify the sign with Br. 8615 as above transcribed? See E. C. 281.

22. The second sign is not *URU* (Thureau-Dangin), but *ḲAL*, Br. 951. A king of *MA-URU-ki* is mentioned in C. T. 12146; comp. above, p. 30, note 1.

(dingir) Nin-gir-su-ra	For Ningirsu,
Lum-ma-dim-šar	the Lummadimshar
mu-na-uš	he established
sag-ku mu-ni-pa-kab	and presented it as a gift.
E-an-na-tum	Eannatum,
à-sum-ma	endowed with power
(dingir) Nin-gir-su-ka-ge	by Ningirsu,
giš-šir-du	on the border
Lum-ma-dim-šar	of the Lummadimshar,
kir-3,600-gur-a-du	a basin (containing) 3,600 gur of water complete
[*mu*]*-ni-ru*	he built.
E-an-na-tum	Eannatum,
(*ga*)*lu enim-ma sig-ga*	to whom eloquence is given
(dingir) Nin-gir-su-ka-ge	by Ningirsu,
dingir-ra-ni	and whose god
(dingir) Dun-gur?	is Dungur?
e-gal Ti-ra-aš	the great house of Tirash
mu-na-ru	he built.

VII. 5. *uš*, Br. 5032, *emêdu*.

6. Br. 5655, *šarâku*, H. W. B. 691, and especially under *širiktu*, ibid. p. 692 = *ana širikti išruk* (Thureau-Dangin). Comp. also E. C. 302 and 67.

10. *giš-šir-du*. The *du* probably stands for *da*; comp. H. W. B. 404, *sub miḫru*; *giš-šir-da* = *miḫir nâri*, K. 247, col. 1, and K. 2022, col. iii. 51.

12. *kir*, Br. 10209, H. W. B. 348. *DU*=*kalâlu*, '*ganz sein*,' and probably also = *kalâlu*, *umfassen*, *umschliessen*; see Br. 9142 and H. W. B. *sub* כלל, pp. 331 and 332.

18. The name of this god has been variously read. Amiaud: *Dun-sir*; Jensen: *Šul-gur*.

The second sign is T. C. 188 = *Dun* and *Šul*. The last sign is not yet identified. Amiaud, who read *ṣir*, identified it with T. C. 154 and 198 *bis*, p. 130. Jensen (K. B. iii[1]. p. 18, note 2; p. 14, note 8) read *gur* = Br. 10808. But see Thureau-Dangin, R. A. iii. p. 119, note 5. The name occurs, among other places, in Cône of Entemena, vi. 2; R. A. ii. p. 149, rev., col. iv. In Tablette A of Entemena the name has an '*AN*' after it. Has this '*an*' to be translated: 'of heaven'? Comp. note to O. B. I. 115, ii. 6.

Col. VIII.

dumu A-kur-gal	He is the son of Akurgal,
pa-te-si	patesi
Šir-la-^{ki}-pur-ge	of Shirpurla ;
pa-giš-bil-ga-ni	his ancestor
Ur-(dingir) Ninâ	is Ur-Ninâ,
pa-te-si	patesi
Šir-la-^{ki}-pur-kam	of Shirpurla.

VIII. 4. *pa-giš-bil-ga-ni.* *giš-bil*, Br. 5713, *abu.* *pa* = any kind of officer (p. 55, 4), Meissner, A. B. P. R. = *amîlu*, *ga* = *alâku.* The whole may be translated: (*amêlu*) *abu âlik* (*maḫri*)-*ia* = 'ancestor.' Because in this place the *pa-giš-bil-ga* is at the same time 'grandfather,' we are not justified in always translating it thus. Comp. Cône of Entemena, col. i. l. 35.

'BRIQUE' OF EANNATUM[1].

Déc. 31, No. 2 *a*, *b*.

Col. I.

(dingir) *Nin-gir-su*	For Ningirsu
E-an-na-tum	Eannatum,
pa-te-si	patesi
Šir-la-pur-^{ki}-ge	of Shirpurla,
mu-pad-da	he who was chosen (called)
(dingir) *En-lil-ge*	by Enlil
	. . . . (comp. Galet A, i. 9)

Col. II.

(dingir) *Ninâ-ge*	by Ninâ,
ga-zi-kù-a	he who was nourished with the milk of life
(dingir) *Nin-ḫar-sag-ge*	by Ninḫarsag,
mu-sà-a	he who was called

[1] The inscription on this brick is apparently not complete. The end of each column is missing. All the expressions occur also in Galet A; it is, therefore, not necessary to give any explanation.

$^{(dingir)}$ *Innanna-ge*	by Innanna,
dumu A-kur-gal	the son of Akurgal,
pa-te-si	the patesi
	of . . . .
	the . . . . .

Col. III.

mu-na-ru	he has built.
$^{(dingir)}$ *Ninâ*	For Ninâ
Ninâ-^{ki}	the city of Ninâ
mu-na-ru	he has built,
E-an-na-tum-e	Eannatum.
Elam ḫar-sag igi-e (sic)-*ga*	Elam, a mountain higher than a temple,
ṭu-ku bi-sig	under the yoke he has put
	. . . . . (comp. Galet A, iii. 17 ff.

Col. IV.

	. . . . .
pa-te-si-bi	its patesi
sag-ba-mu-du	he subdued
ṭu-ku bi-sig	(and) put under the yoke,
saḫar-dul-tag-bi	its dead ones
mu-dub	he buried.
giš-BAN-^{ki}	Gishban
ṭu-ku bi-sig	he put under the yoke,
sa[ḫar-dul-tag-bi]	its dead ones he buried
	(comp. Galet A, iv. 2 ff.),

Col. V.

šu-na mu-ni-gi	to his power he restored it again.
Unug-^{ki}	Erech
ṭu-ku bi-sig	he put under the yoke.
uru ^{ki}-*Az*	The city of Az
mu-ḫul	he destroyed.

Mi-lim-ki (sic)	Milim (*sic*; comp. Galet A, iv. 16)
mu-ĝul	he destroyed.
. . . . . .	Upon . . . .
. . . . . .	(comp. Galet A, vi. 9)
sag-e-ru-sig	he brought distress.
E-an-na-tum	Eannatum,
(ga)lu + sig + enim-ma + ga	he to whom eloquence is given
(dingir) Nin-g[ir-su-ka]	by Ningirsu (comp. Galet A, v. 21 ff. and vii. 17 ff.).

In spite of the solemn promise of Gishban never to invade the territory of Shirpurla again, or to pass over the boundary canal, it very soon—probably at the end of the reign of Eannatum, or better, at the beginning of that of Enannatum I.—becomes rebellious as before. It invades the territory of Girsu under the leadership of a certain Urlumma [1], patesi of Gishban, passes over the boundary canals which Eannatum had made, removes the stèles erected on those canals in honour of Ningirsu, casts them into the fire, and even destroys the sanctuaries which Eannatum had built on one of these canals (i.e. the Namnundakigarra) in honour of Enlil, Ninḫarsag, Ningirsu, and Utu, and lays waste the country (Cône, ii. 28–iii. i.). Enannatum I. promptly arises to chastise 'those dogs' who had dared to break their solemn promise. Whether this battle was decisive or not is not evident. It seems, however, that Enannatum I. gained but a slight victory over Gishban.

[1] This Urlumma, according to the narrative of the 'Cône,' was the son (?) of Enakalli. It is probable that we have, as Thureau-Dangin already indicated, R. A. iv. 40, the same persons as mentioned in le Clercq, ii. pl. x. No 6 (see also Hommel and Menant in P. S. B. A. 1897, p. 89), which reads:

(dingir) EN-KI-gal	i. e.	For the great Enki,
Ur-(dingir) Lum-ma		Urlumma,
lugal TE		king of *TE*,
dumu En-à-kal-li		son of Enakalli,
lugal TE		king of *TE*,
E mu-na-ru		has built a temple.

If this be true, then Urlumma, as well as Enakalli, were both patesis of Gishban and kings of *TE*. (For *TE*, see Strassmaier, Liverpool Collection, Nos. 136 and 149: *irṣit TE-ki ša ki-rib DIN-TIR-ki* (= Babylon).)

For Entemena [1], the son of Enannatum, finds it necessary to renew the war with Gishban. 'He puts Urlumma under the yoke,' i. e. subdues him, forces him to return to his own country, and pursues him to the very midst of Gishban. This triumphant victory began with the decisive battle at the canal Lummaṣirta, in the territory of Shirpurla. 'Of his (i. e. Urlumma's) army sixty men on the side of the Lummaṣirta he left' (Cône, iii. 20, 21). On account of this severe loss Gishban fled. Entemena pursued after it, of which pursuit he records that 'he left the bones of the soldiers (of Urlumma) in the field' (ibid. 22 ff.). Many of these soldiers of Gishban must have fallen, so many, that Entemena was obliged 'to bury their dead in five different places' (ibid. 25 ff.).

Arrived in Gishban, Entemena makes a certain priest of *Innanna-ab-*^{ki} (or *Nin-ab-*^{ki}), Ili by name, patesi of Gishban, probably after having deposed Urlumma (Cône, iii. 28–37). As a compensation for the new dignity thus conferred, Entemena commands Ili to build

[1] Written *En-te-me(n)-na*. *En* = lord; *te-me(n)-na* may be the syllabic writing of the later *temennu*, Br. 7710; comp. H. W. B. 710. The meaning then may be 'The lord of the *temennu*.'

His inscriptions:

Déc. 5, 2. Amiaud, ibid. xxxi.

Déc. 5bis, 1 *a*. Translated by Tablette A, col. i.–iv.

Tablette A. R. A. ii. pp. 148, 149, translated ibid. by Oppert; R. A. iii. p. 59 ff., translation by Heuzey; see also R. A. iv. p. 36 and R. A. iii. p. 119.

Tablettes B-F, not yet published, are said to be essentially the same as Tablette A. Some 'Dispositions différentes' of Tablettes B, C, D are given by Heuzey in R. A. iii. p. 63.

Déc. 31, 3 (brique). Jensen, K. B. iii^1. p. 72 (also translated in R. A. ii. 87, by Oppert).

R. A. ii. p. 82. Jensen, l. c. p. 74, No. 2.

Déc. 43 and 43bis (Vase d'Argent) [comp. Monuments et Mémoires, fondation Eugène Piot, i.]. Translated in R. A. iv. p. 35: comp. with this also Déc. pl. 5bis; Monuments et Mémoires, ii. p. 204; and R. A. iv. 36.

'Cône historique' of Entemena, published by Thureau-Dangin in R. A. iv. No. ii. pl. ii., and translated ibid. p. 37 ff.

O. B. I. Nos. 115, 117, 116; three fragments of the same vase. Comp. Thureau-Dangin, R. S. 1897, p. 172.

British Museum, published by Winckler in Altbabyl. Keilschrifttexte, No. 4, now also in C. T. 12061.

in the territory of Karkar—which latter had also become rebellious—boundary canals and some other buildings (Cône, iv. 13–33). The canal which Eannatum had built 'from the great river (Euphrates?) to the Guedin' (Cône, ii. 1, 2), Entemena prolongs to the Tigris (Cône, v. 9–11), and also repairs the other canals, which had been destroyed more or less by the Gishbanites (Cône, iv. 1 ff.), and dedicates them anew to Ningirsu and Ninâ.

Interesting also is the subscription of this Cône:

'When the men of Gishban the boundary canal of Ningirsu and the boundary canal of Ninâ—for the purpose of ravaging these territories—shall pass over, then may Enlil destroy the men of Gishban and the men of the mountains; may Ningirsu bring his curse over them; may he lift up his great power; may the soldiery of his (Entemena's) city be filled with bravery; may in the midst of the city be courage in their hearts.'

This Cône is indeed a splendid inscription, and of the greatest historical value, giving us an insight into the state of affairs at a period so remote as 4100 B.C. But let us hear the Cône inscription itself:

CÔNE OF ENTEMENA.

Col. I.

(Dingir) En-lil	Enlil,
lugal-kur-kur-ra	king of the lands,
ab-ba dingir-dingir-ru-ne-ge	the father of the gods,
ka-gi-na-ni-ta	upon his righteous command
(dingir) Nin-gir-su	Ningirsu
(dingir) ?-bi	and . . . .

I. 3. *ab-ba*, Br. 3816, *abu* (Semitism !).
dingir-dingir-ru-ne. For *uru* = *ru*, see the Barrel-Cylinder of Urukagina, col. ii. 10.
4. *gi-na* = Br. 2391, *kênu* (Semitism !).
6. The second sign is *LAGABU*, Br. 10151, with inserted *IGI GUNÛ*. It signifies the god of *Gišban-ki*; comp. Lugalzag. ii. 40. *bi* = copula, Br. 5131.

ki-e-ne-sur	marked off the boundary (of the lands) by a well.
Me-silim	Mesilim,
lugal Kiš-^{ki}-ge	king of Kish,
ka $^{(dingir)}$ *Ka-di-na-ta*	upon the command of his god Kadi,
KU gan-bi-ra	on the boundary (?) of their territories,
ki-ba na ne-ru	on that place a stèle he erected.
Uš	Ush,
pa-te-si	patesi
^{giš}-*BAN*-^{ki}-*ge*	of Gishban,
nam-enim-ma-dir-dir-ku	according to evil intentions

7. *sur*, Br. 2975; *masâru*, H. W. B. p. 422. *ki-e-ne-sur = ika irṣitim u(m)aṣṣirû*; so also *ki-e-da-sur*. In *ki-sur* the *ki* forms adjectives and nouns, consequently *ki-sur = miṣru*, H. W. B. 422. *e = iku*. The *da* and *ne* show clearly that we have here a verb-form.

8. *ME-SILIM*. *me = parṣu*, Br. 10374; H. W. B. 544.

Silim, Br. 9534, *šalâmu*. *Silim* has the phonetic compl. *ma* in ii. 7. The whole *Parṣê-ušallim(a)*, R. A. iv. p. 35. For his inscription, see Déc. 1ter, fig. 2. There, as well as here, he is called 'king of *Kiš*.' Here *Kiš* has the sign *ki*, 'place,' but not in Déc. 1ter, fig. 2. This proves that *Kiš* = *Kiš-ki*, and not, as Hilprecht thinks (O. B. I. p. 270), = *kiššatu*.

10. The god Kadi was especially honoured in *Dûr-ilu*, O. B. I. No. 125, obv., 7. At the time of Ur IV. we find very often the proper name *Ur-(dingir) Ka-di*.

11. *gan*, Br. 3177, *eḳlu*. *KU* here is parallel to *ki-ba* in l. 12. Thureau-Dangin = '*Au KU de ces champs (ou de leurs champs)*.' He then translates *KU* = *à la limite* (?).

12. *na*, Br. 1582, *abnu*; comp. O. B. I. No. 127, rev., 2: *mu na-maḫ (dingir) En-lil-la ba-ru*, i. e. in the year when (Gimil-Sin) set up the sublime stone (= probably with an inscription) of Bêl. *Na*, 'stone,' then may stand for 'stone with an inscription,' and because 'this inscribed stone' generally had the form of a stèle it may be translated with Thureau-Dangin = stèle. Indeed it must be taken here = *šiṭir šumi* or *narû*, Br. 1631, 1630, because in l. 18 this *na* is called *na-ru-a*, H. W. B. p. 481.

16. *dir-dir*, Br. 3751; *atâru*, H. W. B. p. 248, with *nam* = abstr. noun. *atâru = uberschüssig sein, über das gewöhnliche Mass hinausgehen*, consequently = ambitious. Lit. according (*ku* = *ana*) to words (*enimma*) that

e-ag	acted.
na-ru-a-bi	That stèle
ni-pad	he took away;
edin Šir-la-pur-^{ki}*-ku*	into the territory of Shirpurla
ni-du	he went.
$^{(dingir)}$ *Nin-gir-su*	Ningirsu,
gud $^{(dingir)}$ *En-lil-la(l)-ge*	the hero of Enlil,
ka-si-di-ni-ta	according to his (Ningirsu's) righteous command,
^{giš}*-BAN-*^{ki}*-da*	with Gishban
dam-ḫa-ra	a battle
e-da-ag	he made (i. e. Mesilim).
ka $^{(dingir)}$ *En-lil-la(l)-ta*	Upon the command of Enlil
sa-šuš-gal ne-šuš	a scourge he brought over (them).
saḡar-dul-tag-bi	The dead ones
edin-na ki-ba ni-uš-uš	in a place of the field he buried.

exceed the measure. *enim-ma*, Br. 518, *amâtu*; this latter, like the Hebrew דבר, has a very wide significance, H. W. B. p. 81.

17. *ag*, Br. 2778, *epêšu*.

18. Partly mutilated. *na-ru-a*; comp. l. 12.

19. *ni-pad*. Thureau-Dangin takes *pad* in the sense of *nasâḫu*, *déplacer*, *enlever*, because in ii. 6–8 it is said that Eannatum *na-ru-a Me-silim-ma ki-bi ne-gi*, i. e. the stèle of Mesilim he brought back to its place (= restored). Comp. also ii. 38, and Déc. pl. 3bis, D^1, col. i. 7: *na-ru-a-bi ba-ra-pad-du*.

20. *edin*, Br. 4529, *ṣêru*.

23. *gud* = *ur-sag* = *ḳardu*, *edlu*; comp. le Clercq, ii. pl. viii. col. i. 2, note.

24. *si-di*, Br. 3461 ff.; *išaru*, H. W. B. 312.

26. *dam-ḫa-ra* = *tamḫaru*. '*Une curieuse trace de sémitisme*' (Thureau-Dangin). Sense: Mesilim, according to the righteous command of Ningirsu, the hero of Enlil, fought a battle with Gishban.

29. *sa-šuš-gal*, in the inscription (Stèle des Vautours), Déc. pl. 3 A, col. i., is translated by Jensen, K. B. iii^1. p. 16, '*der sa des u-gal* (*des grossen* . . .).' Thureau-Dangin takes it as an equivalent of *mamîtu*, '*serment*,' or '*anathème*'; see H. W. B. p. 415. The above-quoted passage he translates: '*Moi Eanadou le serment du roi outou.*' Our passage here he translates: '*un anathème il éleva.*' For *ŠUŠ* = *katâmu*, see Déc. 3bis, D^1, col. i. 14; comp. also col. vi. 23: *šà-ni-šuš*.

30. *saḡar-dul-tag-bi*. The same phrase occurs again in Galet A of Eannatum, col. iii. 15, 21, 25, where Thureau-Dangin translates: '*de la terre*

E-an-na-tum	Eannatum,
pa-te-si	patesi
Šir-la-pur-^{ki}	of Shirpurla,
pa-giš-bil-ga	the ancestor
En-te-me-na	of Entemena,
pa-te-si	patesi
Šir-la-^{ki}*-pur-ka-ge*	of Shirpurla
En-à-kal-li	and, (with) Enakalli,
pa-te-si	patesi
^{giš}*-BAN-*^{ki}*-da*	of Gishban,
ki-e-da-sur	marked off the boundaries of the land by a canal,

en tumulus sur les (cadavres) abandonnés.' In this place he translates *'tells funéraires.'* The signs as they follow mean:

sağar, Br. 5083; *epiru*, H. W. B. 116 = earth, dust.
dul, Br. 9583; *mulû*, H. W. B. 411 = 'the filling, heaping up.'
tag, Br. 1410; *ezêbu*, H. W. B. 34 = to leave, or *rêḫu*, H. W. B. 618 id.
1413; *ḳarâšu*, H. W. B. 598 = ?
1416; *pitû*, H. W. B. 551 = to open.

In R. S. 1897, p. 68, note 4, Thureau-Dangin translates: *'mot à mot: terre monceau-abandonné(s)-le(s) = le tumulus (funéraire) des (cadavres) abandonné;'* while in R. A. iv. p. 43, note 5, he remarks, *'Le sens de "(cadavres) abandonnés" ne peut, je crois, être conservé.'*

Probably we have to take the whole expression in the sense of: those that (*bi* = his: *bi* goes back to *Gišban*) were (are) left (*tag*) for the heaping up (*dul*) with earth (*sağar*) = the fallen ones, those that were slain, the dead. The expression *mu-dub* in Galet A then would be = to bury. The whole might be translated: 'those that fell (in the battle) he buried.' Indeed, *uš-uš* may be considered as a parallel expression to *mu-dub*. *uš*, Br. 5041 = *ridû* = רדה i. in H. W. B. p. 612 (see Delitzsch under רדה ii.) iii [1]. = to make to go. Ll. 30, 31 then might be translated: Its (sc. men = those of *Giš-banki*) that were left for the heaping up with earth on a place of the field he made to go (= buried). The burying of the enemies' dead in the open field may have been considered an additional disgrace (?) that could be brought upon the disturbers of peace.

35. That *pa-giš-bil-ga* cannot mean *'grand-père'* (Thureau-Dangin) is plain from this passage. Entemena was not the 'grandson' of Eannatum, but his nephew. It means 'ancestor'; comp. Galet A, viii. 4.

42. *ki-e-da-sur* = *ki-e-ne-sur*, i. 7.

Col. II.

e-bi id-nun-ta	and a canal from the great river
Gu-edin-na-ku	to the Guedin
ib-ta-ni-ud-du	he made to go.
e-ba na-ru-a	A stèle on this canal
e-me-sar-sar	he inscribed.
na-ru-a	The stèle
Me-silim-ma	of Mesilim
ki-bi ne-gì	to its place he restored.
edin ^{giš}*-BAN-*^{ki}*-ku*	Into the territory of Ġishban
nu-KU	he did not go ravaging.
Im-dub-[ba]	On the Imdubba
$^{(dingir)}$ *Nin-gir-su-ka*	of Ningirsu
Nam-nun-da-ki-gar-ra	and on the Namnundakigarra
bar $^{(dingir)}$ *En-lil-la(l)*	a sanctuary of Enlil,
bar $^{(dingir)}$ *Nin-ḫar-sag-kà*	a sanctuary of Ninḫarsag,
bar $^{(dingir)}$ *Nin-gir-su-ka*	a sanctuary of Ningirsu,
bar $^{(dingir)}$ *Utu*	a sanctuary of Utu,
ne-ru	he built.
še $^{(dingir)}$ *Ninâ*	On corn for Ninâ,
še $^{(dingir)}$ *Nin-gir-su-ka*	on corn for Ningirsu,
1 *gùr-an*	1 karu
(ga)lu ^{giš}*-BAN-*^{ki}	upon the men of Gishḅan

II. 1. *e*, Br. 5841; *iku* H. W. B. 51; Mishna, עוקה.

id-nun. Thureau-Dangin: '*Vraisemblablement l'Euphrate: cf. les expressions* הנהר הגדול, הנהר. *On pourrait encore songer à quelque grand canal.*'

3. *ud-du*, Br. 7873, *aṣû*.

5. *sar*, Br. 4336; *šaṭâru*, H. W. B. 651.

10. *nu-ku*. In col. iii. 1 we have *kur-kur e-ma-ku*. Thureau-Dangin translates the former '*il n'envahit* (?) *pas*,' and the latter '*les contrées il envahit* (?).' *KU*, according to Br. 10526, has the meaning of *ḫalâku*, H. W. B. p. 279 ii^1 = *zu Grunde richten, austilgen, vernichten.*

11, 13. = proper names.

21. *gùr*, Br. 10809, *karû* = a 'ton.' According to Reissner, J. A. O. S. 18, p. 372, equal to 3,600 gur.

ĝar-ku ni-kù	as tax he placed (?)
kud-du ba-uš	and as tribute he put upon.
400 *gal-gùr*	400 great karu (=1,440,000 gur)
ba-tur	he made to bring.
bar še-bi nu-da-sud-sud da-dug	He gave order not to spoil that grain.
Ur-lum-ma	Urlumma,
pa-te-si	patesi
giš-BAN-ki-ge	of Gishban,
e-ki-sur-ra	of the boundary canal
(*dingir*) *Nin-gir-su-ka*	of Ningirsu,
e-ki-sur-ra	of the boundary canal
(*dingir*) *Ninâ*	of Ninâ,
a-e-ni-mi-ud-du	which (Eannatum) had made to go out,
na-ru-a-bi	their stèles
bil ba-sum	into the fire he cast
ni-pad-pad	and took away.

23. *ĝar-ku ni-kù* seems to be parallel to l. 24, *kud-du ba-uš*. *ĝar-(ra)* = *ḫubullu*, Br. 8562. *kud*, Br. 370, *miksu*, 'tribute.' *ba-uš*, *uš*, Br. 5032; *emêdu*, H. W. B. p. 80. Should *kù* have a similar meaning? Thureau-Dangin: '*Le sens de ce cas est obscur.*'

25. Here we have four numbers. Each number is expressed by a large circle with inserted small circle. This, according to Thureau-Dangin, is equal to 10 sar or 36,000 gùr. If 1 gùr = 3,600 gur, as Reissner says, we would get 4 × 36,000 × 3,600 = 518,400,000 gur; comp. R. S. 1897, p. 172. This sum seems almost incredible, especially when we take into consideration that we have here not only gùr(s) in general, but 'great gurs,' gùrgal, which must contain more than gùr alone. This also was felt by Eisenlohr (Z. A. xii. p. 239), who says: '*Wo sie* (that is, the old forms for numerals) *mit karû* . . . *zusammentreffen, bedeutet* ○ *offenbar* 10 × 3,600, *also* 36,000 *gur*, ◎ 360,000 *gur*.' According to this calculation we would have here = 4 × 10 × 10 × 3,600 *gur* = 1,440,000 gur (not gùr = karû); and in iv. 11 = 10 × 3,600 gur = 36,000 gur (not 3,600 gùr = karû).

27. *bar* = *piristu*, H. W. B. 543. *sud-sud* = *raḫâḫu*, H. W. B. p. 617.

31. *e-ki-sur-ra*. Comp. i. 7 and ii. 1.

35. *a* . . . *ud-du* on account of context must be = *ud-du* in ii. 3.

37. *bil* = *išatu*. *sum* = *nadû*, Br. 4417.

38. *pad*. Comp. i. 19.

bar-šub-a dingir-ru-ne	The sanctuaries dedicated to the gods,
Nam-nun-da-ki-gar-ra	(which) on the Namnundakigarra
ab-ru-a	had been built,
ni-gul-gul	he destroyed,

Col. III.

kur-kur e-ma-KU	the lands he ravaged,
e-ki-sur-ra	the boundary canal
(dingir) Nin-gir-su-ka-ka	of Ningirsu
e-ma-ta-bal	he crossed over.
En-an-na-tum	Enannatum,
pa-te-si	patesi
Šir-la-ki-pur-ge	of Shirpurla,
gan šà-gig-ga	in the field . . . .
a-šag-gan (dingir) Nin-gir-su-ka-ka	of the territory of Ningirsu
giš-ur-ur-ku e-da-lal	upon the dogs he poured out his terror.
En-teme-na	Entemena,
dumu ki-ag	the beloved son
En-an-na-tum-ma-ge	of Enannatum,

39. *dingir-ru.* See i. 3. *šub*, Br. 1444; *šarâku*, H. W. B. p. 691.

42. *gul*, Br. 8954; *abâtu*, H. W. B. p. 12.

III. 1. *ku.* Comp. ii. 10.

4. *bal*, Br. 266; *ebêru*, to cross over.

8. The expression *šà-gig* is not quite clear. *GIG* also occurs in several tablets of the E. A. H. collection, designating there 'spelt.' *ŠÀ-GIG* may be here the ripe spelt (*ŠÀ*, Br. 4963 = *enšu*).

10. In Dec. pl. 4 bis, D 2, vi. 1, we have *giš-ur-ur-e e-da-lal.*

For *ur-ur-ku*, comp. Br. 11297, *kalbu* (written *ur-ku*).

For *ur-ur-e*, comp. Br. 11304, *aḫû* = stranger, enemy. *ur* alone = *nakru*, see H. W. B. p. 41; hence this line may also be translated: upon (*ku* = *ana*) the enemies (*giš-ur-ur*; *giš* = *edlu* or *zikaru*) he poured out.

lal, Br. 10112; *šapâku*, H. W. B. 679 = *tabâku*, H. W. B. 699; and compare with this such expressions as: *melammê bêlûtia atbuk*, or *pulḫê melammê elišunu atbuk*.

ṭu-ku ni-ni-sig	put them under the yoke.
Ur-lum-ma	Urlumma
ba-da-kar	he made to return;
šag giš*BAN*-ki-*ku*	up to the very midst of Gishban
e-gaz	he crushed him.
ne-ni erim-60-an	60 men of his army
gu (id)*Lum-ma-ṣir-ta-ka*	on the side of the Lummaṣirta
e-ku-kid	he left;
nam-(ga)lu-ḳal-ba	of that soldiery
gir-pad-du-bi	its bones

14. See Galet A of Eannatum, col. iii. 14, note.

16. *kar*, Br. 7739; H. W. B. p. 46. Thureau-Dangin translates: '*fut payé de retour*'; and adds in the note: '*J'imagine que kar correspond ici comme dans ces contrats* (i. e. *de l'époque de Sargon*, see R. A. iv. No. iii.) *à eṭeru "rembourser." Le sens de "enlever, prendre" aurait difficilement sa place ici.*'

19. *ne*, Br. 9184, *emûḳu*. The numeral, according to Thureau-Dangin, R. S. 1897, p. 172, is = 60.

20. *gu*, Br. 3215; *kišâdu*, H. W. B. 359, '*Ufer*'; comp. כָּתֵף.

21. *kid*, Br. 1410, *ezêbu*. The *ku*, according to Thureau-Dangin, is '*préfixe verbal.*' Comp. also Déc. pl. 31, No. 3, col. iv. 1 ff., which ought to be read *ud-ul-la-ku nam-ti-la-ni-ku* (*dingir*) *Nin-gir-su-ra E-ninnû a-ĝe-na-ku-tum*, and be translated: '*dans les jours à venir pour la vie* (*d'Entéména*) *en l'honneur de Ningirsou dans l'Eninnou puisse* (the *AB-gi* or *Eš-gi*) *subsister.*' Jensen, K. B. iii[1]. p. 74, reads that passage: *ud-ul-la-ku nam-ti-la-ni-ku* (*dingir*) *Nin-gir-ṣu-ra I-ninnû-a* (*ĝi + na + zida + gin, lies dafür*) *ĝi-zida gin-na*; and translates: '[*und der*] *auf ewige Zeiten für sein Leben dem Ningirsu in Ininnu eine* Fülle Korns festgesetzt hat.' Comp. also Jensen, note *, ibid.; see Lugalzaggisi, iii. 33; Déc. 3bis, D[1], col. i. last line, and especially note to C. T. 23287, l. 12.

22. The third sign occurs again in O. B. I. No. 37, col. iii. 24, and by Thureau-Dangin was made equivalent to Br. 951; see E. C. 386. An expression *amêl ḲAL meš* occurs in K. 492, B. A. i. p. 628, viz. *amêl ḲAL meš am-mu-te ni-ḫar-ru-ub*, which Delitzsch translates: '*Jene Soldaten* (?) *werden wir . . .*'; and in his note he remarks: '*Darf vielleicht ḳallê "Diener" spec. "Soldaten"* (comp. B. A. i. p. 244 f. = *tuklâti*, lit. helpers, soldiers) *umschrieben werden?*' Comp. also S. A. Smith in P. S. B. A. x. 164.

23. *gir-pad-du*, Br. 9224; A. L[3]. No. 250 = '*Knochen, Gebeine,*' and Guyard, Notes de Lexicogr. Assyr. § 26.

edin-da e-da-kid-kid	on the plain he left.
sag̃ar-dul-tag-bi	His dead ones (i. e. Urlumma's)
ki-5-a	in five places
ni-mi-dub	he buried.
ud-ba Ili	At that time Ili
sanga Innanna-ab-^{ki}-kam	was priest of *Innanna-ab*.
Gir-su-^{ki}-ta	From Girsu
$^{gi\check{s}}$*BAN-^{ki}-ku*	to Gishban,
kar-dar-ra-a	beating the enemy,
e-du	(Entemena) marched.
Il-li	Ili,
nam-pa-te-si	the patesiat
$^{gi\check{s}}$*BAN-^{ki}-a*	over the Gishbanites,
šu-e-ma-ti	he made to accept.
e-ki-sur-ra	The boundary canal

Col. IV.

(*dingir*) *Nin-gir-su-ka*	of Ningirsu,
e-ki-sur-ra	the boundary canal
(*dingir*) *Ninâ*	of Nina,
Im-dub-ba	the Imdubba
(*dingir*) *Nin-gir-su-ka*	of Ningirsu,
gu (*id*) *Idigna-ku gàl-la*	which goeth to (the side of) the Tigris
gu-gu Gir-su-^{ki}-ka	alongside of Girsu,

24. *edin-da.* *da* = suffix ; comp. Galet of Eannatum, iv. 22, note.
kid. See l. 21.
25. See i. 30.
27. See i. 30.
29. *kam*, suffix = he is (was).
32. *kar-dar*, Br. 6537 ; *sâkipu*, H. W. B. p. 498 ; comp. ii. R. 19, 16, 18 *b*, *kar-dar-mè* = *sa-kip ta-ḫa-zi*. Thureau-Dangin : '*victorieusement.*'
37. *ti*, Br. 1700, *laḳû* ; *šu-ti*, Br. 1701, *maḫâru*. Either 'he received' or '*peut-être šu . . . ti est-il ici pour le shaphel de liqu et faut-il traduire* (*Entéména*) *fit prendre à Ili le patésiat de Gishban.*'
IV. 6. *gàl-la*, Br. 2238, *bašû*, and 2253, *šakânu.*
7. *gu-gu.* Occurs again in Déc. 2ter, fig. 5 ; see iii. 20, and Br. 3212, *idu.*

Nam-nun-da-ki-gar-ra	the Namnundakigarra
(*dingir*) *Nin-ḫar-sag-ka*	of Ninḫarsag
a-e-ni-mi-ud-du	he made to go out.
še Šir-la-ki-pur 10 *gùr-an*	On corn for Shirpurla 10 karu (=36,000 gur)
ni-rug	he added.
En-teme-na	Entemena,
pa-te-si	patesi
Šir-la-ki-pur-ge	of Shirpurla,
bar-e ba-dug	gave an order:
Ili-ku	to Ili,
(*ga*)*lu ĝe-ku gì-gì-a*	a man whom he had brought into prosperity,
Ili	to Ili,
pa-te-si	the patesi
giš-BAN-ki-a	of the Gishbanites,
a-šag-gan Kar-kar	(in) the territory of Karkar,
nin-ne-ru dug-dug-gi	who had pronounced (words of) wickedness,
e-ki-sur-ra	a boundary canal
(*dingir*) *Nin-gir-su-ka*	of Ningirsu,
e-ki-sur-ra	a boundary canal
(*dingir*) *Ninâ*	of Ninâ,
gà-[*kam* ?]	to make
ni-mi-dug	he commanded.
An-ta-sur-ra-ta	From the Antasurra
e (*dingir*) *Gal-dim-zu-ab-ka-ku*	to the temple of Galdimzuab

10. Comp. ii. 35.

11. For numeral, see R. S. 1897, p. 172, but especially note to ii. 25.

12. *rug* = *ruddû*, Br. 168.

18. *ĝe-ku. ĝe*, Br. 4039, *duḫdu*; *gì-gì*, Br. 6331, *târu* = *ša ana duḫdi utirru.*

23. *nin-ne-ru*, Br. 12056; H. W. B. p. 611.
dug-dug-gi = *dabâbu*, H. W. B. 208.

28. *gà*, Br. 5421, *šakânu.* The last sign is not clear. Thureau-Dangin supplies *kam* as above given, and thinks '*kam paraît être ici suffixe verbal.*'

im-ba-ni ud-du-ne	to erect buildings (of clay ?)
ni-mi-dug	he commanded.
(dingir) *En-lil-li*	By Enlil
(dingir) *Nin-ḫar-sag-ge*	and Ninḫarsag
NU na-sum	a decision (?) was given :

Col. V.

En-teme-na	Entemena,
pa-te-si	patesi
Šir-la-ki-pur	of Shirpula,
mu-pad-da	chosen
(dingir) *Nin-gir-su-ka-ge*	by Ningirsu
ka-si-di (dingir) *En-lil-la(l)-ta*.	upon the righteous command of Enlil,
ka-si-di (dingir) *Nin-gir-su-ka-ta*	upon the righteous command of Ningirsu,
ka (sic)-*si-di* (dingir) *Ninâ-ta*	upon the righteous command of Ninâ,
e-bi (id) *Idigna-ta*	a canal from the Tigris
id-nun-ku	to the great river
e-ag	he made.
Nam-nun-da-ki-gar-ra	The Namnundakigarra
ur-bi nà-a mu-na-ni-ru	its foundation with stone he built ;
lugal ki-an-na-ag-ga-ni	unto the king, who loves him,
(dingir) *Nin-gir-su-ra*	viz. unto Ningirsu

32. *im-ba-ni*. Thureau-Dangin : '*im-ba paraît avoir un sens analogue à celui d'im-ru-a qui correspond à pitqu.*' See H. W. B. p. 554 :

. . . *BAR* (?) *AG-A* = *pit-ḳu*.

IM KAK-A = *pit-ḳu*. '*Thon oder Lehmgebilde.*'

36. *nu-nu*, Br. 1969 = *šîru*, 'meat.' *UZU* = *šîru* = 'meat,' but also 'oracle.' It is possible, therefore (as Thureau-Dangin thinks), that *nu* = *šîru* in the sense of 'meat' and 'oracle'; comp. H. W. B. 634 and 655.

V. 8. *ka* (*sic*). The original has *sag*.

13. *ur*, Br. 4832 ; H. W. B. p. 142. *Nà* = Br. 5229 : *abnu*.

14. *ki-an-na-ag-ga-ni*. Comp. Galet A of Eannatum, vi. i.

nin ki-an-na-ag-ga-ni	(and) unto his mistress, who loves him,
(*dingir*) *Ninâ*	viz. Ninâ,
ki-bi mu-na-gì	he restored it.
En-teme-na	Entemena,
pa-te-si	patesi
Šir-la-pur-^{ki}	of Shirpurla,
pa-sum-ma	to whom a sceptre was given
(*dingir*) *En-lil-la*(*l*)	by Enlil,
giš-tug(*-pi*) *sum-ma*	to whom intelligence was given
(*dingir*) *EN-KI-ka*	by Enki,
šag-pad-da	who was chosen by the heart
(*dingir*) *Ninâ*	of Ninâ;
pa-te-si gal	the great patesi
(*dingir*) *Nin-gir-su-ka*	of Ningirsu,
(*ga*)*lu dug dingir-ru-ne tub-ba*	the one who was endowed with the oracles of the gods,

Col. VI.

dingir-ra-ni	his god is
Dun-gur	Dungur.
nam-ti	For the life
En-teme-na-ka-ku	of Entemena,
ud-ul-la-ku	until future days
(*dingir*) *Nin-gir-su-ra*	(in honour) of Ningirsu
(*dingir*) *Ninâ*	and Ninâ,
ĝe-na-me-tum	may (this) stand:

24. *giš-tug*(*-pi*). Comp. Lugalzag. i. 17.

30. *dingir-ru-ne*. Comp. i. 3. *tub-ba*, Br. 10567, *nalbušu*. (*ga*)*lu dug . . . tub-ba* probably = the one who was endowed (*TUB* = *labâšu* iv^1, Br. 10533) with the oracles (*dug*) of . . . Thureau-Dangin: '*l'exécuteur* (?) *des ordres des dieux*.'

VI. 2. See Galet A of Eannatum, col. vii. 18.

5. *ud-ul-la-ku*. Comp. Urukagina, le Clercq, ii. pl. viii. col. v. 1.

8. *ĝe-na-me-tum* (*sic*). Thureau-Dangin reads: *ĝe-na-tum-me*, which also

(ga)lu ^{giš}*BAN*-^{ki}-*a*	when the men of Gishban
e-ki-sur-ra	the boundary canal
$^{(dingir)}$ *Nin-gir-su-ka-ka*	of Ningirsu,
e-ki-sur-ra	and the boundary canal
$^{(dingir)}$ *Ninâ-ka*	of Ninâ
à-zid-ku	—for the purpose of bringing
a-šag-gan tum-ne	this land under their power—
an-ta bal-e-da	should cross over,
(ga)lu ^{giš}*BAN*-^{ki}-*ǧe*	then may he the men of Gishban,
(ga)lu kur-ra-ǧe	and may he the men of the mountain,
$^{(dingir)}$ *En-lil-li*	may he, Enlil,
ǧe-ǧa-lam-me	destroy them ;
$^{(dingir)}$ *Nin-gir-su-ge*	may Ningirsu
sa-šuš-gal-ni	his scourge
šà-ni-šuš	bring over them,
šu-maǧ ne-maǧ-ni	his sublime hand and sublime foot
an-ta ǧe-gà-gà	may be high (he lift up) ;
nam (ga)lu-ḳal uru-na	may the soldiery of his city
šu-šà-na-zi	be (filled) with power ;
šag uru-na-ka	may in the midst of his city
ǧa-ni-gaz-lid-šag-gi	be courage in their hearts !

is possible. *DU* = *tum*, Br. 4884, *kênu kânu* ; comp. Galet A, i. 2. Comp. also Déc. pl. 31, No. 3, col. iv., and Cône, col. iii. 21.

14. *à-zid-ku*, Br. 2312 ; *imnu*. Here = *ana imni-šunu*.

15. *tum*, Br. 9058, *abâlu, babâlu*.

16. *an-ta*, Br. 459, *elû*. *bal*, Br. 266, *ebêru* ; 270, *nabalkutu*, 'to cross over.' *bal-e-da* = *e-da-bal* ; comp. iii. 10.

17. The *ǧe* at the end of ll. 17, 18 stands for *ge*. See Hommel, S. L. p. 142, 4.

20. *ǧa-lam*, Br. 11850 ; *ḫulluḳu*, H. W. B. p. 280.

22. *sa-šuš-gal*. Comp. i. 29.

25. *gà-gà*, Br. 5430, *bašû*.

26. *galu-ḳal*. Comp. iii. 22.

27. *šà* here, as in 23, verbal prefix ; comp. Br. under 'verb-forms.' *šu* = *emûḳu*. *zi*, Br. 2306, *bašû*. The particle of the optative is omitted.

29. *lid-šag*, Br. 8897, *libbu* ; *gaz-lid-šag-gi*, according to Thureau-Dangin *kiṣ libbi* ; see H. W. B. 590, '*Le tout une forme verbale forgée avec gaz-lid-šag-gi*.'

Before we leave this important Cône inscription of Entemena, it will be necessary to say a word or two about the situation of Gishban[1] and Kish.

Hilprecht, in O. B. I. p. 269, asks us to 'throw a glance' upon Sachau's plan of the city of Ḫarran, which is to be found in his Reise in Syrien und Mesopotamien, in order to convince ourselves that Ḫarran was the city which is called here *^{giš}BAN-^{ki}*. He says: 'Sachau, who gave us the first accurate sketch of this city, finds it very natural that "Arabic writers — especially Albîrûnî, edit. Sachau, p. 204—could conceive the idea of comparing it with the form of a half-moon."' And because Hilprecht sees in this half-moon the form of a bow, he concludes *^{giš}BAN-^{ki}*, 'the city of the bow[2],' is the city that looks like a 'half-moon,' as Ḫarran does in Sachau's plan of that city. Nöldeke already in January, 1897, before this Cône was published, remarked on this identification (see Z. A. xi. p. 108):

'*Von Ḫarran, wo von Alters her bis in späte Zeiten der Mondgott besonders verehrt wurde, sagt nämlich Bîrûnî* (*Chronol., arab. Text,* 205, 17) *es habe* (*im Grundplan*) *die Gestalt eines Mondes oder eines Ṭailasan. Der von Sachau* (*Reisen, p.* 223) *gegebene Plan zeigt nach Hilprecht die Aehnlichkeit mit einem Halbmond, also auch mit einem Bogen*: *somit musste Harran die Bogenstadt Kīsh* (sic; read *^{giš}-BAN-^{ki}*) *sein. Aber erstlich steht noch nicht fest, dass Bîrûnî den* Halb*mond meint. Wie ein Ṭailasan—ein Tuch, das über den Turban und* (*resp. oder*) *die Schulter geworfen wird—in Wirklichkeit aussah, ist mir trotz der Beschreibung in Dozy's Dict. des Vêtements, s. v. leider nickt klar geworden. Aus den Umfassungslinien auf dem von Sachau gegebenen kleinen Plan der Stadt lässt sich allerdings* mit einiger Phantasie[3] *die Gestalt eines Halbmondes erkennen, aber* Phantasie gehört dazu[3], *da nirgends eine grössere Rundung erscheint, und mit einem Bogen hat die Zeichnung ziemlich wenig*

[1] For the reading of *^{giš}BAN-^{ki}*, see p. 74, note 1.

[2] The very fact that the second sign is not *BAN* speaks against Hilprecht's identification.

[3] Underlined by me.

Aehnlichkeit. Wollte man die aber auch finden : es giebt genug Städte, deren Grundplan wenigstens ebenso gut einen Bogen darstellt als Ḫarran. Schliesslich ist es doch überhaupt nicht besonders wahrscheinlich, dass die Bezeichnung als "Bogenstadt" auf die Linien der Umfassung gehe.'

So far Nöldeke. He is undoubtedly correct. The Cône inscription of Entemena does not leave any doubt as to the real situation of Gishban. In col. i. 32 ff. we expressly read that Eannatum 'marked off the boundaries of the land' with Enakalli, patesi of Gishban, i.e. they determined the boundaries of their respective territories. After having done this, Eannatum digs a canal from the 'great river' to the Guedin, and makes the Gishbanites swear 'never to trespass this boundary canal.'

From this, then, it follows plainly that Gishban must have been the immediate neighbour of Shirpurla-Girsu. And because this canal went from the 'great river' to the Guedin, and was later on prolonged to the Tigris, it seems very reasonable to suppose that this great river was the Euphrates. Gishban must thus have been situated on or towards the Euphrates. Heuzey recently has published (Rec. de Trav. xix. p. 63) a date of a tablet which he found at *Djokha, à l'ouest de Wasit el-Ḫai* (see the chart in Hommel, Geschichte, p. 274). That tablet is from the time of the fourth dynasty of Ur, and reads :

ud-ba Ur-(dingir) NE-SÙ	i.e.	At that time Ur-Nesu
pa-te-si giš-BAN-ki-kam		was patesi of Gishban,
Mu An-ša-an-ki ba-ĝul		in the year when [Dungi III.] devastated Anshan.

'*Djokha, à l'ouest de Wasit el-Ḫai*,' however, lies north of Shirpurla; consequently Gishban was the immediate northern neighbour of Shirpurla, and Shirpurla being situated east of the Shatt-el-Ḫai, Gishban probably had a territory extending from (the direction of) the Euphrates to the east of the Shatt-el-Ḫai, and north of Shirpurla. The Guedin, the sacred territory of Ningirsu, accordingly, must have been situated between the city of Shirpurla itself and the territory of Gishban east of the Shatt-el-Ḫai[1].

Kish, we have seen, had for some time possession of Shirpurla, and Eannatum in course of time became 'king of Kish.' This Kish mentioned in these oldest texts is undoubtedly identical with the 'city of Kish' referred to in the later inscriptions. According to these inscriptions its position lay east of Babylon. It cannot be without reason that Entemena prolonged the boundary canal between the territories of Gishban and Shirpurla, digged by Eannatum, to the Tigris. No doubt his object was to shut off Kish. Kish must therefore be placed further east of Gishban, whose neighbour it was, but north of Shirpurla and on the river Tigris.

The building operations of Entemena, which it is unnecessary to consider here in detail, are sufficiently described in the inscriptions which follow. By comparison with the inscriptions of Urukagina, it will be seen that the buildings to which Entemena refers were not actually constructed by him, but only repaired.

Special attention should be given to the '*Vase d'Argent*,' an exquisite piece of art, which was presented by Entemena to Ningirsu, and placed upon the 'altar in the sanctuary of the god of Girsu,' as a lasting remembrance of the king's piety and devotion.

ENTEMENA.

Tablette A. R. A. ii. 148, 149; comp. also Déc. 5bis, 1, *a*.

Obverse.

Col. I.

$^{(dingir)}$ *Nin-gir-su*	For Ningirsu,
gud $^{(dingir)}$ *En-lil-ra*	the hero of Enlil,
En-teme-na	Entemena,

[1] This situation of the Guedin, i. e. *north* of Shirpurla, may help us to understand the meaning of the word, because the 'gods were considered to dwell in olden times in the north.'

pa-te-si	patesi
Šir-la-^{ki}*-pur*	of Shirpurla,
dumu En-an-na-tum	son of Enannatum,
pa-te-si	patesi
Col. II.	
Šir-la-^{ki}*-pur-ka*	of Shirpurla,
dumu-ka	grandson
Ur-$^{(dingir)}$ *Ninâ*	of Ur-Ninâ,
gal + (ga)lu	king
Šir-la-pur-^{ki}*-ka-ge*	of Shirpurla—
$^{(dingir)}$ *Nin-gir-su-ra*	for Ningirsu
Ab-bi-ru	the Abbiru
Col. III.	
mu-na-ru	he has built.
2 *ruš*	2 *RUŠ* (towers ?)
e igi-zi-bar-ra,	for the 'house of regard'
mu-na-ru	he has built.
$^{(dingir)}$ *Lugal-Erim-*^{ki}*-ra*	For Lugal-Erim
e-gal Erim-^{ki}*-ka-ni*	his temple of Erim
Col. IV.	
mu-na-ru	he has built.
$^{(dingir)}$ *Ninâ*	For Ninâ
e-zikum + ra + ka-lum-ma	the Ezikum (i.e. 'the house of heaven') for the dates

II. 2. *dumu-ka* is in apposition to Enannatum. Enannatum was the 'grandson' of Ur-Ninâ, the succession being: Ur-Ninâ—Akurgal—Enannatum. *Dumu-šag*, on the contrary, means the 'firstborn.'

7. The *Ab-bi-ru* is mentioned here for the first time. Thureau-Dangin reads: *Ab-dug* (E. C. 380)—so at least in Déc. 5bis. See for the same or a similar *bi* O. B. I. 110.

III. 2. The second sign is that for *ruš* (Br. 8598; T. C. 206; E. C. 261). It has been mistaken for *kiš*, T. C. 204. What it means here is hard to tell. *ruš* = *izzu* and *ḫuššu*. Have we to read *A-RUŠ* and translate: '*A-RUŠ*, the house of his regard he has built?'

3. *igi-zi-bar-ra*. See Lugalzag. i. 13; Gudea B, ii. 10; iii. 7. Heuzey: '*la maison du regard favorable*.'

6. *Erim*. See Jensen, K. B. iii^1. p. 21 to Ur-Ba'u, ii. 2; iv. 8, 9.

IV. 3. The second sign is very doubtful. I would like to identify it with

mu-na-ru	he has built.
(*dingir*) *EN-KI*	For Enki,
gal + (ga)lu	king
Urudug-ki-ra	of Eridu,
zu-ab e-kùr SIR-ra	an abzu for the long canal

Col. V.

mu-na-ru	he has built.
(*dingir*) *Nin-ḫar-sag-ga-ge*	For Ninḫarsag
gi-ka-na	her *gi-ka* (plantation ?)
ter-azag-ga	of the holy forest
mu-na-ru	he has built.
(*dingir*) *Nin-gir-su-ra*	For Ningirsu

Reverse.

Col. I.

An-ta-sur-ra	the Antasurra
E-me (sic)-*ne*(*lam*)-*bi-kur-kur-ra-a-ku*	for an Emenebikurkurra
mu-na-ru	he has built.
(*dingir*) *En-lil-la*(*l*)	For Enlil
e-Ad-da	the Eadda
im-sag-ga	of imsagga

Br. 10221 : *zikum* = *šamû*; comp. also E. C. 451. The *RA* can then be taken as post-position to *ka-lum-ma*. See also R. A. iii. p. 121, and note 4, ibid. If, however, the second sign has to be read *GUR*, the whole line would contain the name of the house.

8. The third sign is '*E*,' with inserted *KÙR-*(*BAB*). It also occurs in Déc. 3bis, D^1, col. i. 4 [*e-*]*kùr-e-bi ki-bal ba-ra-ag-ga*. For *KÙR-E*, see H W. B. p. 51 = *iku*, *palgu*. *RA* = post-position. See also note to Déc. 3bis, D^1, col. i. 4, above.

V. 3. Plantation (Oppert, Heuzey, Thureau-Dangin). But why? *ter*, Br. 7679; *kištu*, H. W. B., p. 359; *ter azag-ga* = *kištu ellîtu*.

Reverse. I. 1, 2. See Urukagina, le Clercq, ii. pl. viii. No. 1, col. ii. 1.

5, 6. Barrel-Cyl. of Urukagina, iii. 2; le Clercq, ibid. col. iii. 8, 9, where we have the *E-Ad-da* of *his* imsagga. *E-Ad-da* = 'the temple of the father.' Comp. also O. B. I. No. 112, and ibid. pp. 263, 264 : *dumu ad-da-ge*; O. B. I. No. 113, 6, and ibid. p. 264 note : *dup-sar ad*(*a*) *e* (*dingir*) *En-lil-ka-ge*.

mu-na-ru	he has built.
e (dingir) *Ga-tum-dug*	The house of Gatumdug

Col. II.

mu-ru	he has built.
(dingir) *Ninâ*	For Ninâ,
šag-pad-da	(who has) chosen (him) in (her) heart,
mu-na-ru	[the . . .] he has built.
(dingir) *Ninâ*	For Ninâ
gi-ka-na mag-ni	her sublime *gi-ka* (plantation)
mu-na-ru	he has built.
ud-ba En-teme-na-ge	At that time by Entemena,

Col. III.

gal + (*ga*)*lu ki-an-na-ag-ga-ni*	for the king who loves him,
(dingir) *Nin-gir-su-ra*	for Ningirsu,
e KAŠ + *GAR* (sic)-*ka-ni* (sic)	his storehouse
mu-na-ru	was built.
En-teme-na	Entemena,

Col. IV.

(*ga*)*lu E-KAŠ* + *GAR*	who the storehouse
(dingir) *Nin-gir-su-ka ru-a*	for Ningirsu has built,
dingir-ra-ni	his god is
(dingir) *Dun-gur-an*	Dungur of heaven.

II. 3. Heuzey: '*la prédilection de son cœur*,' but adds in the note: '*On peut douter s'il s'agit d'œuvre à part ou de la plantation mentionnée à la suite.*' Probably the name of the building is left out here. In Tablette D, vii, we have: For Ninâ, who has chosen him in her heart, 'her holy plantation' he built; we ought to read this here also. For the expression, see Déc. 6, 4, l. 6; Déc. 7, col. i. 9; Gudea B, ii. 8; Déc. 31, 3; ii. 1; iii. 1. See also R. A. iii. p. 119, notes 3 and 4.

III. 3. See le Clercq, ii. pl. viii. col. ii. 6.

IV. 4. Galet A of Eannatum, vii. 17.

ENTEMENA.

Déc. pl. 5, No. 2.

(dingir) Ga-tum-dug	To Gatumdug,
am Šir-la-pur-^{ki}-ra	the mother of Shirpurla,
En-teme-na	Entemena,
pa-te-si	patesi
Šir-la-^{ki}-pur	of Shirpurla,
(ga)lu e-(dingir) Ga-tum-dug ru-a	who has built the house of Gatumdug,
dingir-ra-ni	his god
Dun-gur-an	is Dungur of heaven.

VASE D'ARGENT OF ENTEMENA.

Déc. pl. 43 and 43bis.

(dingir) Nin-gir-su	To Ningirsu,
gud (dingir) En-lil-ra	the hero of Enlil,
En-teme-na	Entemena,
pa-te-si	patesi
Šir-pur-la-^{ki}	of Shirpurla,
šag-pad-da	chosen by the heart
(dingir) Ninâ	of Ninâ,
pa-te-si-gal	the great patesi
(dingir) Nin-gir-su-ka	of Ningirsu,
dumu En-an-na-tum	the son of Enannatum,
pa-te-si	patesi
Šir-pur-la-^{ki}-ka-ge	of Shirpurla—
lugal ki-an-na-ag-ga-ni	to the king who loves him,
(dingir) Nin-gir-su-ra	to Ningirsu,
nigin ku-lağ-ğa zal-da	this vase (recipient) of shining silver,
(dingir) Nin-gir-su-ge ab-ta-gu-e	(which) Ningirsu had commanded (to make),
mu-na-gim	he made.

nam-ti-la-ni-ku	For (the preservation of) his life
(*dingir*) *Nin-gir-su*	unto Ningirsu
E-ninnû-ra	of Eninnû,
mu-na-gub	he presented it.
ud-ba Du-du	At that time Dudu
sanga (*dingir*) *Nin-gir-su-ka-kam*	was priest of Ningirsu.

This Dudu is mentioned again in Déc. 5bis, No. 2 (comp. Hilprecht's translation, O. B. I. p. 253, note 1):

Du-du	Dudu (=proper name: cp. Z. A. xii. p. 344, 9),
sanga-maǵ	high-priest
(*dingir*) *Nin-gir* + *ka* + *su*	of Ningirsu.
(*dingir*) *Nin-gir-su*	To Ningirsu
E-ninnû-ra	of Eninnû,
Du-du	Dudu,
sanga (*dingir*) *Nin-gir-su-ka-ge*	priest of Ningirsu,
URU+inserted *A*[1]-*a*-^{ki}-*ta*	from ?-a
mu-na-ta-DUL-DU (Br. 9593; Hommel, S. L. 361 = *dùd-du* (?))	has brought this,
GAG+*GIŠ*[2]-*ur* (Br. 5191) -*ku*	and into a *GAG-GIŠ* (=*masse d'armes*)-*ur*
mu-na-gim	has made it.

C. T. part V, No. 12061, published also by Winckler, A. B. K., No. 4:

(*dingir*) *Nin-gir-su*	Unto Ningirsu,
gud (*dingir*) *En-lil-ra*	the hero of Bêl,
En-teme-na	Entemena,
pa-te-si	patesi
Šir-la-^{ki}-*pur*	of Shirpurla,
dumu En-an-na-tum	the son of Enannatum,

[1] It is possible that the sign *URU*+inserted *A* is the same as that in Galet A of Eannatum, iii. 17 = *Gišgal*; comp. E. C. 361 and Br. 938.

[2] So Hilprecht and Thureau-Dangin (E. C. 318) = *GAG*+*GIŠ*. Hommel, S. L. 205, still = *Kisal*.

pa-te-si	patesi
Šir-la-pur-^{ki}-ka	of Shirpurla,
(ga)lu AB-GI-GI-ka-ni	who the *AB* of his *GI-GI*
$^{(dingir)}$ *Nin-gir-su-ra*(?)[*ru-a*]	for Ningirsu has built;
dingir-a-ni	his god
$^{(dingir)}$ *Dun+AN+gur*	is Dungur of heaven.

9. In Déc. 31, No. 3, iii. 2, we read: *(ga)lu AB-GI* $^{(dingir)}$ *Nin-gir-su-ka-ru-a*; compare also Urukagina, Déc. 5, i. l. 36, and see note to Déc. 2ter, No. 2, iii. 1. On account of the *KA* we ought to translate as was done above. *Ab*/*Ap*-*ir* probably too stands for *AB-IR-ka*.

10. Only parts of *RA* visible. *RU-A* seems to have been left out.

12. See note to O. B. I. 115, ii. 6.

O. B. I. 115.

Col. I.

. . . . .	
[*En*]*-te-me-na*	Entemena,
[*pa*]*-te-si*	patesi
Šir-la-^{ki}-pur	of Shirpurla,
à sum-ma	to whom power was given
$^{(dingir)}$ *En-lil*	by Bêl,
ga-zi-kù-a	who was nourished with the milk of life
$^{(dingir)}$ *Nin-ḫar-sag-ka*	by Ninḫarsag,
. . . .	. . . .

Col. II.

. . . . . *da-a*	. . . .
a-ni $^{(dingir)}$ *En-lil-la*	his ? of Bêl,
bur-maḫ	a great vase
kur-ta mu-na-ta-en DUL-DU (Br. 9593)	from the mountain he brought
$^{(dingir)}$ *Dun-gur*	to Dungur,
$^{(dingir)}$ *En-temen*[1] (*-an*)	the lord of the temen of heaven

[1] Hardly the beginning of the name Entemena, because this ruler *never* puts '*dingir*' before his name. Probably = *en-temen-an* = 'lord of the foundations of heaven'; comp. also the name $^{(dingir)}$ *Dun-gur-AN*. Hence $^{(dingir)}$ *En-temen-an*, which we ought to read here, is in apposition to $^{(dingir)}$ *Dun-gur*.

O. B. I. 117.

Col. I.

[*ud*-$^{(dingir)}$ . . . . .]	when . . .
[*šag ga*]*lu* 3600-*ta*	among 3,600 men
[*šu*]-*ni ba-ta*-[*tub*-]*ba*[1]	his power he had established,
mag̃ nam-tar-ra	a great fate (destruction)
. . . . .	

Col. II.

. . . . *mu-na-ni-šar*	. . . [a tablet] . . . he inscribed
nam-ti-la-ni-ku	[for] his life

O. B. I. 116.

Col. I.

$^{(dingir)}$ *En-lil-li*	To Bêl
En-lil-^{ki}-*ta*	of Nippur,
En-te-me-na-ra	by Entemena
mu-na-an-[*šub* ?]	it was presented.

Col. II.

. . .

gi . . . .

na . . . .

gi . . . . .

Only two of the inscriptions of Enannatum[2] II., the son of Entemena, have so far been published. The first in Déc. 6, No. 4 = A. B. K. No. 3; see Jensen, K. B. iii¹. p. 17; Hommel, Geschichte, p. 295; and above, p. 13. The second in C. T. 23287. In the former he states that he built, or rather repaired, the storehouse (*E-KAŠ* + *GAR*) for Ningirsu. The latter reads:

[1] See Thureau-Dangin, R. S. 1897, p. 172.

[2] For the meaning of this name, see under Entemena and Eannatum (p. 84). Jensen's objection, K. B. iii¹. p. 17, note 11, that if Enannatum would be = *Bêl-šamê-ukîn*, we should have the determinative 'god' (*dingir*) before *En*, is of no force, because in these early texts we never find the determinative 'god' before a proper name. This custom was first introduced by Sharganisharâli. The expression $^{(dingir)}$ *Ninâ-Ur* is no exception. See under Sharganisharâli.

C. T. 23287.

(Comp. G. Smith, Transactions of the Society of Biblical Archaeology, i. 32; Records of the Past, second series, iii. 7.)

(dingir) Nin-gir-su	Unto Ningirsu,
E-ninnû-ru	of the Eninnû,
En-an-na-tum	Enannatum,
pa-te-si	patesi
Šir-la-ki-pur-ka	of Shirpurla,
gan-'a-ni	his field
bar ki-bad	of a far off sanctuary
sukkal-li	of (his) sukkallu,
nam-ti	for the life
lugal-ni	of his king,
En-an-na-tum + ku + ma	viz. for Enannatum,
a-mu + ku + šub + na	has presented it.

7. *ki-bad* (sic; not *tih* against Thureau-Dangin, E. C. ii. note). See Br. 9659 and 1525; H. W. B. p. 470: *nisû entfernt, fern.*

8. *sukkal.* Written *LUĞ-li*; comp. S^b. 77; Br. 6170; H. W. B. p. 498; and Lugalzag., note to i. 21.

12. *KU* = verbal prefix; comp. Z. A. xii. p. 262: *mu Ša-aš-ru-ki ku* (sic)-*ğul*, and see note to Cône of Entemena, iii. 21.

With Lummadur, the son of Enannatum II, we arrive at the last representative of the house of Ur-Ninâ. Nothing but his name is known to us. From the absence of the title patesi behind his name we may conclude that Enannatum II. was the last patesi of the line of Ur-Ninâ, and that the old enemies Kish and Gishban have finally succeeded in overpowering Shirpurla.

It is hardly possible to look back upon this dynasty of Ur-Ninâ—which, as we have seen, dates from before 4000 B.C.—without being impressed by the high civilization, cult, the many buildings and canals, military skill, and style of writing. Surely such a people as this could not have sprung into existence as a *deus ex machina*; it must have had its history—a history which presupposes a development of several centuries more. We would gladly follow up the history of the successors of Lummadur, but the lack of material prevents us at present from so doing. Passing therefore over an interval of about two hundred years in the history of Shirpurla, we turn now to the enemies of the 'hero Ningirsu,' i. e. KISH AND GISHBAN (or better Gishuḫ).

Kings of Kish and Gishban.

Various changes had befallen the land of Kish. When speaking of Enshagkushanna, we saw that Kish was defeated. It had, however, in course of time again increased in strength[1]. Mesilim was able to establish himself as ruler over Shirpurla at the time of Lugalshuggur. His successors[2] may have retained their glory for a considerable period. They were, however, not able to withstand the mighty weapons of Eannatum. This latter king not only shook off the old yoke which Kish had fastened upon Shirpurla, but even became 'king of Kish.' He must have reduced Kish to total impotence. Hence it came about that Kish was vanquished by another power, of which we shall hear shortly.

Just as Gishban, after its defeat by Eannatum, felt strong enough to disregard the solemn promise never to invade the territory of Shirpurla, so Kish, after its overthrow by Eannatum, seems to have rapidly regained its old power. For we find a certain *En-ne-UGUN*, 'king of Kish,' who is also termed 'king of the hordes of Gishban,' desirous with the help of this latter city to extend the power of his capital. He was however defeated by a certain king of a certain country (the names cannot be read on account of the mutilated

[1] This 'increasing in strength' began already under a certain *U-dug-?* *pa-te-si Kiš*, who presents something (*sag-kab*, comp. Br. 5655; Galet A, vii. 6) to (*dingir*) *Za-[ma-ma]*. Comp. O. B. I. 108, and Hilprecht, ibid. p. 263, note 2. This vase having been found in Nippur, we may suppose therefore that *U-dug-?* was not only in possession of Nippur, but also of Shirpurla.

[2] Among whom may be classed a certain *Lugal-da ?-ak ?* (R. A. iv. p. 111, fig. 18) *lugal Kiš*, whose inscription is to be found on a '*lance votive*,' with a lion engraved on one of its sides, and which was disinterred '*au-dessus du sol d'Our-Nina*.' *Lugal-da ?-ak ?* therefore lived before Ur-Ninâ, and may have been one of the ancestors or successors of Mesilim, having like him sway over Shirpurla.

condition of the tablets). 'His statue'—this unknown victorious king records, while relating his victory over *En-ne-UGUN*—'his shining silver, the utensils, his property, he carried away and presented them to Bêl at Nippur[1].'

[1] Hilprecht, when speaking of this *En-ne-UGUN* (O. B. I. p. 264), thinks that this 'king of Kish' was defeated by a 'king of Kengi,' 'who lived shortly before or after' Enshagkushanna. Both of these statements, however, are without foundation, for—

(1) This inscription, as published by Hilprecht, does not give the slightest trace (*a*) of the name of this victorious king, nor does it say (*b*) that he was an '*EN Ki-en-gi-ki*,' a lord of Kengi. Hilprecht's emendation of line 4 (see O. B. I. p. 264, note 2) is simply imaginary.

(2) Above (p. 11) we have seen that *En-ne-UGUN* must be placed either at the same time or *after* Eannatum (comp. signs *KA*, *KUR*, and *E*).

But may we not assign this inscription to one of the rulers of Shirpurla? The unknown king here reports that he took away '*alanbi*,' 'his (i. e. *En-ne-UGUN's*) statue.' Now we know from the Cône of Entemena that a stèle was erected (*a*) by Mesilim, king of Kish (Cône, i. 12). Ush, patesi of Gishban, removed this stèle (i. 18, 19). (*b*) Eannatum restored this stèle of Mesilim (ii. 8), apparently in a peaceful way (comp. i. 39 ff.—nothing is said of war), and erected a new one on the canal from the great river to the Guedin (ii. 4, 5). Urlumma, patesi of Gishban, casts the stèles of Eannatum into the fire (ii. 36, 37).

Eannatum, no doubt, promptly punishes Urlumma (iii. 10). His victory, however, is only indicated by these words: 'upon the dogs he poured out terror;'—it was therefore probably only a partial victory, or else Entemena would have said that his father '*ṭu-ku bi-sig*' (Galet A, iii. 23, 24) the Gishbanites. The real victory of Gishban was reserved for Entemena; he crushed (*e-gaz*) the power of Urlumma (iii. 13 ff.); he even had strength enough to depose Urlumma and make Ili, a priest of *Innanna-ab-ki*, take his place (iii. 34 ff.). Of course, as might be expected, the Gishbanites were not satisfied with their new patesi; they tried to get rid of him. In order to do this they had to invoke the help of a new power, viz. Kish. At this time there ruled in Kish a 'king'; this king of Kish became thus also 'king of the hordes of Gishban*ki*.' He went against Shirpurla, but was defeated. By what king? If there was a 'king' of Kish at this time (Entemena), a considerable period must have elapsed since that of Eannatum (who himself defeated Kish and became its king). And since Entemena mentions in his Cône only the deposition of Urlumma, it is most probable that 'Gishban, together with Kish,' became hostile at the end of Entemena's, or at the beginning of Enannatum II.'s reign. *En-ne-UGUN*, therefore, lived at about this time, which also is in accordance with the palaeographic evidence.

The tablets which report this victory of a king of Shirpurla (*sic*; see page 119) over *En-ne-UGUN* are published by Hilprecht in O. B. I. Nos. 103, 104, 102, 110, 105—the text of which inscription may be restored as follows (comp. O. B. I. p. 264, note 2, and Winckler, A. F. v. p. 372):—

(ENNE-UGUN.)

[(*dingir*) *En-lil-la*]	To Enlil,
[*lugal-kur-kur-ra*]	king of the lands,
[*Entemena* or *Enannatum*]	. . . . . (Entemena or Enannatum II.)
[*pa-te-si Širpurla-ki*]	(patesi of Shirpurla,)
gal? [+(*ga*)*lu* . . . .] (O. B. I. 103)	king?
ud (*dingir*) [*En-lil-li*]	When Enlil
e-na-ni-ğun-a (O. B. I. 104, 3)	had looked favourably upon him,
Kiš-ki	then Kish
mu-ğul	he infested;
En-ne-Ugun	Enne-Ugun,
gal+(*ga*)*lu Kiš-ki*	king of Kish,

1. Bêl of Nippur is here the chief god, and not Ningirsu, as we would expect on account of Cône of Entemena, i. 1 ff. The division of the territory was made 'upon the righteous command of Bêl.' The fight recorded here resulted from the disobedience to Bel's command, therefore to him this inscription is dedicated. See also l. 24.

2, 3. Supplied according to note 1 on the preceding page. Hilprecht read: X.X. *en Ki-en-gi.*

6. Whether the first sign in l. 6 is the beginning of *lugal* is very doubtful. It may also be *E*; comp. l. 7.

7. The first sign on 104, 3 seems to be *ŠU*, while on 103, 3 it is apparently *E*. The second sign on 103, 3 is *KI*, but has to be read according to 104, 3, *NA*. *ğun*, Br. 10503, *našû ša êni.*

10. *Ugun*, Br. 8861; Z. A. i. p. 57 f.

mu-dur	he cast down.
[*gal*+] (*ga*)*lu erim* ^{giš}*BAN*-^{ki}-*ka-ge* (O. B. I. 102, 2)	The king of the hordes of Gishban,
(*lu*)*gal Kiš*-^{ki}-*ge*	king of Kish,
uru-na ga-ḫul	his city teeming with malignity,
dig-ga	his spoil
. . . . . *bil*	. . . . . he burnt
(Two or more lines are wanting)	. . . . .
mu-ne-gì (O. B. I. 110, 3)	brought back
alan-bi	his statue,
azag-zagin-bi	his shining silver,
giš dig-ga-bi	the utensils, his spoil
$^{\text{(dingir)}}$ *En-lil-la*	to Enlil
[*E*]*n-lil*-^{ki}-*ku*	of Nippur
a-mu-na-šub	he presented.

12. *dur* = *KU*, Br. 10542, *nadû*; K. B. iii^1. p. 48, note **. According to O. B. I. 105 follows upon this line instantly: *alan-bi*, hence ll. 13–20 are left out there.

13. *erim*, Br. 8139, *ṣâbu*. *giš-BAN* = ligature. It seems however to be highly probable that we have to read here, instead of *erim giš-BAN-ki*, *UD* + *BAN-ki*, i. e. simply *UḪ* (Br. 8124). Enne-Ugun then would be king of Uḫ and king of Kish. So already Winckler, A. F. p. 373, note 2. For *UḪ*, see iv. R^2. 38, No. 1, col. i. 12.

15. *ga* stands here for *gan*, Br. 4039, *duḫdu* (*daḫâdu*). The same peculiarity occurs again in O. B. I. 113, 8, *ga-ti-la-ku*, while in l. 4 *gan-ti-la-ku* is written = 'for abundance of'; so also in O. B. I. 98, 6. Comp. also O. B. I. 112, 4 (*ga-ti-la-ku*), and ibid. 106, 3.

16. *dig-ga*. Comp. Enshagkushanna, O. B. I. 92.

17. . . . *bil*, Br. 4575; *ḳalû*, H. W. B. 585.

20. *gì*, Br. 6331; *târu* ii^1, H. W. B. p. 702 *c*. This line is preceded in O. B. I. 110 by . . . *bil-a* = l. 17; hence nothing left out.

21. T. C. 211. *alan*, Br. 7300.

22. *azag*, T. C. 260; *kaspu*. *zagin*, Br. 11773, *ellu*.

26. *šub*. Lugalzag. iii. 40.

In course of time, however—and probably not very long after this defeat—Kish seems to have recovered from this blow.

A certain Urzaguddu[1] must have been very successful in his wars, for in addition to his title 'king of Kish,' he calls himself also 'king of . . . [2].' Unfortunately here again we have a gap, so that we cannot determine of what city he had thus become king.

Very little is known of the next king of Kish, Lugaltarsi. At what time subsequent to Urzaguddu he lived, we cannot tell. So much only is certain, that he reigned some time before Âlusharshid, about 3850 B.C. His inscription—the only one so far known to us—is preserved in the British Museum (C. T. No. 12155)[3], in which he records the building of *BAD-KISAL* in honour of Bêl and Ishtar.

Before speaking of the next two kings of Kish, it would seem

[1] For this reading instead of Ur-Shulpauddu (Hilprecht), see Thureau-Dangin, R. A. iv. p. 74, note 14. His inscription is published in O. B. I. No. 93. Comp. ibid. p. 265, and Winckler, A. F. p. 373, 3. It reads:

[*dingir En-lil*]	To Enlil,
lugal kur-kur-ra	king of the lands,
(*dingir*) *Nin-lil*	and to Ninlil,
nin-an-ki-ra	the mistress of heaven and earth,
nun igi-še-ni-na	who is greater than all its generations,
dam (*dingir*) *En-lil-ra*	the wife of Enlil,
Ur-zag-ud-du	Urzaguddu,
lugal-Kiš-ki	king of Kish,
lugal	king of . . . . . .

[2] The fact that he presents a vase with this inscription to Bêl of Nippur does not prove that Urzaguddu possessed Nippur (Hilprecht). See the Cône inscription of Entemena: The gods of Girsu and Gishban settle, upon 'the righteous command of Enlil, king of the lands,' their boundaries. This does not mean that Nippur was in possession of Shirpurla and Gishban. It is surely a religious matter.

[3] See Thureau-Dangin, R. A. iv. p. 74, note 15. It reads: (*Dingir*) *Lugal-kur-kur-ra* | (*dingir*) *Innanna* | *Nin* (*dingir*) *Innanna-ra* | *Lugal-tar-si* | *lugal Kiš* | *bad-kisal* | *mu-na-ru*, i. e. according to Thureau-Dangin: '*En l'honneur du dieu des contrées et de Ishtar, de la dame Ishtar* (?? Translate: the mistress of the divine Innanna, and comp. p. 84, col. ii. 5), *Lugal-tar-si, roi de Kish, le mur de la terrasse* (?) *a construit.*'

necessary here to remove an objection recently made by Hilprecht (O. B. I. p. 270), who, following Winckler, believes that the expression *lugal Kiš* is equal to *šar kiššati*, i.e. king of the universe (*König der Welt*). By doing this Hilprecht becomes untrue to his first position, stated ibid. p. 23, where he firmly maintained that *LUGAL KIŠ* did not mean anything else but 'king of Kish.' That this latter position is the only true one is evident from a comparison of the inscription of Mesilim quoted above, p. 16, and the Cône inscription of Entemena.

Mesilim, as we have seen, calls himself *LUGAL KIŠ*, while Entemena terms him *LUGAL KIŠ-ki*. Hilprecht probably will not question the identity of the Mesilim mentioned on the 'Masse d'armes aux lions' in Déc. pl. 1 ter, fig. 2, with the Mesilim mentioned by Entemena. If he does not, then *LUGAL KIŠ = LUGAL KIŠ-ki*, and means 'king of Kish' (and not 'king of the world'). In connection with this we would like to draw the attention of the reader to the fact that *the kings of* KISH call themselves only *LUGAL KIŠ*, without the determinative *KI* (comp. inscriptions of Mesilim, Lugal-da?-ak? Lugaltarsi, Manishtusu, Âlusharshid, and O. B. I. 118); while the other kings of Babylonia, when speaking of these kings of Kish, *always* write *KIŠ* with the determinative *KI* (comp. inscriptions of Eannatum, *passim*, Entemena, Enne-Ugun, &c.). One exception, however, seems to occur, viz. the king Urzaguddu, apparently king of Kish, terms himself *lugal Kiš-ki*. This is but an apparent exception. We have seen that Urzaguddu had also another title: 'king of . . .' It seems therefore very probable, notwithstanding the succession of the titles, viz. first 'king of Kish,' and then 'king of . . .' (comp. what has been said under Lugalkigubnidudu about the succession of titles), that Urzaguddu was not originally 'king of Kish,' but 'king of . . .' —a foreigner, who eventually '*became king of Kish*,' and not vice versa.

This objection having been removed, we can now place Manishtusu and Âlusharshid also among the kings of Kish.

Both flourished somewhere about 3850 B.C., i.e. before Sargon I. (see above, p. 18)[1].

When reading the inscriptions of these kings, it is as if a new race were speaking to us, so widely different is the language used by these rulers from that of their predecessors, or of any other kings we have so far met with. We here find for the first time the so-called Semitic-Babylonian inscriptions. It is the same language[2] which is also employed in the inscriptions of Sharganisharâli and his successors, in that of Lasirab, king of Guti, and of Annubânini, king of Lulubu, all of whom were more or less contemporary with these kings of Kish. Scholars who believe that we must postulate two different races among the inhabitants of Early Babylonia, call the kings who wrote in this style, 'Semitic kings,' while the others are referred to the 'Sumerian' population. As a result of this they read the names of these kings in a Semitic way. Manishtusu becomes *MA-AN-iš-tu-irba*[3] (so Winckler!), Urumush becomes *Âlu-ušaršid* (i.e. 'He (some deity) founded the city,' see Br. 5032, 5068, and Hilprecht, O. B. I. p. 20, note 1).

The inscription[4] of Manishtusu, whom we place provisionally before Urumush, runs: 'Manishtuirba, king of Kish, has presented (this) to Bêlit-Malkatu.'

Of more importance, from the historical point of view as well as from the linguistic, is the next ruler, who probably followed soon after the former. This ruler is Âlusharshid. From his inscriptions —to be found in sixty-one fragments of vases, which have been excavated by the expedition of the University of Pennsylvania under Dr. Peters, and partly published by Hilprecht[5]—we learn

[1] Thureau-Dangin places them after Naram-Sin (R. A. iv. p. 74: '*probablement postérieurs à Naram-Sin*').

[2] See under Lugalzaggisi.

[3] The capitals indicate that the scholars do not know how to read the syllables expressed thus in the Semitic language.

[4] Published in Mittheilungen des Akademisch-Orientalistischen Vereins zu Berlin, i. 1887, p. 18; translated by Winckler, K. B. iii[1]. p. 101. Also published in A. B. K. No. 67.

[5] O. B. I. Nos. 5-10, and pl. iii.-v.; see also Déc. pl. 5, 4; C. T. 12161 and 12162; O. B. I. 12, 13.

that he subdued Elam, on the eastern side of the Tigris, and the country of Bara'se (Para'se), from which lands he brought back these marble vases, and dedicated them to his gods at Nippur and Sippara[1]. The longest of these vase-inscriptions, which make known to us these significant historical facts, and thus indirectly give a key for determining the boundaries of Kish, reads (O. B. I. No. 5[2]. Comp. Hilprecht, ibid. p. 20):

A-na	To
(*ilu*) *Bêl* [*EN-LIL*]	Bêl,
Âlu-ušaršid [*URU-MU-UŠ*]	Âlusharshid,
šar	king
Kiš	of Kish—
i-nu [*NI-NU*][3]	after
Elamtu[4]-*ki*	Elam
u	and
Ba-ra-a'-se-ki[5]	Bara'se
inîra [*SAG-GIŠ-RA-NI*][6]	he had subjugated—

[1] For there inscriptions of Âlusharshid have also been found. It is interesting to find that Sippara must have been in existence as early as this (3850 B.C.), and its god must have enjoyed a wide influence.

[2] O. B. I. No. 6 reads:

A-na	To
(*dingir*) *En-lil*	Bêl
Âlu-ušaršid	Âlusharshid,
šar	king
Kiš	of Kish,
A-MU-ŠUB	presented it.

The shorter legends (see O. B. I. Nos. 7, 8; Déc. 5, 4) read:

Âlu-ušaršid	Âlusharshid,
šar	king
Kiš	of Kish.

[3] For *inu* written this way, comp. H. W. B. p. 96. Here a conjunction: 'at the time when.'

[4] Br. 9009.

[5] This line might also be read *Ba-ra-aḫ-se-ki*; *a'* and *aḫ* in Old Babylonian writing fall together. See also S^n. col. i. 7 ff., and A. B. K. 16, 15.

[6] *sag-giš-ra*, Br. 3606; *nêru*, H. W. B. 439. Pract. either *inîr* or oftener *inâr*.

IN NAM-RA-AG[1]	the *IN* of the prince
Elamti-ki	of Elam
iddin [*A-MU-ŠUB*][2]	he presented.

For but a short period subsequent to Âlusharshid does Kish seem to have enjoyed its old power. The might of Kish gave place to that of Agade, as we shall see shortly (comp. also p. 18). Leaving therefore Kish[3] for the present, we turn our attention to the other enemy of Old Shirpurla, viz. Gishban.

At about 4000 B.C.[4], not long after the time of Eannatum, Gishban seems to have acquired new power and might. It directed

[1] Purely Sumerian (*sic*, Hilprecht, O. B. I. 264, note 1), from *nam + ri + ag* (v. R. 20, 13 *c*) = Assyr. *shallatu shalâlu*, Del. Assyr. Gram. § 73, 132. Comp. also O. B. I. p. 20, note 6. *Na-ra-ag* occurs also in Gudea B, vi. 66, and Vase of Naram-Sin, i. R. 3, No. 7, and in R. A. v. No. I. p. 30, fig. 25. Scheil, who recently published some texts, showed that *NAM-RA-AG* must be a name of some kind of an officer. As such it is parallel to *IP-UŠ* (cp. Z. A. xii. 267: *Gimil-Bêl IP-UŠ-GAL; E-ir-Bêl IP-UŠ lugal.* On 368 ibid. *nam-ra-ag* is parallel to *GIR* (= officer). He then translates the passages where this *nam-ra-ag* is found, as follows:—Gudea B, vi. 66: '*il frappa Anšam et amena* son *prince dans le temple de Ningirsu*'; Vase of Naram-Sin (i. R. 3, No. 7): '*A Naram-Sin, roi des quatre régions, vase* du prince *de Magan*'; and our passage here: '*A Bel, après la conquête d'Elam, il consacra* (*ou voua*) *le IN du prince d'Elam.*' This may also help us to understand what *IN* means. *IN* has been translated by 'of' or 'in' (Hilprecht, Winckler). As such it would be a shortened form for *ina*. *IN* here may be just as well something which the prince has; in O. B. I. i. 11 *EN-LIL* is called the *IN* of *EN-LIL-ki*, hence we may think of a 'guard' or 'guardian(s)' of a king or city. Enlil is the 'guardian' of Nippur; in O. B. I. 5 the 'guards' of the prince of Elam are presented to Bêl. Comp. also Sb. 2, 5 in Hommel, S. L. p. 74: *in = pi-il-lum* (*Herr?*); *in = pi-il-tum* (*Herrin?*) Hommel apparently was on the right track. See also note to O. B. I. i. l. 10.

[2] Lugalzag. iii. 40.

[3] To one of the rulers of Kish belongs also the inscription published in O. B. I. 118, which reads:

N. N.	Name X.X.
šarru	king
Kiš	of Kish,
a-na	to
(*ilu*) *Bêl* [(*dingir*) *En-lil*]	Bêl
[*a-*]*mu*[*-šub*] = *iddin*	has dedicated it.

[4] For this date, see the Chronological Table.

K

its chief attention not so much towards Shirpurla as towards the south. Probably the rulers of Shirpurla had at this time been reduced to utter weakness by its old enemies (i. e. Kish and Gishban), of which enemies Gishban was destined to play the most important rôle in the development of ancient Babylonian history.

Lugalzaggisi, the son of Ukush, patesi of Gishban, we find at the head of the armies of Gishban, which he leads victoriously against the south. After Erech had opened its doors, the whole of Babylonia to the Persian Gulf fell an easy prey to the conquering hero. He, although originally only the son of a patesi, becomes king of Erech, nay, even king of the 'whole world.' '*Enlil,* king of the lands, has given to Lugalzaggisi the kingship of the world; *he* has made him to prosper before the world; *he* it was that had placed the lands under his sceptre—the lands "from the rising of the sun even unto the going down of the same." *He* it also was that gave him the tribute of those lands, which he made to dwell in peace, notwithstanding that they had been brought under a new *régime*.' With these words Lugalzaggisi acknowledges, as the kings of Shirpurla did, that Enlil, and Enlil alone, had granted to him so unprecedented a dominion, extending from the lower sea of the Tigris and the Euphrates (i. e. the Persian Gulf) to the upper sea (i.e. the Mediterranean). Constituted thus 'lord of the world,' he now becomes its *summus episcopus*. 'In the sanctuaries of Kengi, as patesi of the lands, and in Erech, as high priest, they (the gods) established him.' To quote Hilprecht (p. 267): 'Babylonia, as a whole, had no fault to find with this new and powerful *régime*. The Sumerian civilization was directed into new channels from stagnation; the ancient cults between the lower Tigris and Euphrates began to revive, and its temples to shine in new splendour.' Thus endowed with the highest temporal and spiritual power, he 'makes Erech to abound in rejoicing.' Nor does he forget the other representative cities of his domain: 'Ur, like a steer, to the top of the heavens he raised.' 'Over Larsa, the beloved city of Shamash, he poured out waters of joy.' His own native town and land receive chief attention: 'Gishban, the beloved city of . . ., to an unheard-of power he raised.' He, as wise ruler and statesman, not only shows his good will and favour towards the larger and more influential cities, but also protects the weaker ones: 'Ki-Innanna-ab' (see Cône of Entemena, iii. 29) 'he kept in an enclosure, like a sheep that is to be shorn[1].'

Indeed, 'Lugalzaggisi stands out from the dawn (?) of Babylonian history as a giant who deserves our full admiration for the work he accomplished' (Hilprecht, O. B. I. p. 268).

The inscription recording these most important events is published by Hilprecht in O. B. I. No. 87; it has 132 lines of text, which were restored by that scholar from 88 fragments of 64 different vases under the most trying circumstances,—indeed a masterpiece of that scholar's skill and learning. The inscription may conveniently be divided as follows:—

(1) Enlil, king of the lands, endows Lugalzaggisi (here follow his titles) (*a*) with the kingship over the world; (*b*) makes the lands to be satisfied with this new reign; (*c*) makes the king also the spiritual head of the newly acquired kingdom; i–ii. 25.

(2) Lugalzaggisi shows his thankfulness, skill, and wisdom by his care for various cities of his realm; ii. 26–iii. 2.

(3) But he does not forget the god from whom he has received all that he is and has; iii. 3–12.

(4) He concludes with a prayer to Enlil, to whom this inscription is dedicated.

The whole reads as follows:—

LUGALZAGGISI.

O. B. I. No. 87[2].

Col. I.

(dingir) En-lil	Enlil (Bêl),
lugal kur-kur-ra	king of the lands,

[1] This is probably the meaning of the passage in ii. 43 ff.

[2] A partial translation, O. B. I. p. 266 ff. Thureau-Dangin first gave a complete translation in R. S. 1897, p. 263 ff.

Lugal-zag-gi-si	to Lugalzaggisi,
lugal Unug-ki-ga	king of Erech,
lugal kalam-ma	king of the world,
išib An-na	priest of Anu,
(ga)lu-maḫ	hero
(*dingir*) *Nidaba*	of Nidaba,
dumu U-kuš	son of Ukush,
pa-te-si giš-BAN-ki	patesi of Gishban,
(ga)lu-maḫ	hero
(*dingir*) *Nidaba*	of Nidaba,
igi-zi-bar-ra	(to him) who was favourably looked upon by the faithful eye
(*dingir*) *Lugal-kur-kur-ka*	of Lugalkurkura,
pa-te-si gal	the great patesi
(*dingir*) *En-lil*	of Enlil (Bêl),
giš-(pi)-tug sum-ma	to whom intelligence was given
(*dingir*) *EN-KI*	by Enki (Ea),
mu-pad-da	who was chosen (called)
(*dingir*) *Utu*	by Utu (Shamash),

I. 6. *išib*, Br. 10352.

9. *kuš*, Br. 6018.

10. Text restored according to ii. 38.

13. *igi . . . bar*, Br. 9297; H. W. B. p. 528: *naplusu*. *igi-zi* = the true faithful eye, opposed to *ḫul* (= *igi-ur* (*nakru*)), the evil eye.

17. *giš(-pi)-tug* and the variant *giš-tug(-pi)*. A phrase which occurs very often among the titles of the patesis of Shirpurla; comp. also Gudea B, col. ix. 24, and see Jensen, K. B. iii[1]. p. 48, note 2, who calls it '*Ideogramm für "Ohr."*' In Galet A of Eannatum, ii. 6, we have *giš-tug(-pi)*; so also in v. R. 61, col. iv. 13: *ana râmânika u-zu-un-ka* (*giš-tug(-pi)*), the syllable *tug* being always written with *KU*. Comp. also the Cône of Entemena, col. v. 24. Hommel, S. L. No. 288, on the other hand, takes *giš-tug* (*KU*) as a phonetic writing for *giš-tug* (Br. 5727), and the *PI* as determinative. See also Br. 7978, *PI-tug*; Br. 5727, *giš-tug*, both = *šemû*; and Br. 5721, *giš-tug* (*KU*) (*-pi*) = *uznu* = understanding, intelligence, H. W. B. p. 37. Comp. also *giš-tug(-pi)-ni* in P. S. B. A. Nov. 1890, p. 63 (where it no doubt stands for Assyr. *mâgiri-šu*), with v. R. 19, 24*a*: *giš-tug ša magâri*, i. e. to hear in the sense of 'to obey.'

19. *pad*, Br. 9422, *zakâru*, *nabû*, *tamû*. *mu* may be = *šumu*.

luǧ-maǧ	sublime minister
(*dingir*) *En-zu*	of Enzu (Sin),
ne-nitaǧ	the shakkanâkku
(*dingir*) *Utu*	of Utû,
u-a (*dingir*) *Innanna*	the fosterer of Innanna (Ishtar),
dumu tu-da	a son brought up
(*dingir*) *Nidaba*	by Nidaba,
ga-zi-kù-a	who was nourished with the milk of life
(*dingir*) *Nin-ḫar-sag*	by Ninḫarsag,
(*ga*)*lu* (*dingir*) *UMU* (*ŠID* ?)	servant of Umu (Shid ?), priest(ess)
sanga Unug-ki-ga	of Erech,
sag eǧi-a	a slave brought up
(*dingir*) *Nin-a-gid-ǧa-du*	by Ninagidǧadu,
nin Unug-ki-ga-ka	mistress of Erech,
iti-maǧ	the great abarakku

21. *luǧ*, Br. 6170, *sukkallu*. Comp. Hilprecht, O. B. I. p. 255, note 6: *sukkallu* = a servant (*gal*) who pours out (*su*) [namely, water over his master's hands and feet]! But see Delitzsch, E. S. p. 98 ff.

23. *ne-nitaǧ*, T. C. 203 + 74. In Gudea B, iv. 13, we have the signs T. C. 203 + 7. Jensen, K. B. iii[1]. p. 30, note 7, transcribes *ne-ura* and translates '*Landvogt*'; comp. also ibid., Kosmol. p. 477. If we are to see in *ne-nitaǧ* the ideogram for *šakkanakku* (generally written T. C. 203 + 8, Br. 9195), we have to suppose that T. C. 74, 7, 8, originally formed one sign. Comp. also Thureau-Dangin, R. S. 1897, p. 270, note 1; Hilprecht, O. B. I. p. 266, note 4. The former reads *kiš-nitaǧ*; the latter *ne-giš*. See also notes to E. C. 26, and l. 8 of O. B. I. 20.

25. *u-a*, Br. 6095; *zâninu*, H. W. B. p. 258.

26. *dumu tu-da*. Comp. Inscription of Gudea, passim. *tu*, Br. 1070, *alâdu*.

28. *ga*, Br. 6114, *šizbu* + *zi* (*napištu*) + *kù*, Br. 882, *akâlu*, and 884, *šuznunu*, H. W. B. p. 258 = nourished with the milk of life.

30. (*dingir*) *UMU*, T. C. 69; Br. 3896. In iv. R. 35[2], No. 2, l. 1, this sign occurs again in the name *Šid-lam-ta-ud-du*; comp. Winckler, K. B. iii[1]. p. 82, No. 8. Should we read with Thureau-Dangin here *Šid* too, and comp. Br. 5974 = god Marduk ? Comp. also Hommel, Geschichte, p. 336 f., on the introduction of Shidlamtauddu into Shirpurla.

31. *eǧi*, Br. 6611; *likûtu*, H W. B. p. 385.

34. *iti*, Br. 9427, *abarakku*. See Galet A, ii. 10; Gudea D, i. 13.

dingir-ri-ne-ra	of the gods—
ud (*dingir*) *En-lil*	when Enlil,
lugal kur-kur-ra-ge	king of the lands,
Lugal-zag-gi-si	to Lugalzaggisi
nam-lugal	the kingship
kalam-ma	of the world
e-na-sum-ma-a	had given,
igi kalam-ma-ge	when he before the world
si-e-na-di-a	had made him to prosper,
kur-kur ne-na	when the lands under his power (rule)
e-ni-sig-ga-a	he had given,
utu ud-du-ta	(and) from the rising of the sun

Col. II.

utu šù-ku	to the going down of the sun
gu-e-na-gar-ra-a	he had subdued (them, i. e. the lands),
ud-ba	then (at that time)
a-ab-ba	from the sea
sig-ga (sic)-*ta*	the lower

41. The first sign is not, as Hilprecht thinks = Br. 5410, *mà*, *ga*, but = Br. 5839, *e*. Comp. above, p. 10; so also Thureau-Dangin in R. S. 1897, p. 68, note 1. This *e* when occurring in verb-forms stands always before n^{a}_{i}. Comp. besides this line: col. i. 43, *si-e-na-di-a*, and ii. 11; i. 45, *e-ni-sig-ga-a*; ii. 2, *gu-e-na-gar-ra*; iii. 11, *e-na-sir-ra*; 12, *e-na-de*.

42. *igi*, Br. 9265, *maḫar*.

43. *si . . . di*, Br. 3461–63; H. W. B. p. 310, *išâru*, *šutešuru*.

44. *ne* = *emûku*, Br. 9184.

46. *utu ud-du* = *ṣît šamši*, Br. 7886.

II. 1. *utu šù*, Br. 7954, *eribu ša šamši*. Here the *ŠÙ* is Br. 8644; it ought to be Br. 10822. Both signs, however, change repeatedly.

2. *gu . . . gar*, Br. 3318, *ḳadâdu*, H. W. B. p. 580 and Br. 3319, *kanâšu ša amêli*, H. W. B. p. 340.

3. *ud-ba* = *ina ûmišuma*, or *ina ûmi šuati* (Br. 113).

4. *a-ab-ba*, Br. 11474, *tâmtu*.

5. *sig-ga-ta*. So should be read. The first *ta* undoubtedly is a mistake of the scribe. *sig*, T. C. 259. *sig-ga*, Br. 11873, *šaplû*, *šaplîtu*.

Idigna	of the Tigris
Buranunu-bi	and the Euphrates
a-ab-ba	to the sea
igi-nim-ma-ku	the upper
gir-bi	his path
si-e-na-di	he straightened.
utu ud-du-ta	From the rising of the sun
utu šù-ku	to the going down of the sun,
(*dingir*) *En-lil-li*	Enlil,
[*lag* ?]-*gar*	the making of gifts
[*šu-ni* ?] *mu-ni-tug*	caused his hands to have,
kur-kur u-sal-la	the lands in peace
mu-da-nà	he caused to dwell (rest),
kalam-e	the world
a ĝul-la mu-da-e	with a water of joy he watered.

6. T. C. 83; Br. 11650.

7. Br. 11663; *bi* – copula, Br. 5131.

9. *igi-nim* (T. C. 157), Br. 9375, *elîtu*. ll. 4-9: *ultu tâmti šaplîti ana tâmti elîti*. The phrase occurs again in Gudea B, v. 25-27.

10. *gir* = *padanu*, *tallaktu*, Br. 9191 and 9207. For *bi* in *gir-bi*, see Thureau-Dangin: '*Dans l'expression gir-bi, bi ne peut d'aucune façon représenter le pronom possessif en rapport avec une personne: il faut donc traduire "sa chemin" ou "leur chemin," c.-à d. le chemin du Tigre et de l'Euphrate.*' So also in Gudea B, v. 25-27. Hilprecht translates: he straightened his path, O. B. I. p. 267. So correctly.

15. Only the second half of the first sign visible. The variant gives a sign which looks something like that in col. i. 30 = *ŠID*; comp. then Br. 5970 = *lag* = *kurbannu*; read *lag-gar*, which would be: the making (*gar*) of gifts (*lag*).

16. Part of *NI* still visible. Probably we have to add, with Thureau-Dangin, *ŠU* before *ni*, and read: *šu-ni mu-ni-tug*. *tug*, H. W. B. 310 = *išû*, to have. Translate: the making of gifts (= revenues) he (Enlil) caused his (Lugalzaggisi's) lands to have = he allowed Lugalzaggisi to receive revenues. Thureau-Dangin: '*les revenus* (?) *lui accorda*.' Hilprecht: and granted him dominion over everything (?).

17. *u-sal-la*, Br. 6086; *aburriš*, H. W. B. p. 10.

18. *nà*, T. C. 261, Br. 8997; *rabâṣu*, H. W. B. p. 610.

20. *a ĝul-la*. The *a* may be either = *mû*, water; or it may be a meaningless (?) prefix to form nouns. *ĝul*, Br. 10884; *ḫadû*, *ḫidûtu*, H. W. B. p. 270. Thus we would get either 'water of joy' or 'joy.'

mu-da-e; *e*, Br. 5844 = *mû*; here with *mu-da* = verb = watered. ll. 19 and 20

bar-bar Ki-en-gi	In the sanctuaries of Kengi,
pa-te-si kur-kur-ra	as patesi of the lands,
ki Unug-ki-gi	and in Erech,
išib nam-nun-ku	as high-priest,
mu-na-gar-e-ne	they established him.
ud-ba	At that time
Unug-ki-gi	Erech
ka (sic) *-zal-a*	in pleasures (joy)
ud-mu-da-zal-zal-li	he made to abound.
Uru-unug-ki-e	Ur,
gud-gim sag-an-ku	like a steer, to the top of the heaven
mu-ru-gur	he raised.
Ud-unug-ki	Larsa,
uru ki-ag	the beloved city

may be translated either: the lands with a water of joy he watered (Thureau-Dangin), or (over) the lands he poured out (*mu-da-e*) joy. Hilprecht, who thinks that *e* = *gà* (= *šakânu*), seems to take these two lines in the sense of: the lands he made joyful. See O. B. I. p. 267, note 4. See also especially l. 36.

21. *bar*, Br. 6878, *parakku*.

24. *nam-nun*, Br. 2143, *rubûtu*.

25. The third sign is probably that of *GAR*, which hangs here on the separating line.

28. The text has for the first sign *sag*; it ought to be *ka*, as the variant gives it. *ka-zal-a*, Br. 668, *tašiltu*, pleasure.

29. *zal-zal*, Br. 5358; *barû*, H. W. B. 184. *ud . . . zal-zal*, Br. 7909, *uštabri*.

31. *gim* = *kîma*; *sag-an-ku* = *ana rêš šamê*; cp. iii. 1.

32. *mu-ru-gur*. The second sign is not that of T. C. 68 = *irû*, 'bronze' (Thureau-Dangin), nor that for *UM*, T. C. 69 (Hilprecht), but that which occurs again in l. 34, *uru-ki-ag*. That the sign *URU* may also have the value of *RU*, see Barrel-Cyl. of Urukagina, col. ii. 10. In verb-forms of our inscription this *URU* = *ṚU* stands, especially in such cases where it is preceded by *MU*; comp. ii. 42; iii. 2, 26, 28. Is this *URU* = *RU* a dialectical variant for *RA?* Comp. also Galet A of Eannatum, col. iv. 24, and vi. 7, 9, in which places we find the expression *sag-e-ru-sig*; and Gudea B, ix. 5: *ĝe-URU* (read *ER*, on account of the *ĝe*, and not *UM* or *IM*)*-kur-ne*. For *gur*, see l. 42.

34. *ki-ag*, Br. 4745, *râmu*.

(dingir) Utu-ge	of Utu,
a-ne ǧul-la	with waters of joy
mu-da-e	he watered.
giš-BAN-ki	Gishban,
uru ki-ag	the beloved city
(dingir) ?-ge	of . . .,
à-maǧ	to a power very high
mu-ru-gur	he raised.
Ki-Innanna-ab-ki-e	*Ki-Innanna-ab,*
ganam sig gur-a-gim	like a sheep whose wool should be shorn,
šeg mu-da-gi-gì	he kept in an enclosure.
Ki-an-ki-ge	Of Kian

Col. III.

gu-an-ku	the 'head' to the heaven

36. *a-ne ǧul-la.* This expression undoubtedly favours the translation of Thureau-Dangin given above in l. 20. *a-ne = a-e-ne = plur.*

40. Comp. Cône of Entemena, col. i. 6. The second sign has not yet been identified.

42. *gur,* T. C. 103; Br. 6148, *našû*; and 6151, *šaḳû.*

43. Thureau-Dangin reads *Ki-Nin-ab-ki-e,* and refers to R. A. iv. No. 1, p. 23. Comp. also Cône of Entemena, iii. 28 ff.

44. The first sign either = Br. 10242, *barun,* or Br. 10256, *ganam.* The second sign is Br. 10781, *šipâtu.* Both these signs occur very often in the E. A. H. texts. Thureau-Dangin remarks to the latter sign: '*C'est exactement l'image d'un métier à tisser.*' The third sign is composed out of *URU,* 'city,' with inserted *GU,* T. C. 172. The whole sign therefore is = Br. 931: *kasâmu,* H. W. B. 344, or *ḳaṣâṣu,* H. W. B. 590, or *maṣâru,* H. W. B. 422, which all mean 'to cut, cut off.' *GU,* according to Thureau-Dangin, R. S. 1897, p. 272, note 8, '*se compose de NI et ǦAL: ceci résulte clairement de la forme que ce signe présente dans les inscriptions d'Our-Nina* (*cf. le nom du père de ce roi, Gu-ni-du, jusqu'ici faussement lu Ni-ǧal-ni-du*).'

45. For *šeg,* comp. Z. A. ii. 211 = Br. 11193; *lipittu,* H. W. B. 383: *Umschliessung, Umhegung.* See also Déc. 2, ii. 2.

gi-gì, Br. 6336; *paḳâdu,* H. W. B. 534. Thureau-Dangin translates: '*Ninab comme une brebis dont on tond la laine* (?) *dans une enceinte il enferma.*'

III. 1. *gu,* Br. 3215 and 3223, *kišâdu, rêšu*; *gu-an-šu*: comp. ii. 31, *sag-an-*

mu-ru-gi	he turned.
Lugal-zag-[gi-si]	Lugalzaggisi,
lugal Unug-[ki-ga]	king of Erech,
lugal kalam-ma	king of the world,
ḳin-ḳin-ma	took care
(dingir) En-lil	of Enlil,
lugal [kur-kur-ra]	king of the lands
En-lil-[ki-a]	the Nippurian;
šukum (dingir) Innanna	sacrifices to Innanna
e-na-gid-[da]	he offered,
a-dug e-na-d[e]	and with good water he watered (them, i. e. the sacrifices).
ŠU-TUR	Prayer:
(dingir) En-lil	'Enlil,
lugal kur-kur-ra-ge	king of the lands,

šu. Both expressions seem to be the same. The *ge* in ii. 46, however, shows that *gu* refers to Kian, which two lines therefore ought to be translated as above.

6. *ḳin*, T. C. 294, Br. 10753; *šipru*, H. W. B. 683. *ḳin-ḳin* may be better taken as a verb: Br. 10754, *šitêu*, H. W. B. 632: '*etwas sich angelegen sein lassen, Sorge für etwas tragen, auf etwas bedacht sein.*' Translate: L. . . . took care of Enlil, and offered up sacrifices for Innanna. The *ma* contains the overhanging vowel; we ought therefore read probably: *gim-gim-ma*.

10. The first sign = T. C. 248, Br. 9928; *kurummatu*, H. W. B. 354.

11. *gid*, Br. 7514; *gaṣâṣu*, H. W. B. 590, Br. 7520; *ḳatâbu*, H. W. B. 599. Both verbs mean 'to cut.' Comp. with this Shalmanassar, Black Obel. l. 84; '*ḳîšâti ana ilâni rabûti ak-kis*; lit. I *cut* presents, i. e. I offered (brought) presents.

12. Second sign, T. C. 190, *dug* = *ṭâbu*. The last sign is probably *DE*: only the beginning is visible. T. C. 117, Br. 6730; *šaḳû ša iḳli*, H. W. B. pp. 685 and 479: *nîḳû*.

13. *ŠU-TUR* occurs again in Gudea B, ix. 12. Jensen translates there: '*zerstückeln*,' and explains in a note, '*tur* = *klein*, *šu-tur* = *klein machen*,' see K. B. iii[1]. p. 48, note ††. Thureau-Dangin translates '*prière*,' and adds: '*le sens de "prière," "invocation," "dédicace," est rendu assez probable par notre passage.*' He is right. In both passages, i. e. in Gudea and here, the verbs follow always with one of the precative particles prefixed (*ḫa-*, *ḫu-*, *ḫe*), except in l. 43; see below. See also Hommel's explanation of *ŠU-nin-TUR-la-bi* in S. L. p. 109.

dingir a ki-ag-mu (sic)	the god my beloved father,
nam-?-mu	my . . .
ĝe-na-bi	may he decree;
nam-ti-mu	to my life
nam-ti	life
ĝa-ba-taĝ-ĝi	may he add;
kur u-sal-la	the land in peace
ĝa-mu-da-nà	may he make to rest;
nam-(ga)lu-ḳal	the soldiery,
u-rig-gim	like flowers (grass),
šu-dagal ĝa-mu-ru-dug	with loving hands may he establish it;
zag an-na-ge	of the heavenly folds (=sanctuaries)
si-ĝa-mu-ru-di	may he take care.
kalam-e	Upon the world

16. *a*, Br. 11324, *abu*. For *ni* read *mu*, on account of the *mu* in ll. 17 and 19, and the *ĝe-men* in l. 36.

17. The second sign has not yet been identified. It also occurs in some of the dates of the E. A. H. collection (Nos. 108, 109), where it has been translated by 'cult.' See Ur IV., uncertain dates, 4.

18. *bi*, Br. 5124; *ḳibû*, H. W. B. 577; *tamû*, H. W. B. 708.

19. *nam-ti* or *nam-ti-la*, Br. 2133, *balâtu*.

21. *taĝ*, Hommel, Sum. Les. No. 151; Br. 4535, *eṣêpu*; H. W. B. 308.

22. Comp. ii. 17.

23. Comp. ii. 18.

24. *nam-(ga)lu-ḳal*. See Cône of Entemena, col. iii. 22. The variant for *ḳal* gives *ra*, comp. i. 35; ought we to translate, therefore, 'The fate (*šîmtu*) for the people may he establish with loving hands like flowers'?

25. *u-rig*, Semitism! Br. 6053, *uriḳitu*, *urḳîtu*; R. A. iv. 74, 2; H. W. B. p. 243.

26. *šu-dagal*. Partly mutilated. *dagal*, Br. 5454, *râmu* = with loving hands. *dug*, Br. 533; *kunnu*, H. W. B. 321. Translate: the soldiery, like herbs (plants), with loving hands may he establish it.

27. *zag*, T. C. 101; Br. 6475, *ešrêti*. *zag-an*, Br. 6499 (*usug*) = *ešrêti*. The *ge* shows that *an-na* = *šamû*. 'Sanctuaries of heaven' = 'heavenly sanctuaries.' E. C. 414 identifies *ZAG* with Br. 5558: *amaš* = *suburu* '*Hürde*.'

28. *si . . . di*, Br. 3461; *išâru* = iii^2, H. W. B. 310.

29. *kalam*. This sign is here separated into two. On account of which, Hilprecht thinks that this sign is composed of *e* (canal) + *gi* (reed), and thus

ki-šag-ga	mercifully
igi-ĝa-mu-da-gab	may he lift up his eye;
nam-šag-ga	mercy,
mu-tar-ri-KU-a	which he has ordained,
šu-na mu-da-ni-ti-e-ne	into their hands (may) they (*e-ne*) receive it.
sib sag-gud-gàl	(I), the shepherd having the head of a steer,
da-er ĝe-men	may I be for ever.'
nam-ti-la-ni-ku	For his life
(*dingir*) *En-lil*	to Enlil,
lugal ki-ag-ni	his beloved king,
a-mu-na-šub	he has consecrated it.

denotes 'a piece of land intersected by canals and covered with reeds' (O. B. I. p. 252, note 9). But see for the present Delitzsch, E. S. p. 142 ff., who takes the very same signs to mean (being composed of three parts): '*grosses Gefüge von Leuten*.'

30. *šag*, T. C. 278; Br. 7291, *damku*.

31. *igi . . . gab*, Br. 9327, *našû ša êni*.

33. *tar*, Br. 381, *šâmu*, 'to ordain, decree.' In the original we have the signs thus: *mu-tar-ri-ku-a*. Probably we ought to read *mu-ku-tar-ri-a*. *ku* then would be verbal prefix; comp. Cône of Entemena, iii. 21. Or have we to suppose with Thureau-Dangin, R. S. 1897, p. 274, note 2, that *KU* is here '*postfixe verbal*'? But see note to C. T. 23287, l. 12. The *a* '*est l'indice de la relativité*.'

34. *ti*, Br. 1700, *laḳû*. Optative particle left out, which we would expect here.

35. *sib sag-gud*, and not *sib-sag-ta* (Thureau-Dangin). *TA* is not written thus; comp. i. 46; ii. 5, et passim. *gàl*, Br. 2238, *bašû*; lit. a shepherd (*sib*) having (*gàl*) the head (*sag*) of an ox (*gud*) = 'the ox-headed shepherd,' a synonym of a king according to Jensen, O. B. I. p. 252, note 4. Thureau-Dangin: '*le pasteur qui se tient à la tête*.'

36. *da-er*, Semitism! Br. 6660, *dârû*, H. W. B. 213. *men*, Br. 10358, *anaku*. *ĝe-men* = *lû anaku*. Hilprecht, p. 269, note 3, translates *da-ur ĝe-me* by = 'he may pronounce (speak) for ever.'

40. *šub*, Br. 1435, 1434, *nadânu*, *nadû*, i.e. to dedicate (comp. נדה נֵדֶה 'gift,' Ezek. xvi. 33); Z. A. ii. 296; K. B. iii[1]. p. 26, note *o; Transactions of the Society of Biblical Archaeology, viii. 350; R. A. ii. p. 62; Tallquist, Babylonische Schenkungsbriefe, p. 9. Not = '*ersehen*,' as Hommel, Gesch. p. 302, translates; see O. B. I. p. 21, note i.

In connection with this text of Lugalzaggisi, Hilprecht, in O. B. I. pp. 266–268, discusses the following important questions:—

(1) The time of Lugalzaggisi.

(2) His nationality.

(3) The situation and identification of *Giš-BAN-ki*.

(4) The meaning of *lugal-kalam-ma* and *nam-lugal-kalam-e* respectively.

As regards the question of time, we have seen (p. 11 ff.) that Lugalzaggisi is not by any means as early as Hilprecht supposes him to be. On the contrary, instead of antedating Eannatum, he rather followed him.

With regard to the situation of Gishban, and its identification (i. e. that Gishban is not Ḫarran, as Hilprecht believes), we have heard, when discussing the Cône inscription of Entemena, that Gishban must be sought in the immediate neighbourhood of Shirpurla-Girsu, it being its northern neighbour, and that its territory extended from the Euphrates (or thereabouts) to the east of the Shatt-el-Ḫai; that the correct reading of its name probably is Gishuḫ, and that it has to be identified with the modern Djokha.

Leaving the fourth point for the present (see Naram-Sin), we proceed to consider the question of the nationality of Lugalzaggisi and his predecessors in the rule of Babylonia. With this is bound up the Sumerian question. Must we assume in Ancient Babylonia two nations, each with its own proper dialect, or was there but one people, using two different modes of writing?

Scholars of great eminence are arrayed on either side.

Among those who maintain that there is only one nation, the Semitic, may be noted especially Halévy and Thureau-Dangin. Scholars who hold that the 'Sumerians' formed the original population of Babylonia are, among others, Sayce, Hilprecht, Hommel, Haupt, Jensen, Lehmann, Delitzsch (Schriftsystem), and Weissbach. According to these authorities, the Sumerians invented the system of cuneiform writing, and had their own (agglutinative) language and grammar; later on, when the barbarians, called Semites, invaded the country, they adopted the system of writing invented by the Sumerians, to express by its help their own language.

Let us hear two scholars who may fairly be cited as representatives of these opposing views.

Hilprecht argues that Lugalzaggisi, although his inscription is written in *Sumerian*, is notwithstanding a *Semite*. He adduces three arguments for this view:—

(1) The Sumerian name Lugalzaggisi was probably adopted by him when he ascended the throne of Erech and of the 'kingdom of the world.' Lugalzaggisi [1], meaning: 'the king is filled with unchangeable power' (O. B. I. p. 265, note 4), must be read in Semitic something like *Sharru-mâlî-emûḳi-kêni*, O. B. I. p. 269 and note 1).

(2) The phrases 'from the lower sea of the Tigris and Euphrates to the upper sea,' 'from the rising of the sun to the setting of the sun,' and others remind us forcibly of the phraseology of the latest Assyrian monarchs. Ibid. p. 269, note 2.

(3) His use of the ideogram *da-er* (col. iii. 36) is doubtless of Semitic origin = *dârû*, 'eternal.'

1. As we are concerned here with texts and inscriptions preceding the time of Sharganisharâli, Naram-Sin, Âlusharshid, and others—who are acknowledged on both sides to be Semitic rulers, and their inscriptions accordingly Semitic—it is necessary to adduce arguments taken from inscriptions of those kings who are disputed as to their nationality, i. e. of the kings who preceded Lugalzaggisi.

The predecessors of Lugalzaggisi bear good Semitic names:—

Mesilim, king of Kish, may be read: *Parṣê-ušallim*, 'he keepeth the commands.'

Lugalshuggur = *šar-kur(um)mat-šamê*, 'the king is food of heaven.'

[1] This name also occurs at the time of Ur IV.; see C. T. 94-10-16, 10, rev. iii: *PA Lugal-zag-gi-si pa-al* (*sabrû*); C. T. 95-10-12, 20, obv. i: *Lugal-sag-gi-si engar*.

In connection with this name, we may invite attention to a remarkable argument of Hilprecht in O. B. I. p. 263, note 1. Hilprecht there endeavours to prove that the title patesi first of all 'characterizes its bearer according to his religious position.' To maintain this, he quotes the inscription of Mesilim, published in R. A. iii. p. 55. Unfortunately in the copy given there the first line was only represented by one sign, namely *DI* (it is, as we have seen, the second part of the name [*Me*]-*DI*=*silim*). 'The inscription,' he says, 'to which I refer had defied the united efforts of Oppert, Heuzey, and myself for a long while. But I am now able to offer the following *correct*[1] interpretation.'

He then reads and translates it as follows:—

Sa!	Decision!
lugal	Ninsugir (l. 6)
Kish	has appointed (l. 7)
sanga	the king (l. 2)
(*ilu*) *Nin-su-gir*	of Kish (l. 3)
(*ilu*) *Nin-su-gir*	to be priest (l. 4)
mu-gin	of Ningirsu (l. 5).
Lugal-kurum-zigum	Lugalkurumzikum
pa-te-si	is patesi
Shir-[*pur*]-*l*[*a-ki*]	of Shirpurla.

And then argues, 'The whole phraseology seems to be Semitic rather than Sumerian (cf. also *sanga*, artificial ideogram composed of *sa*+*ga*). The name means Sharrukurumatshamê, "the king is food of heaven,"' and to make it especially clear that this king is indeed a Semite, he adds in parentheses, '*der König ist Himmelsspeise*.' 'A *foreign*[1] conqueror of Shirpurla, who is already a king, in addition styles himself patesi of Lagash.' So far Hilprecht.

This 'foreign conqueror' is, as we have seen, none other than the patesi of Shirpurla; he is in subjection to the *Sa!* i. e. to [Me]silim, king of Kish, for the inscription should be translated:—

[1] Italicized by me.

1 [Me]silim,
2 king
3 of Kish,
4 high-priest (? or builder) of the house
5 of Ningirsu,
6 to Ningirsu
7 has presented it.
8 Lugalshuggur
9 is patesi
10 of Shirpurla.

The important point in Hilprecht's contention, however, is that he makes Lugalkurumzikum a Semite, who (according to his understanding was king of Kish, but actually) is a very old patesi of Shirpurla. But there are other kings of Shirpurla who bear Semitic names :—

Ur-Ninâ	may be read	*Kalbi*[1]*-Ninâ*, 'servant of Ninâ.'
Eannatum	" "	*Bît-šamê-ukîn*, 'the house of heaven is stable.'
Enannatum	" "	*Bêl-šamê-ukîn*, 'the lord of heaven is righteous' (true, stable).
Entemena	" "	*Bêl-temenn*$^{a}_{i}$, 'the lord is a (or of) foundation.'
Engegal	" "	*Bêl-ḫigalli*, 'lord of riches.'
Enshagkushanna	" "	*Bêl-muštâl(i)-šamê*, 'lord is the wise one of heaven.'
Ur-Ba'u	" "	*Kalbi-Ba'u*, 'servant of Ba'u.'
Gudea	" "	*Nâbiu*, 'preacher.'
Dungi	" "	*Ba'u-ukîn*, 'Ba'u has established.'

Enakalli = *Bêl-emûḳi*[2], 'lord of strength.' Comp. also the writing *Ili* with that of *Il-li*, which latter is undoubtedly the phonetic writing of the former (Cône, iii. 28, 34), the phonetic compl. *iti*(*ti*), Galet A, ii. 10. See also Lugalkigubnidudu = *šarru-manzazu-*

[1] For the reading of *UR* = *Kalbi* or *Kalab*, see Hommel, P. S. B. A. xxi. p. 132.

[2] Or *Bêl-emûḳi-danni*. Comp. however Br. 6597, (*dingir*) *à-kal-maǧ* = *Adar bêl emûḳi*. But if this name is Semitic, then his son (?) Urlumma is also Semitic, probably = *Kalbi-unnubi*?

ušaklil, 'the king has finished the place,' and Lugalkisalsi = *šarru-šâpik-kisalli*, 'the king is the builder of the terrace.'

The above-given names show conclusively that the representatives of the dynasties of Kengi, Shirpurla[1], Gishban, Erech, at this time bore good Semitic names—a fact which, so far as it goes, would lead us to class them under the *Semitic* rulers of *Early Babylonia*.

2. As regards Hilprecht's second argument, that Lugalzaggisi must be a Semite, because certain of his phrases remind us forcibly of those of the latest Assyrian monarchs, it will suffice to call the attention of the reader to a certain passage occurring in the statue B, col. v. 25–27, of Gudea, who is generally regarded as the ruler who '*bezeichnet den eigentlichen Höhepunkt der sumerischen Cultur*' (Hommel, Gesch. p. 312). That passage reads: *a-ab-ba igi nim(a)-ta a-ab-ba sig-ga-ku*, i. e. 'from the upper sea to the lower sea'; comp. Lugalzag. ii. 8, 9, 4, 5.

According to Hilprecht's argument, Gudea would fulfil two requirements which would justify us in calling him a Semite: he has a good Semitic name, and uses good Semitic phrases. And if Gudea is a Semite, clearly his son Ur-Ningirsu must be one also. Thus one (the other is Ur-Ba'u = *Kalbi-Ba'u*) of the representatives of the height of the *sumerische Cultur* becomes a Semite.

3. But how is it with Hilprecht's third argument? Can we similarly adduce *Semitisms* occurring in the inscriptions of the kings of Shirpurla, Kish, &c.? Certainly we can.

Let us begin with *Shirpurla*. The most important for our purpose are:—

ul-la, Urukagina, Clercq, ii. pl. viii. col. v. 3; Entemena Cône, vi. 5.
= Assyr. *ullû*, √ אלה, H. W. B. p. 65; Hebr. עלה, Arab. علا.

e-ḫe-gal-kalam-ma, Urukag. Barrel-Cyl. i. 7.
= Assyr. *bît-ḫigalli-kalâmi*.

[1] If Ur-Ninâ is a Semite, then his son Akurgal is also. How this name may be read in Semitic is hard to say, probably *Amêl* (or *apil* = *a*?)-*Bêl* (*kur-gal*, see above).

zu-ab, Ur-Ninâ, Déc. 2bis, No. 1, passim.
= Assyr. *apsu*; comp. Hebr. אֶפֶס. Comp. Hommel, Neue Kirchliche Zeitung, 1890, p. 410. See however Hilprecht, O. B. I. p. 255, note 6.

da-er, Déc. 4ter, F², iv. 3; Lugalzaggisi, O. B. I. 87, iii. 36; comp. O. B. I. p. 261, note 4; H. W. B. 213.
= Assyr. *dârû* √ דור; comp. دار, تار, طار; Hebr. דּוֹר; Arab. تارة, الدَّهْرُ, דור ודור, Ps. lxi. 7, and בְּכָל־דֹּר וָדֹר, Ps. xlv. 18.

sa-ga, inscript. of Mesilim.
= Assyr. *šangû*. We ought to read, however, here = *e-ru*.

ĝa-lam, Galet A, iv. 19; Cône, vi. 20.
= Assyr. *ḫalâḳu*, see H. W. B. p. 280, under ii[1] ('*künstlich aus ḪALAGGA gebildet*'); comp. Hebr. חָלַק ii.; Aram. חֲלַק, ܫܚܠܩ, חוּלְקָה, ሐለቀ. See also Delitzsch, Assyr. Gram. p. 115, § 49, note.

ab-ba, Cône, i. 3.
= Assyr. *abu*, Hebr. אָב, Aram. אַבָּא, ܐܒܐ; أَب, አብ.

gi-na, Cône, i. 4.
= Assyr. *kênu*, √ כון, H. W. B. p. 321; comp. Hebr. כון, הֵיכִין, كان, ܟܘܢ, ኮነ.

dam-ḫa-ra[1], Cône, i. 26.
≐ Assyr. *tamḫaru*; a T-formation of the √ מחר; contained in the Hebr. מְחִיר.

kalam-ma, Lugalzag. i. 5; comp. Barrel-Cyl. i. 7.
= Assyr. *kalâmu* (?), √ כלה; H. W. B. 329; comp. Hebr. כָּלָה; comp. also כֹּל, كُلّ.

um-ma-an[2], unpublished Cône of Urukag.; see R. A. iv. 73, note 4.

[1] It will be noticed here that in the words *dam-ḫa-ra*, *maš-ga-na*, *u-rig*, *sa-dug*, *zig-ga*, the soft consonants *d*, *g* become later on hard = *t*, *k*, even *ḳ*; comp. also *gu-za* = כִּסֵּא; *li-il-gu-tu* in O. B. I. Nos. 1 and 2 = *lilḳutu*; *A-ga-de* = *Ak*(*k*)*ad*. On the other hand, comp. *u-sa-za-ku-ni*, *zêra-su* (*sub-ú-la-ṭi*), where the older *s* (is this Arabic influence?) becomes later on *š*. The use of ד for ת, ג for ק is probably due to the '*Vulgär-Babylonisch*.'

[2] Comp. also Haupt, Akkadische u. Sumerische Keilschrifttexte, No. 10 (K.

= Assyr. *ummânu*, √ probably = אמם; comp. אֻמָּה, أُمَّة, ܐܘܡܬܐ.

maš-ga-na[1], R. S. 1897, p. 168, col. iv.
= Assyr. *maškânu*; M-formation of שׁכן; Hebr. שָׁכֵן; سكن, ܥܡܪ; comp. מִשְׁכָּן, Aram. מִשְׁכַּן (and מַשְׁכּוֹנָא), ܡܫܟܢܐ (ܡܫܟܢܐ).

u-rig[1], O. B. I. 87, iii. 25 (Lugalzaggisi).
= Assyr. *urḳu, urḳîtu*, ורק, H. W. B. 243; comp. Hebr. יֶרֶק, יָרָק, وَرَاق, ܝܘܪܩܐ. (Originally: *uriḳu, uriḳîtu*, then shortened to *urḳu, urḳîtu*; comp. *epiru, epru*; *gimiru, gimru*; *Arimu, Armu*; *Aribu, Arbu.*)

sa-dug[1], le Clercq, ii. pl. viii. col. iv. 3.
= Assyr. *sattûku*, H. W. B. 513; comp. Hebr. צְדָקָה, Arab. صَدَقَة, Syr. ܙܕܩܬܐ (Hommel).

zig-ga[1], Galet A, Eannatum, iv. 26.
= Assyr. *zâḳu*; comp. Hebr. זיקות, Isa. 50. 11; √ not זנק, nor ܙܢܩ, but זיק, H. W. B. 252. Comp. also ܙܐܩܐ.

šu-nir, Galet A, iii. 17.
= Assyr. *šurinnu.*

But the most important of all is, that we find on a fragment of a marble slab from Abu Habba, published in O. B. I. pl. vi, vii, viii, which is undoubtedly much older than Sargon I.[2] (3800), instead of the so-called 'Sumerian' form *šu-ba-ti* (i.e. 'he (they) received'), the forms:—

im-ḫur, pl. vi. col. ii. 9; ibid. col. iv. 3 (from end), col. v, vi; pl. vii. col. v, vi.
im-ḫur-ru, pl. vi. col. vii. l. 9; pl. vii. col. i; pl. viii. No. 17; and
im-ḫur-ra, pl. vii. col. vi. l. 7.

So large a number and variety of Semitisms to be found in the texts of these kings, who are generally supposed to be Sumerians,

133), 25/26: *ḳar-ra-du-um-bi* = *ḳar-rad-su-ni*; and iv. R. No. 1, obv., 21: *za-ba-lam-a-ni* = *ḫi-ṣib-ša* (personal communication of Prof. Hommel).

[1] See note 1 on previous page.

[2] Comp. e. g. the forms of *ŠU* and *DA*, where 'the thumb is pressed on the fingers'; see p. 8.

surely suffices to show that almost *all* the kings of whom we have any notice may be, and probably are, Semitic kings.

But does this justify us in saying, with Thureau-Dangin, '*nous écarterons l'hypothèse d'une langue non sémitique*,' R. A. iv. p. 73, and call the two modes of writing (the Semitic and the Sumerian) '*l'un où domine le phonétisme, l'autre où domine l'idéographisme*'? It is true, when that scholar says (ibid.): *le phonétisme paraît avoir été dégagé de l'idéographisme dès une très haute antiquité par les habitants de la Babylonie du Nord. . . . Avec les rois d'Agadé le phonétisme se complète et tend en même temps à se répandre de plus en plus, ainsi qu'en témoignent les inscriptions de Kish, qui, idéographiques avec Me-silim, Ur-zag-ud-du, et Lugal-tar-si, deviennent phonétiques avec les rois . . . Uru-mu-uš et Ma-an-iš-tu-su*'—but the difficulty here is this: if the people at so remote a time as 4200 B.C. could use and write and understand two such widely different modes of writing (the '*idéographisme*' and '*phonétisme*'), and if Ḫammurabi (about 2288 B.C.) could write his inscriptions in two columns, the 'ideographic' and 'phonetic' column, how extremely educated and highly civilized must people have been at this distant epoch!

This presupposes a civilization and learning so high and developed as to be without precedent in the history of mankind. For such a development we must in any case postulate a long series of centuries. And further, to call the 'Sumerian' mode of writing 'ideographic' is not quite *ad rem*.

If we have such forms as *ĝul*, *mu-ĝul*, *ba-ĝul*, the first one may be called 'ideographic' and primitive, but the second and third forms cannot. *Mu* and *ba* simply show that *ĝul* has to be taken as a verb, and not as an adjective. *Mu* and *ba* indicate the *person* of the verb and nothing else; they do not belong to the ideogram. And how shall we explain the 'infixes' and 'postfixes,' the verb formation, and all the other peculiarities of this '*idéographisme*'? how the tablets and syllabaries and hymns, and other historical inscriptions occurring in these two modes of writing? All these facts surely prove conclusively enough the existence of two different languages, the Sumerian and the Semitic (see a very able discussion of this subject in Lehmann's Šamaššumukîn, and Weissbach, Die Sumerische Frage, especially pp. 150 ff.). Seeing that Semitisms occur in almost all the earliest inscriptions so far known to us, and that the rulers themselves may have been and probably were Semites—let us confess this—then the other question arises: At what time did the Semites come into the country, so as to induce the original inhabitants to employ expressions foreign to their own language? *Where did they come from?*

To the last question, which has been repeatedly discussed by scholars, different answers have been given. Some make Africa the original home of the Semites; others, Arabia; and Hilprecht, who last spoke of this problem, assigns for this purpose Kish, or better, Ḫarran, in the extreme north of Babylonia.

According to his theory, Lugalzaggisi, the great conqueror from Gishban (Ḫarran), was the first Semite to occupy any territory in Babylonia, and thus opened the way for the Semitic population. But Lugalzaggisi *does not antedate* Ur-Ninâ (see above, p. 9 ff.). Ur-Ninâ is a Semite, as we have seen, consequently Semites were in the country *before* Lugalzaggisi.

Gishban is not Ḫarran, but the neighbouring state of Shirpurla; hence the Semites did not come from Ḫarran, but actually occupied already the whole country of Babylonia. Thus the two questions—when did the Semites invade Babylonia? and whence did they come?—are still awaiting an answer. It is possible that some tablets may give us a key to this problem, but so far these tablets have not been found.

But further, if the Semites at so early a time as 4500 B.C. (Urukagina) had possession of Babylonia and had adopted the old language of the country, which language they interspersed with their own idiom, they must have been for a *long* time resident in the land. This would bring the immigration of the Semites back to at least 5000 B.C. and earlier, when the Sumerian power began to decay. We must therefore push back the height of Sumerian influence to a yet more remote period.

Hence, whatever view we take in regard to the two peoples and their languages, we are led to the same general result. *Civilization and history must go back to at least* 6000 B.C.[1]

The First Dynasty of Ur.

Of Ur[2]—the Biblical 'Ur of the Chaldees'—we have already heard at the time of Eannatum. It was situated on the western side of the Euphrates, opposite the place where the Shatt-el-Ḫai flows into it. Up to the time of Lugalzaggisi it may not have been of very great importance. This latter ruler, however, 'raised it like a steer to the top of the heaven' (col. ii. 30); hence, at no long period subsequent to Lugalzaggisi, we meet two kings, father and son, ruling at Ur. It is not impossible that this dynasty may itself have brought about the overthrow of Lugalzaggisi[3], as to whose successors we have no information[4]. Probably also it took possession of the more northern part of Babylonia (Nippur), for we find that both these kings present vases to Enlil, the 'lord of the lands.'

The names of these two monarchs forming the *first* dynasty of Ur are—

Lugalkigubnidudu[5], and his son[6] (?)
Lugalkisalsi.

[1] For further discussion of the historical relation between the Semitic and Sumerian tongues, see *sub* Kings of Guti and Lulubi, p. 178 ff.

[2] For a history of the excavations that went on at Ur (now called Mugheir), see Taylor's and Loftus' Travels, &c., and Hommel, Geschichte, pp. 113 ff., 212 ff.

[3] If I understand the text correctly, this opinion may be found in the words: 'when Enlil . . . added lordship to kingdom, establishing *Erech* as (the seat of) the lordship.' Erech, which he established as '(the seat of) the *lordship*,' then was *added* to his kingdom.

[4] Among the successors of Lugalzaggisi probably has to be placed a certain Ezuab, king of Gishban-*ki*. See Déc. pl. 5, No. 3. Nothing but the name of this king has come down to us.

[5] His inscriptions are to be found in O. B. I. Nos. 23, 24, 25, 86, and 88; No. 86 translated by Hilprecht, ibid. pp. 271 and 272, note 1.

[6] This is most probable, because in O. B. I. No. 86, pl. 37, both these rulers are mentioned on the same tablet. Comp. also O. B. I. 89; Hilprecht, ibid. p. 272, note 3.

Their dominion extended over Ur, Erech, and Nippur, probably also over Shirpurla, for the kings of the south could not have gained possession of Nippur without passing Shirpurla. This would explain why we know so very little about Shirpurla at this time. It is, however, remarkable that both these kings, in O. B. I. 86, pl. 37, should call themselves first 'kings of Erech' and then 'kings of Ur'; while, on the other hand, Lugalkigubnidudu, in pl. 36, expressly says that Enlil added (*tab*) the lordship (*nam-en*) to the kingship (*nam-lugal*), which lordship so added was, according to ll. 9–11, *Erech*. We would expect that, if he were originally king of Ur, the title 'king of Ur' would come first. Here then we have an analogy to and a confirmation of the argument used in regard to Urzaguddu. The latter king had also two titles, viz. 'king of Kish' and 'king of . . .,' and it was argued that the latter title, 'king of . . .,' was the original, i. e. Urzaguddu became later on 'king of Kish.' So here 'king of Ur' was the original title; Lugalkigubnidudu subsequently became 'king of Erech [1].'

How long this dynasty flourished, how many rulers were comprised in it, and when and by whom it was overthrown, we cannot tell. Probably, however, it was replaced by a mighty kingdom which arose in the north (that of Agade) [2], destined to bear sway over 'the four corners of the world.'

The inscriptions of these two kings follow.

O. B. I. No. 86, according to Hilprecht, reads:

(dingir) En-lil	i. e.	When Enlil,
lugal-kur-kur-ge		king of the lands,

[1] Comp. also the inscription of Enne-Ugun, l. 13 ff., where the title 'king of Kish' follows that of 'king of the hordes of Gishban,' or better, that of 'king of Uḫ' (?).

[2] In the above arrangement, as was already stated, we chiefly follow Hilprecht; our own impression, however, is that the first dynasty of Ur followed *upon* that of Agade, although we are not able to adduce any decisive arguments in favour of this view. See also p. 18, note 3.

Lugal-ki-gub-ni-du-du-ra	to Lugalkigubnidudu—
ud (*dingir*) *En-lil-li*	when Enlil
gu-zi-e (sic)-*na-de-a*	announced life (to him),
nam-en	(when) lordship
nam-lugal-da	to kingship
e (sic)-*na-da-tab-ba-a*	he added,
Unug-^{ki}*-ga*	having made
nam-en	Erech
mu-ag-ge	the (capital of the) lordship,
Uru-um-^{ki}*-ma*	(and) having made
nam-lugal	Ur
mu-ag-ge	the (capital of the) kingship;
Lugal-ki-gu[*b*]*-ni-d*[*u-du-ne*]	then Lugalkigubnidudu
nam-gal-ĝul-la-da	for the great and joyful lot
(*dingir*) *En-l*[*il*]	to Enlil,
lu[*gal-ni*]	his king,
[*a-mu-na-šub*]	presented this.

3. According to Hilprecht, *Sharru-manzazu-ushaklil*, 'the king finished the place.'

5. *sic* Hilprecht. Better: 'Enlil, king of the lands, to Lugalkigubnidudu, when Enlil with a propitious voice had called him.' Comp. R. S. 1897, p. 269, note 2. *gu-de-a* = *nabû*.

8. *tab*. Hommel, Sum. Les. 117 = *radû* ii[1].

15. *ne* = 'this'; comp. O. B. I. 23: (*dingir*) *En-lil-la Lugal-ki-gub-ni-du-du-ne, a-mu-na-šub*; Hilprecht, l. c. p. 260, note 3. O. B. I. Nos. 24 and 25, however, read: (*dingir*) *En-lil Lugal-ki-gub-ni-du-du a-mu-na-šub*, without the '*ne*.'

16. *ĝul* = *ḫadû*, *ḫidûtu*.

O. B. I. 86, pl. 37, may be read:

[(*Dingir*) *En-lil*]	To Enlil,
[*lugal-kur-kur-ra-ge*]	king of the lands,
Lugal-ki-gub-ni-du-du	Lugalkigubnidudu,
lugal Unug-^{ki}*-ga-ge*	king of Erech,
lugal Uru-um-^{ki}*-ma-ka-ge*	king of Ur,

Lugal-si-kisal	and Lugalsikisal,
lugal Unug-^{ki}-gá-ge	king of Erech,
lugal Uru-um-^{ki}-ma	king of Ur,
nam-ti-la-ku	for their life,
$^{(dingir)}$ *En-lil*	to Enlil,
lugal-ni	their king,
a-mu-na-šub	they presented (it).

6. *Lugal-si-kisal* is written in O. B. I. No. 89, *Lugal-kisal-si*. The name means: 'The king is builder of the terrace' = *Šarru-šâpik-kisalli*.

The Patesis of Shirpurla between Lummadur and Ur-Ba'u.

Once more—before we leave southern Babylonia and pass over to the north—we have to direct our attention to Shirpurla. The traces which we possess of the life of Shirpurla and its patesis during this time (i. e. 4100 B. C.—3800 B. C.) are but fragmentary. Only one patesi is known to us from a tablet recently published by Thureau-Dangin in R. A. iv. No. iii. pl. iii. No. 9 (see the translation given on p. 16). This patesi, Lugalanda by name, cannot have lived very long after Lummadur, for the writing of that tablet shows all the palaeographic peculiarities of the inscriptions of Eannatum. Comp. e. g. the sign for 'king,' which is written here *gal+galu*, and the sign for *DA* has still the 'thumb' curved. Probably he belonged to those patesis over whom Lugalzaggisi or his successors may have ruled.

With the next two patesis, Lugalushumgal[1] and his son (?) (see p. 20) Ur-E, we arrive at the time of Sharganisharâli, 3800 B. C. A considerable gap in this period has still to be filled up. Let us

[1] The name *Lugal-ušum-gal* occurs on the following tablets:—

R. A. iv. No. iii. pl. vii. 23; pl. viii. 25, 27, 28; pl. ix. 29, 30; pl. x. 32, 33; pl. xi. 34.

R. A. iv. No. i. p. 5, 8, 11.

Comptes Rendus, 1896 (Dates of Sargon I. and Naram-Sin, by Thureau-Dangin), Reprint, p. 9, 1; p. 10, 3, 4.

hope that the future excavations, combined with the industry of the decipherer, will bring some light into this darkest of all periods in Old Babylonian history.

Mentioning only another patesi that belongs to this period, *Ur-(dingir) Utu* (?)[1]—whose name is followed by [*nam ?*] *patesi Uru-um-ki-ma* (i. e. Ur) (R. A. iv. 78, and note 1; ibid. pl. ix. 31, 8, 9, and xv. 9)—we pass from the south to the north of Babylonia, i. e. to the city of *Agade*.

Kings of Agade.

Agade, near the modern Abu-Habba, formed in olden times, with Sippar, a double city. It was situated near the Euphrates and north of Babylon. As early as 3800 B.C., Semitic kings ruled in this city, extending their sceptres over the whole of Babylonia.

The first king, as far as our knowledge goes, was Sharganisharâli[2],

[1] In any case, whether the name of this patesi of Ur be Ur-Utu or not, it does not matter: this, however, is of historical importance, that at the time of Lugalushumgal and Naram-Sin (Sargon) there were in Ur *patesis*, thus showing that the successors of the kings of the first dynasty of Ur had been reduced to patesis by the king of the 'four quarters of the world.'

[2] For the meaning of his name, see note to O. B. I. No. 1, l. 3.

His inscriptions :—

iii. R. 4, No. 7 (legend); Winckler, K. B. iii[1]. p. 100, Anhang 1.

v. R. 34 (*omina*); Winckler, ibid. p. 102 ff.

O. B. I. Nos. 1, 2, 3; Oppert, R. A. iii. p. 20 ff.; and Hilprecht in the introduction to O. B. I. part i. p. 15.

To the kings of Agade belongs also O. B. I. 119: *A-ga-de-ki* | *a-na* | (*ilu*) *Bêl A-MU-ŠUB* (*iddin*).

Proc. Soc. Bibl. Arch. 1885, p. 68; Winckler, K. B. iii[1]. p. 100, No. 1; A. B. K. No. 64.

Léon Heuzey, R. A. iv. p. 3, with Gilgamish legend. It reads :

Šar-ga-ni-šar-âli	O Sharganisharâli,
šar	king
A-ga-de-ki	of Agade,
. . . *ne-šu-in-ta*	. . . . .
apil Šum-(ilu) Ma-lik	the son of Shummalik

cited by us as Sargon I. He was the son of a certain Itti-Bêl[1]. This latter is neither called a king nor even a patesi. In this we may see a confirmation of the so-called 'legend of Sargon,' according to which this monarch was 'of an inferior birth on his father's side,' and so either a *usurper* or the founder of this dynasty of Agade. This legend—probably written in the eighth century B. C.—purports to be a copy of an inscription found on a statue of this great king, and bears a certain similarity to the Biblical account of Moses. It reads: 'Shargena, the powerful king, the king of Agade, am I. My mother was of noble family (?) (others: was poor), my father I did not know, whereas the brother of my father inhabited the mountains. My town was Azipirânu, which is situated on the bank of the Euphrates. My mother of noble family (? or, who was poor) conceived me and gave birth to me secretly. She put me into a basket of shurru (reeds?), and shut up the mouth (?) of it (?) with bitumen; she cast me into the river, which did not overwhelm (?) me. The river carried me away and brought me to

šakkanâku (Br. 9195)	the shakkanâku
arad-ka (*nitaǧ-zu*)	is thy servant.

On the side: *a-na AL-LA*, i. e. to Alla.

Léon Heuzey, R. A. iv. p. 5 (with 'holy tree'), tablet is directed to Lugal-ushumgal, patesi of Shirpurla.

Ibid. p. 8, '*Lugal-ušum-gal . . . arad-ka.*'

Plans de l'époque de Sargon l'ancien et de Naram-Sin, by Thureau-Dangin, in R. A. iv. p. 20 ff.

C. J. Ball, Light from the East, p. 52.

Contract-tablets of the time of Sargon I. and Naram-Sin, Thureau-Dangin, R. A. iv. No. iii. No. 13–75.

Un Fragment de Stèle de Victoire d'un Roi d'Agadé, Thureau-Dangin, R. S. 1897, p. 166 ff.; also published in Déc. pl. 5bis, No. 3*a*–3*c*.

Inscriptions of Nabû-nâ'id, passim.

Ménant, Cat. de la Collection de le Clercq, i. pl. v. No. 461. It reads: *Šar-ga-ni-šar-âli, šar, A-ga-de-ki, Ib-ni-šarri, dup-sar arad-ka* (*NITAǦ-ZU*); see Hommel, Gesch. p. 302. Also published in A. B. K. No. 65; comp. Winckler, K. B. iii[1]. p. 100, No. 1.

Scheil, Listes onomastiques, rédigées d'après les Textes de Šargani, Z. A. xii. p. 331.

[1] Perhaps shortened from *Itti-Bêl-balâṭu*, 'with Bêl is life'; Hilprecht, O. B. I. p. 15, note 9.

Akki, the drawer of water. Akki, the drawer of water, took me up in . . . Akki, the drawer of water, reared me to boyhood. Akki, the drawer of water, made me a gardener. During my activity as gardener, Ishtar loved me. X + 4 years I exercised dominion, . . . years I commanded the black-headed people (i. e. the Semites) and ruled them,' &c.[1] The rest of this legend tells us something about his campaign against Dûrilu on the borders of Elam; it is however too fragmentary to be coherent.

In connection with this legend we would call the attention of the reader once more to the fact that not merely the identity of this Shargena with our Sharganisharâli[2], his deeds and warlike expeditions recorded in the so-called Tablet of Omens with the date of his rule, have been doubted, but even his very existence[3].

A series of new facts connected with the time of Naram-Sin and Sharganisharâli have since come to light by the publication of a great number of contract-tablets, written during the reign of these kings. These tablets are to be found in R. A. iv. No. iii. Hence it is now impossible to doubt the historicity of Sharganisharâli, as was done by Niebuhr, Chronologie der Geschichte Israels, Aegyptens, Babyloniens, und Assyriens, Leipzig, 1876, p. 75.

Down to the time of Hilprecht's publication of O. B. I. part i, our knowledge of Sargon I. was almost entirely drawn from the 'legend' and the 'Tablet of Omens.' Hence it happened that the great deeds which were attributed to Sargon and Naram-Sin in that 'Tablet of Omens' were said to be 'purely legendary' (so by

[1] See Winckler, K. B. iii[1]. p. 101 f.

[2] See above, p. 6 ff.

[3] This was mainly done because it seemed impossible that there could have existed at about 3800 B. C. (200 years after the Creation according to Usher!) such a mighty monarch. At the present stage of our knowledge of this period we are fully justified in saying, with Hilprecht (O. B. I. p. 241): 'Behind Sargon I. and Naram-Sin there lies a long and uninterrupted chain of development covering thousands of years; and those powerful rulers of the fourth millenium before Christ, far from leading us back to the "dawn of civilization," are at the best but two prominent figures from a middle chapter of the early history of Babylonia.'

Winckler, Geschichte Babyl. und Assyr. p. 38). Others thought that his deeds had been simply projected backwards (so Maspero, Dawn of Civilization, New York, 1895, p. 599: 'Sargon II. is he who is projected backward'); others again, not believing that Sargon I. could have undertaken such expeditions and have become practically the 'king of the four corners of the earth,' invented another king Sargon (so Hommel, Geschichte, Berl. 1883, p. 307, note 4; this Sargon he places at about 2000 B. C.).

Thanks to the excavations at Telloh and the industry and scholarship of Thureau-Dangin, we are now in a position to prove that the statements of the 'Tablet of Omens' are correct in almost every particular.

Let us hear what this 'Tablet of Omens' has to say (see iv. R². 34, and Winckler, K. B. iii¹. p. 103). Eleven of these 'omens' are ascribed to Sargon and three to Naram-Sin. They generally begin with the phrase: 'When the moon was in such and such position,' then Sargon, &c.

The first omen records Sargon's expedition to and subjection of Elam.

The second tells how he marched to the land Aḫarri[1] (i. e. the West-land), and subjected it, and that his army subjugated the *kibrâti irbitta*, i. e. 'the four corners of the world.'

The third (see above, p. 18) tells us that he brought sorrow upon Kish and Babylon, and built a city after the pattern (?) of Agade, and called it *UB-DA-^{ki}*, i. e. 'place (city) of the world.'

The fourth records another expedition against the west and the taking possession of the four corners of the earth. So also the fifth omen.

The sixth omen is too fragmentary to yield any certain sense.

The seventh gives us a fuller account of his expedition against Aḫarri[1]; he crosses the sea of the west and wages war against it for three years, takes it, erects there his statues, and transports the prisoners, whom he had taken, over land and sea.

[1] So Winckler; read *Mar-tu-^{ki}*.

The eighth describes the repairing of one of his palaces, which he calls '*E ki-a-am i-ni-lik*,' i. e. 'the house: "so let us walk."'

In the next we hear of a campaign against a certain Kashtubilla of Kaṣalla, who had revolted. Sargon goes against him, conquers him and his army, and destroys the rebellious country.

The tenth probably is one of the most important. It reads: 'Sargon, against whom under this omen the elders of the whole country had revolted, and in Agade had shut him up—Sargon went out, conquered them and cast them down, subdued their army, and . . .'

The last omen tells us something about Sargon's campaign against the land Suri, how he overcame it and took it, and how he destroyed its army.

The two omens relating to Naram-Sin record a campaign against Apirak (Omen i.) and against Magan (Omen ii.). In both expeditions Naram-Sin was so successful, that he even took captive the kings of these countries, viz. Rêsh-Rammân, king of Apirak, and N. N., king of Magan.

According to this 'Tablet of Omens,' then, Sargon I. subdued Elam, the 'West-land,' brought woe upon Babylon and Kish, conquered the country Kaṣalla, suppressed a revolt which had arisen against him while on his expeditions, and finally subdued the land Suri 'in its totality'; and Naram-Sin was successful in his expeditions against Apirak and Magan.

Can we prove from contemporary inscriptions of Sargon I. and Naram-Sin the correctness of the statements of this 'Tablet of Omens,' which confessedly is a later copy belonging to Ashurbanipal's library, made from an older inscription?

Thanks once more to the publications of Thureau-Dangin in Comptes Rendus, 1896, p. 355 ff., and in R. A. iv. No. iii., we are now in a position to do this. Among them we find tablets (pl. vi. No. 16, envers) which expressly record Sargon I.'s victory—

(*a*) over Elam (comp. Omen i.).

In ištênit ša[tti][1] In the year when

[1] Written *IN I. MU.*

Šar-ga-ni-šar-âli	Sargon I.
KASKAL-MÈ[1] *Elamtu-*[*ki*]	made a warlike expedition against Elam
ù Za-ḫa-ra[*-a ?*]	and against Zaḫara,
in ${}^{b}_{p}$*u-ti*[2] *Uḫ-ki*	opposite to Uḫ,
ù SAG-GUB[3] *iš-ku-*[*nu*][4]	and [when he made] a *SAG-GUB*.

(*b*) over the West-land: Mar-tu-*ki* = Amurru = Aḫarru (Winckler). (Comp. Omen ii.)

L. c. pl. vi. No. 17:

In ištênit šatti	In the year when
Šar-ga-ni-šar-âli	Sargon I.
MAR-TU-am (read *Amurram*)[5]	against the land of the Amorites
[sc. *KASKAL-MÈ ba-gar-ra-a*]	[made a campaign.]

With this compare R. A. iv. p. 78, note 2, where Thureau-Dangin mentions a tablet in the Museum of Constantinople which partly reads: *šu-nigin* 10 *kal* (*ga*)*lu ša Martune-ki-me*, i.e. total: 10 slaves, men from the West-land.

(*c*) over Gutim (Kurdistan), whose king, Sharlak, he takes captive.

L. c. pl. v. No. 15 (written in Sumerian):

Lugal-ušum-gal	Lugalushumgal
pa-te-si	patesi[6].

[1] *KASKAL*, Br. 4454: *ḫarrânu*, H. W. B. 291; *Zug, Feldzug*; *MÈ*, Br. 2804, *taḫâzu*. Thureau-Dangin translates *KASKAL-MÈ iškun* by *le joug . . . a imposé.*

[2] For in ${}^{b}_{p}$*u-ti*, see H. W. B. p. 517 = *ina pûti*.

[3] *SAG-GUB* (= *LI*), Sayce, P. S. B. A., Jan. 1899, p. 22 = 'boundary-stone.' Thureau-Dangin, 'tribute.'

[4] *iškunu*. Thus we should read, according to R. A. iv. iii. pl. v. 13; hence we must supply a *ša* before Sharganisharâli.

[5] According to Thureau-Dangin this line is followed in a variant from the Museum of Constantinople by *in ba-sa-ar šadê*, i. e. '*dans les escarpements des montagnes*' (Compt. Rend., 1896, Reprint, p. 10).

[6] So in a variant from the Museum of Constantinople.

MU KASKAL-MÈ Gu-ti-um-ki ba-gar-ra-a	In the year when (the king) made a campaign against Gutim.

Ibid., No. 13:

In ištênit šatti	In the year when
[Šar]-ga-ni-šar-âli	Sargon I.
[UŠ-SIG[1]*-bî]t (ilu) A-nu-ni-tim*	established the *UŠ-SIG* of the temple of Anunitim
[û UŠ-SIG bî]t (ilu) A-E	and the *UŠ-SIG* of the temple of *A-E*
in Bâb-ili-ki	in Babylon,
iš-ku-nu	and when he
û d. Šar-la-ak	took captive
šar Gu-ti-im-ki	Sharlak (in Assyr. = *Etel-la-ibni*?),
ik-mi-û[2]	the king of Gutim.

(*d*) over Erech and .... *su-ki* (Compt. Rend., 1896, Reprint, p. 10, No. 4[3]).

[1] *UŠ-SIG.* Thureau-Dangin, R. A. iv. p. 22: '*les assises*'; Sayce, P. S. B. A., Jan. 1899, p. 22, note 1: 'platform?' Anunit is, according to iii. R. 66, 3, 24, obv., 5, the bêlit of Akkad.

[2] *ik-mi-û.* Uncontracted form in rel. clause for *ikmû*, √ כמה, H. W. B. 334.

[3] For other dated tablets from the time of Sargon I. and Naram-Sin, comp. Thureau-Dangin, Comptes Rendus, 1896, p. 355 ff., and Sayce, P. S. B. A., Jan. 1899, p. 22; and see R. A. iv. iii. pl. v. No. 14:

In ištênit šatti	In the year when
Šar-ga-ni-šar-âli	Sargon I.
[U]Š-SIG bît (ilu) Bêl	established the *UŠ-SIG* of the temple
[in] Nippur-ki	of Bêl
[iš-ku-nu]	in Nippur.

L. c. pl. vi. No. 18 (written in Sumerian):

mu E-GIŠ-KIN-TI ba-ru.	In the year when the king built the temple of *GIŠ-KIN-TI*.

L. c. pl. vi. No. 19 (comp. R. A. iv. p. 22):

In ištênit šatti	In the year when
(ilu) Na-ra-am-(ilu) Sin	Naram-Sin

Lugal-ušum-gal	Lugalushumgal
pa-te-si	patesi.
mu KASKAL-MÉ	In the year when
Unug-ki-a	a campaign against Erech
ù . . . su-ki-a	and . . . *su*
(sc. *ba-gar-ra-a*)	he (either Sargon I. or Naram-Sin) made.

In these tablets the following lands are mentioned as standing in close business relations either with Shirpurla or with Agade: viz. Magan (bronze from Magan), Meluḫḫa, Elam, Az, Kish (*âlu Kiš-ki*), Nippur (No. 14), Ur (No. 31), Erech (No. 41), and Gishban (see R. A. iv. p. 78, note 6: 1,540 *udu* | 854 *uz* || *šu-nigin* 2,394 *udu-zun* | *udu Giš-ban-ki-kam* || *Ur-šid-e Unug-ki-ku mu-gub-gub*, i. e. 1,540 sheep, 854 (lambs); in all 2,394 sheep, sheep from the land of Gishban, Urshid has brought them to Erech). Among the names of cities which occur are *KA-DINGIR-ki* (= Babylon, No. 13, env. 6), *Ki-nu-nir-ki* (Borsippa), *Innanna-ab-ki* (No. 41, env. 3), *Uḫ-ki* (No. 41, env. 3), *Innanna-Erin-ki*, Sippar[1]; and, what is especially important, the following parts or suburbs of Shirpurla itself: *Gir-su-ki*, *Ninâ-ki*, *Erim-ki*. Hence the statements of this 'Tablet of Omens' can no longer be doubted. The 'ten slaves' from the West-land were undoubtedly the result of the victorious expeditions against the west. That Sargon I. was in possession of Nippur is not only evident from these contract-tablets, but also from O. B. I. No. 3, which reads:

UŠ-SIG bît (ilu) Bêl	established the *UŠ-SIG* of the
in Nippur-ki	temple of Bêl in Nippur,
[*ù*] *bît (ilu) Ištar*	and of the temple of
[*in In*]*nanna-ab-ki*	Ishtar
[*iš-ku-*]*nu.*	in Innanna-ab.

[1] C. J. Ball, Light from the East, p. 52: *Šar-ga-ni-šar-âli, šar, A-ga-de-ki, a-na, (ilu) Šamaš in (dingir) UD-KIB-NUN-ki* (= Sippar. For the sign *dingir*, comp. also O. B. I. 63, 6, 7: *Ka-da-aš-ma-an-Turgu, lugal (dingir) KA-DINGIR-RA-ki*) *A-MU-ŠUB* (= *iddin*).

Šar-ga-ni-šar-âli	i. e.	Sargon,
šar		king
A-ga-de-^{ki}		of Agade,
bâni (*BA-GIM*)		the builder
bît (*E*)		of the temple
$^{(ilu)}$ *Bêl* (^{dingir} *En-lil*)		of Bêl.

We have already seen (p. 7) that he exercised dominion over Shirpurla. Lugalushumgal was at this time patesi of that city. In his inscriptions he calls himself *arad-ka*, 'thy servant' (sc. Sargon's or Naram-Sin's). Indeed, we have some fragments of an inscribed '*stèle d'un roi d'Agadé*,' which—if we accept Thureau-Dangin's view—may refer to this very conquest of Sargon I. over Shirpurla and the dividing up of its territory (see R. S. 1897, p. 166 ff.). The dominion of Agade over Magan in the south-west is also apparent from a tablet of Naram-Sin himself; see i. R. 3, No. 7: *nam-ra-ag Magan*-^{ki}, the 'prince' of Magan. To the north the empire reached even as far as Apirak[1] and Guti, 'the land east of the lower Zâb, in the upper section of the region through which the Adhem and the Dijâlâ rivers flow' (Delitzsch, Parad. pp. 233–237), and over the whole of Armenia. This is evident from a tablet recently published by Thureau-Dangin in Comptes Rendus, 1899, p. 348, pl. 1, which reads:

	$^{(ilu)}$ *Na-ra-am*-$^{(ilu)}$ *Sin*	Naram-Sin,
	da-LUM (= *da-num*)	the mighty
	šar	king
	ki-ib-ra-tim	of the four
5.	*ar-ba-im*	corners of the world,
	SAG-GIŠ-RA (= *nêr*)	the conqueror
	Ar-ma-im-	of Armenia
	ù	and
	....	....

Thus the empire of Sargon I. and Naram-Sin extended from the

[1] This land has to be sought in the north-east of Babylonia; see Hilprecht, O. B. I. p. 22.

uttermost south of Babylonia, Erech, over Ur, Shirpurla, Babylon, Kish, Agade, and northward to Apirak and Guti, from the country of the Elamites in the east, over Dûrilu to Magan (on the eastern boundary of Arabia), and even to the land of the Amorites (Martu, Kaṣalla), which latter, i. e. Kaṣalla, is also mentioned in the inscriptions of Gudea as 'a mountain of Martu.'

So great and extensive a dominion might justly be called a *šarrût kibrat arba'im* (kingdom of the four corners of the world), and yet Sargon himself never assumes this title. He left that for his son, he himself being satisfied with '*šarru dannu šar Agade*,' 'the mighty king, king of Agade,' or '*dannu šar Agade*,' or only '*šar Agade*.' Nabû-nâ'id in his inscriptions calls Sargon I. '*šar Bâbili*,' king of Babylon, probably on account of the buildings erected there by him; comp. R. A. iv. No. 3, pl. v. 13, envers.

In contrast to his father, Naram-Sin assumes the title *šar kibrat arba'i*, 'king of the four quarters of the world.' The meaning of this title is evident. In the 'Tablet of Omens' we saw that Sargon, after having conquered Elam, 'subdued "the land of the west," conquered the four quarters of the world.' In other words: Sargon, being lord over the whole of Babylon (extending from the north to the south), and over Elam in the east, had still to conquer the *west*. Having succeeded in this, his son assumes the title 'king of the four corners of the world,' ruling over a kingdom bounded by the Elamite mountains in the east, the mountains of Armenia in the north, the Mediterranean Sea in the west, and the Persian Gulf in the south. The capital of this mighty kingdom was Agade.

The title '*šar kibrat arba'i*' *may*[1] have the same meaning and carry the same force as that old title of Lugalzaggisi, viz. '*lugal kalama*' (king of the world), which former title was later on translated back into the Sumerian by *lugal an-ub-da-tab-tab-ba*[2], but

[1] For this reason I refer the Semitic inscription of Dungi, which generally has been attributed to Dungi I. of the second dynasty of Ur, to Dungi III. of the fourth dynasty of the same city.

[2] This, however, is very doubtful, we may say even impossible—in spite of

it is not an equivalent of *šar kiššati* (Hilprecht, O. B. I. p. 270), because

(1) such a title is not known in those times; and

(2) *šar kiššati* has to be read *šar Kiš*, i. e. king of Kish (see above, p. 126, and below, p. 214 ff.).

These two rulers were not only mighty conquerors and heroes in war, but also great administrators of their vast dominion. They create high dignitaries, whose office it was to provide for the internal welfare of the country. Among these we find the judge (*daianu*), the *shabrû* (H. W. B. p. 639), and the *shakkanâku.*

Social and commercial life attained to a height it had never reached before. Business relations were maintained throughout all these subject regions. The entertainment of the people was entrusted to the musicians (R. A. iv. No. iii. pl. xi. No. 35, env. 8), while regularly constituted physicians (R. A. ibid. pl. x. No. 32, env. 6) cared for their bodily welfare. In short, we may rightly say, with Thureau-Dangin, l. c. p. 79: '*La remarquable impulsion donnée à toutes les branches de l'activité, par le plein épanouissement et le rayonnement dans toutes les directions d'un art, d'une culture, d'une civilisation dont le lent développement avait rempli les siècles et les millénaires précédents, l'époque de Sargan et de Naram-Sin marque certainement un point culminant dans l'histoire de l'ancien Orient.*'

Before we leave these two rulers, it may be well to notice one or two points of unique interest not previously mentioned. The first is, that these rulers sometimes write their names with the *ilu* (god) sign preceding, and that Naram-Sin—and he only—even calls himself *ilu Agade-ki*, 'god of Agade.' This use of *ilu* in the names $^{(ilu)}$ *Šar-ga-ni-šar-âli* and $^{(ilu)}$ *Na-ra-am-*$^{(ilu)}$ *Sin* is altogether new and unprecedented; even the writing of $^{(dingir)}$ *Ninâ-Ur* is not an exception, for this latter name is written by Eannatum *always*, and

Hilprecht, O. B. I. p. 270, according to whom the *šarrût kiššati* is the 'equivalent' of the Sumerian *nam-lugal-kalama*, which latter 'was translated' by the Semites under Sargon I. into the Semitic *šarrût kibrat arba'im*. 'And the later Sumerian *nam-lugal an-ub-da tab-tab-ba* is simply a translation of the Semitic title back into the sacred Sumerian language of Semitic scribes of the third millennium B. C.'

even by Ur-Ninâ *once* (see Déc. pl. 2bis, No. 1), in this wise: *Ur-*$^{(dingir)}$ *Ninâ*, showing that this latter is the correct way of reading and writing, and that the $^{(dingir = ilu)}$ does not belong to the whole name, but only to the goddess Ninâ [1].

One inscription of Naram-Sin, with this extraordinary title, *ilu A-ga-de-*^{ki}, has been given above, p. 7. Owing to the importance of this subject for the history of religions, we give the other inscriptions also:—

R. A. iv. No. iii. pl. vii. No. 22:

$^{(ilu)}$ *Na-ra-am-*^{ilu} *Sin*	Naram-Sin,
ilu A-ga-de-^{ki}	the god of Agade.

Ibid. No. 23:

$^{(ilu)}$ *Na-ra-am-*$^{(ilu)}$ *Sin*	O Naram-Sin,
ilu A-ga-de-^{ki}	god of Agade,
Šar-ru [2]*-iš-da-gal*	Sharruishdagal
dup-sar	the scribe
arad-ka (*NITAǴ-ZU*)	is thy servant.

In R. A. iv. No. iii. pl. vii. No. 26, we have even only:

ilu A-ga-de-^{ki}	O god of Agade,
Uṛ-da	Urda
dup-sar	the scribe
arad-ka (*nitaǵ-zu*)	is thy servant.

From a comparison of these three inscriptions, it seems beyond question that the 'god of Agade' mentioned in No. 26 is none other than Naram-Sin himself.

But the inscriptions not only call him 'god of Agade,' but also

[1] For the writing $^{(dingir)}$ *En-teme-* . . . (O. B. I. 115), see note 1 on p. 181.

[2] *ru* = sign for *URU*.

EN-MEN-AN-NA; see Rec. de Trav. xix. p. 187. The tablet published there by Thureau-Dangin reads:—

(*ilu*) *Na-ra-am-*(*ilu*) *Sin*	Naram-Sin,
ilu A-ga-de-ki	the god of Agade,
EN-MEN-AN-NA	the . . .

The third line may be translated either the lord (*en*) of the heavenly (*an-na*) tiara (*men* = *agû*, Br. 5511), or the lord (*en*) of the exalted (*an-na* = *ṣîru*) tiara (*men*), and may be read accordingly either as *bêl agê šamâmi*, or *bêl agê ṣîri*.

There hardly can be any doubt that this latter title (*en-men-an-na*) as well as the former (*ilu A-ga-de-ki*) belongs to Naram-Sin, if we compare them with the other titles which this king bears, viz. *šar* (*lugal*) *A-ga-de-ki* (see R. A. l.c. No. 24), or *šar* (Br. 4297) *ki-ib-ra-tim ar-ba-im* (see O. B. I. No. 120, col. ii. 1, 2).

If Naram-Sin could call himself *god*, he might equally well apply to himself the title 'lord of the heavenly tiara.' What induced these kings to put the sign of god before their names, we cannot tell. We know, however, that the same usage prevailed among the later rulers of Babylonia (comp. dynasty of Ur IV. and Isin), who even had temples built in their honour, and compelled the people to offer sacrifices to them (comp. Gimil-Sin, Rec. de Trav. xix. p. 186, and the cult of Gudea under Ur IV., ibid. xviii. p. 64 ff.). Thureau-Dangin *may* be right when he says (ibid. xix. p. 187): '*Shargani et surtout Naram-Sin aient subi, en ce qui touche la conception du caractère royal, l'influence plus ou moins lointaine des idées égyptiennes,*' especially when we remember that the former extended his kingdom as far as Syria-Palestine (the Westland = Martu), and thus may easily have come in contact with the Egyptians [1].

Another point of extreme interest is this. We find on the seals belonging to the time of Sharganisharâli a scene taken from the so-called 'Nimrod Epos.' This scene represents Isdubar or Gilgamish

[1] Comp. however what has been said about the title '*ilu*' under Ur IV.

(the Greek Hercules, the Biblical Nimrod) as fighting a lion. This scene is very often found in later times; and as this epos also contains the 'Assyrian flood-story,' we have every reason to suppose that it was already well known as early as 3800 B.C. The *giš zid-da*, 'the tree of life' (comp. Gen. ii. 17), is represented on another tablet (R. A. iv. p. 5), showing that this symbol was also old.

The execution of both of these works of art is wonderful, and so well conceived that it fills us with astonishment to find it dating from a period as early as 3800 B. C.

In conclusion, let us hear Sargon I. himself, in his two longest inscriptions, published by Hilprecht in O. B. I. Nos. 1 and 2:—

O. B. I. No. 1.

(*ilu*) *Bêl* (*dingir En-lil*)	For Bêl,
U-GAL-BA (=*bêlišu rabû*)	his great lord;
Šar-ga-ni-šar-âli	Sharganisharâli,
da-LUM	the mighty

2. *u-gal-ba*, a pure Sumerian expression for *bêlišu rabû*. *u* = *bêlu*; *gal* = *rabû*; *ba* = *šu*. Or should we read *u-gal-lim* (sic), phonetically for *UD-GAL-LIM*, and comp. H. W. B. 197 *b*, '*grosser Sturmwind*'?

3. Here written without the *ilu*-sign before it. In O. B. I. 2, l. 1, we have (*ilu*) *Šargani-šar-âli*. For the different readings of this name, see note on p. 6. As regards the meaning of the name, only the second part is clear, viz. *šar-âli*, 'king of the city.' With *âlu* = Sum. *URU* are also composed the names *Bin-gani-šar-âli* and *Âlu-ušaršid Uru-ka-gi-na*, and also, at the time of Ur IV., *Lugal-uru-da*, (*dingir*) *Utu-uru-na*, and others. Oppert, in Z. A. iii. 124, translates it by '*fort est le roi de la ville.*' *Šar-ga-nu*, according to v. R. 41, 29 *a*, *b*, means *dannu*. Probably we have here a noun-formation in *ān* (Del. Gram. § 65, No. 35) from the root שׂרג, which may be contained also in the Hebrew proper name שְׂרוּג (Gen. xi. 20–23) and have the meaning 'to be powerful, mighty.' In later times the name was shortened to *Šar-GE-na* (the *GE* was originally pronounced as *ga*; comp. Sum. *kur-gena* = Assyr. *kurkanû*), and when people forgot the true meaning of this word (*šar-ge-na*) they explained it, according to 'folk-etymology,' as Sharru-kênu, 'the true king.' The Hebrew transcribes this name by סַרְגוֹן (with Raphe over the ג); see O. B. I. p. 18, note 4.

4. Here, as in O. B. I. Nos. 2, 3, written *da-LUM*, according to the 'Tablet of Omens,' where we have the same title (*šarru dannu šar Agade-ki*), these signs correspond to '*dan-nu*.' See also Jensen, K. B. iii[1]. p. 116, note 5.

šar	king
A-ga-de-[*ki*]	of Agade,
bâni (*BA-GIM*)	the builder
E-KUR (i. e. *bît šadî*)	of E-kur,
bît	the temple
(*ilu*) *Bêl* (*dingir En-lil*)	of Bêl,
IN EN-LIL-[*ki*] (=*Nippur-*[*ki*])	the guardian (?) of Nippur.
ša duppa	Whosoever this
sú-a	tablet
u-sa-za-ku-ni	shall destroy,
(*ilu*) *Bêl* (*dingir En-lil*)	Bêl

7. *ba-gim* = Sumerian; may be read either *bâni* (partic.) or *ibni* (pret.).

8. *E-KUR*, 'mountain-house.' Among the kings of Babylonia who repaired and added to this '*E-kur*' are to be found: Naram-Sin, Dungi I., Ur-Ninib, Bur-Sin I., Ishme-Dagan, Bur-Sin II., Kurigalzu, Rammân-Shumuṣur, and Esarhaddon. For a good history of the *E-kur*, and the discoveries that have been made there, see Hilprecht, O. B. I. p. 229 ff.

11. For *IN* = 'guard,' 'guardian,' comp. note to O. B. I. 5. It also is found in O. B. I. 120: (*dingir*) *En-ki IN ki-ib-ra-tim ar-ba-im* (which clearly shows that *IN* here cannot be = '*ina*,' but = *bêlu*); R. A. iv. No. iii. 13: (*dingir*) *A-E IN KA-DINGIR ki* (here *IN* probably = '*ina*,' so also above?). Each city had its own *IN* = 'guardian.' For *IN*, an abbreviation for *ina*, see H. W. B. p. 95. So always in the phrase *in ištênit šatti*; comp. dates of Sargon I. and Naram-Sin, and see Ḫamm. Louvre, ii. 7, 15.

13. The first sign has been variously read. Scheil, Rec. de Trav. xv. 62–64, reads it *sig* = *iḫappû*; Oppert, R. A. iii. p. 24, *ḳat* + dual signs = *ḳâtâ*; Hilprecht, O. B. I. p. 13, *shú*. All these identifications are wrong; it is the sign *si-gunnû*, and as such has to be read *sú*; see E. C. 48. So also now Hilprecht (personal communication). *Sú-a* = *šu-a*, which we expect according to the context. *Šu-a* = *shuatum*, see H. W. B. pp. 631, 645; comp. Stèle de Zohâb I., Rec. de Trav. xiv. pp. 100–106, ll. 9–12: 9, *ša ṣa-al-mi-in*; 10, *an-ni-in*; 11, *u DUB BA-AM* (*BA-AM* = *shu'atu* + *am* + *shu'atam*, it being parallel to *annin*); 12, *ù-ša-za-ku*. It occurs again in the inscription of Lasirab, l. 14: *ša duppa sú-a u-sa-za-ku*-ni, Winckler, Z. A. iv. p. 406; in O. B. I. No. 2, l. 14, and No. 120, col. iii. 6. For *s* = *š* comp. *u-sa-za-ku-ni* (= Arabian influence (?); see the Saphel of the South Arabic inscriptions).

14. *u-sa-za-ku-ni*. So also Lasirab, l. 15. In O. B. I. No. 2 the *U* is left out. Stèle de Zohâb I., l. 12, has *u-ša-za-ku*. It is the Shaphel (iii [1]) of the root נזך or נזק; see H. W. B. p. 457, and Hilprecht, O. B. I. p. 14, note 1.

ù	and
(*ilu*) *Šamaš* (*dingir Utu*)	Shamash
ù	and
(*ilu*) *Ištar* (*dingir Innanna*)	Ishtar
išid-su	his foundation
li-zu-ḫu	they may remove,
ù	and
zêra (*ŠE-ZIR*)-*su*	his seed
li-il-gu-tu	they may exterminate.

20. *išdu*, Br. 4811; H. W. B. p. 142.

21. *li-zu-ḫu*. O. B. I. No. 2, l. 21, *li-zu-ḫa*; Lasirab, l. 23, *li-su-ḫa*; √ נסח, H. W. B. 471. Soft *z* becomes hard *s*. Comp. also Delitzsch, Gram. § 90 *c*, for *â* of the third pers. masc. pl.

24. *li-il-gu-tu*. O. B. I. No. 2, 23, *li-il-gu-da*; so also Lasirab, l. 26. Stèle de Zohâb I., *li-il-ku-ṭ[u]*; √ לקת, H. W. B. 385. Hilprecht, l. c., takes as the root of this verb לקט? *g* for *ḳ* = Vulg. Babylonian.

With l. 12 ff. comp. O. B. I. 63, 14 ff., which gives the Sumerian:

(*ga*)*lu-mu-sar-ra-ba*	Whosoever this writing
šu-ne-ib-ur (Br. 7175, *pašâṭu*) *e-a*	shall blot out,
(*dingir*) *En-lil lugal-bi*	Enlil, his king,
lugal kur-kur-ra-ge	king of the lands,
gir-bi ĝe-en-bur-ri	his foundation may he remove
šà kul-bi	and his seed
ĝe-en-til-li	may he destroy.

O. B. I. No. 2.

(*ilu*) *Šar-ga-ni-šar-âli*	Sharganisharâli,
apil It-ti[1]-(*ilu*) *Bêl* (*dingir En-lil*)	the son of Itti-Bêl
da-LUM	the powerful,
šar	king
A-ga-de-ki	of Agade
ù	and

[1] *DA* = *itti*, Br. 6551. *TI* = phon. compl. *It-ti-Bêl*, sc. *balâṭu*, i. e. with Bêl is life. Scheil, Rec. de Trav. xv. 87: *tur* = *banda* = *littu*(*ti*) *pour ilidti*?

sub[1]*-û-la-ti*	of the dominion
(*ilu*) *Bêl* (*dingir En-lil*)	of Bêl,
bâni (*BA-GIM*)	the builder
E-KUR (*bît-šadî*)	of E-kur,
bît (*ilu*) *Bêl* (*dingir En-lil*)	the temple of Bêl,
IN EN-LIL-ki (*Nippur-ki*)	the guardian (?) of Nippur.
ša duppa	Whosoever this
sú-a	tablet
[*u-*]*sa-za-ku-ni*	shall destroy
(*ilu*) *Bêl* (*dingir Enlil*)	Bêl
ù	and
(*ilu*) *Šamaš* (*dingir Utu*)	Shamash
išid-su	his foundation
li-zu-ḫa	they may remove,
ù	and
zêra (*ŠE-ZIR*)*-su*	his seed
li-il-gu-da	they may exterminate.

There is little more to be added in regard to the history of Naram-Sin[3]. That he was the son of Sargon I.[2], we know only

[1] The first sign is not yet understood. Scheil, l. c.: *sag-u-la-ti*; Oppert, R. A. iii. p. 22: '*ris* (*SAK*) *ba-u-la-ti*, "*chef du domaine de Bel.*" *Le signe ba se trouve écrit au-dessus de ris* (*SAK*)?' E. C. 198 = Br. 820. Hilprecht, O. B. I. p. 15, note 6, identifies it with *su* = Br. 802, reads *sûlati* (or pl. *sulâti*), and compares סֹלְלָה (Jer. xxxiii. 34). In all probability we have here the sign *sub* (Br. 856); as such it is the same as Br. 820. (See also H. W. B. p. 350 *b*, *sub sarabu*.) *Sub-u-la-ti* = *šub-ù-la-ti*, pl. of *šub'ultu*, a Shaphel formation of באל; as such it has the same meaning as *ba'ûltu*, pl. *ba'ûlâte*. See H. W. B. p. 162, and comp. *ba'ûlat Bêl*, '*das Reich des Bêl*,' as here. So also Hommel (personal communication).

[2] The wife of Sargon I. is mentioned in R. A. iv. No. iii. pl. xviii. No. 52: *PA lugal-sal*, showing that even queens had their own officers!

[3] Naram-Sin, written (*ilu*) *Na-ra-am-*(*ilu*) *Sin*, i. e. 'the beloved of Sin.'
His inscriptions (comp. also those of Sargon I.):
iv. R. 34 (*omina*); Winckler, K. B. iii¹. p. 107, col. ii. l. 10 ff.
i. R. 3, No. 7; Winckler, ibid. p. 98.
v. R. 64, i. 57, 60: 'the building of the temple of Shamash in Sippar.'

from the inscriptions of Nabû-nâ'id. He, like his father, was not only a great conqueror, but also a great builder. He built—or better continued to build—the temples at Nippur and Agade, and even erected at his own expense the temple Ebarra to the sun-god Shamash in Sippar. This is the temple which later on was repaired by Nabû-nâ'id, and in which he found the 'tablet with the writing of the name of Naram-Sin.' By the help of this discovery we have been enabled to fix the date of Naram-Sin at 3750 B.C.

Only short inscriptions of this king have been found. The longest, but unfortunately a badly mutilated inscription, is published by Hilprecht in O. B. I. No. 120, and reads:

Col. I.

[(*Ilu*) *Na-r*]*a-am-*[*ilu S*]*in*	Naram-Sin,
[*šarru da-LU*]*M*	the mighty king,
. . . .	king of Agade,
	the one who is . . .

Seal-cylinder, Hommel, Geschichte, p. 308; C. J. Ball, Light from the East, p. 53: *Apil* (*dingir*) *Ištar* (?), *apil Ilu-ba-ni, arad* (*ilu*) *Na-ra-am-*(*ilu*) *Sin.*

Déc. pl. 44, fig. 1; comp. Heuzey, R. A. iv. p. 1. It reads:

(*ilu*) *Na-ra-am-*(*ilu*) *Sin*	Naram-Sin,
šar (*lugal*)	king
ki-ib-ra-tim	of the four
ar-ba-im	corners of the world.

Rec. de Trav. xix. p. 187 (Thureau-Dangin).
Heuzey, R. A. iv. 9 (with scene of Gilgamish legend).
Heuzey, ibid. p. 11 (*Lugalušumgal*).
Thureau-Dangin, R. A. iv. No. iii.; comp. Sargon I.
O. B. I. No. 4. It reads:

(*ilu*) *Na-ra-am-*(*ilu*) *Sin*
BA-GIM (*bâni*)
bît (*ilu*) *Bêl* (*En-lil*).

O. B. I. No. 120; Scheil, Rec. de Trav. xv. 62–64; Maspero, Dawn of Civilization, p. 601 f.; Hilprecht, Recent Research in Bible Lands, pp. 87, 88.
Thureau-Dangin, Comptes Rendus, 1899, p. 348, pl. 1 (two inscriptions).
Inscriptions of Nabû-nâ'id, passim.

Col. II.

(ilu) EN-KI	by Enki (Ea),
in ki-ib-ra-tim	the guardian (?) of the four
ar-ba-im	corners of the world,
NA-E	the hero.
-im	
. . . . . .	

Col. III.

KISAL E-KALAM	The foundation of the 'house of the world'
ù	and
KI-GAL	'the great place'
iš-pu-uk[1]	he has heaped up.
ša duppa	Whosoever this
šú-a	tablet
[u]-sa-za-ku-ni	shall destroy,
[(ilu) I]štar	Ishtar and,
. . . . .	&c. . . .
. . . . .	
. . . . .	
[išid-su]	his foundation

Col. IV.

li-zu-ḫu	they may remove
ù	and
zêra [ŠE-ZIR]-su	his seed
li-il-gu-tu	they may exterminate.
. . . . *ni*	
ù	

[1] Root *šapâku*, H. W. B. 679.

Noteworthy also are the words of Thureau-Dangin in R. A. iv. p. 76: '*Le No.* 38 *nomme un certain ERIN-*[*DA*] *qui est qualifié d'esclave de Bi-ga-ni-šar-ali: il est fort possible que ce Bi-ga-ni-šar-ali soit identique au Bi-in-ga-ni-šar-ali, déjà connu comme fils de roi par un cachet publié par M. Menant, et qui, d'après une empreinte encore inédite du Musée du Louvre*[1], *aurait été le propre fils de Naram-Sin.*'

The '*cachet*' above referred to is published by Hommel, Gesch. p. 299, and reads:—

Bi-in-ga-ni-šar-âli	O Binganisharâli,
apil šarri	son of the king,
I-zi-lum	Izilum
dup-sar	the scribe
arad-ka (*nitag-su*)	is thy servant.

That this inscription belongs to this period is unquestionable, and if the *empreinte encore inédite du Musée du Louvre*[1] really shows that a certain Binganisharâli was the son of Naram-Sin, then we can certainly identify him with the above-mentioned 'son of the king.' Whether this Binganisharâli followed his father upon the throne of Agade is not evident from the inscriptions so far published. This much, however, we do know, that Naram-Sin had still another son, Nabe-?-mash, who was patesi of the city of Tutu. Even the name of a granddaughter of his has come down to us; her name was Lipush-Iaum, i.e. 'May Jah (or Jahveh) make.' The interesting inscription which gives us these latter two names is published by Thureau-Dangin in Comptes Rendus, 1899, p. 348, pl. 1, and reads:

Mâr (*ilu*) *Na-ra-am-*(*ilu*) *Sin*	To the son of Naram-Sin
da-LUM	the mighty,

[1] This '*empreinte*' is said to read, according to Thureau-Dangin (Comptes Rendus, 1897, p. 190), as follows:

Naram-Sin, dieu d'Agade;
Bingani-Sarali, ton fils:
Abi-i-sir, scribe, ton serviteur.

Na-be-?-maš	viz. to Nabe-?-mash,
pa-te-si	patesi
Tu-tu-ki	of Tutu,
Li-pu-uš-Ì-a-um	(presents this) Lipush-Iaum,
DIM(?)-di	the altar(?)-keeper
(*ilu*) *Sin*	of Sin
mârat-su	his daughter.

3. The third sign is not yet identified.

5. Comp. (*dingir*) *Tu-tu* = Marduk, Br. 1082.

7. The first sign, which neither Amiaud (T. C. 34) nor Thureau-Dangin (E. C. 46) identified, occurs again in the following passages:—

Gudea, Statue E, iv. 12: *X NIN-AN-DA-GAL-KI mu-na-gim e maḫ-na mu-na-ni-gub*; here this *X* is that of a goddess, is made, and placed in a temple.

Statue B, v. 3: *UŠ-KU-E X nu-gub ir nu-ta-ud-du*, which ought to be translated 'a *kalû* ("*Klagepriester*") did not step to the *X*, and made no lamentation.'

Cyl. B, xi. 1: *X*-$^{g}_{m}$*a-ni* (shows that the sign in question has to end in *G* (Old Sumerian) or *M* (New Sumerian)).

Ibid. xv. 21: *X ki-ag-ni ušum-gal kalam-ma SAG-ba-GIN-na.*

Cyl. A, vi. 24: *X ki-ag-ni ušum-gal kalam-ma GIŠ-KU-DI mu-tug nin-ad-gin-gin-ni.*

Ibid. vii. 24: *X ki-ag-e*, &c., as before.

Ibid. xxviii. 17: *a-ga X a-bi GUD KA-NUN-DI.*

I would like to identify therefore this sign with that of Br. 2737: *DIM*—only that we have here *DIM-gunû*. *DIM* = *markasu, riksu*; comp. also ii. R. 29, 62*a*: *DIM KUR-KUR-RA*; Lyon Sarg. p. 72, No. 54: *DIM-GAL KALAM-MA* with Gudea's *DIM ki-ag-ni UŠUM-GAL KALAM-MA*. A *DIM* then would be something that is 'bound = joined together,' built, and put up in a temple, i. e. it is *an altar*.

DI = Br. 9354: *šalâmu*, and ii[1]. = *unversehrt erhalten, bewahren*, H. W. B. p. 664.

DIM-DI = altar-keeper; and the *E DIM-AN-NA* (Br. 2744) = 'the temple of the heavenly altar.'

9. *Mârat-su* (written *DUMU-SAL-ZU*) we have to read, and not *mârat-ka* (Thureau-Dangin), which latter had to be *DUMU-SAL-ZA*.

With the help of this inscription we can establish the following genealogy:—

Sharganisharâli
|
Naram-Sin
|
Binganisharâli — Nabe-?-mash, patesi of Tutu
|
Lipush-Iaum, his daughter

Whether Binganisharâli was followed by his sons or not, and whether they were able to hold together the vast possessions they had inherited, are at present questions still awaiting an answer. In course of time, however, the successors of Binganisharâli seem to have lost their power—a new kingdom arose, that of Ur II., which latter, no doubt, followed upon that of Agade. Before we, however, go over to the kings of Ur II., we have to direct our attention to two other Semitic rulers in the extreme north of Babylonia, viz. to Lasirab and Anubânini.

The Kings of Guti and Lulubi.

To the same general period as that of Sargon I., i.e. about 3800 B.C., belong also the following two inscriptions, written in the Semitic language:—

(1) That of Lasirab, king of the land of Guti[1], on the east of the lower Zâb;

(2) That of Anubânini, king of Lulubi.

The former is published by Winckler in Z. A. iv. p. 406, and translated and explained by Hilprecht in O. B. I. pp. 13 and 14, note 1. It reads:—

	La-si ?-ra ?-ab ?	Lasirab (?),
	da-LUM	the mighty
	šar	king
	Gu-ti-im	of Guti,
5–10	missing	. . . .

[1] See Delitzsch, Parad. pp. 233–237.

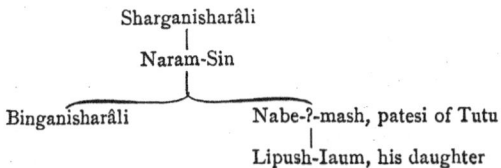

ip-uš (?)-ma	has made and
iddin	presented (it).
ša duppa	Whosoever this
sú-a	tablet
u-sa-za-ku-ni	shall remove,
zikir šum-su	and the mention of his name
i-sa-da-ru (= išaṭaru)	shall write (upon it),
(*ilu*) *Gu-ti-iḿ*	Guti,
(*ilu*) *Ištar*	Ishtar,
ù	and
(*ilu*) *Sin*	Sin
išid-su	his foundation
li-su-ḫa	they may tear up,
ù	and
zêra-su	his seed
li-il-gu-da	they may exterminate,
ù	and
ḫarrân alkat(-kat)-su	whatsoever he undertakes (?)
a i-si-ir (= â îshir)	may not prosper.

Although this inscription is short and badly mutilated, it is still important, for it gives us valuable information in regard to the country north of Babylonia, showing that about 3800 B.C. it was in the hands of a Semitic population. Whether or no this inscription should be placed before those of Sargon I. is hard to say. Seeing, however, that Sargon I. and especially Naram-Sin extended their domain to the furthest north, and that the former ruler actually took captive Sharlak, the king of Gutim (*ù* [d.] *Šar-la-ak šar Gu-ti-im-*[ki] *ik-mi-ù*) (see R. A. iv. iii. pl. v. No. 13), it is likely that these kings of Guti preceded Sargon I., and that by him the kingdom of Guti was overthrown.

The other inscription, viz. that of Anu-Bânini[1], was found in

[1] Comp. now also Hommel in P. S. B. A., March, 1899, p. 115, who identifies this king with a certain *An-ba-ni-ni* mentioned in the 'Kuthaean legend of the Creation' (see Scheil, R. T. xx.; Notes d'Epigraphie, § xxxv; Sayce,

Ser-i-Pul, and is called Stèle de Zohâb (I.). It is published by I. de Morgan and V. Scheil in Rec. de Trav. xiv. pp. 100–106. According to the description there given, it is a '*stèle d'un conquérant, élevée en souvenir d'une victoire comme l'indique la chaîne de captifs que la déesse Ninni* (*Ištar*) *amène au roi Anu-Banini.*' It is written in two columns; the last half of the second column, however, is badly mutilated. It runs:—

Stèle de Zohâb I.

Col. I.

An-nu-ba-ni-ni	Anu-Bânini ('Anu is our begettor'),
šarru da-LUM	the mighty king,
šar Lu-lu-be-ki-im	king of Lulubi,
ṣ[a-l]a-am-šu	his image
ù ṣa-lam (ilu) Ištar (INNANNA)	and the image of Ishtar
i-na ša-du-im	in the mountain
Ba-ti-ir	Padir
uš-zi-iz	has set up.
ša ṣa-al-mi-in	Whosoever this
an-ni-in	image
ù duppa šu'atam (DUB BA-AM)	and this tablet
ù-ša-za-ku	shall remove,
An-nu-um	Anu
ù An-nat (?)	and Anat
(ilu) Bêl (EN-LIL)	and Bêl,
ù (ilu) Bêltum (NIN-LIL)	and Bêltu,
(ilu) Rammân (IM)	Ramman
ù (ilu) Ištar (INNANNA)	and Ishtar,
(ilu) Sin (EN-ZU)	Sin

P. S. B. A. xx. p. 187; Zimmern, Z. A. xii. p. 317), where he and his seven sons are said to have been overcome by an unnamed Babylonian king (a king of Agade?).

ù (*ilu*) *Šamaš* (*UTU*)	and Shamash,
. . . . . *lum*	
. . . .	

Col. II.

(*ilu*) *Nin*	
ù (*ilu*)	
(*ilu*) *En*	
TIL-NIN? . . .	kill . . .
. . . *lu* .	
ù ša	and whosoever
ir-ra-muš	shall destroy it (√ ארם, H. W. B. 134),
li-ru-muš	may he destroy him,
li-ru-ru-uš	(and) may he curse him (ארר, H. W. B. 137),
ṣi-ra-šu[1]	and his seed
li-il-ku-ṭ[*u*]	may he exterminate.

12 ff. The rest is too fragmentary to translate.

With Âlusharshid, Sargon I., Lasirab, Anu-Bânini, we close the first chapter in ancient Babylonian history. The Semites are now not only in possession of the whole of Babylonia, but are also lords of 'the four quarters of the world.' Even allowing for some uncertainty as to whether Sargon I. ruled over Guti[2] and Lulubi, in the north and north-east of Babylonia, the inscriptions of Lasirab and Anu-Bânini at any rate show that Semites held possession of the extreme north. From this fact it has been argued that the Semites invaded Babylonia from the north, but without reason. We have seen that long before the time of Sargon I.—about five hundred years—the dynasty of Ur-Ninâ was undoubtedly Semitic. Even

[1] For the interchange *ṣ* and *z* in Vulg. Babyl. comp. *ḫalṣu* = *ḫalzu* ; *ṣululi* = *zululi* ; *zu-ru-uš-šu* = *ina ṣurri-šu* (O. B. I. No. 84, i. 17).

[2] Comp. however above, p. 159 (*c*).

before Ur-Ninâ, we heard of a certain Lugalshuggur, patesi of Shirpurla (Hilprecht's *Lugal-kurum-zikum*) and contemporary of Mesilim, king of Kish. This patesi was declared to be a Semite even by Hilprecht, and if *he* is a Semite, then also the whole dynasty of which he was a member was Semitic, i. e. the whole dynasty preceding Ur-Ninâ. Unfortunately we have no certain knowledge in regard to the duration of this dynasty. Probably it reigned for about two hundred years. This would give us a Semitic dynasty reigning in Shirpurla at about 4500 B. C. It is not very probable that the Semites, as soon as they invaded Babylonia, became kings or patesis. It is more likely that they had to wait some time before they could seize the sceptre of Shirpurla. Sumerian strength and power had to be weakened first. In this case we might assume a Semitic invasion at about 5000 B. C. This invasion, however, probably came not from the north, but from the south.

Bearing in mind that we find Semites in Babylonia proper from the oldest times—centuries before Sargon I.—we may with much probability conceive of the course of events as follows:—The Semites, having invaded Babylonia from the south, proceeded further northward, till they found a suitable stopping-place. While in Babylonia they adopted the civilization and writing of the old Sumerians, which they developed later on according to their own ideas. Some of these Semitic hordes undoubtedly remained in Babylonia, acquiring in course of time great influence and power. The greater proportion of them, however, settled in the north. For this reason, therefore, at about 3800 B. C. we find Semites all over the north, with a language of their own, but which they express by the Sumerian signs. This is the only reasonable explanation. Or else how could the people of Lulubi and Guti, of Agade and Kish, use a 'mode of writing' which is undoubtedly 'Sumerian[1]'?

We even may go a step further. The Semites in Babylonia

[1] Comp. the following Sumerian forms in Semitic inscriptions: *á-mu-na-šub*, *u-gal-ba*, *ba-gim*, *še-zir*, *sag-giš-ra-ni*, *mu-gim*, *(dingir) En-lil*, &c., &c. The form *nam-ra-ag* is probably not so much Sumerian as Elamitic.

adopted the Sumerian language wholly, with only a chance Semitism here and there (comp. above). The Semites—i. e. of Agade, Kish—who lived nearest to the Sumerians, used generally the Semitic language, employing only now and then Sumerian expressions (comp. note, p. 179), while the Semites living furthest away from the Sumerians—Guti, Lulubi—wrote and spoke their language with scarcely any[1] Sumerian admixture, still using, however, the Sumerian signs.

And if we find in this purest Semitic language (Guti, Lulubi) one or two traces of Sumerian grammar and nomenclature (*še-zir*), is this not evidence enough that the ancestors of the people of Guti and Lulubi lived for some time in Babylonia?

On the other hand, if the ancestors of Guti and Lulubi came from the *north*, how *could* they possibly acquire that mode of writing which at this time is only found in the valley between the Tigris and the Euphrates? But on the assumption that they came from the south, they must have passed through Babylonia, and so have come into contact with the Sumerians, whose writing they adopted. And when they left the valley again, settling down in the north of Babylonia, they took with them the Sumerian mode of writing, by which they were enabled to express their own thoughts and feelings on imperishable clay. *The Semites came from the south*[2].

[1] The names of the gods, as *EN-ZU*, *En-lil*, *Innanna*, which occur in the inscriptions of the kings of Guti and Lulubi are Sumerian, which their ancestors adopted while in Babylonia, and identified them with their own (Semitic) gods: *Sin*, *Bêl*, *Ištar*. The expressions *da-LUM* and *BA-AM* are Semitic. For the former, see Jensen, K. B. iii[1]. p. 116, note 5; for the latter, see Hilprecht, O. B. I. p. 14, note 5: 'perhaps the two characters must be transcribed "*šu-am.*"'

[2] Hilprecht's argument in O. B. I. part ii. that the Semites came from Ḫarran rests on an erroneous identification of this city with Gishban; see above, p. 149. Lehmann also (Zwei Probleme, p. 180) thinks that the Semites came from the north. The invading Semites, according to him, however, are those of Kish; while Hilprecht, as we saw, made Lugalzaggisi from Ḫarran (*giš-BAN-ki*) the first Semitic invader. Lehmann, as well as Hilprecht, failed to see that all the rulers of Shirpurla were Semites who had adopted Sumerian speech and government.

The so-called later Patesis of Shirpurla.

Some 300 years after the time of Sargon I. and about 600 years after that of Eannatum II. we hear of other patesis of Shirpurla, headed by Ur-Ba'u. The period which lies between this ruler and the last of the dynasty of Ur-Ninâ (see Chronological Table) is the darkest in the history of Old Babylonia. Only now and then do we hear of a patesi belonging to this period. The reason for this probably is that the destinies of Babylonia, and especially Shirpurla, were successively in the hands of the Semitic foes from the north (*sic*)[1], beginning with Lugalzaggisi and ending with Naram-Sin. Shirpurla, however, soon after the time of Naram-Sin seems to have acquired new strength, culminating in the reign of Gudea. Although this latter ruler seems to have wielded greater power than perhaps any other ruler of Shirpurla, yet he, in conjunction with his immediate predecessors and successors, only styles himself *patesi* of that city. Many suggestions have been made as to the rulers who exercised supreme sovereignty over Shirpurla. Nothing certain, however, can be said on this point. The most probable view is that the *successors* of the kings of Agade still continued to hold sway over Shirpurla, as they did at the time of Lugalushumgal, a predecessor of Ur-Ba'u, till they were dispossessed by the predecessors of Ur-Gur and Dungi I.[2], who were contemporary with (Ga)lukani I. and Ĝala-Lama.

The first of these later patesis is Ur-Ba'u[3]. Neither the name of his father nor that of his son is known to us. All his inscrip-

[1] Distinguish between assimilated Semites in Babylonia proper and Semites who left Babylonia, settling down in the north and attacking their 'degraded' brethren in the south.

[2] At the time of Naram-Sin there were in Ur only patesis. These patesis in course of time probably succeeded those of Agade in power.

[3] Means 'servant of Ba'u' (*Kalbi-Ba'u*). For Ba'u and her relation to the other gods, see Jensen, K. B. iii[1]. p. 20, note ††. His inscriptions are:

tions are entirely occupied with a record of the building of different temples in honour of his most favoured gods[1]; they do not recount a single campaign. Everything seems to be peaceful. He lived, as Hommel, Gesch. p. 317, says, '*als ein friedlicher Priesterkönig, dem Kultus seiner Götter und Erhaltung ihrer Heiligtümer.*'

Here follow some of his inscriptions:

Déc. pl. 27, No. 2.

(dingir) EN-KI.	For Enki,
lugal-a-ni	his king,
UR-(dingir) Ba-u	Ur-Ba'u
pa-te-si	patesi
Šir-pur-la-ki	of Shirpurla,
dumu tu-da	a son brought up
(dingir) Nin-à-gal-ka-ge	by Ninagal,
e-a-ni	his house
mu-na-ru	he has built.

Déc. pl. 7, Nos. 1 and 2, pl. 8: Amiaud, ibid. iv; A. B. K. p. 2, No. 5; Jensen, K. B. iii[1]. p. 18.

Déc. pl. 26, No. 1 *a*, *b*: Amiaud, ibid. xxxi; Jensen, l. c. p. 24, ii. Comp. Hilprecht, O. B. I. p. 263, note 4.

Déc. pl. 27, No. 2: Amiaud, ibid. xxxi.

Déc. pl. 37, Nos. 1 and 2: Amiaud, ibid. xxxi (*briques*).

Déc. pl. 38, 2 (*Cône*).

[1] Among these gods are to be found—

(dingir) Im-gig(mi)-ĝu-bar-bar (i. e. Ningirsu or the later Ninib), for whom he built the Eninnû (the temple of the number 50); see Jensen, K. B. iii[1]. p. 23, note *†.

Nin-ḫar-sag (i. e. mistress of the mountains; cp. Jensen, Cosmologie, p. 207), the later Bêlit. For her he erects a temple in Girsu. For Ba'u he builds a temple in Uruazag; in another suburb of Girsu, viz. Erim, he erects a temple in honour of Innanna (the later Ishtar); for *EN-KI*, the 'king of Erech,' a temple in Girsu; also Nindara and Ninagal are not forgotten. For *Nin-Mar-ki* (i. e. mistress of Mar) he erects the *Eš-gu-tur*; and for Dumuzizuab (son of Ea), the *nin Ki-nu-nir-ki* (i. e. the lord of Borsippa), a temple in Girsu. See, in general, Jensen, K. B. iii[1]. p. 18 ff.

Inscription on the '*briques*': Déc. 37, No. 1
(No. 2 has the same legend).

(*dingir*) *Nin-gir-su*	For Ningirsu,
gud-lig-ga	the mighty hero
(*dingir*) *En-lil-la(l)-ra*	of Enlil,
Ur-(*dingir*) *Ba-u*	Ur-Bau
pa-te-si	patesi
Šir-pur-la-ki-ge	of Shirpurla
e-a-nị	his house
mu-na-ru	he has built.

Déc. pl. 38, 2 (*Cône*).

Col. I.

[(*dingir*) *Nin-gir-su*]	For Ningirsu,
gud-lig-ga	the mighty hero
(*dingir*) *En-lil-la(l)-ra*	of Enlil,
Ur-(*dingir*) *Ba-u*	Ur-Ba'u
pa-te-si	patesi
[*Šir-pur-la-ki-ge*]	of Shirpurla

Col. II.

(*dingir*) *Im-gig-ĝu-bar-bar*	the temple of Imgigĝubarbar
mu-na-ru	he has built
ki-bi mu-na-gi	and restored it (to its place).

E. A. H. 112 (*Cône*).

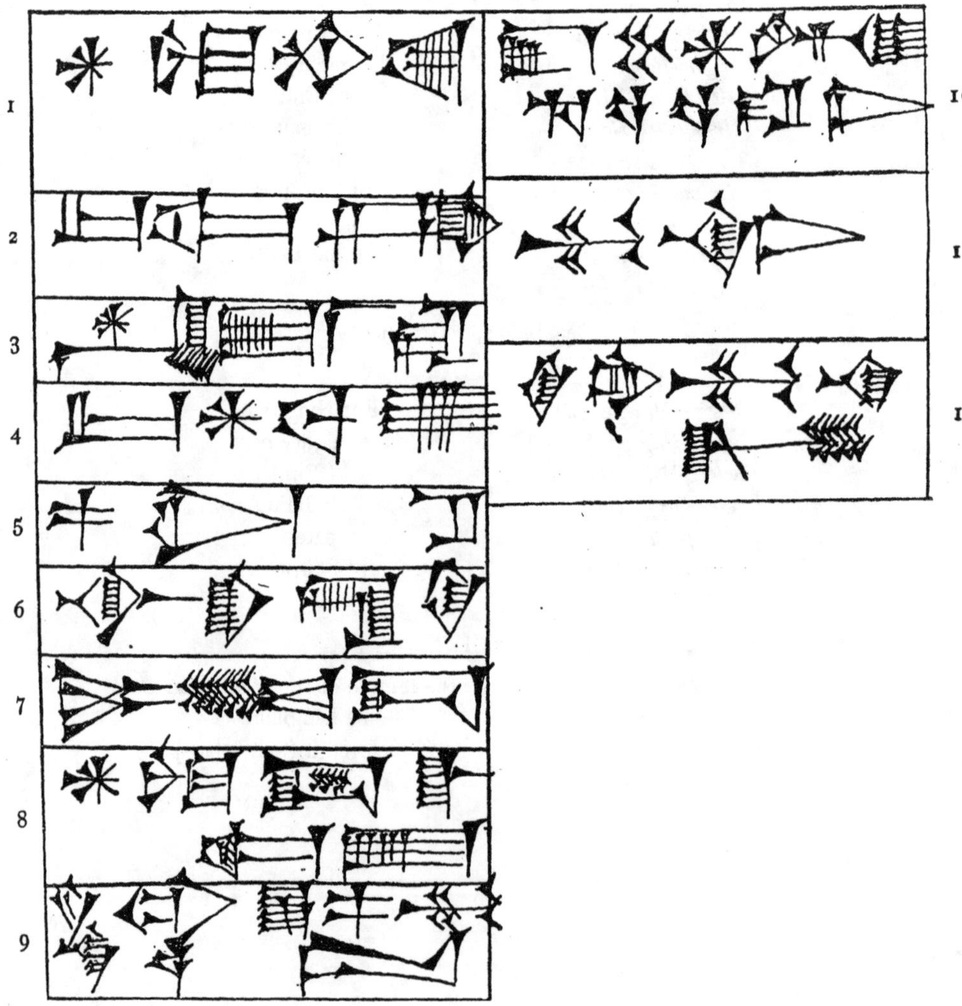

E. A. H. 112, 113.
(*Cônes* of Ur-Ba'u.)

The inscription of both of these *Cônes* is identical, and reads:

(*dingir*) *Nin-gir-su*	For Ningirsu,
gud-lig-ga	the mighty hero
(*dingir*) *En-lil-la(l)-ra*	of Bêl,
Ur-(*dingir*) *Ba-u*	Ur-Ba'u
5 *pa-te-si*	the patesi
Šir-pur-la-ki	of Shirpurla,
dumu tu-da .	a son begotten
(*dingir*) *Nin-à-gal-ka-ge*	by Ninagal,
nin-du-e pa-mu-na-ud-du	he completed the proper thing;
10 *E-ninnû* (*dingir*) *Im-gig-ģu-*	his temple Eninnû-Imgiggu-
bar-bar-ra-ni	barbar
mu-na-ru	he has built
ki-bi mu-na-gì	and restored to its place.

7. *TU = alâdu* ילד, Br. 1070.

8. *Nin-à-gal* = 'lord of great power.' This god, according to ii. R. 58, 58 = Ea, the god of smithery.

9. NI_N^G-*DU-E*; for *UL = DU* comp. Z. A. ii. 83. For the whole expression, comp. Jensen, K. B. iii¹. p. 33, notes *⁰ and **⁰. Jensen, l. c., translates: '*vollendete er (etwas) das Gehörige(s) (Geziemende)*.'

10. *E-ninnû* = 'the temple of the number 50.' 50, according to v. R. 37, 18 = *Ninib*, hence Ningirsu, the later Ninib; as such he is '(*dingir*) *Im-gig-ģu-bar-bar*,' i. e. the god (*dingir*) who may (*ģu*) illuminate (*bar-bar*) the dark (*gig*) heaven (*im*), a name which identifies Ningirsu-Ninib with the 'early sun.' For a fuller account of the building of his temple, comp. Déc. pl. 7 and 8, and Jensen, K. B. iii¹. p. 19 ff. This temple later on was rebuilt and restored by Gudea (comp. E. A. H. 114, 115). According to Statue B, v. 18 ff., he also '*šag-ba gi-gunu ki-ag-ni* (*šim*) *érin-na mu-na-ni-ru*,' i. e. built in its midst a *Gigunu* (Jensen, '*Dunkelgemach*'), which he loves, out of cedar-wood.

Whether the next patesi, *Nammaģni*[1], followed immediately upon Ur-Ba'u or not, is not evident from the inscriptions. On

[1] This name has been misread for a long time. Ledrain first read it *Nam-lugh-ni* and then *Nam-kin-ni*. Hommel (Zeitschrift für Keilschriftforschung, ii. p. 184, and Geschichte, p. 298) read it *Nam-uru(?)-ni*. The name,

p. 19 we saw that he married 'the lady Kandu,' 'a child of Ur-Ba'u'; hence he must have ruled very soon after Ur-Ba'u. We shall not be very far from the truth if we suppose that the immediate successor of Ur-Ba'u was his oldest son, who probably died childless, and that he was succeeded by Nammağni on the throne of Shirpurla. His inscriptions, like those of Ur-Ba'u, are confined to building records, and give us no information about the history of his time. Whether or not he was succeeded by his son, we do not know. From an inscription recently published in C. T. i. No. 96-6-15, 1, it is, however, evident that he must have had a son, for 'his glorious granddaughter' (*dumu-ka azag-ge*), Ninkagina by name, dedicates a tablet for the life of Nammağni, the patesi of Shirpurla. The whole tablet reads:

(dingir) Urdu-zi	To Urduzi,
lugal-a-ni	her king,
nam-ti	for the life
Nam-mağ-ni	of Nammağni,
pa-te-si	the patesi
Šir-pur-la-ki-ka-ku	of Shirpurla,
Nin-ka-gi-na	Ninkagina,
dumu-ka azag-ge	(his) glorious granddaughter (child),
šà nam-ti-la-ni-ku	and for her own life,

1. *Urdu* or *Uri* is the sign *BUR-BUR*, Br. 7304.
7. With *Nin-ka-gi-na*, 'the lady of the true month,' comp. *Uru-ka-gi-na*.
8. *dumu-ka*. Comp. above, p. 13, note 1, and Tablette A of Entemena, note to ii 2. This line hardly contains the name of the father (*dumu KA-AZAG-GE*) of Ninkagina.
9. *šà* = Semitism.

according to Jensen, K. B. iii[1]. p. 69, note 11, means: '*Seine Erhabenheit*' (*ṣîrûtišu*).

His inscriptions are:

Déc. pl. 27, 1; A. B. K. p. 2, No. 6; Jensen, K. B. iii[1]. p. 69, 8.

Déc. pl. 37, 10 (*brique*): (1) *Nam-mağ-ni*, (2) *patesi*, (3) *Širpurla-ki*.

Heuzey, R. A. ii. 79, and Jensen, l. c., p. 74 (inscript. of *nin Kan-du*). Comp. also Heuzey, R. Arch. 1886, pl. vii. No. 4; ibid. p. 203; Ledrain, Rev. Crit. 1883, ii. 220; and above, p. 19.

10 *a-mu-na-šub*	has presented it.
GAG-GIŠ-ba	This *GAG-GIŠ* (= *masse d'armes*):
lugal-mu ba-zig-gi	'My king, look favourably!
ḡe-ma-da-zig-zig	oh! may he look favourably upon it'
mu-bi	is its name.

11. For *GAG-GIŠ*, comp. Inscription of Dudu, Déc. 5bis, No. 2, and Hilprecht, O. B. I, p. 253, note 1.

12. *zig-gi*, Br. 2325: *našû*, here in the sense of *našû ša êni*, 'to look favourably upon,' H. W. B. p. 484. Ll. 12, 13 contain the name of the *GAG-GIS* ('*Schlachtkeule*'). For other names, comp. R. A. ii. 79, 9 ff.: *bur-ba, lugal-mu, nam-ti-mu, ḡe-sud mu*[-*bi*] (sic; see K. B. iii¹. p. 76); iv. R². 35, 2, 9 ff.: *dub-ba* (does not belong to *mu-na-gim*, against Winckler, K. B. iii¹. p. 83, 8) *lugal-mu giš? šag šag-ga-ka-ni, ga-an-ti-il, mu-bi*; i. R. 5, No. xvi. col. ii. 9 ff.: *bad-ba Nannar suḡ ma-da-ge en-gi-en, mu-bi-im* (K. B. iii¹. p. 94, 2); Gudea, Statue A, iii. 4 ff.: *nin an-ki-a nam-tar-ri-ne,* (dingir) *Nin-tu, am dingir-ri-ne-ge, Gu-de-a,* (ga)*lu e-ru-a-ka, nam-ti-la-ni mu-sud, mu-ku mu-na-sa*; B, vii. 14 ff.: *lugal-mu, e-a-ni, mu-na-ru, nam-ti nin-ba-mu, mu-ku mu-na-sa*; C, iii. 18 ff.: *Gu-de-a,* (ga)*lu e-ru-a-ka, nam-ti-la-ni ḡe-sud, mu-ku mu-na-sa*; D, v. 1 ff.: *lugal à-dugud-da-ni, kur-e nu-il-e,* (dingir) *Nin-gir-su-ge, Gu-de-a,* (ga)*lu e-ru-a-ka, nam-dug mu-ni-tar, mu-ku mu-na-sa*; E, ix. 1 ff.: *nin mu ba-zig-gi, nam-ti ba, ud sag gab zal-zal* (sic), *mu-ku mu-na-sa*; H, iii. 1 ff.: *nin dumu ki-ag an-azag-ga-ge, am* (dingir) *Ba-u, E-sil-gid-gid-ta, Gu-de-a, nam-ti mu-na-sum, mu-ku mu-na-sa*.

This inscription testifies strongly in favour of Hommel's argument that we have to supply a gap of about 200 years between Ur-Ba'u and Gudea (see p. 19), during which time the successors of Nammaḡni may have reigned in Shirpurla.

Passing therefore over an interval of several generations, we reach the greatest of these later patesis of Shirpurla.

This patesi is *Gudea*[1] (at about 3400 B.C.). He must have

---

[1] Gudea is rendered into Assyrian (comp. bilingual texts of Ḫammurabi) by *Nâbiu*, 'preacher'; see Jensen, K. B. iii¹. p. 26, note 3.

His inscriptions are:

Statues:

A. Déc. pl. 20 and 15, 5; Amiaud, ibid. p. vi; A. B. K. p. 3, No. 7; and Z. K. i. p. 233.

B. Déc. pl. 16-19; Amiaud, ibid. p. vii; A. B. K. p. 5, No. 12; Jensen, K. B. iii¹. p. 26 ff.

C. Déc. pl. 10 and 13, 1; Amiaud, ibid. p. xvi. Comp. Hommel, Semi-

been a usurper and the founder of a new dynasty [1], for in no

tische Sprachen und Völker, p. 40; Amiaud, Zeitschrift für Keilschriftforschung, i. 156.

D. Déc. pl. 9; Amiaud, ibid. p. xvii; Jensen, l. c., p. 50.
E. Déc. pl. 11 and 13, 2; Amiaud, ibid. p. xix.
F. Déc. pl. 14 and 15, 4; Amiaud, ibid. p. xxiii; Jensen, l. c., p. 55.
G. Dec. pl. 13, 3; Amiaud, ibid. p. xxv, and Z. A. iii. 23 ff.; Jensen, l. c., p. 58.
H. Déc. 13, 4; Amiaud, Z. A. ii. 287.

'Votive tablets:'

(α) Déc. 29, 2, has the same text as Déc. 27, 3. See Amiaud, ibid. p. xxxi.
(β) (*inédite*); Amiaud, ibid. p. xxxi.
(γ) (*inédite*); Amiaud, ibid. p. xxxii.
(δ) Déc. 29, 1; Amiaud, ibid. p. xxxii; A. B. K. p. 4, No. 10.

Bricks:

(α) (*inédite*); Amiaud, ibid.
(β) Dec. 37, 6; Amiaud, ibid.
(γ) Déc. 37, 7; Amiaud, ibid.
(δ) (*inédite*); Amiaud, ibid.
(ε) Déc. 37, 3; Amiaud, ibid.
(ζ) Déc. 37, 4; Amiaud, ibid.
(η) (*inédite*); Amiaud, ibid.
(θ) Déc. 37, 5; Amiaud, ibid.
(ι) (*inédite*); Amiaud, ibid.
P. S. B. A., Nov. 4, 1890, p. 62.

Other inscriptions:

Déc. 26, 2 (vase: Gudea presents it 'for his life').
Déc. 26, 4; K. B. iii [1]. p. 66, ii. (Lugaldur-).
Déc. 26, 7, 9 (fragments).
Déc. 25bis, 1; comp. Revue Archéol. 1891, 3me série, xvii. p. 153 (Heuzey).
Déc. 44, 2 (*vase à libation*).
Clercq, ii. pl. viii. 2 (*Cône*).
Déc. 38, 1, 3, 6, 7.
Déc. 24, 2, 3.
Ménant, Catalogue des Cyl., &c., p. 59; Hommel, Z. A. i. 439 f.; Jensen, K. B. iii [1]. p. 65 *e*; A. B. K. p. 3, No. 8.
Déc. 22bis, 3^{b}.
A. B. K. p. 4, No. 11 *a*, *b*.
R. T. xxi. p. 26 ff., No. xlii.: Scheil, Gudéa sur les cylindres cachets.

Cylinders:

A. Déc. pl. 33, 34, 35; Zimmern, Z. A. iii. p. 232.
B. Déc. pl. 36; Amiaud, R. A. ii. p. 124 and iii. p. 42 (col. xii. 15 to end), transcribed into Assyrian characters. Both these cylinders are now published again by Ira M. Price, in the Assyriologische Bibliothek, vol. xv.

[1] This has already been maintained by Hommel, Geschichte, p. 326. The

inscription—as far as they are known to us—does he give his genealogy [1].

We have seen that a certain Nammagni, in consequence of his marriage with the *nin Kan-du*, a daughter of Ur-Ba'u, became patesi of Shirpurla. The successors of Nammagni—with whom appears to begin a new line of rulers—probably reigned during several generations, till they were overthrown by Gudea. This fact would also account for the difference in the writing as exhibited in the inscriptions of Ur-Ba'u and Gudea respectively (see p. 19). Gudea—powerful as he was—however, seems to have acquired his greatness not so much by leading the armies of Shirpurla against his enemies, as by peaceful commercial intercourse with the neighbouring countries and by erecting a number of temples for his gods—temples distinguished by beauty and magnificence. In this latter work the gods themselves were his inspirers. An old man (*(ga)lu* 1 *a-an*) appeared to him in a *MA-MU* ('vision') and commanded him to build a temple: 'To build his house he commanded me' (Cyl. A, iv. 20). Seeing that he did not know who this man was, the goddess Ninâ informs him: 'My brother the god Ningirsu is this (sc. man). To build his abode, the temple Eninnû, he commands thee' (v. 17 f.). Thereupon the goddess Nidaba, the sister of Ninâ, furnished with the stilus and writing tablet of Ba'u, was presented to him. She—called here (*sal* 1 *a-an*, i. e. a) woman (iv. 23 ff.), or also (*KI-EL*, i. e.) girl (v. 22–26)—makes a drawing in his presence, and puts before him the complete model of the temple Eninnû, i. e. 'the temple of the number 50.'

Gudea—'the *mu-gil-sa* (Jensen, *Schatzspender*), patesi of Shirpurla, the shepherd, chosen by the true heart of Ningirsu, who was favourably looked upon by the faithful eye of Ninâ, to whom power

passage (Cyl. A. iii. 6) on which Hommel based his argument must not be translated: '*eine Mutter hatte ich nicht*,' '*einen Vater hatte ich nicht*,' but just the opposite: 'thou *art* my mother,' 'thou *art* my father.' See Zimmern, Z. A. iii. p. 234.

[1] Consequently he was not the son of Ur-Ba'u; Maspero, Dawn of Civilization, p. 610.

was given by Nindara, a child begotten by Gatumdug, to whom a great dominion and a sublime sceptre were given by Galalim, who was destined by Dunshagga to have courage (life) in his heart and to be of great power, who was triumphantly led into battle by Ningishzidda, his king' (Statue B, ii. 4–iii. 5)—obeys gladly, begins to build this temple, and makes it 'like Erech a holy place' (B, iv. 7).

The building materials for this temple are derived from the most distant countries. From the Amanus mountain (in North-Western Syria) he gets cedar-wood; from the mountain Ibla (=Lebanon?), zabanu-trees and cedars; from Kaṣalla [1], a mountain of the 'West-land [2],' he brings great quarried stones; from another mountain of the 'West-land,' Tidanum [3], he gets shirgal-stones. *KA-GAL-AD-ki* [4], a mountain of Kimash [5], furnishes copper; the mountain of Barsip (near Carchemish), nalua-stone. From the land Meluḫḫa [6] are derived ushu-wood, gold, precious stones, and iron; from Ǵaǵum [7], gold-dust; from Magan [8], dolerite. To sum up in his own words: 'In the power of Ninâ and in the power of Ningirsu for Gudea, to whom a sceptre was given by Ningirsu, have Magan, Meluḫḫa,

[1] Comp. Omen of Sargon I. Jensen reads this name *Sub(mu)-sal(-gal)-la*, K. B. iii[1]. p. 34, vi. 5. See Hommel, Gesch. p. 306; iv. R[2]. 36, No. 1, col. ii. 23; E. A. H. 134, 22; Dungi III., dates, No. 13.

[2] Martu, i. e. the country of the Amorites, whence we get *Amurrû* = 'Amortes' and 'western.' Delitzsch, Parad., '*Für die Länder an der Mittelmeerkuste, besonders also fur Phönizien und Palästina, hatten die Assyrer . . . eine specielle Bezeichnung, nämlich Westland* (*Mar-tu*),' p. 271. For the pronunciation of *Mar-tu-ki* = *Amurrû*, see Hommel, P. S. B. A., 1896, p. 17.

[3] i. e. Dedan, close to Moab; Hommel, Ancient H. Trad. p. 34.

[4] i. e. Assyrian *abullu-abišu* (ii. R. 52, 55), 'the gate of his ancestor' (sc. Nimrod). Is identified by Hommel, A. H. T. p. 35, with the two mountains Aga and Salma.

[5] '*Die grosse syrisch-arabische Wüste, speciell nun, welche die Süd- und Südwestgrenze des Euphrat- und Tigrisgebietes bildet . . . heisst mât MASH*,' Delitzsch, Parad. p. 242. Comp. also the ninth canto of the Gilgamish legend, and Z. A. vi. p. 161 (mentioned there on a cylinder).

[6] i. e. North-Western Arabia; comp. also Jensen, K. B. iii[1]. p. 53, note *o.

[7] A mountainous district near Medina.

[8] i. e. Eastern Arabia.

Gubin[1], and the land Tilmun[2], each of which possesses every kind of tree, brought to Shirpurla ships (laden) with wood for his buildings' (Statue D, iv. 2–12).

Not only, however, did he get stones for his temples, but also for his battle-clubs (*masse d'armes*), called *GAG-GIŠ*, as may be seen from an inscription published Déc. 25bis, 1 *b*. Comp. Heuzey, Revue Arch. 1891, vol. xvii. p. 153, where we read:

(dingir) Nin-gir-su	Unto Ningirsu,
gud-lig-ga	the mighty hero
(dingir) En-lil-[la]	of Bêl,
lugal-a-ni	his king,
Gu-d[e-a]	Gudea,
[pa-te-si]	patesi
Šir-pur-la-ki	of Shirpurla,
ĝar-sag UR-IN-GÌ uru Az [ki]	from the mountain *UR-IN-GÌ* of the city of Az,
a-ab-ba igi-nim-ka	on the upper sea,
(nà) ŠIR-GAL	shirgal-stones
mu-šu ?-ib (?)-lal (?)-a	having fetched
im-ta-DUL-DU	and brought down,
GAG GIŠ gud-III-ku	and to a *GAG-GIŠ gud-III*

8. For *Az*, see above, p. 88, 12.

9. The upper sea = the Mediterranean Sea, see Lugalzag. ii. 9. *Az* therefore has to be sought for in that neighbourhood.

13. Comp. Statue B, vi. 31, 36, and Cyl. 3 xiii. 21.

Such battle-clubs must have been richly adorned. Not only stones furnished the material for them, but also copper, gold-dust, and *KIL-ZA-NIM* (see Statue B, vi. 21 ff.).

---

[1] '*Westlich von Babylon, vielleicht ein Theil von Arabien,*' Jensen, K. B. iii[1]. p. 53, note **†. Amiaud, on the other hand, identifies Gubin with Koptos, near Thebes, in Upper Egypt. From this place Gudea gets ĝalup-trees; these trees then would be the Persea or Lebbakh, which is found growing in Egypt, and is now called by the Syrians '*khalûpa*' (Hommel, A. H. T. p. 35).

[2] On the Persian Gulf. Was identified with Tylos, one of the Baḫrein islands, Jensen, K. B. iii[1]. p. 53, note †*.

mu-na-gim	having made it,
[*a*]-*mu-na-šub*	he presented it.

The fact that so many different countries are mentioned in the inscriptions of Gudea[1] throws a bright light upon the civilization of this period, and furnishes us with welcome information as to the extent of this ruler's dominion or influence. It required no ordinary civilization to quarry stones and cut cedars in such remote countries, and transport them, either on ships or on the back of camels, over these vast distances.

Let us now take a glance at our map and see how wide an extent of country was either actually subject to Gudea, or by alliance accessible to his ships and caravans. This area stretched westward far beyond the Arabian Desert, as far as the Lebanon, the Dead Sea, and probably to Koptos in Egypt. Northwards it went far beyond Borsippa, even to the mountains which separate the valley of the Upper Tigris from that of the Euphrates. In the south it extended over the greater part of Southern Arabia, even into the Persian Gulf to the island of Tylos. In the east the whole of Elam was subject to him. No wonder that he could say, like old Lugalzaggisi, 'Ningirsu, his beloved king, from the upper sea even to the lower sea (i. e. from the Mediterranean even to the Persian Gulf) has opened his way' (B, v. 23–27).

If Gudea actually ruled over all these lands, it appears strange that in all his extant inscriptions we have no mention of his wars. One exception to this is a notice in B, vi. 64–69, of an expedition against Elam: 'The weapons of the city of Ansham in Elam he put down, its *nam-ra-ag* (i. e. prince) he brought to Ningirsu of Eninnû.'

Humble and pious as he was, he did not care to emphasize his worldly achievements, but was satisfied to live wholly for his gods; for he not only built the Eninnû for Ningirsu, but also temples for the other gods.

[1] Especially in Statue B.

Déc. 37, 3 (*brique*): comp. P. S. B. A. Nov. 1890, p. 63, No. ii.

Col. I.

(dingir) *Ninâ*	For Ninâ,
nin-en	the lady mistress,
nin-in-dub-ba	the mistress of the art of writing,
nin-a-ni	his mistress,
Gu-de-a	Gudea,
pa-te-si	patesi
Šir-pur-la-^{ki}-ge	of Shirpurla,

Col. II.

nin-du-e pa-mu-na-ud-du	completed what was proper.
Ninâ-^{ki} uru ki-ag-ga-ni-a	In Ninâ, her beloved city,
E-ud-mà-Ninâ-^{ki}-tag	her temple Udmà-Ninâtag,
KUR-E-ta il-la-ni	which from the *KUR-E* arises,
mu-na-ru	he built.

I. 3. See Jensen, K. B. iii[1]. p. 47, note †.
II. 3. Comp. Br. 7854.
4. *il*, Br. 6146, *elû*, *našû*, *šakû*.
In P. S. B. A. Nov. 1890, p. 63, No. ii., this inscription goes on:

ki-bi mu-na-gì	and restored it to its place;
mà-maǵ-ni	her 'great ship'
. . . *mu-na-ru*	he has built.

Déc. 37, 4 (*brique*).

(dingir) *Nin-dar*[1]*-a*	To Nindara,
lugal-en	the king,
lugal-a-ni	his king,
Gu-de-a	Gudea,
pa-te-si	patesi
Šir-pur-la-^{ki}-ge	of Shirpurla,
E Gir-su-^{ki}-ka-ni	his house in Girsu
mu-na-ru	he has built.

[1] Also read *Nin-si-a*, Jensen, K. B. iii[1]. p. 24, note 1.

The shorter inscriptions of Gudea, recording the building of the temple of Ningirsu, generally run :—

E. A. H. 114.

(Cône.)

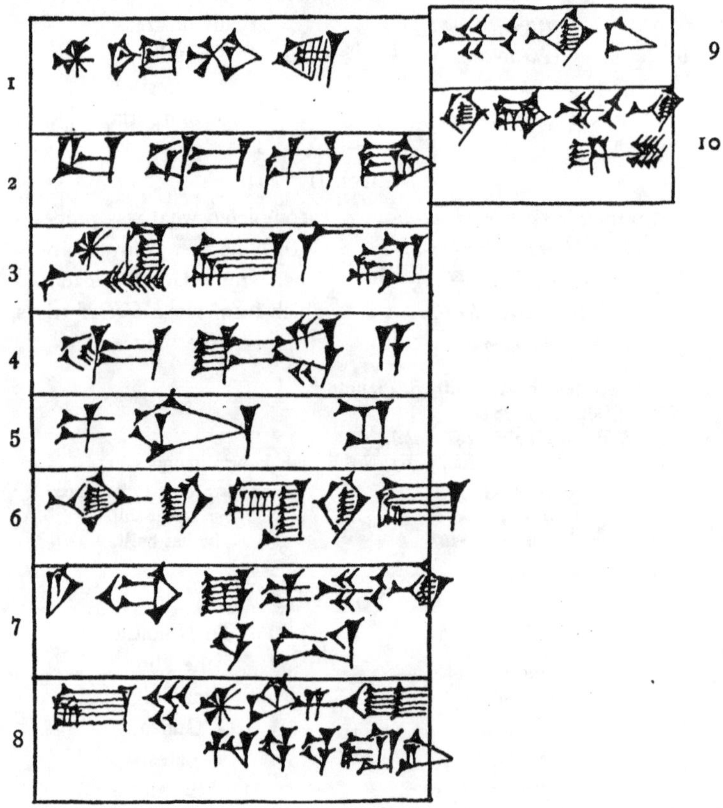

E. A. H. 114, 115 (comp. Déc. 27, 3, and A. B. K. p. 4, No. 10).

E. A. H. 114 is a *cône*, and No. 115 is a small tablet of dolerite (*(nà) KAL*) which Gudea brought from the mountain of Magan (*kur-Mà-gan-ki-ta im-ta-dul-du*). The inscription is the same on both, and reads :—

(dingir) Nin-gir-su	For Ningirsu,
gud lig-ga	the mighty hero
(dingir) En-lil-la(l)-ra	of Bêl,
Gu-de-a	Gudea,
pa-te-si	patesi
Šir-pur-la-ki-ge	of Shirpurla,
nin-du-e pa-mu-na-ud-du	he completed the proper thing,
E-ninnû (dingir) Im-gig-ĝu-bar-bar-ra-ni	his temple Eninnû-Imgigĝubarbar
mu-na-ru	he has built
ki-bi mu-na-gì	and restored to its place.

7. See note to E. A. H. 112, l. 9.
8. See ibid. note 10.

In other inscriptions, see e. g. Déc. 38, 1, 3, 6, he adds to the preceding :—

šag-ba (šim) erin	In its midst, out of cedar-wood,
ki-di-kud-a-ni	his judgement-place
mu-na-ni-ru	he has built.

This judgement-place he called, as we know from B, v. 18, *gi-unu(g)* (Jensen, *Dunkelgemach*, K. B. iii[1]. p. 33, note †*, and Kosmologie, Index. Compare, however, Hommel, Die Astron. der alten Chaldäer (Ausland, 1891/2), who takes it to mean '*Begräbnisplatz.*'

He, like Urukagina, built also a *ki-akkil* for Dunshagga.

Déc. 29, 1 ; A. B. K. p. 4, No. 9.

(Dingir) Dun-šag-ga	For Dunshagga,
dumu ki-ag	the beloved son
(dingir) Nin-gir-su-ka	of Ningirsu,

lugal-a-ni	his king,
Gu-de-a	Gudea,
pa-te-si	patesi
Šir-pur-la-ki-ge	of Shirpurla,
E ki-akkil-li-ni	his temple *Ki-akkil*
mu-na-ru	he has built.

To the same god he also dedicated some kind of a vase 'for (the preservation of) his life.'

Déc. 26, 2.

(Dingir) *Dun-šag-ga*	To Dunshagga,
dumu ki-ag	the beloved son
(dingir) *Nin-gir-su-ka*	of Ningirsu,
lugal-a-ni	his king,
Gu-de-a	Gudea,
pa-te-si	patesi
Šir-pur-la-ki-ge	of Shirpurla,
nam-ti-la-ni-ku	for his life
a-mu-na-šub	he presented it.

Among other dedications has been found a splendid '*vase à libation*' of stone, Déc. 44, 2, with this inscription:

(Dingir) *Nin-giš-zid-da*	To Ningishzidda,
dingir-ra-ni	his god,
Gu-de-a	Gudea,
pa-te-si	patesi
Šir-pur-la-ki-ge	of Shirpurla.

The temples which Gudea built and so beautifully decorated, and which were his delight probably for many years, are to-day mere heaps of stones. Yet the statues, his 'doubles,' which he placed in those different sanctuaries are still preserved. Eight of such statues have come down to us, and are now in the Louvre. In some of these he is represented as 'sitting,' in others as 'standing.' 'The legs brought together, the bust rising squarely from the hips, the hands crossed upon the breast—the right hand always being put into the left—a posture of submission or respectful adoration. The mantle passes over the left shoulder, leaving the right free, and is fastened on the right breast[1].' All these statues have lost their heads. Some of these heads, however, have been recovered. They are completely shaven, and often surmounted by a kind of turban.

Six of these statues have special *names*[2]. From the inscriptions we also learn in what temple these statues have been placed, from what material they were made, and in whose honour they were erected. In some cases Gudea went even so far as to prescribe that certain sacrifices should be offered to this his 'double':—

1 *ga* of drink.
1 *ga* of food.
½ *ga* of flour.
½ *ga nin-ĝur-ra aš-an*[3] (Statue B, i. 8–11). So it then happened that at the time of Ur IV. the statues came to be looked upon as gods, and Gudea—who never called himself (*dingir*) *Gu-de-a*—became 'god Gudea.' See *sub* Ur IV.

The inscriptions in some cases conclude with an invocation of the curse of the gods upon every one who either shall remove the statue or shall blot out the writing upon it. Four (B, D, F, G) of these statues have been translated by Jensen in K. B. iii[1]. p. 26 ff. The others I add for the sake of completeness.

Statue A.

Cartouche.

Gu-de-a	Gudea,
pa-te-si	patesi
Šir-pur-la-ki	of Shirpurla,
(*ga*)*lu E-ninnû*	who the Eninnû
(*dingir Nin-gir-su-ka*	of Ningirsu
in-ru-a.	has built.

[1] Maspero, Dawn of Civilization, p. 612.

[2] Statues F and G have no names. In the latter the space for the name was left free to be filled up at some future time.

[3] For *nin-ĝur-ra* comp. Br. 12123, H. W. B. 626: *ripsu*; √ *rapâsu*, '*dreschen, schlagen, zerschlagen*'; *aš-an* = Neo-Babyl. *aš-a-an* = barley; henc we may see in *nin-ĝur-ra aš-an* 'crushed barley.'

Col. I.

(dingir) Nin-ḫar-sag	For Ninḫarsag,
nin uru da-sar-a	the mistress, who looks favourably upon the city,
am-tur-tur-ne	the mother of the children,
nin-a-ni	his mistress,
Gu-de-a	Gudea,
pa-te-si	patesi
Šir-pur-la-^{ki}-ge	of Shirpurla,
e uru Gir-su-^{ki}-ka-ni	her temple of the city of Girsu
mu-na-ru	he has built,

Col. II.

DUP-PISAN azag-ga-ni	her holy (bright) *DUP-PISAN*
mu-na-gim	he has made,
(giš) DUR-GAR maǵ nam-nin-ka-ni	the sublime throne of her ladyship
mu-na-gim	he has made,
e maǵ-ni a-mu-na-ni-tur	into her great temple he has brought it (them).
kur Mà-gan-^{ki}-ta	From the mountain of Magan

I. 2. *SAR*, Br. 4314: *karâbu*, H. W. B. 350.

3. 'Mother of the children,' sc. of this world = inhabitants.

II. 1. For *PISAN*, see T. C. 93, 99, 135, and E. C. 429 = Br. 6007. As such it has the pronunciation *ALAL*, H. W. B. 476; *PISAN*, H. W. B. 532; *DUBBISAG = dupšarru*, S^{b}. 238. Comp. also Sayce, Transactions of the Society of Bibl. Arch. i. part ii. 1872, and Hommel, P. S. B. A. Jan. 1893, vol. xv. p. 111, and S. L. No. 232. Sayce took *PISAN* = papyrus; Hommel identified it with Aeg. *saḫ*, the picture of the writing-utensils. The sign occurs again Statues B, v. 41, 43; F, iv. 8; T, iii. 10. Amiaud, Z. A. i. p. 247, translates *DUP-PISAN* by '*libatoirs*' (*mot à mot*: libation-vases), *ou peut-être mieux l'* '*autel*' (*la table sur laquelle on plaçait les vases destinés aux sacrifices*). Jensen renders it by '*Opferbecken*' (?), see K. B. iii[1]. p. 57, note ††*.

3. (giš) *DUR-GAR*. See Br. 10663: *kussû*.

5. *TUR* = E. C. 145. Whenever this sign is used it has the value *TUR*, and means *erêbu*, 'to enter'; here = Shaphel, to make to enter = 'to bring (into).'

Col. III.

^(nâ)^ *KAL im-ta-DUL-DU* (Br. 9594)	dolerite he has brought,
alan-na-ni-ku	into his statue
mu-tu	he has formed it.
nin an-ki-a nam-tar-ri-ne	'Oh, mistress that decrees the fates of heaven and earth,
^(dingir)^ *Nin-tu*	oh, Nintu,
am dingir-ri-ne-ge	mother of the gods,
Gu-de-a	of Gudea,

Col. IV.

(ga)lu e-ru-a-ka	who the temple has built!
nam-ti-la-ni mu-sud	his life prolong!'
mu-ku mu-na-sa	he called its name,
e a-mu-na-ni-tur	into the temple he brought it.

Statue C.

Col. I.

^(Dingir)^ *Nin-giš-zid-da*	The god Ningishzidda
dingir Gu-de-a	is the god of Gudea,
pa-te-si	the patesi
*Šir-pur-la-^ki^*	of Shirpurla,
(ga)lu E-an-na	who the Eanna
in-ru-a-kam	has built.

Col. II.

^(dingir)^ *Innanna*	For Innanna,
nin kur-kur-ra	the mistress of the lands,
nin-a-ni	his mistress,

III. 3. *TU*, when written thus (E. C. 147), is = *alâdu, banû.*

4. So also Amiaud. Better probably it might be translated by 'mistress of those that decree the fates of heaven and earth.'

5. ^(dingir)^ *Nin-tu* = *bêlit ilitti* = *am tur-tur-ne* = ^(dingir)^ *Ninḫarsag*; see above, col. i. 1 ff.

Gu-de-a	Gudea,
mu-gil-sa	the mugilsa,
pa-te-si	patesi
Šir-pur-la-ki	of Shirpurla,
(ga)lu E-ninnû	who the Eninnû
(dingir) *Nin-gir-su-ka*	of Ningirsu
in-ru-a	has built,
ud (dingir) *Innanna-ge*	when by Innanna
igi-nam-ti-ka-ni	with the eye of her love
mu-igi-bar-ra-a	he had looked upon,
Gu-de-a	then Gudea,
pa-te-si	patesi
Šir-pur-la-ki	of Shirpurla,
giš-tug(-pi) dagal-a-kam	who has great intelligence,
nitaǧ nin-a-ni	the hero of his mistress,
ki-ag-a-an	her beloved,
ga ù-šub-ba-ka	of the 'situation of the foundation' (?)
giš-ba-ǧar	a draft he made,
ka-al-ka	of *Ka-al*
URU-ba-mul	its *Uru* he has made to shine (?).

Col. III.

im-bi ki-laǧ-laǧ-ga-a	Its clay from a pure place
im-mi-dib	he took,
šeg-bi	its bricks
ki-el-la	on a shining (sacred) place
im-mi-du	he formed,
uš-bi mu-azag	its foundation he made bright,
bil im-ta-lal	and purified it.

II. 5. See Jensen, K. B. iii^{1}. p. 29: '*Schatzspender, wörtlich: Zumesser, Lieferer von Kostbarkeiten*,' and especially note.

12. *igi-nam-ti*, lit. 'the eye of life.'

20 ff. See Jensen, K. B. iii^{1}. p. 56, Statue F, col. ii. 12 ff., and his notes.

III. 1 ff. Jensen, ibid.

temen-bi	Its *Temen*
ni-ir nun-ka	in the *Ni-ir* of the *Nun*
šu-tag ba-ni-dug	he commanded to cast.
e ki-ag-ga-ni	His beloved temple,
E-an-na šag Gir-su-^{ki}-ka	the Eanna in Girsu,
mu-na-ni-ru	he built.
kur Mà-gan-^{ki}-ta	From the mountain of Magan
$^{(nà)}$ *KAL im-ta-DUL-DU*	dolerite he brought down;
alan-na-ni-ku	into his statue
mu-tu	he formed it.
Gu-de-a	'Gudea,
(ga)lu e-ru-a-ka	who has built this temple,

Col. IV.

nam-ti-la-ni ğe-sud	his life may be long!'
mu-ku mu-na-sa	he called its name,
E-an-na-ka	and into the temple of Eanna
mu-na-ni-tur	he brought it.
(ga)lu E-an-na-ta	Whosoever out of the Eanna
ib-ta-ab-ud-du-ud-du-a	shall bring it,
ib-zi-ri-a	and shall break it (?),
mu-sar-a-ba šu-ne ib-ur-a	his writing shall blot out,
$^{(dingir)}$ *Innanna*	Innanna,
nin kur-kur-ra-ge	the mistress of the lands,
sag-ga-ni šun-na	his head may she destroy (?),
nam ğe-ma-tar-e	(his) fate may she decree,
$^{(giš)}$ *gu-za gub-ba-na*	of his established throne
gir-bi	its foundation

15. $^{(nà)}$ *KAL*, Br. 6209 = *ušû*. Jensen, K. B. iii^{1}. p. 61 = dolerite; see also B, vii. 11.

IV. 2. Lit. 'he pronounced it for its name.'

5 ff. Comp. B, viii. 6 ff.

11. *šun*, T. C. 95 = Br. 250.

na-an-gi-ni	may she not uphold,
KUL-a-ni ǧe-til	his seed may she kill,
bal-a-ni ǧe-tar	his dynasty may she cut off.

Statue E.

Cartouche.

Gu-de-a	Gudea,
pa-te-si	patesi
*Šir-pur-la-^ki^*	of Shirpurla.

Col. I.

(*dingir*) *Ba-u*	Unto Ba'u,
sal šag-ga	the gracious lady,
dumu An-na	the daughter of Anu,
nin Uru-azag-ga	the mistress of Uruazagga,
nin ǧe-gàl	the mistress of riches,
nin Gir-su-ki-a nam-tar-ri	the mistress who decrees the fates of Girsu,
nin di-kud uru-na	the judge of her city,
nin sag-e ki-ag	the most beloved mistress,
nin nin-u-gu-de-a	the mistress of those that seek refuge,
nin-a-ni	his mistress,
Gu-de-a	Gudea,
pa-te-si	patesi

I. 1 ff. See also Ur-Ba'u IV., 3 ff.; Gudea, Statues B, viii. 58 ff.: (*dingir*) *Ba'u, nin dumu-sag An-na-ge*; G, ii. 4 ff.; H, i. 1 ff.; and especially E. A. H. 262, 1 ff.: (*dingir*) *SAL* (var. *Nin*)-*IN-SI-NA*, *nin-gal am kalam-ma, zi-gàl kalam dim-dim-me, dumu-sag an-azag-ga*—hence (*dingir*) *SAL* (var. *Nin*)-*IN-SI-NA*, or also (*dingir*) *Nin-in-ni-si-an-na* (Br. 11033) = (*dingir*) *Ba-u*.

6. *nam-tar* = *šîmtu šâmu*, H. W. B. 654; Br. 381.

8. *sag*, Br. 3523; *rêštû*, H. W. B. 607. Amiaud: *dame amie des mortels* (?).

9. For *U-GU-DE*, see Br. 6035 and 6721: *na'butu*, and when with *amêlu* then = *munnabtu*; comp. also H. W. B. p. 13 *sub abâtu* iv. Translate: mistress (*nin*) of those that (*a*) seek refuge (*nin-u-gu-de*). Here apparently an allusion to the name 'Gudea' itself. Amiaud: *dame du trépas* (?).

Šir-pur-la-[*ki*]	of Shirpurla,
(ga)lu E-ninnû	who the Eninnû
(*dingir*) *Nin-gir-su-ka*	of Ningirsu,
E-PA e-ub-7 (imin)	the Epa, a temple of seven spheres,
mu-ru-a	has built.
ud (*dingir*) *Ba-u*	When Ba'u
nin-a-ni	his mistress
šag azag-ga-ni ba-an-pad-da-a	in her glorious heart had called him—

Col. II.

nitaḫ im-tug	he was a wise (circumspect) servant
nin-a-na kam	of his mistress;
nam-maḫ nin-a-na	the greatness of his mistress
mu-zu-zu	he knew—
PI-LUL-da	in his great wisdom
(*dingir* *Ba-u*	to Ba'u
nin-a-na-ku	his mistress
LI-im-ma-ši-TAR	he intrusted himself.
NIN E-ninnû	Just as (it was that) the Eninnû,
e ki-ag-ni	his beloved temple
(*dingir*) *Nin-gir-su*	of Ningirsu,

16. *E-PA.* So Jensen, K. B. iii[1]. p. 50, note 13, according to whom it is = '*Haus des Gipfels.*' Amiaud: *E-GUD* = 'the house of light' (Z. A. iii. 36 ff.). For *e-ub-7*, see Jensen, K. B. iii[1]. p. 51, note **o, and comp. Statue G, i. 13 ff.

II. 1. *im-tug*, Br 8494/5: *nâ'idu, ṭalâḫu.* Amiaud: *en serviteur plein de crainte respectueuse.*

2. Comp. F, ii. 10, 11, where Jensen leaves the *kam* untranslated.

4. *zu-zu*, Br. 130; *idû*, H. W. B. 305. Amiaud: *il a proclamé.*

5. *PI* = *uznu*, Br. 7969; *LUL*, Br. 7269: *dannu*; Br. 7272: *ma'du.*

8. *LI-TAR*, Br. 1122: *paḳâdu*, H. W. B. 534; with *ana* (= *KU*) = '*Jemd. etwas anvertrauen, anbefehlen.*' *Im-ma-ši* = verbal prefix, comp. Déc. 8, iii. 2: *im-ši-gì*, and Hommel, S. L. p. 144.

9. *NIN* and *gim* (l. 13) belong together. *Nin* here = relative particle; comp. iv. R. 7, 30 *a*: *nin MAL-E ni-zu-a-mu* = *ša a-na-ku i-du-ú.* The apodosis begins with l. 21.

	lugal-a-ni	his king,
	mu-na-ru-a-gim	he had built,
	ud (*dingir*) *Ba-u*	when for Ba'u,
15	*dumu An-na*	the daughter of Anu,
	nin Uru-azag-ga	the mistress of Uruazagga,
	nin-a-ni	his mistress,
	E-SIL-GID-GID	the *E-SIL-GID-GID*,
	e ki-ag-ni	her beloved temple,
20	*mu-na-ru-a*	he had built,
	uru mu-azag	so also the city he made to shine
	bil im-ma-ta-lal	and purified it.

Col. III.

	ga giš-šub-ba-ka	Of the 'situation of the foundation' (?)
	giš-ba-ġar	a draft he made,
	ka-al-ka	of *KA-AL*
	(*giš*) *URU ba-mul*	its *URU* he made to shine (?);
5	*im-bi ki-laġ-laġ*	its clay from a pure place
	im-mi-dib	he took,
	šeg-bi ki-el-la	its bricks on a shining (sacred) place
	im-mi-du	he formed;

18. Amiaud: *E-SIL-SIR-SIR* (see Z. A. ii. 297, and ibid. iii. 48), who explains it by 'milky way.'

22. Jensen (see F, iii. 2; and comp. further below, l. 12, and C, iii. 7) translates '*füllte mit Feuerbrand*'; Amiaud, '*il a fait décombrer*.' The sense is 'he purified it,' i. e. he burned up the rubbish by kindling a fire on different places, hence lit. 'he filled (sc. the city) with fire.'

III. 1–8 occur again in F, ii. 12–19, and C, ii. 20–iii. 5; see Jensen, K. B. iii[1]. p. 56 ff.

1. *ga giš-šub-ba-ka* = *ga giš-ù-šub-ba-ka* (F, ii. 12) = *ga ù-šub-ba-ka* (C, ii. 20).
2. F, ii. 13: *giš-ba-an-ġar*.
4. C, ii. 23, has only *URU* without *giš*.
5. F, ii. 16, has *ki-azag-ga*, and C, iii. 1, *ki-laġ-laġ-ga-a*.
7. Forms in C, iii, two lines (3, 4). F, ii. 18: *ki-el-a*

šeg giṣ̌-šub-ba ni-gar	the bricks for the foundation he made,
nin-UL pa-ṅe-ud-du	in splendour he made them to shine;
uš-bi mu-azag	its foundation he made bright
bil im-ta-lal	and purified it;
temen-bi	its *Temen*
ni-ir nun-ka	in the *Ni-ir* of the *Nun*
šu-tag ba-ni-dug	he commanded to cast.
(*dingir*) *Ba-u*	For Ba'u,
nin-a-ni	his mistress,
nin Uru-azag-gi	the mistress who directs
im-si-a-an	Uruazagga,
Uru-azag-ga	in Uruazagga

Col. IV.

ki-laǧ-laǧ-ga-a	on a pure place
e mu-na-ru	a temple he built,
(*giš*) *DUR-GAR maǧ*	the sublime throne
nam-nin-ka-ni	of her ladyship
mu-na-gim	he made,
ki-di-kud-na	in her judgement place
mu-na-tum	he püt it up;
DUP-PISAN azag-ga-ni	her holy (bright) *DUP-PISAN*

9. Lines 9 and 10 are left out in C and F. For *giš-šub-ba*, comp. above, iii. 1.

10. *NIN-UL*=*ulṣu*, Br. 9148; H. W. B. 76: '*Üppigkeit, strotzende Fülle oder Pracht.*' For *pa-ud-du*, see Jensen, K. B. iii[1]. pp. 114, 115, notes 3, 4, and *=*šûpû* '*vollenden*' and '*aufstrahlen lassen.*'

11. Lines 11–15 again in C, iii. 6–10; F, iii. 1–5.

16. Lines 16–19 are left out in F.

19. *Si* or *SI-DI*=ישר, H. W. B. 310. Here=iii[2]: *šutêšuru.*

20–IV. 7=F, iii. 6–11.

IV. 1. Comp. C, iii. 1, and above, iii. 5.

3. See A, ii. 3.

6. Comp. above, i. 7.

8. See A, ii. 1.

	mu-na-gim	he made,
10	*e maġ-a-e*	into her very sublime temple
	mu-na-ni-tur	he brought it;
	DIM(?) *Nin-an-da-gal-ki*	the altar of *Nin-an-da-gal-ki*
	mu-na-gim	he made,
	e-maġ-na	in her sublime temple
15	*mu-na-ni-tum*	he put it up,

10. Remarkable is *maġ-a-E*. Ought we to take *E* in the sense of *rabû* (Br. 5845)?

12. For the reading and signification of the first sign, see above (*sub* Naram-Sin), note 7 to Comptes Rendus, 1899, p. 348, pl. 1. *Nin-an-da-gal-ki* = attribute of Ba'u; the name may be translated 'Mistress (*nin*) of the wide or great (*da-gal*, phonetic writing for *dagal* = *rapšu rapaštu*) heaven (*an*) and earth (*ki*).' Comp. also note to col. i. 1.

Cols. v. 1–vii. 21 are found again in Statue G, col. iii. 5–end. The following differences, however, are noteworthy:

E, v. 15: 7 SAL-GIŠ-SA-*ge*-(ĠU) = G, iv. 9: 7 (ĠU)-SAL-GIŠ-SA-*ge*.

16: 15 KUR-GIG-(ĠU) = G, iv. 10: 15 (ĠU)-KUR-GIG.

18: GIŠ-ĠU-*bi*-15 = G, iv. 12: ditto (Jensen has instead of 15 only 7. But why?).

E, vii. 5: 7 SAL-GIŠ-SA-*ge*-(ĠU) = G, vi. 3: 7 (ĠU)-SAL-GIŠ-SA-*ge*.

6: 15 KUR-GIG-(ĠU) = G, vi. 4: 10 KUR-GIG-(ĠU).

10: 1 TU-ĠA-SUĠUR-A = G, vi. 8: 1 ĠA-SUĠUR-TU.

12: 40 GU-LU-SAR = G, vi. 10: ditto. Jensen only 7! Why?

To E, v. 21, 22, vi. 1, and vii. 12–15 = G, iv. 15–17, vi. 10–12, compare also Hommel, P. S. B. A. May, 1893, p. 292, who reads:

40 *gù dib-sar*
7 *gù gibil-bar*
1 *gù* GIŠ-MA-NU

and translates:

forty receptacles for writing utensils,
seven boxes (or jars) for fire-lighting,
one vessel for wooden staffs (*sic* Hommel!).

Statue E, VII. 22 ff.

e $^{dingir)}$ *Ba-u*	When the temple of Ba'u
ki-bi gì-a-da	had thus been restored;
ǧe-gàl-bi	when in beauty

Col. VIII.

pa-ud-du-AG-da	it had been made to shine;
$^{giš)}$ *DUR-GAR Šir-pur-la-*^{ki}*-ka*	when of the throne of Shirpurla
gir-bi gi-na-da	(its) the foundation had been established;
Gu-de-a	when to Gudea,
pa-te-si	the patesi
Šir-pur-la-^{ki}*-ka*	of Shirpurla,
pa ka-gi-na	a sceptre of truth
šu-na gàl-la-da	into his hand had been put;
nam-ti-la-na	when of his life
ud-bi sud-a-da	(its) the days had been lengthened;
dingir-ra-ni	then his god(s)
$^{(dingir)}$ *Nin-giš-zid-da*	Ningishzidda
$^{(dingir)}$ *Ba-u*	(and) Ba'u
e Uru-azag-ga-na	into their (his, her) temple in Uruazagga
mu-na-da-tur-tur	he (Gudea) brought.

VII. 23. The *DA* in this line, as well as in ll. viii. 1, 3, 8, 10, has to be taken in the sense of *ina* = حِين 'when.' The apodosis follows in viii. 11.

VIII. 1. For *pa-ud-du*, see above, iii. 10. We would expect for *AG-da* either *AG-GA-da* or *AG-a-da*; comp. above, vii. 23, *gì-a-da*; viii. 10, *sud-a-da*, and l. 3, *gi-na-da*; l. 8, *gàl-la-da*.

3. *GIR* = E. C. 306; C, iv. 15.

7. *pa ka-gi-na*, lit. a sceptre (rule) of a truthful (true) mouth.

šag mu-ba-ka	In that very same year
kur Mà-gan-ki-ta	from the mountain of Magan
(nà) *KAL im-ta-DUL-DU*	dolerite he brought;
alan-na-ku	into his statue
mu-tu	he formed it.

Col. IX.

nin-mu ba-zig-gi	'Oh, my mistress, be gracious,
nam-ti ba	give life;
ud sag gab zal-zal (sic)	the days of my life with strength make to overflow and abound!'
mu-ku mu-na-sa	he called its name;
e a-mu-na-ni-tur	into the temple he brought it.
alan	The statue
(ga)lu e (dingir) *Ba-u*	is that of him who the temple of Ba'u
mu-ru-a-kam	has built.
ki-gub-ba-bi	From the place it has been put up,
(ga)lu nu-zi-zi	let no one take it away!

16. In the Temple Records of Ur IV. we sometimes find for *šag mu-ba-ka* also *šag mu-ba* (*ka*) *gàl-a-an.*

IX. Ll. 1–3 contain the name of the statue. Amiaud, who wrongly read *ni-ru* for *zal-zal* (sic, clear on the photo.), was not able to translate it.

1. *ba-zig-gi* occurs again in another name, that of a *GAG-GIŠ* (see C. T. i. No. 96-6-15, 1), and means there 'to look favourably upon' (*našû ša êni*).

2. *BA* has to be taken here in the sense of *ḳâšu*, Br. 107; H. W. B. 584. Comp. also O. B. I. 61: *a-na,* (ilu) *Nin-ib, be-li-šu Kad-diš-man-Tur-gu, apil Na-zi-ma-ru-ut-taš, AŠ-ME* (nà) *zagin IB-BI, u-še-piš-ma, a-na ba-la-ṭi-šu, i-ḳi-iš*, with O. B. I. 49: (dingir) *Nin-lil, Ku-ri-gal-zu, in-na-ba.*

3. *UD*=' *Lebenstage*,' H. W. B. 306; *GAB* is parallel to *ZAL-ZAL.*

GAB, Br. 4474: *daḫâdu*, H. W. B. 214; *strotzen, triefen*, ii^{1} *triefend, strotzend, überfliessend machen. ZAL-ZAL*, Br. 5358: *barû*, H. W. B. 184; *strotzen*, iii^{2}, *strotzen machen, reichlich versorgen. SAG* is obj. to *gab* and *zal-zal. SAG*, according to Br. 3515, may also mean *ḳarnu*, '*Horn*' = Hebr. קרן, in the sense of 'strength.'

9. *DU* if *gub* = *kânu* ii^{1}. Lit. from the place of its having been put up.

10. *Zi-zi* = *nasâḫu*, Br. 2349; H. W. B. 471.

di-ka-bi	This ordinance
(ga)lu la ba-ni-lal-e	let no one set at naught!

11. Lit. 'this word (*di = dabâbu,* Br. 9524) of mouth (*ka = pû*).

12. *Lal,* probably here best = *našû,* Br. 10101; H. W. B. 484: '*wegnehmen. LA* is parallel to *NU,* l. 10, hence it must be = Assyr *lâ,* which latter, when in a prohibitive sentence, is used with the present, Delitzsch, Assyr. Gram. § 144. This present we find even here: *LAL-E.* Thus we have here a remarkable Semitic influence. Comp. also ii. R. 15, 30 *a*: *la ba-an-ši-in-gin = la im-gu-ur,* where *LA* is also to be found for the regular *NU.* Amiaud, who translated *ses prescriptions que personne ne les transgresse,* apparently took *LA* also in the sense of *NU*; see also R. A. ii. p. 19. It is, however, also possible to take *DI-KA* in the sense of *sattûku,* then to be read *SA-DUG* (see Urukagina above, p. 50), col. iv. 3, and to translate it: 'its (i. e. of the statue) appointed offerings let no one take away.'

Statue H.

Col. I.

(*dingir*) *Ba-u*	Unto Ba'u,
sal šag-ga	the gracious lady,
dumu An-na	the daughter of Anu,
nin Uru-azag-ga	the mistress of Uruazagga,
nin ĝe-gàl	the mistress of riches,
dumu an-azag-ga	the child of the bright heaven,
nin-a-ni	his mistress,
Gu-de-a	Gudea,
pa-te-si	patesi
Šir-pur-la-[ki]-ge	of Shirpurla.

Col. II.

ud E-SIL-GID-GID	When the *E-SIL-GID-GID,*
e ki-ag-ni	his beloved temple,
e ĝe-UL Uru-azag-ga	the temple, the beauty of Uruazagga,
mu-na-ru-a	he had built,

I. 1. See E, i. 1 ff.

II. 1. See E, ii. 18.

3. *ĜE = ḫegallu, duḫdu, daḫâdu*; *UL,* see E, iii. 10.

kur Mà-gan-^{ki}-ta	(then) from the mountain of Magan
(*nà*) *KAL* (sic) *im-ta-DUL-DU*	dolerite he brought down ;
alan-na-ni-ku	into his statue
mu-tu	he formed it.

Col. III.

nin dumu ki-ag an-azag-ga-ge	'Oh, mistress, beloved child of the bright heaven !
am (*dingir*) *Ba-u*	Oh, mother Ba'u !
E-SIL-GID-GID-ta	out of the *E-SIL-GID-GID*
Gu-de-a	unto Gudea
nam-ti mu-na-sum	give life !'
mu-ku mu-na-sa	he called its name ;
e Uru-azag-ga-ka	into the temple of Uruazagga
mu-na-ni (sic)-*tur*	he brought it.

6. The original has *PA* for *KAL*.
III. 5. For other names see above, *sub* Nammağni, p. 187, note 12.
8. For *RU* of the original we have to read *ni* !

The buildings of Gudea were too numerous to allow of a complete description ; what has already been given will suffice.

Gudea was married to a certain Gin-Dunpauddu[1], and was followed on the throne of Shirpurla by his son *Ur-Ningirsu*[2].

[1] Ménant, Catal. des Cyl. p. 59 ; K. B. iii^{1}. p. 65 *e*. Jensen reads the name *Gin-*(*dingir*) *Umun-pa-ud-du*. This name was read correctly first by Hommel, Z. A. i. 439 f.

[2] His name means : 'The servant of Ningirsu' (Assyr. *Kalbi-Ninib*). His inscriptions are :

R. A. iii. p. 120.

Déc. 37, 9 ; Jensen, l. c. p. 66 *a* ; A. B. K. p. 7, No. 13.

Le Clercq, ii. pl. ix. 4, and p. 87.

The inscriptions : Déc. 26, 5, identical with Déc. 37, 8, also to be found in A. B. K. p. 7, Nos. 14, 15, see Jensen, K. B. iii^{1}. p. 66 *b* (comp. above, p. 37, note 1) ; and Winckler, U. A. G. p. 157, No. 9 (=C. T. 12218), see Jensen,

Very little can be said of him. He seems to have continued the work of his father in building the Eninnû and the gigunu (*Dunkelgemach*).

After a gap of probably one or more generations, we come to *Ur-*(*dingir*) *Nin-sun*[1]. Our only knowledge in regard to him is that he presented a vase to Ningirsu, the strong hero of Enlil, with the petition to lengthen his life.

After a further gap in the succession of the patesis, we reach the last of the known rulers of Shirpurla, viz. (*Ga*)*lu-ka-ni*. Three inscriptions—as far as I know—mention a patesi (*Ga*)*lu-ka-ni*.

The first—see above, p. 21—records that a certain Gala-Lama, the son of (*Ga*)*lu-ka-ni*, patesi of Shirpurla, dedicates an inscription 'for the life of Dungi, the mighty king, *king of Ur, and king of Shumer and Akkad*.' This (Ga)lukani clearly, then, is a contemporary of Dungi I.

The second—see above, p. 22—on the other hand, tells us that a certain (Ga)lukani, patesi of Shirpurla, dedicates an inscription for Dungi, the mighty hero, *king of Ur*. This inscription we refer to another (Ga)lukani—a contemporary of Dungi II. of the third dynasty of Ur; see above, p. 22, note 2; p. 37, note 2; and *sub* fourth dynasty of Ur.

The third—see Scheil in Rec. de Trav. xviii. p. 74—is in the form of a contract-tablet (a receipt, *šu-ba-ti*, of grain), which has the date: *itu ŠE-IL-LA mu en Eridug-ki ba-a-tug*, together with the following seal-impression:—

(*dingir*) *Utu-a*	Utua,
dumu Ur-	the son of Ur . . .

K. B. iii[1]. p. 68 ii. (comp. above, p. 37), do not belong to Ur-Ningirsu, the patesi of Shirpurla. See above, p. 35 ff. They, however, may be placed under the reign of Dungi II., 'king of Ur.'

[1] Thus we ought to pronounce his name, as has been shown by Scheil, R. T. xii. 208, on the basis of Gudea, Cyl. B, 23, 19: (*dingir*) *Nin-giš-zid-da, dumu-sag* (Price gives *dumu-ka*), *An-na-kam, dingir am-zu* (*dingir*) *Nin-sun-na*.' See also for another *dumu-sag* of Anu, Gudea, Statue E, 1. i, note. *Ur-*(*dingir*) *Ninsun* = Assyr. *Kalbi-Ninsun*, the servant of Ninsun. His inscriptions: Heuzey, R. A. ii. 79; Oppert, ibid.; and Jensen, K. B. iii[1]. p. 77. Comp. above, p. 21.

dup-sar	the scribe (of)
(Ga)lu-ka-ni	(Ga)lukani,
pa-te-si	patesi
Šir-pur-la-^{ki}	of Shirpurla.

This inscription leaves it doubtful whether it refers to (Ga)lukani, the contemporary of Dungi II., or to Dungi III (see *sub* Ur IV.). Hence this much only we can say, that (Ga)lukani, the father of Ĝala-Lama, with whom we are concerned here, was dependent on Dungi I.; so also was his son, who however seems to have lost the position of patesi of Shirpurla altogether, as this title is lacking in his inscription (Déc. 21, 4; Jensen, K. B. iii[1]. p. 70; and above, p. 1)[1].

With (Ga)lukani an important period of Old Babylonian history terminates. Shirpurla-Girsu (also called Lagash) no doubt was *the city*, around which the other cities grouped themselves. These other cities rise into prominence as they become related to or masters of Shirpurla. This naturally produced a chequered and

[1] Scheil published a portion of an inscription, Rec. de Trav. xix. p. 50, 9, which reads:

(Dingir) Dun-gi	To Dungi,
nitaĝ lig-ga	the mighty hero,
&c.	&c. . . . .
Al-la-mu	Allamu,
(dumu) Ur-Sag-ga-mu	the son of Ur-Saggamu,
pa-te-si	patesi.

He adds in a note: '*Elle nous livre le nom d'un nouveau patesi,—de Sirpurla, très vraisemblablement.—Ce cylindre voué à Dungi ne prouve pas que le patesi fût son contemporain. On en vouait aux rois défunts, comme on continuait en Égypte à graver le cartouche de Ramsès II., par exemple, sur les scarabées, jusque vers l'époque ptolémaïque*' (cf. Rec. de Trav. xviii. p. 72, suiv. 1). This opinion rests upon no real foundation. Allamu may be a patesi of any other city. The Dungi—as long as Scheil withholds the remainder of his titles—may be just as well Dungi II. of the third dynasty of Ur, who bore the title *lugal Urum-ki-ma*, or Dungi III. of the fourth dynasty, who calls himself *lugal Urum-ki-ma lugal an-ub-da tab-tab-ba-ge*. Dungi I. (Ur II.) terms himself *lugal Urum-ki-ma lugal Ki-en-gi-ki-Urdu-ge*. It would be well and advisable to publish not only the name of the kings, but also their titles. (See however *sub* Ur IV.)

varied development in the fortunes of Shirpurla. The oldest dynasty, headed by Urukagina, was reduced from the rank of 'kings' to that of patesis by the northern power of Kish. We have already been introduced to three kings of this latter country, viz. U-dug-?, Mesilim, the contemporary of Lugalshuggur, and Lugal-da?-ak?. The struggle lay between *the north* and *the south*. Such conflicts had already taken place before the time of Urukagina. Enshagkushanna, lord of Kengi, had to fight this very same enemy in the north.

Thus, in the earliest recorded period of Babylonian history, we find the question raised: Who shall govern in Babylonia? Shall the north be the master, or shall it be the south? The struggle was protracted. Eannatum, the son of Akurgal, succeeded in throwing off the obnoxious yoke of Kish, placed upon Shirpurla in the time of his predecessors. No doubt Ur-Ninâ, his grandfather, had initiated the conflict, for he terms himself 'king,' which he could not have done if he were still dependent upon Kish. Eannatum, however, dealt the last and decisive blow against Kish, under *Al-zu-zu-a*, whom he burnt, and whose gods he cast into the fire. In consequence of this victory he became himself 'king of Kish.' How long he retained this dignity we cannot tell. It seems, however, that his successors were unable permanently to preserve what Eannatum had left them. Another power acquired in course of time great prominence. This power is Gishban, the northern neighbour of Shirpurla.

Already during the reign of Eannatum we find it filled with a hostile spirit against Shirpurla. This hostility of Gishban against its southern neighbour no doubt resulted from the instigation of Kish, for we find that a certain Enne-Ugun not only was 'king of Kish,' but also 'king of the hosts of Gishban[1].' Probably no

[1] This, however, is true only if we suppose that the reading *erim* (*giš*)*BAN-ki* be correct. If, on the other hand, we read for *erim* (*giš*) *BAN-ki* = Uḫ (which Hommel reads *ṢAB-BAN*=Upi, Opis), we would have to suppose that Kish was not allied with (*giš*)*BAN-ki*, but with Uḫ. But even this alliance was defeated by an unknown king of Shirpurla.

enemy of Shirpurla was as pertinacious as Gishban. Again and again it renewed its hostilities, although repeatedly defeated, and bound by solemn obligations 'never to invade the territory of Shirpurla again.' Gishban was resolved to obtain possession of Babylonia—and it succeeded. Lugalzaggisi, the son of the pateśi Ukush, not only made himself master of the whole of Babylonia (no doubt Shirpurla included), but he also became *lugal-kalam-ma*, 'king of the world,' his empire extending from the Persian Gult to the Mediterranean Sea.

This great empire, however, did not hold its own very long. Although the whole of Babylonia had been temporarily united under one sceptre, yet not very long after the time of Lugalzaggisi we meet with the same disintegration as had previously existed. The great empire was once more split into north and south. The chief *rôle* in the south was taken by Ur under Lugalkigubnidudu, who even succeeded in gaining possession of Erech and Nippur (consequently also Shirpurla). The north is again represented by Kish under Urzaguddu, Lugaltarsi, Manishtusu, and Âlusharshid.

This division, however, did not last long. Agade in the *north*, under Sargon I., obtained the chief power. Sargon I. and his son, Naram-Sin, not only succeeded in bringing the north and the south of Babylonia together, but they extended their dominion in all directions far beyond its confines, so that Naram-Sin could call himself 'king of the four corners of the world'—a title which consequently indicates the extension of the empire *geographically*.

The title 'king of the four corners of the world' *may* mean the same, it was said above (p. 163 ff.), as the Sumerian *lugal-kalam-ma*, 'king of the world.' A closer examination, however, will show that the former *includes more*. 'King of the world' (*lugal-kalam-ma*) does not involve dominion over the extreme north, or over Eastern Arabia and Magan, or over Elam. The expression 'from the rising of the sun to the going down of the sun' is explained by the words immediately following: 'from the lower sea of the Tigris and the Euphrates to the upper sea' (Lugalzag. i. 46; ii. 9). According to this, then, a 'kingship of the world' would be a dominion extending from the Persian Gulf up, between the rivers Tigris and Euphrates (comp. *gir-bi*, Lugalzag. ii. 10 ff.), to the Mediterranean Sea.

The 'gravitation point' of such a kingdom lay in the west, in the countries extending from the Tigris and Euphrates in the north to the Mediterranean.

A 'kingship of the four corners of the world,' on the other hand, not only included the *nam-lugal-kalam-ma*, but in addition to this the lands lying further to the north, as well as those to the east and south. This is clearly shown by an inscription to be found in Peters, Nippur, ii. p. 239 (see below), where we read that Gimil-Sin was called by Nannar to be the

sib kalam-ma
šà an-ub-da tab-tab-ba-ku,

i. e. 'shepherd of the *world and* of the four corners of the world.' If therefore the title *šar kibrat arba'im* was nothing *more* than a *translation* of the *nam-lugal-kalam-ma* (Hilprecht, O. B. I. p. 270), this title here would be meaningless. Gimil-Sin then would simply state the same thing twice, which is very improbable. Hence the title *an-ub-da tab-tab-ba* must include more. Thus we can only maintain that *lugal an-ub-da tab-tab-ba* is = *šar kibrat arba'im*, and that *lugal-kalam-ma* is a title by itself, while a *šar kiššati* does not exist at this time.

How long this 'kingship of the four corners of the world' lasted, we cannot tell. Eventually the successors of Naram-Sin were forced to yield Shirpurla to the kings of the second dynasty of Ur, Ur-Gur and Dungi I.

The Second Dynasty of Ur.

A remarkable change takes place in the titles of these kings. They not only call themselves *lugal Uru-um-ki-ma* [1], i. e. 'king of

[1] Written *Uru-unu(g)-ki-ma* = title of Ur III.

Ur,' but also *lugal Ki-en-gi-ki-Urdu*, i.e. 'king of Shumer and Akkad.' What does this latter title mean?

In the bilingual inscriptions of Ḫammurabi the expression *Ki-en-gi-ki-Urdu* is translated by *Šumerim*[1] *ù Akkadim*[2]. Shumer therefore must correspond to *Kengi* and Akkad to *Urdu*. Is it possible to derive Shumer from *Ki-en-gi*?

The word *Ki-en-gi* is also written *Ki-in-gi*, *Kingin*, and even *Kin-gi-ra* (Lehmann, Shamashshumukin, p. 85, and Winckler, A. O. V. 1887, p. 20). As regards the pronunciation of the signs *BUR-BUR* = Urdu or Uru^{i}_{a}, see Lehmann, l. c. p. 85.

It has been stated above (under Enshagkushanna and Ur-Ninâ) that some scholars derive the word Shumer either directly or indirectly from *SU(N)* + *GIR*. But we must go a step further. There is little doubt that Shumer is derived from Sungir. But can we prove that Sungir is = Kengin, or better Kengir? For the change of *n* to *r*, comp. *Unug* = *Uruk*; *gan* = *kar*, which change undoubtedly occurred under Semitic influence. That *k* in Sumerian can become *š*—when it stands before '*i und i-verwandten Vokalen*'—is proved by a comparison of *KU* = *šu* = *še* (Z. K. p. 99 f.; Lehmann, l. c. p. 86). The form *Kingir* would become consequently *Šingir*, exactly the form which we have in Hebrew שִׁנְעָר[3]; and if we take into consideration the form S^{a}_{i}*ngara*, which occurs in inscriptions of Thutmosis III. (see Tiele, Geschichte, pp. 139, 145), it is evident that the Hebrew שׁ originally was *s*. As was shown above, under Lugalzaggisi, *š* in the oldest inscriptions is represented by *s*; compare such forms as *u-sa-za-ku-ni* (O. B. I. i. 14), *zera-su* (ibid. ll. 20, 23)[4]. From this, then,

[1] Written either *Šu-me-er-im*, *Šu-me-rim*, or *Šu-me-ri-im*, Lehmann, Shamashshumukin, p. 84, note 6.

[2] Written *Ak-ka-di-im*, *Ak-ka-di-i*, *Ak-kad-i*, Lehmann, ibid. p. 84, notes 2 and 3; but also *Ak-di-i*, Lehmann, ibid. p. 73, note 9.

[3] The *a*-sound in Hebrew is probably due to the guttural ע.

[4] It may not be impossible that the pronunciation of *S* for *Š* is due to Arabic influence. This would be only another proof that the Semites originally came from Arabia; for *u-sa-za-ku-ni* and *zera-su* bear marks of South Arabic formation; comp. בנשׂו = بِنُسُو, 'his son,' and ישׂראשׂשׂ = يُسَرْأَشُسْ, 'he went away.'

would follow that the Hebrew שנער is a younger form of Sangar(a), and consequently also of Sungir. The development so far would be $K_{e}^{i}ngin$ = Kingir = $S_{i}^{a}ngar$ = Sungir = שִׁנְעָר. Little or no stress can be laid upon the change of the vowels, as is evident from a comparison of the variety of the forms for Kingin [1].

The next development in these forms is that *ng* becomes *m*; comp. *dingir* = *dimmer*. Sungir then becomes Sumir, and with a softening of the *s* to *š* (as in the Hebrew שנער) Šumir. An *i* before *r* is changed very often to *e* (Haupt, 'The Assyr. E-vowel,' American Journal of Philology, vol. iii. p. 287): Šumir becomes Šumer.

Hence Šumer = Sungir = Kengin. From the inscriptions of Ur-Ninâ we know that the Nin-Su(n)gir was the god of Girsu-Shirpurla. Girsu consequently is only a metathesis of the original Sungir, exactly as *apsu* is that of *zu-ab*, or *lugal* that of *gal*+*ga*(*lu*) [2]. After the metathesis had taken place Girsun became Girsu, losing its final *n*. Girsun would then be the older form for Girsu, as Kengin is the older form for Kengi.

What follows from these considerations? Simply and solely this: *Kengi is the oldest name for Sungir* (= *Girsu-Shirpurla*) [3], *which latter was pronounced by the Semites at the time of Ḫammurabi, Shumer. Enshagkushanna* en Kengi *is the oldest* (*Sumerian?*) *king of Shirpurla!* Now we understand why the kings from Ur-Gur to Dungi I. call themselves '*lugal Kengi*.'

[1] The original pronunciation was Kengin; then, under Semitic influence, it became Kengir (comp. *gan-kar*), and then further Sengir. The *e* of the syllable Sen was pronounced halfway between *a* and *i*—hence the name of Thutmosis III. (comp. e.g. *aš-te-mu-šu* for *ištemušu*, Amarna, 121, 20. *aš* = *àš* = *eš* = *iš*). The Semites in Babylonia proper pronounced Sungir, which again was heard as שִׁנְעָר by the Canaanites (comp. Amarna, 121, 13: *iš-ta-ḫa-ḫi-in* for *uštaḫaḫin* in Assyr. *iknuš* and *ikniš*. *u* = *ü* = *i*).

[2] Comp also in Semitic languages: כרב = *karâbu* = Hebr. בָּרַךְ; Assyr. *laḫru* = Hebr. רָחֵל, Arab. رخل, &c.

[3] The very fact that we have a *KI*, = 'place,' after Kengi speaks for our explanation. Quite different is Hommel's view (P. S. B. A., May, 1894, p. 209), who reads *KI-Imgi KI-Urra.*

We know from the inscription of Ġala-Lama that Dungi I. was in possession of Girsu-Shirpurla (K. B. iii[1]. p. 71, 9). He, writing in the Sumerian dialect, uses for Girsu-Shirpurla only the original Sumerian name Kengi in contradistinction to Urdu.

Further, if Kengi-Shumer is the city (land) of Girsu, and *lugal Kengi* means 'king of Girsu,' then *lugal Urdu* must mean 'king of the city (land) of Urdu.' This latter word, as we have seen, is translated in Semitic by Akkad. Akkad undoubtedly is the later pronunciation for Agad(e); the soft *g* has been changed to *k*[1]. If Shumer-Sungir are the later forms for Kengi, then Agade-Akkad *must be* the later forms for Urdu; this would clearly follow from the analogy of the case. *How* Agade-Akkad can be derived from Urdu (*BUR-BUR*) is still a secret. And if *lugal Kengi* means nothing less and nothing more than 'king of Girsu-Shirpurla,' it follows from the parallelism in the title that *lugal Urdu* must mean 'king of Agade-Akkad.'

We have seen why the kings from Ur-Gur to Dungi I. called themselves *lugal Ki-en-gi*, i.e. king of Kengi-Sungir-Shumer (Girsu), viz. because they were in possession of Shirpurla. Hence if they also call themselves *lugal Urdu*, i.e. king of Urdu-Agade-Akkad, they must also have ruled over this latter city. It is true that this statement cannot yet be substantiated from the inscriptions. We know, however, that they possessed *Kutha*[2] (i.e. the modern Tell Ibrâhîm, not far east of Babylon, Delitzsch, Parad. p. 217 ff.). Since Agade lies a little further to the north of Kutha it seems probable that they held sway over Agade also.

The question now remains, why should these kings adopt such a title as '*lugal Ki-en-gi-ki-Urdu-ge*'? We have already called the attention of the reader to the protracted struggle between the north and the south, stretching back to the earliest period of Babylonian history. The south up to this time was mainly represented by

[1] The writing *Ak-ka-di-i* with double *k* results from its being syllabically written. But comp. also *Ak-di-i*.

[2] Mittheilungen des Akad.-Or. Ver. zu Berlin, i. p. 16; Winckler, K. B. iii[1]. p. 81, 5.

Girsu-Shirpurla. This was the case under Enshagkushanna, lord of Kengi (i. e. Girsu), under Ur-Ninâ and his successors, and also the later patesis of Shirpurla. The north, on the other hand, was represented sometimes by Kish, sometimes by Gishban, or by Kish and Gishban together, and last of all by Agade-Akkad. The victories of Kish were partial and intermittent. Even the supremacy of Gishban under Lugalzaggisi exercised no such wide influence over Babylonia as did that of Agade under Naram-Sin[1]. Thus finally the kingdom of Agade became the true representative of the north, in the same way as Shirpurla had been of the south, and this was especially the case under Ur-Gur or possibly before. Ur-Gur ruled over Shirpurla and over Urdu-Akkad, thus for the first time uniting the two representative states or cities under one sceptre. That Ur-Gur should thus use Urdu-Agade-Akkad to represent the whole north is due to the fact that Agade had overcome Kish and Gishban. Hence Agade had become, shortly before the time of Ur-Gur, the true representative of the north.

We have seen that in the north (Gishban, Kish, Agade) from the very beginning Semitic kings ruled, mostly using in the inscriptions their own language. In the south, on the other hand, Semitic (*sic*) kings reigned—it is true—but these kings spoke the Sumerian language, at least used it in their inscriptions, and thus had become 'acclimatized,' i. e. had become 'naturalized Sumerians.' Ur-Gur in using the title *lugal Ki-en-gi-*^{ki}*-Urdu-ge* wished to indicate that he was king both of the north, where the Semitic language was spoken, and of the south, where the Sumerian language was used; in other words, he was king both of the Sumerians ('pure' and 'naturalized') and of the Semites. For the same reason also Ḫammurabi, who had obtained possession of the *šarrût Kengi-*^{ki}*-Urdu* in consequence of his victory over Rim-Sin, and thus was able to call himself 'king (lord) of the *KALAM Šumerim û Akkadim*,' wrote his inscriptions in the two languages, thus claiming that he was king alike over the Sumerians (in the largest sense) and the Semites.

This consideration supplies the key to the right understanding

[1] Notice also the difference between *lugal-kalam-ma* and *šar kibrat arba'im*!

of the perpetual conflicts between the north and the south. The north represented the *pure* Semitic race, pure at least to this extent, that they spoke their own language. The south, originally inhabited by a Sumerian population, passed gradually under the rule of those Semites, who had remained there after the greater part of them had left it to settle down in the north. These Semites assimilated themselves to the Sumerians, accepted their language, which they in the earlier or earliest period mingled with a 'goodly lot' of Semitisms (time of Eannatum, Entemena, Lugal-zaggisi, &c.), but later on were able to write it comparatively well (time of Gudea); nay, they even succeeded in acquiring the sovereignty of Shirpurla. The south therefore represents the old Sumerians under the rule of assimilated Semites.

No wonder that the Semites of the north should be filled with enmity towards their degraded brethren in the south.

From the above-given facts it is evident that it matters very little what derivation we ascribe to the actual term, 'Kengi or Urdu'; whether we give to Kengi the meaning of 'the land of reeds and rushes' (Hilprecht), or 'land κατ' ἐξοχήν' (Lehmann), or '*Tiefland*' (Winckler), and to Urdu or *BUR-BUR* the 'land of the strangers' (Amiaud: *bur-bur* = βάρ-βαρ-(ος) and perhaps = בל־בל = בבל, Gen. iii. 9; see B. O. R. 123 f.), or 'the land of the two rivers' (Lehmann, Shamashshumukin, p. 92), or 'highland' (Tiele, Geschichte, p. 76 f. Comp. also Winckler's idea: *Kengi-ki-Urdu* = *Hochland und Tiefland*).

Only so much is certain, that Kengi = Sungir = Shumer = Girsu-Shirpurla, and Urdu = Agade = Akkad, both cities taken as the representative cities of the north and of the south of Babylonia, where the Semitic and the Sumerian languages were used respectively. Hence, once more, '*lugal Kengi-ki-Urdu-ge*' *means the king of the two cities Girsu and Akkad, which are the representatives of the Sumerian* (*or southern*) *and the Semitic* (*or northern*) *people and language*; it is therefore a geographic as well as ethnic title.

In conclusion we may note the views of earlier scholars with regard to the meaning of this title.

Pognon showed first that Kengi and Urdu denote two districts of a territory subject to the kings of Babylon—Akkad on the confines of Assyria, and Shumer, whose site is unknown (L'Inscription de Bavian, pp. 125–134).

Winckler, on the other hand, tried to prove that Kengi-Urdu at this time had a more restricted application to a kingdom of Southern Babylonia, of which Ur was the capital. Hence the phrase is not geographical but political. The capital of this small Southern Babylonian kingdom, according to Winckler, later on became Isin, then Larsa, &c. See 'Sumer und Akkad,' in Mittheilungen des Akad.-Orient. Vereins, vol. i. p. 6 ff.; U. A. G. p. 65 ff.; Geschichte, p. 19 ff.

Lehmann, however, has called this opinion in question. According to him, Shumer-Akkad had a geographical meaning as well as a gentilic. See Shamashshumukin, p. 68 ff.

Two rulers, Ur-Gur and his son, combined those two hostile elements of Shumer and Akkad under one sceptre, thus restoring in Old Babylonia the peace which had been disturbed for many centuries, nay, even from the time of the original Semitic invasion. No wonder, then, that the later Assyrian kings should ascribe to themselves this very same title. In this way they desired to proclaim themselves 'princes of peace,' doing justice to all classes of men and to all nationalities. Ur-Gur's[1] capital was situated in Ur (Ur of the Chaldees). His greatness is seen in the building of temples rather than in war[2]. The temple Teimila of $^{(dingir)}$ *Uru-*

[1] No name in all Old Babylonian history has been read in as many ways as this king's name. See Maspero, Dawn of Civilization, p. 617, note 1. The name means 'the servant of the god *GUR*.'

His inscriptions:

i. R. 1, No. i. 5, 6, 7, 8, 9; Winckler, A. B. K. p. 8, No. 21; p. 9, Nos. 22, 23, 25, 26; and K. B. iii[1]. p. 78, Nos. 4, 8.

O. B. I. Nos. 14, 121, 122.

Comp. also i. R. 68, No. 1; Peiser, K. B. iii[2], p. 95.

[2] If, however, we suppose that Ur-Gur II. is identical with Ur-Gur I.—which may very well be possible (see Ur III.)—we would have to say that he was first 'king of Ur,' and later on, in consequence of successful wars, became also 'king of Shumer and Akkad.'

ki (i. e. Nannar, the moon-god) in Ur, and the temple Eanna (i. e. 'house of heaven') of the goddess Innanna (i. e. Ishtar) in Uruk (Warka), owe their origin to him. For Shamash (the sun-god) he built the temple Ebarra at Larsa; for Ninlil (the wife of Enlil) or Bêlit, one at Nippur; and for Enlil (Bêl) he restored the old Ekur ('house of the mountain') which was built by Sargon I. and Naram-Sin. See O. B. I. No. 121:

$^{(Dingir)}$ *En-lil*	For Bêl,
lugal kur-kur-ra	the king of the lands,
lugal-a-ni	his king,
Ur-$^{(dingir)}$ *Gur*	Ur-Gur,
nitaǵ lig-ga	the mighty hero,
lugal Uru-um-^{ki}-*ma*	king of Ur,
lugal Ki-en-gi-^{ki}-*Urdu-ge*	king of Shumer and Akkad,
E-kur	the Ekur,
e-ki-ag-ga-ni	his beloved house,
mu-na-ru	he has built.

and O. B. I. No. 122:

Ur-$^{(dingir)}$ *Gur*	Ur-Gur,
lugal Uru-um-^{ki}-*ma*	king of Ur,
lugal Ki-en-gi-^{ki}-*Urdu*	king of Shumer and Akkad,
(*ga*)*lu e* $^{(dingir)}$ *En-lil-la*(*l*)	the one who the house of Bêl
in-ru-a	has built.

Also for the goddess Ninḫarsag he built or restored a temple; see O. B. I. No. 14:

$^{(Dingir)}$ *Nin-ḫar-sag*	For Ninḫarsag,
nin-a-ni	his mistress,
Ur-$^{(dingir)}$ *Gur*	Ur-Gur,
nitaǵ lig-ga	the mighty hero,
lugal Uru-um-^{ki}-*ma*	king of Ur,

lugal Ki-en-gi-ki-Urdu-ge	king of Shumer and Akkad,
. . . *AN-DUG+PA-KI*[1]	the . . .,
[*e*]-*ki-ag-ga-ni*	her beloved house,
mu-na-ru	he has built.

According to Nabû-nâ'id, Ur-Gur, as well as his son[2] Dungi, built also the *E-lugal-gud-si-di*, the *ziḳ-ḳur-rat* of the temple *E-giš-šir-gal* in Ur.

Ur-Gur was followed by his son Dungi[3], who continued the work of his father; completed the sanctuaries of the moon-god, and the Eanna of Ishtar; erected temples in honour of *Nin-Mar-ki* (i. e. the

[1] Before the sign *AN*, which is partly mutilated, something seems to have been broken away, probably an *A*. The sign after *AN* is not yet assimilated; it is *DUG* with an inserted *PA*, or better *NAGID*. As such it might mean 'the house of the good shepherd.'

[2] So it was said above, p. 24. We may however be doubtful whether the Dungi mentioned by Nabû-nâ'id is really our Dungi here, for he calls Ur-Gur only '*šarru ša maḫri*,' without giving his full title. Assuming that he meant Ur-Gur, 'king of Ur, king of Shumer and Akkad,' we are justified in calling Dungi his son.

[3] Dungi, according to Winckler, K. B. iii[1]. p. 80, note 3, = Semitic *Ba'u-ukîn*.

His inscriptions:

Winckler, U. A. G. p. 157, 9; K. B. iii[1]. p. 69, 11.

Winckler, A. F. vi. p. 547, 8.

i. R. 2, ii. 1-4; Winckler, K. B. iii[1]. p. 80, 1-4; A. B. K. p. 10, Nos. 28-31.

Mittheilungen des Akademisch-Orientalischen Vereins zu Berlin, i. p. 16; Winckler, l. c., p. 80, 5. Also published by Winckler, Altbabyl. Keilinschriften, No. 35. Nos. 2 and 3 are also to be found in C. J. Ball, Light from the East, p. 63.

Lenormant, Textes inédit. p. 163, No. 69; Winckler, l. c. p. 82, 7 (doubtful).

C. T. 12217 (doubtful).

Collection de Clercq, No. 86 (?); Amiaud, Z. A. ii. p. 295.

O. B. I. Nos. 16, 123.

Déc. pl. 28, 1; pl. 29, 3, 4 = A. B. K. p. 11, Nos. 32, 33.

Déc. pl. 38, 4; Jensen, K. B. iii[1]. p. 70, No. 9; and above, p. 21.

Hommel, Geschichte, p. 334. Two patesis of Nippur (p. 30, 1) dedicate the seal to (*dingir*) *Nusku*, *luḫ-maḫ*, (*dingir*) *En-lil-la*(*l*) for the life of Dungi I.

(The inscription of Dungi given above, p. 22, belongs to Dungi II.)

mistress of Mar) in Girsu [1], of Nergal [2] in Kutha [3], of Ninâ [4] and of Ningirsu [5] in Girsu.

To these should be added the Ekarzida of the goddess *Nin-Uru-um-ki-ma*, i. e. the mistress of Ur; see O. B. I. No. 16:

(*Dingir*) *Nin-Uru-um-ki-ma*	For Nin-Ur,
nin-a-ni	his mistress,
Dun-gi	Dungi,
nitaǵ-lig-ga	the mighty hero,
lugal Uru-um-ki-ma	king of Ur,
lugal Ki-en-gi-ki-Urdu-ge	king of Shumer and Akkad,
e Kar-zi-da-ka-ni	her house of *KAR-ZI-DA*
mu-na-ru	he has built.

the temple of the goddess *Dam-gal-nun-na*, i. e. the great wife of Nun or Ea, at Nippur; see O. B. I. No. 123:

(*Dingir*) *Dam-gal-nun-na*	For Damgalnunna,
nin-a-ni	his mistress,
Dun-gi	Dungi,
nitaǵ-lig-ga	the mighty hero,
lugal Uru-um-ki-ma	king of Ur,
lugal Ki-en-gi-ki-Urdu-ge	king of Shumer and Akkad,
e-En-lil-ki-ka-ni	her house in Nippur
mu-na-ru	he has built.

and a temple for Ea himself (Winckler, A. F. p. 547, 8 = C. T. i. 7287):

(*dingir*) *En-ki*	For Ea,
lugal-a-ni	his king,

[1] For her he built the Esalgilsa, i. e. according to Jensen, K. B. iii [1]. p. 29, note * = *bît šukutti*, '*Schatzhaus*.'

[2] Nergal is called here *Šid-lam-ta-ud-du*, and the temple which he built the E-Shidlam. See Hommel, Gesch. p. 336 ff.

[3] For Kutha, written *TIK-GAB-A-ki*, see Delitzsch, Parad. p. 217 f.

[4] For her—called here the *nin-in-dub-ba*, *nin-en*, *nin-a-ni*, i. e. 'the mistress of the art of writing'—he built the *E-URU-URU-e-ga-ra*, Déc. 29, 4; Hommel, Geschichte, p. 321. For *uru*, comp. Jensen, K. B. iii [1]. p. 12, note 4.

[5] The Eninnû, Déc. 29, 3.

Dun-gi	Dungi,
lugal Uru-um-ki-ma	king of Ur,
lugal Ki-en-gi-ki-Urdu-ge	king of Shumer and Akkad,
e-a-ni	his house
mu-na-ru	he has built.

The buildings erected in honour of different gods by Ur-Gur and Dungi indicate that they held sway over the whole of Babylonia, i. e. over Erech, Larsa, Girsu, Nippur, and Kutha.

Thus Ur-Gur and Dungi stand out as two mighty figures, the ancestors[1] of a long line of kings ruling over the Semites and Sumerians, i. e. over Agade (Akkad) and Kengi (Shirpurla)—the patesis of which latter city they reduced in course of time to utter powerlessness (Ǵala-Lama, comp. above, p. 21).

At the present, however, we have no knowledge in regard to the names either of their predecessors or their successors. It seems, however, that these kings of Ur very soon lost Uruk or Warka, for we find not long after their time certain kings calling themselves *lugal Unug-ki-ga lugal Am-na-nu-um*, i. e. *king of Erech, king of Amnanu*[2].

Kings of Erech.

Two rulers belong to this latter dynasty, Singâshid[3] and Singâmil[4]. Both bear pure Semitic names.

[1] Or successors ?

[2] Lehmann (Zwei Probleme), Winckler, and Hommel put this dynasty after Ur IV.

[3] Probably = (*ilu*) *Sin-ḳâšid*, 'Sin exalteth'; comp. Nabû-nâ'id.

His inscriptions:

i. R. 2, No. viii. 1, 2; Winckler, K. B. iii[1]. p. 82, 1, 2; and A. B. K. Nos. 38, 39.

iv. R. 35, 2; Winckler, l. c. p. 84, 3; comp. also Babylonian and Oriental Records, i. pp. 8–11, and Winckler, A. B. K. Nos. 40 and 41.

[4] (*ilu*) *Sin-gâmil* = 'Sin spares, protects.' His inscription:

British Museum, 82, 7–14, 181; Winckler, K. B. iii[1]. p. 84 *b*.

To this period also belongs:

Ménant, Glyptique orient. i. p. 104, table iii. 1; Winckler, ibid. p. 84 *c*; Hommel, Gesch. p. 206; A. B. K. No. 42; and O. B. I. 26; comp. Hommel, A. H. T. p. 129, and Winckler, A. F. p. 274.

That we should find kings with such pure Semitic names in Southern Babylonia (Erech) at this time (about 3100 and 3000 B.C.) is undoubtedly the result of uniting under one sceptre the Semitic population in the north with the more or less Sumerian in the south. Semites had free intercourse, during the reign of the kings of *Kengi-ki-Urdu*, with the Sumerians, and could move freely throughout their dominions. Thus they would settle down in the most southern part of Babylonia, and in process of time make themselves independent kings, taking for their capital Erech, and erecting there their royal palace: *e-gal nam-lugal-la-ka-ni mu-ru* says *(dingir) Sin-ga-šid*, i. R. 2, viii. 2. Singâshid, therefore, was probably the founder of this dynasty. They were, however, not content with Erech alone, but tried to extend their power further towards the east over Amnanum, of which country they eventually became kings.

Winckler's theory, Mittheil. des Akad.-Orient. Vereins, p. 13, that at this time there existed three kingdoms in Old Babylonia, viz.

(1) the kingdom of Babel in the north,

(2) the kingdom of Shumer and Akkad in the south, and

(3) the kingdom of Amnanum with the capital Erech, situated between that of Babel and Shumer and Akkad,

is undoubtedly wrong, as has been shown by Lehmann, Shamash-shumukin, pp. 40 and 75 ff., according to whom Amnanum is '*ein an Babylonien angrenzender elamitischer Bezirk.*' So also Hommel, Geschichte, p. 342.

Besides erecting his royal residence, Singâshid repaired the temple Eanna of Ishtar (see Ur-Gur and Dungi I.), and built that of Kankal in honour of Lugalbanda and Ninsun his wife.

(Dingir) Sin-ga-mi-il is only known from an inscription of a certain *AN-A-AN-Giš-dub-ba* [1], the son of *Nab-še-me-a* [2], who records that he 'for the life of Singâmil' built a temple for Nergal [3], *lugal*

[1] Has probably to be pronounced *Ilû-ma-Gišdubba.*

[2] This *Nab-še-me-a* is also mentioned in a tablet published by Hilprecht, O. B. I. 26; see also his Assyriaca, where he is said to be the father of

[3] Written *(dingir) NER-UNU-GAL*, K. B. iii[1]. p. 84 *b*.

u-ur (?)-*ra-ki* (i.e., according to Winckler, '*König der Unterwelt*').

It is impossible to translate with Winckler, l.c. p. 85 *c*, the inscription of a seal-cylinder published by Ménant, Glypt. orient. i. p. 104, C. J. Ball, Light from the East, p. 45, as follows:—

BIL-GUR-	(*Dir, o*) *Bil-gur-aḫi*,
aḫi (?) *šar*	*König*
Urug-ki	*von Uruk*,

a certain *DINGIR-A-AN* (pronounced *Ilû-ma*). Hommel, A. H. T. p. 130, thinks that *Ilû-ma* is only an abbreviation of *Ilû-ma-Gišdubba* ('God is *Gišdubba*' = *Gilgamish*). That inscription reads:

Dingir-a-an	*Ilû ma*,
ab-ba (= *šibu*, Br. 3821) *ki-su-lu-ku-gar* = *ummânu*, Br. 9649, H. W. B. p. 87)	the sheikh of the people
Unug-ki-ga-ge	of Erech,
dumu Nab-še-me-a	the son of Nabshemea,
bad Unug-ki-ga	the wall of Erech,
nin-dim-dim-ma (Br. 12141)	an old building
labar-ra (Br. 9463)	
(*dingir*) *Giš-bil-ga-miš-ge*	of Gilgamish (comp. C. T. 94-10-16, 4, obv., ii.; *GIR Ur-(dingir) Gi(š)-bil-ga-miš dumu Al-la*)
ki-bi ne-in-gi-a	has restored.

If *Ilû-ma* = *Ilû-ma-Gišdubba*, we would have here the first example of an abbreviated name. Such examples occur especially very often in Neo-Babylonian contract-tablets. Winckler, A. T. p. 274, who misread the last sign in line 3 (*iš* or *mil* for *ge*, comp. l. 7), transcribed that line *URU-KI-ga-mil* (*URU-KI* = *Nannar* = *Sin*), i.e. Singâmil, thus making Singâmil, who is not said here to be a king, the son of Nabshemea. The sign, however, is clear. *Ilû-ma* or *Ilû-ma-Gišdubba* was apparently only a general in the royal army of Erech, and as such he restores the wall of the royal capital, fortifying it against its enemies. Winckler, l. c., translated our inscription: '*Der Gottheit A-AN, dem ältesten der Künstler, hat Sin-gamil, Sohn des Nabshemea, Uruk, den alten Bau des Gilgamesh wieder erbaut.*' Hommel also wants to identify this *Ilû-ma* or (*Ilû-ma-Gišdubba*) with the well-known *Ilû-ma-ilu* (or also written only *Ilû-ma*) of dynasty B of Babylon, thus making—

1. The sheikh of the people of Erech also king of Babylon;

2. This dynasty of Erech to have existed at the time of Babylon B, which latter, however, he thinks to be apocryphal, with the exception of just this *Ilû-ma-ilu*, whom he puts somewhere at the beginning of dynasty A. '*Aber das glaube wer will!*'

Q 2

dup-sar	*der Schreiber*
íri-zu	*dein Diener.*

If *aḫi* were a part of the name of the king, it could not be separated from *Bil-gur* by a line! Hence *Bil-gur-aḫi* is no king of Uruk, but *'a brother' of a king*[1] of Erech. It has to be translated:—

O Bil-gur,
brother (*aḫu*) of the king
of Erech,
the scribe
is thy servant.

We have scarcely realized the existence of a Semitic kingdom in Southern Babylonia before we are compelled again to leave it in darkness. The name of the kingdom disappears, and the title *lugal Amnanum* is borne by no other king up to the time of Shamashshumukin (669–647 B.C.), who accepts this title again, apparently as a reminiscence of ancient days[2].

Kings of Isin.

The uniting of the Sumerian and Semitic population at the time of Ur-Gur I. and Dungi I. brought with it another calamity. The independence of Erech under Singâshid was soon paralleled by that of Isin[3], a little further to the north, apparently also under Semitic rulers. These kings, at first[4] ruling only over Isin, extended their dominion over Nippur, Ur, Eridu, and Erech, thus putting an end to the dynasty of the last-named city[5]. From their bearing the title *na-gid Uru-um-ki-ma*, it is evident that the

[1] See also Lehmann, Zwei Probleme, p. 175, note 3, and Z. D. M. G. 49, p. 309 f.

[2] Lehmann, Shamashshumukin, i. p. 75; Winckler, A. F. pp. 231, 232.

[3] The situation of Isin is not yet made out, but comp. for the present Delitzsch, Parad. pp. 190, 225. It probably has to be sought near the Shatt-el-Kehr, between Uruk and Nippur; see Hommel, Geschichte, p. 474. For the pronunciation of *Ni-si-in-ki-(na)* = Isin, see Bezold, Z. A. iv. p. 430.

[4] Comp. the title of the different rulers.

[5] Hence we have to put the dynasty of Erech before that of Isin, contrary to Lehmann, Zwei Probleme, p. 175.

second dynasty of Ur had by this time ceased to exist. Nay, further, they even took the title originally held by Ur-Gur I. and Dungi I., calling themselves 'king of Shumer and Akkad.' By this step they proclaimed their intention of dealing out equal justice to Sumerians and Semites alike, to 'Jew and Gentile,' thus once more seeking to appease any hostile feeling between these two nations.

The first king with the title 'king of Isin, king of Shumer and Akkad,' is Libit-Anunit[1]. If the inscription of a cylinder published by Scheil in R. T. xix. p. 48, belongs to this Libit-Anunit, this latter king would be the son of a certain *Ia-lu-un-a-šar*. That inscription reads:—

Li-bi-it-Anunit	To Libit-Anunit,
apil Ia-lu-un-a-šar[2]	the son of Ialunashar,
Ardi-(*ilu*) *Na-bi-um*	Ardi-Nabium (presents this).

Another ruler with the title 'king of Isin' only[3] is mentioned on a much mutilated tablet published in iv. R². 35, 7. The name of this king has been generally read (*dingir*) *Iš-bi-gir-ra*. Against this reading Scheil, Rec. de Trav. xix. p. 48, says: '*Protestons ici contre la lecture Išbi-Girra du nom du prince d'Isin. . . . Cette lecture est erronée et doit être modifiée en Išgaš-Girra, c'est-à-dire "Girra a assommé" (verbe šagašu)*,' see H. W. B. p. 687. He also mentions in corroboration of this reading a name *Išgum-Girra*, '*le dieu Girra a rugi*' (√ *šagâmu*). But against the reading of *Iš-gaš* is to be said that the praet. of *šagâšu* is not *išgaš* but *išgiš*.

[1] Also read Libit-Ishtar. Libit-Anunit = 'the work of Anunit.'
His inscriptions:
i. R. 5, No. xviii; Winckler, K. B. iii¹. p. 86 *b* (where l. 11, *lugal Ki-en-gi-ki-Urdu*, is left out!); A. B. K. p. 14, No. 44.
Scheil, Rec. de Trav. xix. p. 48, 3.

[2] To this name Scheil, l. c., remarks: '*Yalunašar n'a pas l'aspect babylonien. Une lecture Yalunasar serait également correcte. Yalun pourrait être le phénicien Elôn. Ašar, asar rendrait-il l'araméen asar pour Assur, Osir, ou celui qui est indûment employé dans Šalman-asar, Tiglatpil-asar?*'

[3] Should this (*dingir*) *Iš-bi-gir-ra* belong to another *later* dynasty? If so, I would like to put him after Ur IV. and before Babylon I. His title would speak strongly in favour of this view.

A third king belonging to this dynasty is Ur-Ninib[1]. He calls himself (O. B. I. No. 18):—

(Dingir) *Ur-*(dingir) *Nin-ib*	Ur-Ninib,
sib nin-nam-ila	the glorious shepherd
En-lil-ki	of Nippur,
na-gid	the shepherd
Uru-um-ki-ma	of Ur,
me-šú-íl	he who delivers the commands
Urudug-ki-ga	of Eridu,
en še-ga	the gracious lord
Unug-ki-ga	of Erech,
lugal Ni-si-in-ki-na	king of Isin,
lugal Ki-en-gi-ki-Urdu	king of Shumer and Akkad,
dam igi-il-la	the beloved husband
(dingir) *Innanna*	of Ishtar.

2. =*rê'u tanadâti.*
4. =*nâḳidu*, Hebr. נקד.
6. *me-šú-il* corresponds here to *me-a-tum-ma* in O. B. I. 19, 6; *tum* and *il* = *abâlu*, 'to bring, deliver.'
7. Read also *Eridug-ki-ga.*
12. *igi-il-la = nišit ênâ.*

Among these kings of Isin has also to be placed a so-called Bur-Sin I[2].

[1] Thus this name has to be pronounced, Hilprecht, O. B. I. p. 27, and in Z. A. vii. p. 315, note 1.
His inscriptions:
iv. R. 35, 5; Winckler, K. B. iii[1]. 84 *a*, identical with O. B. I. No. 18; see Hilprecht, l. c. p. 27: 'i. R. 5, No. xxiv, erroneously ascribed to Ishme-Dagan, is obviously the lower half of this same legend.'

[2] He is called Bur-Sin I. to distinguish him from another Bur-Sin II. of the fourth dynasty of Ur. Although the pronunciation of these two names is the same, yet the writing is not. In Bur-Sin I. the sign *BUR* is that of Br. 6971, while in Bur-Sin II. it is written with Br. 9068: *bûru = amar.* The former is only the phonetic writing for the latter. Both mean, according to Delitzsch

The inscription of Bur-Sin I., published in O. B. I. No. 19, reads :—

$^{(dingir)}$ *Bur-*$^{(dingir)}$ *Sin*	Bur-Sin,
sib šag En-lil-^{ki} *dug-dug*	the good shepherd of Nippur,
engar-lig-ga	the powerful shepherd
Uru-um-^{ki}*-ma*	of Ur,
giš-kin Urudug-^{ki}*-ga ki-bi-gi*	the restorer of the oracle tree of Eridu,
en me-a-tum-ma	the lord who delivers the commands
Unug-^{ki}*-ga*	of Erech,
lugal Ni-si-in-^{ki}*-na*	king of Isin,
lugal Ki-en-gi-^{ki}*-Urdu*	king of Shumer and Akkad,
dam me-te-ma ?-azag $^{(dingir)}$ *Innanna*	the glorious . . . husband of Ishtar.

2. The *dug-dug* apparently belongs to *sib*, and corresponds to the *nin-nam-il-la* in Ur-Ninib. *DUG* also = *šar* = *gitmalu*, 'perfect.'

3. *engar* = *ikkaru* = Hebr. אִכָּר ; comp. Hilpr. O. B. I. p. 28, note 3.

5. For *giš-kin*, see Jensen, Kosmol. pp. 99 ff., 249 note.

6. For this line, see Ur-Ninib, l. 6.

10. The *me-te-ma ?-azag* corresponds to the *igi-il-la* in Ur-Ninib and the *ki-ag* in Ishme-Dagan; see Winckler, K. B. iii [1]. p. 84 *a*, l. 12, and p. 86 *d*, l. 10. Comp. also the *me-ad-azag* in Déc. 37, 8.

It is more than probable that a certain $^{(dingir)}$ *Idin* $^{(dingir)}$ *Dagan* (='Dagan judgeth'), whom Hilprecht (R. R. B. L., p. 84) refers to the fourth dynasty of Ur, belongs to the kings of Isin, on account of the *rôle* which Shumer and Akkad plays in his inscription. Unfortunately the tablet is so greatly mutilated that hardly any coherent sense can be made out of it. Besides that it has

(B. A. ii. p. 622), 'the son of Sin.' Better probably is the rendering, 'a young ox is Sin.' For a different reading of this name, see Lehmann, B. A. ii. p. 598 ff.

His inscriptions :

O. B. I. No. 19; comp. Hilprecht, ibid. p. 28.

Lehmann, B. A. ii. p. 598 ff.

been published by Scheil in Neo-Assyrian characters—a habit which ought to be discontinued once for all, for it cuts off all control. The inscription is in the form of a dedication ending with a prayer for Idîn-Dagan. It has been published in R. T. xvi. p. 187 ff. (1894), and reads:

Obverse.

. . . .

dub-ba-uš-sa se-gi . . .	The younger (?) brother, the one who overpowers . . .
Ki-en-gi-ki-Urdu an-kuš dagal . . .	Shumer and Akkad, the great protection (or protector?) of . . .
kalam-e ú nir-gàl KA-šà-ne- . . .	of the lands, the wise hero, who . . .
(*dingir*) *En-lil-li id-bi mu-da-* . . .	of Enlil, who on his side . . .
(*dingir*) *I-dîn-*(*dingir*) *Da-gan sib šag-ga* . . .	To Idîn-Dagan, the shepherd called by the true heart of . . .
gu-zi-de-a (*dingir*) *En-lil* . . .	the true prophet of Enlil . . .
(*dingir*) *En-ki-ge giš-tug*(*-pi*) *dagal nin-* . . .	by Enki, to whom great intelligence was given by . . .
kin igi-gàl gi-ka uk ta . . .	the circumspect one, the wise one, to whom a sceptre of . . .
(*dingir*) *I-dîn-*(*dingir*) *Da-gan* . . .	To Idîn-Dagan, the . . .
kur-kur-ri . . .	of the lands . . .
dumu ù-tu-da (*dingir*) . . .	a son, born by . . .
(*dingir*) *I-dîn-*(*dingir*) *Da-gan* . . .	to Idîn-Dagan . . .

Obv. 1. *dub-ba-uš-sa*, Br. 3942 = *duppussû*, 'younger' (?) brother. Comp. H. W. B. 226; Shalm. Black Ob. 74; and Z. A. i. p. 392.

se-gi, Br. 4404; *sapânu*, H. W. B. 508.

2. *an-kuš*, Br. 6368; *ṣalûlu* and *ṣalmu*.

3. *ú*, Br. 6024; *le'u*. *nir-gàl*, Br. 6290, *etellu*.

5. Probably *zipad-da* (*dingir*) . . . to be added.

6. *gu-de-a* = *nâbiu*; *zi* = *kênu*.

7. *nin-ba sum-ma* (*dingir*) . . . This line probably continued.

8. *kin*, Br. 10754; *šite'u*; *igi-gal*, Br. 9306; *mudu*, A. L[3]. 253; *igêgallu*, '*offenäugig, allwissend*'; *gi-ka*, Br. 2413; *šibṭu*, H. W. B. 638. For *uk*, see Br. 3862; *šarru* and *uk-dur*, ibid. = *maliku*.

zal-li nin . . .	the hero . . .
(dingir) En- . . .	of (by) En . . .

Reverse.

Ki-en-gi . . .	Shumer [and Akkad]
(dingir) I-dîn (dingir) Da-gan . . .	Idîn-Dagan . . .
nin-dug-ga . . .	thy commands may be . . .
inim-ma (dingir) . . .	the words of . . .
ka-ta ud-du-a-zu (dingir) . . .	what goeth out of thy mouth may . . .
dug-ga (dingir) En- . . .	the commands of En- . . .
igi-bar-ra-zu (ga)lu mu-un . . .	what thy eyes look upon, a man may . . .
ka-ba-zu (ga)lu mu-un- . . .	when thy mouth openeth itself, a man may . . .
dug-ga-a-zu (dingir) EN-GUBUR-[RA] . . .	thy commands *EN-GUBUR-RA* may . . .
šag-gi-gin-zu (dingir) NIN-GUBUR-RA . . .	the desires of thy heart *NIN-GUBUR-RA* may . . .
sib (dingir) EN-GUBUR-RA iti . . .	[thou art] the shepherd of *EN-GUBUR-RA*, the abarakku of . . .
. . . .	. . . .

13. *zal-li*, Br. 5328; *zikaru*.
Rev. 3. *nin-dug-ga*, Br. 532; *ḳibîtu*.
4. *inim-ma*, Br. 508; *amâtu*.
5. *ka-ta ud-du-a* = *ṣît pî-ka*.
8. *ka-ba* = *pît pî*, Br. 555.
10. For *ŠAG-gi-DU* (= *gin*), comp. Br. 8008; *ŠAG-GI* (= *gin*)-*na* = *bibil libbi*, H. W. B. 166.
11. *iti* = Br. 9427, *abarakku*. For *(dingir) EN* (and especially *NIN*)-*GUBUR-RA*, see Br. 6225 and 6176.

The last king of the dynasty of Isin is *(dingir) Iš-me-(dingir) Da-gan*[1]. Nothing besides his titles is known of him.

Fragmentary as the inscriptions of the kings of Isin are, they

[1] The name means, 'Dagan hears.'
i. R. 2, No. 5, 1 and 2; Winckler, K. B. iii^{1}. p. 86 *d*.
O. B. I. No. 17: a fragment, which gives only the name of this ruler.

however suffice to show that Libit-Anunit probably was the first, and Ishme-Dagan the last ruler. Of how many members this dynasty consisted, and how one succeeded the other, are questions which still await an answer. The kings of Isin were at length succeeded by the rulers of the third dynasty of Ur, headed by Gungunu.

The Third Dynasty of Ur.

The kings of this dynasty, in contradistinction to those of the second, always call themselves or are called 'king of Ur.'

Gungunu, the founder of this dynasty, put an end to that of Isin, for Enannatum, the son of Ishme-Dagan, built several temples 'for the life of Gungunu, the mighty hero, the king of Ur'; hence the son of Ishme-Dagan sat no more on the throne of Isin, but acknowledged openly his dependence on the king of Ur, applying to himself only religious titles (K. B. iii[1]. p. 87, 4, 1, 2)[1].

On account of the difference in the titles of Gungunu and, e.g., Bur-Sin II. on one hand and Dungi I. on the other, we have to distinguish between the second, the third, and the fourth dynasties of Ur. This has already been hinted at above, p. 37, note 2. Reserving for the present a full discussion of Winckler's theory (see O. L. Z. i. 238), we shall go on with the enumeration of the other kings, who are called or call themselves 'king of Ur' only.

Besides Gungunu[2], two other kings bear the title *lugal Uru-um-ki-ma*, viz., Ur-Gur II. and Dungi II.—so called by us, to distinguish them from Ur-Gur I. (second dynasty of Ur) and Dungi III. (fourth dynasty of Ur). Whether Ur-Gur II. preceded Dungi II. is not certain, nor do we know whether the latter is the immediate successor of the former.

[1] Comp. i. R. 2, No. vi. 1; 36, No. 2; and A. B. K. 47, (1) and (2).

[2] Does the date mentioned by Scheil, R. T. xxi. 125: *mu Gu-un-gu-nu ba-til*, i. e. 'the year when Gungunu died,' belong to Gungunu, king of Ur? Schiel remarks to that date: *Que signifie, dans notre cas, l'absence de tout titre? Ce prince avait-il usurpé la royauté? ou, sur la fin de sa vie, avait-il perdu la souveraineté, mais non la popularité?*

Ur-Gur II.[1] built for *(dingir) Uru-ki* (= Nannar-Sin, the moon-god of Ur) the temple Te-im-ila [2], and for *(dingir) Lugal-dingir-ri-ne* (i. e. for the god who is the 'king of the gods') the temple Nun-maĝ. He was in possession of the city Ishkun-Sin—the situation of which is not yet made out—for its patesi, Ḫashḫamir, acknowledges, in an inscription to be found on a seal-cylinder, that he is the 'servant of Ur-Gur, king of Ur' (see above, p. 30, note 1, and C. J. Ball, Light from the East, p. 50).

The enemies of Ur must have been troublesome, for Ur-Gur II. finds it necessary to fortify the wall of his royal capital (*bad Uru-um-ki-ma mu-na-ru*, K. B. iii[1]. p. 76 *a*, 2).

The third king who belongs to this dynasty is Dungi II.[3] Of this king we possess no inscriptions written *by himself*, he being known only from votive inscriptions of certain patesis or other people, who dedicated those inscribed tablets 'for the life of Dungi, king of Ur.'

Among the patesis who thus acknowledged their dependence upon Dungi II. are to be found :

[1] It seems, however, more probable that Ur-Gur II. is the same as Ur-Gur I. (see *sub* Ur II.). The inscriptions in which Ur-Gur is called 'king of Ur' only are the following :—

i. R. 1, No. 1, 1 = A. B. K. No. 17 ; Winckler, K. B. iii[1]. p. 76 *a*, No. 1 ; also in C. J. Ball, Light from the East, p. 63.

i. R. 1, No. 1, 3 = A. B. K. No. 19 ; Winckler, K. B. iii[1]. p. 76 *a*, No. 2.

i. R. 1, No. 1, 4 = A. B. K. No. 20 ; „ „ „ No. 3.

iv. R. 35, 1 = A. B. K. No. 27 ; „ „ p. 78, No. 9.

i. R. 1, 1, No. 10 = A. B. K. No. 24 ; „ „ p. 80, No. 10.

[2] This temple was also built by Ur-Gur I. ; see K. B. iii[1]. p. 78, 4. Notice the difference in the titles of god Nannar and Ur-Gur respectively.

[3] His inscriptions :

iv. R. 35, No. 2 = A. B. K. No. 36 ; Winckler, K. B. iii[1]. p. 82, 8 ; Amiaud, Z. A. ii. p. 292.

O. B. I. No. 15 ; Hilprecht, ibid. p. 31.

C. T. Part v. No. 12218 = U. A. G. p. 157, 9 ; Jensen, K. B. iii[1]. p. 68, ii., and above, p. 37.

R. A. iv. iv. p. 90 ; above, p. 22.

C. T. 12217 (doubtful, because 'for Dungi' only).

Lenormant, Textes inédits, p. 163, No. 69 ; Winckler, K. B. iii[1]. p. 82, 7 (doubtful, because Dungi has no title).

(*a*) (Ga)lukani, a patesi of Shirpurla, who presented his tablet to Ningirsu; see above, p. 22.

(*b*) A certain *Si-a-tum* (O. B. I. No. 15), who dedicated his inscription to goddess Ishtar for the life of his sovereign. This latter tablet being interesting in more than one respect, we give its transcription and translation here (comp. also Hilprecht, O. B. I. p. 31).

O. B. I. No. 15, obverse (written in Sumerian).

(*dingir*) *Innanna*	Unto Ishtar,
nin-a-ni	his mistress,
nam-ti	for the life of
Dun-gi	Dungi,
nitaǧ lig-ga	the mighty hero,
lugal Uru-um-ki-ma-ka-ku	king of Ur,
Si-a-tum	Siatum
. . . . . *-ni*	[the . . . . of . . . .]*ni*
[*a-mu-na-šub*]	[has presented it].

Reverse; see O. B. I. No. 43 (written in Semitic).

Ku-ri-gal-zu	Kurigalzu,
šar Ka-(u)ru-du-ni-ia-aš	king of Karduniash,
êkalla (*E-GAL*) *ša* (*âlu*) *Ša-a-ša-ki*	from the palace of Susa
ša Elamti (*NIM-MA*)*-ki*	in Elam
ik-šu-ud-ma	has taken, and
a-na (*ilu*) *Bêltum* (*NIN-LIL*)	to Bêlit,
be-el-ti-šu	his mistress,
a-na ba-la-ṭi (*DI*)*-šu*	for his life
i-ḳi-iš	has presented (this tablet).

'This tablet,' to use Hilprecht's words, 'tells its own story. Siatum presented it for the life of Dungi, king of Ur. At the time of the Elamite invasion, Kudurnanḫundi carried the image of the goddess Ishtar, with all that belonged or was dedicated to it, into Elam. Kurigalzu, of the Cassite dynasty, after he had conquered Susa, brought it back and presented it to Bêlit of Nippur. There, in the sanctuary of Bêlit, it remained till it was again taken by the excavators at Nippur and transferred to the Museum of the University of Pennsylvania.'

Among the *other persons* who dedicated tablets to certain gods 'for the life of Dungi, king of Ur,' are to be found:

(*a*) *Ki-lul-la-gu-za-lal*, the son of a certain *Ur-Ba-bi* (= *Ur-Bayi* = *Ur-Ba'i*), who presented a seal-cylinder to (*dingir*) *Šid-lam-ta-ud-du*[1] *lugal à zi-da Šir-pur-la-ki-ge* (iv. R. 35, No. 2; Hommel, Geschichte, p. 336).

(*b*) (*dingir*) *Ba-u-nin-a-an*, who made the *ZABAR-KU* of *Ur-(dingir) Nin-gir-su* to be a *ǴI-LI* (ornament) for Ninlil (*Bêlit*); see above, p. 37. It is interesting to note that Ur-Ningirsu, mentioned here, has exactly the same title as the one mentioned in Déc. 37, No. 8, and Revue Arch. 1886, pl. 7, No. 2, viz. *en ki-ag* (*dingir*) *Ninâ-ka-ge*; they are one and the same person, and must therefore also be differentiated from Ur-Ningirsu, patesi of Shirpurla; see above, p. 37 (*d*).

[1] For Shidlamtauddu = Nergal, see Winckler, K. B. iii[1]. p. 80, 5, and Hommel, Geschichte, p. 336 ff. The god Shidlamtauddu is also mentioned in C. T. 12217, which reads:

(*dingir*) *Šid-lam-ta-ud-du-a*	Unto Shidlamtauddu,
dingir-a-ni	his god,
(*Ga*)*lu-ligir-e* (= (*amêl*) *Nâgir-bîti*, Br. 6968)	the Nâgir-bîti
nam-ti	for the life
Dun-gi-ku	of Dungi
a-mu-na-šub	has presented it.

Who this Dungi was, we cannot tell.

It should be noticed here that it was Dungi I. who built for Shidlamtauddu a temple called *E-ŠID-LAM*, which temple was situated in *TIK-GAB-A-ki* (= Kutha); see K. B. iii[1]. p. 80, 5. Nergal, whose original home was in the north (Kutha)—time of Dungi I.—was made later on also *lugal à-zi-da* of Shirpurla—time of Dungi II. (Comp. also time of Ur IV., C. T. 17758, iii. 10, and ibid. 94-10-15, 3, obv., ii. 16: *a-šag* (*dingir*) *Nin-gir-su à-zi-da* (*dingir*) *Ninâ*.) This undoubtedly was the result of the uniting of the north and south of Babylonia under one sceptre (comp. Ur II. and Isin). Even Dungi III. in a Semitic inscription reports that he built, or better, rebuilt, the same temple of Nergal; see K. B. iii[1]. p. 82, 6.

The Fourth Dynasty of Ur.

Before we go over to the fourth dynasty of Ur, headed by another Dungi—called by us Dungi III.—it would seem necessary to say a few words with regard to the theory of Winckler in O. L. Z. i. 238, viz. that all three rulers bearing the name Dungi are one and the same person, thus making the second, third, and fourth dynasties of Ur only *one*, i. e. the second.

Winckler bases his theory upon the following arguments:—

1. Dungi, 'king of Ur, king of Shumer and Akkad,' must be the same as Dungi, 'king of Ur, king of the four corners of the world,' '*da die beiden Inschriften*[1] *welche von Bauten Dungi's am Nergaltempel in Kutha sprechen, und in deren beiden er die beiden Titulaturen führt*, nur von einer Person herrühren können.'

2. '*Die gleichzeitigen Patesis von Lagaš erweisen die Identität beider Personen: vgl. die Angaben Thureau-Dangin's oben, Sp.* 172, 173.'

On this place referred to by Winckler, Thureau-Dangin mentions two tablets:

(*a*) R. T. xviii. pp. 73, 74, where a seal-inscription to be found on a tablet dated *itu ŠE-IL-LA mu en Eridug-ki ba-a-tug* has the following legend:—

(dingir) Utu-a dumu Ur-
dup-sar
(Ga)lu-ka-ni
pa-te-si
Šir-pur-la-ki

(See also above, p. 211.)

(*b*) R. A. iv., iv. p. 90 (see above, p. 22), where a certain (Ga)lukani, patesi of Shirpurla, dedicates an inscription to Ningirsu for the life of '*Dungi, king of Ur.*'

[1] These are K. B. iii[1]. p. 80, 5, and ibid. p. 82, 6. See also note on preceding page.

I. A careful examination of Winckler's position exhibits the most careless and illogical argument.

Let us begin with statement No. 2: 'The contemporary patesis of Lagash prove the identity of *both persons*,' the *persons* being: 'Dungi, king of Ur, king of Shumer and Akkad,' and 'Dungi, king of Ur, king of the four corners of the world' (see above *sub* 1); their contemporary patesi of Lagash is said to be (1) (Ga)lukani, (2) Gudea and Ur-Ningirsu (so also Lehmann, Zwei Probleme, p. 176, and Winckler, U. A. G. p. 35; see above, p. 34. *The two inscriptions referred to by Winckler and quoted above sub (a) and (b) do not say a single word that (Ga)lukani was either a contemporary of 'Dungi, king of Ur, king of Shumer and Akkad,' or of 'Dungi, king of Ur, king of the four corners of the world.'* But let us examine those two inscriptions more closely.

From the inscription quoted *sub* (*b*), only this much can be derived: (Ga)lukani was a contemporary of a certain '*Dungi, king of Ur.*' Apparently Winckler bids us to believe—without any arguments on his part—that the plain title 'king of Ur' is the same as 'king of Ur' PLUS 'king of Shumer and Akkad,' or PLUS 'king of the four corners of the world.' Here lies the fallacy of Winckler's theory. As long as Winckler does not see fit to prove either the one or the other, just so long our objection holds. But what does Winckler do with Gungunu, king of Ur? Does this latter ruler's title also imply a dominion over Shumer and Akkad, or even over the four corners of the world? 'No,' he informs us, '*Gungunu ist beiseite zu stellen, und wir haben in ihm nichts anderes zu sehen, als einen Königssohn, der mit oder gegen den Willen seines Vaters in Ur ein Stadtkönigtum besass.*' If Gungunu is permitted by Winckler's graciousness to possess a '*Stadtkönigtum*,' may we not rightly ask, why is he so hard on Dungi, king of Ur, whom he not only denies a '*Stadtkönigtum*,' but whom he even wipes out of existence? No, if Gungunu was 'king of Ur' and possessed a '*Stadtkönigtum*'—as the title attributed to him by Enannatum indicates—then Dungi, king of Ur, as well as Ur-Gur (?)[1], king of

[1] See note 1 on p. 235.

Ur, have to be classed together with Gungunu, i. e. they too were kings of Ur and possessed a '*Stadtkönigtum*.'

Or does Winckler think, with Thureau-Dangin (O. L. Z. i. 172 and 174, i.), that the title 'king of Ur' to be found in connection with Dungi II. is '*une formule simplement abrégée*'? If so, how is it with Gungunu's title? Thureau-Dangin, l. c. p. 174, i., tells us: "*Gungunu aurait relevé le titre de roi d'Ur à une époque très postérieure aux rois classés jusqu'ici dans la "seconde (maintenant la troisième) dynastie d'Ur*,"' thus making Gungunu belong to *another* dynasty. May we not ask here, too, if the title 'king of Ur' in Gungunu's case is *not* '*une formule simplement abrégée*,' why should it be in Dungi's case? No, the title 'king of Ur' *cannot* be an *abbreviation*. For—

1. In votive inscriptions, where one person dedicates something for the life of a king, the person thus dedicating is always careful to give the *exact* and *complete* titles of his king.

Dungi, 'king of Ur, king of the four corners of the world,' belongs to the same dynasty as Bur-Sin II., Gimil-Sin, and Ine-Sin.

Among all the votive and seal inscriptions so far published and known to me, I have not yet found a *single inscription* where Bur-Sin II., or Gimil-Sin, or Ine-Sin are simply called 'king of Ur[1].' And as long as we have no inscriptions proving that, e. g.,

[1] But I *have* found votive and seal inscriptions giving *always* the *full titles* of Bur-Sin II. and the other rulers. Comp. for Bur-Sin II., R. A. iv. pl. xxxi. No. 80:

I. *(dingir) Bur-(dingir) Sin*
nitaǵ lig-ga
lugal Uru-um-ki-ma
lugal an ub-da tab-tab-ba
II. *Nam-ǵa-ni luǵ*
dumu UD (?) a-a-mu
nitaǵ-zu

For Gimil-Sin, comp. iv. R. 35, 4; i. R. 3, No. xi.; K. B. iii[1]. p. 90, 3, and R. A. iv. pl. xxxi. No. 81:

I. *(dingir) Gimil (dingir) Sin*
lugal lig-ga

'Bur-Sin, king of Ur, king of the four corners of the world,' is equal to 'Bur-Sin, king of Ur,' just *so long* we are *not justified* in making 'Dungi, king of Ur,' equal to 'Dungi, king of Ur, king of the four corners of the world.'

2. It is a well-known fact that kings, in their inscriptions, were rather inclined to use the most comprehensive titles, thus claiming dominion over a greater territory than they really possessed. This, e.g., was the reason why the kings of Kish would express this latter title by '*lugal Kiš*' or '*šar Kiš*,' without *KI*, while their contemporary kings or patesis of Shirpurla always term them *lugal Kiš-ki*. They wanted to claim silently a dominion over the universe (= *Kiš* = *kiššatu*), while the kings of Shirpurla simply narrowed the title down to a '*Stadtkönigtum*' (*šar Kiš-ki*).

Hence a king, if he were 'king of Shumer and Akkad,' and even 'king of the four corners of the world,' would surely prefer these latter titles before that of 'king of Ur' only, especially if he himself were enumerating his own titles.

lugal Uru-um-ki-ma
lugal-an-ub-da tab-tab-ba
II. *Eri-(dingir)-Uru-ki* = *Ardi-Nannar* (*Sin*)
luǧ-maǧ
dumu Ur-(dingir) Dun-pu-ud-du
nitaǧ-zu

or Ine-Sin, comp. R. A. iv. pl. xxxi. No. 82:
I. *(dingir) I-ne-(dingir) Sin*
lugal lig-ga
lugal Uru-um-ki-ma
— break —
II. *(Ga)lu-(dingir) Nin-gir-su*
dup-sar
dumu (Ga)lu-(dingir) Ba-[u]

or ibid.:
I. *(dingir) I-ne-(dingir) Sin*
lugal lig-ga
lugal Uru-um-ki-ma
lugal an-ub-da tab-tab-ba
II. *(Ga)lu-(dingir) LAGAB* + inserted *IGI-gunû LUǦ*
nitaǧ-zu

For Dungi, see E. A. H. 61, further below, and R. T. xviii. p. 73.

Perhaps some one might say, the different titles which Dungi bears clearly indicate the development in the history of his time, he being first 'king of Ur,' and in consequence of some successful wars became 'king of Shumer and Akkad,' and later on even 'king of the four corners of the world.' This might be possible. In that case we would, however, have to imagine that Ur-Gur, originally king of Ur only, later on became also 'king of Shumer and Akkad'; his son Dungi lost, in the beginning of his reign, some of the territory conquered by his father, but regained it again, and even extended it far beyond that of his father—conquered a 'kingdom of the four corners of the world.' If this were true, we have, however, to explain why Dungi, when building the temple *E-ŠID-LAM*, should have called himself, at one and the same time, in one inscription '*lugal Uru-um-^{ki}-ma lugal Ki-en-gi-^{ki}-Urdu*' (K. B. iii[1]. p. 80, 5), and in another '*šar Uru-um-^{ki} ù šar ki-ib-ra-tim ar-ba-im*' (K. B. iii[1]. p. 82, 6), seeing that both tablets record one and the same building. Winckler also gives to this question an answer. '*Ich habe,*' he says, O. L. Z. i. 239, '*das von jeher so erklärt, dass er in Nordbabylonien den Titel "König der vier Weltgegenden," im Süden "König von Sumer und Akkad" bevorzugte.*' What Winckler must have thought when he wrote the above statement is beyond my imagination. Does not the Sumerian inscription of Dungi prove clearly that he called himself, even in the *north*, 'king of Shumer and Akkad'? How then could he have '*bevorzugt*' the title 'king of Shumer and Akkad' in the south? We see then that Winckler's explanation is absurd—Dungi could not attribute to himself at one and the same time two different titles; and if not, we have to refer those two inscriptions recording the building of *E-ŠID-LAM* to two different Dungis, i. e. to Dungi I. and Dungi III. For—

3. As long as we do not find inscriptions which prove that, e. g., Bur-Sin II., or Ine-Sin, or Gimil-Sin bore *also* the title 'king of Shumer and Akkad,' just so long we are not allowed to make the title 'king of Shumer and Akkad' equal to the much more

comprehensive 'king of the four corners of the world'; for be it remembered that among the thousands of dated tablets belonging to Bur-Sin II., &c., not a single one can be found where he has the title 'king of Shumer and Akkad.' (Bur-Sin I. only calls himself king of Isin and king of Shumer and Akkad.)

II. The fact that a tablet published in R. T. xviii. pp. 73, 74, bears the seal-inscription of a certain Utu-a, the scribe of (Ga)lu-kani, patesi of Shirpurla, does not prove anything either.

Only this much we can say about that tablet:

1. The date to be found on that tablet occurs both under the reigns of Dungi III. (see date No. 31) and Bur-Sin II. (date No. 9), hence that tablet may just as well have been written under the latter king's reign.

2. Suppose, for the sake of argument, the date belongs to Dungi III. If that were true we could make the equation Utu-a contemporary of (Ga)lukani and Dungi III., but we are not justified in making, without any more stringent arguments, (Ga)lu-kani the contemporary of Dungi III. The former might have died long ago. This is especially illustrated by E. A. H. 61, which is a case-tablet dated *mu* ^(giš)^ *gu-za* ^(dingir)^ *En-lil-la(l) ba-gim* —a date found so far *only* among those of Bur-Sin II. (see No. 4). It bears the seal-impression of a certain Ur-Galalim, which he dedicated to 'Dungi, king of Ur, king of the four corners of the world' (see below). What equation could we make on the basis of this tablet? Of course only the following:

Ur-Galalim, contemporary of Dungi III. and Bur-Sin II.; but it would be absurd to make Dungi III. now also the contemporary of Bur-Sin II. But just this absurdity is committed by Winckler. As long as Winckler does not bring in more convincing arguments that (Ga)lukani *must* have been the contemporary of Dungi III., we cannot follow him.

The occurrence of that seal-impression on the tablet dated *mu en Eridug-ki ba-a-tug* may be explained, either—

(*a*) By supposing that also under the reign of Dungi II. tablets were dated. This is not hard to imagine if we bear in mind that this practice occurs as early as Sargon I. In this case (Ga)lukani would be a contemporary of Dungi II. Or,

(*b*) By supposing that the seal of Utu-a was a family treasure, and as such handed down from generation to generation until it was used again at the time of Dungi III. or Bur-Sin II. At any rate no definite argument can be built upon R. T. xviii. pp. 73, 74.

III. Winckler's first argument in favour of the identity of Dungi I. and Dungi III. was already answered by Thureau-Dangin, O. L. Z. i. 173: '*Ce fait n'est pas concluant: il est en effet très admissible que deux rois du même nom aient successivement travaillé à la construction d l'E-ŠID-LAM.*'

But how is it with the other patesis of Shirpurla, viz. Gudea and Ur-Ningirsu his son, who are said to be contemporaries of Dungi (i. e. of Dungi I., Dungi II., and Dungi III.—all these supposedly one and the same Dungi)? The occurrence of such names as Gudea patesi (at Ur IV.), (Ga)lukani patesi (at Ur III. and Ur II.), and Ur-Ningirsu *en ki-ag* ^(dingir)^ *Ninâ* (at Ur III.), might seem to justify Winckler's theory, and in some measure corroborate it.

Let us first of all enumerate all those patesis, who either are called directly '*pa-te-si Girsu-ki*' (= Shirpurla, see time of Urukagina), or who are thought to be such, occurring in connection with the name Dungi. We arrange them according to the succession given in our Chronological Table, above, p. 30.

1. *Gu-de-a pa-te-si* (always without the name of the city!):

R. A. iv., iii. pl. xxvii. No. 76—a tablet with the date of Bur-Sin II. No. 4.

R. A. iii. p. 135—date of tablet not given.

R. T. xviii. p. 65 ff.: '*Toutes ces tablettes mentionnant le patési sont datées, explicitement ou implicitement, des rois de la II*[e] (read *IV*[e]) *dynastie d'Ur, soit Gimil-Sin, Bur-Sin, et Ibil-Sin*' (i. e. Ine-Sin). In these tablets the name occurs sometimes written as '*Gu-de-a pa-te-si*' or '(*dingir*) *Gu-de-a pa-te-si.*' As such it is found in connection with different gods—among whom also is (*dingir*) *Dun-gi*—and also in connection with a certain *Ur-*(*dingir*) *KAL pa-te-si.*

2. Ur-Ningirsu *en ki-ag*(dingir) *Ninâ* (hence not called patesi) supposed to be Gudea's son:

(*a*) a contemporary of 'Dungi, king of Ur'; see C. T. 12218, and above, p. 37.

(*b*) Dec. 37, 8; see above, p. 37, note 1, where this Ur-Ningirsu has the same title as that *sub* (*a*).

3. (*a*) (Ga)lukani; see above, p. 211.

(*b*) Ǵala-Lama, son of a certain (Ga)lukani; see above, p. 21.

To these ought to be added now—

4. *Al-la-mu*, the son of *Ur-Sag-ga-mu*, patesi (the city is left out); see above, p. 212, 1.

5. *Ur-*(dingir) *KAL* (pronounce Kalbi-Lamassi), mentioned on the following tablets of C. T., viz.:

94-10-15, 5,	with	date No.	16	of	Dungi III.
15324, col. iv.	,,	,,	34 *b*	,,	,,
94-10-15, 4	,,	,,	38	,,	,,
94-4-10, 3 } 19024, col. xii. }	,,	,,	47 *b*	,,	,,
12231, col. x.	,,	,,	48 *a*	,,	,,

21340, l. 152 ff.: *nin-šid-ag-ga* | *Ur-*(dingir) *Ba-u dumu URU-DUR-DUR* | *itu ŠU-KUL-ta* | *itu ZIB-KÙ-ku* | *itu* 2 *kam* | *bal-bi* 1 *a-an* | *Ur-*(dingir) *KAL* | *pa-te-si* | *mu Ki-maš-ki Ḫu-mur-ti-ki ba-ḫul* = No. 49 of Dungi III.

18346, col. viii.: No. 50 *b* of Dungi III.

Comp. also 18933, 12913, and O. B. I. 124, where the dates are broken away.

A. O. 2512 (see above, p. 28): *Ur-*(dingir) *KAL pa-te-si* (dingir) *Bur-*(dingir) *Sin lugal* = date 1 of Bur-Sin II.

C. T. 13138, rev., with date No. 3 *b* of Bur-Sin II. (see there).

This *Ur-*(dingir) *KAL* is called *pa-te-si Gir-su-ki* (= Shirpurla, see time of Urukagina) in R. A. iv., iii. pl. xxix. No. 78, env., 10, which tablet has the date No. 47 *a* of Dungi.

Hence we may rightly say that *Ur-*(dingir) *KAL*, patesi of Girsu-Shirpurla, was a contemporary of Dungi III. and reigned *at least* forty years (from date No. 16 of Dungi III. to date No. 3 *b* of Bur-Sin II)[1].

6. Two sons of a patesi are mentioned:

(*a*) C. T. 18343, col. vii. 7 (with date No. 47 *a* of Dungi III.): *GIR Ur-(dingir) Nun-gal dumu pa-te-si.*

(*b*) C. T. 18958, l. 12 (with date No. 18 of Dungi III., may also be date No. 11 of Bur-Sin II): *Ur-(dingir) Ba-u dumu pa-te-si.*

Both these sons were probably those of *Ur-(dingir) KAL.*

If there is only *one* Dungi, then all the above-given patesis must have been his contemporaries.

If *Ur-(dingir) KAL* was patesi of Girsu during the last thirty-six years of Dungi and the first four years of Bur-Sin II. we would be obliged to put Gudea, together with his son, *before Ur-(dingir) KAL*, i. e. they would have been patesis of Girsu-Shirpurla during the first fifteen years of Dungi's reign. But where are we to place (Ga)lukani? Of course also *before Ur-(dingir) KAL*, and either *after* Ur-Ningirsu or before Gudea. We would have in this case the following succession:—

[(*Ga*)*lukani*]
. . . . .
Gudea
|
Ur-Ningirsu
. . . . .
(*Ga*)*lukani*
} during the first fifteen years of } Dungi III.
. . . . .
Ur-(dingir) KAL : during the last thirty-six years of Dungi III. and also during the first four years of Bur-Sin II.

But still one patesi is unaccounted for, i. e. Allamu, whom Scheil (*très vraisemblablement*, above, p. 212, 1) and Thureau-Dangin (*peut-être*, O. L. Z. i. 173, note 4) think to be a patesi of Shirpurla! In this case he, too, had to precede *Ur-(dingir) KAL*; hence we

[1] In E. A. H. 91—a tablet dated from the reign of Gimil-Sin, date No. 1—*Ur-(dingir) KAL*, patesi, is mentioned in the body of the tablet. Should he have been patesi even during the whole reign of Bur-Sin II., till the first year of Gimil-Sin? In that case he must have reigned *at least* fifty years. From this it would follow further that Gudea II. was not patesi of Girsu, but of another city. See below, p. 248.

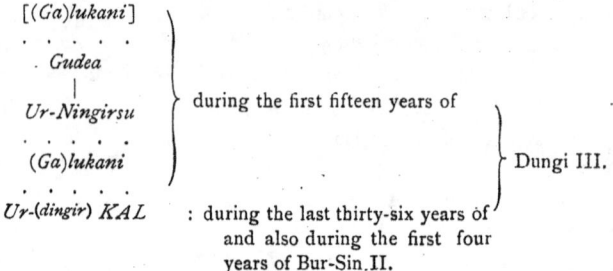

would have to crowd *four patesis into the first fifteen years of the reign of Dungi*[1]! Their respective patesiates must have been very short; one patesi followed quickly upon the other! Could Gudea have built all those temples and statues in such a short time—in less than fifteen years? But let us reason a moment.

We have seen that at the time of Bur-Sin II. (see above, p. 244, *sub* 1) there was a '*Gu-de-a pa-te-si*' or '*(dingir) Gu-de-a pa-te-si*.' From R. T. xviii. p. 66, No. 2, we know that this *(dingir) Gu-de-a* must also have been a contemporary of Gimil-Sin. Who is this *Gu-de-a pa-te-si* or *(dingir) Gu-de-a pa-te-si*? Do these names stand for one and the same person? Suppose they do. In this case *Gu-de-a* or *(dingir) Gu-de-a* would have been a patesi for at least eleven years (from fifth of Bur-Sin II. to first of Gimil-Sin). Of what city was our Gudea here a patesi? The tablets do not give the name of the city. But we know already of one patesi of Shirpurla called Gudea, hence we might be inclined to connect both and make them one person. In this case Gudea would be a contemporary of Dungi, Bur-Sin II., and Gimil-Sin. But this is not possible, for in that case Gudea must have been a patesi of Shirpurla together with Ur-Ningirsu his son, *Ur-(dingir) Kal*, and probably also with (Ga)lukani, Allamu, and Ur-Ninsun—*five patesis over one and the same city*! Hence we have to differentiate between Gudea, the father of Ur-Ningirsu, and Gudea, the contemporary of Bur-Sin II. We still have to go a step further. We also have to distinguish between *Gu-de-a pa-te-si* and *(dingir) Gu-de-a pa-te-si*. The former has nothing to do with the latter. We know from the inscriptions of Gudea of Shirpurla that he placed 'statues' in different temples and ordered sacrifices to be offered unto them. A great number of these statues are still preserved at the Louvre, hence they also must have been in existence at the time of Ur IV. So it then happened that the people of Ur IV. considered the statue of Gudea of Shirpurla as a god, and called him outright *(dingir) Gu-de-a*. While Gudea was living he never called himself 'god'; this title,

[1] And if Ur-Ninsun belongs also after Ur-Ningirsu (see Chronological Table) then even five patesis!

as we shall see, was preserved for kings only. We arrive then at the following result:—Gudea, the father of Ur-Ningirsu, who had put up statues of himself in different temples, was worshipped by the people of Ur IV. as god = $^{(dingir)}$ *Gu-de-a*; but this Gudea has to be distinguished from the other Gudea (Gudea II.), a contemporary of Bur-Sin II. and Gimil-Sin. If we bear this distinction in mind all difficulties disappear. If we suppose that Allamu, together with Gudea II., were patesis of Girsu-Shirpurla, which by no means is certain[1], we might arrange them as follows:—

Allamu, patesi (of Girsu?) during the first fifteen years of Dungi III.

Ur-^{dingir} *KAL*, patesi of Girsu during (at least) the last thirty-six years of Dungi III., and the first four years of Bur-Sin II.

Gudea II., patesi (of Girsu?) during the remainder of the reign of Bur-Sin II., and (at least) during the first year of Gimil-Sin.

It might be objected that on some tablets published by Scheil in R. T. xviii. p. 65, *Ur-*$^{(dingir)}$ *KAL* and *Gu-de-a pa-te-si* (not $^{(DINGIR)}$ *Gu-de-a pa-te-si*) are mentioned together, hence they must have been contemporaries.

Upon this I would answer:

1. They *may have* been contemporaries: *Ur-*$^{(dingir)}$ *KAL* was patesi of Girsu-Shirpurla, and Gudea of some other city. See also R. T. xix. p. 63, where Scheil mentions *Ur-*$^{(dingir)}$ *NE-SÙ*, patesi of Gishuḫ, living at the time of Dungi III. (dates 37, 38).

2. If Gudea should really have been a patesi of Girsu-Shirpurla, he took, probably during the end of *Ur-*$^{(dingir)}$ *KAL's* patesiat, the latter's place, seeing that he (*Ur-*$^{(dingir)}$ *KAL*) was at least for forty years a patesi[2].

We have seen then that Winckler's arguments are weak, to say the least, and as long as we are not convinced that

(*a*) the title 'king of Shumer and Akkad' is the same as 'king of the four corners of the world';

[1] See above, p. 246, 1.

[2] Two more patesis are known to me, viz. *Ur-gar*, patesi, E. A. H. 91 (p. 327), and $^{(dingir)}$ *GUG-KAM*, O. B. I. 126 (p. 413). To what cities these two patesis belong I am not prepared to say.

(*b*) the title 'king of Ur' is an abbreviation of either 'king of Ur' PLUS 'king of Shumer and Akkad' or PLUS 'king of the four corners of the world';

we are justified in distinguishing three Dungis:

Dungi I., a contemporary of (Ga)lukani I., the father of Ġala-Lama;

Dungi II., a contemporary of (Ga)lukani II., and probably also of Ur-Ningirsu, the *en ki-ag* (*dingir*) *Ninâ*;

Dungi III., a contemporary of Allamu and *Ur-*(*dingir*) *KAL*; and hence have to differentiate the third dynasty of Ur from the second as well as from the fourth[1].

The kings of the fourth dynasty of Ur bear the proud title 'king of Ur, king of the four corners of the world,' and are the following: Dungi III., Bur-Sin II., Gimil-Sin, Ine-Sin, and Idîn-Dagan (according to Hilprecht)[2].

[1] We should even claim five dynasties on the basis of R. A. iv. No. iii. pl. ix. No. 31, where a (*n*)*am-patesi* of Ur is mentioned; hence there also must have been at the time of Sargon I. *patesis* of Ur, who preceded Ur-Gur and Dungi I.

[2] Inscriptions: General—

Rec. Trav. xvii; xvii. p. 64 ff.; xix. p. 47 ff., p. 186.

R. A. iii. No. iv. p. 118 ff.

R. A. iv. No. iii. pl. xxvii. Nos. 76–81.

Z. A. xii. pp. 258–268.

W. R. Arnold, Ancient Babylonian Temple Records in the Columbia University Library, New York, 1896.

Winckler, A. F. vi. p. 546, 6.

C. T. parts i, iii, v, vii.

C. T. 12031.

Inscriptions of Dungi III.:

Winckler, A. F. vi. p. 547, No. 7; C. T. No. 17288 (Semitic); comp. with Z. D. M. G. xxix. p. 37, and K. B. iii[1]. p. 83, 6 (both in Semitic).

O. B. I. No. 124.

All tablets with the dates of Dungi given below.

Le Clercq, ii. pl. viii. No. 3.

Z. A. iii. p. 94.

Un poids de deux mines. Museum of Constantinople. Unpublished.

Lenormant, Textes inédits, p. 163, No. 69 (doubtful).

Scheil, R. T. xviii. p. 73.

Scheil, R. T. xix. p. 50, 9. (The titles after Dungi are doubtful!) See also *sub* Ur II.

[Inscriptions of Bur-Sin II.:—

As regards Dungi III., it has been noticed above (p. 27) that he preceded Bur-Sin II. He must not be confounded with the older Dungi, Dungi I. of the second dynasty, or with Dungi II. of the third dynasty of Ur.

Thureau-Dangin's statement in R. S. 1897, p. 74, that Dungi III. preceded Bur-Sin II., is confirmed by another tablet published in Rec. Trav. xviii. p. 73, by Scheil. It reads:—

Gir Lugal-aš (?)-tur-ri
Mu en-maǧ-gal An-na en [dingir Uru-ki] ba-a-tug

The date given here apparently puts *Lugal-aš-tur-ri* during the reign of Bur-Sin II. (comp. E. A. H. 70; O. B. I. 127, 4). On another tablet published by Scheil, ibid., we find that the same *Lugal-aš-tur-ri* is the servant of a certain Dungi, king of Ur, king of the four corners of the world. That tablet reads:—

(Dingir) Dun-gi
nitaǧ lig-ga
lugal Uru-um-ki-ma
lugal an-ub-da tab-tab-ba
Lugal-(aš ?)-tur-ri
dumu Ba-a-mu
nitaǧ-zu

Inscriptions of Bur-Sin II.:
O. B. I. Nos. 20–22, 126, 127.
i. R. 5, No. xix; Winckler, K. B. iii[1]. p. 89, 1.
i. R. 3, No. xii. 1 and 2; Winckler, K. B. iii[1]. p. 89, 1.
i. R. 3, No. xii. 2; Winckler, K. B. iii[1]. p. 89, 1.
All inscriptions with the dates of Bur-Sin II. given below.
Rec. Trav. xx. p. 67.
Inscriptions of Gimil-Sin:
O. B. I. No. 12.
iv. R. 35, 4; Winckler, K. B. iii[1]. p. 88 c, No. 1.
i. R. 3, No. xi.; Winckler, K. B. iii[1]. p. 91, 2.
Sitzungsberichte d. Berl. Akad. d. Wiss. 17. März, 1879; Winckler, K. B. iii[1]. p. 91, 3; also in Hommel, Geschichte, p. 341.
Peters, Nippur, vol. ii. p. 239; also in Hilprecht, Bible Helps, pl. 25.
Inscriptions of Ine-Sin:
O. B. I. No. 125.
All the tablets with the dates of Ine-Sin given below.

Scheil remarks on this text: '*Il est clair que ce Lugal-aš(?)-tur-ri vivant sous la IIe* (ought to be *IVe*) *dynastie d'Ur ne pouvait être le contemporain de Dungi.*' Certainly he could not be the contemporary of Dungi I. of the second dynasty of Ur, but he might be made the contemporary of Dungi III., a predecessor of Bur-Sin II. Since this *Lugal-aš-tur-ri* lived during the reigns of both Dungi III. and Bur-Sin II., it follows that the latter ruler succeeded the former.

Having thus established the existence of a certain Dungi III., we are justified in referring the Semitic Babylonian inscription—generally ascribed to Dungi I.—to Dungi III. (see K. B. iii[1]. p. 82, and Winckler, A. B. K. No. 37). In this inscription Dungi has the title:—

da-LUM
šar Uru-um-ki
ù šar
ki-ib-ra-tim
ar-ba-im

which corresponds exactly to the Sumerian:—

nitaĝ lig-ga
lugal Uru-um-ki
šà lugal
an-ub-da
tab-tab-ba.

Compare this Sumerian title with the seal found on E. A. H. 61—a tablet dated at the time of Bur-Sin II. (*mu* (*giš*) *gu-za* (*dingir*) *En-lil-la(l) ba-gim*)—where this very same Dungi is mentioned:—

(*dingir*) *Dun-gi*	O Dungi,
nitaĝ lig-ga	the mighty hero,

lugal Uru-um-^{ki}*-ma*	king of Ur,
lugal an-[ub-da tab-tab-ba]	king of the four corners of the world,
Ur [^{dingir} *Gàl-alim]*	Ur-Galalim,
di . . . .[1]	the . . .
nitaḫ-zu	is thy servant.

Another inscription belonging to Dungi III. is to be found in Clercq, ii. pl. viii. No. 3, which records the 'restoring' (. . . *na-gì*) of a certain temple to $^{(dingir)}$ *Uru-ki*, and also in Winckler, A. F. vi. p. 547, No. 7 (identical with C. T. 17288)—a Semitic inscription, and as such similar to that in Winckler, A. B. K. No. 37. The former reads:—

A-na	To
$^{(ilu)}$ *A-GUR* (= *Náru*)	*A-GUR*,
be-li-su (*BE-NI-SU*)	his lord,
Dun-gi	Dungi,
šar Uru-um-^{ki}	king of Ur,
š[ar ki-ib-ra-ti]m	[king of the four corners]
[ar-ba-im]	[of the world,]
[iddin]	[has presented it.]

Only comparatively very few historical documents belonging to these rulers have come down to us. The dates, however, to be found in the temple records written during their respective reigns give us the means to form a clear conception of the 'mighty deeds' of these several rulers. These dates, in addition to the enumeration of buildings erected in honour of certain favoured gods, give us also the names of the cities and countries against which the armies of Ur were led to victory.

Dates of Dungi III.

In C. T. 18358 (comp. Thureau-Dangin, O. L. Z. i. 163) a tablet is published which is dated:

[1] Probably = *DI-KUD* = *daianu*: judge.

itu GAN-MAŠ
mu-uš-sa e IP ša (*dingir*) *Iši-Da-gan ba-ru*
mu-uš-sa-bi-ta
itu ŠE-IL-LA
mu Ur-bil-lum-^{ki} *ba-ĝul-ku*
itu 62 ^{kam}
itu-dir 2-*a-an šag ba-ni-gàl*

The tablet, as such, is a *NIN-ŠID-AG* (*epuš nikasi*), covering a period of sixty-two months, among which are two intercalary months, hence five years. These five years are the following:—

(*a*) Col. i. 5: *mu-uš-sa mu-uš-sa-a-bi*, which, according to col. vi. 5, is only an abbreviation[1] of *mu-uš-sa e IP ša* (*dingir*) *Iši-Da-gan ba-ru mu-uš-sa-bi*.

(*b*) Col. i. 13: *mu Ša-aš-ru-um-*^{ki} *ba-ĝul.*

(*c*) Col. i. 18: *mu en* (*dingir*) *Uru-ki maš-e-ni-pad.*

(*d*) Col. ii. 1: *mu Si-mu-ùr-ru-um-*^{ki} *Lu-lu-bu-um-*^{ki} *a-du X-lal-I-kam-ru ba-ĝul.*

(*e*) Col. ii. 7: *mu Ur-bil-lum-*^{ki} *ba-ĝul.*

Nos. (*a*)–(*c*) of these dates we find again on the reverse of O. B. I. 125, last three lines. Hence in C. T. 18358 we have the continuation of O. B. I. 125.

Again, in C. T. 18957, dated *mu Ki-maš-*^{ki} *ba-ĝul*, are mentioned, of the above-given dates: No. (*c*) in col. i. 5; No. (*d*) in col. ii. 35, iii. 60, and iv. 108 (shorter form); No. (*e*) in col. iv. 113. From this it follows that the date *mu Ki-maš-*^{ki} *ba-ĝul* follows upon (*e*). Further, according to Constantinople, 622 (see Thureau-Dangin, R. S. 1897, p. 74), dates Nos. (*d*) and (*e*) are followed by:

(*f*) *mu Ki-maš-*^{ki} *ba-ĝul.*

(*g*) *mu-uš-sa Ki-maš-*^{ki} *ba-ĝul.*

(*h*) *mu Ḫa-ar-ši-*^{ki} *ba-ĝul.*

(*i*) *mu* (*dingir*) *Bur-*(*dingir*) *Sin lugal.*

(*k*) =O. B. I. 127, obverse, 2, &c.

[1] Such abbreviations are very common. Comp., among others, C. T. 14608 with 16370; C. T. 18422 with E. A. H. 1–3, &c.

From this it will be seen that dates (*a*)–(*h*) belong to the predecessor of king Bur-Sin II., i. e. to Dungi III.; see above, p. 27 ff. O. B. I. 125, which contains the dates preceding that of No. (*a*), has therefore to be referred to Dungi III., against Scheil, R. T. xviii. 37 ff., and Hilprecht, O. B. I. p. 244, who referred it to the reign of Ine-Sin. The beginning of the obverse and the end of the reverse of that most interesting tablet are unfortunately broken off. We were, however, able to adduce five dates—Nos. (*d*)–(*h*)—which must have followed the last one given on the reverse of O. B. I. 125, i. e. date (*c*); hence we must supply also a lacuna of about five dates, which preceded the first one given on the obverse of the same tablet.

We would like then to restore O. B. I. 125 as follows:—

(1) *mu* (*dingir*) *Dun-gi lugal-e*
(2) . . . .
(3) *mu* (*dingir*) *Dun-gi-ra à sum-ma*
(4) . . . .
(5) [*mu E-ŠID-LAM ba-ru*]
(6) Begins O. B. I. 125, obverse, l. 1.

O. B. I. 125, obverse, l. 2 ff.

(7) *mu gir En-lil-ki* . . . . In the year when (the king) . . . *gir* of Nippur.

1. Restored according to the analogy of the first date of Bur-Sin II. and Ine-Sin. Instead of *lugal-e*, we might have also *lugal* only, or *lugal-a-an*; comp. O. B. I. 127, 1.

3. This date I found when looking over a collection of case-tablets in the possession of Mr. Noorian, former superintendent of the University of Pennsylvania Expedition to Nippur.

5. Hypothetically enumerated according to K. B. iii[1]. p. 83, 6. The building of *E-ŠID-LAM* undoubtedly was important enough to warrant us in placing it here, seeing that such a date has no other place in O. B. I. 125.

7. The first sign is that of T. C. 303 and Br. 9178, and not that for *ANŠU*. It is the same which is used in the composition *GIR-SIG-GA* (comp. R. A. iii. p. 142, env.) = *manzaz pâni*, Br. 9201. *GIR* alone occurs very often in the E. A. H. tablets before proper names, and signifies there an officer connected with the granaries; see below, p. 424. In Z. A. xii. p. 268 *a*, *GIR-UNUG-ki* stands in parallelism to *NAM-RA-AG UNUG-ki*. The end of this line, as well as that of No. 3 and No. 8, is broken away.

(8) *mu lugal-e Uru-um-ki-[ma . . . .]*	In the year when the king of Ur . . .
(9) *mu mà(?)* (*dingir*) *Nin-lil-la(l) ba-gab*	In the year when (the king) consecrated a ship to Bêlit.
(10) *mu* (*dingir*) *Uru-ki Te-zi-da e-a ba-tur*	In the year when (the king) brought Nannar-Karzida into (his) house.
(11) *mu E-ḫar-sag lugal ba-ru*	In the year when (the king) built the royal Eḫarsag.
(12) *mu* (*dingir*) *Ka-di Dûru-rab-ilu-ki e-a ba-tur*	In the year when (the king) brought Kadi into his house in Durrabilu.

9. The sign for *MÀ = elippu* is not certain. For *GAB*, see Gimil-Sin date No. 2.

10. *Te-zi-da*, according to No. 39, where it is written *Te-zi-da-ki*, is a place. (*dingir*) *Uru-ki* = Nannar = Sin. Comp. with this also E. A. H. 89 (Bur-Sin dates, No. 11): (*dingir*) *Uru-ki*-Kar-*zi-da*, and note to it. This *TE* here and in No. 39 is probably a mistake of the scribe. Comp. also Scheil, Rec. Trav. xvii. 38 ff., who reads here: *Mu an Nannar-te-a-zi-da ba-an-tur*, but *TE-A = KAR*.

For *TUR*, comp. Gudea B, vii. 19, 20: (*alan*) *E-ninnû a-mu-na-ni-tur*, 'the statue he brought into the temple Eninnû,' and D, v. 9, 10. The god Nannar of Karzida is brought twice into his temple, No. 10 and No. 39.

11. *E-ḫar-sag* = 'mountain house'; comp. (*dingir*) *Nin-ḫar-sag* and the city *Ḫar-sag-kalam-ma*. Jensen, K. B. iii[1]. p. 22, note 5, reads *Ur-sag* for *ḫar-sag*. The *lugal* here is the gen. to *E-ḫar-sag* = the royal Eḫarsag.

12. The god Kadi we met already at the time of Entemena; comp. Cône, i. 8-12: *Me-silim lugal Kiš-ki-ge ka* (*dingir*) *Ka-di-na-ta ku gan-bi-ra ki-ba na ne-ru*. Comp. also 'Babyl. Chron.' col. iii. ll. 44, 45; iii. R. 68, 53*b*, 54*b*, 57*b*, and K. 4629, rev., iii. 10 (Reissner, Sum. babyl. Hymnen, p. 135), but especially Winckler, Altbabyl. Keilschrifttexte, No. 16, which reads:

(*ilu*) *Mu-ta-bil*	Mutabil,
NITAḪ LIG-GA	the mighty hero,
mi-gir	the favoured one
(*ilu*) *Ka-di*	of Kadi,
na-ra-am	the beloved
(*ilu*) *Ištar*	of Ishtar,
šakkanakku	the shakkanakku
Dûr-ilu-ki	of Dûrilu,
ma-ḫi-is	the one who puts down
ḳa-ḳa-ad (written *ga-ga-ad*)	the heads

(13) *mu* (*dingir*) *NU-KU-SIR-DA KA-ṢAL-LU.* *ki* *e-a ba-tur*	In the year when (the king) brought *NU-KU-SIR-DA* into his temple in Kaṣalla.
(14) *mu E-ĠAL-BI lugal ba-ru*	In the year when (the king) built the royal Eḫalbi.
(15) *mu* (*dingir*) *Uru-ki En-lil-ki* *e-a ba-tur*	In the year when (the king) brought Nannar of Nippur into (his) house.

E. A. H. 94.

(16) *mu en NIR-ZI An-na en* (*dingir*) *Uru-ki MAŠ-e ni-pad*	In the year when (the king) was declared by a decision to be high-priest and true protector of Anu and of Nannar.

um-ma-an	of the troops
An-ša-an-ki	of Anshan,
Elam-tim	Elam,
Si-maš-ki-im	Simashku,
ù ri-iṣ	and who helps
Ba-ra-aḫ-si-im-ki (comp. p. 128, 5)	Baraḫse.

If this god Kadi is the god of Mesilim, and Mesilim is the king of Kish, it is very probable that Dûrilu or Dûrrabilu, the place where the god was especially worshipped, was situated in the kingdom of Kish. *Dûru-rab-ilu-ki* written in Sum. = *bad-gal-dingir-ki*. A proper name, *Ur-*(*dingir*) *Ka-di*, is very common at this time.

13. The reading of the name of the god is merely hypothetical. The name of the city ought to be read *KA-ṢAL-LU*. The copy gives for *LU*=*KU*. Comp. E. A. H. 134, 22; and see for the present, above, p. 158, and iv. R. 36, No. 1, obv., col. ii. 23.

14. The *E-ĠAL-BI* is probably a 'house of his (*BI*) *Ġal*' = an officer mentioned in the E. A. H. texts in connection with the herds; see p. 414 (*g*).

16. For *en*, see Jensen, K. B. iii[1]. p. 67, note *†. The sign transcribed by *MAŠ* is that of Br. 2024 (=*uriṣu*). Scheil, in Rec. Trav. xix. p. 56, No. 66, mentions a tablet which has the inscription *KI*-Br. 2024-*ki*, which stands for '*le nom de la ville KI-MAS-ki*.' Indeed, sometimes our date runs: *Mu en* [*NIR-ZI*] [*An-na*] (*dingir*) *Uru-ki MAŠ* (=Br. 1726)-*e ni-pad*; see E. A. H. 94. It is therefore evident that Br. 2024 =*MAŠ* (Br. 1726). *MAŠ*=*parâsu*, Br. 1785. *MAŠ-E*=a noun, which in connection with *PAD* (=*tamû*, Br. 9417) may mean 'to declare by a decision or oracle,' and should be translated passively: 'In the year when the king was de-

(17) *mu alan* $^{(dingir)}$ *Nin-lil-la(l) ba-[ru]*	In the year when (the king) built the statue of Bêlit.
(18) *mu en NIR-ZI An-na en* $^{(dingir)}$ *Uru-ki ba-tug-ga*	In the year when (the king) was invested high-priest and true protector of Anu and high-priest of Nannar.
(19) *mu NI-KIŠ (?)-MI-DA-ŠU dumu-sal lugal nam-nin Mar-ḫa-ši-*^{ki} *ku ba-il*	In the year when (the king) raised . . . the princess (=the daughter of the king) to the lordship over Marḫashi.

clared by a decision to be the *EN*,' &c. This is justified not only by E. A. H. 94, where we have *MAŠ-E*-RU, but also by date No. 18, where we read instead of *MAŠ-E ni-pad* = *ba-tug-ga*. Hence, in No. 15 the king 'was declared to be the *En*,' in No. 18 'he is invested *EN*.' E. A. H. 94 is also against Thureau-Dangin's translation (O. L. Z. i. 167), who takes *maš-pad* in the sense of '*élire, choisir*.' But *maš-pad* is more than *pad* only, it implies that 'the choosing, electing, declaring' was done on the strength of some oracle or decision by the gods. See also Gudea B, iii. 14; and note to Déc. 2ter, No. 2, iii. 3–6. This is also the reason why we translate: 'The king *was* declared by a decision,' &c., and not with Thureau-Dangin: 'The king chose a high-priest.' Every king, be it remembered, is *patesi-gal* of his gods, and was made such at the beginning of his reign. *NIR*, Br. 6283, 6282: *etellu, edlu*; *ZI*=*kênu*. The *NIR-ZI* probably is parallel to the *en-MAĜ-GAL* (Bur-Sin dates, No. 5), and may be translated 'lord and true protector of.' Comp. also Scheil, Rec. Trav. xvii. 38 ff., who refers a date similar to this to Gimil-Sin. Comp. also No. 46. In C. T. 13164 this date reads: *mu en* $^{(dingir)}$ *URU* (sic, without *KI*; comp. p. 269, note 11) *ib-pad*.

17. Thureau-Dangin, O. L. Z. i. 167, reads *na(d)*, Br. 8986, E. C. 368, but incorrectly. *Nad* looks somewhat different; comp. O. B. I. 124, obv., iii. l. 11 from the end; iv. 4; v. 3 from the end. He translates: '*fit le lit*.'

19. The sign for *KIŠ* is not certain; it is that of T. C. 203 = *GIR* + a small *DI* put under it. The *NI-KIŠ (?)-MI-DA-ŠU* is probably the proper name of the daughter of the king. Scheil, Rec. Trav. xix. p. 55, note 1, translates: '*année où . . . la fille du roi fut élevée à la souveraineté de Marḫashi*.' If this translation be correct, we should have here an instance of women sitting on the throne in these times over certain dominions and cities. Comp. however note to No. 33. The expression *NAM-NIN*, the lordship (of a woman), in opposition to the *NAM-EN*, lordship (of a man), undoubtedly speaks for Scheil's position (against Hilprecht, O. B. I. p. 245, note 5): '*que des princesses aient occupé de hautes dignités civiles à cette époque*.' *Marḫashi* = Mar'ash, in Northern Syria (Hommel, A. H. T. p. 37). See iv. R^{2}. 36, No. 1, col. i. 17.

(20) *mu bad-ki ki-bi ba-ab-gi*	In the year when (the king) restored the wall of the place.
(21) *mu dumu Uru-um-ki-ma (ga)lu GIŠ-BU DUR-DUG ba-ab-šer*	In the year when (the king) assembled the inhabitants of Ur, strong and mighty soldiers.
(22) *mu (dingir) Nin-ib pa-te-si-gal (dingir) En-lil-la(l)-ge*	In the year when [the king] . . . Ninib, the great patesi of Bêl . . .
(23) [*mu (dingir) En-lil-la(l) (dingir) Nin-lil-la(l)-ge*	In the year when . . . of Bêl and Bêlit . . .
(24) . . . . . *ba-dug-ga*	. . .

O. B. I. 125, Reverse.

(25) *mu uš*	One year after . . .
(26) *mu lugal*	In the year when the king . . .

20. The *bad-ki* is the wall of the place *κατ' ἐξοχήν*, i. e. the wall of Ur. Thureau-Dangin, l. c., reads *Ubara-ki* (Br. 4398) = Uruk?

21. *Šer* = E. C. 365 = *kaṣâru*, H. W. B. 590: *zusammenbringen, versammeln*; compare also such expressions as *kaṣâru taḫâza, kaṣâru ušmânu*. (*Ga*)*lu GIŠ-BU*, as well as *DUR-DUG*, is in opposition to *dumu Uru-um-ki-ma*. *GIŠ=zikaru*; *BU=gitmalu*. For *DUR-DUG*, comp. Br. 10574, *kibû ša amêlu*, H. W. B. p. 346; here undoubtedly in the sense of 'to bend down,' trans. = 'to oppress,' 'to cast down.' The (*ga*)*lu DUR-DUG* then would be 'people that cast down' = soldiers. In K. 4395, col. iv. 31–33, we have the following expressions: *amêl râb DUR-DUG-ŠER* and *amêl DUR-DUG-ŠER*, which are explained by *amêl râb ka-ṣir* and *amêl ka-ṣir*. Delitzsch, H. W. B. p. 591, says: '. . . *noch unsicher ist, welche Bedeutung kaṣâru in den beiden Berufsnamen kâṣir und rab kâṣir hat.*' Our passage here explains Delitzsch's difficulty. A (*ga*)*lu DUR-DUG* is a soldier, one whose business it is 'to oppress, to cast down' = Arabic مُقَاتِل; and if this soldier is a (*DUR-DUG-*)*ŠER* he is an *enlisted* soldier, one that was called to his post by the king, and *amêl râb DUR-DUG-ŠER* is the captain of the enlisted soldiers.

22. A god (*sic*) is called here *pa-te-si-gal!* With this Ninib, the great patesi of Bêl, comp. (*dingir*) *Nin-gir-su* (= Ninib) *gud lig-ga* (*dingir*) *En-lil-la*(*l*).

23. This date apparently is not complete.

24–26 are mutilated.

(27) *mu Kar-ḫar-ki ba-ğul*	In the year when (the king) devastated Karḫar.
(28) *mu [Si]-mu-ru-um-ki ba-ğul*	In the year when (the king) devastated Simuru.
(29) *mu Si-mu-ru-um-ki a-du-II-kam-ma-ru ba-ğul*	In the year when (the king) devastated Simuru for the second time.
(30) *mu Ḫa-ar-ši-ki ba-ğul*	In the year when (the king) devastated Ḫarshi.
(31) *mu en Eridug-ki-ga ba-tug-ga*	In the year when (the king) was invested lord of Eridu.
(32) *mu-uš-sa en Eridug-ki-ga ba-tug-ga*	One year after (the king) was invested lord of Eridu.

E. A. H. 95.

(33) *mu dumu-sal lugal pa-te-si An-ša-an-ki-ge ba-tug*	In the year when the daughter of the king *became* (*sic*) patesi of Anshan.

27. According to Thureau-Dangin, O. L. Z. i. 168, a king of Karḫar is mentioned in le Clercq, No. 121, whose name is *AN-KI-SA-A-RI.*

29. *a-du-II-kam-ma-ru.* For *A-DU,* see Delitzsch, H. W. B. p. 23. The *RU* clearly indicates that we have not to translate 'twice,' but 'for (*ru*) the second time.' This also follows from Nos. 28 and 36, where it is said that the king devastated Simuru (sc. for the first time), and for the third time respectively. Hence the expression *a-du-10-lal-1-kam,* either with or without *RU,* cannot mean '*neuf fois simultanément*' (Scheil, Rec. Trav. xix. p. 55, note 1), but 'for the ninth time.' See further below. That the events, which happened more than once, are quoted in their consecutive order is a proof that this tablet is arranged chronologically (O. B. I. p. 244, note 6).

30. Thus the name of this city has to be read. The signs for *Ḫa* + *ar* are not clear.

33. Anshan in Elam, Delitzsch, Parad. p. 321. The whole may be translated: '*année où la fille du roi* devint *patesi dans le pays d'Anshan*' (Scheil, Rec. Trav. xvii. p. 38, note 6, and ibid. xix. p. 55, note 1). Hilprecht, O. B. I. p. 245, note 5, rejects this translation 'on the ground that there is no evidence that in ancient Babylonia women were permitted to occupy the highest political or religious positions independently,' and translates: 'In the year when the patesi of Anshan married a daughter of the king' (*tug* =

E. A. H. 96.

(34 *a*) *mu Kar-ḫar-^{ki} a-du-II-kam-ru ba-ǧul*	In the year when (the king) devastated Karḫar for the second time.
(34 *b*) *mu Kar-ḫar-^{ki} a-du-III-kam-ru ba-ǧul*	In the year when (the king) devastated Karḫar for the third time.

E. A. H. 97.

(35) *mu Si-mu-ru-um-^{ki} a-du-III-kam-ru ba-ǧul*	In the year when (the king) devastated Simuru for the third time.
(36) *mu-uš-sa Si-mu-ru-um a-du-III-kam-ru ba-ǧul*	One year after (the king) devastated Simuru for the third time.
(37) *mu An-ša-an-^{ki} ba-ǧul*	In the year when (the king) devastated Anshan.

E. A. H. 98.

(38) *mu-uš-sa An-ša-an-^{ki} ba-ǧul*	One year after the king devastated Anshan.
(39) *mu $^{(dingir)}$ Uru-ki Te-zi-da-^{ki} a-du-II-kam-ru e-a ba-tur*	In the year when (the king) for the second time brought Nannar-Karzida into (his) house.
(40) *mu Bad-Ma-da-^{ki} ba-ru*	In the year when (the king) built Dûr-Mada.

aḫâzu, 'to take a wife, to marry,' H. W. B. p. 42). Both translations are grammatically possible. Date No. 19, however, seems to be evidence enough that women actually did occupy such high political positions. See note to No. 19. The fact that Anshan very soon after this (comp. No. 37) was devastated by Dungi III. also speaks for Scheil's translation. Dungi III. having put his daughter on the throne of Anshan, the people of that city rebelled; Dungi III. had to subdue them.

34 *b*. This date, so far found only in C. T. part vii. No. 15324, col. iv., is left out in O. B. I. 125. Whether it belongs here is doubtful. So much only is certain, that it is one of the dates of Dungi III., because immediately preceding the date *Ur-$^{(dingir)}$ Kal* patesi is mentioned. See, however, note to date 48.

40. *Bad-Ma-da* cannot be translated here = 'the wall of the land,' on account of the *KI*, which shows that *Bad-Ma-da* (= Semitic *Dûr-Mati*) is a place. Comp. E. A. H. 99, 100; C. T. 18389.

E. A. H. 99, 100.

(41) *mu-uš-sa Bad-Ma-da-ki ba-ru*	One year after (the king) built Dûr-Mada.

E. A. H. 101.

(42) *mu e IP ša Iši (dingir) Da-gan-na ba-ru*	In the year when the damḳâr of Ishi-Dagan built a temple (sc. for Dungi).

42. The following variations of this date may also be found:

C. T. 12927, col. i. 22: *mu (uš-sa) e IPša Iši Da-an* (sic)*-gan ba-ru* (*mu-uš-sa-bi*).

C. T. 18358, vi. 5: *mu(uš-sa) e IP ša (dingir) Iši-Da-gan ba-ru.*

C. T. 14594—a tablet from the time of Bur-Sin II—*mu IP Iši-Da-gan ba-ni* (sic).

E. A. H. 101: *mu IP ša Iš (dingir) Dagan e (dingir) Dun-gi-ra ba-ru.*

If we compare the above-given dates with C. T. 94-10-16, 25, obv. iii., and C. T. 95-10-12, 8, obv. ii., where a scribe (*dup-sar*) *Ur (dingir) Iši (dingir) Ba-u* is mentioned, and with C. T. 19740, iii. 70, 18371, and 18422, where we find a *Pa* (= officer) *Ur-(dingir) Iši-(dingir) Ba-u*, then there cannot be any doubt that *Iši-(dingir) Dagan*, or *(dingir) Iši Dagan*, or *Iši-Dagan*, or *Iši-Da-an-gan*, or possibly also *(dingir) Iši-(dingir) Dagan* belong together, and are an analogy-formation to [*Ur*]*-(dingir) Iši-(dingir) Ba-u*. *Ur-(dingir) Iši-(dingir) Ba-u* is a proper name, and if translated would mean 'the servant (lit. dog, *kalbu*) of Ishi-Ba'u.' *Iši-Ba'u*, then, is another proper name. Such proper names formed out of another proper name with *Ur* or *Lugal* or *Eri* or (*Ga*)*lu* preceding it are very often found at this time; comp. *Ardi-Naram-(ilu) Sin* (R.T. xix. p. 47), *Lugal-(dingir) Dungi ni-ku* (C. T. 94-10-16, 3, obv. iii.), (*Ga*)*lu Šir-pur-la-ki* (C. T. 48427), (*Ga*)*lu-Ki-nu-nir-ki* (C. T. 17757), *Ur-E-ninnû*, and *Ur-E-INNANNA-GE*. From this it follows that we have to take *Iši-Dagan* with or without *dingir* before *Iši* or *Dagan* as a proper name. The sign for *Iši* is *IŠ*, Br. 5079. I transcribe *Iši* instead of *IŠ*, because we have here undoubtedly a 'phonetic writing' for *I-ši-Dagan*; hence also a Semitism. Comp. with this the phonetic writing of the name of king Bur-Sin I. The name *Iši-Dagan* would mean: 'O Dagan, lift up.' Comp. also Hilprecht, vol. ix., 3 *a*, 5, where the following name is found: *Bêl-zêr-iddina apil-šu ša I-ši-(dingir) KUR-GAL*. That the sign *dingir* should sometimes be found before *Iši* is not strange; comp. *(dingir) Iš-me-(dingir) Dagan*. Further below we shall see that the sign *dingir* is found either (*a*) before the names of kings, or (*b*) before the names of certain old patesis who erected

(43) *mu-uš-sa e IP ša Iši-*(*dingir*) *Da-gan-na ba-ru*	One year after the damḳar of Ishi-Dagan built a temple (*sc.* for Dungi).
(44) *mu-uš-sa e IP ša Iši-*(*dingir*) *Da-gan-na ba-ru* [*mu-uš-*] *sa-*[*a-bi*]	Two years after the damḳar of Ishi-Dagan built a temple (*sc.* for Dungi).
(45) *mu Ša-aš-ru-*[*ki*] *ba-ḡul*	In the year when (the king) devastated Shaṣhru.

statues of themselves and put them up in certain temples. If that be true, then (*dingir*) *Iši-*(*dingir*) *Ba'u* and (*dingir*) *Iši-*(*dingir*) *Dagan* are or were either *kings* or celebrated old patesis, whose statues were still in existence at the time of Ur IV, and in whose honour certain persons were named. The identification of the third sign is not yet certain. Scheil (R. T. xvii. p. 38) and Thureau-Dangin formerly identified it with Br. 802; see E. C. 199 and 200, both of which forms occur in our passage. Sayce, who translates our passage by: 'In the year when the temple at the edge (= *šaptu*, Br. 803) of the mound of Dagan was built,' follows them (P. S. B. A. xxi. p. 21). Thureau-Dangin (O. L. Z. i. 168) transcribes our sign now by Br. 820. King, in his copy of C. T., gives sometimes a form which resembles Br. 855. Comp. also the different forms as given in ll. 43 and 44, and in E. A. H. 101.

Scheil, in Rec. Trav. xix. p. 55, 3, mentions a name which is written either *IP ŠA* (*dingir*) *En-lil*, or our sign in question, + *ŠA* + (*dingir*) *En-lil*. From this he concludes correctly: '*cette variante nous donne la valeur IP pour ce dernier signe qui est ou le No.* 810 *ou le No.* 812 (*Ibira*) = *damḳâru de Brunnow*.' The latter identification is undoubtedly the correct one. For *damḳâru* (H. W. B. p. 222), comp. Jensen, Z. A. vi. 349, and Hilprecht, O. B. I 262, and note 6. The very fact that *ŠA* after *IP* may be omitted, as is actually done in C. T. 14594, shows that it is neither a part of *IP* nor of *Ishi-Dagan*—it is nothing more than the *ša* which is sometimes employed in Assyrian to express the genitive; hence we have here another Semitism. Compare also *IP ša Bêl* above. E. A. H. 101, as well as C. T. 14594, show that the subject of the whole sentence is *IP*—'they (he) built.' Our date can be translated only as has been done above. Thureau-Dangin (O. L. Z. 168) translates: *année où il construisit le temple* Br. 820-*ŠA-IŠ de Dagan*.' The fact that *dingir* is found sometimes before *IŠ* makes that translation impossible For such a 'temple of Dungi,' comp. among other places C. T. 12912, obv., iii. 24, and especially C. T. 94-10-15, 4, where the amount of grain is mentioned that was offered unto Dungi in such a temple. E. A. H. 5 mentions 60 + *X gur 7 ḳa gar-zid lugal ŠAG-GAL IP ša Iši-Dagan* (food for the *damḳar* of Ishi-Dagan). See, however, also Index *sub* nom. propr. beginning with *IP-ša*...

44 The *sa* in this line has to be completed to read either *mu-uš-sa-bi* or *mu-uš-sa-a-bi*, or even *mu-sa-a-bi*, C. T. 18358, i. 5.

(46) *mu en* ^(dingir)^ *Uru-ki maš-e-ni-pad*	In the year when the king was declared by a decision to be high-priest of Nannar.

E. A. H. 1–3.

(47 *a*) *Mu Si-mu-ru-um-^ki^ Lu-lu-bu-um-^ki^ a-du-*10*-lal-*1*-^kam^-ru ba-ḫul*	In the year when (the king) devastated Simurru and Lulubi for the ninth time.

46. That dates 46 ff. belong here has been shown above. It is however remarkable that Dungi III. should once more be declared 'high-priest of Nannar,' seeing that he not only had been 'declared' already, but even 'invested high-priest of Nannar.' Comp. above, dates Nos. 16 and 18. Should we have to divide the dates given on O. B. I. 125 between two rulers? This seems to me more than probable, or else there hardly would have been any necessity of stating one and the same thing twice. If this date read *mu en* ^(dingir)^ *Uru-ki a-du-II-kam-ru maš-e ni-pad* it would be intelligible, but not so otherwise. I would therefore assign hypothetically the last few dates to the predecessor of Bur-Sin II., i.e. to Dungi III, while the earlier dates may belong to some unknown ruler. If Winckler's theory—see above—could be proved to be correct, we might refer the earlier dates to Ur-Gur I.; but this is still an open question. We have a similar case in O. B. I. 127, where the earlier dates belong to Bur-Ṣin II., while the later ones belong to Gimil-Sin.

47 *a*. Simurru (= سمرّة). The situation of this country is not yet certain. Scheil (R. T. xvii. p. 38 and xix. p. 55, note 1) places it in the neighbourhood of Lulubi; comp. above, 'king *An-nu-ba-ni-ni* of Lulubi.' Hommel (Aus der babylonischen Altertumskunde, p. 9), whom Hilprecht (O. B. I. p. 245, note 4) follows, identifies it with Simyra in Phoenicia, between Arvad and Tripolis. (See also Hommel, A. H. T. p. 38.)

In E. A. H. 3 we have *Si-mu-ru-um-RU*, which latter *RU* undoubtedly is a mistake for '*ki*.' On other tablets I found these names written also *Si-mu-ùr-ru-(um)* and *Lu-lu-bu*, either with or without *KI*. In C. T. 18422 we find *mu Si-mu-ùr-um-^ki^ Lu-bu* (sic), &c.

*a-du-*10*-lal-*1*-^kam^-ru*. For 10-*lal*-1 = 9, see below, p. 340, under *LAL-NI*. That *A-DU* = 'time' is proved by O. B. I. 125, rev. 4, 5. This expression 'for the ninth time' presupposes the first, second, &c., devastation of the same cities. But no such first, second, &c., devastation of these cities is mentioned in O. B. I. 125. Only three devastations of Simurru alone were enumerated above, ll. 28, 29, 35, 36, and no mention is made at all of the fourth to eighth devastation either of Simurru alone or of Simurru and Lulubu together. We have to suppose, therefore, that the author of O. B. I. 125 either left Lulubu

(47 *b*)	[*Mu-u*]*š-sa mu* [*Si-mu-ru-u*]*m-ki* *Lu-lu-*[*bu-um-ki* *a-d*]*u-10-lal-1-kam-*[*ru ba-*]*ǵul*	One year after (the king) devastated Simurru and Lulubi for the ninth time.

E. A. H. 4, 5.

(48)	*Mu Ur-bil-lum-ki ba-ǵul*	In the year when (the king) devastated Urbillum.

unmentioned in ll. 28, 29, 35, 36, or that 'for the ninth time' has to be referred to Simurru alone. But, as already stated, we have no fourth to eighth devastation of Simurru either. The reason for this probably is that these latter devastations occurred *late in the year* when the other events enumerated above in ll. 37–46 had taken place already, or else we would have here an apparent discrepancy, especially when we take into consideration date No. 47 *a*. This date *must* be *identical* with the date No. 48, or else the reckoning of C. T. 18358 (above, p. 253) would be wrong, i. e. from date No. 44 to No. 48 would not be a space of five years plus *itu dir 2-a-an*, but one of six years. The same may be said of date No. 50 *b*, which is the same—only the earlier one—as date No. 51. This probably is also the case with date No, 34 *b* = 35. The truth of this could be easily established if we compare the names of the months given on tablets dated according to No. 47 *b* with those dated according to No. 48. The months to be found on tablets dated according to No. 47 *b* had to be the earlier ones.

47 *b*. I found this so far only on C. T. 19024, xii., and 96-4-10, 3, where it is preceded by *Ur-(dingir) KAL pa-te-si*. The wording of this date is noteworthy, showing that the expression *mu-uš-sa Simurru*, &c., is an abbreviation of the fuller form *mu-uš-sa mu Simurru*, &c., i. e. the year (*mu*) that follows (*uš-sa*) the year (*mu*) when, &c.

48. E. A. H. 4 has only *Ur-bil-lum*, without *ki*. C. T. 12231, x., gives this date more fully: *Ur-(dingir) KAL pa-te-si, mu (dingir) Dun-gi, nitaǵ lig-ga, lugal Ur-um-ki-ma lugal an-ub-da tab-tab-ba-ge, Ur-bil-lum-ki, Si-mu-ru-um-ki, Lu-lu-bu-ki, šà Kar-ḫar-ki-ra, KUL(?) KU-SAG* + inserted *IŠ* (comp. E. C. 394)-*bi šu-bur-ra im-mi-ra*, i. e. in the year when Dungi III., &c., of Urbillum, Simurru, Lulubu, and Karḫar . . . their soldiers (read *KU-KA* = *dur-dug*, comp. above, l. 21) drove together (lit. gathered together with the hand, *BUR* = *paḫâru*, Br. 343; H. W. B. 520) and cast them down (*RA* = *raḫâṣu*, H. W. B. 617). It is possible that because Karḫar is mentioned in this longer date No. 34 *b* belongs here, it being the third devastation of that city! (Comp. Nos. 27 and 34.)

E. A. H. 6–8.

(49)	*Mu Ki-maš-^{ki} (Ḫu-mur-ti-^{ki}) ba-ǧul*	In the year when (the king) devastated Kimash (and Ḫumurti).

E. A. H. 9–17.

(50 *a*)	*Mu-uš-sa Ki-maš-^{ki} (Ḫu-mur-ti-^{ki}) ba-ǧul*	One year after (the king) devastated Kimash (and Ḫumurti).

E. A. H. 18–24.

(50 *b*)	*Mu-uš-sa Ki-maš-^{ki} (Ḫu-mur-ti-^{ki}) ba-ǧul mu-uš-sa-a-bi*	Two years after (the king) devastated Kimash (and Ḫumurti).

E. A. H. 25 and 104.

(51)	*Mu Ḫa-ar-ši-^{ki} Ḫu-mur-ti-^{ki}) ba-ǧul*	In the year when (the king) devastated Ḫarshi and Ḫumurti.

49. *Ki-maš*, later on pronounced *MAŠ*, is situated in Central Arabia, Delitzsch, Parad. p. 242; Hommel, A. H. T. p. 38. In E. A. H. 8 *ba-ǧul* is omitted.

50 *a*. For the meaning of *uš-sa* = 'joined to,' 'following,' see Hilprecht, O. B. I. 244, note 6, and Br. 5060, *emêdu*. The lit. translation then would be: In the year that follows (the year) when, &c., i.e. 'one year after'; see above, date No. 47 *b*.

50 *b*. *Mu-uš-sa-a-bi* = its following year to the year that follows (*mu-uš-sa*) the year when, &c., i.e. 'two years after.' The following forms of this date occur: *mu-uš-sa Ki-maš-ki ba-ǧul mu-uš-sa-a-bi*, E. A. H. 18; or the same with *ba-ǧul* left out, E. A. H. 19–22; or only *mu-uš-sa mu-uš-sa-a-bi*, E. A. H. 23, 24. These two latter dates may also belong to No. 44. C. T. 18346, viii., gives this date more fully: *Ur-$^{(dingir)}$ KAL, pa-te-si, mu $^{(dingir)}$ Dun-gi, nitaǧ lig-ga, lugal Uru-um-^{ki}-ma, lugal an-ub-da tab-tab-ba-ge, Ki-maš-^{ki} Ḫu-mur-ti-^{ki}, šà ma-da-bi ud-I mu-ǧul, mu-uš-sa-a-bi*, i.e. in the year when Dungi III., &c., devastated on one day (or at one time) Kimash, Ḫumurti, and their lands. That this date is the same as No. 51 has been shown above; see note to date No. 47.

51. It will be noticed that in dates Nos. 49 to 51 Ḫumurti is sometimes mentioned in connection with Kimash and sometimes with Ḫarshi. Compare also Uncertain Dates, No. 6, where we find Ḫarshi, Kimash, and Ḫumurti mentioned together. Comp. further the shorter form, *mu Ḫa-ar-ši-^{ki}* (C. T. 21338, vii. 162), with the longer, *mu Ḫa-ar-ši-^{ki} Ḫu-mur-ti-^{ki} ba-ǧul* (ibid., col. viii. 185).

The immediate[1] successor of Dungi III. was Bur-Sin II[2]. (Comp. above, Dates of Dungi III., *sub* (*h*) and (*i*).)

Dates of Bur-Sin II.

Among the dates belonging to this ruler are to be found the following (comp. also O. B. I. 127, obv., and Thureau-Dangin, R. S. 1897, p. 73, and O. L. Z. i. 170):—

E. A. H. 27–32.

(1)	*Mu* (*dingir*) *Bur*-(*dingir*) *Sin lugal*	In the year when Bur-Sin became king.

E. A. H. 33, 34.

(2)	*Mu-uš-sa* (*dingir*) *Bur*-(*dingir*) *Sin lugal*	One year after Bur-Sin became king.

E. A. H. 35–54.

(3 *a*)	*Mu* (*dingir*) *Bur*-(*dingir*) *Sin lugal-e Ur-bil-lum*-*ki mu-ḫul*	In the year when king Bur-Sin devastated Urbillum.

1. In E. A. H. 27 the sign *BUR* has not the determinative of god (*dingir*). All the other tablets exhibit the sign of *DINGIR* before that of *BUR*. The absence of the sign *dingir* is either due to the carelessness of the scribe, or it may have been made illegible by the seal-impression, which has been rolled all over the tablet, so that even the dividing lines are no more visible. See p. 424.

2. This date does not occur in O. B. I. 127, and is not given by Thureau-Dangin in R. S. 1897, p. 73, and in O. L. Z. i. 170. The same is true of dates Nos. 3 *b* and 10.

3 *a*. The devastation of Urbillum has already been recorded under Dungi III. The sign *lugal* generally has an *E* after it, except in E. A. H. 47, 48, 51, 54.

---

[1] Scheil, Rec. Trav. xvii. p. 38, note 3, places Bur-Sin II. after Ine-Sin. Hilprecht—who follows Scheil—arranges these rulers: Ine-Sin—Bur-Sin—Gimil-Sin (O. B. I. p. 244, note 6).

[2] The sign for *Bur* is here = *AMAR*, Br. 9065. *Bur* = st. constr. of Assyr. *bûru*. Bur-Sin has not to be read = Amar-Sin, because these rulers are Semites. Comp. also what has been said about the name of Bur-Sin I. The name signifies, not 'child of Sin,' Delitzsch, B. A. p. 623, but 'a young ox is Sin.'

(3 *b*)	*Mu-uš-sa Ur-bil-lum-ki ba-ĝul*	One year after (the king) destroyed Urbillum.

E. A. H. 55–67.

(4)	*Mu (giš) gu-za (dingir) En-lil-la(l) ba-gim*	In the year when (Bur-Sin) erected the throne of Bêl.

E. A. H. 68–73.

(5)	*Mu en-maĝ-gal An-na ba-tug*	In the year when (the king) was invested priest most high of Anu.

3 *b*. This date so far is to be found only in C. T. (part vii.) 13138, rev. It cannot belong to the reign of Dungi III. (see date 48), because there the succession is established not only by C. T. 18957, but also by Constantinople, 622 (see above). Besides this, we know that in O. B. I. 125 the *mu-uš-sa* dates are mentioned—as a rule—while in O. B. I. 127 they never occur! Until this year *Ur-(dingir) KAL* was patesi of Girsu.

4. The sign for *GIŠ* is sometimes omitted before *GU-ZA*. So in E. A. H. 55, 64, 65, 67.

In some texts, however, we read: *Mu (giš)-gu-za-maĝ (dingir) En-lil-la(l) ba-gim*, i. e. In the year when (the king) erected the sublime throne of Bêl; comp. E. A. H. 62, 63, 65.

For *GIM* or *DIM* = *banû*, 'to build,' see Br. 9112.

5. For the pronunciation of *KU*=*tug*, see Hommel, S. L. 402; and comp. E. A. H. 87 (*sub* (9)), where it is followed by *ga*. For *ba-tug*(*-ga*) we also have *ba-a-tug*, comp. E. A. H. 76; or *in-tug* (O. B. I. 126, col. vii.).

The subject of *TUG* must be in all cases the king, as is evident from O. B. I. 126, col. vii.: *mu (dingir) Bur-(dingir) Sin nitaĝ lig-ga lugal Uru-um-ki-ma lugal an-ub-da tab-tab-ba-ge en te-unu-gal (dingir) Innanna in-tug.*

TUG. Either Br. 10523, *ašâbu*, here = *Šaphel ušešib*, 'make to sit,' H. W. B. p. 245; or better, Br. 10533: *labâšu*, H. W. B. p. 371. Hence we have here a certain 'investiture,' and must translate: 'in the year when the king was invested.' For *en* = priest, high-priest, see Dungi III. dates, No. 16; Scheil, Rec. Trav. xvii. p. 37; and Thureau-Dangin, R. A. iv. p. 142. In some tablets we find this date given only by *Mu en-maĝ-gal An-na ba-tug*; comp. E. A. H. 68, 69. E. A. H. 70–73, on the other hand, state that Bur-Sin was invested 'priest most high' of Ishtar and priest of Nannar (*dingir Uru-ki*) = Sin, the moon-god, who is called in i. R. 5, xix., 'king of Ur.' The formula then runs: *Mu en-maĝ-gal An-na en (dingir) Uru-ki ba-tug*. Curious is also the variant of C. T. 14606: *mu en-nun-gal An-na ki-ag (dingir) Bur-(dingir) Sin en Eridug-ki ba-tug*, which ought to be translated (against

E. A. H. 74–77.

(6)	*Mu en-te-unu-gal* (*dingir*) *Innanna ba-tug*	In the year when (the king) was invested high-priest of the great abode of Ishtar.

E. A. H. 78–86.

(7)	*Mu* (*dingir*) *Bur-*(*dingir*) *Sin lugal-e Ša-aš-ru-um-ki ba-ĝul*	In the year when king Bur-Sin devastated Shashru.

O. B. I. 127, obv. 7.

(8)	*Mu Ḫu-uḫ-nu-ri-ki ba-ĝul*	In the year when (the king) devastated Ḫuḫnuri.

Thureau-Dangin, O. L. Z. i. 170, note 9), 'in the year when he (i.e. the king) was invested priest most high of Anu, beloved of Bur-Sin, lord of Eridu.' It is remarkable that Bur-Sin should be called here already 'lord of Eridu'—a position to which he was raised only later on; comp. date No. 9. Should this justify us in referring this latter date to the 'uncertain dates,' and in ascribing it to his successors, i. e. either Ur-Ba'u II. or Gimil-Sin? See note 8*c* to Uncertain Dates.

6. The sign for *UNU*(*G*) is here that for *AB* with the *gunu*-signs = Br. 4790. It is the same sign which occurs in the name for *Ur* = *Uru-unu*(*g*)-*ki-ma*, which latter name we always transcribe as *Uru*-um-*ki-ma* on account of the *MA*. For *TE-UNU*, see Syl.° 93 = *unu* = *makânu* (Br. 7722), H. W. B. p. 323. O. B. I. 127, obv., 5, has for *en-te-unu-gal* only *en-ĝar-gal*. Thureau-Dangin translates this latter passage in R. A. iv., note 1, '*année où le grand-prêtre du grand TE-UNOU de INNANNA a été installé*,' but corrects himself in R. S. 1897, p. 73, and O. L. Z. i. 170, where he renders it: '*année où* (*Bur-Sin*) *a été investi seigneur de la grande Demeure d'Ishtar*,' which latter translation is undoubtedly to be preferred.

7. The forms *Ša-aš-ru-ki* and *Ša-aš-ru-um-ki* occur side by side. Some tablets give the name of king Bur-Sin (comp. E. A. H. 78, 79), others do not (see E. A. H. 80–84). Once the *KI* after *Šašrum* is left out (E. A. H. 84).

8. This date does not occur in the E. A. H. tablets. The copy of Hilprecht has *Ri-ban-nu-ḫu-ki*—apparently a mistake of the scribe, see note 3 to Uncertain Dates.

E. A. H. 87.

(9)	*Mu en Eridug-ki ba-tug-ga*	In the year when (the king) was invested lord of Eridu.

E. A. H. 88.

(10)	*Mu-uš-sa en Eridug-ki ba-tug*	One year after (the king) was invested lord of Eridu.

E. A. H. 89.

(11)	*Mu en (dingir) Uru-ki-kar-zi-da ba-tug*	In the year when (the king) was invested high-priest of *Nannar-KAR-ZI-DA.*

9. *NUN-ki*, when followed by *ga*, as is sometimes the case, has to be read *Eridug-ki-ga, Urudug-ki-ga.* E. A. H. 87 has *ba-a-tug*; E. A. H. 88 only *ba-tug.*

10. This date so far is only found in the E. A. H. collection.

11. The *Kar-zi-da*, on the one hand, is a temple (*E*) built or rebuilt by Dungi I. for (dingir) *Nin-Uru-um-ki-ma*, i.e. the Bêlit of Ur; it was therefore probably situated in Ur (comp. O. B. I. 16): on the other a place, see Dungi III. dates, No. 10.

Scheil, in Rec. de Trav. xx. p. 67, published a text in Assyrian characters, which mentions the introduction of *Nannar*-Karzida into his temple. As such it is probably identical with date 10 of Dungi III., where, however, Hilprecht's copy (O. B. I. 125) has *TE-ZI-DA*, which ought to be read therefore *KAR-ZI-DA*. See the note to that date. The text above referred to reads:

(dingir) *URU*	For Nannar-
KAR-ZI-DA	Karzida = '*Lebensburg*,'
lugal ki-ag-ga-ni-ir	his beloved king,
(dingir) *Bur-*(dingir) *Sin*	Bur-Sin,
En-lil-ki-a	of Nippur,
(dingir) *En-lil-li*	by Bêl
mu-pad-da	called
SAG-UŠ	to be the *SAG-UŠ*
e (dingir) *En-lil-li*	of the temple of Bêl;
an-zi	for the god of life,
an-ud kalam-ma-na	the divine light of his world,
lugal lig-ga	the powerful king,
lugal Uru-um-ki-ma	king of Ur,
lugal an-ub-da tab-tab-ba-ge	king of the four corners of the world.

To these dates may be added:

(12)	*Mu-uš-sa Bur-Sin-lugal-e bad gal é Ur ku ki li bi da tig ? ga mu-ru* (so Scheil, Rec. Trav. xix. p. 59, No. 338)	*Année qui a suivi celle où le roi Bur-Sin a construit la grande enceinte de Bît Kalbu-(ki)?* . . .

It may be stated right here, that the above-given dates, as well as those that follow, by no means cover the whole reign of their respective kings. This, e. g., is evident from two tablets (i. R. 5, xix.; i. R. 3, xii. 1, 2) which record that Bur-Sin II. 'renewed' (*BIL*) his city (i. e. Ur), and built for (*dingir*) *En-ki* (= Ea) an apsu. Probably we may find in the near future some tablets which are dated from these two years. (Comp. also date 11 with Rec. Trav. xx. 67.)

To the above-mentioned buildings has to be added the *KI-ŠAG-ĠUL-LA*, which occurs in O. B. I. 20. The inscription reads:

(*dingir*) *En-lil*	For Bêl,
lugal kur-kur-ra	the king of the lands,
KAR-ZI-DA	In the Karzida
ud-ul-ru-a-ku (= *anâ ûmê ṣâti*, Br. 9154)	for ever,
MI-KISAL GUD . . . ru-a	the builder of . . .
en-nu-un (Br. 2838, *naṣâru*) *ti-la-a* . . .	for the preservation of his life,
(*dingir*) *Bur-*(*dingir*) *Sin*	Bur-Sin,
ki-ag (*dingir*) *URU-ge*	the beloved of Nannar,
MI-KISAL azag-ga-ni	his splendid . . .
mu-na-ru	he has built;
DURU-ki-ag-ga-ni	into his beloved abode
mu-na-ni-tur	he has brought it.
(*dingir*) *Bur-*(*dingir*) *Sin*	Bur-Sin,
ud im-da-ab-gid-da	for long days to come
nam-ti-la-ni-ku	for his life,
mu-na-ru	he has built it.

12. This date, published by Scheil, apparently belongs to Bur-Sin II. The *uš-sa* predicates another year (= *mu* simple) to Bur-Sin II.

lugal-a-ni-ir	his king,
(*dingir*) *Bur-*(*dingir*) *Sin*,	Bur-Sin,
En-lil-ki-a	by the Nippurian
(*dingir*) *En-lil-li*	Bêl
mu-pad-da	called
SAG-UŠ	to be the *SAG-UŠ*
e-(*dingir*) *En-lil-ge*	of the temple of Bêl,
nitaǵ lig-ga	the mighty hero,
lugal Uru-um-ki-ma	king of Ur,
lugal an-ub-da tab-tab-ba-ge	king of the four corners of the world,
nitaǵ-azag	the glorious hero
(*dingir*) *En-lil-la*(*l*)	of Bêl,
KI-ŠAG-ǴUL-LA	the *KI-ŠAG-ǴUL-LA*
(*dingir*) *Bur-*(*dingir*) *Sin-ka-ka*	of Bur-Sin
mu-na-an-DU	he has erected.

4, 5. *Bur-Sin En-lil-ki-a.* The *A* after *En-lil-ki* has here to be taken for *a*—*a* = ـِيّ = ִי—, the gentilic ending: '*der Nippursche*,' Winckler translates: '*Bur-Sin aus Nippur*' may also be possible. Sometimes, as in O. B. I. 21, 6, *En-lil-ki-a* stands after (*dingir*) *En-lil-li*, which shows that *En-lil-ki-a* does not belong to Bur-Sin, but to Bêl.

8. For *SAG-UŠ*, see Br. 3581–85. Here probably a title designating 'protector.' Comp. also *SAG-GIŠ*, i. R. 2, No. 5, 1, 2, 3; *NE-GIŚ* (=*nitaǵ*), Lugalzag. i. 23—all similar titles to the Assyr. *šakkanakku*.

15. The third sign is doubtful. Most probably it is the sign *ǵul* = *ḫidûtu*, 'joy.' *KI-ŠAG-ǴUL-LA* would be the place of 'the joy of his heart,' which he erected (*DU*=*gub*=*nazâzu*, Br. 4892) in honour of Bêl. With this building comp. also the *E-ǴUL-ǴUL* of Nâbû-na'id.

O. B. I. 21 records the building of another house—a storehouse for the sacrifices—as follows:—

(*dingir*) *En-lil*	For Bêl,
lugal kur-kur-ra	the king of the lands,
lugal ki-ag-ga-ni-ir	his beloved king,
(*dingir*) *Bur-*(*dingir*) *Sin*	Bur-Sin,

(dingir) En-lil-li	by Bêl
En-lil-ki-a	of Nippur
mu-pad-da	called
SAG-UŠ	to be the *SAG-UŠ*
e-(dingir) En-lil-ka	of the temple of Bêl,
lugal lig-ga	the mighty king,
lugal Uru-um-ki-ma	king of Ur,
lugal an-ub-da tab-tab-ba-ge	king of the four corners of the world—
E LAL NI-NUN	the house for honey, cream,
šà GEŠTIN	and wine,
ki-SIGIŠŠE-SIGIŠŠE-ra-na	a place for his sacrifices—
NU-SILIG-GI	for the most powerful one
mu-na-an-ru	he has built.

13, 14. *LAL*=E. C. 357: Br. 3339, *dišpu*, '*Honig*.' The last two signs are a ligature=*NI-NUN*; see Br. 5349, *ḫimêtu*, cream.

GEŠTIN. This sign occurs again in Ur-Ba'u, vi. 5; see also Jensen, K. B. iii^{1}. p. 24, note 4. It is given in T. C. *sub* No. 85 as '*non assimilé*.' Thureau-Dangin formerly (R. A. iv. p. 71, note 1) identified it with Br. 3338=*LAL*; so also Amiaud. The former scholar, however, identifies it now correctly with Br. 5006 =*karânu* (see E. C. 372 and note)—as such it is not identical with the sign *AL*, occurring in Déc. 2ter, 4, 16, or even with the *BI* in *mà giš ru-a-bi* (Gudea D, iv. 11)—against Hilprecht, O. B. I. p. 253, note 1. Lines 13 and 14 may be translated into Assyrian by *bît dišpi ḫimêti ù karâni*, i. e. 'the house for honey, cream, and wine'; comp. also Abel and Winckler, Keilschrifttexte, Nabonidus, ii. 1.

15. The second and third signs = Br. 9094; comp. Syl.^{b} 158 = *sigišše* = *nikû*, H. W. B. p. 479, 'sacrifice.' The *RA* contains the 'overhanging' vowel. The correct reading of this sign, ending in *R*, is not yet known.

16. The second sign is *SILIG*, Br. 919. Comp. with this Br. 1965, *(dingir) NU-SILIG-GA*; R. A. iv. No. 3, pl. i. No. 1, env., iv. 3, *LUGAL-NU-SILIG* (= a proper name); also Gudea, Cyl. B, iv. 1, and Thureau-Dangin, R. A. iv. p. 71, note 1. *Nu-silig-gi* here undoubtedly refers back to Bêl; as such then it takes up l. 1: For Bêl . . . for the *NU-SILIG* he has built. *NU*, Br. 1964, *zikaru*; *SILIG*, Br. 920, *šagapûru*, H. W. B. 640, *mächtig*, *stark*, *Machthaber*.

To these texts has now to be added :—

E. A. H. 26 (soapstone), from Warka; has the same inscription as C. T. 12156.

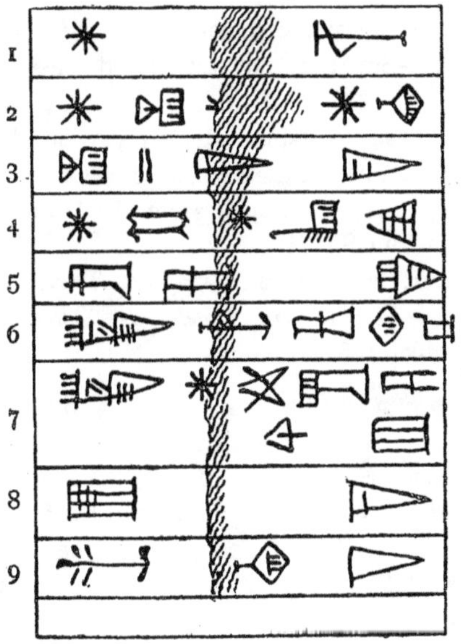

(dingir) *Innanna*	To Ishtar,
(dingir) *nin-dingir-si-an-na*	the mistress of divine (exalted, heavenly) power,
nin-a-ni-ir.	his lady,
(dingir) *Bur-*(dingir) *Sin*	Bur-Sin,
nitaḡ lig-ga	the mighty hero,
lugal Uru-um-ki-ma	king of Ur,

2. For the expression (dingir) *nin-dingir-si-an-na*, comp. O. B. I. 16, 1: *Dingir nin-Uru-um-ki-ma.* The usual phrase is only *nin-si-an-na* (without *dingir*), which is according to Br. 11028 = *Ištar.*

3. *nin-a-ni-ir.* Thus I prefer to read. The line is somewhat mutilated. Possibly there stood only *nin-a-ni.*

6. In ll. 6 and 7 only a few signs are visible.

lugal an-ub-da tab-tab-ba-ge	king of the four corners of the world,
e-a-ni	her house
mu-na-ru	he has built.

Whether Gimil-Sin was the direct successor (Hilprecht, O. B. I. p. 244, 16) of Bur-Sin II. is not yet settled; see however above, p. 27.

From O. B. I. 127—a tablet which gives on the obverse the dates of Bur-Sin II. and on the reverse some of those of Gimil-Sin (comp. especially l. 4)—it would seem that Gimil-Sin followed immediately upon Bur-Sin II [1].

Scheil, however, has published in Rec. Trav. xix. p. 49 '*une empreinte de cylindre sur une tablette de Telloh, iie* (read *ive*) *dynastie d'Ur,*' which reads:

(dingir) Bur-(dingir) Sin	Bur-Sin,
nitag lig-ga	the mighty hero,
lugal Uru-um-ki-ma	the king of Ur,
lugal an-ub-da tab-tab	king of the four corners of the world,
Ur-(dingir) Ba-u	Ur-Ba'u
dumu-ni	his son.

Here then we have a son of Bur-Sin II., whose name is Ur-Ba'u. Whether this son ever ascended the throne of Ur is not evident. We may however hypothetically place this Ur-Ba'u—whom we call Ur-Ba'u II. to distinguish him from the older Ur-Ba'u, a patesi of Shirpurla—among the kings of this dynasty of Ur. His reign may

[1] It should also be borne in mind that O. B. I. 127 does not give any '*mu-uš-sa*' dates, while with the help of the E A. H. collection we were able to bring in at least two of them. Besides this, O. B. I. 127 does not seem to give *all the dates* belonging to Bur-Sin II.; see above, dates Nos. 2, 3 *b*, 10, 12, and note. It is, therefore, very well possible that Ur-Ba'u II. has to be placed between Bur-Sin II. and Gimil-Sin, or that we have to supply a gap between these two latter rulers, notwithstanding R. A. iv. p. 142; for the dates to be found on that tablet occur almost under any ruler. Comp. e. g. Dungi III. dates No. 31 and No. 10 with Bur-Sin II. date No. 2 and note.

have been very short. Probably some of the doubtful dates (see below) may belong to this Ur-Ba'u II.

However this may be, it is evident that no long interval could have elapsed between Bur-Sin II. and Gimil-Sin [1] (comp. O. B. I. 127, 4).

Dates of Gimil-Sin.

The following dates of the reign of Gimil-Sin have so far come to light (comp. R. S. 1897, p. 73, and O. L. Z. i. 170):—

E. A. H. 91.

(1) *mu* $^{(dingir)}$ *Gimil*-$^{(dingir)}$ *Sin lugal*	In the year when Gimil-Sin became king.
(2) *mu mà-dara-zu-ab ba-ab-gab*	In the year when the king consecrated the ship *DARA-ZU-AB*.

. . . . gap . . . .

1, 2. These dates, together with Nos. 9 and 11 of the reign of Bur-Sin II., are mentioned on a tablet published by Thureau-Dangin in R. A. iii. p. 144. Date No. 10 of Bur-Sin II. is not mentioned. It is therefore possible that other dates, also lying between No. 11 of Bur-Sin II. and No. 1 of Gimil-Sin, have to be postulated, which must then be referred to Ur-Ba'u II., son of Bur-Sin II.

2. The identification of the sign *DARA* was for a long time doubtful. Thureau-Dangin, R. A. iii. p. 143, l. 8, thought '*c'est peut-être une variante du No.* 261 *du tableau d'Amiaud.*' This latter sign, however, occurs in its *regular* form on a tablet of Dungi III. (O. B. I. 124, v. 20) in the expression *AMAR-ANŠU-NA(D)-A*; see below, under *ANŠU*. Scheil, on the other hand, identified it with *KIN*; see Rec. Trav. xvii. 38 ff. Thureau-Dangin, in O. L. Z. i. 179, reads '*dara*,' thus identifying it correctly with Br. 2946; see also E. C. 149 and p. 110.

GAB. Thureau-Dangin thinks that the meaning of *GAB* is here = *šurru* (H. W. B. 689, *eröffnen, einweihen*): '*délier, c'est-à-dire entreprendre,*

---

[1] Gimil-Sin = 'present of Sin,' not Ḳat-Sin, 'hand of Sin,' is the pronunciation of this name. See Delitzsch, B. A. ii. p. 624; Thureau-Dangin, R. A. iii. p. 124, l. 6, against Hilprecht, Z. A. vii. 315, note 1, and Assyriaca, p. 104, note 1.

(3) (a) *mu Si-ma-LUM-ki ba-ĝul*	(a) In the year when (the king) devastated Simanu.
(b) *mu- uš-sa Si-ma-nu-um* (*ba-ĝul*)	(b) One year after (the king) devastated Simanu.

E. A. H. 93.

(4) *mu bad-mar-tu ba-ru*	In the year when (the king) built the west wall.
(5) *mu-uš-sa bad-mar-tu ba-ru*	One year after (the king) built the west wall.

O. B. I. 127, rev. 2.

(6) *mu na-maĝ (dingir) En-lil-la ba-ru*	In the year when (the king) made the sublime inscription of Bêl.

commencer.' *GAB*, according to Br. 4489 = *pitû*. 'To open a ship' may be = to make it ready for navigation. Comp. however O. B. I. 125, 4: *mu mà (?) (dingir) Nin-lil-la(l) ba-GAB*. Here *MÀ-GAB* is equivalent to 'to open a ship for Ninlil' = to consecrate it to her. The sense 'to consecrate' has also to be postulated here. K. 4378, v. 28, mentions a (*giš*) *MÀ-DARA-ZU-AB*, which it translates by: *elip Ea*. This 'ship of Ea' we find also in a variant of our date here, viz. C. T. 18427: *mu mà-dara-zu-ab (dingir) En-ki ba-ab-gab*.

3, 4. These dates are found on a tablet published by Thureau-Dangin in R. A. iii. p. 144.

The right reading of the city *Si-ma-LUM* is *Si-ma-num*, as is evident from 3 *b* and Rec. Trav. xix. p. 57, No. 210. Comp. also *da-LUM* = *da-num*.

5. This date reads as follows on a tablet published by Thureau-Dangin in Rec. Trav. xix. p. 186:—

mu-uš-sa (dingir) Gimil-(dingir) Sin lugal Uru-um-ki-ma-ge bad-mar-tu mu-ri-iḳ Ti-id-ni-im mu-ru, i. e. one year after Gimil-Sin built the wall of the west (called) '*muriḳ Tidnim*,' i. e. which keeps away (off) Tidnu. With Tidnu, which is according to Hommel = Tidanum, comp. Gudea B, vi. 13, *Ti-da-num ĝar-sag Mar-tu*, and ii. R. 48, 12 *c, d*; ibid. 50, 58 *c, d*.

6. This date also occurs in the following forms: *mu na ba-ru* (Constantinople 762); *mu (dingir) Gimil-(dingir) Sin lugal Uru-um-ki-ma-ge na-maĝ (dingir) En-lil šà (dingir) Nin-lil mu-ne-ru*, and with the variant *na-ru-a* for *na*, Scheil, Rec. Trav. xvii. p. 38 ff. *na-ru-a* = Assyr. *narû*.

(7) *mu* (*dingir*) *Gimil-*(*dingir*) *Sin lugal Uru-um-ki-ma-ge ma-da Za-ap-ša-li-ki mu-ĝul-a*	In the year when Gimil-Sin, king of Ur, devastated the land of Zapshali,
(8) *mu* (*dingir*) *Gimil-*(*dingir*) *Sin lugal Uru-um-ki-ma-ge mà-gur-maĝ* (*dingir*) *En-lil* (*dingir*) *Nin-lil-ra mu-ne-gim*	In the year when Gimil-Sin, king of Ur, built the sublime bark for Bêl and Bêlit.
(9) *mu e* (*dingir*) . . . *ba-ru*	In the year when the king built the temple of . . . . (= the god for *Giš-uḫ-ki*).

7. *ma-dâ* = Assyr. *màtu*. Zapshali, Hommel, A. H. T. p. 37 = 'Zapsha of the Van inscriptions, and therefore probably situated in Cilicia or Armenia.' Hilprecht's translation, 'In the year when (Gimil-Sin became king and) Gimil-Sin brought evil upon the land of Zapshali' (O. B. I. p. 245, note 6), is inaccurate, because this year is not the first year of Gimil-Sin's reign.

8. Thus this date occurs in R. A. iii. p. 124. Sometimes we have only *mu mà-gur-maĝ ba-ru.*

GUR = T. C. 201. *MÀ-*(*GUR*) = bark; see Gudea D, iii. 3, and Jensen, K. B. iii¹. p. 52, note 1 and *.

9. The temple which Gimil-Sin built is that of the god of Gishuḫ. Indeed some tablets bear the following inscription: *Mu e* (*dingir*) *? Giš-uḫ-ki ba-ru.* How the sign, which is composed of a square with inserted *IGI*, which latter has the *gunu*-signs, and which stands for the god of Gishuḫ, ought to be pronounced, we do not know as yet. Comp. Cône of Entemena, col. i.

To the above-given dates ought also to be added one year in which Gimil-Sin built for *Uru-ki* the *E-MU-RI*(?)*-A-NA-BA* . . ., as testified to by Peters, Nippur, ii. p. 239; also in Hilprecht, Bible Helps, pl. 25:

(*dingir*) *Uru-ki*	For Nannar,
dumu-sag	the firstborn
(*dingir*) *En-lil-la*(*l*)	of Bêl,
lugal ki-ag-ga-ni-ir	his beloved king,
(*dingir*) *Gimil-*(*dingir*) *Sin*	Gimil-Sin,
ki-ag-(*dingir*) *Uru-ki*	the beloved of Nannar,

lugal (dingir) [En]-lil-li	a king whom Bêl
šag-ga-na	in his heart
in-pad	has called
sib kalam-ma	to be the shepherd of the world
šà an-ub-da tab-tab-ba-ku	and of the four corners of the world,
lugal lig-ga	the mighty king,
lugal Uru-um-ki-ma	king of Ur,
lugal an-ub-da tab-tab-[ba-ge]	king of the four corners of the world,
E MU-RI (?)-A-NA-BA	the . . .
e ki-ag-ga-ni	his beloved house
mu-na-ru	he has built.

Dates of Ine-Sin.

The successor of Gimil-Sin was Ine-Sin[1]. In R. A. iii. p. 144, Thureau-Dangin published a tablet which mentions the following dates:—

mu mà-gur-maḫ ba-ru (=Gimil-Sin No. 8).
mu e (dingir) ? ba-ru (=Gimil-Sin No. 9).
mu (dingir) I-ne-(dingir) Sin [lugal].

Hence 'the year when Ine-Sin became king' follows upon date No. 9 of the reign of Gimil-Sin. This succession is corroborated by Constantinople No. 762 and No. 831 (see R. S. 1897, p. 74; R. A. iii. p. 144).

The following dates may occur during the reign of Ine-Sin, according to Constantinople No. 762:—

[1] The correct reading of this name is not yet certain. Hilprecht, Assyriaca, p. 104, note 1, reads: *I-ne-Sin*, 'the eye of Sin.' Others, *I-bil-Sin* or *I-bi-Sin*. See Delitzsch, B. A. ii. 626; Thureau-Dangin, R. A. iii. p. 126.

(1) *mu* $^{(dingir)}$ *I-ne-*$^{(dingir)}$ *Sin lugal*	In the year when Ine-Sin became king.
(2) *mu en* $^{(dingir)}$ *Innanna ba-tug*	In the year when (the) king was invested high-priest of Ishtar.

. . . .

Uncertain Dates.

The following dates also belong to the members of the third dynasty of Ur, but cannot yet be referred to definite kings :—

E. A. H. 105.

(1) [*mu du*]*mu-sal lugal pa-te-si* [*Za-a*]*p-ša-li-*^{ki}*-ge ba-an-tug*	In the year when the daughter of the king became (*sic*) patesi of Zapshali.

E. A. H. 106.

(2) *mu-uš-sa Lu-lu-bu-um-*^{ki} *ba-ḫul*	One year after (the king) devastated Lulubu.

E. A. H. 107.

(3) *mu Ḫu-ḫu-nu-ri-*^{ki} *ba-ḫul*	In the year when (the king) devastated Ḫuḫunuri.

1. Comp. Dungi III. dates, No. 33, where a daughter of Dungi III. becomes patesi of Anshan. Zapshali was devastated by Gimil-Sin (date No. 7); here a daughter of one of our kings becomes its patesi. Hommel, A. H. T. p. 37, refers this date to Dungi III.

2. For Lulubu, comp. Dungi III. dates, No. 47 *a*, where it is mentioned in connection with Simuru. The *mu-uš-sa* presupposes a year in which the actual defeat took place.

3. For the name *Ḫu-ḫu-nu-ri-*^{ki} the following variants may be found (Scheil, Z. A. xii. p. 258): *Ḫu-ḫu-nu-ru-*^{ki}, *Ḫu-ḫu-ru-*^{ki}, *Ḫu-UD + BAN* (?)-*nu-ri-*^{ki}, *Ḫu-BAN* (?)-*nu-ri-*^{ki}. Scheil therefore concludes that the sign in question—which also occurs in ^{giš}*-BAN* (?)-^{ki}—has to be read *UḪ*; *Ḫu-BAN*(?)*-nu-ri-*^{ki} = *Ḫu-UḪ-nu-ri-*^{ki}, and *Giš-BAN-*^{ki} he wants to read *Giš-uḫ-*^{ki}. See also above, p. 74, note 1, and comp. also the note in Delitzsch, A. L^{4}. p. 28, where, according to K. 3622 and 4871, the pronunciation of *UḪ* is

E. A. H. 108, 109.

(4) *mu-en nam-? (dingir) Dun-gi-ra-ge ba-DU ba-tug*	In the year when (the king) was appointed and invested high-priest of the cult (?) of Dungi.

Reç. Trav. xvii. p. 38.

(5) *mu-uš-sa Ḫarši-ki Kimaš-ki Ḫumurti-ki ba-ḫul*	One year after (the king) devastated Ḫarshi, Kimash, and Ḫumurti.

Rec. Trav. xix. p. 60, No. 615.

(6) *mu en-gu-gal An-na (dingir) Innanna ba-tug*	In the year when (the king) was invested lord most high of Anu and Ishtar.

ki-is-ša and *ki-e-ši* ! This same sign *BAN*(?) occurs also in O. B. I. 127, 7 (see dates of Bur-Sin, No. 8): *Ri-BAN-nu-ḫu-ki*. Scheil, l. c., wishes to read this name = *Ḫu-uḫ-nu-ri-ki*. So very correctly. Apparently the scribe misplaced the two signs *RI* and *ḪU*. Hommel, P. S. B. A. xxi. p. 135, reads for *NU* = *tar*. The *NU* however is clear here.

4. The sign after *NAM* occurs also in O. B. I. 87, iii. 17: *(dingir) En-lil . . . nam-?-mu ge-na-bi*, which Thureau-Dangin translates: '*que Enlil . . . mon sort décrète*'; but adds in a note: '*traduction est hypothétique.*' Further also in Gudea, Cyl. B, viii. 10; xi. 13; and in C. T. 18343, xi. 37: *a-šag La-za-pi šà a-šag nam-? gub-ba*. Here it is said that our king was *ba-DU* and invested 'high-priest of the *nam-?*' The *(dingir) Dungi*, as we shall see, is Dungi III., who was deified and received worship, as also was the case with Bur-Sin II. and Gimil-Sin. *Nam-?* may therefore mean worship, cult, and the *en-nam-?* = the one who had to arrange this worship. This also would be in accordance with Lugalzaggisi's prayer that Bêl may honour him with a certain cult.

DU = *gub* = *nazâzu*, i. e. 'to put up' in the sense of 'to appoint.' Comp. also *DU* = *gin* = *kânu*. *BA-DU BA-TUG* = '(when the king) was appointed, and invested lord,' &c.

5. Ḫarshi and Ḫumurti were mentioned together above, dates of Dungi III., No. 51; Kimash and Ḫumurti under Dungi III. dates, No. 49. Ḫarshi and Ḫumurti are probably situated in the neighbourhood of Kimash, i. e. Central Arabia.

6. *GU-GAL*. See Br. 3284, *ašaridu*; 3285, *gugallu*, H. W. B. 194. Hence *en-gu-gal* may be parallel to *en-maḫ-gal*. Comp. Bur-Sin II. dates, No. 5.

Rec. Trav. xix. p. 61.

(7) *mu KIB-KIB-ŠE Šir-pur-la-ki GIŠ-NE-RA-A*	*Année où l'abondante moisson de Shirpurla fut anéantie par l'inondation.*

To these uncertain dates ought to be added also the following :—

(8 *a*) *mu e-gal (dingir) Bur-(dingir) Sin ki-ag (dingir) en Eridug-ki ba-tug*	In the year when (the king) was installed in the palace of Bur-Sin, the beloved of the divine lord (i. e. the god) of Eridu.
(8 *b*) *mu en-nun-ni (dingir) Bur-(dingir) Sin-ra ki-ag en Eridug-ki ba-a-tug*	In the year when (the king) was installed by Bur-Sin, the beloved of the lord of Eridu, to be his (i. e. Bur-Sin's) high-priest.
(8 *c*) *mu en-nun-gal An-na ki-ag (dingir) Bur-(dingir) Sin en Eridug-ki ba-tug*	In the year when (the king) was installed priest most high of Anu, beloved of Bur-Sin, the lord of Eridu.

7. Thus Scheil translates and compares *KIB-KIB-KI*: *duḫḫudu. ša mirsi*; *RA*: *raḫâšu*, Br. 5219, 6361.

8 *a*. This date occurs on C. T. 94-10-16, 5. It is clearly against Thureau-Dangin's translation, i. e. the king himself does not install, invest, but *is installed*; see also above, dates of Dungi III., No. 16. Apparently this date is only a variant of No. 8 *b*. The post-position *RA* shows clearly that a king was installed or invested *by* Bur-Sin. Hence we have here the important historical fact that Bur-Sin II. had during his reign a '*Mitregent*,' which latter may have been his son Ur-Ba'u II.

8 *b*. Occurs on C. T. 95-10-12, 20. *En-nun-ni*. If the *NI* be correct we only can translate: (to be) his high-priest. This is favoured by date No. 8*c*.

8 *c*. Occurs on C. T. 14606, and is an amplification of Nos. 8 *a* and *b*, telling us in what the *(nam)-en-nun* consisted, viz. in the high-priestship of Anu. If we would combine *a–c* we possibly might read: *mu e-gal (dingir) Bur-(dingir) Sin ki-ag dingir en Eridug-ki en-nun-gal-ni An-na (dingir) Bur-(dingir) Sin-ra ba-(a)-tug*, i. e. in the year when (the king, i. e. Ur-Ba'u II.) was installed in the palace of Bur-Sin, the beloved of the divine lord of Eridu, by Bur-Sin, to be his (Bur-Sin's) priest most high before Anu. See also what has been said *sub* Bur-Sin II. dates, No. 5, note, and compare also the shortened form of

· No. 8 *c* in C. T. 94-10-16, 59: *mu en-nun-ra ba-tug*, i.e. in the year when (the king) was installed as (*ra*) high-priest.

From the above-given dates it is evident that we must postulate for the reign of Dungi III. at least fifty-one years, and if we take Nos. 47 *b* and 50 *b* as representing two *independent* years, we would have to presuppose a reign of fifty-three years for this ruler. He, like Bur-Sin II., paid more attention to the gods than to the hostile nations, yet was, no doubt, the greatest of all the rulers of this dynasty. We have to see in him not only a notable builder and military hero, but also a great statesman. After having performed his obligation towards his gods by building or restoring temples in their honour, and by taking upon himself the different offices connected with the cult of his favoured gods, he placed one of his daughters on the throne of the city of Marḫashi (=Mar'ash in Northern Syria), probably in order to make peace with that city, after having waged war against it. He repeated this experiment with Anshan (in Elam). But the Elamites could not endure this 'new queen'; they promptly rebelled, and four years later Dungi III. found it necessary to subdue the revolt. The enemies of Ur must have succeeded in reaching even the walls of the royal capital, for Dungi III. 'restores the wall of the place,' and assembles or enlists all the inhabitants of Ur, 'great and mighty soldiers,' in order to drive away the enemy from his royal capital. However, peace was very soon again disturbed. Karḫar and Simurru—both places were situated in the west—rebelled. Also Ḫarshi—probably the neighbouring state to Simurru—could not bear any longer the 'lordship' of the daughter of the king; it rebelled, but was severely punished. These victories do not seem to have been permanent, for very soon the king found it necessary to punish Simurru again. Having subjugated the west, he now turned his attention to the east, i.e. Elam, and especially Anshan. Peace supreme seems to have reigned for a short time, giving the king time to continue his buildings and perform his religious obligations. His victories over Anshan must have been so decisive that even 'a temple' was built for him, where he was to be worshipped as 'god Dungi.' However, for only six years did he enjoy this quietude. Shashru rebelled, but was subjugated. This rebellion of Shashru gave a new stimulus to Simurru, which however felt too weak to undertake the rebellion alone, seeing that it had been defeated eight times. It therefore incited Lulubu in the north to lift up arms, thus trying to split up the armies of the king, and make him wage war on two different places at the same time. The king became master of the situation. He not only overpowered the west (for the ninth time), but even the north had to yield to his mighty weapons. After one year's peace, during which time the king no doubt strengthened his armies, he felt strong enough to complete the conquest of the four corners of the world. He had, as we have seen, already conquered the west, the east, and the north. Only the south remained. Thus it happened that he had to lead his victorious armies also against Kimash in Southern Arabia. Kimash allied itself with Ḫumurti; both are overcome. The four corners of the world do homage to Dungi III.

Of the reign of Bur-Sin II. we covered fourteen years. (Date No. 12, e. g., shows that another year has to be postulated.) Hilprecht may not be wrong when he says (O. B. I. 245, note 6): 'Bur-Sin . . . in all probability . . . reigned sixteen or eighteen years. He seems to have been a peaceful prince, devoting himself chiefly to buildings and religious functions. Only three campaigns occurred during his reign, viz. against Urbillum, Shashru, and Ḫuḫnuri.' His last years were taken up by religious duties. If our translation of 'uncertain dates,' No. 8 *a–c*, be correct, it would seem that he had a co-regent during the latter years of his reign. This co-regent was in all probability Ur-Ba'u II., of whom in other respects we know absolutely nothing.

Gimil-Sin found it necessary after a certain number of years to fortify the royal city again against his enemies—probably Elam (O. B. I. 246 ff.), in which country several of the cities and districts against which these kings made war were also situated. During his reign, which probably covered a period of fifteen years (of ten years we have dates), two campaigns occurred, viz. against Simanu and Zapshali.

For Idîn-Dagan, whom Hilprecht (R. R. B. L. p. 84) places here, see above *sub* Nisin.

Of the 'uncertain dates' some may belong to the rulers above mentioned, others to those not yet known [1].

From these different dates we can now determine accurately the extent of the dominion of the rulers of this dynasty.

The title of these kings clearly indicates, if taken literally, a dominion as extensive as that of Naram-Sin. Naram-Sin called himself *šar ki-ib-ra-tim ar-ba-im* (O. B. I. 120, ii.), thus claiming to be ruler over a territory which extended from the Persian Gulf in the south to the mountains of Armenia in the north, from the Elamite mountains in the east to the Mediterranean Sea in the west. Can we prove that the representatives of this dynasty, who also, like Naram-Sin, ascribed to themselves the proud title, *šar ki-ib-ra-tim ar-ba-im* (Dungi III.), or in Sumerian *lugal an-ub-da tab-tab-ba*, really possessed a dominion as extensive as that of Naram-Sin, i. e. a kingship of the four corners of the world? Hommel, in A. H. T. p. 36, maintains: 'It is evident that they (i. e. the kings of the fourth dynasty of Ur) only held sway over a smaller part of Babylonia; they no longer possessed Ingi (i. e. Kengi), and had lost Akkad as well. . . . They made up for this loss, however, by extending their rule over Elam, Arabia, and the countries of the west, and for this reason described themselves by the proud title of "kings of the four cardinal points."'

That these kings held sway not only over a 'smaller part,' but over the whole of Babylonia, is evident from the following facts:—

Bur-Sin II. tells us that he was invested 'lord of *Eridug-ki*,' i. e. Eridu (E. A. H. 87, 88, dates Nos. 9, 10; comp. also Dungi III. dates, Nos. 31, 32). Eridu being situated in the extreme south of Babylonia, on the Persian Gulf, was thus under the sway of these rulers. Girsu, Erim, and Ninâ—all of which are parts of Shirpurla

[1] A king's son I found mentioned also on C. T. 21335, vi. 175: *MU-E-AN-NA dumu lugal.*

—were in their possession (comp. E. A. H. 14, 28, *šag Gir-su-ki* and *šag Nina-ki*, and C. T. 95-10-12, 20). And if we accept the identity of Kengi = Girsu [1] (as was shown above), these kings also ruled over Kengi. But even if this were not the case, we can show that their dominion extended over the whole of South Babylonia. The representative cities of South Babylonia are, besides Girsu and Eridu, Uruk, Mar, Gishuḫ, Nippur.

For Uruk, comp. Z. A. xii. p. 268 *a*, and see above, E. A. H. 26; for Mar, comp. E. A. H. 36, 16–28; for Gishuḫ, E. A. H. 134, 5; for Nippur, O. B. I. 20, 21, and passim. All these cities are mentioned on tablets dated from the reigns of the different members of this dynasty. It is evident, therefore, that these kings possessed the whole of South Babylonia from Nippur down to Eridu.

But in addition to the south they included also the north in their wide dominion. Among the North Babylonian cities mentioned on the E. A. H. tablets we find *Ki-nu-nir-ki* = Borsippa, *KA-DINGIR-ki* = Babylon, and Kutha. It is true that no mention occurs in these tablets of the city of Agade, but E. A. H. 27 is a tablet dated from Lulubu in the extreme north of Babylon (comp. also the different campaigns against Lulubu). This would seem to justify us in holding that these kings possessed the whole of North Babylonia, their dominion extending to the mountains of Armenia. They also held sway over Elam (Anshan), Arabia (*Ki-MAŠ*), even over Syria and the countries of the west (*KA ṢAL-LU*). Hence their kingdom was indeed 'a kingdom of the four corners of the world,' comprising the whole of Babylonia south and north, consequently also Shumer and Akkad, and thus it was in no way unlike that of Naram-Sin (comp. also Hilprecht, O. B. I. 246, 4).

How long this kingship of 'the four corners of the world' remained unharmed we can only conjecture. For it seems that at about 2400 B.C. (Lehmann, Zwei Probleme, Tabelle i., 2360 B.C.) this 'kingship of the four corners of the world' was overthrown by

[1] But notice especially *Ur-(dingir) KAL*, the patesi of Girsu, and see above.

a certain Sumuabi, the first king of the dynasty of Babylon, and a predecessor of Ḫammurabi. Encouraged by the success of the north (Babylon), the south also rebelled, under Nûr-Rammân, who in consequence of his victories founded the *kingdom of Larsa.* Nûr-Rammân was succeeded by his son Siniddina (K. B. iii[1]. p. 91), who calls himself 'king of Larsa and king of Shumer and Akkad.' This is noteworthy. The kings of Babylon, as well as Nûr-Rammân, confined their rebellion primarily to their own respective cities. Siniddina was not content with this; he wanted to extend his dominion over Shumer and Akkad, and succeeded in doing this. However his success was to be checked. Elam, which for a long time had been the deadly enemy of Dungi III. and his successors, was bound to take a hand in the game that went on in Babylonia. It had acquired in the meantime some strength, and invaded the south of Babylonia under Kudurnanḫundi I. at about 2300 B.C., and under Kudurdugmal[1] (כְּדָרְלָעֹמֶר (?)). They even succeeded in establishing in Larsa a kingdom of their own under Rim-Sin (= Eri-Aku = אַרְיוֹךְ), a contemporary and former satrap of Kudurdugmal[2], and who adopted the same title which Siniddina bore. This invasion took place while Siniddina was sitting upon the throne of Larsa, and while Ḫammurabi (= אַמְרָפֶל, 2288–2223; Lehmann, 2248–2194) was reigning in Babylon. Siniddina in his distress implores the help of Ḫammurabi; the latter grants it, and overpowers Rim-Sin (K. B. iii[1]. p. 127, No. 1): 'In the month Shebat, on the twenty-third (twenty-second) day, in the year when king Ḫammurabi in the power of Anu and Bêl established his (their?) shéga, and when his hand cast down to the ground the adda of Iamudbalum' (see Winckler, l. c., p. 127, note *, and ibid. p. 95, 2, col. i. 9) 'and the king Rim-Sin.'

Thus we see that the 'kingship of the four corners of the world' was torn up by Babylon in the north, and by Larsa in the south.

[1] His name is written either *KU-KU-KU-mal* (= *Ku-dur-dug-mal*) or *KU-KU-KU-KU-mal* (= *Ku-dur-dug-gu-mal*). The syllables '*dug-mal*' are in all probability only a variant for '*Lag*(*a*)-*mar*.'

[2] And of Kudurnanḫundi I.

This confusion brought in the Elamites, who tried to establish in Southern Babylonia a new kingdom, but were defeated by Ḫammurabi and Siniddina, which former ruler then eventually became king of the whole of Babylonia, nay, even 'king of the four corners of the world,' and thus a successor of the fourth dynasty of Ur in extent of dominion as well as in title.

The Names of the Months.

In connection with the dates of these rulers, it would be of interest to notice the names given to the several months of the year. Three distinct nomenclatures seem to have been current at this time. The following months, which we arrange according to Thureau-Dangin in R. A. iv. p. 83 (comp. also Journal Asiatique, mars—avril, 1896, p. 339 ff., and R. A. iv. No. iii, tablet 77), occur most often in the subscription to be found on the tablets of the E. A. H. Collection; and a comparison with those of the time of Sargon I. will show that they are to a large extent relics of the oldest nomenclature:

Time of Sargon I.	Time of the fourth dynasty of Ur.
Itu EZEN ŠE-IL-LA	*Itu ŠE-IL-LA*; E. A. H. 76.
Itu EZEN GAN-MAŠ	*Itu GAN-MAŠ*; Nos. 82, 145, 146.
Itu EZEN GUD-DU-NE-SAR-SAR [1]	*Itu GUD-DU-NE-SAR-SAR*; No. 144.
Itu EZEN (*dingir*) *NE-SÙ* [2]	*Itu EZEN* (*dingir*) *NE-SÙ* [3].

[1] Sometimes also *Itu GUD-NE-SAR*-[*SAR*] or *Itu GUD-A-NE-SAR*-[*SAR*].

[2] Thureau-Dangin, l. c.: '*Pour la place de ce mois et celle du suivant, f. Rec. Trav. xix. p.* 186, *note* 2. *Le signe que je transcris SÙ se confond dans l'écriture postérieure avec le signe DAR.*'

[3] Thus in E. A. H. 27, 57, 143, 151; or only *Itu* (*dingir*) *NE-SÙ*, as in E. A. H. 88, 96.

5	*Itu ŠU-KUL*[1].
Itu EZEN ZIB-KÙ	*Itu ZIB-KÙ*; Nos. 75, 77, 81, 139.
Itu EZEN (*dingir*) *DUMU-ZI*	*Itu EZEN* (*dingir*) *DUMU-ZI*; Nos. 12, 17, 66, 95, 152.
. . . .	*Itu EZEN* (*dingir*) *DUN-GI*; Nos. 68, 78, 84, 149.
Itu EZEN (*dingir*) *BA-U*	*Itu EZEN* (*dingir*) *BA-U*; Nos. 113, 141, 148.

[1] Thus in E. A. H. 107, 140, 142, 150. In E. A. H. 61 we have *Itu-ŠU-KUL-LI*. In later Assyrian times this month was the *fourth*. Thureau-Dangin, Rec. Trav. xix. p. 186, note 2, thought: '*les places des mois ŠU-KUL et EZEN* (*dingir*) *NE-SÙ doivent être interverties*.'

That the month *ŠU-KUL* has to retain its place *after* the month *itu EZEN* (*dingir*) *NE-SÙ* is evident from C. T. 18343, col. ix. 25 ff.:

40 (*ḳa*) *itu EZEN* (*dingir*) *NE-SÙ-ta*
150 (*ḳa*) *itu ŠU-KUL-ta*
60 (*ḳa*) *itu EZEN* (*dingir*) *Dun-gi-ta*
60 (*ḳa*) *itu EZEN* (*dingir*) *Ba-u-ta*
itu ŠE-IL-LA-ku
še-bi 9 *gur* 20 (*ḳa*)
itu 11 *kam*
itu-dir Ia-an šag-ba-ni-gàl

which latter passages can only be translated as follows:—

40 (*ḳa* of grain = *še*) from the month *EZEN* (*dingir*) *NE-SÙ* (*scil.* for every month up to *ŠE-IL-LA*), i. e. for eleven months; hence 40 × 11 = 440

150 (*ḳa* of grain) from the month *ŠU-KUL* (*scil.* for every month up to *ŠE-IL-LA*), i. e. for ten months; hence 150 × 10 = 1500

60 (*ḳa* of grain) from the month *EZEN* (*dingir*) *Dun-gi* (*scil.* for every month up to *ŠE-IL-LA*), i. e. for seven months; hence 60 × 7 = 420

60 (*ḳa* of grain) from the month *EZEN* (*dingir*) *Ba-u* (*scil.* for every month up to *ŠE-IL-LA*), i. e. for six months; hence 60 × 6 = 360

Summa (= its grain is) = 9 *gur* 20 *ḳa* or 1 *gur* = 300 *ḳa* (see A. B. P. R. p. 101) = 2720 *ḳa*

during eleven months, among which is one intercalary month (i. e. the *Itu DIR ŠE-KIN-KUD*). If *itu ŠU-KUL* were put *before itu EZEN* (*dingir*) *NE-SÙ*, the '*summa*' would be quite different.

10 *Itu MU-ŠU-GAB* — *Itu MU-ŠU-UL*; Nos. 92, 117.
Itu EZEN AMAR-A-SI — *Itu AMAR-A-A-SI*; Nos. 7, 59, 99, 149.
. . . . — *Itu ŠE-KIN-KUD*; Nos. 2–6, 8, 11, 70–72, 85, 147.
. . . . — *Itu DIR ŠE-KIN-KUD*; No. 67.

To the period of Sargon I. belong also the following names :—

(1) *Itu ŠE-ŠE-KIN-A*, which probably is another form (Thureau-Dangin) for *Itu ŠE-KIN-KUD*; (2) *Itu ŠID-EN-DU-ŠE-A-NÀ* (see R. A. iv. No. iii. tablet No. 42); (3) *araḫ Ḫa-ni-i*; (4) *araḫ Ba-ḫi-ir arkû*; (5) *araḫ Za-bi-tum*, '*qui*' (i.e. Nos. 3–5) *peuvent être considérés comme les noms en usage plus au nord en pays d'Accad*' (Thureau-Dangin, l. c., p. 84).

A glance over the above-given dates will show that the names of the months—to a great part at least—are chosen according to the *season* in which they fell. Comp. e. g. *GAN-MAŠ*, 'field (in) blossom'; *ŠU-KUL*, 'sowing'; *ŠE-KIN-KUD*, 'grain harvest'; *ŠE-IL-LA*, 'grain-grown.' A similar nomenclature—where the months are called after the season—has come down to us in four Canaanitish names. They are:

1. יֶרַח הָאֵתָנִים (1 Reg. viii. 2), generally explained as '*der Monat der fliessenden Bäche*'; was originally the first, later on the seventh month = תִּשְׁרִי.

2. יֶרַח בּוּל 1 Reg. vi. 38—בּוּל; here either nom. propr. (comp. זבדבול, בולברך) or *proventus*, '*Erzeugnis, Frucht*'; originally the second, later the eighth month = מַרְחֶשְׁוָן.

3. אָבִיב, or more completely חֹדֶשׁ הָאָבִיב (Ex. xiii. 4; xxiii. 15; xxxiv. 18; Deut. xvi. 1), i.e. 'the month of the ears of the corn.' It was originally the seventh, but later on became the first month of the year = נִיסָן.

4. זִו (1 Reg. vi. 1, 37), or more fully, according to Targ., יֶרַח זִיו,

נִצָּנִיא, 'the month of the beauty (of the flowers)'; originally the eighth, but later on became the second month = אִיָּר.

What seasons or, better, months of our time would correspond to the names of the months above given?

A good starting-point for determining this is given by the month *ŠE-KIN-KUD*.

ŠE-KIN-KUD, or harvest-month, is made the same by the later Assyrians as *Addarû* (comp. Delitzsch, A. L[3]. p. 93). The Hebrews, who adopted the nomenclature of the Assyrians, called it אֲדָר (see Schrader, Keilinschriften und das Alte Testament, p. 379); the same name is also to be found in E. A. H. 134 (see below). We know however that the month *Addaru*, אֲדָר, fell in February–March (see Hommel, article 'Babylonia' in Hastings' Dictionary of the Bible, vol. i. p. 217). The month *ŠE-IL-LA*, which follows upon *ŠE-KIN-KUD*, corresponding to the Assyr.-Hebrew *Nisannu*, נִיסָן, would fall in March–April, and *GAN-MAŠ* = Assyr.-Hebrew *Airu*, אִיָּר, in April–May. With this agrees exactly the Canaanitish nomenclature. We have seen that נִיסָן corresponds to the old אָבִיב, hence it must be also = *ŠE-IL-LA*, which is also proved by the meaning of the respective names: *ŠE-IL-LA*, 'grain-grow(n),' אָבִיב, '(month of) the ear of the grain'; and *Airu*, אִיָּר = *GAN-MAŠ* = 'field (in) blossom' = זִו, 'beauty (of the flowers).' We have to establish the following two important similarities between the Canaanitish and our nomenclature here:—

1. In both we have the same succession, viz.:

ŠE-KIN-KUD	*ŠE-IL-LA*	*GAN-MAŠ*
[אֲדָר]	אָבִיב	זִו

2. In both the same meaning:

'grain-harvest'	'grain-grow(n)'	'field in blossom'
	'ear of the corn'	'beauty (of flowers)'

These similarities lead us to suppose that:

אֵתָנִים = *ilu EZEN-(dingir) Dumu-zi* = September–October.

בּוּל = *ilu EZEN-(dingir) Dun-gi* = October–November.

In the Assyrian nomenclature we meet again the following names :—

ŠE-KIN-KUD = *Addàru*, אֲדָר
ŠU-KUL = *Du'uzu*, תַּמּוּז.

But here we have one difficulty. Above we have seen that :

ŠE-KIN-KUD = אֲדָר, *Addaru* = February–March.
ŠE-IL-LA = אָבִיב = נִיסָן, *Nisannu* = March–April.
GAN-MAŠ = זִו = אִיָּר, *Airu* = April-May.

Hence if we continue the successive six months as given on hand by Ur IV., we would have

GUD-DU-NE-SAR-SAR = סִיוָן, *Simânu* = May–June.
EZEN (*dingir*) *NE-SU* = June–July.
ŠU-KUL = *Du'uzu*, תַּמּוּז = July–August.

But *Du'uzu*, תַּמּוּז, is = June–July!

Now it might be said that we ought not to make the month *ŠE-KIN-KUD* the starting-point in determining the *season* which corresponds to the names of the month, but the month *ŠU-KUL*. In this case we would get the following equation :—*ŠU-KUL* = *Du'uzu*, תַּמּוּז = June–July, and because, according to Ur IV., we have six months between the former and *ŠE-KIN-KUD*, this latter falls in January–February, but it ought to be in February–March. Hence if we want to keep *ŠU-KUL* = *Du'uzu* = תַּמּוּז = fourth month = June–July, and *ŠE-KIN-KUD* = *Addaru* = אֲדָר = twelfth month, we have to suppose that at some time the above-given arrangement of the months was changed, i. e. that the time from *ŠU-KUL* to *ŠE-KIN-KUD* embraced seven instead of six months, or that *ŠU-KUL* became the fourth month of the year.

The above indicated difficulty is increased by E. A. H. 143, which gives us a completely different nomenclature for the months. Thureau-Dangin (l. c.) already mentioned this fact, giving the two names *Itu À-ki-ti* and *Itu Ezen* (*dingir*) *An-na* with the remark, '*on trouve cependant la trace d'une nomenclature différente.*'

E. A. H. 134 is remarkable in more than one respect. It gives us the names of twelve months, every month being assigned to the patesi of a different city[1]. During this month the patesi so mentioned had probably to perform certain religious duties. So we find, e. g., that during the month of the festival of Dungi the 'patesi of the festival of Dungi,' *PA ? MU-Ù-LU*, the mighty *LUĠ*, officiated (see rev. 13, 14). The patesi of *Girsu-ki* was performing religious duties during four months (see ll. 1–3 and 10–12). Once we meet, instead of the patesi, the *PA-ÀL*= *šabrû* as the officiating person. This *pa-al* was that of Ur; he officiated in the 'month of the great festival.' This statement is significant (ll. 17, 18). Every king is also a patesi. The patesi of Ur would be the king of Ur, but he does not officiate; he has his servants; hence the *PA-AL* of Ur takes the king's place.

It is also remarkable that this tablet begins with the month *ŠE-KIN-KUD*, which in the above-given arrangement (called by us List A) we put last. Supposing, as we must do, that E. A. H. 134 (called by us List B) is arranged according to a certain order—the repetition of '*pa-te-si Girsu-ki*' shows this—we find the following difference between A and B:—

In A, *ŠE-KIN-KUD* = 12th,
In B, " " 1st,

both nomenclatures having been used at one and the same time, as is apparent from E. A. H. 87: *itu Ezen-maǵ mu en Urudug-ki ba-tug-ga*; E. A. H. 109: *Itu KI-KIN* (?) *(dingir) Nin-a-zu mu en nam- ? (dingir) Dun-gi-ra-ge ba-DU ba-tug*; and R. A. iv. iii. pl. xxix. No. 78, Endroit 6, 7: *itu À-ki-ti mu Si-mu-ru-um-ki Lu-lu-bu-um-ki a-du X-lal-1 ba-ǵul-a*. This latter tablet is interesting. Only three months are mentioned there: *À-ki-ti*, *ŠE-KIN-KUD*, and

[1] Comp. a similar arrangement of the months according to *lands* in ii. R. 49, 1, cols. 1 and 2, ll. 7 ff.:

Itu BÀR-AZAG (sic)-*GAR*	*itu GUD NIM-MA* (i. e. *Elamtu*)-*ki*
Itu [broken away]	*itu MAR-TU-ki*
[*Itu* broken away]	[*itu*] *KU ? GU-TI-I*
[*Itu* . . . .]	[*Itu* . . . .] *GIM*
[*Itu* . . . .]	[*Itu* . . . .] *IS*

DIR ŠE-KIN-KUD, i. e. the seventh and first (first intercalary) months.

How can we then reconcile A with B, or which of the months was the first?

In List A, where the succession is established beyond doubt, Thureau-Dangin formerly made—without giving further reasons—the month *ŠE-IL-LA* the first (R. A. iv. 83), but later on changed his view and began the year with *itu GAN-MAŠ* (O. L. Z. i. 163 ff.), because certain tablets of C. T. reckoned: *itu GAN-MAŠ-ta* . . . *itu ŠE-IL-LA-ku* (see e. g. C. T. 18358, col. vi.; 18343, col. iii. 30, 35, 40–45, &c.).

That the year could not have begun with *GAN-MAŠ*, but must have commenced with *ŠE-IL-LA*, is apparent from the following reasons:—

1. In legal documents or records any month of the year may be made the starting-point for determining a certain period. Thus, e. g., in Neo-Babylonian contract-tablets the months differ according to the contents of those respective tablets: when dates are to be returned *Tišrîtu* is the month; when grain, *Airu*; and when figs and grapes, *Du'uzu*.

2. One tablet is known to me which reckons (C. T. 17752, iv. 5): *Itu Amar-a-a-si Ša-aš-ru-um-ki ba-gul-la itu Amar-a-a-si mu en (dingir) Uru-ki maš-e-ni-pad-ku*, but it would be wrong to make, on account of that, the month *Amar-a-a-si* the first one of the year.

3. Above we have seen that only two months are common to A and B, viz. *ŠE-KIN-KUD* and *EZEN (dingir) Dun-gi*. In trying to reconcile both lists we might take as basis either the former or the latter month.

ŠE-KIN-KUD, it may be said, is in later times the twelfth month, hence probably also at this period. If that were true we would get the following equation:—

ŠE-KIN-KUD=twelfth month=A 12=B 1, which latter would have to be put at the end of that list. But against this is—

(*a*) The arrangement of List B itself.

(*b*) *EZEN* (*dingir*) *Dun-gi* of B would become the seventh, while in A it is the eighth month.

(*c*) v. R. 43—a list of months written in two columns.

On the left side (first column) of this list we find, with the exception of the first, six names for every month, which are identified on the right side (second column) with the Neo-Assyrian months. A closer examination of the first of those six names (called by us List C) reveals our List B—showing that *ŠE-KIN-KUD* must have been the first, *EZEN* (*dingir*) *Dun-gi* the eighth, and *EZEN-ME-KI-GÀL* the last or twelfth month respectively. Also the third names (called by us List D) are interesting. We have to see in them a relic of List A, and of the names that were in use at the time of Gudea. May I be allowed to give the transcription of Lists C and D, with their Neo-Assyrian equivalents, here:

v. R. 43.

Column II: Neo-Assyrian names.	Column I, List C.	Column I, List D.
1. *BÀR-AZAG* = *Ni-sa-an-nu*	Broken away	Name not given
	Has to be completed, according to B, to *ŠE-KIN-KUD*.	Is *Itu GAN-MAŠ* to be supplied?
2. *GUD-SI-DI* = *A-a-ru*	. . . *KÙ*	. . . *SI* (!) - *SAR-SAR*
	Has to be completed to *BAR-AZAG-KÙ*.	In this name we recognize no doubt the *GUD-NE-SAR-SAR*—only the *second* half of *NE* being preserved in the copy!
3. *ŠEG-GA* = *Si-ma-nu*	*SI-I-TAN* (written *UR*)	*EZEN* (*dingir*) *Nin-si-na*
	This is the only month which is not to be found in List B. It corresponds to *DUN-DA-KÙ*.	Probably the same as *EZEN* (*dingir*) *NE-SÙ*.

Column II: Neo-Assyrian names.	Column I, List C.	Column I, List D.
4. *ŠU-KUL-NA* = *Du-'-u-zu*	*ŠÀ*(sic)-*NE-RI*(sic)-*MU*(sic)	*ŠU-KUL*; ditto in List A
	Thus the copy gives! Here apparently the writer or the copyist misread several signs. *ŠÀ* was not the first sign, but that which we transcribe hypothetically by *ĜU+SI*; the third is *ĜU*, not *RI*—a mistake easily made—and the *MU* is only the beginning of *KÙ*! Read *ĜU+SI-NE-ĜU-KÙ*.	
5. *BIL-BIL-GAR* = *A-bu*	*KI-EL* *(dingir)* *Nin-* . . .	*EZEN* *(dingir)* . . .
	(dingir) *Nin-* . . . is to be completed to *Nin-[a-zu]*. In B we have for *KI-EL* = *KI-SIG* or *KIN* (?)—the latter sign being not yet identified.	From this month onward the names do not agree any more with List A.
6. *KIN* *(dingir)* *In-nanna* = *U-lu-lu*	*EZEN* *(dingir)* *Nin-a-zu*; ditto in List B	*KI-E[L]* *(dingir)* *Ba-u*
7. *DUL-AZAG* = *Tiš-ri-tu*	. . . *KI-IT*	*[EZEN]* *(dingir)* *Ba-u*
	To be completed to [*À*]-*ki-it* = *À-ki-ti* of B. The name (which means 'New Year's festival,' see H. W. B. p. 123) shows that this month must have been at one time the first of the year (see also List D). Later on the *Àkitu* or New Year's festival was celebrated in the month *Nisan*.	This month was at the time of Gudea the first of the year; see Statue G, iii. 5, 6: *ud zag-muezen* *(dingir)* *Ba-u*. As such it corresponds to the *À-ki-ti* of Lists B and C. This also shows that already at Gudea's time, whose caravans so often visited the Lebanon, the Canaanites must have adopted the Babylonian calendar.
8. *ENGAR-GAB-A* = *A-ra-aḫ-šam-na*	*EZEN* *(dingir)* . . . *gi*	*E* . . . *AN*(sic)
		Has to be completed, according to Gudea, Cyl. B, iii. 7, to *E-BA-BA-A-LIL*!
	Has not to be read with Br. 4351 = *EZEN* *(dingir)* *BIL* (*NE*)-*GI*, but according to List B = *EZEN-* *(dingir)* *Dun-gi*.	

Column II: Neo-Assyrian names.	Column I, List C.	Column I, List D.
9. *ĠAN-ĠAN-NA* = *Ki-si-li-mu*	Broken away Read *ŠU(?)-PEŠ(?)-ŠA* (List B).	Broken away
10. *AB-BA-UD-DU* = *Ṭe-bi-tum*	Broken away Read *EZEN-MAĠ* (List B).	Broken away
11. *AŠ-A-AN*=*Ša-ba-ṭu*	*EZE*$^{N}_{M}$*-MA AN-BA* (sic) The *MA* after *EZEN* contains the overhanging vowel; as such it is a later form of *EZEN-NA*. Comp. the later gloss *ALAM* with the older (time of Gudea) *ALAN-NA*, and see Hommel, Z. K. i. p. 173. In *AN-BA* the *BA* was misread for *NA*. Read *EZE*$^{N}_{M}$ *AN-NA* (List B).	*EŠ-GA-ZU*
12. *ŠE-KIN-KUD* =*Ad-da-ru*	*EZEN-ME-DI*(sic)-*GÀL* The *DI* was again misread for *KI*. This is evident from Lists B and D.	*ME-E-KI*-(*ga*)-*GAL*-(*al*) Here the *KI* was read correctly. The sign *GAL*, written here *SAL*, has two phonetic complements: (*ga*) and (*al*). For a similar case, see Strassen, Cyrus, 277, 19: *i-KAR-ir*=*iṭṭir*.

The above-given lists show clearly that the month *EZEN ME-KI-GÀL* was the last (twelfth), *EZEN* (*dingir*) *Dun-gi* the eighth, and *ŠE-KIN-KUD* the first month; hence we cannot take *ŠE-KIN-KUD* as our basis in trying to reconcile both lists[1], but must begin with *EZEN* (*dingir*) *Dun-gi*. If this be true we might make the following equation:—

[1] For if *ŠE-KIN-KUD* of A were the first, then *EZEN* (*dingir*) *Dun-gi* would be the ninth month, while in B it is the eighth!

ŠE-KIN-KUD = *ŠE-IL-LA* = *Nisan* = first month.

À-KI-TI = *EZEN* ^(dingir)^ *Dumu-zi* = *Tišrîtu* = seventh month.

EZEN ^(dingir)^ *Dun-gi* = *EZEN* ^(dingir)^ *Dun-gi* = *Araḫ-šamna* = eighth month.

EZEN ME-KI-GÀL = *ŠE-KIN-KUD* = *Addaru* = twelfth month.

That this is the only possible way of reconciling A and B—notwithstanding the fact that *ŠE-KIN-KUD* of B = *ŠE-IL-LA* of A, and *ŠE-KIN-KUD* of A = *EZEN ME-KI-GÀL* of B—is also proved by the Canaanitish names.

Above we saw that אָבִיב, although originally the seventh, became in later times = נִיסָן or first month. But אָבִיב corresponds, as regards its meaning, to *ŠE-IL-LA*; hence also *ŠE-IL-LA* must have been in the oldest times the seventh, and later on the first month of the year. *GAN-MAŠ*, it was said, corresponds to זִו, which latter again became later on the second = אִיָּר; hence also *GAN-MAŠ* must have been originally the eighth, and later on became the second month.

The different position of the 'harvest-month' (*ŠE-KIN-KUD*) in Lists A and B is probably due to *local circumstances*. The year, as we know, began with the twenty-first of March. The harvest of B then would fall in March–April, and that of A in February–March—consequently *earlier*. It may therefore be quite possible that List A was in use further south, while A was employed further north.

The result then is:

1. The year originally began with *À-ki-ti* = *Ezen* ^(dingir)^ *Dumu-zi* = *Ezen* ^(dingir)^ *Ba-u* = אתנים = תִּשְׁרִי.

This is proved by—

(*a*) The name *À-ki-ti* itself, which means 'New Year's festival.'

(*b*) By the fact that at the time of Gudea this seventh month was called *EZEN* (*dingir*) *Bà-u*, which again was the *ZAG-MU*, 'the New Year,' Gudea G, iii. 5, 6.

(*c*) The Canaanitish reckoning, according to which the month אתנים was the *first*. It is highly probable that the word אתן (sing. of אתנים) contains or is a corruption of *EZEN*, *isin*, *išin*, i. e. the festival κατ' ἐξοχήν, the 'New Year's festival'—in which case we would have the same phonetic law as in *šûru*, שׁוּר, ثَوْر, ܬܘܪܐ.

(*d*) The habit of the modern Jews, who still make תִּשְׁרִי their New Year's month.

2. At some time after Gudea the New Year was changed from *À-ki-ti*, &c., to *ŠE-KIN-KUD* = *ŠE-IL-LA*; hence *À-ki-ti*, &c., had to become the seventh = time of Ur IV.

3. At a still later time (Ḫammurabi dynasty?) the *ŠE-KIN-KUD* = *ŠE-IL-LA* was made the last. This seems to be indicated—

(*a*) by v. R. 43, List D: *X* (= *GAN-MAŠ*?); [*GUD-N*]*E-SAR-SAR*; *EZEN* (*dingir*) *Nin-si-na* (= *EZEN* (*dingir*) *NE-SÙ*); *ŠU-KUL*.

(*b*) by *BAR-AZAG-KÙ* of List B, which may be the same as *BÀR-AZAG-GAR* = *Nisannu* of later times.

While these changes took place it happened that new months were introduced, as e.g. the *EZEN* (*dingir*) *Dun-gi*—time of Ur IV. (Comp. in our calendar July and August). Others lost their original place, as for instance *ŠE-KIN-KUD* and *ŠU-KUL*. (So also with our calendar, September, October, &c.) The history of this latter month is especially interesting. In List A it is the fifth; in List D, on the other hand, the fourth. In the Assyrian period, or possibly before, it was even thrown together with the eighth month: *EZEN* (*dingir*) *Dumu-zi* (= *Duṃu-zi* = *Du'uzi* = *Dûzi* = תַּמּוּז). Thus it happened that the month of 'sowing' (*ŠU-KUL*) became the 'child of life' or 'true child' (*Du'uzu*, תַּמּוּז).

E. A. H. 134. Comp. v. R. 43.

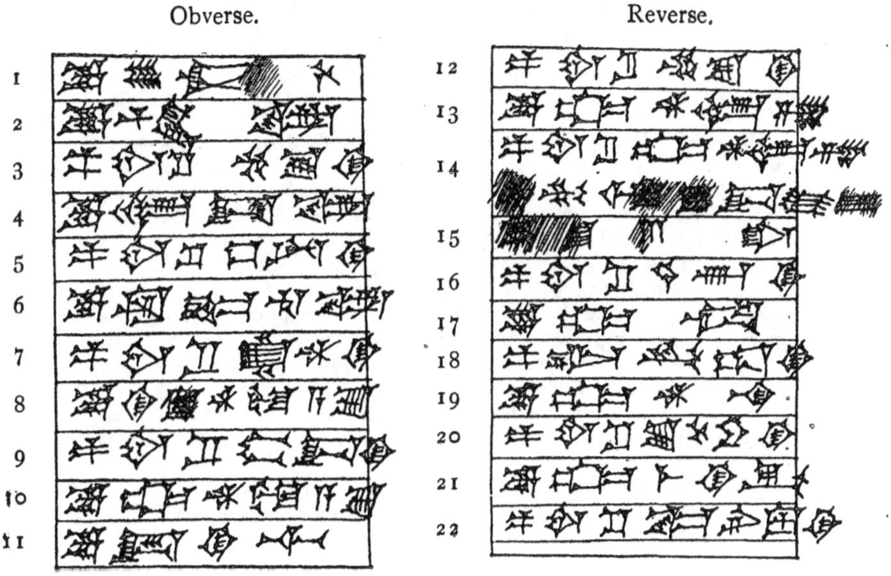

I. 1. *Itu ŠE-KIN-KUD.*
II. 2. *Itu BAR-AZAG-KÙ*
3. *pa-te-si Gir-su-ki.*

I. The month *ŠE-KIN-KUD* corresponds, according to v. R. 43, to *Nisannu.* After this month we should expect the *Itu DIR ŠE-KIN-KUD*, which, however, is left out. Comp. also above, List A, Nos. 12, 13, and Delitzsch, A. L³. p. 93.

II. The *Itu BAR-AZAG-KÙ* (= *BÀR-AZAG-GAR ?*) corresponds to the *A-a-ru* or the *Itu* (*EZEN*) *GAN-MAŠ.* During both of these months the patesi of Girsu was the officiating priest, probably in the temple of Bêl at Nippur, for it cannot be denied that Bêl even at this time exercised the chief influence. Comp. e. g. O. B. I. 20 and 21; and the expression *SAG-UŠ E* (*dingir*) *En-lil-ka.*

III. 4. *Itu DUN-DA-KÙ*
5. *pa-te-si Giš-BAN-ki.*
IV. 6. *Itu ĠU-SI-NE-ĠU-KÙ*
7. *pa-te-si KA-DINGIR-ki.*
V. 8. *Itu KI-KIN (? SIG) (dingir) NIN-A-ZU*
9. *pa-te-si MARAD-DA-ki.*

III. *Itu DUN-DA-KÙ* so clearly here. In E. A. H. 97 we find a month called *Itu URU* (*ŠES*, Br. 6435)-*DA-KÙ*, which tablet is dated: *Mu a-du-III-kam-ru Si-mu-ru-um-ki ba-ĝul*, hence evidently it belongs to this period. Are these two months identical? If so, the sign *DUN*(*ŠUL*) must have also the value *URU*-(*ŠES*). This would correspond to *Itu EZEN GUD-DU-NE-SAR-SAR*. The patesi of *Giš-uḫ-ki* officiated. For the situation of *Giš-uḫ-ki*, see under Eannatum and Entemena, p. 110, and under 'Uncertain Dates,' note 3. The name of one patesi of *Giš-uḫ-ki* is known to us; he ruled at the time of Dungi III.; see Scheil, Rec. Trav. xix. p. 63: *Ud-ba Ur-(dingir) NE-SÙ* (*sic*, not *KÙ*) *pa-te-si Giš-uḫ-ki-kam mu An-ša-an-ki ba-ĝul* (= Dungi III. dates, Nos. 37 and 38). In C. T. 96-6-12, 3 (= Scheil, R. T. xxi. 125), a tablet of a certain (*Ga*)*lu-(dingir) Utu* (= *Amêl-Šamaš*), patesi of *Giš-uḫ-ki*, is published, which in all probability belongs also to this period. It reads:

(Dingir) Nin-ḫar-sag	For Ninḫarsag,
am dingir-ri-ne-ra	the mother of the gods,
(*Ga*)*lu-(dingir) Utu*	Amêl-Shamash,
pa-te-si	the patesi
Giš-uḫ-ki-ge	of Gishuḫ,
nam-ti-la-ni-ku	for his life,
dingir-gi dingir ki-ag-na	viz. for the queen (Br. 10073, comp. Jensen, Kosmologie, p. 207), his beloved goddess,
e mu-na-ru	a temple he has built.
uš-bi mu-dug	Its foundations (may she) make good,
temen-bi mu-si	its temen (may she) establish,
sib-bi šag-bi-a	the priesthood in its midst
si-im-ma-ni-di	(may she) direct.

IV. The sign after *Itu* is uncertain. It may be a ligature of *ĠU* + *SI*; comp. E. C. 37. It corresponds to *Itu EZEN (dingir) NE-SÙ* and to *Dû'zu*. The patesi of *KA-DINGIR-ki* officiates. *KA-DINGIR-ki* apparently is the Semitic writing for *BÂB-ILI-ki* = Babylon. Comp. also R. A. iv. No. iii. pl. v. 13, env. 6.

V. *KI-KIN* (*? SIG*) (*sic*), as testified to by E. A. H. 109 and by E. C. 463; it stands here in the same relation to the following as *EZEN* (l. 10) does.

VI. 10. *Itu EZEN (dingir) NIN-A-ZU.*
VII. 11. *Itu À-KI-TI*
12. *pa-te-si Gir-su-ki.*
VIII. 13. *Itu EZEN-(dingir) DUN-GI*
14. *pa-te-si ezen (dingir) Dun-gi*
PA (?) Mu-ù-lu (?) da-LUM LUǴ.
IX. 15. *Itu ŠU (?)-(P)EŠ-ŠA*
16. *pa-te-si UD-NUN-ki.*

In v. R. 43 we have for *KI-SIG = KI-EL*. Or should we read here *KI-KIN*, and comp. *Itu KIN (dingir) Innan-na = Ululu*, Delitzsch, A. L[3]., p. 92, 4, l. 6? *KI-SIG (? KIN)* corresponds to the *Itu ŠU-KUL*, which later on became the fourth month, but here it is the fifth = *A-bu*. For the pronunciation *MARAD-DA-ki*, see Br. 9079. Marad, according to Smith = 'Αμορδοκαία (Ptol. v. 20, 3), south of Borsippa. Comp. also NiMRoD with *Nu-MaRaD* (= the man from Marad); see Delitzsch, Parad. p. 220, and iv. R[2]. 36, No. 1, col. ii. 22.

VI. *Itu EZEN-(dingir) NIN-A-ZU = itu ZIB-KÙ = U-lu-lu = KIN (dingir) Innanna.*

VII. With *À-KI-TI* begins the second half. During this and the preceding month the patesi of Girsu again officiates. *À-ki-ti = DUL-AZAG = Tiš-ri-tu* יֶרַח הָאֵתָנִים = *EZEN (dingir) Dumu-zi = EZEN (dingir) Ba-u* (of Gudea).

VIII. This month we find again in List A, and is, according to v. R. 43, = *Araḫ-šamna.*

The *Dun-gi* here mentioned is Dungi III.; see further below.

The officiating priest was the *pa-te-si EZEN (dingir) Dun-gi.* Here then we have a new class of patesis, e.g. one of a festival. It is evident that patesi can mean in this connection only as much as '*Vorsteher*,' or 'arranger,' an officer specially appointed for this occasion. Line 14 *b* is much mutilated by a petrified mass, only the signs *MU-Ù* and *da-LUM LUǴ* are clear. The first sign may be *PA* or *BA* or *AŠ*; the fourth either *ŠU* or *KU* or *LU*. The reading *PA MU-Ù-LU* seems to be the most probable. *PA* = officer; *MU-Ù-LU* = the name of the officer (= patesi). *Da-LUM = da-num* (see notes to O. B. I. 1). This shows that the whole tablet ought to be read in an Assyrian way. *LUǴ = sukallu*, Br. 6170, H. W. B. 498, and O. B. I. part ii. p. 41, note 6. Comp. also C. T. 12231, ii. 20: *GIR Ezên (dingir) Dun-gi (ga)lu-im* (= *šanû*, Br. 4821).

IX. The sign after *Itu* may be either *ŚU, KU,* or *LU?*, or even *SIG*. The next sign is the number '3.'

Itu ŠU ?-(P)EŠ-ŠA = Itu EZEN (dingir) BA-U of List A = *Ki-si-li-mu.*

For *UD-NUN-ki*, comp. iv. R[2]. 36, 1, obv. 5, 6, mentioned between Ur and Isin.

X. 17. *Itu EZEN-MAǴ*
18. *PA-AL Uru-um-ki.*
XI. 19. *Itu EZEN AN-NA*
20. *pa-te-si SU-KUR-RU-ki.*
XII. 21. *Itu EZEN ME-KI-GÀL(IK)*
22. *pa-te-si KA-ṢAL-LU-ki.*

X. The month of the 'great festival' = *Itu MU-ŠU-GAB* (Sargon) = *Itu MU-ŠU-UL* (List A) = *AB-BA-UD-DU* = *Ṭe-bi-tum*. The *pa-al* (= Assyr. *šabrû*) of *Ur* officiated.

XI. 'Festival of Anu' = *Itu (EZEN) AMAR-A-(A)-SI* = *Ša-ba-ṭu*. According to Br. 223 the *(ilu) SU-KUR* is = Marduk, ii. R. 54, 49 *g*. In iii. R. 68, 8 *c*, the *(ilu) SU-KUR-RU* is mentioned. This month is also on E. A. H. 87.

XII. This month, written in List D *ME-E-KI-(ga)-GAL(SAL)-(al)*, is according to v. R. 43 = *ŠE-KIN-KUD* or *Ad-da-ru*, i.e. the twelfth month.

For *KA-ṢAL-LU*, comp. Br. 670 and 675, and Dungi III. dates, No. 13; iv. R. 36, No. 1, obv. ii. 23; and above, pp. 158, 163, 190, 256.

Traces of a third nomenclature, which is the beginning of the later or Assyrian already in use at the time of Ḫammurabi, give us the following months:—

Itu AŠ-A, E. A. H. 90. This tablet is dated: *Mu en Uru-ki-Kar-zi-da ba-tug*, belongs therefore to this period (comp. Dates of Bur-Sin, No. 11). This month clearly corresponds to the Assyr. *Šabaṭu* (eleventh month).

Itu GIŠ-ENGAR-GAB-A is to be found on E. A. H. 106, with the date *Mu-uš-sa Lu-lu-bu-um-ki ba-ǵul* (Uncertain Dates, No. 2). Apparently this writing is only the fuller form for the *ENGAR-GAB-A* = *A-ra-aḫ-šam-na* (eighth month), Delitzsch, A. L.[3]. p. 92.

Itu INNANNA on E. A. H. 108 (*mu en nam-? (dingir) Dun-gi-ra-ge ba-DU ba-tug*; see Uncertain Dates, No. 4). This probably is only an abbreviation for *Itu* [*EZEN* or *KIN (dingir)*] *INNANNA*; comp. also above (arrangement A) *sub* No. 4: *Itu EZEN (dingir) NE-SU* and *Itu (dingir) NE-SÙ*. The month *Ululu* is called the *itu KIN (dingir) INNAN* (Br. 3051)-*NA*. The *itu*

Innanna then is = *Itu* (*dingir*) *Innanna* = *Itu KIN* (*dingir*) *Innan-NA* = *Ululu* = the sixth month.

For *Itu URU-DA-KÙ*, comp. above, note III.

We see then that at the time of Ur IV. there were in use three distinct nomenclatures for the months. The year consisted of twelve months; sometimes a thirteenth month, called *DIR ŠE-KIN-KUD* (or *araḫ Baḫir arkû*, time of Sargon I.), was added, and according to C. T. 18358 it might happen that in a period of five years two such intercalary months could be put in.

This is important in more than one respect—important not only for the question of how many days the month consisted, but also for that of the intercalary months themselves.

From iii. R. 52, 37 b, *XII arḫi pl. ša šatti* 1 *gan VI UŠ* (= 360) *ûmê pl. ša mi-na-at ZAG-MUG ina šû* . . ., we know that the year consisted of 360 days, or twelve months of thirty days. We know further that the names of three intercalary months are preserved: the second *Nisan*, *Elul* (ואליל), and *Addar* (ואדר)[1], and that the month *Abu* was that of dry heat, while *Šabaṭu* was that of snow and cold (*šalgu kuṣṣu araḫ AŠ dannat kuṣṣi ul âdur*, iii. R. 15, i. 14). This latter passage—occurring very often in Assyrian inscriptions—proves that the people at that time must have reckoned according to sun-years. If therefore the year consisted of 360 days, and they notwithstanding reckoned according to sun-years, it was necessary for them to intercalate *one month* every six years, or else within thirty-six years the *Šabâṭu* would have become the month of dry heat, and *Abu* that of snow and cold. Thus the existence of one intercalary month might be explained. But there were *three* such months.

From C. T. 18358, see above *sub* Dates of Dungi III, p. 252, we learn that it could happen that in a period of five years two such intercalary months were sometimes put in. On the supposition that the year consisted of 360 days, such a thing could happen only every 120 years. With us every four years a twenty-ninth of February is intercalated. If this were not done, then in

[1] See among other places also iii. R. 56, No. 5.

30 × 4 years we should be back one month in our time. If this explanation be admissible, then we have to suppose that within those five years enumerated by C. T. 18358 one such one hundred and twentieth year was to be found. In this way we possibly could account for the existence of two intercalary months, but never for that of three[1]. This shows that at some time the Babylonians or Assyrians were in need of three intercalary months. How then can we explain the existence of *three* intercalary months?

Lists A and B again give us the key. Above it was argued that the year originally began with *Àkiti* = *Ezen* *(dingir)* *Dumu-zi* = *Tišrîtu* = אתנים = *Ezen* *(dingir)* *Ba'u* (List D, time of Gudea). If this be true then the month *ŠE-KIN-KUD* (List B) = *ŠE-IL-LA* (List A) must have been the seventh. Unfortunately no tablet has come down to us so far which shows that they had at that time e. g. a *DIR ŠE-KIN-KUD,* although we know that on one of the tablets belonging to Sargon I.'s period an *araḫ Baḫir arkû* (= a second *Addar*?) is mentioned. We saw also that at some time after Gudea the beginning of the year must have been changed from *Àkiti* to *ŠE-KIN-KUD* = *ŠE-IL-LA*, which arrangement we find at the time of Ur IV. In R. A. iv. iii. pl. xxix. No. 78—a tablet reckoning according to List B—a *DIR ŠE-KIN-KUD* is mentioned, see env. ii. 9 ff.: *NIN-ŠID-AG, bal Ur-*(*dingir*) *KAL pa-te-si Gir-su-*[*ki*], *itu ŠE-KIN-KUD-ta, itu DIR ŠE-KIN-KUD-ku, itu* 2[*kam*]. *ŠE-KIN-KUD* being in List B the first month = *Nisan*, we should have here a *second Nisan*[2]. The *DIR ŠE-KIN-KUD* to be found among other places also in R. A. iv. iii. pl. xxviii. No. 77, env., i. 1—

[1] According to the above-given supposition, the one hundred and twentieth year must have had *two* intercalary months: one that was put in every six years, and the other that of every one hundred and twenty years. But one year with *two* intercalary months is improbable—yes, impossible. Hence they could not have invented a second *Elul* alongside of a second *Addar*.

[2] And because a *second Nisan*, we must postulate also a second *Tišrîtu*. This would follow from the analogy of the second *Elul*.

a tablet reckoning according to List A—is not the second *Nisan*, but the *second Addar* (ואדר), because in List A *ŠE-KIN-KUD* is the twelfth month.

But WHY was there also a second *Elul* (ואלול)?

C. T. 18358 again gives us the answer! It reckons according to List A, and states expressly that among sixty-two months, or five years, two intercalary months are to be found (*itu* 62 *kam itu-dir 2-a-an šag-ba-ni-gàl*), hence among every thirty-one months, or $2\frac{1}{2}$ years, *one* intercalary month, which must have been the *second Elul*. True it is that I have not yet seen mentioned, on any of the tablets belonging to this period, a second *Elul* (which would have been called according to List A *DIR ZIB-KÙ*, or possibly also *ZIB-KÙ* 2 *gan* (*kam*)), but that does not prove that it did not exist at all[1]. The fact however that such a second *Elul* is known proves enough—at least, so much that it was felt necessary to intercalate a month in the middle of the year. It was no doubt *intended* to have a year of 360 days, as is apparent from iii. R. 52, 37^b, but in fact it must have had less, so that every five years two months could be intercalated. On this supposition we would get the following equation: $5 \times 360 = 5 \times 360 - 60$ for five years, and for one year $= \frac{5 \times 360}{5} = \frac{5 \times 360 - 60}{5}$, i.e. the year had only 348 days; hence every two and a half years one month had to be added: $2\frac{1}{2} \times 360 = 2\frac{1}{2} \times 348 + 30$.

Another fact, however, has to be taken into consideration. Such names as *ŠE-KIN-KUD* = 'harvest,' *ŠE-ÍL-LA* = 'grain grown,' *GAN-MAŠ* = 'field in blossom,' *ŠU-KUL* = 'sowing,' show clearly enough that the people at this time (Ur IV.) must have had a *sun-year*, or else every thirty-six years the harvest month, e. g., would be exactly six months too early; hence we must suppose that still a third month had to be intercalated every six years. In the following I give a survey of thirty years; the

[1] At the time of Ḫammurabi such a second *Elul* (ואלול), written *itu KIN (dingir) Innanna* 2 *kam*, was in existence; see King, Letters of Ḫammurabi, No. 14. (Personal communication of Prof. Hommel.)

large numbers show the years when thirty days were added at an interval of thirty months, while the *underlined* numbers give those years when one month was intercalated in order to keep up with the sun: 1, 2, **3**, 4, **5** | 6, 7, **8**, 9, **10** | 11, 12, **13**, 14, **15** | 16, 17, **18**[1], 19, **20** | 21, 22, **23**, 24, **25** | 26, 27, **28**, 29, **30** |. (With 31 ff. the same arrangement begins over again.)

This survey shows that if the people of Ur IV. reckoned according to sun-years, the five years of C. T. 18358 could only have fallen within the period of Nos. 7–11 (or 37–41, &c.) of the above-given scheme. If, on the other hand, they did not reckon according to sun-years, those five years might embrace any period of that length.

Further, if it be true that the year had only 348 days instead of 360, it might be natural to suppose that each month had 29 days. But against this is E. A. H. 152: *itu EZEN* *(dingir)* *Dumu-zi ud* 30 *kam*; and Arnold, Ancient Babylonian Temple Records, No. 2: *itu EZEN* *(dingir)* *Ba-u ud* 30 *kam*, showing that there must have existed some months of 30 days. Hence we may say, if it be admitted that the year had 348 days, the months must have had 30 and 28 days alternately. The month *ZIB-KÙ*, with 28 days, is mentioned in C. T. 13889, and *GUD-DU-NE-SAR* is mentioned with 29 in C. 13892. According to List A, the *EZEN* *(dingir)* *Dumu-zi* is the seventh, and *EZEN* *(dingir)* *Ba-u* the ninth month; hence we may say that at the time of Ur IV. all months with uneven numbers had 30, while the others had only 28 days[2]. This seems to us the most reasonable explanation. The result then is:

A year consisted of 348 days, and the months had alternately

[1] This year as well as No. 30 ought to have two intercalary months! In all probability this was avoided, and one month was added to the following year, i. e. nineteenth or thirty-first year.

[2] At the time of Ḫammurabi this arrangement has been changed—it being probably due to the fact that the year did not begin with *ŠE-KIN-KUD* = *ŠE-IL-LA*, but with *BAR-AZAG-KÙ* = *GAN-MAŠ*, see above—for we find a 30th *Araḫšamna*, A. B. P. R. No. 66; a 30th *Nisan*, ibid. No. 107; a 29th *Tišritu*, ibid. No. 119; a 30th *Addar*, King, Letters of Ḫammurabi, No. 40, 6, 13.

Sargon I.	IV. Dynasty of Ur.			Assyrian.		Day
1 *Itu EZEN ŠE-IL-LA*	1 *Itu ŠE-IL-LA*	1 *Itu ŠE-KIN-KUD*[2] / [*Itu DIR ŠE-KIN-KUD*]	. . . .	1 *BÀR-AZAG-GAR*[3]	1 *Ni-sa-an-nu*[3] (7. אביב)	30
2 *Itu EZEN GAN-MAŠ*[1]	2 *Itu GAN-MAŠ*[1]	2 *Itu BAR-AZAG-KÙ*	. . . .	2 *GUD-SI-DI*	2 *A-a-ru* (8. זו)	28
3 *Itu EZEN GUD-DU-NE-SAR-SAR*	3 *Itu GUD-DU-NE-SAR-SAR*	3 *Itu DUN-DA-KÙ*	3 *Itu URU-DA-KÙ*[2]	3 *ŠEG-GA*	3 *Si-ma-nu*	30
4 *Itu EZEN* (*dingir*) *NE-SÙ*	4 *Itu EZEN* (*dingir*) *NE-SÙ*	4 *Itu ĠU-SI-NE-ĠU-KÙ*	. . . .	4 *ŠU-KUL-NA*	4 *Du-'-u-zu*	28
5	5 *Itu ŠU-KUL*	5 *Itu KI-KIN* (?) (*dingir*) *NIN-A-ZU*	. . . .	5 *BIL-BIL-GAR*	5 *A-bu*	30
6 *Itu EZEN ZIB-KÙ*	6 *Itu ZIB-KÙ*	6 *Itu EZEN* (*dingir*) *NIN-A-ZU*	6 *Itu Innanna*[3]	6 *KIN* (*dingir*) *Innanna*	6 *U-lu-lu*	28
7 *Itu EZEN* (*dingir*) *DUMU-ZI*	7 *Itu EZEN* (*dingir*) *DUMU-ZI*	7 *Itu À-KI-TI*	. . . .	7 *DUL-AZAG*	7 *Tiš-ri-tu* (1. אתנים)	30
8	8 *Itu EZEN* (*dingir*) *DUN-GI*	8 *Itu EZEN* (*dingir*) *DUN-GI*	8 *Itu GIŠ-ENGAR-GAB-A*[3]	8 *ENGAR-GAB-A*	8 *A-ra-aḫ-šam-na* (2. בול)	28
9 *Itu EZEN* (*dingir*) *BA-U*	9 *Itu EZEN* (*dingir*) *BA-U*	9 *Itu ŠU* (?)-(*P*)*EŠ-ŠA*	. . . .	9 *ĠAN-ĠAN-NA*	9 *Ki-si-li-mu*	30
10 *Itu MU-ŠU-GAB*	10 *Itu MU-ŠU-UL*	10 *Itu EZEN-MAĠ*	. . . .	10 *AB-BA-UD-DU*	10 *Ṭe-bi-tum*	28
11 *Itu EZEN-AMAR-A-SI*	11 *Itu AMAR-A-A-SI*	11 *Itu EZEN AN-NA*	11 *Itu AŠ-A*	11 *AŠ-A-AN*	11 *Ša-ba-ṭu*	30
12	12 *Itu ŠE-KIN-KUD*	12 *Itu EZEN ME-KI-GÀL*	. . . .	12 *ŠE-KIN-KUD*	12 *Ad-da-ru*	28
	Itu DIR ŠE-KIN-KUD			13 *DIR ŠE-KIN-KUD*	13 *ar-ḫu maḫ-ru ša Ad-da-ru*	30

[1] If numbered according to C. T. 18343 *Itu GAN-MAŠ* would be the first and *ŠE-IL-LA* the last.
[2] Numbering according to Ur IV. B, on the basis of E. A. H. 134 and v. R. 43.
[3] Numbering according to the more modern Assyrian arrangement of months, based upon Delitzsch, A. L.[3], p. 92.
[4] Numbering according to Canaanitish tradition, based upon the Bible.

30 and 28 days. The year, although intended to be a sun-year, was a combination of a sun- and a moon-year. Every two and a half years an intercalary month was put in: the second *Elul* (ואלול) and the second *Addar* (ואדר).

For the sake of completeness I may be permitted to mention a third possibility of the mode of reckoning at this time. From the Hebrew calendar we know that the months had alternately 30 and 29 days; the year therefore consisted of 354 days. According to this, every five and every six years an intercalary month had to be put in—the former to make it harmonize with iii. R. 52, 37^b (equation: $5 \times 360 = 5 \times 354 + 30$), the latter to make the year agree with the course of the sun or seasons. The following scheme shows the years when one month was intercalated; the large numbers indicate that of every five years, and the underlined that of every six years: 1, 2, 3, 4, **5** | 6, 7, 8, 9, **10** | 11, 12, 13, 14, **15** | 16, 17, 18, 19, **20** | 21, 22, 23, 24, **25** | 26, 27, 28, 29, **30**[1] |. According to this scheme the five years of C. T. 18358 could fall into any period of that length—no doubt a great advantage over the supposition that the year consisted of 348 days only. However, if this latter were true, there would have been no need whatever to have a second *Elul*, which, as we saw, exists already at the time of Ḫammurabi. If therefore it be true that a second *Elul* could and had to be put in some time—which cannot be denied—we are forced to the conclusion that the year originally must have had only 348 days. Later on it may have been changed. To show when and why this old arrangement was abolished is the task of future investigation.

In conclusion, I have prepared a comparative table of the names of the months during this period (see opposite).

The sign of 'god' before certain proper names.

The attention of the reader has already been drawn to the remarkable fact that up to the time of Sargon I. the kings of Early

[1] See note 1, p. 306.

Babylonia never prefixed to their names the sign of god ('*dingir*'). From that time on, till the fourth dynasty of Ur, and even later, the kings were considered, or better considered themselves, as emanations of the deity, i. e. as 'gods.'

True it is that the kings before the time of Sargon I. acknowledged or emphasized their belief that the wisdom and power which they displayed were given them by the different gods.

Eannatum expressly says that 'he was nourished with the milk of life by Ninḫarsag, was endowed with power by Nirgirsu, that his intelligence was given him by Enki' (Galet A, i. and ii.), but he does not yet go so far as to say that he is the son of a specified god, or still further 'god' himself[1]. This bold idea was first propounded by Lugalzaggisi, who claims to be 'a son begotten by Nidaba, nourished with the milk of life by Ninḫarsag, a slave brought up by Ninagidǵadu' (O. B. I. 87, i. 26 ff.). Lugalzaggisi, although clearly maintaining that he was of divine origin, a בן אלהים, refrains however from styling himself directly 'god Lugalzaggisi.'

The first who ventured to claim the divine appellation was Sargon I. (O. B. I. 2, 1[2]). His son Naram-Sin goes even a step further. Not only does he invariably term himself 'god Naram-Sin' (*ilu Na-ra-am-*(*ilu*) *Sin*), but even 'god of Agade' (*ilu Agade-ki*); nay, even *en men anna*, i. e. in Assyr. either = *bêl agê šamâmi*, 'lord of the heavenly disk,' or = *bêl agê ṣîri*, 'lord of the exalted disk.'

This is significant. Above we have seen that some of the Semites after they had invaded Babylonia remained in their new home; others, leaving it again, settled down in the north. Among those Semites that remained in Babylonia must be reckoned Eannatum. To those that settled down in the north belong Lugalzaggisi and

[1] That the expression (*dingir*) *En-temen-* . . . has not to be referred to Entemena, who thus would call himself here 'god,' but that it is in apposition to (*dingir*) *Dun-gur*, who sometimes is also called (*dingir*) *Dun-gur-an*, see above, p. 118, note 1 to O. B. I. 115, and also p, 92, note 18.

[2] Only here. In all the other inscriptions of this king the sign for god is not written before his name.

Sargon I. Hence we see that to the *Semites* of the north[1] was restricted this particular belief, that the king was an emanation of the deity. But here again we should distinguish between those Semites situated nearest to the Sumerians (i. e. Lugalzaggisi) and those that were more remote (i. e. Sargon I.). If we compare the peculiar belief of these two latter kinds of Semites with that of those who actually lived among the Sumerians (i. e. Eannatum) we shall find the reason for this variety of phraseology. Originally all the Semites believed that their head, the king, was a son of god; nay, even a god himself. This belief was later on—when the Semites had invaded Babylonia and had come into contact with the old Sumerians—to some extent modified. Those Semites that were in daily intercourse with the Sumerians lost in course of time this faith, being content with stating that they were endowed with divine power. Those nearest to the Sumerians (Gishuḫ : Lugalzaggisi) modified it so far that they looked upon their king as 'a son of god,' but did not directly claim for him the divine title. The Semites who lived furthest away from the Sumerians kept their original faith undefiled. Their king was their god. It is however remarkable that the name of Sargon I. is written only once *ilu Šar-ga-ni-šar-âli*, and that of Naram-Sin always *ilu Naram-ilu Sin*. Why? It has been stated above (p. 166) that Thureau-Dangin (Rec. Trav. xix. p. 187) holds '*que Shargani et surtout Naram-Sin aient subi, en ce qui touche la conception du caractère royal, l'influence plus ou moins lointaine des idées égyptiennes.*' This hypothesis he bases upon the fact '*que Sargon l'Ancien a étendu son empire jusqu'en Syro-Palestine*,' and had thus come into contact with Egyptian ideas.

We know however that Lugalzaggisi had also extended his domain as far as Syria-Palestine; comp. e. g. in O. B. I. 87, ii. 4 ff., the phrase, 'from the lower sea of the Tigris and the Euphrates to

[1] They did not assimilate themselves to such a degree to the old Sumerians as did those of their kinsmen who remained among the old inhabitants of ancient Babylonia.

the upper sea,' and his statement that he made conquests 'from the rising of the sun even to the going down of the same.' It would therefore be natural to suppose that he too would have come into contact with Egyptian ideas. He would have had no reason for refusing the title of god, seeing that he already claimed to be 'a son begotten by Nidaba.' Hence it seems that the reason why Sargon I. and Naram-Sin should call themselves 'god' must be sought elsewhere. True it is that the kingdom of Agade was the most remote from Sumerian influence, consequently it also kept the old faith purest. But this reason alone would not account sufficiently for the facts. What then was the chief cause which should induce Sargon I. to call himself 'god'? We have seen that Sargon I., and especially his son Naram-Sin, not only conquered the west but also Arabia (see p. 162). But Arabia was the original home of the Semites. Here among the Semites of the Arabian Desert the old Semitic faith was preserved in all its purity. Sargon I., himself being a Semite, was only too glad to 'renew' the old faith of the Semites—which to some extent was still lingering among his people—especially because it contributed so much to his own honour. He is followed in doing this by his son Naram-Sin, who even goes a step further, not only calling himself 'god Naram-Sin,' but also 'god of Agade'; nay, even 'lord of the heavenly disk.' Thus we also understand why Lugalzaggisi did not call himself 'god.' Simply because he was only a *lugal-kalamma*, and not a *šar kibrat arba'im*, not having subjugated Arabia and thus not having come into contact with the *old* Semitic faith[1].

The conception of the king as a 'son of god' is found also among the later patesis of Shirpurla. No doubt this was a result of the reign of Sargon I. and Naram-Sin over the whole of Babylonia.

Ur-Ba'u calls himself 'a son begotten by Ninagal' (i. e. Ea, see E. A. H. 112, 7, 8); Gudea is begotten by Gatumdug (Statue

[1] This also explains why the kings of Kish do not call themselves 'god'—simply because they had not come into contact with the old Semites of the Arabian Desert.

B, ii. 16). This latter patesi even goes beyond all his predecessors. He makes a statue of himself, places it in the temple of Ningirsu, and orders that 1 *ḳa* of fermented drink (*gaš*), 1 *ḳa* of food (*gar*), ½ *ḳa* of fine flour (*zid-dub-dub*), ½ *ḳa* of crushed barley (*nin-ĝur-ra aš-an*) (Statue B, i. 8–11) should be offered yearly (?) to it.

This action of Gudea is somewhat remarkable, seeing that he does not call himself god[1]; nor do any of the later patesis of Shirpurla ascribe to themselves this arrogant title. The reason for this probably is that the title 'god' could only be ascribed to kings; hence, being a patesi, he could not call himself 'god.' For this deficiency he made up by at least trying to get the worship of a god.

During the time of the second dynasty of Ur[2] the title 'god' disappears. It reappears, however, with the kings of Isin in South Babylonia. We can explain this as follows:—Under Ur-Gur and Dungi I. the Semitic and the Sumerian populations were joined under one sceptre in the *nam-lugal Kengi-ki-Urdu*, i. e. in the kingship of Shumer and Akkad. Semites had free intercourse with the Sumerians. They could go to and fro, settle down wherever they pleased. Those who settled down in Isin were able to seize in course of time the power and kingship of Babylonia. They naturally brought all their ideas about king and kingship with them. Their ancestors had been living in the north of Babylonia, where the king was 'god.' Hence those Semites who eventually became kings of Isin ascribed to themselves the title of god. Thus, then, the title 'god,' which had its original home in Arabia, and with the

[1] The writing *dingir Gu-de-a* in Statue C is not an exception. The *dingir* there refers back to (*dingir*) *Nin-giš-zid-da*, and has to be connected with *kam* in l. 6. See the translation above, p. 199.

[2] The name of Dungi I. occurs sometimes written (*dingir*) *Dun-gi*; comp. i. R. 2, ii. 1; K. B. iii[1]. p. 80, Nos. 1 and 4. Winckler, l. c. note 3, makes the following remark to this *AN*: '*Dieses AN* (= *dingir*) *scheint* nicht *das vor den Namen spaterer Konige gesetzte Gottesdeterminativ zu sein, welches auch vor dem Namen Ur-Gur's nicht steht, sondern sich nur auf das DUN zu beziehen. AN-DUN ist aber nach v. R.* 44, 20 = *Ba'u, der Name DUN-GI also semitisch, wohl als Ba'u-ukîn oder ahnlich zu deuten.*'

use of which the subjugation of that country may have been connected originally, lost at length its signification and became a mere 'ornamental[1]' appendage to the names of these kings.

Enannatum, the son of Ishme-Dagan, is not king, consequently also not styled 'god[2]'.

Too little so far is known about the rulers of the third dynasty of Ur to justify us in making any conclusions, but the representatives of the fourth dynasty of Ur all[3] call themselves 'god': *(dingir) Dun-gi*[4] (E. A. H. 61); *(dingir) Bur-(dingir) Sin*[5]; *(dingir) Gimil-(dingir) Sin*; *(dingir) I-ne-(dingir) Sin*—the first '*dingir*' being only there to deify the persons.

Scheil, in Rec. Trav. xviii. 64 ff., published a number of tablets—all written during the time of the fourth dynasty of Ur—which give us the 'appointed portions' for the following gods and persons: for *(dingir) Dun-pa-ud-du*, for *(dingir) Dun-gi*, for *(dingir) Nin-giš-zid-da*, for *(dingir) Gu-de-a pa-te-si*, for *Gudea the patesi*, and for *Ur-(dingir) KAL the patesi* (comp. also Thureau-Dangin, R. A. iii. p. 135—a tablet which mentions the same names).

[1] That the name or sign 'god' is a mere ornament is evident from the names themselves; comp. *(dingir) Ur-(an) Ninib*; *(dingir) Iš-me-(an) Dagan*, &c., where the first *dingir* is apparently meaningless.

[2] The kings of Erech, Singâshid and Singâmil, have also the sign of 'god' before their names, but here it is clearly the determinative before 'Sin.'

[3] Excepting Ur-Ba'u II. The reason for this undoubtedly is that in the places where he is mentioned (Rec. Trav. xix. 49) he appears not yet as 'king,' consequently also not as 'god.'

[4] The sign of 'god,' however, is left out in the Semitic-Babylonian inscription of Dungi III. published by Winckler, A. B. K. No. 37, and translated by the same in K. B. iii[1]. p. 83. Above it has already been stated that this tablet belongs not to Dungi I., but to Dungi III., on account of the 'title.' The reason why the sign of 'god' is left out here is that the 'scribe who made this copy forgot to put it there,' for there can be no doubt that that tablet is simply a copy of an older one. This is expressly stated on another tablet (belonging to Dungi I.), copied also from an older one found in the temple at Kutha: *šâ êli (abnu) na-ru-a labiri ša E-Šid-lam ki-rib Kutâ. Dup-pu ša Bêl-uballi-iṭ dup-sar* (Winckler, A. B. K., No. 35).

[5] It is also left out on a tablet dated from Lulubi, E. A. H. 27. See for the reason of this note 1 to dates of Bur-Sin, p. 266.

Scheil, l. c.[1], thinks, because the patesi Gudea is mentioned on those tablets, that this Gudea is the old patesi of Shirpurla who had erected his statue in the temple of Ningirsu, and had ordered that certain sacrifices should be brought to this statue. The (*dingir*) *Dun-gi*, then, he takes to be Dungi I., king of Ur (second dynasty), he being a contemporary of Gudea (Winckler, U. A. G. 157, 9). He is partly right and partly wrong. The very fact that Gudea, the old patesi of Shirpurla, never called himself directly 'god' leads us to discriminate between (*dingir*) *Gu-de-a pa-te-si* and *Gudea patesi*. All Gudea of Shirpurla could do was to erect certain statues—some of which have come down to us and are preserved in the Louvre—and order that sacrifices should be brought to these 'statues.' Undoubtedly these statues were still in existence at the time of Ur IV. The people, seeing the statues in their temples, came to look upon them in course of time as 'gods,' and thus it happened that we have here a (*dingir*) *Gu-de-a pa-te-si*. But this does not necessarily imply that the old Gudea was still living. Besides this, we saw above that Gudea, having instituted certain specific sacrifices in honour of 'his double,' adds: 'A patesi who should retract this, who should hinder the command of Ningirsu, his sacrifices may be retracted from the house of Ningirsu and his commands may be bound!' (B, i. 13–20). A comparison of the above instituted sacrifices with those actually brought—mentioned on the tablets above referred to—will show that these sacrifices did not agree with those commanded by Gudea I. We can hardly suppose that the people of the fourth dynasty, if they were contemporaries of the Gudea of Shirpurla, would set at nought his express command, and in defiance of his curse would offer to him whatever they pleased.

Hence we have to distinguish between (*dingir*) *Gu-de-a pa-te-si*, who is the old patesi of Shirpurla—dead, to be sure, for a long time, but still living in the statues he had erected, and which statues were looked upon in course of time as '*gods*[2]'—and between Gudea

[1] And R. T. xxi. 26 ff.: Le culte de Gudea.

[2] Hence it also happened that we find at the time of Ur IV. such names as

patesi, a contemporary of the kings of Ur IV[1], viz. Bur-Sin II. to Gimil-Sin, see p. 244 ff. Whether this latter was also a patesi of Girsu-Shirpurla is by no means certain. This latter Gudea we call Gudea II.; comp. also Thureau-Dangin, R. A. iii. p. 139, l. 18. Furthermore, if this distinction holds, we cannot say very well that sacrifices were offered to Gudea patesi and *Ur-*(*dingir*) *Kal pa-te-si.* Sacrifices are only for gods[2].

There is further nothing to lead us to suppose that the (*dingir*) *Dun-gi* mentioned in those tablets is Dungi I. At the time when Scheil wrote his article, he was not aware of the existence of a Dungi III., and thus, because Gudea and Dungi were mentioned together, he, like Lehmann (Zwei Probleme), thought they must be Dungi I., king of Ur, and Gudea, patesi of Shirpurla (see above, pp. 34 and 347).

We have already seen, when considering the names of the months, that under Dungi III. (or the fourth dynasty of Ur) the eighth month was called *Itu EZEN* (*dingir*) *DUN-GI*—a new name, for it only occurs during this period. Hence it is natural to suppose that Dungi III. himself had dedicated this month as a festival in his own honour, in which, under the patesi *EZEN* (*dingir*) *Dun-gi,* sacrifices were to be offered to him as god. In addition to this, the day of the new moon and the fifteenth day of each month were also 'sacred to him.' Sacrifices offered on these days were

(*Ga*)*lu* (*dingir*) *Gu-de-a*, R. T. xviii. p. 72; also *Amat* (*GIN*)-(*dingir*) *Gu-de-a*, ibid.

[1] The name Gudea is very common at this time; comp. e.g. C. T. 12231, x., two Gudeas mentioned.

[2] This is clear from the analogy of the case. Thureau-Dangin has published a similar tablet in R. A. iii. p. 135. Among the parties for whom *GAR*, *KAŠ*, *KU*, *ZAL* were appointed are to be found the *GIR-ǦAL*, the slaves *ǦU-NI-BAR*, the slaves of Anshan, the slaves of Shimash, the slaves of Kimash, the *KUR-BI SANGU DU-GAB*, the slaves of Marḫashi, the (*ga*)*lu KIN-GI-A* (=*mâr šipri*, Br. 10768), the asses *ZI-LUM*, Gudea the patesi, god Dunpauddu, and lastly god Dungi. This tablet shows that the grain, &c., were appointed not as sacrifices for Gudea—or else he had to be a (*dingir*) Gudea—but simply as a kind of food (*šag-gal*) or sustenance, as in the case of the different slaves.

called *AB-AB UD-SAR UD-XV*, i.e. 'offerings (?) on the new moon (and) on the fifteenth day.' This is proved by the subscription of the tablets above referred to, in which mention is made of the following months in this connection: *ŠU-KUL*, *EZEN* *(dingir) Dun-gi*, *ŠE-IL-LA*, *GAN-MAŠ*, *ZIB-KÙ*, *MU-ŠU-UL*, *AMAR-A-SI*. The incompleteness of the tablets leads us to suppose that the same was true of the other months.

Thus we see that during this time (Ur IV.) kings were looked upon as 'gods[1]'; that a special month was dedicated to them (as in the case of Dungi III.); and that on the new moon (= first day) and on the fifteenth day of each month special sacrifices were to be offered to them.

After the death of Dungi III., the eighth month was retained as 'the festival of Dungi[2].' The first and fifteenth day of each month, however, were reserved for the special service in honour of the individual king that might happen to reign.

It is self-evident that the king was not worshipped *in persona*, but—like Gudea of old—he made statues of himself and placed them in different temples, commanding the people to sacrifice to 'this double.' Clearly the king could not be in all the different places of his realm, hence the necessity for this expedient. This is clearly corroborated by a tablet published by Thureau-Dangin in Rec. Trav. xix. 186, which reads:

4 *gir-lam* 3 *ḳa giš-ma*
statue of Gimil-Sin (in) the temple of Ningirsu
4 *gir-lam* 3 *ḳa giš-ma*
statue of Gimil-Sin (in) the temple of Ba'u
4 *gir-lam* 3 *ḳa giš-ma*

[1] Nay, even directly called 'god.' See e.g. C. T. 94-10-16, 4, rev. iii.: *a-šag (dingir) Bur-(dingir) Sin dingir-ni ki-ag*, the field of Bur-Ṣin, his beloved god. Comp. also such names as *(dingir) Dun-gi-zi-kalam-ma*, *(Ga)lu-(dingir) Dungi*, *Lugal-(dingir) Dungi* in C. T., and *(dingir) Dungi-bâni*, *Mêr-Dungi*, *Dungi-ili* in R. T. xviii. p. 72, and especially C. T. part vii. No. 12939.

[2] This follows from the fact that even at the time of *Gimil-Sin* the month *Itu EZEN (dingir) Dun-gi* occurs. See C. T. 13882.

temple of Gimil-Sin

Offerings (*AB-AB*) on the new moon, and on the fifteenth day of the month *ŠU-KUL*.

One year after Gimil-Sin had built the wall of the east (called) '*muriḳ Tidnum*' (i. e. which keeps away Tidnum).

It is, however, remarkable that the successors of Dungi III should retain the eighth month as the *EZEN* (*dingir*) *DUN-GI*, while they appointed the fifteenth day of each month to their own worship. Surely this fact gives to Dungi III. a special significance. He stood out as the 'hero-god' during this whole period. Are we not justified in regarding him as the founder of this new dynasty whose memory had to be kept sacred? This, I think, is the only solution, or else would not his successors have been anxious also to set apart a special month for their own honour? But they do not do it, and because they do not do it they *ipso facto* testify to the greatness of this king—the king who founded their dynasty, and who, during a reign of at least fifty-one years, was able to seize the kingship of the four corners of the world[1].

In course of time, and probably not very long after the reign of such a 'god-king,' the kings seem to have been worshipped under the form of a '*star*.' Scheil recently published a remarkable tablet (Z. A. xii. p. 265), which states expressly that 2 *ḳa* (of grain) were given to (*dingir*) *Bur*-(*dingir*) *Sin*, the *MUL AMAR-UD*, i. e. to Bur-Sin, who is the star Marduk.

Thus then we see that the kings of this dynasty assumed for themselves the title of 'god,' built temples in their honour, placed their statues in the different sanctuaries, appointed certain offerings in honour of their 'doubles,' instituted a certain month (the eighth), and besides this the first and fifteenth day of each month, as times on which sacrifices were to be offered to them. Certain officers were appointed to conduct these services: for the eighth month (*EZEN* (*dingir*) *Dungi*), the patesi *EZEN* (*dingir*) *Dungi*, and for the first

[1] This also speaks against the theory of Winckler, that our Dungi III was the same as Dungi son of Ur-Gur.

and fifteenth day of each month, the *ḲA-ŠU-GAB* (see Scheil, Rec. Trav. xviii. 71 ff.)—apparently an officer of minor importance, and as such standing under the supervision of the patesi, whose duty clearly it was to officiate before 'the statues' (hence *ḲA-ŠU-GAB* (*dingir*) *Gu-de-a*).

From these considerations it follows:

(1) That only kings could call themselves 'god,' and be worshipped as such while still living.

(2) That in course of time the statues of any ruler—be he patesi or king—were looked upon, because they had been placed in the temples, as gods, which were to be worshipped and to which sacrifices were to be offered [1].

[1] Hence such names as (*dingir*) *Iši-* (*dingir*) *Dagan* (p. 262, 42); (*dingir*) *Iši-* (*dingir*) *Ba-u* (ibid); (*dingir*) *Ur-*(*dingir*) *Dun-pa-ud-du* (E. A. H. 91; see p. 327); (*dingir*) *Ur-*(*dingir*) *En-zu-na* (v. R. 52, 29 *a*; iii. R. 68, 20 *c*); (*dingir*) (*Ga*)*lu-An-na* (iii. R. 68, 11 *a*); (*dingir*) (*Ga*)*lu-*(*dingir*) *Nin-ib* (iii. R. 67, 54 *a*); (*dingir*) *Ur-gu-ru* (!) (ii. R. 55, 8, 9 *c d*), &c., stand either for old kings or old patesis, whose names—with the exception of probably (*dingir*) *Ur-gu-ru* (= Ur-Gur I ?)—have not yet been found on tablets written by themselves.

APPENDIX

THE E. A. HOFFMAN COLLECTION

OF BABYLONIAN CLAY-TABLETS IN THE GENERAL THEOLOGICAL SEMINARY NEW YORK CITY

THE E. A. HOFFMAN COLLECTION
OF BABYLONIAN CLAY-TABLETS IN THE GENERAL THEOLOGICAL SEMINARY NEW YORK CITY

In the year 1896 the Very Rev. E. A. Hoffman, D.D., LL.D., D.C.L., Dean of the General Theological Seminary, New York City, bought from Mr. Noorian, formerly interpreter for the Pennsylvania Expedition to Nippur, a collection of old and modern Babylonian clay-tablets. In 1898 the same benefactor purchased six more tablets of singular beauty and interest, which proved to be from the time of Ur-Ba'u (two *cônes*, E. A. H. 112, 113), Gudea (one *cône* and one dolerite tablet, E. A. H. 114, 115) (both of whom were patesis of Shirpurla-Telloh), Rim-Aku or Rim-Sin, a contemporary of Abraham (E. A. H. 262), and one tablet antedating even the so-called Monument Blau; see above, p. 12, note 1.

The whole collection now comprises 262 tablets and fragments. Dr. Body, who was present when these tablets were bought, and who showed special interest in ascertaining whence they came, reports that the places where these documents have been found are Telloh, Borsippa, Warka, and Nippur.

The whole collection may be conveniently divided into two parts—

I. Old Babylonian, E. A. H. 1–194, 261, 262.

II. New Babylonian, E. A. H. 195–260.

The oldest ruler of the Old Babylonian period, as represented in this collection, is Ur-Ba'u, patesi of Shirpurla, 3500 B.C., and the youngest of the New Babylonian is Philip—written either *Pi-il-ip-su šar matâti* (E. A. H. 199) or *Pi-li-ip-su šarru* (*šattu* 2[kam], E. A. H.

245). The whole collection therefore covers a period of over 3,000 years.

I. **The Old Babylonian Period** may be classified again under the following heads:—

(*a*) Representatives of the *later patesis of Shirpurla-Telloh*[1]—

α. Ur-Ba'u, E. A. H. 112, 113.

β. Gudea, E. A. H. 114, 115.

(*b*) Tablets belonging to a certain patesi of *Ash-nun-na-ki*, Ur-Ningishzidda by name, E. A. H. 110, 111.

(*c*) The fourth dynasty of Ur, E. A. H. 1–109, and also E. A. H. 116–157. Among the rulers belonging to this dynasty we find the following mentioned:—Dungi III.[2], Bur-Sin II., and Gimil-Sin. E. A. H. 1–109 are dated, and may be arranged as follows:—

α. Tablets belonging to Dungi III., E. A. H. 94–103, 1–25, and 104.

β. Bur-Sin II., E. A. H. 26–90.

γ. Gimil-Sin, E. A. H. 91–93.

δ. Tablets containing dates, which cannot as yet with certainty be referred to any of the rulers of this dynasty, E. A. H. 105–109.

ε. Tablets which palaeographically belong to the fourth dynasty of Ur, E. A. H. 116–157.

ξ. Fragments belonging to this period, E. A. H. 158–173.

α. With regard to the arrangement of these tablets, see above *sub* 'dates of Dungi III.,' where it will be seen that O. B. I. 125—on the basis of which we put E. A. H. 94–103 *before* E. A. H. 1–25—does not belong to the reign of Ine-Sin, but to that of Dungi III.

Among the tablets belonging to Dungi III. we have eleven 'case-tablets'—mostly receipts (*šu-ba-ti*) of grain (*ŠE*). This grain in most cases is designated by *lugal* = *prima sorte*. Sometimes

[1] These have been translated and explained above under the two rulers respectively. See pp. 184 and 194.

[2] Only in a seal-impression of a tablet dated from the reign of Bur-Sin II. See p. 251.

the tablets also state the price of the grain and for whom it was bought. Comp. E. A. H. 1:

10 *gur. še lugal*
gur UD-KA-BAR-[1]*la*
ŠAG-GAL[2] *gud-ku.*

The recipient of the grain is generally the *ENGAR*. Comp. E. A. H. 3:

8 *engar* 3 × 60 + 30 (sc. *ḳa*) *še-lugal-la*
še-bi 5 *gur* 3 × 60 (sc. *ḳa*).

These case-tablets are all 'sealed,' which seals give the name of the writer (*dup-sar*), and that of his father, together with the latter's title—whenever he held an office. Comp. seal of E. A. H. 4:

(*Ga*)*lu-Šir-pur-la-ki*
dup-sar
dumu Ur-(*dingir*) *Ninâ*
nu-banda-[*gud*].

Sometimes the seal-inscription is in the form of an invocation. Comp. E. A. H. 25:

A-tu
PA-AL (= *šabrû*) *lugal*
Lugal-ka-gi-na
dup-sar
nitaǧ-zu.

These seal-inscriptions are invariably accompanied by the well-known legend peculiar to the fourth dynasty of Ur: The moon-god sitting upon the throne accepts the devotions of the *dup-sar*, who is led on his left hand by a minor god before the city-god of Ur, lifting up his right hand in prayer.

E. A. H. 5 is interesting, because on it occurs the name *IP ša IŠI-DA-GAN*. Comp. O. B. I. 125, rev., fourth line from the end, and what has been said under 'dates of Dungi III.' Although this case-tablet is somewhat mutilated, yet we may restore that portion as follows:—

[1] Pronounce *ZA-BAR* = *siparru*, Br. 7819.
[2] *ŠAG-GAL*; comp. ii. R. 39, 54 *c*, *d* = *ukullû*, H. W. B. p. 54.

60 + *x-gur* 7 *ḳa gar-zid lugal*
ŠAG-GAL IP ša Iši-Da-gan

i. e. feed for the damḳar of Ishi-Dagan. (See however Index, nom. pr. *sub* IP-ša . . . .)

Besides receipts, we find also expenses (*zig-ga*) of grain (E. A. H. 7). Among those containing lists of expenses should probably be classed tablets like E. A. H. 9:

5 × 600 + 9 × 60 + 7 *gur* 120 (*ḳa*) *še-lugal*
SAR[1] *UD-DU-A*
ŠAG-bi-ta
5 × 600 + 9 × 60 + 7 *gur* 120 (*ḳa*) *še-lugal*
NI-DUB (= *šapâku*).

E. A. H. 11 is also extremely interesting. After stating how many *GIN* (shekels) of money (*ku-babbar*) flowed into the treasury from different persons:

12 *gin IGI-3-GÀL* (= ¾) *ku-babbar*
ki-Ur-(dingir)*-Ninâ dumu Ur-*(dingir) *Ba-u-ta*
9 *gin ki-Nam-ḫa-ni-ta*, &c.,

it gives, on rev., l. 1, the total:

ŠU-NIGIN ½ *ma-na* 8 *gin*
lal-igi-6-gàl ku-babbar,

and goes on (l. 2):—

šag-bi-ta
½ *ma-na ku-babbar*
še-bi 27 (?) *gur*, &c.,

thus stating how much grain was bought for the money received.

E. A. H. 18 has two dates: *mu-uš-sa Ki-maš-ki ba-ḫul* and *mu-uš-sa Ki-maš-ki ba-ḫul mu-uš-sa-a-bi*, thus showing that the explanation of *mu-uš-sa-a-bi* given above is correct.

The remaining tablets are simply accounts of herds, which will be explained further below. Tablets like these we shall call '*MU-GUB ZIG-GA*' tablets.

E. A. H. 94 is interesting and important, proving that the expression *ŠAG-bi-ta* . . . *NI-DUB* is = *ŠAG-bi-ta* . . . *ZIG-*

[1] Thus to be read most probably, and not *ŠE-GIŠ*.

GA, which latter we find on this tablet. It also has two dates: *Mu Ša-aš-ru-um-*^{ki} *ba-ǵul* and *MU EN* $^{(dingir)}$ *URU-KI MAŠ-E-RU(M) NI-PAD.*

E. A. H. 95 is a receipt (*šu-ba-ti*) of *ZID*, (*ZID*)-*GIG*[1], and *ŠE*. The recipient is (*GA*)*LU*-^{dingir}-? (? = the sign for the god of *GIŠ-UḪ*-^{ki}).

E. A. H. 97, *Lugal-ka-gi-na* receives *ŠE*.

E. A. H. 101 states how many *gur* and *ḳa* of *še*. different *ENGAR-RI-NE ŠU-BA-AB-TI.*

E. A. H. 102, 103 are '*šag-bi-ta*' tablets, the latter having two dates: *MU EN* $^{(dingir)}$ *URU-KI MAŠ-E NI-PAD* and *MU Ša-aš-ru*-^{ki} *ba-ǵul*. For the date of E. A. H. 104 see *sub.* Dungi III., p. 265, 51.

β. Tablets from the time of Bur-Sin II.

Among these tablets we find 27 case-tablets, mostly 'receipts of grain,' but also of

GUNIN-UD (= *kupru*), E. A. H. 63;
ZAL + *GIŠ* (*šamnu*), E. A. H. 70;
ZID (*ḳêmu*), E. A. H. 87;
KA-LUM-ŠIG ('sweet dates,' *suluppu damḳu*) *lugal*, E. A. H. 60;
NI-NUN (= *ḫimêtu*), E. A. H. 72, &c., &c.

By far the greater number are *MU-GUB ZIG-GA* tablets; some are accounts of wool (*SIG* = *šipatû*), all of which are treated of in full further below.

Of special interest seems to be E. A. H. 55. This tablet is dated from the *E-GAL* of Bur-Sin II., and gives an account of how many *ḲA* of dates (*KA-LUM*) were received for the sustenance (*KǓ*) of different servants (*KAL*) at different times (*A-DU*):—

116 *KAL KA-LUM* 2 *ḳa-ta*
8 *KAL* 5 *ḳa-ta*

[1] In Neo-Babylonian contract-tablets *GIG* is written either *GIG-BA* (sometimes with *ŠE* before it, and sometimes not), *GIG-BI*, or *GIG-A-BA* (Strassen, Darius, 198, ll. 18, 20). It is mentioned *after ŠE-BAR* (wheat) and *AŠ-AN* (barley). Hilprecht wants to read it *GUL-BA*, comparing the Talmudic גולבא, and translate it by "spelt."

KA-LUM-bi 272 *ḳa*
a-du 1 ^{kam}
118 *KAL* 3 *ḳa-ta*
KA-LUM-bi 1 (*gur*) 54 *ḳa*
a-du 2 ^{kam}, &c.

Most of these tablets having been translated further below, we now turn to—

γ. Those of Gimil-Sin.

Only three tablets belong to the reign of this ruler, E. A. H. 91–93.

E. A. H. 91, however, is the largest tablet in this collection, measuring 280 × 270 × 45 mm. Originally it was inscribed on obverse and reverse; the former side, however, is almost completely destroyed. On the reverse we have nine columns, with an average inscription of fifty lines. The beginning of Col. i. on reverse, which apparently is the continuation of Col. ix. on obverse, reads:—

40 ^{giš}-*GUG-A*
ki-Ur-Ba-bi-ta
PA NI-NA-NA
80 ^{giš}-*GUG-A*
GIR UR-KA-?-KI
ki-GU-U-MU-*ta*
50 *ḳa-lum*
200 ^{giš}-GUG-A
$^{(\text{dingir})}$ *Nin-sun*
50 *ḳa-lum*
ki-Amêl-ili (*UR-DINGIR-RA*)-*ta*
PA NI-NA-NA
50 *ḳa-lum*.

Besides this ^{giš}-*GUG* (=Br. 6912?)-*A* and the *KA-LUM* are also mentioned the ^{giš}-*MA*, ^{giš}-*MA-AM-A*, all of which are measured according to *GUR* and *ḲA*.

From the above-given example it is evident that l. 9 indicates 'the person for whom' = 'For Ninsun'; l. 11, the 'place from which,' or the 'person from whom,' the *KA-LUM* were brought; l. 13

gives the 'total'; l. 12 probably is the officer (*PA*) who receives the *KA-LUM* for Ninsun.

Among other gods who thus received *giš-GUG-A* or *KA-LUM* are to be found: *(dingir) Ur-(dingir) Dun-pa-ud-du*; *(dingir) Ninâ*; *(dingir) Nin-Mar-ki*; *(dingir) Nin-ḫar-sag*; *(dingir) Innanna*; *(dingir) Nin-giš-zid-da*; *(dingir) En-ki*; *(dingir) Im*; and also the following persons: *Ur-(dingir) KAL pa-te-si*; *Ur-gar pa-te-si*; *Gu-de-a*; *AMAT-Dun-pa-ud-du*; *Ur-(dingir) Ba-u*; and the following houses or temples: the *Ti-ra-aš* (see Ur-Ninâ); *An-ta-sur-ra* (see Enannatum); *(dingir) Dun-pa-ud-du E-GAL*; *E-BAR-BAR*, &c., &c.

This tablet being extremely interesting on account of the names, places, cities, and houses mentioned, I purpose to give a transcription and translation elsewhere.

E. A. H. 92 is a receipt of 'dates,' and E. A. H. 93 one of 'money.'

δ. Among the tablets belonging to this section, E. A. H. 108 is important.

We find on this case-tablet the same seal-impression as on E. A. H. 25, which latter tablet belonged to the reign of Dungi III. Should the date of E. A. H. 108, *mu EN-NAM-? (dingir) Dun-gi-ra-ge ba-DU ba-tug*, therefore be referred to the reign of Dungi III.? If this were true, then the king would be the *EN* (lord) of his own *nam-?* (cult), which however is hardly possible. We have seen above that the successor of Dungi III. was Bur-Sin II., but among the dates of Bur-Sin II. we do not find any mention of this date. The tablet is also important because on it two items (*GU-GAL* and *GU-TUR*) are mentioned, not found elsewhere in this collection. The whole inscription is as follows:—

Obv. 11 *gur* 30 *ḳa ZID lugal*
4 *gur* 3 × 60 + 10 (= *BAR*) + 1 *ḳa* (*ZID*)-*GIG*
Seal.
120 + 30 GU-GAL-GAL 120 + 30 GU-TUR-TUR [1]
. . . . . *ki-UR-NIGIN* (Br. 9251)-*GAR-ta*

[1] Comp. R. A. iv. No. iii. pl. xv. No. 44, where *gu-gu-gal-gal* and *gu-gu-tur-tur* are mentioned as being *im-ḫur*, 'received.' They are the great *GU* and the small *GU*, i. e. '*Hülsenfrüchte*'; hence probably, as Hilprecht thinks, 'beans' (the large ones) and 'lentils' (the small ones).

Rev. *DUB* (= tablet of) *Lugal-ka-gi-na-ka*

Seal.

Itu Innanna.

Date.

ε. Among these are four case-tablets. The majority of the tablets are receipts or expenses of grain, flour, &c., &c. Some are accounts of herds (*mu-gub zig-ga*), others 'skins,' and others again of 'wool.'

Of special interest are E. A. H. 139–153, all belonging to the same class. They are lists of expenses (*zig-ga*) of 'date wine,' 'flour,' 'food,' and 'oil.' E. A. H. 140, e. g., reads partly:—

5 *ḳa kaš*
I-šar-a-a-DUG dumu nu-banda
1 *kaš lugal*
eri An-sha-an-^{ki}*-me*
Gir I-šar-a-DUG dumu nu-banda
An-sha-an-^{ki}*-ta DU-ni.*

The *eri An-sha-an-*^{ki}*-me* (*me* = pl. sign) here referred to are undoubtedly the prisoners made by the kings of the fourth dynasty of Ur.

(*d*) The dynasty of the kings of *Larsa* (Rim-Sin), E. A. H. 262—which tablet is also published in C. T. part I, No. 96-4-4, 2.

(*e*) The dynasty of the Kassites, E. A. H. 175–194. Of the representatives of this dynasty we find in the E. A. H. collection the following mentioned:—

Bur-na-bu-ri-ia-aš, E. A. H. 175.

Na-zi-Mu-ru-ut-ta-aš, the fourth year (E. A. H. 176) and the thirteenth year (E. A. H. 177), i.e. 1290 and 1281 B.C. respectively.

Ka-diš (sic)-*man-Tur-gu*, the third year (E. A. H. 178), i.e. 1265 B.C., and the thirteenth year, i. e. 1255 B.C. (E. A. H. 179).

$^{(dingir)}$ *Ku-dur-ri-*$^{(dingir)}$ *EN-LIL* (= *Turgu*), the eighth year, i.e. about 1364 B. C., E. A. H. 180.

ŠIBIR (Br. 8847) *šarru*, E. A. H. 181; comp. *Ašurnaṣira-pal* II, Annals, col. ii. 84: 'Sibir, king of Karduniash.'

According to the analogy of the subscriptions already found, we would refer E. A. H. 182 to this period, which mentions, after the date *mu* 10 *kam*, a certain *GIR-RI-A-AB-BA*. Is this latter to be classed among the kings of this dynasty? The absence of the sign for *Lugal* would not tell against this, for both Burnaburiash and Nazi-Muruttash have not the sign for *Lugal* after their names.

Some of these tablets are receipts (*ma-ḫi-ir*) of *ŠE*, others lists of grain-income paid to various temples in a certain city during specified months. Comp. e.g. E. A. H. 177:

ŠE GIŠ-BAR-GAL ša i-na libbi (*ŠAG*) *Te-li-ti-ki ša šatti* 12 *kam Na-zi-Mu-ru-ut-ta-aš iš-tu* (*arḫu*) *Tišrîti* (*DUL-AZAG*, Br. 9608) *ša šatti* 12 *kam a-di* (*arḫu*) *Nisannu* (*BÀR*) *ša šatti* 13 *kam i-na ZA-RAD-IM-ki nàd-nu* (*SE-NU*).

The body of the tablet then further states the various items received or given by sundry persons for the different gods. At the end it gives the 'total':

napḫaru (Br. 1145) *ŠE nàd-nu ištu* (*TA*) (*arḫu*) *Tišrîti adi* (*EN*) (*arḫu*) *Nisannu* (*BAR-ZAG-A*) *i-na ZA-RAD-IM-ki nàd-nu šattu* 13 *kam Na-zi-Mu-ru-ut-ta-aš*.

Others have a shorter heading. Comp. E. A. H. 178:

ŠE GIŠ-BAR-GAL ša i-na KAR-UD-NUN-ki ištu (*TA*) (*arḫu*) *Nisannu* (*BÀR*) *adi* (*arḫu*) *Ululu* (Br. 10758) *ša šatti* 3 *kam Ka-diš-man-Tur-gu a-na ŠE-BA* (or *TU?*) *nàd-nu*.

Or we find only:

ŠE-GIŠ-BAR-GAL MU-BI-IM

(i.e. which was expended yearly).

II. Modern Babylonian Tablets.

The tablets written during this period are very varied as regards their contents:

(*a*) Astronomical texts, E. A. H. 195, 196.

(*b*) Lists of gods, E. A. H. 197–200.

E. A. H. 197, 198 are identical. They have three columns; e. g.

A | *A* | ^(ilu)^ *A-nu-um*, &c.

E. A. H. 197 has a long inscription on the reverse, the beginning of which is much mutilated.

(*c*) Contract-tablets from the reigns of the following rulers:—

a. *Šamaš-šum-ukîn*, the thirteenth year of his reign, E. A. H. 202.

Bêl-uballi-it brings a lawsuit against *Nabû-u-ṣal-li* and *Šamaš-nâṣi-ir*, to return to him the *f. Il-'-e-tu* and the *amêlu ḳin-ni-ši*. The two defendants are not willing to do this, but offer 5 *ma-na* of money for those slaves. *Bêl-uballi-iṭ* refuses to accept this money, goes to a *dâinu*, and complains. The judge decides in favour of *Bêl-uballi-it*, and orders that the slaves be given back to the original possessor. *Nabû-u-ṣal-li* and *Šamaš-nâṣi-ir* recognized their evil action, and '*ud-da-ru mimma a-na Bêl-uballi-iṭ i-nam-di-nu*,' i. e. 'they felt sorry for that which they had done to *Bêl-uballi-iṭ*."

The tablets of this period are generally sealed, which seal is attested by the scribe. Comp. e. g. E. A. H. 227, left side:

Kunuk Marduk-zêr-ib-ni dup-sar.

The same seal-inscription is also found on the right side. Sometimes we find, besides the *kunuk*, also the *ṣu-pur*, i. e. 'nail-imprints' of certain *(amêlu) mu-kiñ-nu*,' or 'witnesses,' who are always mentioned in these contract-tablets. Comp. e. g. E. A. H. 202:

ṣu-pur Nabû-u-ṣal-li u Šamaš-nâṣi-ir kîma kunukki-šu-nu, i. e. 'nail-imprints of N. and Š. instead of their seals.'

These nail-imprints—generally three in number—are put in most cases on the four sides of the tablet. After the witnesses have been mentioned—who are introduced either by:

(1) *ina ku-nuk duppi MU-meš* (= *šu'ati*) followed by *pâni* (or *maḫir* = *ŠI*), or by only

(2) *amêlu mu-kin-nu*, or even shortly

(3) *ina pâni*—then follows the *amêlu šangu ša-ṭir duppi*, or often shortly represented by the simple *dup-sar*, i. e. the writer. Then

follows the place, where the tablet was written, ending with the month, day, and year of the specific king of Babylon under whose reign the business was transacted. Comp. E. A. H. 202:

Bar-sip-^*ki* *(arḫu) Tišrîtu ûmu* 13 ^*kam* *šattu* 13 ^*kam* *Šamaš-šum-ukîn šar DIN-TIR-*^*ki* (i. e. Babylon).

Sometimes it happens that some persons are present at a certain business transaction, who are not witnesses, '*amêlu mu-kin-nu*,' in a legal sense. These persons are introduced generally by '*ina a-ša-bi*,' 'in the presence of.'

Among other kings mentioned on these tablets we find:

β. *Nabû-kudur-uṣur šar DIN-TIR-*^*ki*, the fourteenth year of his reign, E. A. H. 203, 204.

γ. *Nergal-šar-uṣur šar DIN-TIR-*^*ki*, the first year of his reign, E. A. H. 205.

δ. *Nabû-nâ-'-id šar DIN-TIR-*^*ki*, the third and fourth year of his reign, E. A. H. 206, 207.

ε. *Ku-ra-aš šar DIN-TIR-*^*ki* *šar matâti*, the seventh year of his reign, E. A. H. 208.

ξ. *Kam-bu-zi-ia šar DIN-TIR-*^*ki* *šar matâti*, the first and sixth year of his reign, E. A. H. 209, 210.

η. E. A. H. 211–232 are tablets dating from the different years of king Darius, who generally bears the title *šar DIN-TIR-*^*ki* (or *KA-DINGIR-[RA]-*^*ki*) *šar matâti* (written either *KUR-*^*meš* or *KUR-KUR* or even *KUR-KUR-*^*meš*). The *first* year is the earliest and the thirty-fifth is the latest mentioned. Remarkable also are the different forms in which the name Darius occurs:

Da-ri-'-a-muš
Da-ri-'-uš-šu
Da-ri-'-ia-muš
Da-ri-ia (=Br. 12190)-*a-muš*
Da-ri-ia (Br. 12190)-*muš*
Da-a-ri-ia (*I*+*A*)-*muš*
Da-ri-ia (*I*+*A*)-*muš*
Da-ri-'-šu

Da-ri-a-muš
Da-ri-'-muš
Da-ri-'-a-mu-uš
Da-ri-ia (I + A)-a-muš
Da-a-ri-muš
Da-a-ri-ia (I + A)-'-uš-šu
Da-ri-ia (I + A)-mu-uš
Da-ri-a-mu-uš

θ. The second year of *Iḫ-ši-ia-ar-ši* (Xerxes), 'king of Babylon, king of the lands,' E. A. H. 233.

ι. Tablets belonging to Artaxerxes, whose name is written either *Ar-tak-šat-su* or *Àr-tak-šat-su.* He bears the title of *šarru* only. The tablets are dated from the years between the third and thirty-ninth inclusive, E. A. H. 234–244.

κ. Two tablets from the time of Philip, E. A. H. 199 and 245.

λ. E. A. H. 246–260 are fragments of New Babylonian tablets.

The contents of these New Babylonian tablets cover almost everything which may happen in the daily intercourse of men. There we have *bequests* (*ina ḫu-ud libbi-šu. ik-nu-uk-ma pâni u-ša-ad-gil*); *selling* (*a-na kaspi iddin*) of shares, lands, property of various kinds, &c., &c.; statements that one person owes another (*ina eli* or *ina muḫḫi*) dates, figs, wine, or money, which latter has to be paid back either with or without interest. Sometimes it is also stated that if the debtor fails to pay by a certain date, then the money shall bear interest (*ki lâ iddannu irabbi*). Rents for houses or gardens, lawsuits, and many other interesting 'contracts' are also to be found among the tablets of this collection.

Most of these tablets are dated from Borsippa, the old *Ki-nu-nir-ki*; others come from *Gir-su-ki*; *Tik-ab-ba-ki*, *Ninâ-ki*, *Uru-um-ki-ma*, *En-lil-ki*, *Unug-ki-ga*, &c., &c. Dr. Body's statement (see above) is therefore fully corroborated by the subscriptions of these tablets.

It may be well to supplement this general description with a more detailed account of the Old Babylonian tablets, especially with those belonging to the fourth dynasty of Ur. They give us a fair representation of the daily life of the people of Babylonia some 500 years before the time of Abraham. It will be seen that almost all of them are related to what may be called the 'rural life' of the Old Babylonians, thus showing that the chief occupation of the people at that time was 'to till the ground and to raise cattle.'

Tablets called 'MU-GUB ZIG-GA.'

E. A. H. 13–16, 19-24, from the time of Dungi III.

E. A. H. 28–31, 35–46, from the time of Bur-Sin II.

The above-given tablets are 'lists of cattle,' and state—

1. How many of those cattle, which compose the flock of a certain shepherd (*ENGAR* or *NI-KU*), whose name is given generally at the bottom of each tablet, are 'present' (*MU-GUB*).

2. How many were in some way or another 'removed' from the flock. This 'removal' of the flocks may be caused either by—

(*a*) expenditure (*ZIG-GA*), or

(*b*) sacrifices (*RIG-RIG-GA*) or some 'malady' called *ID-PA*, or

(*c*) *LAL-NI*, or

(*d*) death (*BA-TIL*).

In this paragraph we very often find that only the formulas are given, without actually stating the number of the sheep which thus were either 'consumed' or 'snatched away[1].' Sometimes we also find that the number was given, but erased again.

Following this, the sum total (*ŠU-NIGIN*) gives us the whole number of the cattle that either are present or removed.

Then follows the name of the shepherd (*ni-ku* or *engar*) to whom the flock belongs; sometimes also the name of the chief shepherd (*nu-banda-gud*) or overseer (*PA*), under whose supervision the shepherd stands. The tablet concludes with the name of the city

[1] This shows that the *dupsar* wrote ahead while the cattle were counted, leaving the spaces blank, if the result of the counting required it.

(introduced by *ŠAG*) where it is written, followed by the date (*MU*).

Without going further into detail here, it will be advisable to explain—

(1) the expressions used in these tablets, and

(2) the different names of the cattle.

This will be followed by a list of names to be found in the above-given tablets, together with a translation of four of them—E. A. H. 14, 19, 35, 37—which will be sufficient for our purpose.

1. *MU-GUB.*

(*a*) With this expression the first paragraph of these lists concludes. In the *šu-nigin* paragraph the expression is repeated, but has the form *GUB-BA*. It signifies the 'cattle' that 'are there,' 'are existing,' 'are present.' *GUB*, Br. 4893=*nazâzu*, H. W. B. 455.

In E. A. H. 15, rev., 2, we have: *šu-nigin* 117 *udu gub*, consequently only *GUB* for *GUB-BA*. The expression *UDU* is remarkable here, showing that under the *UDU* were classed *ganam*, *udu-uš*, *sal-puḫâdu*, *puḫâdu-uš*, and the *uriṣu-sag*. In none of the other tablets does *UDU* occur in this *šu-nigin* paragraph.

For *MU-GUB* we sometimes find in these tablets *GUB-BA-A-AN*, apparently with the same meaning. Comp. R. A. iii. p. 122 and p. 123, note to line 4, and below, 6, 1, 2.

(*b*) In some tablets *GUB-BA-A-AN* has the meaning 'to furnish,' 'to deliver'=*kânu* ii [1].

(*c*) In the expressions:

gud-engar-GUB-BA
(dingir) Nin-Mar-ki-ka, E. A. H. 33, 27, 28

(comp. also E. A. H. 34, 26, 27), the *GUB-BA* means only *kânu*= كان 'to be' (notice: *GUD-ENGAR*, not = *ENGAR-GUD*; see under Engar), and may be translated: 'oxen of the shepherd (who is in the service) of the goddess *Nin-Mar-ki*,' or 'oxen belonging to the shepherd employed by the goddess *Nin-Mar-ki*,' i. e. oxen of the shepherd of the goddess *Nin-Mar-ki*, or 'oxen employed for the tilling of the ground belonging to (كان ل) the goddess *Nin-Mar-ki*'; for *ENGAR* may belong also to *GUD*, explaining what kind of *GUD* they are. The latter seems to be the more probable explanation, because we find also such expressions as *DUP-SAR-GUD-ENGAR*.

ENGAR, according to Br. 1023, = *erēšu*, H. W. B. p. 140, and *irrišu*. The *GUD-ENGAR* then would be 'the oxen that are employed for the tilling of the ground,' '*bœufs employés à la culture*.'

(*d*) Such expressions as:

UZ GUB-BA
e-gal ša dingir-ri-ne
šag Ninâ-ki, R. A. iii. p. 126, and ibid. p. 124:
udu-? GUB-BA
e-gal ša dingir-ri-ne
šag Ninâ-ki

also occur. Here *GUB-BA* undoubtedly has the meaning كان ل = 'to belong': 'cattle belonging to "the temple of (*ša* = Semitism!) the gods" in Ninâ.' Thureau-Dangin, l.c., translates both passages with '*actif en chèvres*' and '*actif en moutons*.' But why? The translation '*appartenant*,' ibid. p. 131, is much better, and the only correct one.

2. *ZIG-GA*.

ZIG, according to Br. 2303, means *našû*, H. W. B. 484, 'to take,' 'take away,' and *nasâḫu*, H. W. B. 471, 'to take away,' 'carry away.'

ZIG-GA then signifies those cattle which 'were taken away' from those that 'were present,' i.e. from the herd. It may not be impossible that the animals which are said to be *ZIG-GA* are those that 'were consumed,' in contradistinction to those that were '*rig-rig-ga*.'

ZIG-GA then may stand for 'consumed,' 'expended,' 'expenditure' in general.

ZIG-GA—

(*a*) is found alone, without any subject. This is generally the case; comp. E. A. H. 19, 10.

(*b*) with a subject, stating who it was that 'took away,' 'expended' the sheep; e.g. E. A. H. 35, 8–10.

3. *RIG-RIG-GA.*

Br. 2594 gives for *RIG-RIG-GA* the Assyr. *laḳâtu*, H. W. B. 385, 'to take away,' 'snatch away.' Comp. ii. R. 38, 11, *e, f*, *amêlu* *LAG RIG-RIG-GA* = *la-ḳit kur-ba-an-ni* = *Gabensammler*, Delitzsch, H. W. B. 351, *sub* '*kurbannu*.' If *ZIG-GA* signifies the cattle that 'were consumed,' 'expended,' *RIG-RIG-GA* may denote those that were either—

(*a*) 'snatched away' for the purpose of *sacrifices*—so in the most cases where *RIG-RIG-GA* stands alone, i.e. *RIG-RIG-GA* = *maḳâtu* (Br. 2595), H. W. B. 424. Comp. also Sm. 2148 (in Delitzsch, W. B. p. 196; Z. K. ii. 6), 8–11:

GANAM ǴAD (sic?) *BI RIG-RIG-GA-MU*, i. e. *laḫ-ra ŭ pu-ḫad-sa ú-šam-ka-tu*;

UZ Br. 2030-*BI RIG-RIG-GA-MU*, i. e. *en-za ŭ la-la-ša ú-šam-ka-tu*;

or (*b*) that were 'killed,' 'snatched away' by some malady. In this latter case *RIG-RIG-GA* is followed by *ID-PA* (or *À-SIG*) = *ašakku*, H. W. B. 144. Comp. R. A. iii. p. 125, l. 12.

4. *LAL-NI.*

A. That this expression must signify 'cattle, which in some way or another are *not existing*,' is evident from the *ŠU-NIGIN* paragraph. There we find the cattle that are *LAL-NI* enumerated after those that were *ZIG-GA* and *RIG-RIG-GA*.

The places where *LAL-NI* occurs are:

(*a*) In O. B. I. 126, iii. 7–9, *LAL-NI* is found after *BA-TIL*:

1 (*sic*, read 2) *anšu-uš BA-TIL*
LABAR-A-AN
LAL-NI-2.

Ibid. iv. 16–18:

1 *anšu-uš BA-TIL*
LABAR-A-AN
LAL-NI-1

(*b*) after *RIG-RIG-GA*; see O. B. I. 126, v., the last four lines:

2 *anšu-sal*
1 *anšu-uš*
RIG-RIG-GA
LAL-NI-3

(*c*) Compare with the above O. B. I. 126, vii. 3 ff.:

a. 2 *lid*-[*al*]
1 *gud*-[*giš*]
RIG-RIG-GA
LABAR-A-AN
1 *gud-giš*
NIN-ŠID NA-DA-TUM-ta[1]
LAL-NI-2.

and ibid. col. vi. 21 ff.:

β. 1 *gud-giš*
1 *gud-I*
RIG-RIG-GA
LABAR-A-AN
2 *gud-giš*
NIN-ŠID NA-DA-TUM-ta.

From the above-given examples it is evident that *LAL-NI must* have some such meaning as '*minus*,' for in (*a*) 2 (*sic*, not 1) are said to be 'dead' (*BA-TIL*), hence we have a 'minus' of two (*LAL-NI*-2). In (*b*) three animals are said to be *RIG-RIG-GA*, 'taken away,' hence 'a minus of 3' (*LAL-NI*-3). In (*c*) *a.* three animals are said to be *RIG-RIG-GA*, but *one* animal was received from the estate (*NIN-ŠID*=*nikasu*) of Nadatum, thus diminishing the 'minus of 3' by one, hence we have only *LAL-NI*-2. In (*c*) *β.*

[1] For *NIN-ŠID* = *nikasu*, see Br. 12082; H. W. B. 463. For the nom. pr. *NA-DA-TUM*, see O. B. I. 124, obv., ii. 9. Translate: 'From the estate of Nadatum.' Nadatum seems to have been a man of wealth, as is apparent from O. B. I. 124, 126, in both of which tablets he is mentioned frequently, however with this distinction, that in O. B. I. 124 the expression always runs, *Na-da-tum-ta*, showing that he must have been living at the time (Dungi III.) when that tablet was written. In O. B. I. 126 we always find *NIN-ŠID NA-DA-TUM-ta* (at the time of Bur-Sin II. Nadatum was dead).

two animals are *RIG-RIG-GA*, but two others were received from the estate of *NADATUM*, hence no 'minus' (*LAL-NI*) is given. The examples under (*b*) and (*c*) confirm this explanation of *LAL-NI*; hence we would read in (*a*), instead of 1 *anšu-uš BA-TIL* = 2 *anšu-uš BA-TIL*. Such mistakes in the numerals seem, however, to be frequent in O. B. I. 126; comp. e. g. reverse, ii. 12–17 (l. 12 ought to be 6 *gud-giš*), ibid., obv., col. v. 16–21 (l. 16 ought to be 3 *gud-giš*). The above-given explanation is confirmed by the following other passages: O. B. I. 126, iv. 16–18; iv. 24–end; R. A. iii. p. 130, 11, 12.

We are thus justified in postulating for *LAL-NI* or *LAL-NI-A-AN* (only another form for *LAL-NI*; see 6, 1, 2) the meaning 'minus' or 'not existing.' The loss may have been caused either by the 'death' (*BA-TIL*) of the animal, or by a 'malady' (*Á-SIG*), or some other cause. Thus we understand why in the E. A. H. tablets the *LAL-NI* paragraph should in most cases give only the names for the cattle, without stating how many were lost. Comp. e. g.

E. A. H. 16, rev. 1, *LAL-NI* (erasure) *udu-uš*, none were lost.

E. A. H. 13, rev. 4–6, *ganam udu-uš*
puḫâdu
LAL-NI-A-AN.

This also throws light upon the following passage, E. A. H. 22, obv. 11, and rev. 1 ff.:—

LAL-NI 1 *ganam* 3 (erasure)[1]
LAL-NI-A-AN LABAR-A-AN
LAL-NI 22 *udu RUG-RUG IM-MA*,

i. e. Minus (loss) 1 ewe 3 mature sheep.
Deficit.
Minus 22 sheep, bodies (flesh = meat) of the *IM-MA*.

[1] The cattle after the numeral 3 ought not to have been erased, for the *ŠU-NIGIN* gives 26 *LAL-NI*. The traces on the tablet indicate 3 *udu-uš*.

The *LAL-NI* here then indicates the 'loss' which arose from the fact that the official, called *IM-MA*, 'took away' from the herd those twenty-two sheep which were *his* (sc. bodies) = *RUG-GA IM-MA*.

It is however important to note that the expression *LAL-NI* occurs *very often* just before the animals (sheep) called *RUG-GA* [*IM-MA*]; see E. A. H. 19, rev. 1; 20, rev. 5; 24, rev. 1; 29, rev. 1; 37, 9; 40, rev. 4, &c., &c. Now officials 'take away' or 'diminish' the herds only by those sheep which are paid them as 'their hire,' which are 'due to them,' which are their rightful 'income.' Indeed this latter signification is the only correct one here. With this agrees exactly a statement like this, which also occurs very often in the E. A. H. tablets:—

XX GIN KU-BABBAR
LAL-NI RUG-GA,

i. e. so and so many shekels of silver, minus their income (=interest), were received, &c.

If this be true, then the animals called *RUG-GA* served as a kind of compensation for the officials of the herds.

B. (*a*) Of similar meaning is another *LAL-NI*, occurring in those documents which state the *income* and the *expenditures* of certain things (e. g. grain, dates, flour, &c., &c.). After the expenditures have been subtracted from the income, and if there remains still a 'remainder,' this 'remainder' is marked by *LAL-NI*. The Neo-Babylonian equivalent is = *LAL-DI*, as has been shown by Oppert in Z. A. x. p. 49. *LAL-NI* then marks 'the balance on hand'='its remainder (is).'

This is the signification of the *LAL-NI* occurring in E. A. H. 37, 9 ff.:

5 *puḫádu-UŠ LAL-NI rug-ga sag-udu-uš-ku*
Ur-Gu-la ni-ku
zig-ga,

i. e. 5 he-lambs, remainder of the *RUG-GA* ('income'), exchanged
for the 'mature' sheep
Ur-Gula, the chief shepherd,
has taken away.

(*b*) If on the other hand the expenditures *exceed* the income, the sign *DIR* is used (*DIR*=Br. 3729, *atâru*, H. W. B. 248). *DIR* then is the opposite of *LAL-NI,* and means literally 'to go over the measure,' 'to exceed it.'

Note: *DIR* among other places is also used in E. A. H. 43, 6: 7 *puḫâdu-UŠ DIR.* Here *DIR* states 'the over and above' of the *puḫadâti* that were *MU-GUB,* for the very same *puḫâdu-UŠ* were mentioned already in l. 4.

C. *LAL,* when standing between two numerals, means 'minus,' lit. 'there remaineth.' E. g.

20-*LAL*-1 = 20 there remaineth (= minus) one = 19; comp. Lat. *un-de-viginti*

20-*LAL*-2 = 18 = Lat. *duo-de-viginti*

10-*LAL*-1 = 9, &c., &c.

Comp. Jensen, Kosm. p. 106, 2; Reissner, J. A. O. S. 18, p. 374.

5. In some of these tablets we find the expression *BA-TIL* = Hebr. מות, 'to die'; see R. A. iii. p. 127, l. 14: 1 *gud-giš ba-til,* i. e. is dead; and ibid. p. 130: 1 *lid-al ba-til.* This *BA-TIL* then signifies another class of 'not existing' cattle.

6. Very often we also meet in these texts the expression *LABAR-A-AN.*

In order to understand the force of this expression it will be well to enumerate the places where it is found and in what connection it stands.

(*a*) *Alone* it occurs in E. A. H. 29, rev. 2. In line 1 we have:

LAL-NI 10 *udu-uš RUG-RUG IM-MA*;

then follows a line left blank, and after this

LABAR-A-AN (see K).

(*b*) After *LAL-NI,* E. A. H. 29, obv. 11:

LAL-NI 37 *udu-uš*
LABAR-A-AN.

(*c*) After *LAL-NI-A-AN,* E. A. H. 20, rev. 1 ff.:

LAL-NI 25 *ganam* 18 *udu-uš*

6 *puhâdu*
LAL-NI-A-AN
LABAR-A-AN.

This is the most common occurrence. Comp. E. A. H. 21, rev. 3, 4.

(*d*) *LABAR-A-AN* with *LAL-NI-A-AN* is to be found in *one* line. Comp. E. A. H. 22, obv. 11 and rev. 1:—

LAL-NI 1 *ganam* 3 [*udu-uš*]
LAL-NI-A-AN LABAR-A-AN.

(*e*) After *ZIG-GA* in E. A. H. 19, obv. 10, 11:

ganam 1 *udu-uš*
(line left blank)
ZIG-GA
LABAR-A-AN.

(*f*) After *RIG-RIG-GA*, R. A. iii. p. 130, l. 4:

1 *anšu-sal-II*
1 *anšu-sal-I*
RIG-RIG-GA
LABAR-A-AN.

Comp. with this also E. A. H. 40, obv. 8–10:

So and so many animals,
RIG-RIG-GA
LAL-NI-A-AN
LABAR-A-AN.

(*g*) After *BA-TIL.* Comp. R. A. iii. p. 127, ll. 14, 15:

1 *gud-giš BA-TIL*
LABAR-A-AN.

(*h*) In some texts *GUB-BA LABAR-A-AN* is only another form or variant for *GUB-BA-A-AN* (R. A. iii. p. 128, l. 15). Comp. with this also (*c*) and (*d*).

(*i*) From these examples we see that—

(1) *LABAR-A-AN* is found behind all verb-forms occurring in these tablets, such as—

GUB-BA (*h*)
ZIG-GA (*e*)
RIG-RIG-GA (*f*)
BA-TIL (*g*)
LAL-NI (*b*)

and because we have (2) such forms as

LAL-NI-A-AN
LABAR-A-AN (*c*)

as well as

LAL-NI-A-AN LABAR-A-AN (*d*)

on one hand, and

GUB-BA-A-AN

with the variant

GUB-BA LABAR-A-AN (*h*)

on the other, hence we conclude—

(*a*) That the verb-forms ending in *A-AN* are of the same meaning as those without this ending; comp. *GUB-BA* = *GUB-BA-A-AN* (*h*). The ending *A-AN* therefore is only an emphatic ending; comp. Br. 11401.

(*b*) That *LABAR-A-AN* is some kind of an emphatic verbal postfix, which may be rightly compared with the Assyr. *-ma.* Hence

GUB-BA or *GUB-BA-A-AN* = *izzazû,*
GUB-BA-LALAR-A-AN = *izzazû-ma.*

7. *SAG-KU.*

In v. R. 51, 51 ff. we have:

SAG-e-eš ga-ra-ab-PA-KAB-du-ga, which is translated *ana širikti lûšarikšu.* Comp. with this Gudea D, iii. 12: *SAG-KU im-mi-PA-KAB-DU*[1], which Jensen translates '*und schenkte . . . zum Geschenk.*' Comp. also Br. 3526. *SAG* therefore = *širiktu,* 'a present,' H. W. B. p. 692. *SAG . . . KU* then would be 'a present for . . .,' and this in the sense of 'exchange for . . .' = *šupiltu* in Neo-Babylonian contracts; see Tallquist, Spr. d. Contr. p. 113, sub פאל, and comp. Thureau-Dangin in R. A. iii. p. 123, l. 12, and H. W. B. p. 514.

[1] See also Eannatum, Galet A, vii. 6; O. B. I. 109, 4.

E. A. H. 16, 6:

10 *ganam SAG-udu-uš-KU* should therefore be translated:

10 ewes (a) present for (*ku*) sheep that are of age, or

10 ewes received (=present *SAG*) instead of (*ku*) sheep that are of age, i. e. '10 ewes exchanged for mature sheep.'

The following cattle are mentioned in these tablets:—

8. *GANAM.*

This sign is composed out of *LAGABU* (Br. 10151) with the sign for *GUD* or *GUD-GUD* inserted; hence it is equivalent to Br. 10256 or 10252. For the reading of these signs, see Z. A. iii. p. 203. The latter occurs in O. B. I. 87, ii. 44; the former in Gudea F, iv. 1; see also Hommel, S. L. No. 383.

The Assyrian pronunciation is not *udru* = Hebr. עֵדֶר (Br. l. c.), 'a herd,' nor *par-ru* = ܦܪ̈ܐ (Z. A. iii. p. 202), for ܦܪ̈ܐ according to Nöldeke (Z. A. l. c. note 1) is = כבשה, and is explained in Efr. i. 174 *c* by [illegible]. Nor is it '*junges Schaf*' = Arab. فَرِيرٌ فُرَارٌ ('*Lamm, junge Gazelle*')[1], but it is the Hebrew רָחֵל, comp. رَخِل, رِخْل, and means an 'ewe, *Mutterschaf, brebis*'; see Hommel, Z. D. M. G. 46 (1892), p. 566. This is evident from Sm. 2148 (Lotz, T. P. 171; Delitzsch, A. W. 196), ll. 4, 5, where we have *GANAM-ĠAD* (sic?)-*BI*=*laḫ-ra ù pu-ḫad-sa*, i. e. 'the ewe and its lamb.' See also Br. 10252; H. W. B. p. 375. For *GANAM*=*im-mir-tum* (Z. A. iii. p. 203), see Hommel, S. L. No. 384, and notice that *GA-NAM* stands for original *GA-NAG* (Gudea, Cyl. B, x. 4, *uz-azag uz-ga-nag*) = 'milk-drinking.' This animal always is at the head of these lists, and is never found with any distinguishing addition. Hommel thinks that the Arab. غَنَم is = *GANAM.*

9. *UDU.*

This animal is generally mentioned immediately after the *GANAM.* For the pronunciation of this sign, see Hommel, S. L. No. 403: *ugug, udub, udu, idib.* Comp. also Gudea G, v. 14, 15; Jensen, K. B. iii[1]. p. 62; A. L[3]. 289; Br. 10673.

According to E. A. H. 15, rev. 2 (see above under 1 (*a*)), *UDU* comprise the *GANAM, UDU-UŠ, SAL-puḫâdu, puḫâdu-UŠ,*

[1] Nor is it = the Hebr. פָּרָה, פַּר, 'young cow.'

urisu-SAG. From this then it is evident that *UDU* is the general expression for *cattle*—including *all kinds* of *sheep* and *goats*—standing here not only for Assyr. *immeru* (H. W. B. p. 92), '*Lamm, Schaf*' (comp. Arab. إِمَّرٌ, '*agnus*'), but for Hebr. צֹאן, '*cattle*,' '*Kleinvieh*' (comp. Arab. ضَائِنٌ, ضَائِنَةٌ), H. W. B. 556. According to E. A. H. 104 the *udu*, however, stand also in contradiction to goats, hence must have also a more restricted or specific meaning, i. e. they signify 'sheep'=Arab. ضَأْن. See below, p. 365, note to l. 28.

In the *GUB-BA* paragraph *UDU* is never found alone, but has either the sign for *GAL* or *UŠ* after it; comp. E. A. H. 29, 2, 3.

We have to distinguish therefore between the (*a*) *UDU-UŠ* and the (*b*) *UDU-GAL*.

(*a*) *UDU-UŠ*.

The sign for *UŠ* is here always that of T. C. 7, which, as Amiaud, l. c., says, '*semble avoir été employé surtout dans l'expression complexe DUMU-UŠ* "*enfant mâle*."' In Gudea G, iv. 1, we have the sign *UŠ* as given in T. C. 74. Jensen, K. B. iii[1]. p. 60, translates *UDU-UŠ* (T. C. 74) by '*geschlechtsreife Schafe*,' and adds in note [o]: '*Männlich kann UŠ* (T. C. 74) *hier nicht heissen, da es, wie Amiaud bemerkt, nicht* das *Zeichen ist, welches nach DUMU = Kind* "*männlich*" *bezeichnet*.'

That even this sign used here (=T. C. 7) cannot mean 'male'—although it is that which is used after *DUMU* to express the idea 'male'—seems to be evident from E. A. H. 28, 3, 2 *UDU-UŠ BAR-RUG-GA*, compared with iv. R. 28, 52 *a*, *RUG SAL-AŠ-ḲAR UŠ-NU-ZU*, which latter is translated by: *mašak û-ni-ki la pi-ti-ti*. *UŠ-ZU* then is = *pitû*, Br. 5050, H. W. B. p. 552, 'to open'; *maška pitû*, 'to open the skin' with regard to sexual intercourse = the Hebr. ידע.

BAR, according to ii. R. 39, 4 *a* (comp. Br. 1791, *ḲA-BAR-RA*), means also *pitû*, 'to open.'

An *UDU-UŠ BAR-RUG-GA* then would be an animal (*UDU-UŠ*) that is 'opened (*BAR*) as regards its skin (*RUG*),' i. e. '*ein Thier, das besprungen ist*.' Hence it follows that *UŠ* (although = T. C. 7) cannot mean 'male,' and thus *UDU-UŠ* must mean a (feminine) sheep (*udu*) that is *UŠ*. Indeed in E. A. H. 40, rev. 2, we have *UDU-UŠ-GÀL* (*IK*), which *GÀL* shows clearly that *UŠ* is something which the sheep either *is* or *has*. And if the *UDU-UŠ* are said 'to be covered' (= *besprungen* = *BAR-RUG-GA*), then *UŠ* can only mean a sheep which *can* or *may* be 'covered' = '*ein geschlechtsreifes Schaf*,' i. e. *UŠ* = *ridû* (H. W. B. p. 614; Z. A. iii. p. 201, 4; Amiaud, Z. A. iii. 44: '*uš doit répondre ici à l'assyrien ridû et signifier quelque chose comme* "*adulte*" *ou* "*domestique*"'). Jensen therefore is undoubtedly right when he says (K. B. iii [1]. p. 60, note o): '*Vielleicht bezieht sich . . . UŠ auf die weibliche Geschlechtsreife.*' Hence

UDU-UŠ = '*ein* (*weibliches*) *geschlechtsreifes Schaf*,'

UDU-UŠ BAR-RUG-GA = ditto, which is 'covered' (*besprungen*).

(*b*) *UDU-GAL*.

In all the lists where this animal is mentioned, it precedes the *UDU-UŠ*.

In iv. R. 23, No. 1, col. i. 8, 9, we have *GUD-GAL GUD-MAǴ* explained by *gu-gal-lum gu-maḫ-ḫu*; comp. also iv. R. 20, No. 1, 26, 27: *GUD-GAL-GAL-LA* = *gumaḫḫe*.

The *UDU-GAL* may be therefore the 'great sheep,' κατ' ἐξοχήν, i. e. the Assyr. *lulîmu* or *ailu* = Hebr. אַיִל, the 'ram,' '*Schafbock*,' '*bélier*.' Comp. also *uriṣu-GAL*.

(*c*) In Gudea G, iii. 1 (from below) we also find the expression: *udu ŠE*, which *ŠE*, according to Jensen (K. B. iii [1]. p. 60, note ††), signifies '*die männliche Geschlechtsreife*,' in contradistinction to *udu-UŠ*; see above, 9 *a*.

10. The *UDU*, 'sheep,' are followed by the 'lambs.' The sign for 'lamb' is that to be found in Br. 5489. The Sumerian pronunciation of this sign is doubtful (Jensen, K. B. iii [1]. p. 60, note 7, and Gudea G, iv. 2); comp. however Hommel, S. L. No. 199 = *ǵad*. We transcribe this sign always by its Assyrian equivalent: *puḫâdu*. See H. W. B. p. 170.

The following *puḫadâti* are mentioned:

(*a*) *puḫâdu-UŠ*, E. A. H. 13, 4.

(*b*) *SAL-puḫâdu*, E. A. H. 13, 3.

(*c*) *puḫâdu-BA-UR*, E. A. H. 19, 4.

(*d*) *puḫâdu-NU-UR*, E. A. H. 19, 5.

UŠ and *SAL* no doubt are used with regard to gender, *BA-UR* and *NU-UR* with regard to age.

(*a*) *puḫâdu-UŠ*. The *UŠ* sign is the same here as that used behind *UDU-UŠ*. Here however it retains its original meaning 'male'; the *SAL* shows that clearly. *Puḫâdu-UŠ* is therefore = male lamb.

(*b*) If *puḫâdu-UŠ* = he-lamb, then *SAL-puḫâdu* = she-lamb = *puḫattu*, H. W. B. 170. Notice also that the *SAL-puḫâdu* precedes the *puḫâdu-UŠ*!

(*c*) A little more difficult are the expressions *BA-UR* and *NU-UR* (*UR*=Br. 11887). As *UŠ* is the opposite of *SAL*, so is BA-*UR* the opposite of NU-*UR*. In all those texts in which the *puḫâdu-BA-UR* (-*NU-UR*) are mentioned, the *puḫâdu-UŠ* (*SAL*) are omitted. It is evident that the expressions *puḫâdu-BA-UR* (*NU-UR*) are only used with regard to age, and not with regard to gender—for which latter the expressions *UŠ* and *SAL* are employed.

This statement is corroborated by E. A. H. 56; see the notes to that tablet. According to that tablet the *puḫâdu-BA-UR* were shorn, while the *puḫâdu-NU-UR* were not. The *puḫâdu-BA-UR* must therefore have been *older* than the *puḫâdu-NU-UR*. Lambs when very young 'suck,' but when older they are 'weaned' and 'give wool.' It is highly probable that *puḫâdu-BA-UR* denotes *those lambs* which are *weaned* = Hebr. גָּמוּל, hence older and thus 'give wool'; while the

(*d*) *puḫâdu-NU-UR* signify those lambs which are *not* (*NU*) weaned, i. e. those that 'suck' = Hebr. יוֹנֵק. Comp. with this also Thureau-Dangin, R. A. iii. p. 123, l. 3.

11. To these lists of cattle belong also the 'goats' and their 'kids,' as is evident from E. A. H. 14, 5, 6. The sign for 'goat' is that given by Amiaud, T. C. No. 31, as '*non assimilé*.' Later on, however, he identified it with Br. 3707; see Z. A. iii. p. 198 and 210, γ. As such it has to be pronounced

UZ (Syl.[b] 286) and corresponds to the Assyr. *enzu*, 'a goat' (H. W. B. p. 99; Z. A. iii. 204; Gudea F, iv. 5); comp. the Hebr. עֵז, pl. עִזִּים (√ ענז), Aram. עִזִּין (Ezra vi. 17); Arab. عَنْز; Syr. ܥܙܐ.

12. The 'kid' is represented here by the sign Br. 2030. The Sumerian pronunciation is not yet known; Hommel, S. L. 64 (*lal?*); Z. A. iii. 204; Delitzsch, A. L[2]. 49. It is equivalent to the Assyr. *uriṣu* = Arab. عَرِيض (iv. R. 26, 20 *b*; H. W. B. 137), as well as to *lalû* (H. W. B. 377).

In Sm. 2148, 6, 7, we have *UZ*-Br. 2030-*BI* explained by *enza ù la-la-ša*, i. e. 'the goat and its kid' (see Delitzsch, A. W. 196); and comp. with this *laḫ-ra ù pu-ḫad-sa* (see *sub* 8). *Uriṣu* and *lalû* then means 'the young goat,' the 'kid.' We transcribe this sign always by *uriṣu*.

The following 'kids' are mentioned in these texts:—

(*a*) *uriṣu-GAL*, R. A. iii. p. 125, 2.
(*b*) *uriṣu-UŠ*, E. A. H. 46, 10.
(*c*) *sal-aš-ḳar*, E. A. H. 104, 31.
(*d*) *uriṣu-ŠAG-DUG*, E. A. H. 14, 6.
(*e*) *uriṣu-SAG*, E. A. H. 15, 5.

(*a*) *Uriṣu-GAL.*

If uriṣu is = *lalû*, then *uriṣu-GAL* would be 'the great kid.' It seems, however, that *uriṣu* is the general expression for 'goat,' just as *UDU* is that for 'sheep.' *Uriṣu-GAL* then is parallel to *UDU-GAL*, and signifies the 'he-goat, buck,' '*Ziegenbock*,' '*bouc*,' and corresponds to the Hebrew תַּיִשׁ (ܬܝܫܐ, תַּיְשָׁא, تَيْس) or to the שְׂעִיר עִזִּים (Gen. xxxvii. 31). In all those lists in which this *uriṣu-GAL* is mentioned, a small number only is to be found in comparison with that of the 'other goats.' So in R. A. iii. 125 only thirty-eight *uriṣu-GAL* come upon 450 goats.

(*b*) *Uriṣu-UŠ.*

The *UŠ* (T. C. 7) signifies here, as in *puḫâdu-UŠ*, 'male.' *Uriṣu-UŠ* then would be 'the young he-goat,' Heb. גְּדִי (ܓܕܝܐ, גַּדְיָא, جَدْى).

(*c*) The 'young she-goat,' however, is not expressed here by *sal-uriṣu*—according to the analogy of *SAL-puḫâdu*—but by the following three signs: *SAL-AŠ-ḲAR.* The signs *SAL-AŠ* in modern Babylonian script are written together, and pronounced *ṢU*; see Hommel, S. L. 419. Comp. also the form for *ṢU* in Gudea B, iv. 18: *SIG GIŠ-ṢU-AG*, i.e. wool that is made from the young goat. *ṢU* (= *SAL-AŠ*)-*ḲAR* corresponds to the Assyr. *unîḳu* (not *unîku*, H. W. B. p. 101; comp. Arab. عَنَاق), and undoubtedly means 'a *young* she-goat.' Comp. iv. R. 5, col. 3, 32, 33, 34, 35, where *SAL-AŠ-ḲAR* is parallel to *SAL-puḫâdu*:

SIG SAL-AŠ-ḲAR UŠ-NU-ZU SIG SAL-puḫâdu UŠ-NU-ZU = *ša-rat u-ni-ḳi la pi-ti-ti ša-rat pu-ḫat-ti la pi-te-te.*

Just as *SAL-puḫâdu* (= *puḫattu*) signifies the *she*-lamb, so does *SAL-AŠ-ḲAR* signify the '*young she-goat.*'

(*d*) *Uriṣu-ŠAG-DUG.*

The 'kids' thus called follow the *uriṣu-UŠ*; see E. A. H. 46, 11; R. A. iii. 125, l. 5.

Literally the whole expression means: Kid-heart-good, i.e. 'a kid of a good (= *tendre*) heart.' It is highly probable that we have here the 'kids that suck,' Thureau-Dangin: '*chevreaux à la mamelle*' (R. A. iii. p. 126, l. 5). If this be true, then *ŠAG-DUG* here would correspond to the *NU-UR*, when used of the *puḫadâti*. Comp. also E. A. H. 14, 6, where the *uriṣu-ŠAG-DUG* follow immediately upon the *UZ*.

(*e*) *Uriṣu-SAG.*

The *SAG* at the first sight suggests the idea of *strength* or *age* (comp. Assyr. *ašaridu* and *rêšu*) rather than that of gender. Clearly the idea of 'gender' must be excluded here, because we have seen that the young *he*-goats were called *uriṣu-UŠ*, and the young *she*-goats had the name *SAL-AŠ-ḲAR*. We are therefore inclined to understand by the *uriṣu-SAG* those 'kids' which are 'weaned.' Hence *SAG* may be used of the *uriṣu* as opposed to *ŠAG-DUG* (= *NU-UR*). As such it would be = *BA-UR*, when used of a *puḫâdu*.

13. *RUG-RUG.*

This expression occurs in the E. A. H. tablets in the following compositions:—

17 *udu RUG-RUG-GA IM-MA*, E. A. H. 20, rev. 5. The *GA* shows that we have to pronounce *RUG.*

22 *udu RUG-RUG IM-MA*, E. A. H. 22, rev. 2.

1 *gud-giš RUG-GA ENGAR*, E. A. H. 34, 3.

If we compare with this:

1 *gud-giš RUG-GA PA-AL* (=*šabrû*), O. B. I. 126, i. 9;

1 *gud-giš RUG-GA NU-BANDA-GUD*, ibid. ii. 7;

1 *anšu-uš RUG-GA Ur-(dingir) Ba-u dup-sar-gud*, ibid. iv. 8;

1 *gud-I RUG-GA IM-MA UR-E-ninnû-ra* (sic), ibid. col. iv. 4th line from end; comp. also col. vi. 18;

it will be evident that *RUG-RUG-GA*, or *RUG-RUG*, or *RUG-GA* signifies a certain class of animals. Interesting is also the *ŠU-NIGIN* paragraph of O. B. I. 124, rev., col. v. There we read:

9	*ŠU-NIGIN*	15 *lid-al.*
10	„ „	74 *gud-giš.*
	„ „	11 *gud RUG-RUG.*
	„ „	5 *lid-II-giš-tug.*
	„ „	3 *gud-II-giš-tug.*
	„ „	4 *lid-II.*
15	„ „	2 *gud-II.*
	„ „	2 *lid-I.*
	„ „	2 *gud-I.*
	„ „	1 *lid-amar-ga.*
	„ „	2 *gud-amar-ga.*
20	„ „	1 *gud-šu-gì.*

After these 'cows' and 'oxen' the same paragraph enumerates the 'asses' as follows:—

21	*ŠU-NIGIN*	35 *anšu.*
	„ „	3 *anšu RUG-RUG.*

ŠU-NIGIN 48 *anšu-uš.*
" " 3 *anšu-uš-RUG-RUG.*
25 " " 3 *anšu-II-giš-tug.*
" " x + 1 *anšu-uš-II.*
" " 5 *anšu-I.*
" " 5 *anšu-uš-I.*
" " 7 *anšu-amar-ga.*
30 " " 1 *anšu-uš-amar-ga.*
" " 1 *anšu-šu-gì.*
" " 2 *anšu-uš-š[u-gì].*
" " *gub-ba-[a-an].*

Comp. also O. B. I. 126:

Rev., col. ii.

ŠU-NIGIN 26 *lid-al.*

Rev., col. iii.

ŠU-NIGIN 2 *lid-al RUG-GA.*
" " 1 *lid-II giš-tug.*
" " 1 *lid-II-giš-tug sag-lid-al-ku.*
" " 50-*lal*-2 *gud-giš.*
5 " " 14 *gud-giš RUG-GA.*
" " 5 *nu-gud-giš RUG-GA.*
" " 4 *gud-I RUG-GA sag-gud-giš-tug.*
" " 2 *gud-giš RUG-GA sag-lid-al-ku.*
" " 3 *gud-giš sag-lid-al-ku.*
10 " " 1 *gud-I sag-gud-giš-ku.*
11 " " 1 *gud-I RUG-GA sag-anšu-uš-ku.*
12 " " 1 *gud-II RUG-GA sag-lid-al-ku.*
18 " " 1 *anšu-sal RUG-GA.*
20 " " 1 *anšu-uš-II RUG-GA sag-anšu-sal-ku.*

These examples show sufficiently that the expression *RUG-RUG-GA* may be applied to oxen, cows, sheep, which may be either masculine or feminine, great or small, old or young. Notice (*a*) that *RUG-RUG-(GA)* is generally found in the tablets after the mention of more animals than *one* (the only exception is O. B. I. 126), thus showing that *RUG-RUG-GA* is a plural form, while *RUG-GA* stands generally when *one* animal only is referred to, hence it is the singular; (*b*) that the expression *RUG-GA* has *always*—excepting in the *ŠU-NIGIN* paragraph, which gives only the 'total' of the animals signified by *RUG-GA*—either a 'title' (comp. *En-gar, PA-AL, NU-BANDA-GUD*) or a 'name' after it (comp. *Ur-*$^{(dingir)}$*-Ba-u dup-sar-gud, IM-MA Ur-E-ninnû-ra*). The last example is interesting. O. B. I. 126, iv. l. 4 from the end, 1 *gud-I RUG-GA IM-MA UR-E-ninnû-ra*, can be translated only: 1 ox of one year *RUG-GA* belonging to (*ra* = postposition) the *IM-MA Ur-E-ninnû*. That *RA* must be taken here as postposition is proved by O. B. I. 126, vi. 18, where we have *KU*. If we compare *IM-MA* with *Engar, Nu-banda-gud, Pa-al, dup-sar-gud*, which expressions are all titles occurring after *RUG-GA*, we should be inclined to take *IM-MA* for a 'title' too, signifying *a certain officer* connected in some way or other with the 'herds,' probably a certain class of the shepherds. This may be corroborated by Br. 8358, where *IM-MA* has the meaning *bêlûtu*, 'lordship' (comp. also Br. 8362, *IM*=*emûku*, which *IM* however in this case is pronounced *NI*; see Syl.^{c} 286).

But what does *RUG-GA* mean in this connection? The postpositions *RA* and *KU*, which we meet, show clearly that the animals signified by *RUG-GA* belong *to* or *are for* somebody.

RUG, according to Br. 170, is=*šîru*, 'body, flesh,' or Br. 172, *zumru*='body.' One of these two meanings we would postulate here. Hence E. A. H. 20, rev. 5, 17, *udu RUG-RUG-GA IM-MA*, may be translated: 17 sheep, bodies (flesh) belonging to the *IM-MA* (an officer). If we remember that in Germany, even up to the present day, the *shepherd* of a landlord receives at the yearly '*Zahltag*' one or more sheep, we shall understand why we should meet here such expressions as 'bodies or body (flesh) belonging to.' The animals called *RUG-GA* are thus implied to be the 'income' of some (kind of) officer or shepherd. Comp. also above, under *LAL-NI*.

14. Sometimes we also meet the expression *NU-ZU* in connection with *RUG-GA*; see E. A. H. 24, rev. 1, *LAL-NI* 22 *RUG-RUG NU-ZU IM-MA*, and comp.

1 *NU-gud RUG-RUG NU-ZU* (sic) *Ur-*[*(dingir)*] *KAL dumu* (*Ga*)*lu-*[*(dingir)*] *EN-ZU*, R. A. iii. 127, 16;

1 *gud RUG-RUG NU-ZU IM-MA NIN-U-RU*(*M*) *PA-AL*, O. B. I. 126, rev. ii. 10.

This *ZU* is sometimes written with the sign for *RUG* (just as *RUG* is sometimes represented by *ZU*). *ZU*, Br. 130 = *idû*, 'to know' = Hebr. ידע, which root is used in Hebrew either of a 'man' = *cognovit vir mulierem*, i.e. *concubuit cum ea* (comp. Gen. iv. 25: וַיֵּדַע אָדָם עוֹד אֶת־אִשְׁתּוֹ), or of a 'woman' = *experta est virum* (comp. Gen. xix. 8: בָּנוֹת אֲשֶׁר לֹא־יָדְעוּ אִישׁ). The same is the case with *ZU*; when used of a female *UŠ* is prefixed = *UŠ ZU* = *penis* + *cognoscere*; comp. iv. R. 28, 52 *a*: *SAL-AŠ-ḲAR UŠ-NU-ZU*. In this case *UŠ ZU* is = *BAR-RUG*, and *UŠ-NU-ZU* would be lit. *penem* + *non* + *cognovit*. When used of a 'male' *ZU* is used *alone*. Hence *NU-ZU* (= *non* + *cognovit*) may be translated here 'undefiled.'

15. Scheil recently published in Z. A. xii. p. 260 ff. some tablets enumerating cattle. There the *UDU* and the *puḫâdu* occur in the following compositions:—

T. C. 272-*UDU* as opposed to T. C. 272-*puḫâdu*.

ZU-UDU as opposed to T. C. 272-*UDU*.

ZU-puḫâdu as opposed to T. C. 272-*puḫâdu*.

From this he concludes that T. C. 272 (see Gudea B, iv. 2) is = (*ga*)*lu-ŠE* (*ŠI*) = *marû* (Br. 6419), '*qui indique la puberté chez le mâle*'; see also above, p. 344 (*a*). E. C. 290 takes it as (*ga*)*lu-gunû*.

15. The following proper names (with their titles) occur in these tablets:—

(Time of Dungi III.)

1 *LUGAL-BAR-ZU*, E. A. H. 13, rev. 12 (*na-gid*).

2 (*Pa*) *DUG-GA-ZID-DA*, E. A. H. 13, rev. 14; 14, rev. 9; 15, rev. 8; 16, rev. 9.

3 *NAM-ĠA-NI*, E. A. H. 14, rev. 8.
4 *LU-Ù-ŠAG-GA*, 15, rev. 6.
5 *LUGAL-KA-GI-NA*, 15, rev. 7 (*na-gid*).
6 *UR-(dingir) PA-SAG*, 16, rev. 7.
7 *UR-(dingir) NIN-TU*, 19, rev. 6 (*na-gid*).
8 *LUGAL-U-KAŠ-ŠU-E*, 20, rev. 9 (*na-gid*).
9 *UR-(dingir) DUMU-ZI dumu DUG-GA-ZID-DA*, 21, rev. 9 (*na-gid*).
10 (*GA*)*LU-(dingir) NA-RU-A*, 22, rev. 6 ((*ga*)*lu KU na-gid*).
11 (*GA*)*LU-KA-*[*NI*], 23, 10.
12 *LUGAL-ŠI-GAR-E dumu ŠAG-DA*, 23, rev. 6 (*na-gid*).
13 *LUGAL-EZEN* (= *Šarru-ikrub ?*), 23, rev. 7 (*ni-ku*).
14 *LUGAL-KA-KI-NA*, 24, rev. 5 (*pa-*[*al*] *dagal-ĝe*).

(Time of Bur-Sin II.)

15 (*GA*)*LU-DINGIR-RA* (=*Amêl-ili*), 28, rev. 6.
16 *A-LA* (?)-*URU*, 29, rev. 4.
17 *UR-ŠID*, 29, rev. 8 ab (Br. 3819, H. W. B. 140).
18 *UR-GU-LA dumu* [*A-l*]*u*, 30, 5 (*na-gid*).
19 *UR-ŠAG-GA dumu* (*GA*)*LU-(dingir) NA-RU-A*, 31, rev. 8.
20 *AB*, 35, 8 (*ni-ku*); 36, 8; 37, 8; 38, 9.
21 *UR-GU-LA*, 35, 9 (*ni-ku*); 36, 9; 37, 10; 38, 10.
22 (*GA*)*LU-ME-NE* (= *melammi*), 35, rev. 6; 40, rev. 9 (*na-gid ?*).
23 *LUĠ-DI-NE*, 36, rev. 9.
24 *LUGAL-EZEN* (= *Šarru-ikrub ?*), 37, rev. 9.
25 *NAM-MAĠ*, 38, rev. 7.
26 *A-DA*, 39, rev. 8 (*na-gid*).
27 *ŠÚ-E* (?)-*A-NI-ŠA*, 40, rev. 10 (*na-gid*).
28 *LA-NI-MU*, 41, rev. 10 (*na-gid*).
29 *UR-(dingir) KAL* (≐ *Kalbi-Lamassu*) *dumu AMAR-?-a*, 42, R. 7.
30 -*NUN*, E. A. H. 43, rev. 8.
31 [*NIN*]-*GIŠ-ZI-DE* (sic)-*A*, 44, rev. 9.
32 *LUGAL-ME-NE* (= *melammi*), 45, rev. 10.
33 *UR-(dingir) IM* (=*Kalbi-Rammânu*), 46, rev. 4.

Among the cities[1] mentioned in these tablets are to be found :—

Ki-nu-nir-^{ki} = Borsippa.
Gir-su-^{ki} = a part of Shirpurla (Telloh).
Tik-ab-ba-^{ki}[2].
Ninâ-^{ki} = a part of Shirpurla (Telloh).

E. A. H. 14.

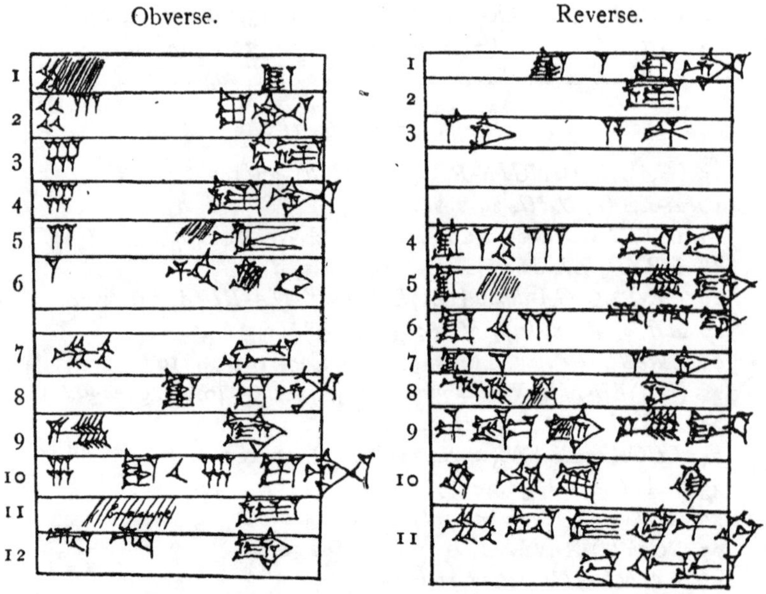

[1] The cities are always introduced by *ŠAG* = (*ina*) *libbi* = in (the midst of). In E. A. H. 31, rev. 9, we have *ŠAG-Ninâ-ki*-ka = in the midst of (*ka*) *Ninâ-ki*. Sometimes we also find : *ŠAG . . . gàl-la-a-an*, E. A. H. 54.

[2] Pronunciation is hypothetical. May also be read : *Gu-ab-ba-ki* (= 'sea-side'). The situation of this city is not yet known. See, however, iv. R^2. 31, No 1, col. ii. 12, where it is mentioned before *DIN-TIR-ki*.

E. A. H. 14.

Obverse.

43 *ganam*	43 ewes
43 *udu-uš*	43 'mature' sheep
7 *sal-puḫădu*	7 she-lambs
7 *puḫădu-uš*	7 he-lambs
3 *uz*	3 she-goats
1 *urișu šag-dug*	1 sucking kid
mu-gub	were present
ganam udu-uš	ewes mature sheep
zig-ga	expended
6 *ganam* 17 *udu-uš*	6 ewes 17 mature sheep
puḫădu	lambs
rig-rig-ga	snatched away

Reverse.

ganam 1 *udu-uš*	ewes 1 mature sheep
puḫădu	lambs
lal-ni-a-an	*lal-ni-a-an* (were lost)
šu-nigin 103 *gub-ba*	Total: 103 present
šu-nigin zig-ga	Total: expended
šu-nigin 23 *rig-rig-ga*	Total: 23 snatched away
šu-nigin 1 *lal-ni*	Total: 1 *lal-ni* (lost)
Nam-ḫa-ni	Namḫani (shepherd)
Pa Dug-ga-zid-da	Overseer: Duggazidda
šag Gir-su-^{ki}	Girsu
Mu-uš-sa Ki-maš-^{ki} *ba-ḫul*	One year after (the king) devastated Kimash.

E. A. H. 19.

Obverse.

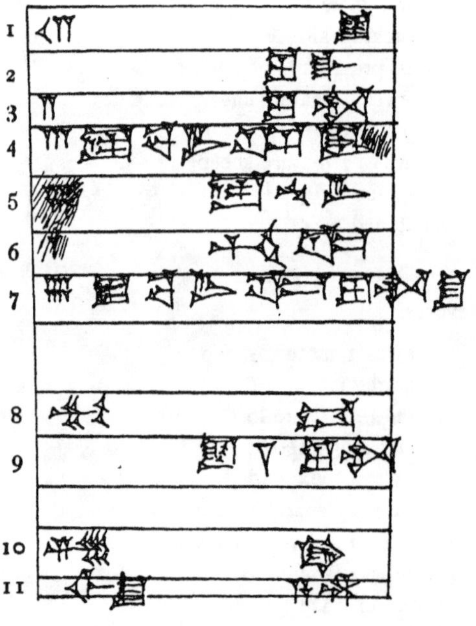

Reverse.

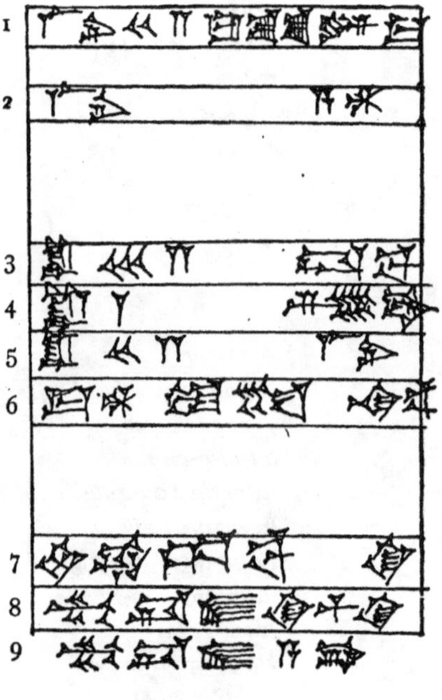

E. A. H. 19.

Obverse.

12 *ganam*	12 ewes
udu-gal	rams
2 *udu-uš*	2 mature sheep
3 *puḫádu-ba-ur sag-ganam-[ku]*	3 weaned lambs exchanged for ewes
6 *puḫádu-nu-ur*	6 sucking lambs
1 *uriṣu-sag*	1 weaned kid
8 *puḫádu-ba-ur sag-udu-uš-ku*	8 weaned lambs exchanged for mature sheep
mu-gub	were present
ganam 1 *udu-uš*	ewes 1 mature sheep
zig-ga	expended
LABAR-a-an	

Reverse.

lal-ni 22 *udu rug-rug im-ma lal-ni-a-an*	Lost were 22 sheep, income of the *Im-ma*
šu-nigin 32 *gub-ba*	Total: 32 present
šu-nigin 1 *zig-ga*	Total: 1 expended
šu-nigin 22 *lal-ni*	Total: 22 lost
Ur-$^{(dingir)}$ *Nin-tu na-gid*	Ur-Nintu, shepherd
šag Tik-ab-ba-^{ki}	Tikabba
Mu-uš-sa Ki-maš-^{ki} *mu-uš-sa-a-bi*	Two years after (the king) devastated Kimash.

E. A. H. 35.

Obverse.

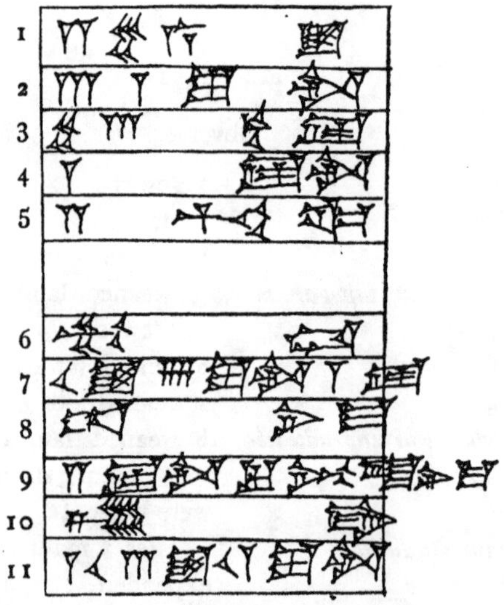

Reverse.

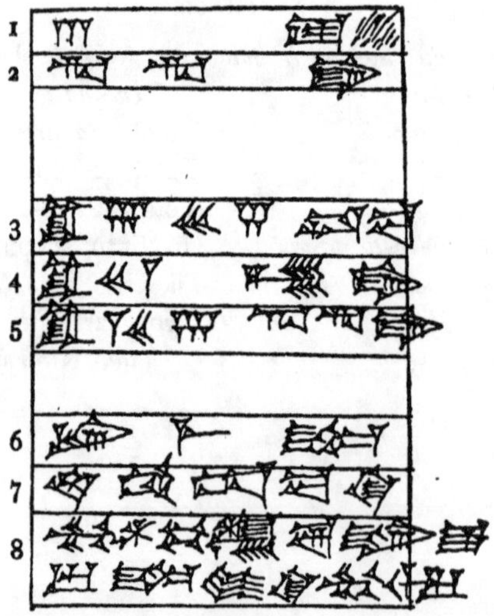

E. A. H. 35.

Obverse.

169 *ganam*	169 ewes
181 *udu-uš*	181 mature sheep
43 *sal-puḫádu*	43 she-lambs
60 *puḫádu-uš*	60 he-lambs
2 *uriṣu-sag*	2 weaned kids
mu-gub	were present
10 *ganam* 8 *udu-uš* 1 *puḫádu*	10 ewes 8 mature sheep 1 lamb
Ab ni-ku	Ab, the chief overseer
2 *puḫádu-uš Ur-Gu-la ni-ku*	2 he-lambs Ur-Gula, the chief overseer
zig-ga	took away
73 *ganam* 11 *udu-uš*	73 ewes 11 mature sheep

Reverse.

3 *puḫádu*	3 lambs
rig-rig-ga	were ravished
šu-nigin 455 *gub-ba*	Total: 455 present
šu-nigin 21 *zig-ga*	Total: 21 taken away
šu-nigin 87 *rig-rig-ga*	Total: 87 ravished
(*Ga*)*lu-me-ne* (*lam*)	(Ga)lumene (*lam*)
šag Tik-ab-ba-ki	Tikabba
mu (*ilu*) *Bur-*(*ilu*) *Sin lugal-e Ur-bil-lum-ki mu-ĝul*	In the year when king Bur-Sin (II.) devastated Urbillum.

E. A. H. 37.

Obverse.

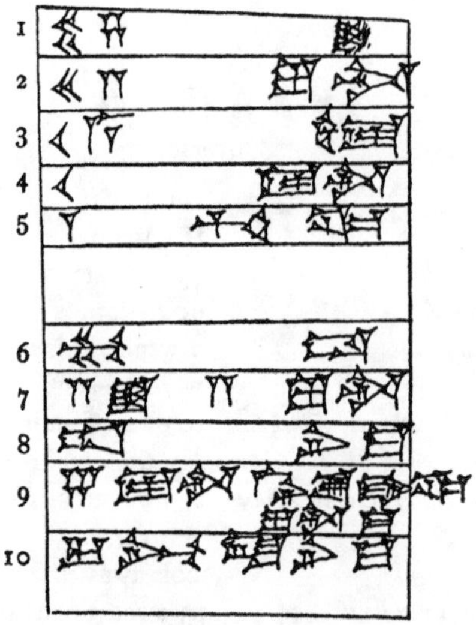

Reverse.

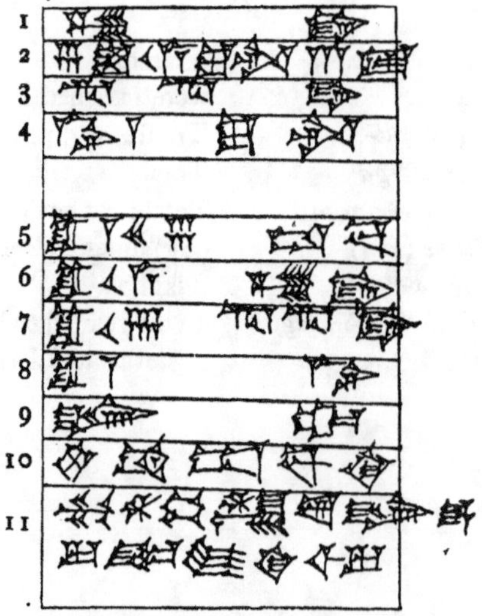

E. A. H. 37.

Obverse.

44 *ganam*	44 ewes
22 *udu-uš*	22 mature sheep
9 *sal-puḫâdu*	9 she-lambs
10 *puḫâdu-uš*	10 he-lambs
1 *uriṣu-sag*	1 weaned kid
mu-gub	were present
2 *ganam* 2 *udu-uš*	2 ewes 2 mature sheep
Ab ni-ku	Ab, the chief overseer
5 *udu-uš lal-ni rug-ga sag-udu-uš-ku*	5 he-lambs, remainder of the income, exchanged for the mature sheep
Ur-Gu-la ni-ku	Ur-Gula, the chief overseer

Reverse.

zig-ga	has taken away
6 *ganam* 9 *udu-uš* 3 *puḫâdu*	6 ewes 9 mature sheep 3 lambs
rig-rig-ga	were ravished
lal-ni 1 *udu-uš*	Loss: 1 mature sheep
šu-nigin 86 *gub-ba*	Total: 86 present
šu-nigin 9 *zig-ga*	Total: 9 taken away
šu-nigin 18 *rig-rig-ga*	Total: 18 ravished
šu-nigin 1 *lal-ni*	Total: 1 lost
Lugal-ezen	Lugalezen
šag Tik-ab-ba-ki	Tikabba
Mu (ilu) Bur-(ilu) Sin lugal-e Ur-bil-lum-ki ḫul	In the year when king Bur-Sin (II.) devastated Urbillum.

To the preceding tablets belongs also E. A. H. 104. The understanding of this tablet depends on the *KU* in line 27, which carries its force also to ll. 12, 20, 22, and 24; hence we have to supply before those lines an '*ana*,' i. e. 'to,' 'for.' A verb is not expressed. The postposition *KU*, however, demands some such word as '*nadânu*,' 'to give.' Thus, then, this tablet states the income (*NIN-ŠID*, cp. *epuš nikasi*) of the following five (5 *NIN-ŠID-ta*) temples or persons:—

(*a*) the temple of Dungi, l. 12.
(*b*) Ur-Ba'u of the *bît šabrî*, l. 20.
(*c*) the shâbrû of Ningirsu, l. 22.
(*d*) the temple of Ba'u, l. 24.
(*e*) Munabašag (=*Šumi-šu-mudammiḳ*), l. 27.

E. A. H. 104 Obverse.

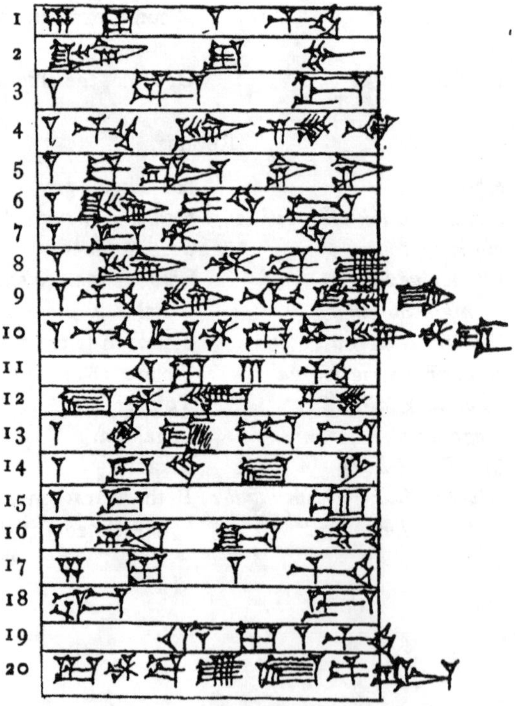

E. A. H. 104.

Obverse.

6 *udu* 1 *uriṣu*	6 sheep 1 kid
Lugal-dib-bu	from Lugaldibbu
Sag-ṭu	1 (sheep) from the Sagṭu
1 *uriṣu* (*Ga*)*lu-gin-na*	1 kid from Amêlukîn
5 1 (*udu*) *Ba-al-ni-ni*	1 (sheep) from Balnini (= *Bâl-ili*)
1 (*udu*) *Lugal-pa-ud-du*	,, ,, Lugalpauddu
1 (*udu*) *Ur-*(dingir) *Utu*	,, ,, Ur-Utu (= Kalbi-Shamash)
1 (*udu*) (*Ga*)*lu-*(dingir) *Ba-u*	,, ,, from Amêl-Ba'u
1 *uriṣu* (*Ga*)*lu-Bal-šag-ga*	1 kid from (Ga)lu-Balshagga
10 1 *uriṣu* *Ur-*(dingir) *KAL* *dumu* (*Ga*)*lu-dingir-ra*	,, ,, Kalbi-Lamassu, the son of Amêl-ili
11 *udu* 3 *uriṣu*	(Total) 11 sheep 3 kids (should be 4 kids!)
E-(dingir) *Dun-gi*	for the temple of Dungi
1 (*Gudu*) *ar* (?)-*ra-ab-du*	1 (sheep) from Ḫarrabdu
1 (*udu*) *Ur-Nigin-gar*	,, ,, Ur-Nigingar
15 1 (*udu*) *Ur-šid*	,, ,, Urshid
1 (*udu*) *Ad-da-mu*	,, ,, Addamu
5 *udu* 1 *uriṣu*	5 sheep 1 kid
Sag-ṭu	from the Sagṭu
10-*lal*-1 *udu* 1 *uriṣu*	(Total) 9 sheep 1 kid
20 *Ur-*(dingir) *Ba-u e-pa-al*	for Ur-Ba'u of the *bît-šabrî*

3. SAG-ṬU is the name of an officer; comp. Rec. Trav. xix. p. 51, 10: *Lugal-uru-da SAG-ṬU dumu À-zi-da SAG-ṬU*.

13. The first sign is not clear; it may also be *LID* (Br. 8982), or *ŠIR* (Hom. S. L. 301).

14. The sign *NIGIN* is that of Br. 9251. *Nigin-gar* here no doubt is a god, and probably the same as that mentioned in ii. R. 60, 13 *a*: (dingir) *PAP* (*KUR*)-*NIGIN-GAR-RA šarru ša UD-UNUG* (= *Larsa*)ki. According to ii. R. 57, 57 *c*, he is = (ilu) *Nin-ib*.

20. *PA-AL* is the Assyr. *šabrû*, an officer; comp. S b. 217; H. W. B. p. 639.

E. A. H. 104.

Reverse.

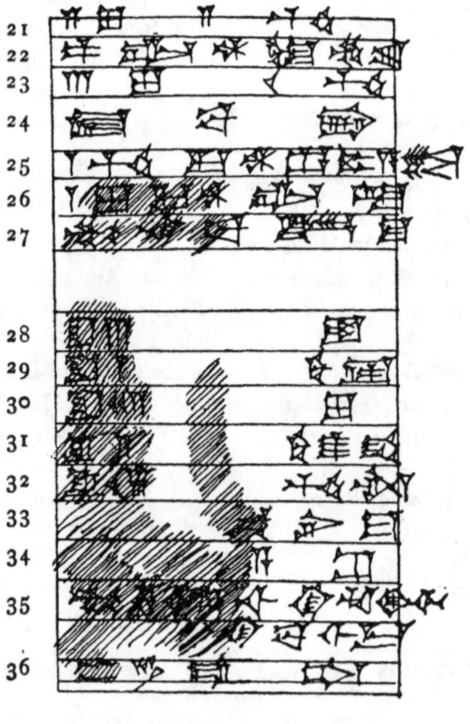

E. A. H. 104.

Reverse.

2 udu 2 uriṣu	2 sheep 2 kids
Pa-al (*dingir*) *Nin-gir-su*	for the shâbrû of Ningirsu
3 udu 10 uriṣu	3 sheep 10 kids
E-Ba-bi	for the house of Ba'u
1 uriṣu Ur-(*dingir*) *KAL dumu A-tu*	1 kid from Kalbi-Lamassu the son of Atu
1 udu Ur-(*dingir*) *Al-la*	1 sheep from Ur-Alla
Mu-na-ba-šag-ku	for Munabashag
šu-nigin 3 ganam	Total: 3 ewes
šu-nigin 1 sal-puḫâdu	Total: 1 ewe-lamb
šu-nigin 22 udu	Total: 22 sheep
šu-nigin 2 sal-aš-ḳar	Total: 2 young she-goats
šu-nigin 16 uriṣu-uš	Total: 16 young he-goats
. . . . . *maĝ ni-ku*	. . . . *-maĝ* the chief overseer
[*Itu Amar-a-*]*a-si*	In the month of Amarasi
[*Mu Ḫa*]*-ar-ši-ki Ḫu-mur-ti-ki ba-ĝul*	In the year when (the king) devastated Ḫarshi and Ḫumurti
5 *Nin-šid-ta*	Five incomes (revenues).

24. *E-Ba-bi* = *E-Ba-vi* = *E-Ba-i*, which latter is the gen. of Ba'u, i.e. 'for the house (temple) of Ba'u.'

28. The *ŠU-NIGIN* paragraph is remarkable. It shows that *UDU* on one hand means *cattle* (צאן); on the other, 'sheep' (= Arab. ضَأْن; comp. 1 Sam. xxv. 2), in contradistinction to goat; for in the body of the tablet only *UDU* are mentioned (= צאן), which again are divided into *ganam*, *sal-puḫâdu*, *and UDU* (= sheep as such, ضَأْن). The numerals are not clear on the tablet, but 3 + 1 + 22 = 26 *udu* = 11 (l. 11) + 9 (l. 19) + 2 (l. 21) + 3 (l. 23) + 1 (l. 26) = 26 *udu*.

36. The first sign is not clear, but it must be the numeral 5. The *TA* probably is only an abbreviation of *TA-A-AN*. For *NIN-ŠID* see above, pp. 253, 337, 1.

E. A. H. 33, 34, 121.

These tablets are similar to those of the *UDU*, sheep. They are accounts of the herds composed out of 'asses' (*anšu*), 'cows' (*lid*), and 'oxen' (*gud*), and state how many were present (*gub-ba-a-an*), how many were 'taken away' (*zig-ga*, E. A. H. 121, 20, 30), or were *LAL-NI* (E. A. H. ibid. b 31, 43), or 'are dead' (*ba-til*, E. A. H. ibid. 21).

The general expression for 'cow' is *LID*. That this sign (Br. 8866) had already at the time of Ur-Ninâ the syllabic value *LID* is evident from the name of the eldest son of Ur-Ninâ, who is called *LID-DA* (Déc. pl. ii. bis, No. i.). We are justified therefore in reading this sign=*LID*, and not *AB* (Jensen, K. B. iii [1]. 58, to Gudea F, iii. 16). *AB*, Syl. b 254 = Assyr. *arḫu*, H. W. B. 132; *LID*=Assyr. *littu*, 'cow,' which is the fem. of *lû* (Arab. لَأًى), 'ox,' 'bull,' H. W. B. 364; comp. Hebr. לֵאָה, Arab. لَآةٌ. 'Ox' is *GUD* = Assyr. *lû* [or *alpu*] (Br. 5739, 5737). *LID* and *GUD* then would correspond to the Hebrew[1] פָּרָה (1 Sam. vi. 7 ff.) and פַּר respectively. The *LID* always precedes the *GUD*.

The sign for 'ass' = Br. 4984; see Z. A. iii. 205. Sum. = *anšu*; Assyr. = *imêru* (H. W. B. 91); Hebr. חֲמוֹר. When the sign for *anšu* is used alone, it always signifies the she-ass = Assyr. *atânu* (H. W. B. 158), Hebr.. אָתוֹן, أَتَان, ܐܬܢܐ. Comp. E. A. H. 33, l. 1, *anšu*, as being opposed to *anšu-uš*; l. 3, *anšu-II*, with l. 4, *anšu-uš-II*. In O. B. I. 124, on the other hand, *anšu* is never found alone, but has either *SAL* or *UŠ* after it; comp. ibid. col. iv. 1 ff. Hence *anšu-UŠ*=*imêru*=חֲמוֹר, while *anšu* or *anšu-sal* = *etânu*, אָתוֹן, the 'she-ass.'

The following *LID*, *GUD*, and *ANŠU* may occur :—

[1] The Hebrew אלף is gen. comm. embracing both *LID* and *GUD*.

	LID	*GUD*	*ANŠU*	
1.	(*a*) *lid-AL*	(*b*) *gud-GIŠ*	(*c*) *anšu-(sal)*	(*d*) *anšu-UŠ*
2.	(*a*) *lid-AL-(RUG-GA)*	(*b*) *gud-GIŠ-(RUG-GA)*	*anšu-(sal) (RUG-GA)*	*anšu-uš-(RUG-GA)*
3.		*NU-gud-GIŠ-(RUG-GA)*		
4.	*lid-(RUG-GA)*	*gud-(RUG-GA)* *NU-GUD-(RUG-GA)* (see under 3)		
5.	*lid-II GIŠ-TUG*	*gud-II (GIŠ-TUG)*	*anšu-II GIŠ-TUG*	
6.	*lid-II*	*gud-II*		*anšu-uš-II*
7.		*gud-II (RUG-GA)*		*anšu-uš-II (RUG-GA)*
8.	*lid-I*	*gud-I*	*anšu-(sal)-I*	*anšu-uš-I*
9.		*gud-I (RUG-GA)*		
10.	*lid-amar-ga*	*gud-amar-ga*	*anšu-(sal)amar-ga*	*anšu-uš-amar-ga*
11.	*lid-šu-gì*	*gud-šu-gì*	*anšu-šu-gì*	*anšu-uš-šu-gì*
12.			*ànšu-amar-NÀ*	

This arrangement is based chiefly upon the *ŠU-NIGIN* paragraph in O. B. I. 124, rev. col. v., supplemented by that of O. B. I. 126, rev. col. ii. fol., and the above-mentioned tablets of the E. A. H. collection.

1. *LID-AL*; *GUD-GIŠ*; *ANŠU-(SAL)*; *ANŠU-UŠ*. As regards the meaning of *UŠ* as opposed to *SAL* in O. B. I. 126, rev. iv. 14, it is evident that the former (*UŠ*) can only mean = *zikaru*, 'male.' As such it is like the *UŠ* occurring in connection with *puhâdu* (not = that which is found after *UDU*). *ANŠU-UŠ* then would be the 'he-ass,' *ANŠU-(SAL)* the 'she-ass.' And because these two always head the lists of the asses, which lists generally are concluded with the *ANŠU-AMAR-GA* (= sucking asses, see there), we may rightly suppose that these two expressions signify the 'full-grown' asses, the he- and she-asses, κατ' ἐξοχήν. As such they would correspond to the *LID-AL* and the *GUD-GIŠ*. The meaning of the *AL* is not yet certain. The *LID-AL*, however, head the lists of the *LID*, as do the *GUD-GIŠ* those of the *GUD*, both of which lists are again concluded by the *LID-*

AMAR-GA and the *GUD-AMAR-GA* respectively. *GIŠ* may mean *edlu*, *zikaru*, *rabû*, Br. 5702, 5707, 5704, suggesting at once the idea of 'strength.' *AL*, being parallel to *GIŠ*, undoubtedly has a similar meaning. *LID-AL* then is = *littu rabîtu*, *GUD-GIŠ* = the *lû rabû*, the 'great' (i. e. 'full-grown') cow, the 'great' (i. e. 'full-grown') bull. That *AL* must have here some such meaning is evident from E. A. H. 135, 2 (unpublished), where we find the *LID-GAL* (= *rabû*) preceding those called *LID MU-IV*.

2. *LID-AL-RUG-GA* (O. B. I. 126, rev. iii. 1); *GUD-GIŠ RUG-GA*, *ANŠU-(SAL) RUG-GA*, *ANŠU-UŠ RUG-GA*. The *RUG-GA* clearly indicates—because found behind cows and bulls as well as behind he- and she-asses—a certain *quality* common to *all animals*. We have seen that it is also to be found after the 'sheep,' and this irrespective of age; comp. No. 7, *gud-II RUG-GA*; No. 9, *gud-I RUG-GA*. *RUG-GA alone* occurs only in the *ŠU-NIGIN* paragraph, while in the body of the tablet this expression is always followed by the signs for *ENGAR* or *NU-BANDA* or *PA-AL*, or even proper names (see above, under *RUG-GA*, p. 349 ff.). The *RUG-GA*, then, signifies here as well as there the *bodies* (the flesh = meat) belonging to somebody, the 'income.'

3. *NU-GUD-GIŠ*, or also *NU-GUD* (R. A. iii. 127, 16). In O. B. I. 126, iii. 6, this animal is mentioned immediately after the *GUD-GIŠ* (l. 4) and followed by the *GUD-I*. In O. B. I. 126, no *GUD-II* are mentioned; if they were, the *NU-GUD-GIŠ* would no doubt have been placed between the *GUD-GIŠ* and the *GUD-II*. The literal translation of these signs would be: Not-bull. It is hardly probable that the *NU* negates the *GIŠ*; if this were the case we would expect *GUD-NU-GIŠ*, i. e. a bull which is not *GIŠ*, 'full-grown.' Besides this, the expression would be too general, for every *GUD* that is not *GIŠ* is *NU-GIŠ*, 'not full-grown'; hence it might be applied to all *GUD*, whether they be one or two years old. No, the *NU* negatives the *GUD* or *lû*, for we have also the expression *NU-GUD*. *Lû* is the masc. of *littu* and means 'bull.' A *NU-GUD* then would be an 'ox,' in

contradistinction to bull, and a *NU-GUD-GIŠ* is a 'full-grown ox.' As such he is *RUG-GA*, i. e. the income of a shepherd (O. B. I. 126, iii. 6; comp. also R. A. iii. 127, 16). In this latter place the *NU-GUD RUG-RUG* is followed by *NU-ZU*, and as such he belongs to *Ur-*^(dingir)^ *KAL dumu* (*GA*)*LU-*^(dingir)^ *EN-ZU*. *NU-ZU*, it was maintained (see above, p. 352), is = *non-cognovit*, sc. any *LID*. The *NU-GUD NU-ZU* then mentioned here would be an 'ox' which *never* (*NU*), even when he was not yet a *NU-GUD*, did *ZU*, i. e. an undefiled ox.

4. *LID; GUD.*

LID and *GUD*, when used alone, signify the 'cow' and the 'bull' in general. As such they precede the *LID-II* and the *GUD-II*. A calf or young bull came to be signified by *LID* and *GUD* when they were three years old; hence they are placed after the *LID-AL* and the *GUD-GIŠ*, which latter must have reached the age of four years, if they deserved to be called *AL* or *GIŠ* respectively.

5. *LID-II GIŠ-TUG* (written *KU*); *GUD-II GIŠ-TUG; ANŠU-II GIŠ-TUG.*

The expression *GIŠ-TUG*, as is evident from these examples, must be a *general* expression, applicable to cows, bulls, she-asses (and by analogy also to he-asses), to male and female. So far I have found this expression only after the numeral II, which indicates the age of the animal according to years, standing as such for *MU-II* (see E. A. H. 135, 2 ff., *lid-MU-IV*, *lid-MU-III*, &c.; and E. A. H. 121, 40, *anšu-uš RUG-RUG NU-ZU MU-III*). These *GIŠ-TUG* animals are enumerated between the *LID*, *GUD* and the *LID-II*, *GUD-II*. The force of this expression is not yet clear to me. Has it anything to do with the *time* when these animals either want 'to cover' or 'be covered'? Their being mentioned between the *LID*, *GUD* and *LID-II*, *GUD-II*, &c., would make this idea probable.

6–8. Animals followed by a number.

This number indicates, as has already been said under (5),

the years, standing for *MU-II* or *MU-I*. A *Lid-II* would be a 'heifer,' a *lid-I* a 'calf' of one year, &c., &c.

10. *LID-AMAR-GA; GUD-AMAR-GA; ANŠU-(SAL)-AMAR-GA; ANŠU-UŠ-AMAR-GA.*

GA, Br. 6114, *šizbu*, H. W. B. 649, 'milk'; or Br. 6115: *tulû*, H. W. B. 707. *AMAR*, Br. 9098 = *bûru*, H. W. B. 169, 'the young one' (of animals and men). What precedes *AMAR* is determinative, indicating what kind of *AMAR* it is, whether it belongs to the cows (*lid*), bulls (*gud*), she-asses (*ANŠU-(SAL)*), or he-asses (*ANŠU-UŠ*). *LID-AMAR-GA*, lit. translated cow-young-(of) milk, i.e. *bûru ša eli tu-lu-u*, which still 'sucks.' The expression *AMAR-GA* then would correspond to the *urišu-ŠAG-DUG* or to *puḫâdu-NU-UR*.

In the *NIGIN-BA* paragraph (lit. *its* (*ba*) grand total) of O. B. I. 126, rev. vi., the *LID-AMAR-GA* and *GUD-AMAR-GA* are comprised under the title *AMAR-GUD-ṢUN*, i. e. *bûrê ša alpê* (*gud* = *alpu*, as such comprising also the *LID*), and the *ANŠU-(ŠAL)-AMAR-GA* and *ANŠU-UŠ-AMAR-GA* are mentioned as *AMAR-ANŠU-ṢUN*, i. e. *bûrê ša imêrê*.

11. Very often occur also the so-called *LID-ŠU-GÌ*, *GUD-ŠU-GÌ*, *ANŠU-ŠU-GÌ*, *ANŠU-UŠ-ŠU-GÌ*. Whenever these animals are mentioned, they follow the *AMAR-GA*.

GÌ here = Br. 6307. In these old texts *GÌ* stands very often for *GI* (Br. 2385). *ŠU-GI*, Br. 7129 = *šâbu*, H. W. B. 652, '*grau sein' oder 'werden,' 'alt, greis sein.*' Comp. also *ŠU-GI* = *šêbu*, Br. ibid., H. W. B. ibid.

The animals thus signified then would be the 'old' animals. Thureau-Dangin, '*hors d'âge*'; see R. A. iii. p. 130, l. 9.

12. In O. B. I. 124 also occur the so-called *AMAR-ANŠU-NÀ-A* (iii. 25; v. 20) or *ANŠU-AMAR-NÀ-A* (iv. 4).

NÀ = T. C. 261 = Br. 8990, *iršu*, 'bed'; 8997, *rabâṣu*, H. W. B. 610 (*utûlu*, H. W. B. 158 and 438 *sub* נאל), 'to lie down.' The young asses thus called are those that 'lie down in the yard,' either on account of sickness (comp. also *KI-NÀ* = *tapšaḫu*) or because they are still too young to join the herd. Comp. also O. B. I. 124, rev. iv., last line, where we seem to have [*AMAR-ANŠU*]-*A-NÀ*.

13. In the enumeration of these cattle we not only hear of certain animals as being exchanged (*SAG-KU*) for others, but also as being *AZAG-TA-ŠAM*. Comp. O. B. I. 124, i. 17, 1 *anšu AZAG-TA-ŠAM*; ibid. ii. 11, 1 *gud AZAG-TA-ŠAM*. For this expression, see Br. 9903, *šîmatu*, and A. B. P. R. p. 126, '*das durch Kauf erworbene Besitztum*,' lit. 'a thing paid for with money.'

After these introductory remarks it will suffice to give a transcription and translation, as far as possible, of the above-mentioned tablets.

E. A. H. 33.

Obverse.

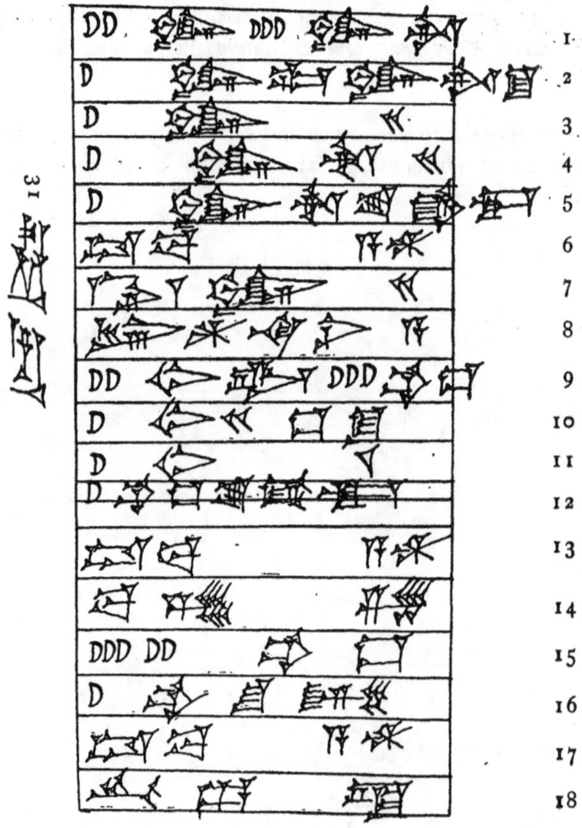

E. A. H. 33.

Obverse.

2 *anšu* 3 *anšu-uš*	2 she-asses 3 he-asses
1 *anšu sag-anšu-uš-ku*	1 she-ass exchanged for a he-ass
1 *anšu-II*	1 she-ass of 2 years
1 *anšu-uš-II*	1 he-ass of 2 years
1 *anšu-uš RUG-GA EN-GAR*	1 he-ass the income of the shepherd
gub-ba-a-an	are present
lal-ni 1 *anšu-II*	Minus 1 she-ass of 2 years
(*Ga*)*lu-*(*dingir*) *Na-ru-a*	(Ga)lu-Narua (shepherd)
2 *lid-al* 3 *gud-giš*	2 great cows 3 great bulls
1 *lid-II giš-tug*	1 cow of 2 years *GIŠ-TUG*
1 *lid-I*	1 cow of 1 year
1 *gud-giš RUG-GA EN-GAR*	1 great bull the income of the shepherd
gub-ba-a-an	are present
Ba-zig-gi	Baziggi (shepherd)
5 *gud-giš*	5 great bulls
1 *gud-šu-gì*	1 old bull
gub-ba-a-an	are present
Uru-kal-la	Urukalla (shepherd)

Left side.

31 *Ad-da*	Adda.

E. A. H. 33.

Reverse.

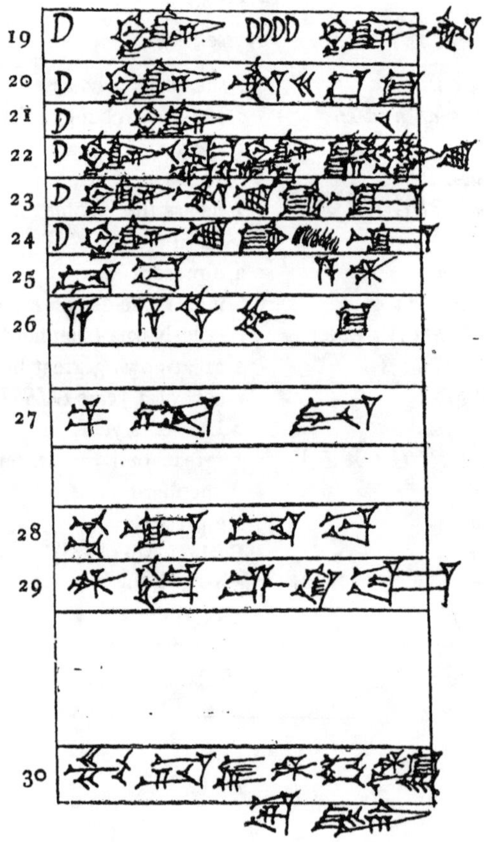

Reverse.

19	1 *anšu* 4 *anšu-uš*	1 she-ass 4 he-asses
20	1 *anšu-uš-II giš-tug*	1 he-ass of 2 years *GIŠ-TUG*
	1 *anšu-I*	1 she-ass of 1 year
	1 *anšu-I sag-anšu-ku MU-IN-RUG KA-PI-GAR-MA BA-A-TIL-KU*	1 she-ass of 1-year exchanged for a she-ass . . .
	1 *anšu-uš RUG-GA EN-GAR*	1 he-ass the income of the shepherd
	1 *anšu RUG-GA ENGAR*	1 she-ass the income of the shepherd
25	*gub-ba-a-an*	are present
	A-a-ud-bu-ku	Aaudbuku (shepherd)
	Pa Ad-da	Overseer: Adda
	gud-engar-gub-ba	Oxen employed for the tilling of the ground belonging
	(dingir) *Nin-Mar-ki-ka*	to *Nin-Mar-ki*
30	*Mu-uš-sa* (ilu) *Bur-*(ilu) *Sin lugal*	One year after Bur-Sin (II.) became king.

22. The signs of this line are so crowded that it is very difficult to distinguish one from the other.

The signs for *MU-IN-RUG*, however, are clear. The sign for *RUG* sometimes also stands for *ZU* (and vice versa). Have we perhaps to read *MU-IN-ZU* (*ZU* = ידע), and to translate, '1 she-ass of one year exchanged for a she-ass that has been covered'? The next four signs probably stand for a proper name. *PI* is not clear; it might also be *ŠI*. The two signs read above *BA-A* (= two strokes) might also be read *LUǴ*. For *TIL-KU*, comp. Br. 1577: *TIL-KU-DA* = *nîtu*, H. W. B. 460: '*Zurückhaltung, Hemmung.*' Probably we have to read here *LUǴ-BE-ZID*, and see in this a certain office, that of a shepherd. The whole line then might be translated: '1 she-ass of one year exchanged for a she-ass that has been covered, belonging to *KA-PI-GAR-MA*, the *LUǴ-BE-ZID* (= servant of the pasture)?' Comp. with this the parallel passage in E. A. H. 34, 22, in which line the signs are just as crowded as here.

27. For *PA*, see under 'officials,' p. 411 (*e*) ff.

28. See p. 334, 1 (*c*).

E. A. H. 34.

Obverse.

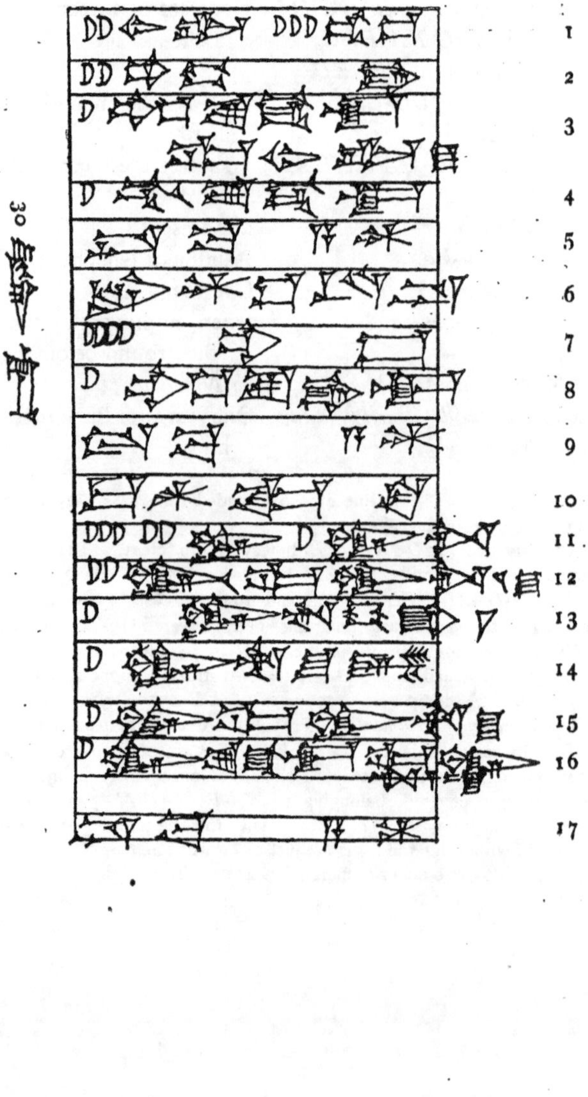

30

E. A. H. 34.

Obverse.

2 *lid-al* 3 *gud-giš*	2 great cows 3 great bulls
2 *gud-amar-ga*	2 bulls that suck
1 *gud-giš RUG-GA EN-GAR sag-lid-al-ku*	1 great bull the income of the shepherd exchanged for a great cow
1 *gud-I RUG-GA ENGAR*	1 bull of 1 year the income of the shepherd
gub-ba-a-an	are present
(*Ga*)*lu-*(*dingir*) *Giš-bar-ud-du*	(Ga)lu-Gishbaruddu (shepherd)
4 *gud-giš*	4 great bulls
1 *gud-giš RUG-GA EN-GAR*	1 great bull the income of the shepherd
gub-ba-a-an	are present
Ur-(*dingir*) *Ka-di*	Ur-Kadi (shepherd)
5 *anšu* 1 *anšu-uš*	5 she-asses 1 he-ass
2 *anšu-I sag-anšu-uš-I-ku*	2 she-asses of 1 year exchanged for a he-ass of 1 year
1 *anšu-uš amar-ga-I*	1 he-ass that sucks, 1 year old
1 *anšu-uš šu-gi*	1 old he-ass
1 *anšu sag-anšu-uš-ku*	1 she-ass exchanged for a he-ass
1 *anšu RUG-GA ENGAR sag-anšu-uš-I-ku*	1 she-ass the income of the shepherd exchanged for a he-ass of 1 year
gub-ba-a-an	are present

Left side.

Lugal-engar	Royal shepherd.

E. A. H. 34.

Reverse.

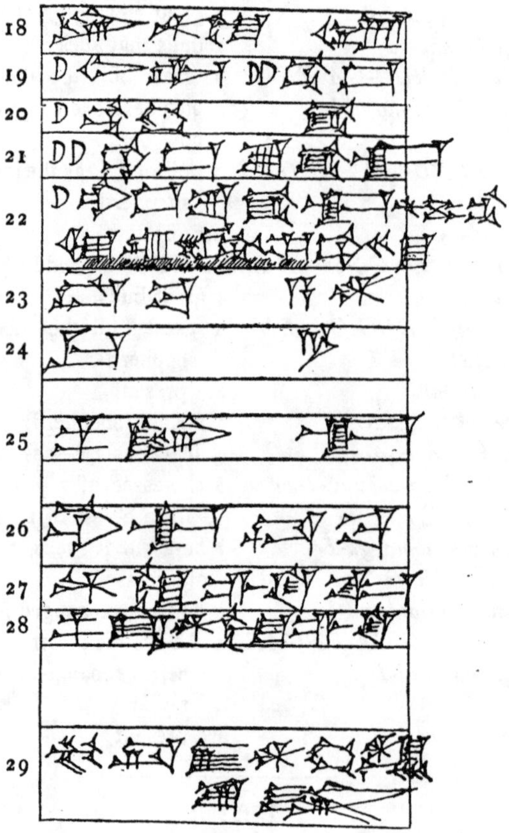

Reverse.

18	(*Ga*)*lu*-(*dingir*) *Nin-sun*	(Ga)lu-Ninsun (shepherd) -
	1 *lid-al* 2 *gud-giš*	1 great cow 2 great bulls
20	1 *gud-amar-ga*	1 bull that sucks
	2 *gud-giš RUG-GA EN-GAR*	2 great bulls the income of the shepherd
	1 *gud-giš RUG-GA EN-GAR nu-banda-gud ù dup-sar gud-I*[1] *sag-gud-II-ku*	1 great bull the income of the chief shepherd and scribe, of the oxen that are 1 year old instead of the oxen that are 2 years old
	gub-ba-a-an	are present
	Ur-Gar	Ur-Gar (shepherd)
25	*PA lugal-engar*	overseer of the royal shepherds
	gud-engar-gub-ba	Oxen employed for the tilling of the ground belonging to
	(*dingir*) *Nin-Mar-ki-ka*	*Nin-Mar-ki*
	PA-SANGA (*dingir*) *Nin-Mar-ki*	high-priest of *Nin-Mar-ki*
	Mu-uš-sa (*ilu*) *Bur*-(*ilu*) *Sin lugal*	One year after Bur-Sin (II.) became king.

[1] Comp. R. A. iii. p. 129: 1 *anšu-uš RUG-GA dup-sar gud-X*; '1 *âne Rug-ga du bouvier-scribe* (*chef*) *de* 10 *bœufs*.'

E. A. H. 121.

Obverse.

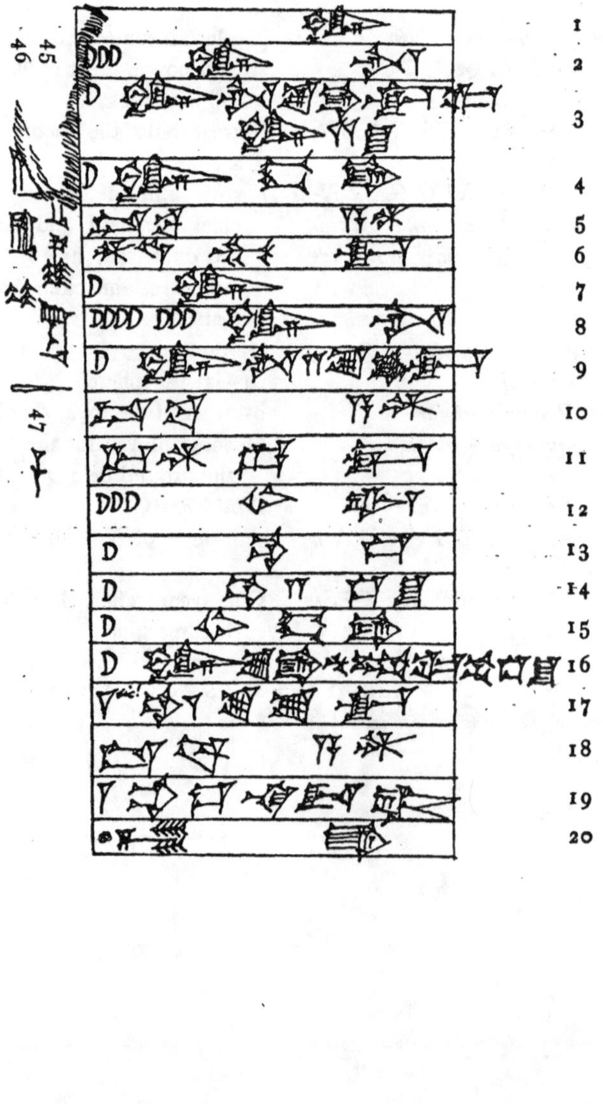

E. A. H. 121.

Obverse.

anšu	she-asses
3 *anšu-uš*	3 he-asses
1 *anšu-uš RUG-GA engar-I sag-anšu-II-ku*	1 he-ass the income of the shepherd, 1 year old, exchanged for a she-ass of 2 years
1 *anšu-amar-ga*	1 she-ass that sucks
gub-ba-a-an	are present
(*dingir*) *Utu-MU engar*	*Utu-MU* (Shamashiddin), shepherd
1 *anšu*	1 she-ass
7 *anšu-uš*	7 he-asses
1 *anšu-uš-II RUG-GA engar*	1 he-ass of 2 years the income of the shepherd
gub-ba-a-an	are present
Ur-(*dingir*) *KAL engar*	Kalbi-Lamassu, shepherd
3 *lid-al*	3 great cows
1 *gud-giš*	1 great bull
1 *gud-II giš-tug*	1 bull of 2 years *GIŠ-TUG*
1 *lid-amar-ga*	1 calf that sucks
1 *anšu RUG-GA nu-bandu-gud sag-gud-giš-ku*	1 she-ass the income of the chief shepherd, exchanged for a great bull
1 *gud-I RUG-RUG engar*	1 bull of one year the income of the shepherd
gub-ba-a-an	are present
1 *gud-giš Na-da-tum*	1 great bull Nadatum (see p. 337, 1)
zig-ga	has taken away

Left side.

[*Ur-*(*dingir*) *Nin-g*]*iš-zid-da*	[Ur-Ning]ishzidda
Ur-E-ninnû	and Ur-Eninnû
Ğal	the Ğal.

E. A. H. 121.

Reverse.

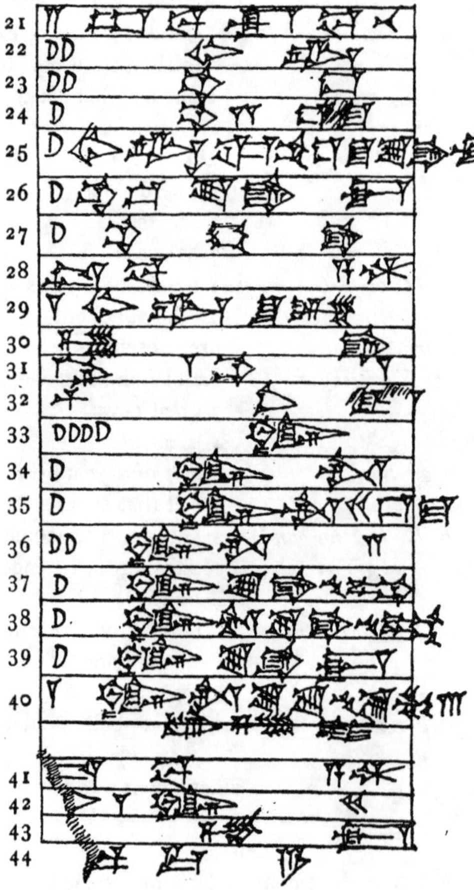

Reverse.

2 *Ab-ba engar ba-til*	2 belonging to Abba the shepherd are dead
2 *lid-al*	2 great cows
2 *gud-giš*	2 great bulls
1 *gud-II giš-tug*	1 bull of two years *GIŠ-TUG*
1 *lid-al sag-gud-giš-ku RUG-GA engar*	1 great cow, exchanged for a great bull the income of the shepherd
1 *gud-giš RUG-GA engar*	1 great bull the income of the shepherd
1 *gud-amar-ga*	1 bull that sucks
gub-ba-a-an	are present
1 *lid-al šu-gi*	1 old great cow
zig-ga	is taken away
lal-ni 1 *gud-I*	minus 1 bull of one year
Bar-ru engar	Barru, shepherd
4 *anšu*	4 she-asses
1 *anšu-uš*	1 he-ass
1 *anšu-uš-II giš-tug*	1 he-ass of two years *GIŠ-TUG*
2 *anšu-uš-II*	2 he-asses of two years
1 *anšu RUG-GA nu-banda-gud*	1 she-ass the income of the chief shepherd
1 *anšu-uš RUG-GA nu-banda-gud*	1 he-ass the income of the chief shepherd
1 *anšu RUG-GA engar*	1 she-ass the income of the shepherd
1 *anšu-uš RUG-RUG NU-ZU mu-III (Ga)lu-zi-lum*[1]	1 he-ass, an income, never having covered, three years old, belonging to (Ga)luzilum
gub-ba-a-an	are present
[*lal-n*]*i* 1 *anšu-II*	minus 1 she-ass of two years
-gi engar	-gi, shepherd
PA Ur-Gar	Overseer: Ur-Gar

[1] For this name see also R. A. iii. p. 135: *ŠAG-GAL anšu ZI-LUM*, 'food for the asses *ZI-LUM*,' and ibid. p. 139, l. 14.

E. A. H. 47, 48, 49, 122.

These tablets are accounts of wool (*SIG*). It is no wonder that the people at this time were very particular in keeping account of their sheep—how many of them were present, and thus were able to yield a certain measure of wool, and how many were absent, thus a clear loss to the owners of the herds. The people were chiefly shepherds. Among other things, wool was the most favoured article that the shepherds dealt in, because it furnished the material for the clothes (*SIG-KU*) of the people. The wool is arranged according to *quality*. Four qualities are distinguished; then comes the common wool (*DU*), after this the black (*GIG*), and lastly the wool called *LUM*. The *ŠU-NIGIN* gives the total income of the wool according to talents and manas. That each of these tablets is simply an account of the wool gotten from one particular herd is evident from the fact that the name of the shepherd (*NA-GID*) to whom the herd belongs is almost always given.

The expressions which occur in these tablets are the following:—

1. *SIG*. This sign we have already found in O. B. I. 87, ii. 44. T. C. 293, '*non assimilé*.' But see Jensen, K. B. iii[1]. p. 30, note 10 (Gudea B, iv. 42). *SIG*=Assyr. *šipâtu*, Br. 10781, H. W. B. 678, 'wool.'

SIG-KU=*šipâtu ana lubuštum* (comp. Nbr. 754, 6), 'wool for clothes.' The following 'kinds' of this *SIG-KU* (or only *KU*, in which case we ought to add a *SIG*; comp. E. A. H. 48, 1, 2, *SIG-KU*; in ll. 3, 4, 5 only *KU* = (*SIG*)-*KU*. In E. A. H. 49 we have *SIG-KU* only in l. 1, but in the following lines *KU* = an abbreviation for *SIG-KU*, so everywhere in these tablets where *KU* stands alone) are mentioned:—

(*a*) *SIG-KU LUGAL*.
(*b*) *SIG-KU UŠ-LUGAL*.
(*c*) (*SIG*)-*KU III-kam-UŠ*.
(*d*) (*SIG*)-*KU IV-kam-UŠ*.

(*e*) *SIG-DU.*
(*f*) *SIG-DU-GIG.*
(*g*) *SIG-GIG.*
(*h*) *SIG-LUM.*

(*a*) Wherever the *SIG-KU LUGAL* is mentioned, it stands first. It is therefore the 'wool' (*SIG*) of 'royal quality' = the highest excellence.

(*b*) Next to it is the *SIG UŠ-LUGAL.* *UŠ*, Br. 5032, *emêdu*, H. W. B. 79. The 'wool' *UŠ-LUGAL*, then, is the wool that 'stands' (*UŠ*) nearest to that of royal quality, i. e. here as much as 'second quality.'

(*c*), (*d*) If *UŠ-LUGAL* is = 'second kind,' then *III-kam-UŠ* and *IV-kam-UŠ* are the third or fourth kinds respectively. Lit. the wool (*sig*) which stands (*UŠ*) third (*III-kam*), &c., in quality. In some cases the *kam* is left out.

(*e*) *SIG-DU.* The wool thus signified always follows in those tablets that of the 'fourth' quality; it must be therefore of a less quality than the *IV-kam-UŠ.* Thureau-Dangin may be right in supposing for *DU* some such sense as '*commun, ordinaire*,' R. A. iii. 136.

(*f*), (*g*) *SIG-GIG.* For this expression, see iv. R. 8, iii. 28, 29. *SIG-UD SIG-GIG* = *ši-pa-a-te pi-ṣa-a-te ši-pa-a-te ṣal-ma-a-te.* *SIG-GIG*, then, is the 'black wool.' *SIG-DU-GIG* = the common black wool.

(*h*) *SIG-LUM* occurs in E. A. H. 48, 5: 3 *gûnu* 38 *ma-na* *LUM*-4-*uš*—here *LUM* alone, neither *SIG* nor *KU* stands before it; E. A. H. 47, 5: 6 *gûnu KU-LUM*-4-*uš*; E. A. H. 51, 4: [*GU-ŠUR*] *KU-LUM*-4-*uš*. Comp. with this latter E. A. H. 50, 6: 1 *GUŠUR SIG-DU-GIG.* It will be noticed here that whenever this *LUM* is mentioned, '*kam*' after the numeral 4 is omitted. This *LUM*-wool follows after that of the 'fourth quality,' but stands before the *SIG-DU.* Ought we to see in this *LUM* only another expression for *GIG*? E. A. H. 51, 4, compared with E. A. H. 50, 6, would favour this.

LUM = *unnubu* and *uššubu*, 'to sprout,' H. W. B. pp. 97 and

141. Could we derive from this the signification of 'young' wool in the sense of wool that is not yet grown long?

2. Sometimes we find after the qualities mentioned *sub* (*a*)–(*è*) also the expression *IGI-NU-SAG-*(*ge*). With what meaning?

3. In some texts we also are told from what particular part of the sheep's body this wool was taken. Comp., e. g., R. A. iii. 131, 1: 2 *ma-na* 15 *ṬU SIG* GU-UDU *KU-LUGAL IGI-NU-SAG-ge.*

The sign for *GU* here is that of Br. 3202. For the meaning of it, see Delitzsch, Ass. St. pp. 122 and 138, and comp. such expressions as *eṣen ṣîru*, *eṣen ṣîr elippi*, H. W. B. 121. The *SIG-GU-UDU*, then, is the 'wool taken from the *back* (*GU*) of the sheep (*UDU*).' See Thureau-Dangin, R. A. iii 132, 1.

4. *GU* or *GÛNU* (Br. 3199, here apparently an abbreviation of Br. 3334, *GUN*) = *biltu.* 1 *GU* = 60 *MA-NA*; 1 *MA-NA* = 60 *ṬU* (shekel); 1 *ṬU* = 180 *ŠE.* See Reissner, J. A. O. S. 18, p. 372.

5. *SIG BA-LAL. LAL*=*šaḳâlu*, H. W. B. p. 685: 'the wool was paid for,' sc. 'with money' (see A. B. P. R. p. 95).

E. A. H. 47.

Obverse. Reverse.

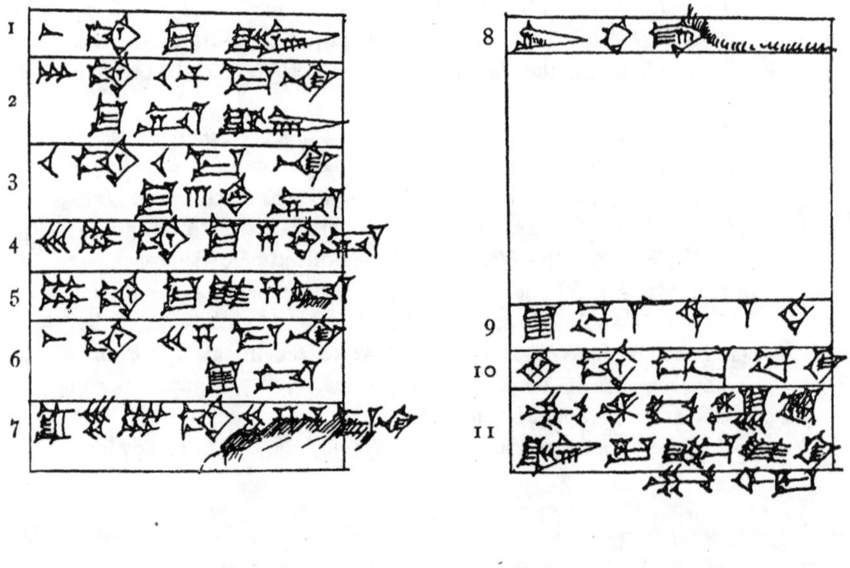

E. A. H. 47.

1 *gûnu ku-lugal*	1 talent of (wool for) clothing, royal quality
3 *gûnu* 10½ *ma-na ku-uš-lugal*	3 talents 10½ manas of (wool for) clothing, second quality
10 *gûnu* 10 *ma-na ku-III-kam-uš*	10 talents 10 manas of (wool for) clothing, third quality
36 *gûnu ku-IV-kam-uš*	36 talents of (wool for) clothing, fourth quality
6 *gûnu ku-LUM-IV-uš*	6 talents of (wool for) clothing, *LUM*, fourth quality
1 *gûnu* 24 *ma-na sig-du*	1 talent 24 manas of common wool
šu-nigin 57 *gûnu* 44½ *ma-na* [*SIG-ṢUN*]	Total: 57 talents 44½ manas of wool
Ir-dug-ga [*na-gid*]	Irdugga [shepherd]
sig ba-lal ud-I-kam	The wool was paid for on the first day
šag Tik-ab-ba-^{ki}	*Tik-ab-ba-*^{ki}
Mu $^{(ilu)}$ *Bur-*$^{(ilu)}$ *Sin lugal Ur-bil-lum-*^{ki} *mu-ḫul*	In the year when king Búr-Sin (II.) devastated Urbillum.

E. A. H. 48.

Obverse.

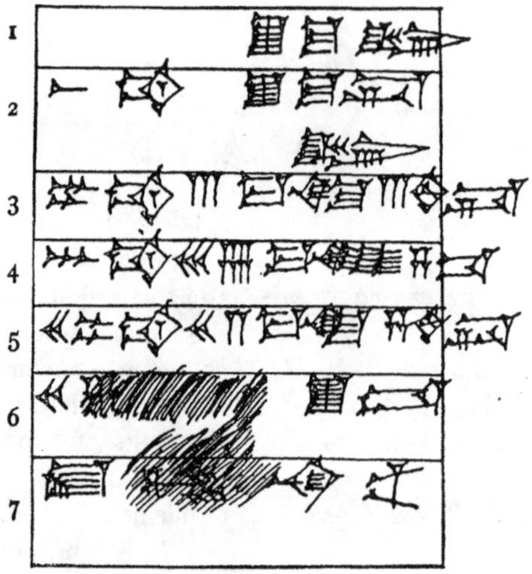

Reverse.

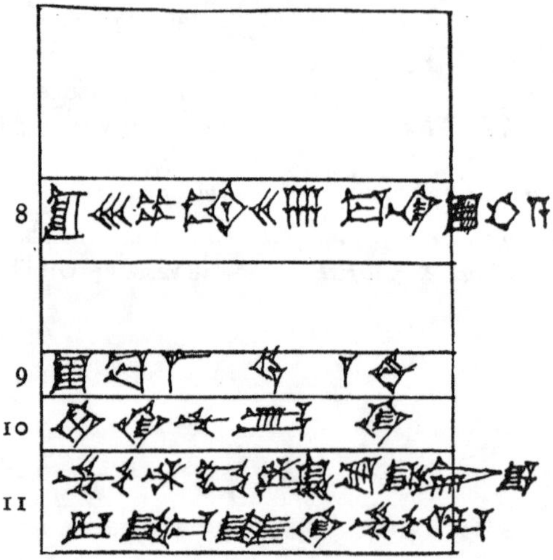

E. A. H. 48.

Sig-ku-lugal	Wool for clothing, royal quality [1]
1 *gúnu sig-ku-uš-lugal*	1 talent of wool for clothing, second quality
5 *gúnu* 3 *ma-na ku-III-kam-uš*	5 talents 3 manas of (wool for) clothing, third quality
24 *gúnu* 22 *ma-na ku-IV-kam-uš*	24 talents 22 manas of (wool for) clothing, fourth quality
3 *gúnu* 37 *ma-na ku-LUM-IV-uš*	3 talents 37 manas of (wool for) clothing, *LUM*, fourth quality
2[6 *ma-na*] *sig-du*	2[6 manas] of common wool
E-zi na-gid	Ezi, shepherd
šu-nigin 34 *gúnu* 28 *ma-na sig-ṣun*	Total: 34 talents 28 manas of wool
sig ba-lal ud-I-kam	The wool was paid for on the first day
šag Ki-nu-nir-^{ki}	Borsippa
Mu $^{(ilu)}$ *Bur-*$^{(ilu)}$ *Sin lugal-e Ur-bil-lum-*^{ki} *mu-ḫul*	In the year when king Bur-Sin (II.) devastated Urbillum.

[1] The amount of wool in this line is left out. Comp. also E. A. H. 51, where the *GUŠUR-KU-LUGAL* is left out, and E. A. H. 52, 6, where we have only *GUŠUR-SIG-DU* 1 *gúnu*.

E. A. H. 49.

Obverse.

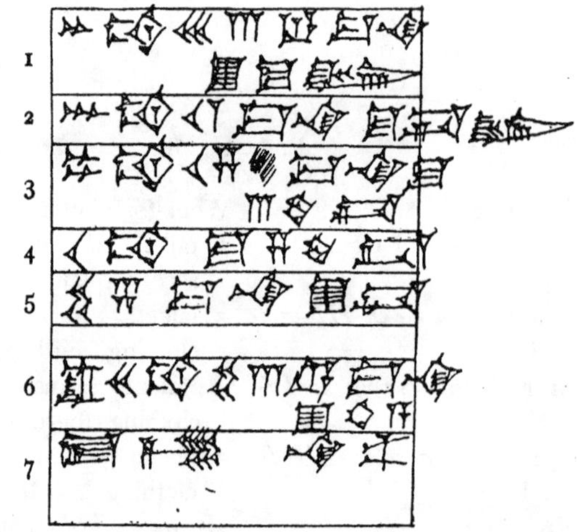

Reverse.

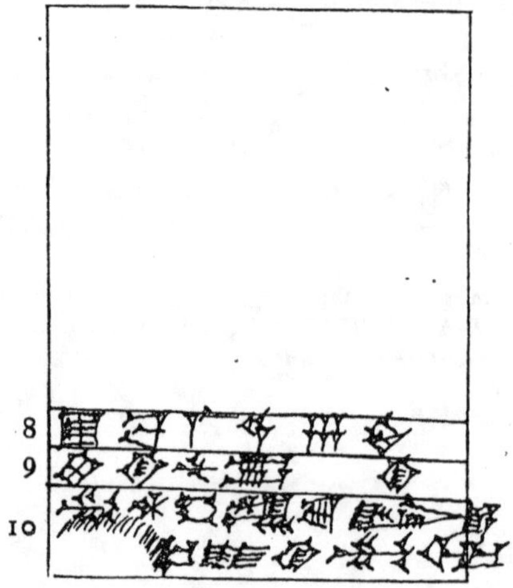

E. A. H. 49.

2 *gúnu* $33\frac{5}{6}$ *ma-na sig-ku-lugal*	2 talents $33\frac{5}{6}$ manas of wool for clothing, royal quality
3 *gúnu* 11 *ma-na ku-uš-lugal*	3 talents 11 manas of (wool for) clothing, second quality
4 *gúnu* 14 *ma-na ku-III-kam-uš*	4 talents 14 manas of (wool for) clothing, third quality
10 *gúnu ku-IV-kam-uš*	10 talents of (wool for) clothing, fourth quality
45 *ma-na sig-du*	45 manas of common wool
šu-nigin 20 *gúnu* $43\frac{5}{8}$ *ma-na sig-ṣun*	Total: 20 talents $43\frac{5}{8}$ manas of wool
E-zi na-gid	Ezi, shepherd
Sig ba-lal ud-6-kam	The wool was paid for on the sixth day
šag Ki-nu-nir-ki	Borsippa
Mu (ilu) Bur-(ilu) Sin lugal-e [Ur-bi]l-lum-ki mu-ĝul	In the year when king Bur-Sin (II.) devastated Urbillum.

E. A. H. 122.

Obverse.

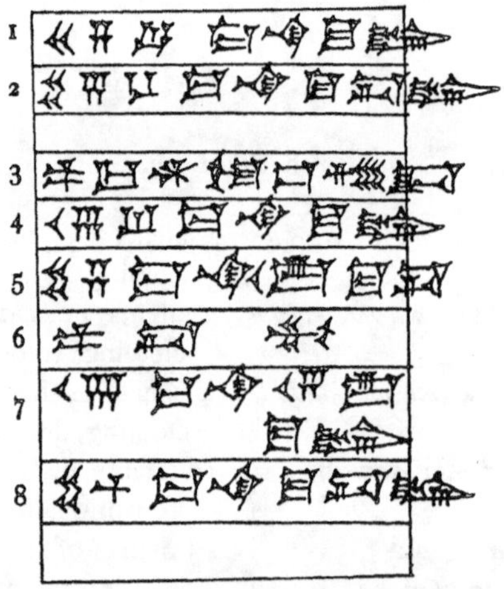

Reverse.

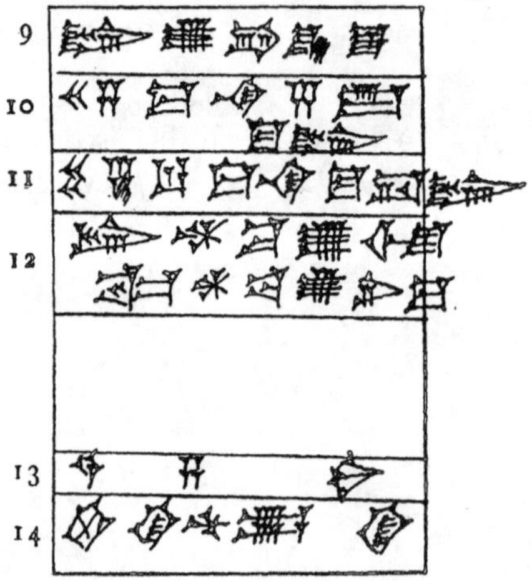

E. A. H. 122.

$24\frac{5}{8}$ *ma-na KU-lugal*	$24\frac{5}{8}$ manas of (wool for) clothing, royal quality
$45\frac{1}{3}$ *ma-na KU-uš-lugal*	$45\frac{1}{3}$ manas of (wool for) clothing, second quality
PA Ur-(dingir) Nin-giš-zid-da	Overseer: Ur-Ningishzidda
$16\frac{2}{3}$ *ma-na KU-lugal*	$16\frac{2}{3}$ manas of (wool for) clothing, royal quality
44 *ma-na* 10 *ṬU KU-uš*	44 manas 10 shekels of (wool for) clothing, second quality
PA UŠ-MU	Overseer: *UŠ-MU*
17 *ma-na* 15 *ṬU KU-lugal*	17 manas 15 shekels of (wool for) clothing, royal quality
$40\frac{1}{2}$ *ma-na KU-uš-lugal*	$40\frac{1}{2}$ manas of (wool for) clothing, second quality
LUGAL-U-KAŠ-ŠU-E	*Lugal-u-kaš-šu-e*
24 *ma-na* 5 *ṬU KU-lugal*	24 manas 5 shekels of (wool for) clothing, royal quality
$45\frac{5}{8}$ *ma-na KU-uš-lugal*	$45\frac{5}{8}$ manas of (wool for) clothing, second quality
(Ga)lu (dingir) Ba-u ù Enim-(dingir) Ba-u ni-ku	(Ga)lu-Ba'u and Enim-Ba'u, shepherds
ud 4-kam	On the fourth day (the wool was paid for)
šag Ki-nu-nir-ki	Borsippa.

E. A. H. 50.

Obverse.

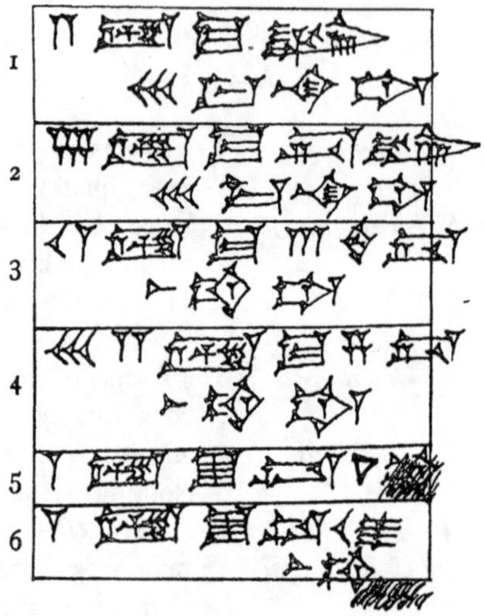

Reverse.

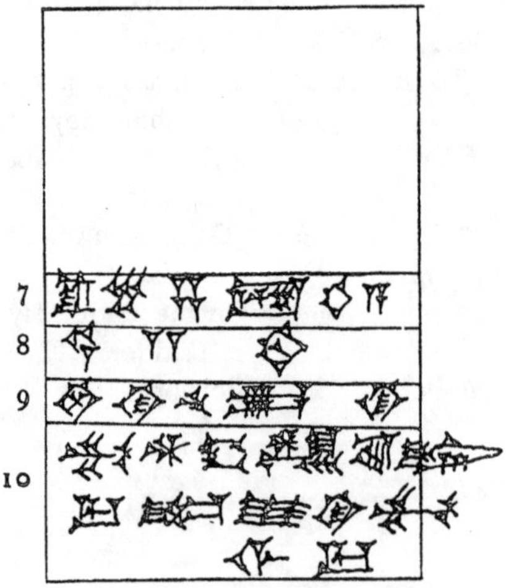

Similar in contents to the preceding are E. A. H. 50–52. They treat of some 'stuff' or 'wool' furnished for clothes. The sign transcribed by us with *GUŠUR* is by no means certain; by reading it *GUŠUR*, I would like to identify it with Br. 5500, *šinṭu*; see H. W. B. 670, '*šintu, eine bestimmte Art Thierpelz oder* Wollstoff.' This latter meaning probably has to be taken here. The *TA* at the end of each line = *ana*, 'for' so and so many manas, sc. of money. Hence these tablets would be accounts of the buying (*ta*) of a certain kind of stuff (*GUŠUR*), to be worked up by the so-called *GIN-UŠ-BAR*, '*Weberfrauen*.' Just as the preceding tablets state the selling (*lal*) of the wool by the shepherd, so these tell us the buying of that wool for the *UŠ-BAR* ('*Weberei*'), in which the *GIN-UŠ-BAR* (*Weberfrauen*) are employed.

E. A. H. 50.

2 *gušur-ku-lugal* 30 *ma-na-ta*	2 gushur for clothing, royal quality, for 30 manas
7 *gušur-ku-uš-lugal* 30 *ma-na-ta*	7 gushur for clothing, second quality, for 30 manas
11 *gušur-ku-III-kam-uš* 1 *gûnu-ta*	11 gushur for clothing, third quality, for 1 talent
32 *gušur-ku-IV-kam-uš* 1 *gûnu-ta*	32 gushur for clothing, fourth quality, for 1 talent
1 *gušur sig-du* 1 *gunû*[*-ta* ?]	1 gushur of common wool, for 1 talent
1 *gušur-sig-du-gig* 1 *gûnu-*[*ta*]	1 gushur of common wool, black, for 1 talent
šu-nigin 54 *gušur-ṣun*	Total: 54 gushur
ud-2-kam	The second day
šag Ki-nu-nir-ki	Borsippa
Mu (*ilu*) *Bur-*(*ilu*) *Sin lugal Ur-bil-lum-ki mu-gul*	In the year when king Bur-Sin (II.) devastated Urbillum.

E. A. H. 51.

Obverse.

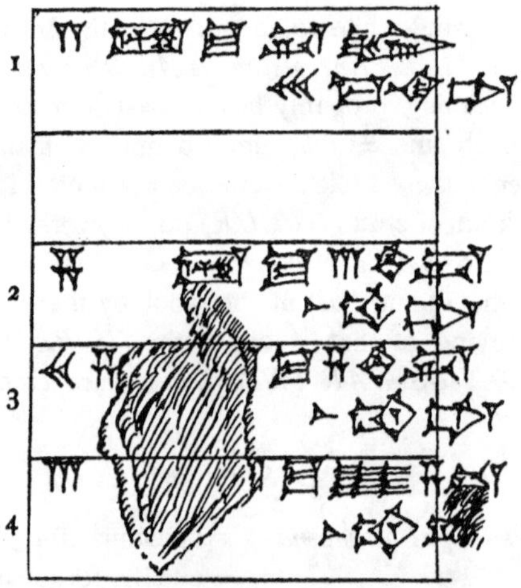

Reverse.

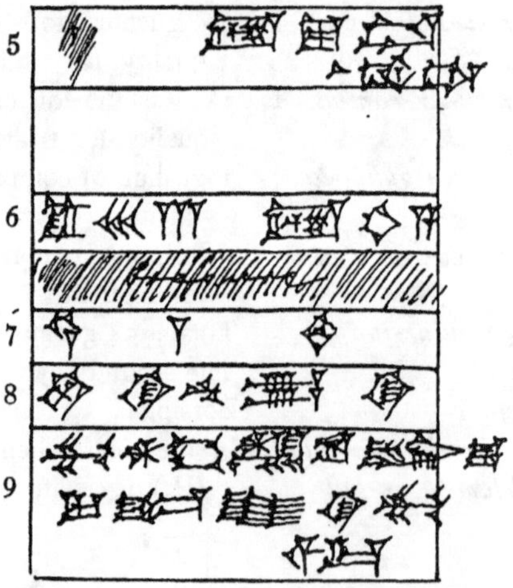

E. A. H. 51.

2 *gušur-ku-uš-lugal* 30 *ma-na-ta*	2 gushur for clothing, second quality, for 30 manas
4 *gušur-ku-III-kam-uš* 1 *gûnu-ta*	4 gushur for clothing, third quality, for 1 talent
24 [*gušur*]-*ku-IV-kam-uš* 1 *gûnu-ta*	24 [gushur] for clothing, fourth quality, for 1 talent
3 *gušur-ku-LUM* 4-*uš* (sic) 1 *gûnu-ta*	3 [gushur] of wool, that is *LUM*, fourth quality, for 1 talent
gušur-sig-du 1 *gûnu-ta*	gushur of common wool, for 1 talent
šu-nigin 33 *gušur-ṣun*	Total: 33 gushur
ud-1-kam	The first day
šag Ki-nu-nir^{ki}	Borsippa
Mu $^{(ilu)}$ *Bur-*$^{(ilu)}$ *Sin lugal-e Ur-bil-lum*^{ki} *mu-ḫul*	In the year when king Bur-Sin (II.) devastated Urbillum.

E. A. H. 52.

Obverse.

Reverse.

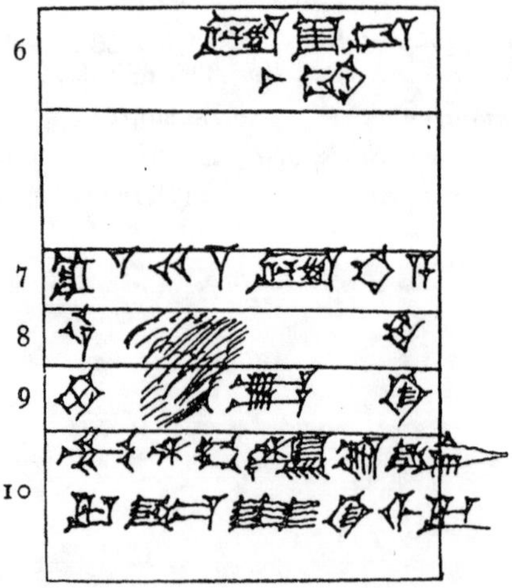

E. A. H. 52.

gušur [*-ku-lugal*] 30 *ma-n*[*a-ta*]	3 gushur for clothing, royal quality, for 30 manas
7 *gušur-ku-uš-lugal* 30 *ma-na-ta*	7 gushur for clothing, second quality, for 30 manas
25 *gušur-ku-III-kam-uš* 1 *gûnu-ta*	25 gushur for clothing, third quality, for 1 talent
1 *gušur-ku-NIN-LAM*[1]*-III-kam-uš gûnu*	1 gushur for 'splendid' clothing, third quality, for . . . talent
45 *gušur-ku-IV-kam-uš* 1 *gûnu-ta*	45 gushur for clothing, fourth quality, for 1 talent
gušur-sig-du 1 *gûnu*	gushur of common wool, for 1 talent
šu-nigin 81 *gušur-ṣun*	Total: 81 gushur
ud-[1 ?]*-kam*	The . . . day
šag [*Ki-n*]*u-nir-ki*	Borsippa
Mu (*ilu*) *Bur-*(*ilu*) *Sin lugal-e Ur-bil-lum-ki mu-ĝul*	In the year when king Bur-Sin II. devastated Urbillum.

E. A. H. 56 enumerates the cattle which furnished the wool (*SIG*). The cattle that could be shorn were the *ganam*, *udu-gal*, *udu-uš*, and *puḫâdu-ba-ur*. The latter more or less comprised the *sal-puḫâdu* as well as the *puḫâdu-uš*. The *puḫâdu-nu-ur* are always enumerated separately. They, although belonging to the 'herds' as such, were not shorn—a corroboration of the correctness of the meaning '*nu-ur*'='not weaned'='sucking.'

The numerals at the end of ll. 5, 10, 14, 20, 24, 29, 33, refer to the number of animals that furnished the wool—the *puḫâdu-nu-ur* excepted. The sum total of these animals is given in l. 38 : 796. It ought to be, however, 795; the adding together of the above-given numerals as well as those given in ll. 34, 35 shows this. L. 34 gives the number of the *udu*, i.e. the *ganam*, *udu-gal*, and *udu-uš*; l. 35 the number of the *puḫâdu-ba-ur*. And because all

[1] For *KU-NIN-LAM*, see Br. 12055, *lamḫuššû*, H. W. B. 380: *Pracht- oder Staatskleid*.

the *udu* are '*ba-ur*,' i. e. weaned, they are counted together with the *puḫâdu-ba-ur*, and called in l. 39 simply *udu-ba-ur*, the number of which is 795 (*sic*), not 796, as the tablet gives.

L. 36 gives the whole amount of the wool received from the flocks of the seven following shepherds:—Tiggil, Lugal-an-azaggi, Abbaginna, Baziggi, Ur-Gula, Ur-Ba'u, son of Atu, and Shuna. Ll. 18 and 22 are rather mutilated, so that it is impossible for me to determine exactly how many *gûnu* and *ma-na* of wool the flocks of Baziggi and Ur-Gula yielded; 6 *gûnu* and 55 *ma-na*, however, have to be divided among these two flocks. The tablet reads:

E. A. H. 56.

Obverse.

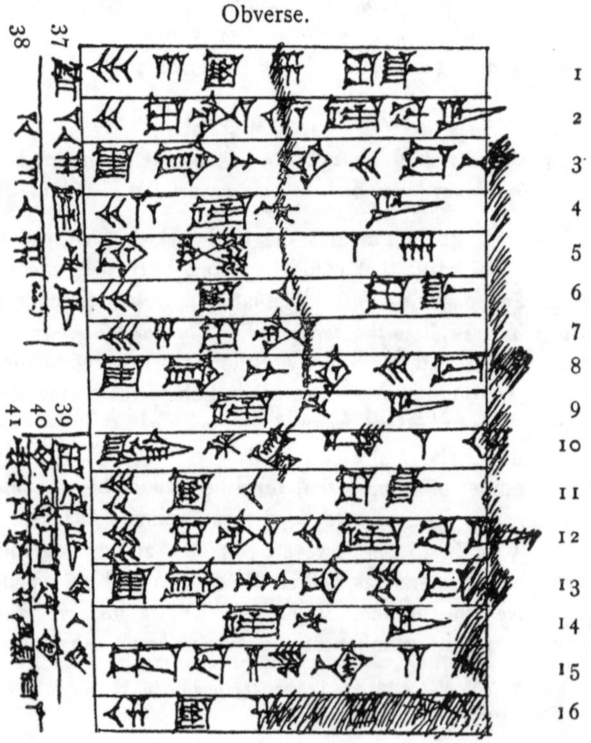

E. A. H. 56.

Obverse.

33 *ganam* 6 *udu-gal*	33 ewes, 6 rams
20 *udu-uš* 10-*lal*-1 *puḫâdu-ba-ur*	20 mature sheep, 9 weaned lambs
síg-bi 2 *gûnu* 20 *ma-na*	furnished on wool (lit. its wool is) 2 talents 20 manas
20-*lal*-1 *puḫâdu-nu-ur*	19 sucking lambs
Tig-gil 68	Tiggil (shepherd) 68
30 *ganam* 10 *udu-gal*	30 ewes, 10 rams
35 *udu-uš*	35 mature sheep
síg-bi 2 *gûnu* 30 *ma-na*	furnished on wool 2 talents 30 manas
puḫâdu-nu-ur	sucking lambs
Lugal-an-azag-gi 75	Lugal-Anazaggi (shepherd) 75
50 *ganam* 10 *udu-gal*	50 ewes, 10 rams
50 *udu-uš* 20 *puḫâdu-ba-ur*	50 mature sheep, 20 weaned lambs
síg-bi 4 *gûnu* 50 *ma-na*	furnished on wool 4 talents 50 manas
Ab-ba-gin-na 130	Abbaginna (shepherd) 130
puḫâdu-nu-ur	sucking lambs
14 *ganam* 6 *udu-uš*	14 ewes, 6 rams

Left side.

šu-nigin 76 *puḫâdu-nu-ur*	Total: 76 sucking lambs
796 (sic)	796 (*sic*. Read 795)
udu-ba-ur ud 10 *kam*	weaned sheep. The tenth day
šag Tik-ab-ba-^{ki}	Tikabba
Mu $^{(giš)}$*-gu-za* $^{(dingir)}$ *En-lil-la*(*l*)	In the year (when king Bur-Sin II. erected) the throne of Bêl.

E. A. H. 56.

Reverse.

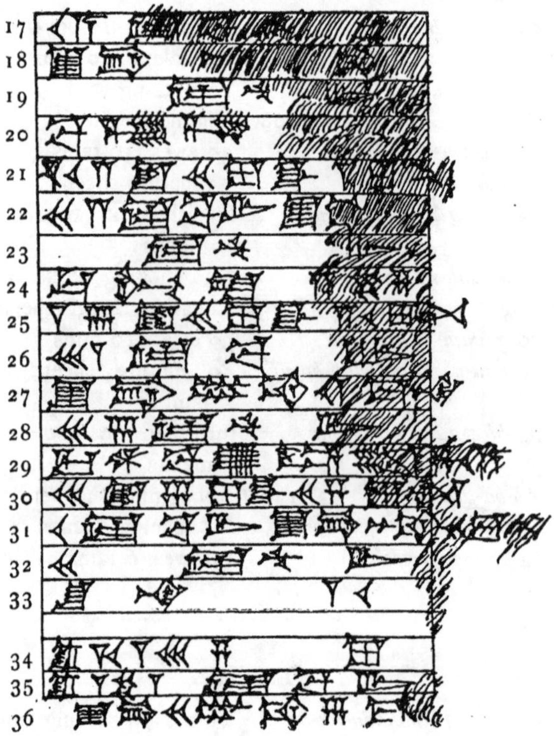

Reverse.

10-*lal*-1 *puḫádu-ba-ur*	9 weaned lambs
síg-bi	furnished on wool . . .
puḫádu-nu-ur	sucking lambs
Ba-zig-gi 29	Baziggi (shepherd) 29
72 *ganam* 20 *udu-gal* 60 *udu-uš*	72 ewes, 20 rams, 60 mature sheep
22 *puḫádu-ba-ur síg-bi* . . .	20 weaned lambs furnished on wool . . .
puḫádu-nu-ur	sucking lambs
Ur-Gu-la 174	Ur-Gula (shepherd) 174
68 *ganam* 20 *udu-gal* 130 *udu-uš*	68 ewes, 20 rams, 130 mature sheep
31 *puḫádu-ba-ur*	31 weaned lambs
síg-bi 8 *gúnu* 11 *ma-na*	furnished on wool 8 talents 11 manas
37 *puḫádu-nu-ur*	37 sucking lambs
Ur-(*dingir*) *Ba-u dumu A-tu* 250-*lal*-1	Ur-Ba'u, the son of Atu (shepherd) 249
30 *ganam* 6 *udu-gal* 24 *udu-uš*	30 ewes, 6 rams, 24 mature sheep
10 *puḫádu-ba-ur síg-bi* 2 *gúnu* 20 *ma-na*	10 weaned lambs furnished on wool 2 talents 20 manas
20 *puḫádu-nu-ur*	20 sucking lambs
Šu-na 70	Shuna (shepherd) 70
Šu-nigin 694 *udu*	Total: 694 sheep
šu-nigin 101 *puḫádu-ba-ur*	Total: 101 weaned lambs
síg-bi 27 *gúnu* 6 *ma-na*	Wool furnished: 27 talents 6 manas

E. A. H. 107.

Not only in wool dealt the shepherds at that time, but also in skins (*RUG*=*mašku*). Among the skins mentioned here are those of the *UDU* (= sheep), of the *UDU-AL* (for *AL*, see under *LID-AL*, p. 367, 1) = full-grown sheep, and of the *UZ* (goats). The

E. A. H. 107.

Obverse.

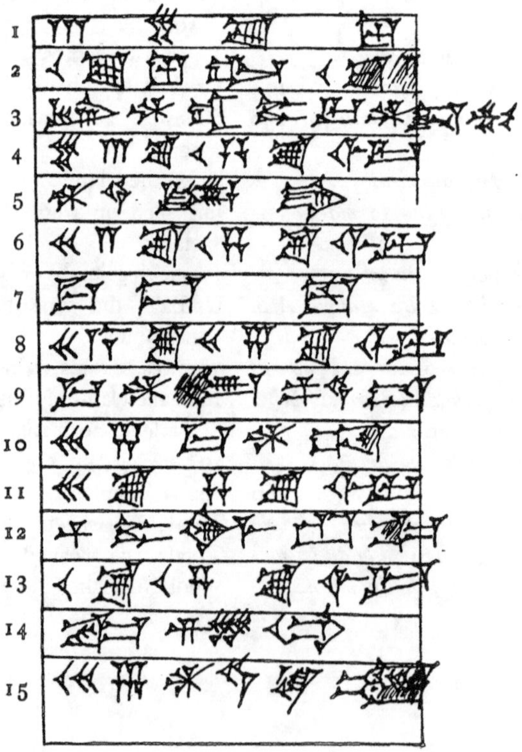

RUG-ĠUL probably are the 'bad' skins, which were not as good as the others. For ĠUL, see Br. 9500 = ḳalâlu, H. W. B. p. 585. ĠUL is apparently adj. = ḳallu, 'gering,' also 'klein, schwach'; comp. also ĠUL = limnu, 'schlecht,' H. W. B. 380. The best signification, however, may be derived from the original meaning of the sign ĠUL = eye + bad = 'bad looking.'

The 'total' of the skins of the sheep is too small by 20, for 586 sheepskins are mentioned in the body of the tablet.

The tablet reads:

E. A. H. 107.

Obverse.

230 rug udu	230 skins of sheep
10 rug udu-al 10 rug-II	10 skins of full-grown sheep, 10 skins (of sheep) two years old
(Ga)lu-dingir-ra dumu Ur-(dingir) Da-mu	Amêlili, the son of Ur-Damu (shepherd)
53 rug 14 rug-ġul	53 skins, 14 bad skins
5 (dingir) Utu-šag-ga	Utushagga (shepherd)
22 rug 14 rug-ġul	22 skins, 14 bad skins
Ur-Giš-mar	Ur-Gishmar (shepherd)
19 rug 25 rug-ġul	19 skins, 25 bad skins
Ur-(dingir) Dun-pa-ud-du	Ur-Dunpauddu (shepherd)
10 35 Ur-(dingir) Ninâ	35 (skins), Ur-Ninâ (shepherd)
30 rug 4 rug-ġul	30 skins, 4 bad skins
Bar dumu Uġ-me-uru-sag	Bar, the son of Uḫmeurusag
10 rug 14 rug-ġul	10 skins, 14 bad skins
Dug-gi-ul	Duggiul (shepherd)
15 36 (dingir) Utu-ki-ag	36 (skins), Utukiag

E. A. H. 107.

Reverse.

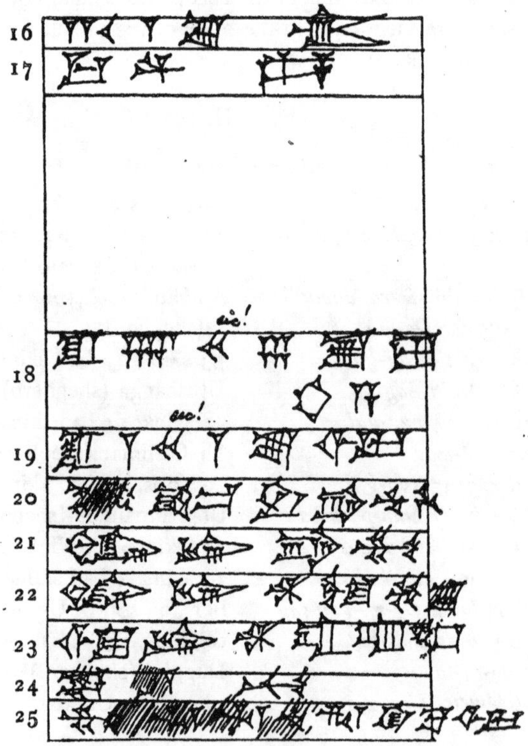

Reverse.

16	131 *rug uz*	131 skins of goats
	Ur-(dingir) Kal (Kalbi-Lamassu)	Kalbi-Lamassu
	Šu-nigin 566[1] *rug udu-ṣun*	Total: 566 skins of sheep
	šu-nigin 71 *rug-ĝul*	Total: 71 bad skins
20	*Nam-ne-ru-bi-nu-kud*	Namnerubinukud[2]
	Gir (Ga)lu-bi-mu	The Gir (Ga)lubimu
	Gir (Ga)lu-(dingir) Nin-gir-su	The Gir (Ga)lu-Ningirsu
	ù (Ga)lu-dingir-ra dup-sar	and Amêlili, the scribe
	Itu Šu-kul	In the month Shukul
25	*mu Ḫu-ḫu-nu-ri-ki ba-ĝul*	In the year when (the king) devastated Ḫuḫunuri.

E. A. H. 152 gives us an account of feed consumed by the flocks of the different shepherds during a whole month, or thirty days.

The measure according to which the account is given is *ḲA*. 1 *ḲA* = 60 *GIN*; 300 *ḲA* = 1 *GUR*; 3,600 *GUR* = 1 *karû* (Reissner, J. A. O. S. 18, p. 373). The feed consists in grain (*ŠE*).

The fuller expression for '80 *udu* $1\frac{1}{2}$ *ḳa*' would be '80 *udu* $1\frac{1}{2}$ *ḳa-ta*,' i. e. 80 sheep, every one receives during a month (*ud*-30-*kam*) $1\frac{1}{2}$ ḳa, which of course is as much as '80 sheep, at $1\frac{1}{2}$ ḳa a head monthly.' If 1 sheep receives $1\frac{1}{2}$ ḳa of grain during 30 days, it receives daily 3 gin of grain. Sheep fed with 1 ḳa monthly receive daily 2 gin. If 12 lambs receive 6 ḳa of grain during the whole month, one lamb receives daily 1 gin, and during a month 30 gin or $\frac{1}{2}$ ḳa. Hence we have to translate l. 20 as given below. Of the 10 oxen mentioned in l. 21, every one receives daily 16 gin, while those mentioned in l. 22 receive daily only 12 gin. The oxen, therefore, receive 4 to 8 times as much as the sheep.

[1] *Sic.* Read 586.

[2] See Br. 2182. In Assyrian this line would be = *Mamît-su(nu ?)-lâ-itami(û)*, i. e. 'His (their) oath(s) he (they) shall not swear.' Is this a nom. propr., or does it refer to ll. 21–23?

Instead of 190 ḳa in ll. 3, 6, 9, 12, we ought to read 193 ḳa, for $80 \times 1\frac{1}{2} (=120)+73 = 193$ ḳa. *ŠE-BI,* lit. = its grain = makes (sc. for the whole month) so and so many ḳa.

In l. 17 the numeral 77 is written 60+*MAŠ*. For *MAŠ*=10, see V. A. 2596, col. ii. 1 in A. B. P. R. p. 58 (texts).

E. A. H. 152.

Obverse.

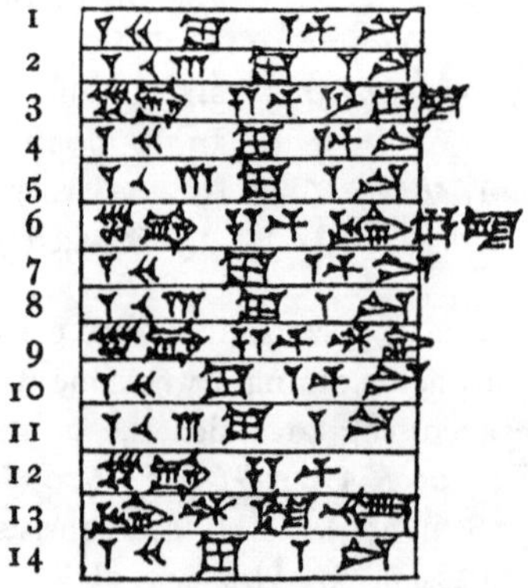

Reverse.

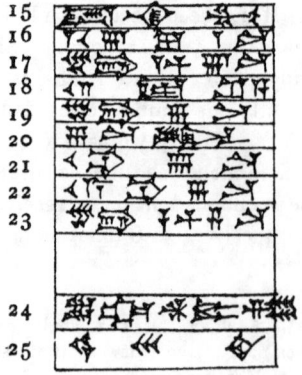

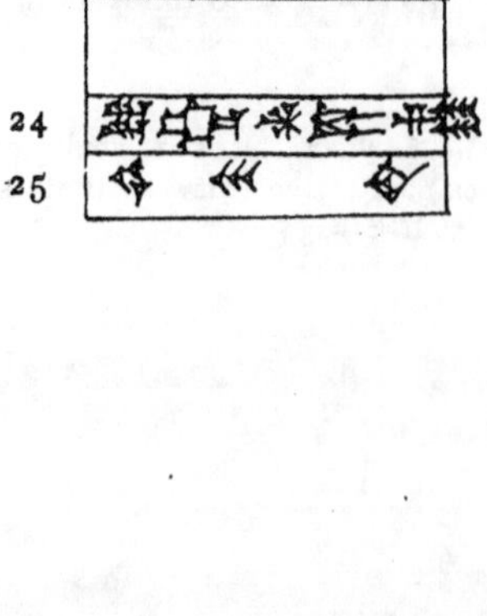

E. A. H. 152.

80 *udu* 1½ *ḳa*	80 sheep at 1½ ḳa
73 *udu* 1 *ḳa*	73 sheep at 1 ḳa
še-bi 190 *Nin-kal-la*	makes 190 (ḳa), Ninkalla (shepherd)
80 *udu* 1½ *ḳa*	80 sheep at 1½ ḳa
73 *udu* 1 *ḳa*	73 sheep at 1 ḳa
še-bi 190 (*Ga*)*lu-kal-la*	makes 190 (ḳa), (Ga)lukalla
80 *udu* 1½ *ḳa*	80 sheep at 1½ ḳa
73 *udu* 1 *ḳa*	73 sheep at 1 ḳa
še-bi 190 *An-ni*	makes 190 (ḳa) Anni
80 *udu* 1½ *ḳa*	80 sheep at 1½ ḳa
73 *udu* 1 *ḳa*	73 sheep at 1 ḳa
še-bi 190	makes 190 (ḳa)
(*Ga*)*lu*-(*dingir*) *Nin-šul*	(Ga)lu-Ninshul (see p. 57)
80 *udu* 1 *ḳa*	80 sheep at 1 ḳa
À-na-mu	Anamu
77 *udu* 1 *ḳa*	77 sheep at 1 ḳa
še-bi 77 *ḳa*	makes 77 ḳa
12 *puḫâdu-dir*	12 lambs over and above
še-bi 6 *ḳa*	makes 6 ḳa
6 *ḳa kiš maš*	6 ḳa for all, ½ (for one)
10 *gud* 8 *ḳa*	10 oxen at 8 ḳa
9 *gud* 6 *ḳa*	9 oxen at 6 ḳa
še-bi 134 *ḳa*	makes 134 ḳa
Itu Ezen-(*dingir*) *Dumu-zi*	Ezen-Dumuzi
Ud-30-*kam*	For 30 days.

Officials.

From 1 Sam. xxi. 8 (אַבִּיר הָרֹעִים אֲשֶׁר לְשָׁאוּל) we know that at the time of Saul there existed among the shepherds a certain hierarchy. The same is true with regard to this time. Not only do we find a certain gradation among the shepherds, but also among all the other officials—may they be connected with the temple-service or the granaries?

The traces of such officials can be followed up even to the oldest times. The attention of the reader has been drawn from time to time to this fact. Comp. e.g. *dam-kar-gal* ('chief agent,' Hilpr. O. B. I. 262), which occurs l.c. No. 94, ⁽*dingir*⁾ *Nin-din-dug* (so Hilprecht, better: ⁽*dingir*⁾ *Innanna-edin*) *Ur-*⁽*dingir*⁾ *En-lil dam-kar-gal á-mu-šub,* with *dam-kar* in l.c. No. 95: [*Dingir N*]*in-din-dug-ga Ur-Ma-ma dam-kar* (so only!) [*dingir E*]*n-*[*lil*] *a-mu-na-šub; pa-te-si* with *pa-te-si-gal* (Déc. 6, No. 4, l. 8). At the time of Sargon I. we had the *PA-AL* (=*šabrû*), *DI-KUD daianu*), *A-ZU.*

Also Gudea (Statue B, iv. 13 ff.) mentions the following officials: *ne-ur, nu-banda, pa,* (*ga*)*lu-zi-ga, kin-a-ra-ba-ba, sig-giš-ṣu-ag nam-sig šu-ba mu-gàl-a-an,* which Thureau-Dangin, R. A. iii. p. 129, 1, translates: '*le préfet, l'intendant, le surveillant, le soldat, celui qui tisse des laines de différentes couleurs, ont chômé*' (see also Jensen, K. B. iii[1]. p. 31, and notes, ibidem).

Among the officials connected in some way or another with the herds occur in the E. A. H. texts the following: (*a*) *engar;* (*b*) *na-gid;* (*c*) *sib;* (*d*) *nu-banda-gud;* (*e*) *pa* (*luǧ-maǧ*); (*f*) *ni-ku;* (*g*) *ǧal;* (*h*) *dup-sar-gud* or *dup-sar-gud-engar* or *dup-sar-gud-X,* &c., &c.

(*a*) *ENGAR* (Br. 1024; Z. A. iii. p. 199 ff.). This word occurred already in O. B. I. 19, 3: ⁽*dingir*⁾ *Bur-*⁽*dingir*⁾ *Sin . . . engar lig-ga. Engar* is the Hebrew אִכָּר, Assyr. *ikkaru* (a Semitic word adopted by Sumerian language, Zimmern, Babylon. Busspsalmen, p. 5, 1); as such it means 'a farmer' (Z. A. iii. p. 199 sq.; Delitzsch, Assyr. Wörterbuch, p. 400). It is a synonym of *erêšu,* Talm. אריסא (Br. 1023; Z. A. iii. p. 200), as well as of *nâkidu, rîd alpê;* hence it is parallel in Gudea F, iii. 14, with *utul* (l. 18), *sib* (iv. 3), *na-gid* (iv. 12). *Engar* may therefore be translated by 'farmer' or 'shepherd,' because farmers 'till the ground' and 'raise the stock,' Hilprecht, O. B. I. p. 28, 3. Distinguish, however, between

ENGAR-GUD='shepherd of the oxen,' and *GUD-ENGAR*= 'oxen employed for tilling of the ground'; see above, p. 334, 1 (*c*).

(*b*) *NA-GID*. The sign for *GID* is not = *PA*, but = Br. 2702 (Z. A. iii. 208). It, too, is a Semitic word taken into the Sumerian language = Hebr. נֹקֵד. Comp. O. B. I. 18: *(dingir) Ur-(dingir) Nin-ib . . . na-gid Uru-um-*^{ki}*-ma*. In Gudea F, iv. 12, it is parallel to *engar*; see *sub* (*a*). *NA-GID* in the E. A. H. texts occurs only on tablets which mention *UDU* (cattle) or *SIG* (wool, E. A. H. 48, 7).

(*c*) *SIB*, Br. 5688, *rê'u*, although not mentioned as an official name, yet occurs sometimes before proper names. Another word for 'shepherd' is also *utul*, Gudea F, iii. 18, which however does not occur in the E. A. H. texts.

(*d*) *NU-BANDA*. According to Jensen, K. B. iii[1]. p. 31, note **o, it is composed out of *NU* = '*Aufseher, Verwalter*,' and *BANDA etwa* = '*stellvertretender Aufseher*.' According to ii. R. 51, 44, *NU-BANDA* is = *labuttû* = صَاحِبُ ٱلأَمْرِ = '*Vorsteher, Wortführer, Gebieter*,' H. W. B. p. 373.

NU-BANDA-GUD = *labuttû ša alpê*. As such he had under him '*deux bouviers*' (Thureau-Dangin, R. A. iii. p. 129).

(*e*) *PA*. In Z. K. ii. pp. 301 and 302, *PA* is = *aklu* or *šâpiru*. That *PA* must signify a certain official is evident from Gudea B, iv. 13 ff. Comp. also iv. R. 38, iii. 1; Hilprecht, Assyriaca, p. 16, No. 1; and p. 55, under *pa-te-si*. Meissner, A. B. P. R. p. 126, maintains that *PA*=*amêlu*. That *PA* cannot be=*amêlu*, Thureau-Dangin already has shown, R. A. iii. p. 129, according to whom expressions such as *PA-DAM-KAR*, *PA-ŠU-ḪA* are = *maître marchand, maître pêcheur*. The *PA-MAR-TU* of A. B. P. R. No. 107 is undoubtedly parallel to *RAB (dingir) MAR-TU* (A. B. P. R. No. 110), and '*sans doute quelque employé du temple de MAR-TU*.' The *PA* occurs in the following compositions:—

PA E (dingir) Dumu-zi-ge, E. A. H. 106, 3, which can be translated only the *PA* (*aklu*, *šâpiru*) of the temple of Dumuzi. Comp. also the seal, ibid.

PA-SANGA, p. 379 (E. A. H. 104, 22), 'high-priest.'

PA-LUGAL-ENGAR, 'the *PA* of the royal shepherds,' p. 379 (E. A. H. 34, 25).

According to E. A. H. 33, 34, 121, the *PA* must have had four *engar* under him. This is corroborated by O. B. I. 126, where the following *PA* are mentioned:—

(1) *PA Ur-*(dingir) *NIN-ZU* (*sic*; read *Nin-a-zu*) *nu-banda-gud* (ii. 4).

(2) *PA Lugal-ni-šag nu-banda-gud* (iii. 17).

(3) *PA Ur-Ma-ma nu-banda-gud* (iv. 20).

(4) *PA Al-la nu-banda-gud* (vi. 15).

(5) *PA Ab-ba nu-banda-gud* (rev. i. 7).

(6) *PA* (dingir) *Utu-kam nu-banda-gud* (rev. ii. 19).

Every one of these six *PA* had four *engar* under him.

To No. 1 belong—

Ur- . . . . . (i. 19).
AZAG- . . . . . (i. 24).
UR-ŠID dumu Ur-(dingir) *Ninâ* (i. 31).
ĠE-ŠAG-MU engar (ii. 3).

To No. 2 belong—

. . . . (ii. ? . .).
E-GIŠ-MI engar (iii. 2).
(dingir) *Utu-MU*[1] *engar* (iii. 11).
Lugal (dingir) *Utu engar* (iii. 16).

To No. 3 belong—

Lugal-KAR-ZI engar (iii. last line).
(dingir) *Ninâ-MA-AN-UD-DIŠ engar* (iv. 5).
À-NE-MI engar (iv. 10).
Lugal-EZEN engar (iv. 19).

To No. 4 belong—

(Ga)lu-(dingir) *NIN-ŠUL engar* (v. 1).
(Ga)lu-(dingir) *PA-SAG engar* (v. 11).
Ur-(dingir) *Nin-giš-zid-da engar* (v. 23).
Ga(lu)-KA-ṢAL engar (vi. 14).

[1] = *Šamaš-iddina*.

To No. 5 belong—
   (Ga)lu (dingir) AN (=Anu) engar (vi. 4 from end).
   IGI-ŠAG-ŠAG engar (vii. 10).
   A(?)-NAM-URU-NA engar (vii. 5 from end).
   Ur-(dingir) PA-SAG engar (rev. i. 6).

To No. 6 belong—
   Lugal-ENGAR engar (rev. i. 14).
   ZA (ĠA ?)-BA-ZI-ZI engar (rev. ii. 1).
   Ur- dingir) Nin-giš-zid-da engar (rev. ii. 9).
   Ur-GAN-NE (BIL) engar (rev. ii. 18).

The six *PA*, however, were subordinate to another *PA*, *Ur-*(dingir) *NIN-GIR* (=*Almu*, Br. 11070) by name (rev. ii. 22, and especially rev. vii. 3), who in his capacity as 'chief overseer' was an officer of (dingir) *GUG-KAM*, the patesi. It is evident therefore—

(1) That the patesi was the highest official of the king (in O. B. I. 126 apparently of Bur-Sin II.).

(2) That the patesi had, again, an official under him, who is called *PA*. This *PA* undoubtedly is the same as the *LUĠ-MAĠ pa-te-si*, which official occurs generally (instead of *this PA*) on these tablets (comp. R. A. iii. pp. 124, 126, 131), and as such has to be distinguished from the other *PA* (No. 3). Thureau-Dangin, l. c., remarks about this *LUĠ-MAĠ*: 'le *LUḤ* ou soukkalou, c'est le מלאך, le ministre, le fac-totum. Peut-être le soukkalou maḫḫou était-il une sorte d'administrateur des domaines du temple sur lesquels le patesi, en sa qualité de chef religieux, aurait eu la haute main.'

(3) That *this PA* or *LUĠ-MAĠ* had, again, at least six other *PA* under him (as in O. B. I. 126. This *PA* = overseer).

(4) That O. B. I. 126 is an account of *all* the herds of the different *PA* (overseers), while E. A. H. 33, 34, 121, give us an account of only one *PA*.

(5) That this one *PA* was an official who had four *engar*, 'shepherds,' under him; the title must therefore be translated 'overseer.' According to this the *PA E* is = overseer of a temple;

PA-SANGA = overseer of the priests = high-priest; *PA lugal-engar* = overseer of the royal shepherds.

(6) That expressions like *PA Ab-ba nu-banda-gud* can only mean *Ab-ba*, the overseer (*PA*) of the *nu-banda-gud*.

(*f*) *NI-KU*. Composed out of *NI* (= *rabû*, *zikaru*, Br. 5323, 5328) and *KU* (= *rubû*, Br. 10547). The *NI-KU* then would be a high official. According to Thureau-Dangin, R. A. iii. p. 129, '*cinq NOU-BANDA-GUD étaient soumis à un NI-KOU.*' I do not know upon what text that scholar bases his assertion; this much only I can say, that this official occurs on the E. A. H. texts only in connection with the *UDU* (cattle). These latter tablets, however, are too small to base any conclusion upon them, they being generally the account of the herd of one *NA-GID*. If I may venture to make a suggestion, I would assign to the *NI-KU* not five but six *NU-BANDA-GUD*, provided that the former official was also connected with the 'oxen.' In that case we would get, according to O. B. I. 126, the following arrangement:—

King
Patesi
1 *LUĠ-MAĠ* or *PA* who had under him =
2 *NI-KU* or (*ĠAL*) =
6 *PA* =
12 *NU-BANDA-GUD* =
24 *engar* or *na-gid*.

(*g*) *ĠAL*. The reader will have noticed that the highest official is always mentioned last (comp. O. B. I. 126: *engar—PA—PA* (= *luĝ-maĝ*)—*pa-te-si—lugal*; and R. A. iii. p. 131: *PA—NI-KOU—LUG-MAĠ—pa-te-si—lugal*). In E. A. H. 121, 47, where this official occurs, he is mentioned after the *PA*. That tablet being an account of the *GUD* of four shepherds under the supervision of the 'overseer,' *PA UR-GAR*, it is natural to suppose that the *ĠAL* was also an official connected in some way or another with the *GUD*, and he, being mentioned after the *PA*, undoubtedly has the same rank as the *NI-KU*; see under (*f*). Probably the *ĠAL* was of the same rank among the *ENGAR* as was the *NI-KU* among the *NA-GID*, i.e. the *ǴAL* of the *GUD* (oxen) would be called *NI-KU* if he presided over the shepherds of the cattle. *ǴAL*, according to Br. 82, = *šâbu*, *šêbu*, H. W. B. p. 652, which meaning (*alt sein*, *Alter*, *Greis*) undoubtedly indicates his high rank.

(*h*) *DUP-SAR-GUD-ENGAR* (R. A. iii. p. 130).
DUP-SAR-GUD-X (O. B. I. 126, iv. 8).
DUP-SAR-GUD-I sag-gud-II-ku (E. A. H. 34, 22).

The literal translation of these passages would be:—

scribe—oxen—employed for tilling the ground.
scribe—oxen—10.
scribe—oxen-I exchanged for oxen-II.

This latter passage is remarkable. It has been shown above that when a numeral follows *GUD* or any other animal, that numeral indicates the *age*. *GUD-I*, *GUD-II* therefore can only mean ox of one year, ox of two years; hence *GUD-X* must mean ox ten years old. Thureau-Dangin, R. A. iii. p. 129, translates '*DUP-SAR GUD-X*' by '*bouvier-scribe* (*chef*) *de* 10 *bœufs*.' Against this translation may be said—

(1) that 'ten oxen' are not expressed in these texts by *GUD-X*, but by *X Gud*.

(2) According to that scholar's translation, we ought to translate E. A. H. 34, 22, by '*bouvier-scribe* (*chef*) *de* 1 *bœuf reçu en échange contre deux bœufs*,' which of course is not possible, and without any sense. Hence we can translate this latter passage only by 'scribe of the oxen that are one year old, instead of those that are two years old.'

From this, then, it follows that the oxen (or asses or other cattle) had to be counted, or better 'booked,' by certain officials, called *DUP-SAR* (scribe). Those that were one year old had one scribe, as well as those that were two years old and that were already able to till the ground. The old oxen (*GUD-ŠU-GǏ*), to which class the *GUD-X* belong, were 'booked' by a *DUP-SAR* especially appointed for that business, who is called the 'scribe of the oxen that are ten years old.'

E. A. H. 96 and 109.

E. A. H. 96 is a case-tablet in the form of a receipt (*šu-ba-ti*) of grain. *Šu-ba-ti* is the common expression for Assyr. *imḫur*, both of which forms occur already side by side on contract-tablets from the time of Sargon I. and Naram-Sin; see R. A. iv. No. iii. No. 41–44; also O. B. I. pl. vi. No. 15. For *ŠU-TI* = *maḫâru*, see Br. 1701 and H. W. B. p. 400: to receive, i. e. to buy.

The person *from which* the grain (or any other article) is received is indicated by *KI-* . . . *-TA*, lit. 'from (*ta*) the estate (*ki*) of.' The *ŠU-BA-TI* has to be translated here 'passively,' on account of the *GE* (tablet, l. 3), it being a postfix signifying the genitive.

Lugalkagina, the recipient, is, according to the seal, the scribe (*dup-sar*) and servant (*nitaĝ*) of a certain Atu, who is the *PA-AL*= *šabrû* of the king Dungi III.—for this tablet dates from that king's reign. This seal shows that the *šabrû* of a king must have been a very high official of the king. On the case we find the sign *DUB* before Lugalkagina. *DUB* here='tablet'; comp. E. A. H. 27, 12, where we have *DUB Ur-(dingir) Gàl-alim DUP-SAR-ku.* Lugalkagina lived in Nippur (E. A. H. 109, 5). The date given on E. A. H. 96 makes him a contemporary of Dungi III.; the date on E. A. H. 109 belongs to the 'uncertain dates'; it may therefore be very probable that this latter date has to be referred to that king too.

It will also be noticed that the 'verb' is left out on the case. So on all case-tablets. In this way case-tablets are made to be *private* transactions, for nobody knows whether the grain was 'bought' or 'sold.' Hence we find on the cases:

(1) The subject matter (grain, flour, dates, &c.);
(2) The person to whom this 'letter' is directed;
(3) The person from whom (*ki-ta*) it comes;
(4) Date.

In the enumeration of the *GUR* and the *ḲA* of grain, it will be noticed that the sign for *GUR* always follows the *ŠE*. The sign for *ḲA* generally is not given, but whenever it is given it precedes the sign for *ŠE*. Where the numeral of the *GUR* ends, and where that of the *ḲA* begins, can only be distinguished by the writing of the numerals themselves. The full expression of E. A. H. 96, l. 1, would be :—

3 × 60 + 30 + 2 | 120 (see A. B. P. R. p. 100) + 30 (= *AŠ*) *ḲA še GUR lugal*, i.e. 212 *GUR* | 150 *ḲA še-lugal.*

The tablets read :—

E. A. H. 96.

Case.

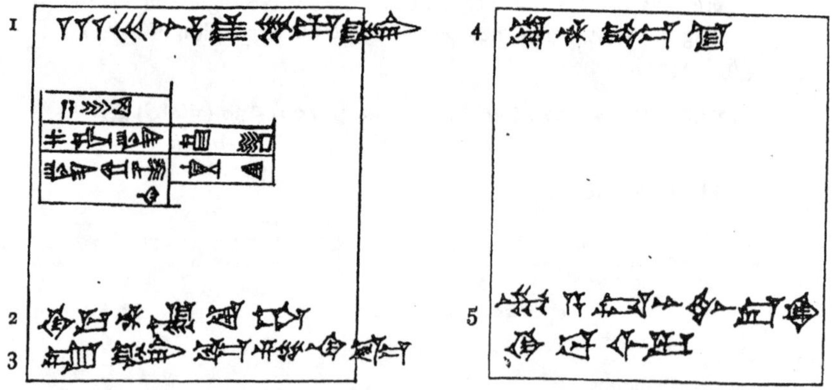

Tablet.

Obverse. Reverse.

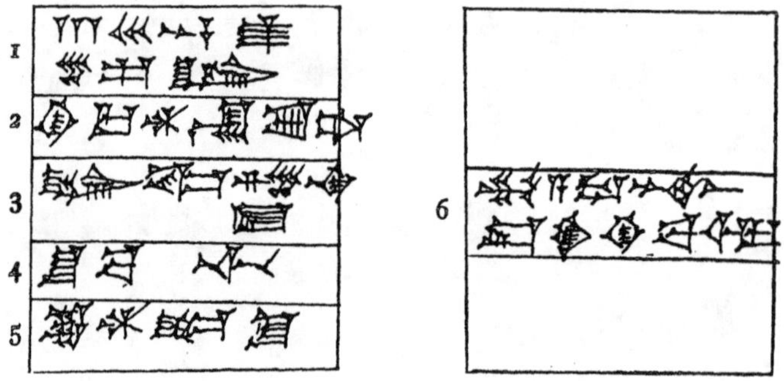

E. A. H. 96.

Case.

212 gur 150 [1] *(ḳa) še-lugal*	212 gur 150 ḳa of grain, royal quality,
ki-Ur-(dingir) En-zu-ta	from Kalbi-Sin.
DUB Lugal-ka-gi-ṇạ-ka	Tablet of Lugalkagina (&c. were received).
Itu (dingir) Ne-sù	Month (of the festival of) Nesu,
mu a-du-II-kam-ru Kar-ḫar ba-ǧul	The year when (the king) devastated Karḫar for the second time.

Seal.

A-tu	(O) Atu,
Pa-al lugal	shabrû of the king,
Lugal-ka-gi-na	Lugalkagina,
dup-sar	the scribe,
nitaǧ-zu	(is) thy servant.

Tablet.

212 gur 150 (ḳa) še-lugal	212 gur 150 ḳa of grain, royal quality,
ki-Ur-(dingir) En-zu-ta	from Amil-Sin,
Lugal-ka-gi-na-ge	by Lugalkagina
šu-ba-ti	were received.
Itu (dingir) Ne-sù	Month (of the festival of) Nesu,
mu a-du-II-kam-ru Kar-ḫar ba-ǧul	The year when (the king) devastated Karḫar for the second time.

[1] 150 is written 2 × 60 + *AŠ*; *AŠ* = 30: Meissner, A. B. P. R. p. 100.

E. A. H. 109.

Obverse.

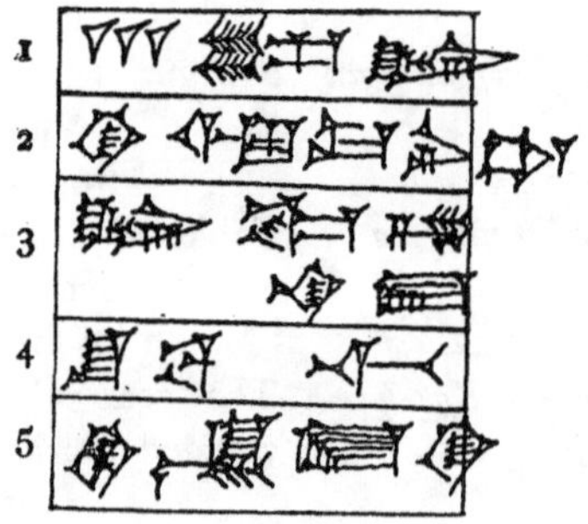

Reverse.

180 *gur še-lugal*	180 gur of grain, royal quality,
ki-Ú-ma-ni-ta	from Umani,
Lugal-ka-gi-na-ge	by Lugalkagina
šu-ba-ti	were received.
šag En-lil-ki	Nippur,
Itu Ki-kin(?)-dingir Nin-a-zu	in the month Abu,
mu en nam-? (dingir) Dungi-ra-ge	in the year when (the king) was
ba-DU ba-tug	appointed and invested high-priest
	of the cult (?) of Dungi.

E. A. H. 87.

This tablet states that Lugalkagina (see preceding tablets) received from a certain *Ur-Nigin-gar*:

ZID-ŠE-lugal, i. e. wheat-flour, of royal quality.

ZID, flour (Assyr. *ḳêmu*, H. W. B. 586).

GIG. This *GIG* we have found already in the Cône of Entemena, iii. 8: *En-an-na-tum pa-te-si Šir-la-pur-^{ki}-ge gan šà-GIG-ga.* For *GIG*, Br. 9235, which occurs again on E. A. H. 95, 2: '3 *gur GIG*,' on both of which places it is mentioned *after ZID*, see above, p. 325, 1.

GAŠ-TIN (*sic*). The second sign is not *ḪAR-*, for that is written differently (comp. O. B. I. 125, rev., 10), but *TIN* (Br. 9852). *GAŠ-TIN* = *GIŠ-TIN* (comp. Z. A. i. 185) = *kurunnu* (Br. 5156; H. W. B. 355) = sesam-wine.

NI-NUN. *NI* = *šamnu*, 'oil' (Br. 5325) + *NUN* = *ḫimêtu* (Br. 5349; H. W. B. p. 280) = חֶמְאָה, 'butter.'

This tablet must be read:—

Obverse.

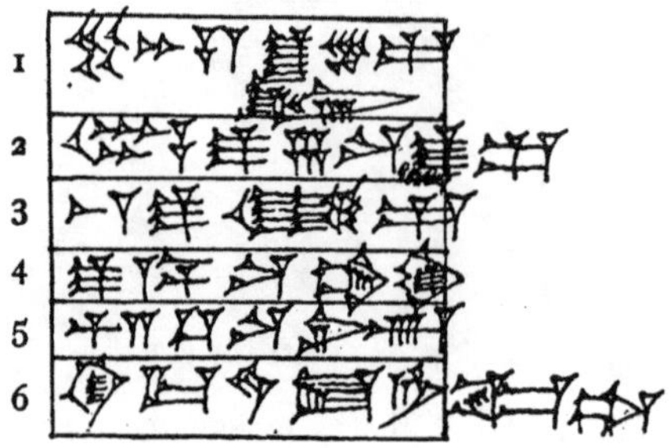

Reverse.

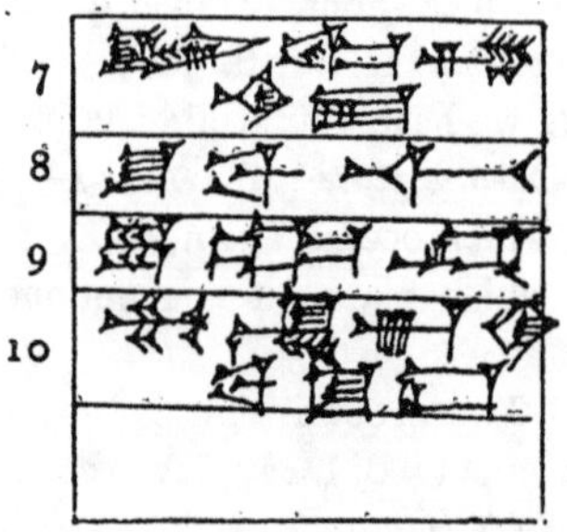

52 *gur* 180 (*ḳa*) *zid-še-lugal*	52 gur 180 ḳa of wheat-flour, royal quality,
15 *gur* 156 *ḳa zid*	15 gur 156 ḳa of flour,
1 *gur* 90 (*ḳa*) *GIG*	1 gur 90 ḳa of spelt,
29½ *ḳa GAŠ-TIN*	29½ ḳa of sesam-wine,
12⅓ *ḳa NI-NUN*	12⅓ ḳa of butter,
ki-UR-NIGIN-GAR-ka[1]*-ta*	from *UR-NIGIN-GAR*
Lugal-ka-gi-na-ge	by Lugalkagina
šu-ba-ti	were received.
Itu EZEN-MAĠ	In the month of the great festival
mu en Eridug-ki ba-tug-ga	of the year when (Bur-Sin II.) was invested lord of Eridu.

[1] The *ka* is remarkable. Should we read here = *Kalbi-NIGIN-GAR,* and translate 'the servant of (god) Nigingar'?

E. A. H. 27.

This tablet states how many gur and ḳa of flour (*ZID*) were sent (*mà-a sig-ga*) by different people (*KI-ta*) to Nippur.

MÀ-A = *clippu* ; *SIG-GA* = 'to be full.' Hence *MÀ-SIG* = a shipful = shipload = cargo.

l. 8. The *IP-UŠ* are some kind of officers. *IP*, Br. 10484 = *lâgittu*. In ii. R. 34, No. 3, 32, we have *la-gi-in i-sit-ti*, which according to Scheil, Rec. Trav. xix. p. 55, is '*le chef de la fête*.' *Lâgittu* then would be = *lâgin-tu*, and *IP* = *Lâgittu* (fem.) and *lâginu* (masc.). In this sense *IP* is pronounced = *URAŠ*, S^{c}. 2, 4; H. W. B. p. 373. The *URAŠ-UŠ* then would be the mighty (*UŠ*) *lâginu*. In Z. A. xii. p. 267, the *IP-UŠ* is parallel to the *NAM-RA-AG*. That tablet reads:

IP-UŠ ù NAM-RA-AG	For the *IP-UŠ* and the *NAM-RA-AG*
9 *GUR* 180 *ḲA KAŠ-ŠIG*	9 gur 180 ḳa of fine date-wine,
36 *GUR* 4×60+50+10 (*sic* in copy) *ḲA KAŠ-DU*	36 gur 300 (*sic*) ḳa of common date-wine
IP-UŠ-ME	for the *IP-UŠ*
UD-1-ta UD-22-^{kam}	from the first day to the twenty-second day.

It is evident therefore that the *IP-UŠ* as well as the *NAM-RA-AG* are officers. Comp. also above, under Âlusharshid. The *ME* at the end of this line signifies the plural; comp. R. A. iii. p. 134:—

120 *KAŠ* 120 *ZID* 2 *ḲA ZAL*
UŠ AN-ŠA-AN-^{ki} *ME*

i. e. to the slaves from Anshan; and Gudea, Cyl. B, xi. 11, 12:—

dumu-nitağ-7 $^{(dingir)}$ *Ba-u ME*
banda en $^{(dingir)}$ *Nin-gir-su-ka ME*

(Thureau-Dangin, R. A. iii. p. 137, l. 71). We should expect here: *KI-ip-uš pa-te-si-me-TA*.

The *GIR* in l. 13 seems to have been an officer resembling very much a 'quarter-master.' He had to look after the food of the royal officers as well as that of the priests, and even of the royal flocks.

Obverse.

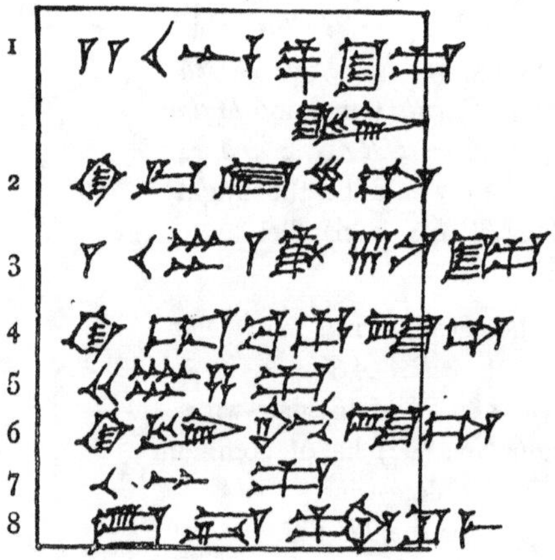

Reverse.

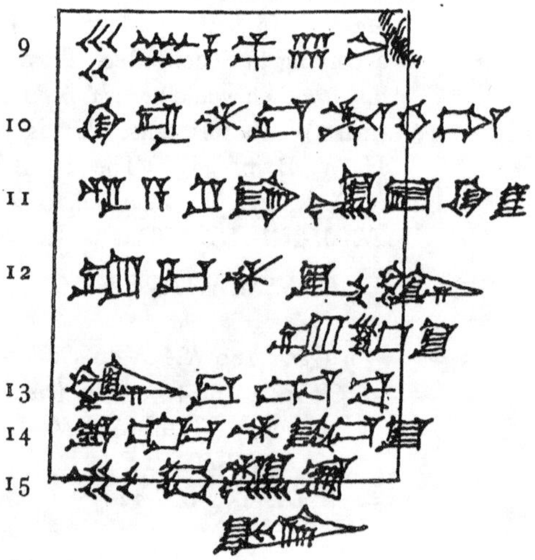

Seal.

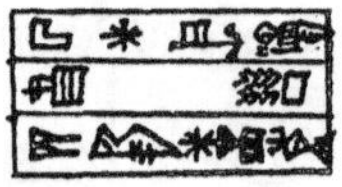

E. A. H. 27.

132 *gur* 150 (*ḳa*) *zid-lugal*	132 gur 150 ḳa of flour, royal quality,
ki-Ur-E-ninnû-ta	from Ur-Eninnû,
75 *gur* 117 *ḳa zid*	75 gur 117 ḳa of flour
ki-Ab-ba-kal-la-ta	from Abbakalla,
27 *gur* 240 (*ḳa*)	27 gur 240 ḳa
ki-(Ga)lu-Gu-la-ta	from (Ga)lu-Gula,
12 *gur*	12 gur
Ip-uš pa-te-si-me	from the *IP-UŠ* of the patesi,
57 *gur* 148 *ḳa*	57 gur 148 ḳa
ki-Sanga (*dingir*) *Ga-tum-dug-ta*	from the priest of Gatumdug,
mà-a sig-ga En-lil-ki-ku	cargo to Nippur.
DUB Ur-(*dingir*) *Gàl-alim dup-sar-ku*[1]	Tablet of Ur-Galalim, the scribe.
Gir Ur-Ab-ba	The Gir Ur-Abba.
Itu Ezen-(*dingir*) *Ne-sù*	In the month of the festival of Nesu,
mu Bur-(*dingir*) *Sin lugal*	in the year when Bur-Sin became king.

Seal.

Ur-(*dingir*) *Gàl-alim*	Ur-Galalim,
dup-sar	scribe,
dumu (*Ga*)*lu-*(*dingir*) *Nin-gir-su*	the son of (Ga)lu-Ningirsu.

[1] The *KU* here is noteworthy.

E. A. H. 54.

This tablet gives an account of the grain (*še*) belonging to (*ra*) Ur-Ba'u (l. 14), stating how many gur and ḳa were given to the several houses (*e*) of certain persons. Besides the *ŠE* are also mentioned the *GU-GAL*, for which see above, p. 327, 1.

The tablet is written in Lulubu. Notice the expression *gàl-la-a-an* in l. 15. *GÀL*=*bašû*, hence lit. the being (*GÀL*) in the midst (*šag*) of (*ka*) Lulubu, i. e. in the city of Lulubu it was.

l. 2. *SAR*, Br. 4315 = *kirû*.

In l. 12, instead of 264 gur, read 266 gur.

Obverse.

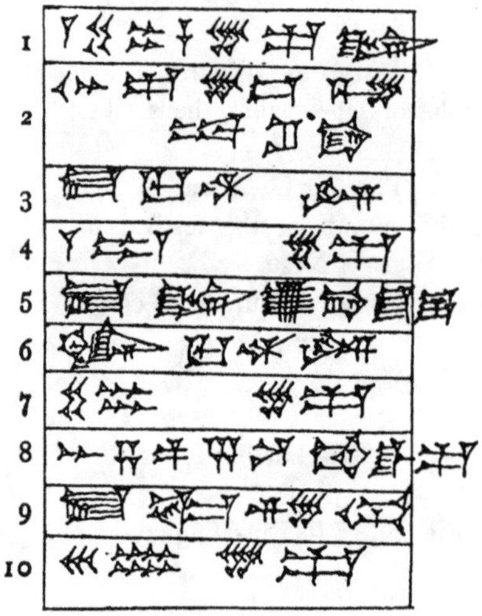

Reverse.

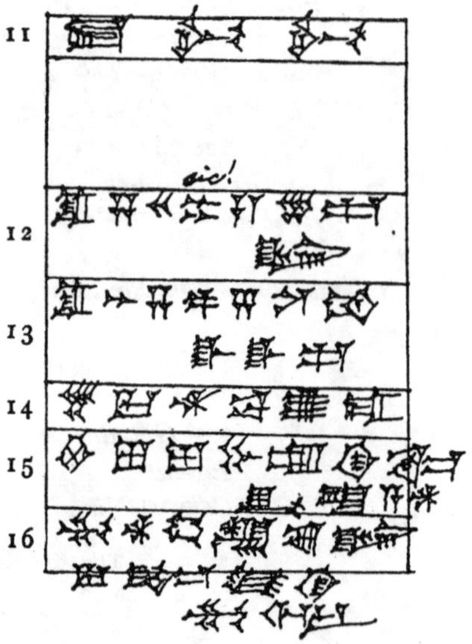

E. A. H. 54.

104 *gur* 120 (*ḳa*) *še-lugal*	104 gur 120 ḳa of grain, royal quality,
12 *gur sar Gi-tab-ba-sig-ga*	12 gur from the field of Gitabba-sigga,
E-Ur-(dingir) Im	for the house of Kalbi-Rammânu.
64 *gur* 60 (*ḳa*) *še*	64 gur 60 ḳa of grain
E-Lugal-u-kaš-šu-e	for the house of Lugalukashshue.
Gir Ur-(dingir) Im	*GIR* Amêl-Rammânu.
46 *gur še*	46 gur of grain,
2 *gur* 265 *ḳa gu-gal*	2 gur 265 ḳa of beans,
E-Dug-gi-ul	for the house of Duggiul.
38 *gur še*	38 gur of grain
E-Gu-gu	for the house of Gugu.
Šu-nigin 264 (sic) *gur* 180 (*ḳa*) *še-lugal*	Total: 264 (read 266) gur 180 ḳa of grain, royal quality.
šu-nigin 2 *gur* 265 *ḳa gu-gal*	Total: 2 gur 265 ḳa of beans.
Še[1] *Ur-(dingir) Ba-u-ra*	Grain for Ur-Ba'u.
šag Lu-lu-bu-um-ki-ka gàl-la-a-an	In Lulubi (it was).
mu (dingir) Bur-(dingir) Sin lugal Ur-bil-lum-ki mu-ḫul	In the year when king Bur-Sin devastated Urbillum.

[1] Notice that the *GU-GAL* belong to the class of *ŠE*!

E. A. H. 106.

A receipt (*šu-ba-ti*) of *KIN*. This '*kin*' is 'measured' according to *MA-NA*. What *KIN* as such may mean here is not evident. I would like to take the *KIN* as another form for *SIG*, Br. 10781, *SIG* being the *KIN* with *gunu*-signs. *SIG* = *šipâtu*, wool. Comp. also the first half of the sign in E. C. 465, and the month *KI-KIN* (?) (*dingir*) *Nin-a-zu*.

In the seal, after *dumu Ur-ud* (?)*-azag-ga*, we would expect some such title as *PA E* (comp. l. 3), and translate:

the son of Urudazagga,
the *PA* of the temple
of Dumuzi
(and) the *PA* of the temple
of Rammânu.

The name of the *PA E* in l. 3 is apparently Lugaliddazi the scribe.

Obverse. Reverse.

1
2
3
4

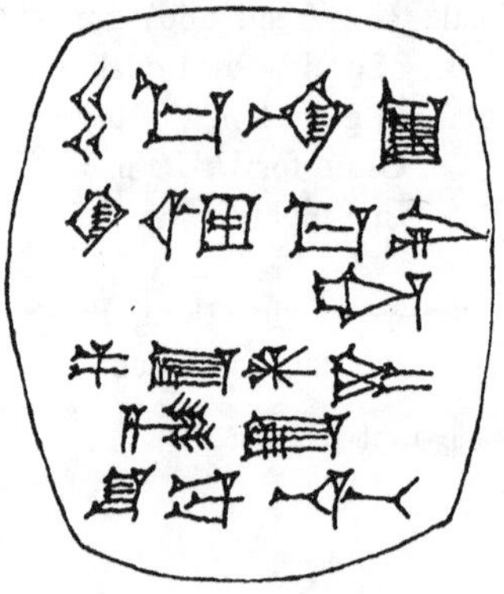

5
6

E. A. H. 106.

40 *ma-na KIN*	40 mana of wool
ki-Ù-ma-ni-ta	from Ùmani
Pa E-$^{(dingir)}$ *Dumu-zi-ge*	by the *PA* of the temple of Dumuzi
šu-ba-ti	was received.
Itu Giš-engar-gab-a	In the month Araḫshamna,
mu-uš-sa Lu-lu-bu-um-^{ki} *ba-ḫul*	one year after (the king) devastated Lulubi.

Seal.

Lugal-id-da-zi	Lugaliddazi,
dup-sar	scribe,
dumu Ur-ud (?)-azag-ga	the son of Urudazagga, (the *PA* of the temple)
$^{(dingir)}$ *Dumu-zi*	of Dumuzi (l. 3)
pa E	and the *PA* of the temple
$^{(dingir)}$*-Im-ra*	of Rammânu.

E. A. H. 100, 102.

The arrangement of these two tablets is similar.

1. The amount of grain in the granary being stated first.

The *MU-GUB* apparently belongs to l. 1, and should be translated: so and so many gur (ḳa) of grain is on hand (*GUB*= *nazâzu*, 'to be present').

2. The *šag-bi-ta* = *ultu ḳirbi-šu*, states how much of this was expended. If it happened that the expenditure exceeded the amount on hand, this was indicated by *DIR* (= *atâru*). So in E. A. H. 100: 265 ḳa of grain only should have been expended, but instead of that 1 gur of grain (1 gur = 300 ḳa) left the granary, hence a deficit (*DIR*) of 35 ḳa.

3. *NIN-ŠID-AG*. For *NIN-ŠID*, see pp. 253; 337, 1; 365, note 36.

AG = *epêšu*; and *NIN-ŠID-AG* = *êpuš nikasi*, which Thureau-Dangin, O. L. Z. i. 163, translates by *revenus encaissés*.

Here however *nothing* was *encaisse*, but on the contrary 1 gur of grain was expended. Hence it seems better to take *nin-šid-ag* in a more general sense = to transact business.

4. *MA-DU-DU*, Br. 3698: *malaḫu*.

5. *IGI-DU*, Br. 9336 ff., *maḫru*, *ašaridu*, *âlik maḫri*.

E. A. H. 100.

Obverse. Reverse.

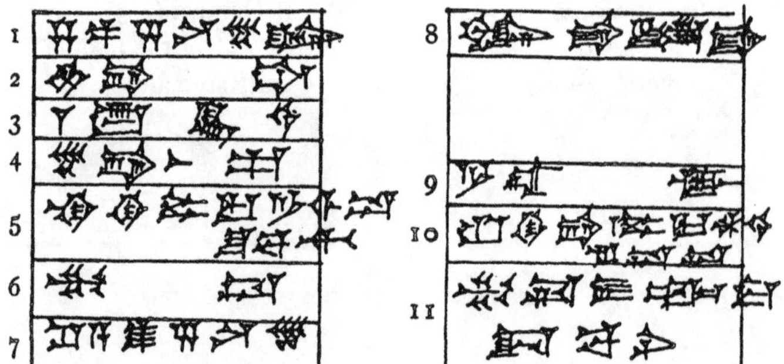

E. A. H. 100.

265 *ḳa še-lugal*	265 ḳa of grain, royal quality—
šag-bi-ta	of which,
1 *gin kubabbar*	for 1 gin of silver,
še-bi 1 *gur*	on grain 1 gur
Na-ki dumu Ur-Gar igi-du	Naki, the son of Ur-Gar, formerly
šu-ba-ti	has received—
mu-gub	(is the grain) on hand.
Dir 35 *ḳa še*	Deficit = 35 ḳa of grain.
Gir Ga-šag-ga	Gir Gashagga
nin-šid-ag	transacted the business (with ?)
Uru-ki-bi dumu Ur-(*dingir*) *Utu*	Urukibi, the son of Ur-Utu the
mà-du-du	sailor.
mu-uš-sa BAD-Ma-da ba-ru	One year after (the king) built Dûr-Mada.

E. A. H. 102.

Obverse. Reverse.

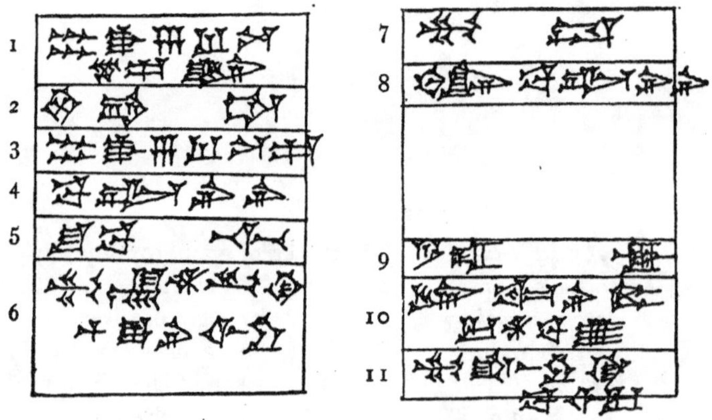

6 *gur* $46\frac{2}{3}$ *ḳa še-lugal*	6 gur $46\frac{2}{3}$ ḳa of grain, royal quality—
šag-bi-ta	of which
6 *gur* $46\frac{2}{3}$ *ḳa*	6 gur $46\frac{2}{3}$ ḳa
Ba-al-ni-ni	Balili
šu-ba-ti	has received
mu en (*dingir*) *Uru-ki maš-e ni-pad*	in the year when the king was declared by a decision to be the high-priest of Nannar—
mu-gub	is the grain on hand.
Gir Ba-al-ni-ni	Gir Balili,
nin-šid-ag	transacted the business (with ?)
(*Ga*)*lu-ka-ni dumu Ur-*(*dingir*) *Ba-u*	(Ga)lukani, the son of Ur-Ba'u.
mu Ša-aš-ru-ki ba-gul.	In the year when the king devastated Shashru.

E. A. H. 110, 111 (comp. also Pognon, Le Muséon, 1892, p. 253, No. ii.).

The inscription on these two pieces is stamped upon sun-dried bricks. They came, according to Dr. Body, from Nippur. *Aš-nun-na-ki*, the city where *Ur-Nin-giš-zid-da* was patesi, must therefore be sought in the neighbourhood of that city, and thus Scheil's statement (Rec. Trav. xix. p. 55, No. 11), '*le site de cette ville n'est pas à trop grande distance de Niffer,*' is corroborated. The writing *Aš-nun-na-ak* or *Eš(AB)-nun-nak*, which also occurs, would point, however, towards Elam. Notice also (*dingir*) *TIŠPAK!* The patesi of that city, although bearing a Sumerian name (*Ur-(dingir) Nin-giš-zid-da*, i.e. the servant of the lord of the tree of life), was a Semite, or at least spoke Semitic-Babylonian, otherwise he would have used for *NA-RA-AM* the Sumerian *KI-AG*. The name of the god is not (*dingir*) *U+DAR* = *Ištar* (so Pognon and Pinches, B. O. R. 1892, B. vi. No. 3, p. 67), but (*dingir*) *Tišpak* (Br. 3022), i.e. Ninib, who was, according to iii. R. 66, the god of Ashnunna! The inscription reads:—

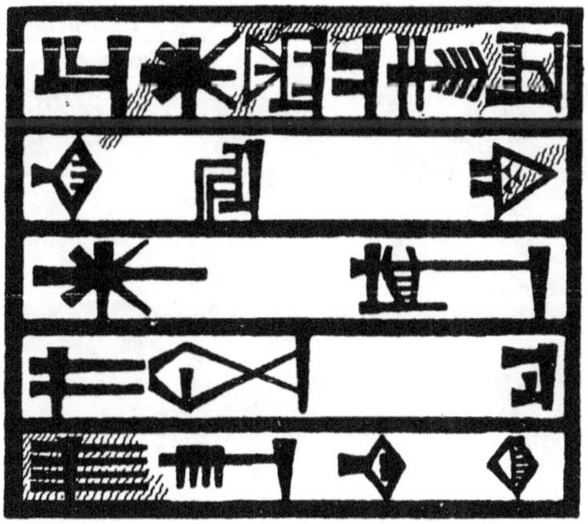

Ur-(dingir) *Nin-giš-zid*(sic)*-da*	Ur-Ningishzidda,
na-ra-am	the beloved
(dingir) *TIŠPAK*	of Ninib,
pa-te-si	the patesi
*Aš-nun-na-*ki	of Ashnunna.

Besides the above-given inscription, Pognon, l. c., has published also three others, giving us the names of three more patesis—all of whom may have been contemporaries of the kings of the fourth dynasty of Ur. For a translation of the inscriptions, see also Pinches, l. c. They read:—

Muséon, 1892, p. 253, No. iv.

[. . .]*ma-šú*
[*na-ra-*]*am*
[(dingir)] *TIŠPAK*
[*pa-te-*]*si*
[*Aš-nun-*]*na-*ki

Ibid. No. iii.	Ibid. No. i.
Til(?)*-la-ku*	*I-ba-al-pi-el*
na-ra-am	*na-ra-am* (dingir) *TIŠPAK*
(dingir) *TIŠPAK*	*patesi*
pa-te-si	*Aš-nun-na-*ki
*Aš-nun-na-*ki	

INDICES

I. PROPER NAMES

[d. = dupsar; dr. = daughter of; e. = engar (p. 410 *a*); f. = father of; g. = gir (p. 424); gd. = grand-daughter of; k. = king of; n. = niku (p. 414 *f*); n. b. g. = nu-banda-gud (p. 411 *d*); ng. = nagid (p. 411 *b*); nin = lady; nt. = note; O. = Obverse; p. = patesi of (p. 55, 4); pa = overseer (p. 411 *e*); R. = Reverse; s. = son of; sh. = shepherd; š. = šabrû; w. = wife of.]

A.

A-a-ud-bu-ku, sh., 375, 26.
Ab, n., 353, 20; 359, O. 8; 361, O. 8.
Ab-ba, e., 383, 21; pa and n. b. g., 412, 5.
Ab-ba-gin-na, sh., 400; 401, 14.
Ab ba kal la, 425, 4.
Abi-i-sir, d., 173, 1.
Abraham, 1, 321.
A-da, ng., 353, 26.
Ad-da, 373, 31; pa, 375, 27.
Ad-da-mu, 363, 16.
A-kur-gal, s. Ur-Ninâ, k. and p. Shirpurla, 12, 14, 65, 66, 68, 73, 85, 87 nt., 93, 94; 145, 1; 213.
A-la (?)-uru, 353, 16.
Al-la, 155 nt.; pa and n. b. g., 412, 4.
Al-la-mu, s. Ur-Sag-ga-mu, p. Girsu (?) 212, 1; 245, 246, 248.
Âlu-ušaršid, k. Kish, 18, 23, 125–129, 178, 214. *See also* Uru-mu-uš.
Al-zu-zu-a, k. Kish, 17; 82, 4; 213 (comp. Zu-zu).
Amar-?-a, f. Ur-(dingir) KAL, 353, 29.
AMAT-, *see* Gin-.
Amraphel, *see* Ḫammurabi.
An-a-an, *see* Ilû-ma.
À-na-mu, 409, 15.
À(?)-nam-uru-na, e., 413.
An-ba-ni-ni, k., 176, 1.
À-ne-mi, e., 412.
À-ni-kur-ra, s. Ur-Ninâ, 68.
À-ni-ta, 66, 68.
An-ki-sa-a-ri, k. Karḫar, 259, 27.
An-ni, 409, 9.
An-nu-ba-ni-ni, k. Lulubi, 127, 175–178; 263, 47 *a*.
Apil-(ilu) Ištar, s. Ilu-ba-ni, 171 nt.
Apil-Sin, k. Babylon, 30.
Ardi-(ilu) Na-bi-um, 229.
Ardi-Naram-(ilu) Sin, 261, 42.
Arioch, *see* Rim-Sin.
Ar-tak-šat-su, k. Babylon, 332.
A-tu, š., 323, 416, 419.
—— f. Ur-(dingir) Ba-u, 400; 403, 29.
—— f. Ur-Gu-la, 353, 18.
—— f. Ur-(dingir) KAL, 365, 25.
Azag-, e., 412.
À-zi-da, f. Lugal-uru-da, 363, 3, nt.

B.

Ba-al-ni-ni, 363, 5; 432, 3 (= Bâl-ili?).
Ba-a-mu, f. Lugal-aš(?)-tur-ri, 250.
Ba-lip, 66, 68.
Bar, s. Uǵ-me-uru-sag, 405, 12.
Bar-ru, e., 383, 32.
(dingir) Ba-u-nin-a-an, 37, 237.
Ba-zi, k. Al, 30, nt. 1.
Ba-zig-gi, sh., 373, 14; 400; 403, 20.
Bêl-uballi-iṭ, d., 312, nt. 4; — 330.
Bi-ga-ni-šar-âli, 173.
Bi-in-ga-ni-šar-âli, s. Naram-Sin, k. Agade, 23, 173, 175.
Bil-gur, 227, 228.
Bur-na-bu-ri-ia-aš, k. Babylon, 328.
(dingir) Bur-(dingir) Sin I., k. Isin, 26, 29; 168, 8; 230, 231.
(dingir) Bur-(dingir) Sin II., k. Ur, 27–29; 168, 8; 230, 2; 240–247, 249, 253, 266–275, 316, 322, 325, 333, 359, 361, 375, 379, 387, 389, 391, 395, 397, 399, 410, 425, 427.

D.

Darius, k. Babylon, 331.
Dingir-a-an, *see* Ilû-ma.
Du-du, high priest of Ningirsu, 117.
Dug-ga-zid-da, pa, 352, 2; 355, R. 9.
—— f. Ur-(dingir) Dumu-zi, 353, 9.
Dug-gi-ul, sh., 405, 14; — 427, 9.
Dun-gi or (dingir) Dun-gi I., k. Ur, s. Ur-Gur, 21, 29; 37, 1; 39, 144; 168, 8; 211, 212, 215, 217, 218, 223–225, 228, 229, 234; 237, 1; 239, 242, 249, 311.
Dun-gi or (dingir) Dun-gi II., k. Ur, 22, 26, 28, 29; 37, 1; 144, 211, 212, 234–236, 239, 240, 243, 249.
(dingir) Dun-gi III., k. Ur, 27, 28, 29; 37, 1; 144, 212, 234; 237, 1; 238–251; 264, 48; 265, 50*b*; 282, 286, 312, 315, 333, 416.
Dun-gi, 237, 1.
(dingir) Dungi-bâni, 315, 1.
Dungi-ili, 315, 1.
(dingir) Dun-gi-zi-kalam-ma, 315, 1.

E.

E-an-na-tum, s. Akurgal, k. and p. Shirpurla, 12, 71–95, 99, 113, 121; 122, 1; 126, 129, 144, 153, 213, 220, 308, 309.
E-giš-mi, e., 412.
En-à-kal-li, f. Ur-lum-ma, p. Gishuḫ, k. TE, 75; 94, 1; 100.
En-an-na-tum I., s. Akurgal, p. Shirpurla, 13, 14, 72, 95, 103, 116, 117, 144.
En-an-na-tum II., s. Entemena, p. Shirpurla, 13, 119, 120; 122, 1; 144.
En-an-na-tum, s. Ishme-Dagan, 25, 26, 29, 234, 239, 312.
En-ǵe-gal, k. Shirpurla, 16, 54, 144.
Enim-(dingir) Ba-u, n., 393, 12.
En-ne-Ugun, k. Kish and Uḫ(?), 17, 121–124, 126; 151, 1; 213.
En-šag-kuš-an-na, lord of Kengi, 43, 45, 121; 122, 1; 144, 213, 217, 219.
En-teme-na, s. En-an-na-tum I., p. Shirpurla, 13, 96–119; 122, 1; 123; 125, 2; 126, 144, 220.
Eri-Aku, *see* Rim-Sin.
Erin-da, 173.
Eri-(dingir) Uru-ki, s. Ur-(dingir) Dun-pa-ud-du, 240, 1.
E(?)-ud-bu, s. Ur-Ninâ, 68.
E-zi, ng., 389, 7.
E-zu-ab, k. Gishuḫ, 23; 150, 4.

G.

(Ga)lu-(dingir) An, e., 413.
(dingir) (Ga)lu-An-na, 317, 1.
(Ga)lu-Bal-šag-ga, 363, 9.
(Ga)lu-(dingir) Ba-u, 363, 8; 393, 12.
—— f. (Ga)lu-(dingir) Nin-gir-su, 240, 1.

(Ga)lu-bi-mu, g., 407, 21.
(Ga)lu-dingir-ra, 353, 15; d., 407, 23.
—— s. Ur-(dingir) Da-mu, 405, 3.
—— f. Ur-(dingir) Kal, 363, 10.
(Ga)lu-(dingir) Dun-gi, 315, 1.
(Ga)lu-(dingir) En-zu, f. Ur-(dingir) Kal, 352, 369.
(Ga)lu-gin-na, 363, 4.
(Ga)lu-(dingir) Giš-bar-ud-du, 377, 6.
(Ga)lu-(dingir) Gu-de-a, 313, 1.
(Ga)lu-Gu-la, 425, 6.
(Ga)lu-kal-la, 409, 6.
(Ga)lu-ka-ni I., f. Ǵa-la-Lama, p. Shirpurla, 21, 23, 29, 211, 246, 249.
(Ga)lu-ka-ni II., p. Shirpurla, 22, 29, 212, 236, 238, 243, 244, 246, 249.
—— s. Ur-(dingir) Ba-u, 432, 10.
(Ga)lu-ka-[ni], 353, 11.
(Ga)lu-Ka-ṣal (= Amêl-Kaṣalli, 'the man from Kaṣallu'), e., 412.
(Ga)lu-Ki-nu-nir-ki, 261, 42.
(Gal)u-(dingir) Lagab + inserted igi-gunû (= god of Gishuḫ), 240, 1; 325.
(Ga)lu-ligir-e, 237, 1.
(Ga)lu-me-ne(lam), 353, 22; 359, R. 6.
(Ga)lu-(dingir) Na-ru-a, (ga)lu KU, ng., 353, 10; 373, 8.
—— f. Ur-Šag-ga, 353, 19.
(Ga)lu-(dingir) Nin-gir-su, s. (Ga)lu-(dingir) Ba-u, 240, 1.
—— f. Ur-(dingir) Gàl-alim, 425, 12.
—— g., 407, 22.
(dingir) (Ga)lu-(dingir) Nin-ib, 317, 1.
(Ga)lu-(dingir) Nin-sun, sh., 379, 18.
(Ga)lu-(dingir) Nin-šul, 409, 13; — e., 412.
(Ga)lu-(dingir) Pa-sag, e., 412.
(Ga)lu-Šir-pur-la-ki, 261, 42.
—— d., s. Ur-(dingir) Ninâ, 323.
(Ga)lu-(dingir) Utu, p. Gishuḫ, 30, 1; 300, III.
(Ga)lu-zi-lum, 383, 40.
Ga-šag-ga, g., 431, 8.
. . . . gi, e., 383, 43.
(dingir) Gimil-(dingir) Sin, k. Ur, 27, 28, 215, 240 and nt., 247, 249, 274–278, 312; 315, 2; 322.
Gin-(dingir) Dun-pa-ud-du, w. Gudea I., 210; — 327.
Gin-(dingir) Gu-de-a, 313, 1.
Gir-ri-a-ab-ba(?), 329.
Gi-tab-ba-sig-ga, 427, 2.
Gu-de-a I., f. Ur-(dingir) Ningirsu, p. Shirpurla, 20, 23, 31, 39, 144, 187–210, 220, 244, 246, 247, 295, 297, 301, 304, 310, 311, 313, 321, 322.
Gu-de-a II., p. Girsu (?), 144, 244, 247, 248.
(dingir) Gu-de-a, p., 244, 247. *See* Gudea I.
Gu-de-a, 327.
(dingir) Gug-kam, p. Girsu (?), 248, 2; 413. (The sign for Gug is not yet assimilated. It may possibly be read also AGA, Br. 6949 = agû.)
Gu-gu, 427, 11.
Gu-nam-mi-de (?), p. Gishuḫ, 75.
Gu-ni-du, f. Ur-Ninâ, 12, 58, 64–66; 137, 44.
Gur-sar, f. Gunidu, 12, 58, 61.
Gu-u-mu, 326.
Gu-un-gu-nu-um, k. Ur, 25, 28, 29, 234, 239, 240.

Ǵ, Ḫ.

Ḫa-aš-ḫa-mi-ir, p. Ishkun-Sin, 30, 1; 235.
Ǵa-la-Lama, s. (Ga)lukani I., 21, 23, 29, 39, 211, 212, 218, 225, 249.
Ḫammurabi, k. Babylon, 1, 32, 216, 217, 219, 286, 298, 302; 305, 1.
Ǵar(?)-ra-ab-du, 363, 13.
Ǵar-sag-ku-al, 66, 69.
Ǵe-šag-mu, e., 412.

I.

Ia-lu-un-a-sar, f. Libit-Anunit, 26, 29, 229.
I-ba-al-pi-el, p. Ashnunna, 434.

Ib-ni-šarri, d., 155 nt.
$^{(dingir)}$ I-din-$^{(dingir)}$ Da-gan, k. Isin (?), 27, 29, 231, 232, 249, 312.
Igi-šag-šag, e., 413.
Iḫ-ši-ia-ar-ši, k. Babylon, 332.
$^{f.}$ Il-'-e-tu, 330.
Ili or Il-li, p. Gishuḫ, 96, 105, 106; 122, 1; 144.
Ilu-ba-ni, f. Apil-$^{(ilu)}$ Ištar, 171 nt.
Ilû-ma, s. Nab-še-me-a, 226, 2.
Ilû-ma-Giš-dub-ba, s. Nab-še-me-a, 226.
$^{(dingir)}$ I-ne-$^{(dingir)}$ Sin, k. Ur, 27–29; 240 nt., 249, 278.
Ip-ša-$^{(dingir)}$ En-lil, 261, 42.
Ip-ša-$^{(dingir)}$ Innanna-Erin-$^{(ki)}$, p. Innanna-Erin-^{ki}, 30, 1. (The sign IP is that mentioned already on p. 261, 42, occurring there in the date mu e IP ša Iši-$^{(dingir)}$ Da-gan-na ba-ru. The fact that IP-ŠA forms here part of a nom. pr. may make it probable that we have to take IP-ša-Iši-$^{(dingir)}$ Da-gan-na as *one* name, i. e. that of the temple. In this case Ip-ša would be parallel to Ur or Ardi, comp. Ur-$^{(dingir)}$ Iši-$^{(dingir)}$ Ba-u = Ip-ša-$^{(dingir)}$ Iši-Da-gan, comp. also Ardi-Naram-$^{(ilu)}$ Sin. E. A. H. 101 might be translated: In the year when the 'Ip-ša-Iši-$^{(dingir)}$ Da-gan'—a house for Dungi—was built. The ŠAG-GAL Ip-ša-Iši-Dagan mentioned on E. A. H. 55 (p. 323) shows that if this explanation be correct, Ip-ša-Iši-Dagan must still have lived at the time of Bur-Sin II., for E. A. H. 55 has the date No. 4 of that king. What IP-ŠA when forming nom. pr. means is not yet certain.)
Ip-ša-$^{(dingir)}$ Iši-Da-gan, 312; 317, 1; 261, 42, and above; 324.
Ir-dug-da, ng., 387, 8.
I-šar-a-(a)-dug, g.; 328.
Iš-bi-gir-ra, k. Isin, 26, 29, 229.
$^{(dingir)}$ Iši-$^{(dingir)}$ Ba-u, 261, 42; 317, 1.
Iš(?)-mà-l-lum, p. Dun-til-^{ki}-la, 30, 1.
$^{(dingir)}$ Iš-me-$^{(dingir)}$ Da-gan, f. Enannatum, k. Isin, 25, 26, 29; 168, 8; 233.
Itti-$^{(ilu)}$ Bêl, f. Sargon I., 155, 169.
I-zi-lum, d., 173.

K.

Ka-da-aš-ma-an-Tur-gu, k. Babylon, 161, 1.
Kad-diš-man-Tur-gu, k. Babylon, 208, 2; 328, 329. (The same as preceding.)
Kam-bu-zi-ia, k. Babylon, 331.
Kan-du, dr. Ur-Ba'u, nin, 19, 186, 189.
Kashtubilla, 158.
Ki-lul-la-gu-za-lal, s. Ur-Ba-bi, 237.
Ku-dur-dug-mal, 30, 32.
Kudur-Lagamar = (?) Ku-dur-dug-mal, 30, 286.
Ku-dur-nan-ḫun-di I., 30, 236, 286.
Kudurnuḫgamar, wrong reading for Ku-dur-dug-mal, *see* there.
$^{(dingir)}$ Ku-dur-ri-$^{(dingir)}$ En-lil (= Turgu), k. Babylon, 328.
Ku-ra-aš, k. Babylon, 331.
Ku-ri-gal-zu, k. Karduniash, 168, 8; 236.
Ku (?)-uru-$^{(dingir)}$ Utu, k. Ma-uru-^{ki}, 30, 1.

L.

La-ni-mu, ng., 353, 28.
La-si-ra-ab, k. Guti, 127, 175, 178.
$^{(dingir)}$ Li-bi-it-Anunit, k. Isin, 26, 29, 229.
Lid-da, s. Ur-Ninâ, 68, 366.
Li-pu-uš-Ì-a-um, dr. Na-be-?-maš, 173, 175.
Lugal-an-azag-gi, 400, 401.
Lugal-an-dà, p. Shirpurla (?), 16, 135.

Lugal-aš(?)-tur-ri, s. Ba-a-mu, 250, 251.
Lugal-bar-zu, ng., 352.
Lugal-da(?)-ak(?), k. Kish, 17; 56, 2; 121, 2; 126, 213.
Lugal-dib-bu, 363, 2.
Lugal-(dingir) Dun-gi, n., 261, 42; 315, 1.
Lugal-dur-, 188.
Lugal-engar, e., 413.
Lugal-ezen (or šir?), 353, 24; 361, R. 9; — e., 412.
Lugal-id-da-zi, s. Ur-ud(?)-azag-ga, 428, 429.
Lugal-ka-gi-na, d., 323, 325, 328, 416, 419–421; 422, 5; — ng., 353.
Lugal-kal-la, f. Ur-(dingir) AN-MAǴ, p. Nippur, 30, 1.
Lugal-kar-zi, e., 412.
Lugal-ki-gub-ni-du-du, k. Ur, 18, 23, 144, 151–153, 214.
Lugal-kisal-si, k. Ur, 18, 23, 145, 150; 153, 6.
Lugal-me-ne(lam), 353, 32.
Lugal-ni-šag, pa and n. b. g., 412, 2.
Lugal-pa-ud-du, 363, 6.
Lugal-si-kisal, *see* Lugal-kisal-si.
Lugal-ši-gar-e, s. Šag-da, ng., 353, 12.
Lugal-šir (or ezen?), s. Ur-Ninâ, 66, 68; — 89, 2.
Lugal-šug-gur, p. Shirpurla, 16, 56, 74, 121, 142, 179, 213.
Lugal-tar-si, k. Kish, 23, 125 and nt. 3, 126, 147, 214.
Lugal-u-kaš-šu-e, 353, 8; 393, 9; 427, 5.
Lugal-uru-da, s. À-zi-da, 363, 3.
Lugal-ušum-gal, p. Shirpurla, 7, 23, 153, 159, 161, 162.
Lugal-(dingir) Utu, e., 412.
Lugal-zag-gi-si, s. Ukush, k. Erech, 17, 23, 31, 130, 134, 138, 149, 153, 214, 219, 220; 280, 4; 308–310.
Luǵ-bar-ǵe-gid(?)-dul, 66.
Luǵ-di-ne, 353, 23.
Lum-ma-dur, s. Enannatum II., 15, 1; 120, 153.
Lu-ù-šag-ga, 353, 4.

M.

Ma-an-iš-tu-su, k. Kish, 18, 23, 126, 127, 148, 214.
Marduk-zêr-ib-ni, 330.
Mêr-Dungi, 315, 1.
Me-silim, k. Kish, 15, 55, 74; 98, 8; 99, 101, 121; 122, 1; 126, 142, 148, 179, 213; 255, 12.
MU-E-AN-NA, dumu lugal, 284, 1.
Mu-na-ba-šag, 365, 27.
Mu-ri-kur-ta, s. Ur-Ninâ, 66, 68.
(ilu) Mu-ta-bil, šakkanâku of Dûr-ilu-ki, 30, 1; 255, 12.
. . . . maǵ, n., 365, 33.
. . . . ma-šu, p. Ashnunna, 434.

N.

Na-be-?-maš, s. Naram-Sin, f. Lipuš-Iaum, p. Tutu, 173, 175.
Nab-še-me-a, f. Ilû-ma or (and?) Ilû-ma-Giš-dub-ba, 226; 226, 2.
Nabû-kudur-uṣur, k. Babylon, 331.
Nabû-nâ'id, k. Babylon, 4, 171, 223, 331.
Nabû-u-ṣal-li, 330.
Na-da-tum, 337 and nt., 381.
Na-ki, s. Ur-Gar, 431, 5.
Nam-ǵa-ni, 324; 353, 3; 355, R. 8.
—— s. Ud(?)-a-a-mu, luǵ, 240, 1.
Nam-maǵ, 353, 25.
Nam-maǵ-ni, p. Shirpurla, 19, 23, 39, 185, 186, 189.
Nam-ne-ru-bi-nu-kud(?), 407, 20.
Nam-tum, d., 66.
(ilu) Na-ra-am-(ilu) Sin, s. Sargon I., k. Agade, 7, 23, 31; 90, 18; 160, 3; 164–166; 168, 8; 170, 171; 173, 1; 175, 176, 214, 215, 219, 284, 308, 310.

Na-zi-Mu-ru-ut-ta-aš, k. Babylon, 328, 329.
Nergal-šar-uṣur, k. Babylon, 331.
.... ne-šu-in-ta, s. Šum-(ilu) Ma-lik, šakkanâku, 154, 2.
Ni-ǵal-la, 66.
Ninâ-ku-tur-à, 68.
(dingir) Ninâ-ma-an-ud-diš, e., 412.
Ni-na-na, pa, 326.
[Nin]-giš-zi-de-a, 353, 31.
Nin-ka-gi-na, gd. Nammaǵni, 186.
Nin-kal-la, sh., 409, 3.
Nin-kiš (?)-mi-da-šu, dr. Dungi III., 257, 19.
.... nun, 353, 30.
Nun-pad, s. Ur-Ninâ, 68.
Nûr-Rammân, k. Larsa, 30, 286.

P.

Pi-il-ip-su or Pi-li-ip-su, k., 321, 332.

R.

Rêsh-Rammân, k. Apirak, 158.
Rim-Sin, k. Larsa, 286, 321, 328.

S.

Sag-an-tug, 68.
Si-a-tum, 236.
(ilu) Sin-gâmil, k. Erech, 29, 225, 226; 312, 2.
(ilu) Sin-gâšid, k. Erech, 29, 225, 228; 312, 2.
Sin-i-din-na, 30, 286.
Sin-muballiṭ, k. Babylon, 30.
Sumuabi, 286.
Sumulan, k. Babylon, 30.

Š.

Šag-da, f. Lugal-ši-gar-e, 353, 12.
Šamaš-nâṣi-ir, 330.
Šamaš-šum-ukîn, k. Babylon, 330, 331.
Šar-ga-ni-šar-âli or (ilu) Šar-ga-ni-šar-âli (only once) (= Šar-ge-na of Nabû-nâ'id), s. Itti-Bêl, k. Agade, 7, 23, 127, 154–164, 167, 169, 170, 175, 176, 178, 179, 214, 289, 308–310.
Šar-la-ak, k. Guti, 159, 160, 176.
Šar-ru-iš-da-gal, d., 165.
Šibir, k., 329.
Šú-e (?)-a-ni-ša, ng., 353, 27.
Šum-(ilu) Ma-lik, f. .... ne-šu-in-ta, 154, 2.
Šu-na, sh., 400; 403, 33.

T.

Tig-gil, sh., 400; 401, 5.
Til(?)-la-ḳu, p. Ashnunna, 434.
.... tum, 66.

U.

Ud (?)-a-a-mu, f. Nam-ǵa-ni, 240, 1.
U-dug-?, p. Kish, 55, 2; 121, 1; 215.
Uǵ-me-uru-sag, f. Bar, 405, 12.
U-kuš, f. Lugalzaggisi, p. Gishuḫ, 130, 132, 214.
Ù-ma-ni, 420, 2; 429, 2.
Ur-, 412.
Ur-ab-ba, g., 425, 13.
Ur-(dingir) Al-la, 365, 26.
Ur-(dingir) AN-MAǦ, s. Lugal-kal-la, p. Nippur, 30, 1.
Ur-Ba-bi, f. Ki-lul-la-gu-za-lal, 237; — 326.
Ur-(dingir) Ba-u, p. Shirpurla, 19, 23, 31, 39, 144, 181–185, 310, 321, 322.
Ur-(dingir) Ba-u II., s. Bur-Sin II., 28, 29, 144, 274, 312, 3.
Ur-(dingir) Ba-u, dumu patesi, 246; — 327, 427.
—— d., 349, 351.
—— s. A-tu, 400, 403, 29.
—— f. (Ga)lu-ka-ni, 432, 10.
—— f. Ur-(dingir) Ninâ, 324.
—— s. Uru-dur-dur, 245.
Ur-da, d., 165.
Ur-(dingir) Da-mu, f. (Ga)lu-dingir-ra, 405, 3.

Ur-(dingir) Dumu-zi, s. Dug-ga-zid-da, 353, 9.
(dingir) Ur-(dingir) Dun-pa-ud-du, 317, 1; 327.
Ur-(dingir) Dun-pa-ud-du, f. Eri-(dingir) Uru-ki, 240, 1; — 405, 9.
Ur-dingir-ra, 326.
Ur-E, p. Shirpurla, 20, 23, 153.
Ur-E-Innanna-ge, 16; 261, 42.
Ur-E-ninnû, 261, 42; 349, 351; 425, 2; — ĝal, 383, 46.
Ur-(dingir) En-lil, dam-kar-gal and p. Nippur, 30, 1; 44, 4; 410.
Ur-(dingir) En-zu, 419, 2.
(dingir) Ur-(dingir) En-zu-na, 317, 1.
Ur-(dingir) Gàl-alim, d., 416, 252.
— d., s. (Ga)lu-(dingir) Ningirsu, 425, 12.
Ur-gan-ne (bil), e., 413.
Ur-Gar, sh., 379, 24; — p., 248, 2; 327; — pa, 383, 44.
— f. Na-ki, 431, 5.
Ur-Giš-mar, sh., 405, 7.
Ur-Gu-la, n., 339; 359, O. 9; 361, O. 10; 400; 403, 24.
— s. A-tu, 353, 18.
Ur-Gur I., k. Ur, 24, 29; 37, 1; 39, 215, 217, 219, 221, 222, 228, 229, 234, 242; 263, 46; 311; 317, 1.
Ur-Gur II., k. Ur (probably the same as Ur-Gur I.), 26, 28, 29; 37, 1; 234, 235.
(dingir) Ur-Gu-ru, 317, 1.
Ur-Ĝa-lu-ub, 73, III. 2.
Ur-(dingir) Im, 353, 33; — g., 427, 6.
Ur-(dingir) Iši-(dingir) Ba-u, 261, 42.
Ur-(dingir) Ka-di, 98, 10; 256 nt.; — sh., 377, 10.
Ur-Ka-?-ki, 326.
Ur-(dingir) KAL, p. Girsu, 27, 245–248; 260, 34 *a*; 264, 47 *b*, 48; 265, 50 *b*; 267, 3 *b*; 304, 312, 327.
— s. Amar-?-a, 353, 29.
— s. A-tu, 365, 25.
— s. (Ga)lu-(dingir) Enzu, 352, 369.
— s. (Ga)lu-dingir-ra, 363, 10.
U-r(dingir) KAL, e., 381, 11; — 407, 17.
Ur-lum-ma, s. En-à-kal-li, p. Gishuḫ, k. ṬE, 95, 1; 96, 102, 104, 105; 122, 1.
Ur-Ma-ma, damkar, 30, 1; 410; — pa and n. b. g., 412, 3.
Ur-(dingir) NE-SÙ, p. Gishuḫ, 111, 248; 300, III.
Ur-Nigin-gar, 327; 363, 14; 421; 422, 6.
Ur-(dingir) Ninâ, s. Gunidu, k. Shirpurla, 12, 56–58, 61, 64–66, 93, 113, 144, 164, 178, 213, 217, 219, 366; — 405, 10.
— f. (Ga)lu-Šir-pur-la-ki, 323.
— s. Ur-(dingir) Ba-u, 324.
— f. Ur-Šid, 412.
Ur-(dingir) Nin-gir, 413.
Ur-(dingir) Nin-gir-su, s. Gudea, 20, 23, 39, 145, 210, 244.
— priest of Ninâ, 37, 237, 244, 245, 249.
Ur-(dingir) Nin-giš-zid-da, e., 412, 413; — 381, 45.
— p. of Ashnunna, 433.
(dingir) Ur-(dingir) Nin-ib, k. Isin, 26, 29; 168, 8; 230; 312, 1; 411.
Ur-(dingir) Nin-sun, p. Shirpurla, 21, 23, 29, 211; 247, 1.
Ur-(dingir) Nin-tu, ng., 353, 7; 357, R. 6.
Ur-(dingir) Nin-zu (*sic*), 412, 1.
Ur-(dingir) Nun-gal, dumu patesi, 246.
Ur-(dingir) Pa-sag, 353, 6; — e., 413.
Ur-Sag-ga-mu, f. Allamu, 212, 1; 245.
Ur-Šag-ga, s. (Ga)lu-(dingir) Na-ru-a, 353, 19.
Ur-Šid, 353, 17; 363, 15.
— s. Ur-(dingir) Ninâ, 412.
Ur-ud (?)-azag-ga, f. Lugal-id-da-zi, 428, 429.
Uru-dur-dur, f. Ur-(dingir) Ba-u, 245.
Uru-ka-gi-na, k. Shirpurla, 47–54, 213.
Uru-kal-la, sh., 373, 18.
Uru-ki-bi, s. Ur-(dingir) Utu, 431, 10.
Uru-mu-uš, *see* Âlu-ušaršid.

Ur-(dingir) Utu, f. Uru-ki-bi, 431, 10; — 363, 7.
—— p. (?) Ur, 20, 3; 23, 34, 154.
Ur-zag-ud-du, k. Kish, 23, 125 and nt. 2, 126, 147, 151, 214.
Uš, p. Gishuḫ, 74, 98; 122, 1.
Uš-mu, pa, 393, 6.
(dingir) Utu-a, s. Ur-, d., 211, 238, 243, 244.
(dingir) Utu-ki-ag, 405, 15.
(dingir) Utu-mu, e., 381, 6; 412.
(dingir) Utu-šag-ga, 405, 5.

Z.

Za-ba-si-si, e., 413.
Zu-zu, k. Uḫ, 82, 89 (comp. Al-zu-zu-a).

II. GODS

ALSO NOMINA PROPRIA AND CITIES PRECEDED BY THE SIGN FOR *DINGIR* (*ILU*).

[n. pr. = nomina propria.]

A.

(ilu) A-E, 160.
(dingir) AGA, *see* n. pr. (dingir) GUG-kam.
ilu A-ga-de-ki, 7, 165, 166.
(ilu) A-GUR, 252.
(dingir) Al-la, *see* n. pr. Ur-(dingir) Al-la. So probably also ii. R. 57, 71 *a*.
AMAR-UD, Bur-Sin II. was worshipped as the MUL-AMAR-UD, 316.
(dingir) An, *see* n. pr. (Ga)lu-(dingir) An.
(dingir) An-maǵ, *see* n. pr. Ur-(dingir) An-maǵ.
An-na, 132, 202, 204, 209, 211, 1; 250, 256, 257, 267, 280, 281, 291, 296, 302. *See also* n. pr. (dingir) (Ga)lu-An-na.
An-nat (?), 177.
An-nu-um, 177. *See also* n. pr. An-nu-ba-ni-ni.
(ilu) A-nu-ni-tim, 160. *See also* n. pr. (dingir) Li-bi-it-Anunit (Ištar).
(ilu) A-nu-um, 330.

B.

(ilu) Bâb-il$^{u}_{1}$-ki, *see* (dingir) Ka-dingir-ra-ki.
(dingir) Ba-u, 44, 4; 50, 53, 65; 182, 1; 202-205, 207-209, 288, 295, 297, 298, 301; 311, 2; 315, 365, 423. *See also* n. pr. (dingir) Ba-u-nin-a-an, Enim-(dingir) Ba-u, (Ga)lu-(dingir) Ba-u, Ur-Ba-bi (always without dingir), Ur-(dingir) Ba-u, Ur-(dingir) Iši-(dingir) Ba-u.
(ilu) Bêl, *see* (dingir) En-lil and n. pr. Itti-(ilu) Bêl.
(ilu) Bêltum (Bêlit), *see* (dingir) Nin-lil.
(dingir) Bur-(dingir) Sin, n. pr.

D.

(dingir) Da-gan, *see* n. pr. Ip-ša-Iši-(dingir) Da-gan, 261, 42.
(dingir) Dam-gal-nun-na, 224.
(dingir) Da-mu (Br. 6662 = Ba-u), *see* n. pr. Ur-(dingir) Da-mu.
Dingir-(ra), *see* n. pr. (Ga)lu-dingir-ra, Ur-dingir-ra.
(dingir) Dumu-zi, 288, 297, 298, 301, 411, 429. *See also* n. pr. Ur-(dingir) Dumu-zi.
(dingir) Dumu-zi-zu-ab, 84; 182, 1.
(dingir) Dun, *see* n. pr. (dingir) Dun-gi and p. 311, 2.
(dingir) Dun-gi, 288, n. pr. *See also* the compositions: (dingir) Dun-gi-ba-ni-

(dingir) Dun-gi-ili, (dingir) Dun-gi-zi-kalam-ma, (Ga)lu-(dingir) Dun-gi, Lugal-(dingir) Dun-gi, Mêr-(dingir) Dun-gi, and especially p. 315, 1; and C. T. No. 12939.

(dingir) Dun-gur, 92, 18; 108, 118 and nt. 1; 308, 1; or (dingir) Dun-gur-an, 115, 116, 118 ((dingir) Dun + AN + gur), 308, 1.

(dingir) Dun-pa-ud-du, 312; 314, 2. *See also* n. pr. Gin-(dingir) Dun-pa-ud-du, Ur-(dingir) Dun-pa-ud-du.

(dingir) Dun-šag-ga, 49, 53, 190, 195, 196.

E.

(dingir) En-, 178, 233.

(dingir) En-gubur-ra, 233.

(dingir) En-ki, 80; 81, 1; 84, 95, 108, 114, 132, 172, 182, 224, 232, 270; 275, 2; 308, 327.

(dingir) En-lil, 14; 30, 1; 44, 45, 50, 51, *et passim*; written also

(dingir) En-lil-la, 118, 123, 124; or

(dingir) En-lil-la(l), 19, 21, 22; 89, 22; 99, 101, *et passim*; or

(dingir) En-lil-li, 107, 109, 119, 123, 135, 152, 191, 278, *et passim*. *See also* n. pr. Ip-ša-(dingir) En-lil, Kad-diš-man-Tur-gu (= Enlil), (dingir) Ku-du-ri-(dingir) En-lil (= Turgu), Ur-(dingir) En-lil.

(dingir) En-temen[-an], 118; 308, 1.

(dingir) En-zu, 81, 1; 133; 180, 1. *See also* n. pr. (Ga)lu-(dingir) En-zu, Ur-(dingir) En-zu.

(dingir) En-zu-na, *see* n. pr. Ur-(dingir) En-zu-na.

G.

(dingir) Gàl-alim, 49, 51, 190. *See also* n. pr. Ur-(dingir) Gàl-alim.

(dingir) Gal-dim-zu-ab, 106.

(dingir) Ga-tum-dug, 58, 64, 65, 115, 116, 190, 310, 425.

(dingir) Gim-nun-ta-ud-du-a, 54.

. . . . gir, 52.

(dingir) Giš-bar-ud-du, *see* n. pr. (Ga)lu-(dingir) Giš-bar-ud-du.

Giš-dub-ba, *see* n. pr. Ilû-ma-Giš-dub-ba.

Gišuḫ, god of, *see* (dingir) Lagab + inserted igi-gunû.

(dingir) Gu-de-a, 312 ff. *See also* n. pr. (Ga)lu-(dingir) Gu-de-a, Gin-(dingir) Gu-de-a.

(dingir) Gug, *see* n. pr. (dingir) Gug-kam.

Gu-la (always without dingir), *see* n. pr. (Ga)lu-Gu-la, Ur-Gu-la.

(ilu) Gu-ti-im, 176.

I.

Ilu, *see* n. pr. Ilu-ba-ni, Ilû-ma, Ilû-ma-Giš-dub-ba, Iš-mà-i-lum, and also *sub* dingir-(ra).

(dingir) Im, 327, 429. *See also* n. pr. Ur-(dingir) Im.

(dingir) Im-gig-ĝu-bar-bar, 182, 1; 183, 185, 195.

(dingir) Im-pa-ud-du, 53.

(dingir) I-ne-(dingir) Sin, n. pr.

(dingir) Innanna, 90, 94, 133; 180, 1; 182, 1; 199, 200, 201, 222, 230, 236, 237, 268, 273, 279, 280, 295, 301, 302, 327.

(dingir) Innanna-ka, 'goddess of Innanna,' 84. Comp. also

(dingir) Innanna nin (dingir) Innanna, 'Innanna, the mistress of the divine I.,' 125, 3. *See also* n. pr. Ur-E-Innanna-ge.

(dingir) Innanna-edin, 44, 4; 87 note, 410.

(dingir) Innanna-Erin-ki, *see* n. pr. Ip-ša-(dingir) Innanna-Erin-ki.

(dingir) Iši-(dingir) Ba-u, n. pr. *See* n. pr. Ur-(dingir) Iši-(dingir) Ba-u.

(dingir) Iši-Da-gan, n. pr. *See* n. pr. Ip-ša-(dingir) Iši-Da-gan.

(dingir) Iš-me-(dingir) Da-gan, n. pr.
(ilu) Ištar, 160, 3; 169, 172, 177; 180, 1; 182, 1; 226; 255, 12. *See also* (dingir) Innanna, and n. pr. Apil-(ilu) Ištar, (dingir) Li-bi-it-Anunit (Ištar).

K.

(dingir) Ka-di, 98, 255. *See also* n. pr. Ur-(dingir) Ka-di.
(dingir) Ka-dingir-ra-ki, 161 nt.
(dingir) KAL, *see* n. pr. Ur-(dingir) KAL.
(dingir) Ku-dur-ri-(dingir) En-lil (= Turgu), n. pr.
Ḳur-gal, *see* n. pr. A-kur-gal.

L.

(dingir) Lagab + inserted igi-gunû = god of Gišuḫ, 28, 97; 101, 22; 137. *See also* n. pr. (Ga)lu-(dingir) Lagab + inserted igi-gunû.
(dingir) Li-bi-it-Anunit, n. pr.
(dingir) Lugal-ban-da, 226.
(dingir) Lugal-dingir-ri-ne, 235.
(dingir) Lugal-Erim-ki, 85 (written gal + (ga)lu + dingir-Erim-ka), 113.
(dingir) Lugal-kur-kur-ra, 132.

M.

(ilu) Ma-lik, *see* n. pr. Šum-(ilu) Ma-lik.
Ma-ma, *see* n. pr. Ur-Ma-ma (without dingir).
(ilu) Marduk, 133, 30 (written (dingir) ŠID). *See also* AMAR-UD, Su-kur, and Tu-tu.
(dingir) Mar-tu, 411.
(ilu) Mu-ta-bil, n. pr., 30, 1; 255, 12.

N.

(ilu) Na-bi-um, *see* n. pr. Ardi-(ilu) Na-bi-um.
(ilu) Nannar, 225. *See also* (dingir) Uru-ki.
(ilu) Na-ra-am-(ilu) Sin, n. pr. *See* n. pr. Ardi-Naram-(ilu) Sin.
(dingir) Na-ru-a, *see* n. pr. (Ga)lu-(dingir) Na-ru-a.
(ilu) Nergal (written (dingir) NER-UNU-GAL), 226, 3. *See also* (dingir) Šid-lam-ta-ud-du.
(dingir) Ne-sù, 287; 288, 1; 294, 298, 300, 302, 419, 425. *See also* n. pr. Ur-(dingir) Ne-sù.
(dingir) Nidaba, 132, 133, 308, 310.
(dingir) Nin-, 178.
(dingir) Ninâ, 58, 61, 62, 64, 66, 68; 82, 4; 84, 87 nt., 93, 94, 97, 101, 102, 105–109, 113, 115, 116, 189, 193, 224, 237, 327. *See also* n. pr. Ninâ-ku-tur-à, (dingir) Ninâ-ma-an-ud-diš, Ur-(dingir) Ninâ.
(dingir) Nin-à-gal, 182, 185, 310.
(dingir) Nin-a-gid-ǵa-du, 133, 308.
Nin-an-da-gal-ki, 206.
(dingir) Nin-a-zu, 292, 295, 300, 301, 420. *See also* (dingir) Nin-zu.
(dingir) Nin-dar-a, 182, 1; 190, 193.
(dingir) Nin-din-dug, 44, 4; 89, 22; 410.
(dingir) Nin-gir, *see* n. pr. Ur-(dingir) Nin-gir.
(dingir) Nin-gir-su, 14, 19, 21, 22, 48, 51, 52, 58, 66, 68, *et passim*;
written (dingir) Nin-su-gir, 16, 58, 64, 66, 68, 143, 217;
or (dingir) Su-nin-gir, 16.
See also n. pr. (Ga)lu-(dingir) Nin-gir-su, Ur-(dingir) Nin-gir-su, and comp. (dingir) Im-gig-ǵu-bar-bar.
(dingir) Nin-giš-zid-da, 190, 196, 199, 207; 211, 1; 311, 1; 312, 327. *See also* n. pr. [Nin]-giš-zi-de-a and Ur-(dingir) Nin-giš-zid-da.
(dingir) Nin-gubur-ra, 233.
(dingir) Nin-ḫar-sag, 81, 1; 84, 93, 95, 101, 106, 107, 114, 118; 133, 1; 182, 1; 198, 222, 308, 327.
(dingir) Nin-ib, 258; *and see* n. pr. Ur-(dingir) Nin-ib.

(dingir) Nin-in-(ni)-si-(an)-na, 202, I. 1. *See also* (dingir) Nin-si-na.
(dingir) Nin-ki, 81, 1.
(dingir) Nin-lil, 37; 89, 22; 125, 1; 177; 182, 1; 222, 236, 237, 277; written (dingir) Nin-lil-la(l), 255, 257, 258; 275, 2; 277.
(dingir) Nin-Mar-[ki], 59, 14; 182, 1; 223, 327, 334, 375, 379.
(dingir) Nin-sar, 52, 54.
(dingir) Nin-si-na, 294, 298. *See also* (dingir) Nin-in-(ni)-si-(an)-na.
(dingir) Nin-sun-na, 211, 1; 226, 326. *See also* n. pr. Ur-(dingir) Nin-sun.
(dingir) Nin-šul-li(l), 51. *See also* n. pr. (Ga)lu-(dingir) Nin-šul.
(dingir) Nin-Uru-um-[ki]-ma, 224; 269, 11.
(dingir) Nin-zu, *see* n. pr. Ur-(dingir) Nin-zu, and comp. (dingir) Nin-a-zu.
(dingir) Nu-ku-sir-da, 256.
(dingir) Nun, *see* (dingir) Dam-gal-nun-na.
(dingir) Nun-gal, *see* n. pr. Ur-(dingir) Nun-gal.
(dingir) Nu-silig-ga, 276, 16.
(ilu) Nusku, 223, nt. 3.

P.

(dingir) Pap-nigin-gar-ra, 363, 14. *See also* n. pr. Ur-Nigin-gar.
(dingir) Pa-sag, 85. *See also* n. pr. (Ga)lu-(dingir) Pa-sag.

R.

(ilu) Rammân, 177. *See also* n. pr. Rêsh-Rammân, and comp. (dingir) Im.

S.

(dingir) Sal-in-si-na = (dingir) Nin-in-(ni)-si-(an)-na.
(ilu) Sin, 174, 176, 178, 180. *See also* n. pr. Apil-(ilu) Sin, (ilu) Sin-gâmil, (ilu) Sin-gâšid, and comp. (dingir) En-zu and (dingir) Uru-ki.
(dingir) Su-kur, 302, XI. *See also* (ilu) Marduk.
. . . . šag . . . , 53.
(ilu) Šamaš, 169, 170, 171, 177, 222. Comp. (dingir) Utu.
(ilu) Šar-ga-ni-šar-âli, 169.
(dingir) ŠID, 133.
(dingir) Šid-lam-ta-ud-du, 133, 30; 224; 237, 1.

T.

Tur-gu, *see* (dingir) En-lil.
(dingir) Tu-tu, 174, 5. *See also* (ilu) Marduk.

U.

(dingir) UD-KIB-NUN-[ki], 161, 1.
(dingir) Umu, 133.
(dingir) Urdu-zi, 186.
(dingir) Ur-Gu-ru, n. pr., 317, 1.
(dingir) Uru (for (dingir) Uru-ki), 256, 16; comp.
(dingir) Uru-Kar-zi-da, 269, 11.
(dingir) Uru-ki, 25, 222; 226, 2; 234, 250, 253, 256, 257, 263; 267, 5; 277, 293, 325, 432. *See also* n. pr. Eri-(dingir) Uru-ki, and comp. (ilu) Nannar and (ilu) Sin.
(dingir) Uru-ki En-lil-[ki], 256.
(dingir) Uru-ki-Kar (sometimes also written TE)-zi-da, 27, 255, 260, 269, 302. *See also* Kar-zi-da-[ki].
(dingir) Utu, 25, 76, 77, 83, 95, 101, 132, 133, 137, 161. *See also* n. pr. Lugal-(dingir) Utu, Ur-(dingir) Utu, (dingir) Utu-a, (dingir) Utu-ki-ag, (dingir) Utu-mu, (dingir) Utu-šag-ga, and comp. (ilu) Šamaš.

Z.

(dingir) Za-ma-ma, 55, 2; 121, 1. *See also* (dingir) Ma-ma.
(dingir) Za-za-ru, 53.

III. BUILDINGS

[For the temples see also under GODS.]

A.

Ab-bi-ru, 113.
ab-dug, 113, nt. to II. 7.
ab-gi, 62, nt. to III. 1; 118, nt. 9.
ab-gi-gi, 118.
ab-Gir-su, 64, 4; 64, 6 (ab-Su-gir).
ab-zu, *see* zu-ab.
alan, 61, 62, 199, 201, 208, 210, 257.
. . . . an-dug + nagid-ki, 223.
An-ta-sur-ra, 48, 51, 53, 89, 91, 106, 114, 327.
a$^{p}_{b}$-ir, 62; 118, nt. 9.
A-RUŠ, 113, nt. to III. 2.

B.

bad gal ê Ur ku ki li bi da tig? ga, 270, 12.
bad-ki ki-bi ba-ab-gl, 258, 20. *See also* Ubara-ki.
bad-kisal, 125, 3. *See also* kisal, mi-kisal.
bad-pur + la + Šir, 59, nt. 16; 63 (bad Šir-pur-la).
bad Uru-azag-ga, 85.
bad Uru-um-ki-ma, 235.
bad-mar-tu mu-ri-iḳ Ti-id-ni-im, 276, 5; 316.
bar, 101, 14 ff.
bît (ilu) Bêl, 162, 171 nt. *See also* E-KUR.
bur-maǵ, 118.
bur-sag, 50.
bur-še-gaz, 14.

D.

DIM(?) Nin-an-da-gal-ki, 206.
Dul-nir, 60, 64.
[duppa] ip-uš(?), 176, 119 (mu-na-ni-šar).
DUP-PISAN, 198, 205.
(giš) DUR-GAR, 198, 205.

E.

e: e-bi ib-ta-ni-ud-du, 101.
e-ab . . . . 52, 63, III. 1.
e-ad-da im-sig-ga-(ka), 50, 54, 114.
E-an-na, 199, 201, 222, 223, 226.
Ḙ-bar-bar, 80, 327.
E-bar-ra, 52, 171, 222.
e-dam, 59, 65.
edin: min edin mu-ru, 63.
e-gal (dingir) Dun-pa-ud-du, 327.
e-gal Erim-ki, 113.
e-gal nam-lugal-la-ka, 226.
e-gal Ti-ra-aš-(ka), 48, 51, 53, 65, 92, 327.
e-geštin, 272.
E-giš-kin-ti, 160, 3.
e-giš-me-ra, 49.
E-giš-šir-gal, 223.
e-gur-ra kalam-ma, 113.
e-ǵal-bi, 256.
e-ǵar-sag, 255.
e-ǵe-gàl-kalam-ma, 49, 51, 53.
E-ǵi-li-a-ni-in-ru, 25.
E-ǵul-ǵul, 271, 15.
e-igi-ni (written igi-e-ni), 65.
e-igi-zi-bar-ra, 113.
e Ip-ša-Iši-(dingir) Da-gan, 261, 42.
e kalam, 172.
e Kar-zi-da-ka, 224. *See also* 27; 269, 11; 270.
e KAŠ + GAR, 49, 115, 119.
e ki-a-am i-ni-lik, 158.
e ki-akkil-li, 196. *See also* 49, 53.

E-KUR, 168, 170, 222. *See also* bît (ilu) Bêl.
e lal, 272.
E-lugal-gud-si-di, 223.
E-me-gal-kiš(ǵuš)-an-ki, 50.
e-me-ne(lam)-bi-kur-kur-ra, 49, 52, 114; = e-ne-bi-kur-kur-ra, 49.
E-MU-RI(?)-A-NA-BA . . . ., 277, 278.
E-ninnû, 14, 50, 117, 120; 182, 1; 185, 10; 195, 197, 200, 203, 211.
e ni-nun, 272.
E-nun-maǵ, 235.
E-pa, 61, 23; 63. *See also* e-ub-imin-na.
e-sa-dug, 50.
E-sal-gil-sa, 224, 1.
E-sar-gub-a-ni-in-ru, 25.
E-sil-gid-gid, 204, 209, 210.
e . . . . šag . . . ., 53.
eš-gu-tur, 182, 1.
E-šid-lam, 224, 2; 237, 1; 242, 244, 254; 312, 4.
e-ub-imin-na, 61, 23; 203. *See also* E-pa.
E-ud-mà-Ninâ-ki-tag, 193.
e-uru-uru-e-ga-ra, 224, 4.

G.

GAG-GIŠ, 117, 187, 191.
Gi-gunu, 185, 10; 195, 211.
gi-ka, 114.
Gir-su-ki ki-bi mu-na-gi, 85.

I.

Ib-gal, 60, 64.
im-ba-ni, 107.
Im-dub-ba, 105.

K.

Kankal, 226.
Kar-zi-da, 27; 269, 11; 270.
ki-akkil, 49, 53. *See also* 196.
ki-di-kud, 195.
ki-gal, 172.
kisal e-kalam, 172. *See also* bad-kisal, mi-kisal.
ki-SIGIŠŠE-SIGIŠŠE-ra, 272.
Ki-šag-ǵul-la, 270, 271.
KI-U, 60, 21. *See also* Dul-nir.
KUR-E, 193.

M.

mi-kisal gud . . . ., 270. *See also* bad-kisal, kisal.

N.

na, 98, 12.
Nam-nun-da-ki-gar-ra, 106, 107.
na-ru-a, 101, 4. 6.
nigin ku-laǵ-ǵa zal-da, 116.
Ninâ-ki, 85, 94.

R.

RUŠ, *see* A-RUŠ.

Ṣ.

Ṣa-la-am-šu ù ṣa-lam (ilu) Ištar, 177.

T.

Te-im-ila, 221, 225.
Ti-aš-ra, 65. *See also* e-gal Ti-ra-aš-ka.

U.

Ubaia-ki, 258, 20. *See also* bad-ki.
uru (= Ur), 270.
uru (ŠES)-ni, 66, 69.

Z.

zu-ab, 270.
zu-ab e-kùr sir-ra, 114.
zu-ab-gal, 64, nt. 4.
zu-ab-tur-da, 64, nt. 4; 66, 68, 69.

IV. CITIES, LANDS, ETC.

Erech, 17; 44, 3; 130, 145, 151, 161, 162; 182, 1; 214, 225, 226, 228. *See also* U^{n}_{r}ug-ki-g^{a}_{i}, Uruk.
Eridu, written NUN-ki, *see* Urudug-ki and
Eridug-ki, 211, 228, 238, 243, 259; 267, 5; 269, 281, 284, 422.
Erim-ki, 46, 113, 161; 182, 1; 284.
Euphrates, 111, 130, 214, 215, 309. *See also* Buranunu and Id-nun.

G.

Gir-su-ki, 46, 51, 63, 64, 85, 88, 105, 161; 182, 1; 193, 198, 201, 202, 217, 224, 225, 245, 284, 292, 299, 304, 332, 354, 355. Also written Su-gir, 64, 216. *See also* Šir-pur-la-ki.
Giš-ban-ki, 74, 1; 213, 1. *See also* Giš-uḫ-ki.
Gišgal-ki, 75, 86; 91, 18. *See also* URU + inserted A-a-ki.
Giš-uḫ-ki, 15, 2; 30, 1; 74, 1; 76 ff., 110 ff., 129; 279, 3; 285; 300, III., *et passim*. *See also* Ḫarran.
Giš-uḫ-ki-a, 79, 28; 81, 105, 106, 109.
Γόμορρα, 58, 6.
Gubin, 191, 1. *See also* Koptos.
Gu-edin(-na), 75; 82, 2; 86, 87 nt., 88 nt., 97, 101, 111 ff.
Gu-ti-im, 175. Gu-ti-um-ki, 160. *See also* 127, 159, 162, 163, 180; 292, 1, and Kurdistan.

G, Ḫ.

Ḫa-ar-ši-ki, 253, 259, 265, 280, 282, 365.
Ġa-ĝum, 190.
חֲנוֹךְ, 54, III., 6.
Ḫarran, 110, 2; 141, 149. *See also* Giš-ban-ki and Giš-uḫ-ki.
Ḫu-mur-ti-ki, 245, 265, 280, 283, 365.
Ḫu-uḫ-mu-ri-ki, 74, 1; 268, 283; written also
Ḫu-ḫu-nu-ri-ki, 74, 1; 279, 407.

I.

Ibla, mountain, 190. *See also* Lebanon.
Idigna, 105, 107, 135. *See also* Tigris.
Id-nun, 'great river'; הנהר הגדול, 97; 101, II., 1; 107, 111; 122, 1. *See also* Buranunu and Euphrates.
Im-dub-ba, 83, 101, 105.
Innanna-ab-ki, 96, 105; 160, 3; 161; written also Ki-Innanna-ab-ki, 131, 137. (Comp. Ki-an-ki, Ki-en-gi-ki-Urdu, Ki-maš-ki, Ki-(dingir)-Utu, and Ki-Unug-ki-gi, 136.)
Innanna-Erin-ki, 30, 1; 161.
Isin, 25, 228, 3; 234. *See also* Ni-si-in-ki-na.
Iš-ku-un-Sin, 30, 1; 235.

K.

Ka-dingir-ra-ki, *see* Babylon.
Ka-gal-ad-ki, 190. *See also* Aga and Salma.
Kar-ḫar-ki, 259, 260, 264, 282, 419.
Kar-kar, 97, 106.
KAR-UD-NUN-ki, 329. *See also* Nun-ki, Ud-kib-nun-ki, and Ud-nun-ki.
Kar(TE)-zi-da-ki, 260, 39. *See also under* 'Buildings' and (dingir) Uru-ki-Kar-zi-da.
Ka-ṣal-lu-ki, 158, 163, 190, 256, 285; 302, XII.
Ki-an-ki, 137.
Ki-en-gi (alone), 45, 46; 82, 3; 136; 122, 1; 145, 213, 216, 217, 220.
Ki-en-gi-ki-Urdu, 21, 25; 30, 1; 45, 216, 222–225, 230–233, 242. *See also* Shumer and Akkad.
Ki-Innanna-ab-ki, 131, 137. *See also* Innanna-ab-ki.
Ki-maš-ki, 27, 190, 245, 253, 265, 280, 283, 285; 314, 2; 324, 355, 357.

Ki-nu-nir-^{ki}, 161; 182, 1; 285, 332, 354, 389, 391, 393, 395, 397, 399. *See also* Bar-sip-^{ki}, Borsippa.
Kîš-^{ki}, 45, 46; 82, 4; 91, 98, 110, 112, 123, 125, 129, 143, 161 (âlu Kîš-^{ki}), 163; 180, 2; 212, 241; 255, 12, *et passim*.
Kîš (without ki), 16, 121; 125, 3; 128, 213, 219.
Kîš-edin-na, 82, 2; 83.
Ki-$^{(dingir)}$ Utu, 82, 88. *See also* Larsa.
Koptos, 191, 1; 192. *See also* Gubin.
Kurdistan, *see* Gu-ti-im.
Kutha, 218, 224, 225, 238, 285; 310, 4. *See also* TIK-GAB-A-^{ki}.

L.

Lagash, 47. *See also* Šir-pur-la-^{ki}.
Larsa, 130, 222, 225, 286, 328. *See also* Ki-$^{(dingir)}$ Utu and UD-UNU(G)-^{ki}-(GA).
Lebanon, 73, 191. *See also* Ibla.
Lulubi, 127, 175, 180, 266 nt. 1; 312, 5; written
Lu-lu-be-^{ki}-im, 177; or
Lu-lu-bu-^{ki}, 264, 48; or
Lu-lu-bu-um-^{ki}, 253; 263, 47 *a*; 264, 279, 283, 285, 292, 302, 427, 429; or
Lu-bu, 263, 47 *a*.
Lum-ma-dim-šar, 83, 90; 92, 4, 11.
Lum-ma-gir-nun-ta-šag-azag-gi-pad-da, 83, 88 nt.
Lum-ma-ṣir-ta, 83, 96, 104.

M.

Mà-al, 59, 63, 68.
Mà-gan-^{ki}, 59, 16; 89, 7; 158, 161–163, 190, 198, 203, 210, 214.
Ma-ḳal-^{ki}, 91, 22. *See also* Ma-uru-^{ki}.
Mar-^{ki}, 285. *See also* $^{(dingir)}$ Nin-Mar-^{ki}.
Marad-da-^{ki}, 300, V. *See also* Ἀμορδοκαία.
Mar'ash =
Mar-ḫa-ši-^{ki}; 257, 19; 282; 314, 2.
Mar-tu-^{ki}, 157, 163, 166, 190, 276; 292, 2.
Mar-tu-am, 159. *See also* Amurru.
Ma-uru-^{ki}, 30, 1; 91, 22. *See also* Ma-ḳal-^{ki}.
Mediterranean Sea, 130, 214, 215, 284.
Meluḫḫa, 161, 198.
Mi-lim-^{ki}(-me), 82, 88, 95.
Mugheir, 46; 150, 2. *See also* Uru-um-^{ki}-ma.
. . . . mu-tuk . . . . -^{ki}, 30, 1.

N.

הנהר הגדול : נהר, *see* Id-nun.
נוֹר, 63, 7. *See also* A-idinna.
Nam-nun-da-ki-gar-ra, 83, 101, 103, 106, 107.
Nim(-ma)-^{ki}, 30, 1; 236. *See also* Elamtu-^{ki}.
Ninâ-^{ki}, 46, 54, 85, 161, 193, 284, 332, 335, 354.
Ninâ-^{ki}-tum-ma, 54, 82.
Nippur, 46, 122, 150, 151; 160, 3; 161, 171, 214, 222–225, 228, 285; 299, II.; 321, 416. *See also* En-lil-^{ki}.
Ni-si-in-^{ki}-na, 25; 228, 3; 230, 231. *See also* Isin.
NUN-^{ki}, 269, 9. *See also* Eridug-^{ki}, Urudug-^{ki}.

P.

Padir, 177. *See also* Ba-ti-ir.
Palestine, 309.
Persian Gulf, 130, 214, 215, 284.

S, Ṣ, Š.

Salma, mountain, 190, 4. *See also* Ka-gal-ad-^{ki}.
Sangara, 214. *See also* שִׁנְעָר.
Ser-i-Pul, 177.

Shatt-el-Ḫai, 46, 111, 112, 150.
Shatt-el-Kehr, 228, 3.
Shimash, 314, 2.
Shumer and Akkad, 216, 284, 285, 286. *See also* Ki-en-gi-^{ki}-Urdu.
Si-ma-LUM(num), 276, 283.
Si-maš-ki-im, 255, 12.
Si-mu-ru-um-^{ki} (سمرّة), 259, 260, 263, 264, 282, 283, 292, 300; written also
Si-mu-ùr-ru-um-^{ki}, 253; or
Si-mu-ùr-um-^{ki}, 263, 47 *a*; =
Simyra, 263, 47 *a*.
Sippar, 154, 161, 171. *See also* UD-KIB-NUN-^{ki}.
. . . . su-^{ki}, 161.
Su-kur-ru-^{ki}, 302, XI.
Su(n)-gir, 216. *See also* Gir-su-^{ki}.
Suri, 158.
Susa, *see* Ša-a-ša-^{ki}.
Syria, 285, 309.
Ṣab-ban-^{ki}, 213, 1. *See also* Uḫ-^{ki}, Upi (Opis).
Ša-a-ša-^{ki}, 236. *See also* Susa.
Ša-aš-ru-^{ki}, 262, 283, 325, 432; also written
Ša-aš-ru-um-^{ki}, 253, 268, 293, 325.
Šaǵ, 91, 17.
. . . . ši, 30, 1.
שִׁנְעָר, 58, 6; 216. *See also* Sangara and Shumer and Akkad.
Šir-pur-la-^{ki}, 46 ff., 181 ff., 281, *et passim*; written without ki, 63, 64; also
Pur-šir-la, 55.
Pur-la-šir, 59, nt. 16.
Šir-la-^{ki}-pur, 84, 85, 106, 107, 113, 116, 117, 118, 120.
Šir-la-pur-^{ki}, 108, 113, 116.
ŠIT-TAR-^{ki}, 30, 1.

T.

TE(-^{ki}), 95, 1.
Te-li-ti-^{ki}, 329.
Tell Ibrâhîm, 218. *See also* Kutha.
Tell-Loh, 46, 321. *See also* Lagash and Šir-pur-la-^{ki}.
Te-zi-da-^{ki}, 255, 10; 260, 39. *See also* Kar-zi-da-^{ki}.
Tidanum, mountain, 190; =
Ti-id-ni-im-^{ki}, 276, 4; 316.
Tigris, 97, 111, 130, 214, 215, 309. *See also* Idigna.
Tik-ab-ba-^{ki}, 332, 354, 357, 359, 361, 387, 401.
TIK-GAB-A-^{ki}, 224, 3; 237, 1. *See also* Kutha.
Tilmun = Tylos, 191, 2.
Tripolis, 263, 47 *a*.
Tu-tu-^{ki}, 174.

U.

Ubara-^{ki}, 258, 20.
UB-DA-^{ki}, 18, 1; 157.
UD-KIB-NUN-^{ki}, 161, 1. *See also* Sippar.
UD-NUN-^{ki}, 301, IX.
UD-UNU(G)-^{ki}(-GA), 80, 136. *See also* Larsa.
Uḫ-^{ki}, 82, 89, 91; 124, 13; 159, 161, 213, 1. *See also* Ṣab-ban-^{ki} and Upi.
Unug-^{ki}-a, 161. *See also* Erech and Warka.
U$^{n}_{r}$ug-^{ki}-ga, 27, 29; 44, 3; 82, 87, 94, 132, 133, 138, 152, 153, 225, 230, 231, 332.
Unug-^{ki}-gi (*sic*), 136.
ki-Unug-^{ki}-gi, 136. (For this latter writing, *see* Innanna-ab-^{ki}.)
Upi = Opis, 213, 1. *See also* Ṣab-ban-^{ki} and Uḫ-^{ki}.
Ur, written Uru-unu(g)-^{ki}-(ma) and transcribed by us: Uru-um-^{ki}-(ma), 21, 22, 25, 27, 30, 1; 88, 221, 222, *et passim*. Once
Uru-unu(g)-^{ki}-e, 136.
Ur-bil-lum-^{ki}, 253, 264, 266, 283, 359, 361, 387, 389, 391, 395, 397, 399, 427.

Urdu, 216, 220. *See also* A-ga-de-^{ki}, Bur-bur, and Shumer and Akkad.
Ur-in-gl, 191.
Uru-azag-ga, 46, 75, 83, 85; 182, 1; 202, 204, 205, 207, 209, 210. Once Uru-azag-gi, 205.
Uru + inserted A-a-^{ki}, 117; = Gišgal?
Urudug-^{ki} (written NUN-^{ki}), 114, 230, 231, 292. *See also* Eridug-^{ki}.
Uruk, 285. *See also* Erech, U$^{n}_{r}$ug-^{ki}-g$^{a}_{i}$.

W.

Warka, 27, 29, 46, 82, 273, 321. *See also* U$^{n}_{r}$ug-^{ki}-g$^{a}_{i}$.
Wasit-el-Ḫai, 111.

Z.

Za-ap-ša-li-^{ki}, 27, 277, 279, 283.
Zâb, 162, 175.
Za-ḫa-ra-[a?], 159.
Za-rad-im-^{ki}, 329.

www.ingramcontent.com/pod-product-compliance
Lightning Source LLC
Chambersburg PA
CBHW081144290426
44108CB00018B/2434
* 9 7 8 1 5 9 7 5 2 3 8 1 3 *